KINDERGARTEN
SCHOOL EDITION

MW00650887

God Loves Us

CATECHIST MANUAL

AUTHORS
Sisters of Notre Dame
Chardon, Ohio

LOYOLA PRESS.
A JESUIT MINISTRY
Chicago

Nihil Obstat: Reverend Jeffrey S. Grob, S.T.L., J.C.L., Censor Deputatus, November 10, 2006
Imprimatur: Reverend John F. Canary, S.T.L., D. Min., Vicar General, Archdiocese of Chicago, December 1, 2006

The *Nihil Obstat* and *Imprimatur* are official declarations that a book is free of doctrinal and moral error. No implication is contained therein that those who have granted the *Nihil Obstat* and *Imprimatur* agree with the content, opinions, or statements expressed. Nor do they assume any legal responsibility associated with publication.

God Loves Us of the *God Made Me Everything* Series
found to be in conformity
The Ad Hoc Committee to Oversee the Use of the Catechism, United States Conference of Catholic Bishops, has found the doctrinal content of this manual, copyright 2008, to be in conformity with the *Catechism of the Catholic Church.*

ACKNOWLEDGMENTS

Excerpts from *Catechism of the Catholic Church.* English translation of the *Catechism of the Catholic Church* for the United States of America copyright © 1994, United States Catholic Conference, Inc.—Libreria Editrice Vaticana.

Excerpt from the English translation of *Directory for Masses with Children from Documents on the Liturgy,* 1963–1979: Conciliar, Papal, and Curial Texts © 1982, International Committee on English in the Liturgy, Inc. All rights reserved.

Excerpts from the *General Directory for Catechesis* © 1997 Libreria Editrice Vaticana-United States Conference of Catholic Bishops, Inc., Washington, DC. All rights reserved.

Excerpts from the English translation of *The Liturgy of the Hours* © 1974, International Committee on English in the Liturgy, Inc. (ICEL); excerpts from the English translation of *The Roman Missal* © 2010, ICEL; excerpts from the English translation of *A Book of Prayers* © 1982, ICEL; excerpts from the English translation of *Book of Blessings* © 1988, ICEL. All rights reserved.

Excerpts from the *National Directory for Catechesis.* Copyright © 2005 United States Conference of Catholic Bishops, Inc., Washington, DC. No portion of this text may be reproduced by any means without written permission from the copyright holder.

Excerpts from the *New American Bible* with Revised New Testament and Psalms Copyright © 1991, 1986, 1970 Confraternity of Christian Doctrine, Inc., Washington, DC. All rights reserved. No portion of the New American Bible may be reprinted without permission in writing from the copyright holder.

Excerpt from *Welcome and Justice for Persons with Disabilities.* Copyright © 1998, United States Catholic Conference, Inc. Washington, DC. All rights reserved.

Excerpts from Vatican conciliar, postconciliar, and papal documents are from the official translations, Libreria Editrice Vaticana, 00120 Citta del Vaticano.

"God Made a Flower" by Janice Driscoll is reprinted with permission from *Religion Teacher's Journal,* P.O. Box 180, Mystic, CT 06355, 800-321-0411.

"Choosing" from *Eleanor Farjeon's Poems for Children* by Eleanor Farjeon, copyright © 1933, renewed 1961 by Eleanor Farjeon. Reprinted by permission of Harold Ober Associates Inc.

"Handprints" by T. Lambert, Jr. © T. Lambert, Jr. May 1978, from Creative Kids at Home, www.creativekidsathome.com.

Excerpt from *Dag Hammarskjöld: The Man and His Faith* by Henry P. Van Dusen. Copyright © 1967 by Henry P. Van Dusen. Reprinted by permission of HarperCollins Publishers.

Every effort has been made to determine copyright owners. In the case of any omissions, the publisher will be pleased to make suitable acknowledgments in future editions. Unless otherwise acknowledged, photos are the property of Loyola Press. Credits are supplied in sequence, left to right, top to bottom. Page positions are abbreviated as follows: (t) top, (c) center, (b) bottom, (l) left, (r) right.

Illustration Credit references student edition folio.
Nan Brooks: 2, 3, 23, 48, 85, 119, 128 Susan Tolonen: 6, 7, 44, 45, 54, 55, 108, 110 Yoshi Miyake: 113, 117, 131, 137 Cheryl Arnemann: 49, 88, 93, 96 Mike Muir: 11, 15, 59, 133 Robert Voigts: 75, 81, 89, 97 Eileen Mueller Neill & Kelly Neill: 127 Proof Positive: 123 Martin Erspamer, OSB.: 111 Ida Pearl: 32 Robert Crawford: 37 Laura Fry: 104–105

Photography Credit references student edition folio.
UNIT 1: 1 Mike Timo/Stone/Getty Images. **4** (tl)Jose Ortega/Stock Illustration Source/Getty Images. **6**(tr) Camille Tokerud/Photographer's Choice/Getty Images. **8** Stephanie Howard/Stone/Getty Images. **8**(tr) © The Crosiers/Gene Plaisted OSC. **9**(b) Christoph Wilhelm/Taxi/Getty Images. **10** David Young-Wolff/Photographer's Choice/Getty Images. **10**(tl) © The Crosiers/Gene Plaisted OSC. **14**(tl) Aaron Graubart/Iconica/Getty Images. **14**(tr) Altrendo/Altrendo Images/Getty Images. **18**(tr) Eri Morita/Stone/Getty Images. **18**(tlc) PIER/Stone/Getty Images. **19**(tr) Camille Tokerud/The Image Bank/Getty Images. **22**(b) Ariel Skelley/CORBIS. **24**(tr) Kevin Hatt/Photonica/Getty Images. **27**(trl) © The Crosiers/Gene Plaisted OSC. **28**(br) © The Crosiers/Gene Plaisted OSC. **29**(tr) © The Crosiers/Gene Plaisted OSC. **30**(tr) © The Crosiers/Gene Plaisted OSC. **31** Altrendo/Altrendo Images/Getty Images. **35**(br) Randy Faris/CORBIS. **35**(tl) © The Crosiers/Gene Plaisted OSC. **36**(b) Dave Nagel/Taxi/Getty Images. **43** Yellow Dog Productions/The Image Bank/Getty Images. **47** Karen Kapoor/Taxi/Getty Images. **50**(tl) © The Crosiers/Gene Plaisted OSC. **51**(bl) Mark Hall/Photonica/Getty Images. **53** Ronnie Kaufman/CORBIS. **56**(tr) © The Crosiers/Gene Plaisted OSC. **57** Anne-Marie Weber/CORBIS. **58** Ariel Skelley/CORBIS. **60**(tl) © The Crosiers/Gene Plaisted OSC. **61** © Mark Grimberg/Getty Images. **62** © The Crosiers/Gene Plaisted OSC. **63**(tc) bread & butter/Photographer's Choice/Getty Images. **63**(tl) Elyse Lewin/Photographer's Choice/Getty Images. **65** Grace/zefa/CORBIS. **67** © The Crosiers/Gene Plaisted OSC. **72**(tr) © The Crosiers/Gene Plaisted OSC. **73**(t) The Crosiers/Gene Plaisted OSC. **73**(b) Andersen Ross/Getty Images. **77**(lc) © The Crosiers/Gene Plaisted OSC. **81**(tr) Phil Martin Photography. **83** Steven Puetzer/Solus Photography/Veer. **84**(lc) Phil Martin Photography. **84**(tr) © The Crosiers/Gene Plaisted OSC. **87** Peter Rodger/Workbook Stock/Getty Images. **90**(tr) © The Crosiers/Gene Plaisted OSC. **92**(tl) © Bill Wittman Photography. **92**(br) Agnus Images. **94**(tr) Phil Martin Photography. **95** Mark Gamba/CORBIS. **96** © The Crosiers/Gene Plaisted OSC. **97**(tr) © The Crosiers/Gene Plaisted OSC. **98**(cr) © The Crosiers/Gene Plaisted OSC. **99** Joe McBride/Taxi/Getty Images. **100**(tc) Siri Stafford/Stone/Getty Images. **100**(bc) Emmanuel Faure/Taxi/Getty Images. **101**(br) Joe Polillio/Photographer's Choice/Getty Images. **101**(tl) © The Crosiers/Gene Plaisted OSC. **102**(tr) © The Crosiers/Gene Plaisted OSC. **107**(cl) Phil Martin Photography. **107**(cr) © The Crosiers/Gene Plaisted OSC. **112**(br) Gary Gay/Photographer's Choice/Getty Images. **113**(tl) Annie Engel/zefa/CORBIS. **114**(br) © The Crosiers/Gene Plaisted OSC. **115**(tl) © Bill Wittman Photography. **116**(tr) © Bill Wittman Photography. **119**(tr) © The Crosiers/Gene Plaisted OSC. **120**(l) © The Crosiers/Gene Plaisted OSC. **121**(tr) © The Crosiers/Gene Plaisted OSC. **122**(tr) © The Crosiers/Gene Plaisted OSC. **123**(tr) © The Crosiers/Gene Plaisted OSC. **124**(tr) © The Crosiers/Gene Plaisted OSC. **125**(trl) © The Crosiers/Gene Plaisted OSC. **126**(br) © Bill Wittman Photography. **127**(tr) © The Crosiers/Gene Plaisted OSC. **128**(br) © Office Central de Lisieux. **129**(tr) © The Crosiers/Gene Plaisted OSC. **130**(tl) © The Crosiers/Gene Plaisted OSC. **131**(tr) © The Crosiers/Gene Plaisted OSC. **132**(bl) Paul C. Pet/zefa/CORBIS. **133**(tr) © The Crosiers/Gene Plaisted OSC. **134**(tl) © The Crosiers/Gene Plaisted OSC. **135**(tr) © The Crosiers/Gene Plaisted OSC. **136** Courtesy Sisters of Notre Dame. **137**(tl) © The Crosiers/Gene Plaisted OSC. **138**(tr) © The Crosiers/Gene Plaisted OSC.

Credit references teacher edition folio.
OV-14(b) Mike Timo/Stone/Getty Images. **OV-19**(b) Mike Timo/Stone/Getty Images. **OV-20** Ariel Skelley/CORBIS. **OV-27**(tl) Annie Engel/zefa/CORBIS. **OV-27**(br) © Bill Wittman Photography. **T1** Mike Timo/Stone/Getty Images. **T296**(tr, c, b) © The Crosiers/Gene Plaisted OSC. **T297**(tl) Courtesy Sisters of Notre Dame. **T298**(m) © The Crosiers/Gene Plaisted OSC. **T299**(m) © The Crosiers/Gene Plaisted OSC. **T300**(tr) Alamy **T300**(c) © Office Central de Lisieux. **T301**(c) © The Crosiers/Gene Plaisted OSC.

Acknowledgments continued on page T386

For more information related to the English translation of the *Roman Missal, Third Edition,* see www.loyolapress.com/romanmissal.

Design: Loyola Press, Judine O'Shea
Cover Art: Susan Tolonen

ISBN 10: 0-8294-2402-4, ISBN 13: 978-0-8294-2402-7

Manufactured in China.

11 12 13 14 RRD/China 10 9 8 7 6 5 4 3 2

LOYOLA PRESS.
A JESUIT MINISTRY

3441 N. Ashland Avenue
Chicago, Illinois 60657
(800) 621-1008
www.loyolapress.com

DEDICATION

THE SISTERS OF NOTRE DAME GRATEFULLY REMEMBER
PERSONS FROM THEIR PAST WHOSE MINISTRY
OF CATECHESIS THEY ARE PRIVILEGED TO CONTINUE
IN THE PRESENT.

Sister Maria Aloysia Wolbring (1828–1889) foundress of the Sisters of Notre Dame of Coesfeld, Germany, and the first sisters of this new community, were formed in the spiritual and pedagogical tradition of Reverend Bernard Overberg. God, our loving and provident Father, was presented not only as caring for persons more than anyone else ever could, but also as challenging them to a responsible love for themselves, for all other people, and for creation. One of Sister Aloysia's students recalled: "Her religious instructions meant more to us than the sermons preached in church. She spoke from deepest conviction and tried to direct our hearts to God alone. Best of all, she did not require too much piety of us. 'Children,' she would say, 'always follow the golden middle way—not too little, not too much.'"

Reverend Bernard Overberg (1752–1826) began his life work of shaping teacher formation and catechesis in 1783 in the diocese of Munster, Germany. Reverend Overberg sought to present the Church's faith and teaching in such a way as to lead children and adults toward a deep, mature relationship with God in Jesus Christ. Faith, experienced through the lens of salvation history and related to everyday life, was to touch both the mind and the heart, calling forth reflection, prayer and active response. His approach to catechesis was the way the Coesfeld Sisters of Notre Dame were led to know God in their childhood, and how they were later formed as catechists.

Saint Julie Billiart (1751–1816), foundress of the Sisters of Notre Dame de Namur, was the source of the Rule by which the Coesfeld Sisters of Notre Dame were formed. With Christian education designated as the main work of the congregation, the sisters had a framework within which to continue the mission they had begun as lay teachers. As they learned more about Julie, the sisters were inspired by the story of how this simple French woman became a remarkable catechist who helped renew the people's faith after the chaos of the French Revolution. As a young girl, Julie's deep faith and love impelled her to share the Good News with others. During a twelve-year period in which she suffered a crippling illness, Julie devoted herself to catechizing women and children. Julie's confidence in the goodness and provident care of God remained unshaken in the face of misunderstandings on the part of some bishops, priests and even her own sisters. Always open to the Spirit, she courageously carried out her ministry and taught others to proclaim the Good News. The more the Coesfeld Sisters of Notre Dame came to know about Julie, the more they desired to make known God's goodness. "How good God is." Today they regard her as their spiritual mother.

Contents

God Loves Us

Unit 4: Celebrating God's Love

Welcome to *God Loves Us*

The *God Loves Us* program recognizes that young children have a readiness to learn about God. The program integrates Scripture and doctrine in each lesson to help children and their catechists relate the richness of our Catholic faith to their every day lives.

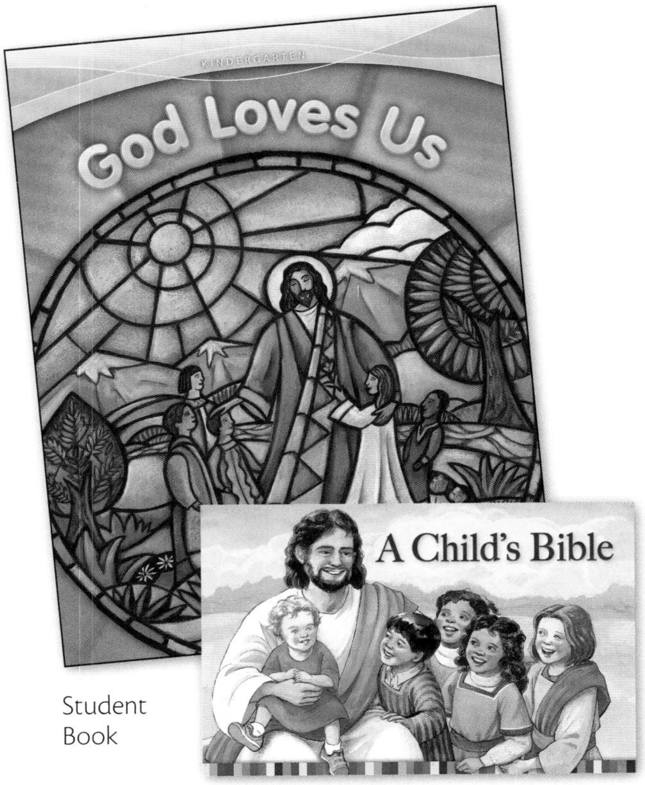

Student Book

A Child's Bible

Parish Catechist's Manual

School Catechist's Manual

Music CDs (2 discs)

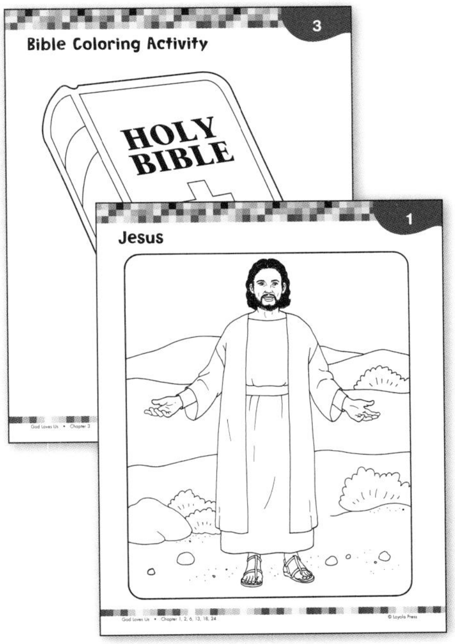

Blackline Masters

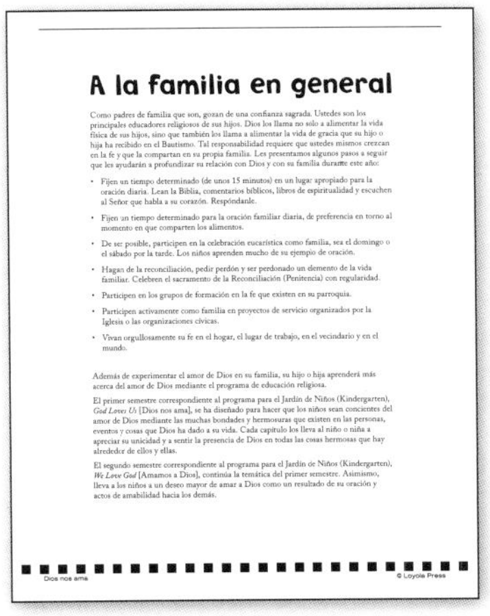
A la familia en general

Family resources in Spanish (online only)

Posters, 17"x22" (10)

Student Book

- **Faith content** is developed throughout with Scripture integrated into each lesson
- **Parent and family resources** connect family and faith to enrich the children's experience
- **Traditional and familiar prayers** invite personal and communal prayer
- **Punchouts** bring the content to life in fun hands-on activities
- **Parish Religious Education and Catholic school** needs are met using the same Student Book
- ***A Child's Bible*** is free with every Student Book

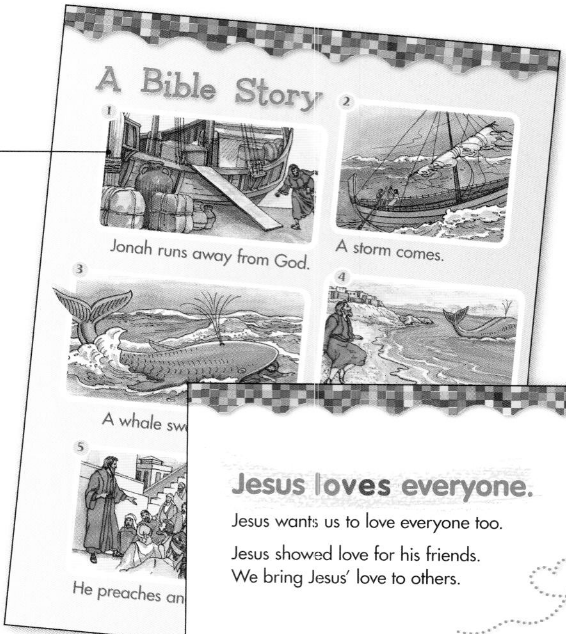

Jonah runs away from God.

A storm comes.

A whale sw

He preaches an

Appealing art and graphics capture young children's attention

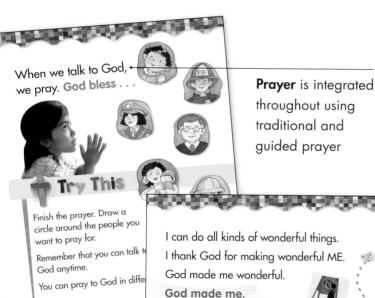

Prayer is integrated throughout using traditional and guided prayer

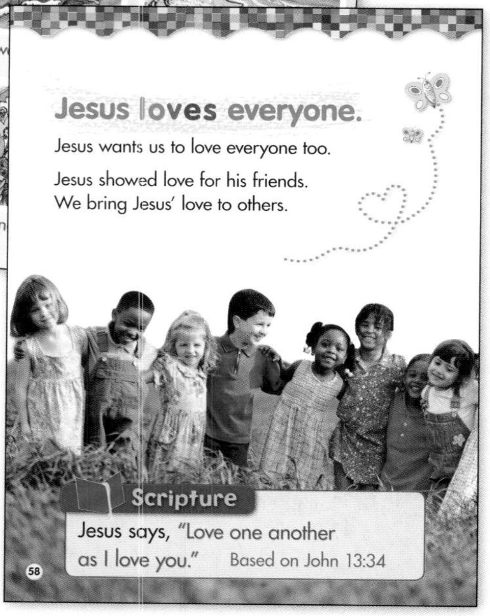

I can do all kinds of wonderful things.
I thank God for making wonderful ME.
God made me wonderful.
God made me.
God loves me.
Scripture
I thank you, O Lord, for the wonder
of myself. Based on Psalm 139:14
32

Scripture and doctrine help children learn the traditions of the faith and know the Bible as God's Word

Summary of the lesson involves parents in each chapter

Bridge to the home offers ideas and activities to reinforce learning and involve the family

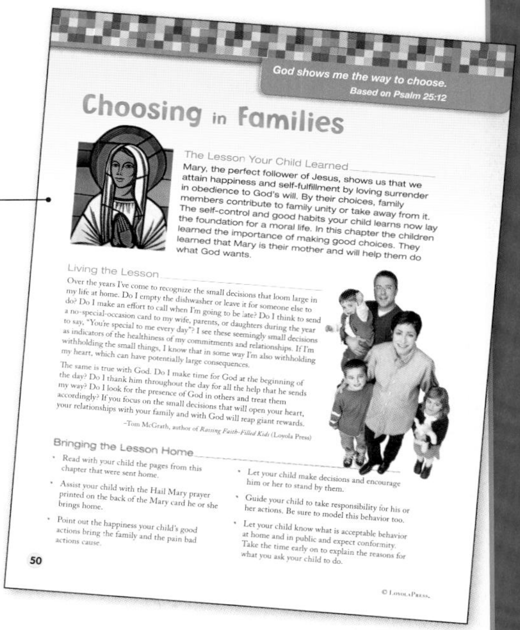

Family features at the end of each unit offer additional support for parents of young children

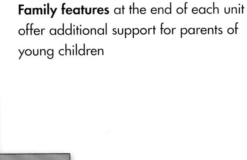

A special section provides lessons for **liturgical seasons** and **saints' feast days**

Punchouts in the back of the book provide fun, hands-on activities

School Catechist's Manual

- **Faith Focus** is introduced in first lesson and enriched in remaining lessons
- **Two music CDs** provide over 30 songs for children
- **Flexible structure** adapts easily to include liturgical seasons and special feast days
- **Comprehensive children's literature and music resource lists** provide teachers with over 400 recommendations of age-appropriate resources
- **Catechist's Handbook** is included in every manual
- **Preparing the Faith Experience** offers background resources and supports catechists' spirituality
- **Special Seasons and Days** section provides lessons on litugical seasons and saints' feast days
- **Web support and resources** are featured at http://godlovesus.loyolapress.com
- **Teacher-scripted for new teachers**, with flexibility built in for experienced teachers
- **Lessons written for a 4–5 day per week** school program

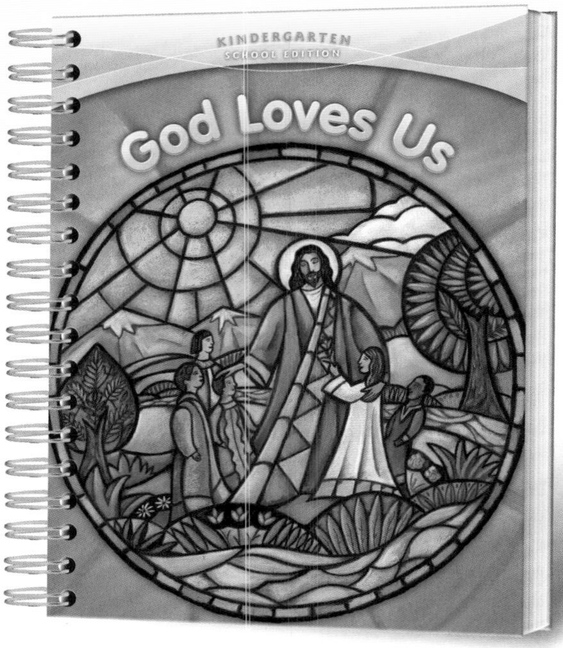

Free components with every Catechist's Manual

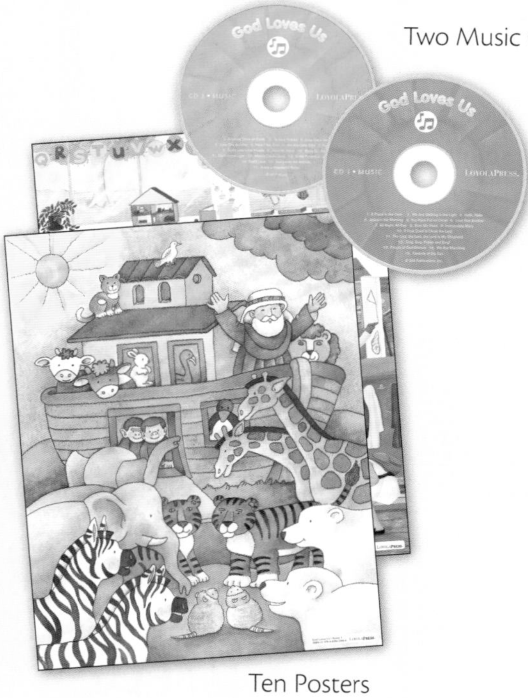

Two Music CDs

Ten Posters

Over 30 Blackline Masters

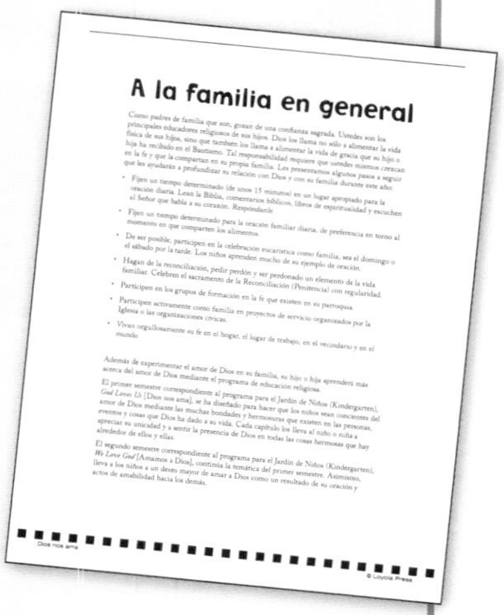

Family resources in Spanish (online only)

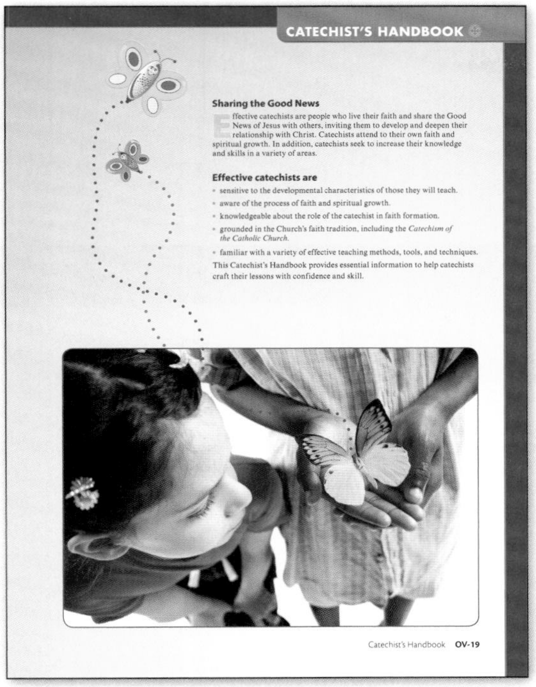
CATECHIST'S HANDBOOK

Sharing the Good News

Effective catechists are people who live their faith and share the Good News of Jesus with others, inviting them to develop and deepen their relationship with Christ. Catechists attend to their own faith and spiritual growth. In addition, catechists seek to increase their knowledge and skills in a variety of areas.

Effective catechists are

- sensitive to the developmental characteristics of those they will teach.
- aware of the process of faith and spiritual growth.
- knowledgeable about the role of the catechist in faith formation.
- grounded in the Church's faith tradition, including the *Catechism of the Catholic Church.*
- familiar with a variety of effective teaching methods, tools, and techniques.

This Catechist's Handbook provides essential information to help catechists craft their lessons with confidence and skill.

Catechist's Handbook OV-19

Catechist's Handbook

The *God Loves Us* Catechist's Handbook is included in every teaching manual. It provides essential information to help catechists build their program on a strong foundation.

- **Catechist's important role** in faith formation is featured as central
- **Planning calendar** suggests ways to structure year-long plans and incorporate liturgical seasons and special feast days
- **Music and children's literature list** provide over 400 age-appropriate resource recommendations
- **Teaching techniques, tools, and methods section** offers ideas for variety and creativity
- **Background on kindergartners'** developmental stages and areas of growth in faith and spirituality supports cathechist's effectiveness
- **Cutouts** provide visual aids for engaging children's attention.

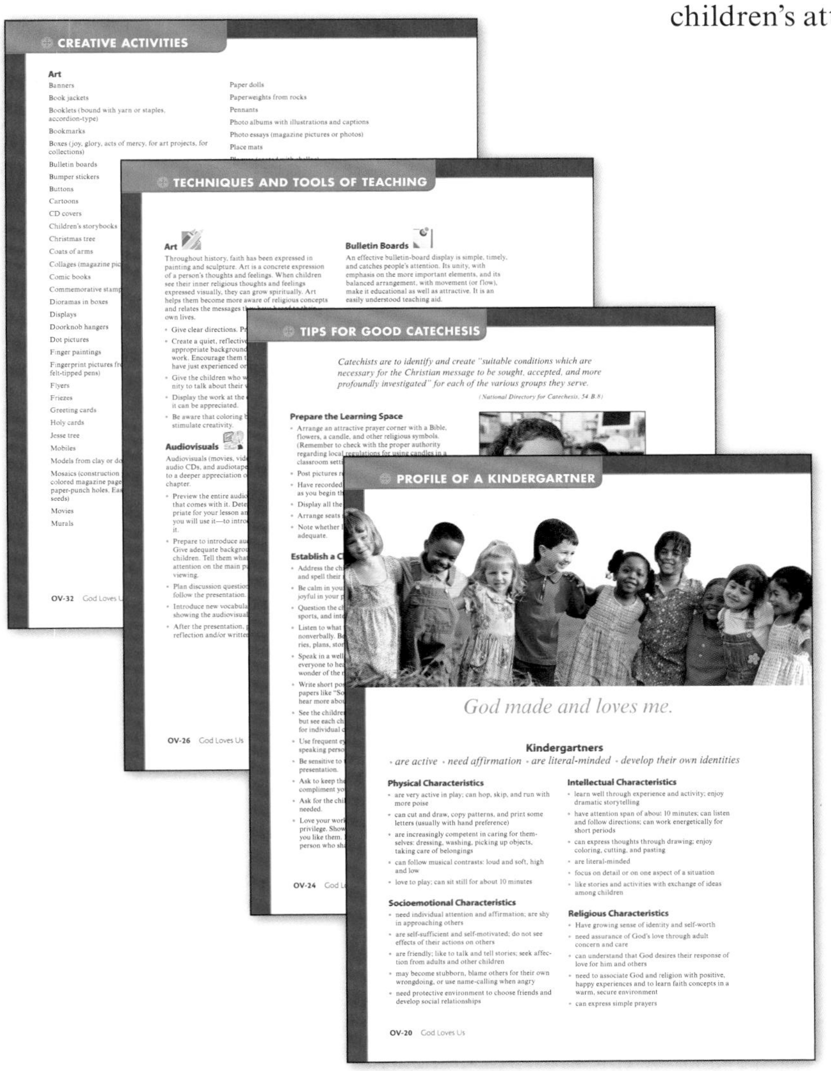
CREATIVE ACTIVITIES

OV-32 God Loves Us

TECHNIQUES AND TOOLS OF TEACHING

OV-26 God Loves Us

TIPS FOR GOOD CATECHESIS

Catechists are to identify and create "suitable conditions which are necessary for the Christian message to be sought, accepted, and more profoundly investigated" for each of the various groups they serve. (National Directory for Catechesis, 54 B.8)

OV-24

PROFILE OF A KINDERGARTNER

God made and loves me.

Kindergartners

• are active • need affirmation • are literal-minded • develop their own identities

Physical Characteristics

- are very active in play; can hop, skip, and run with more poise
- can cut and draw, copy patterns, and print some letters (usually with hand preference)
- are increasingly competent in caring for themselves: dressing, washing, picking up objects, taking care of belongings
- can follow musical contrasts: loud and soft, high and low
- love to play; can sit still for about 10 minutes

Socioemotional Characteristics

- need individual attention and affirmation; are shy in approaching others
- are self-sufficient and self-motivated; do not see effects of their actions on others
- are friendly; like to talk and tell stories; seek affection from adults and other children
- may become stubborn, blame others for their own wrongdoing, or use name-calling when angry
- need protective environment to choose friends and develop social relationships

Intellectual Characteristics

- learn well through experience and activity; enjoy dramatic storytelling
- have attention span of about 10 minutes; can listen and follow directions; can work energetically for short periods
- can express thoughts through drawing; enjoy coloring, cutting, and pasting
- are literal-minded
- focus on detail or on one aspect of a situation
- like stories and activities with exchange of ideas among children

Religious Characteristics

- Have growing sense of identity and self-worth
- need assurance of God's love through adult concern and care
- can understand that God desires their response of love for him and others
- need to associate God and religion with positive, happy experiences and to learn faith concepts in a warm, secure environment
- can express simple prayers

OV-20 God Loves Us

Cutouts

Preparing the Faith Experience

Two teacher-preparation pages introduce the background and preparation steps for each chapter. The preparation begins with the FAITH FOCUS which provides the theme of the lesson and its scriptural basis.

Preparing the Faith Experience encompasses a consistent three-step preparation process—**Listening, Reflecting, Responding**.

Listening: A Scripture passage related to the Faith Focus invites the catechist to listen to God's Word

Reflecting: A reflection on the theme provides background and links the Faith Focus to the catechist's own faith life

Responding: A question and prayer starter relates the chapter theme to the catechist's role and invites a personal response to the Faith Focus of the lesson

Chapter 7
Families Are Good

FAITH FOCUS
In God, we are all brothers and sisters. Luke 2:39–40

Lesson 11 on the Holy Family in SPECIAL SEASONS AND DAYS can be correlated with this chapter.

PREPARING THE FAITH EXPERIENCE

LISTENING

Those who share God's Word with others must also be fed by God's word found in Sacred Scripture. Share some time of quiet prayer with God, listening to God's Word. Ask God to fill you with his presence and nourish you by his holy Word.

"This is how you are to pray:

Our Father in heaven,
hallowed be your name,
your kingdom come;
your will be done,
on earth as in heaven.
Give us this day our daily bread;
and forgive us our debts,
as we forgive our debtors;
and do not subject us to the final test,
but deliver us from the evil one.

If you forgive others their transgressions,
your heavenly Father will forgive you.
But if you do not forgive others, neither
will your Father forgive your transgressions."
Matthew 6:9–15

REFLECTING

The names we use to address people express our relationships with them. We use intimate terms to address those we love. We use more formal terms to speak to business associates. When Jesus told us to call God "our Father" and gave us the Our Father prayer, he said a great deal about our relationship to God and to one another. This prayer is also called the Lord's Prayer because Jesus himself taught it to us.

Nothing is left unsaid in the Our Father. With Christ, we acclaim God as our heavenly Father and offer him our praise and love. We express our desire for the Father's kingdom and for the fulfillment of his will. We acknowledge our dependence on God and his loving, forgiving, faithful care for us. We declare our confident trust that our heavenly Father, the source of our very being, provides all that we need for our human sustenance. We express our solidarity with the human family and note how our personal well-being is inseparably linked to our forgiving and selfless concern for others. How fitting it is that the Lord's Prayer introduces the communion rite of the Mass! It is a kind of "meal prayer." We unite as a community to plead for our true nourishment. We come humbly, recognizing that we can be united with the Lord only when we are truly one with our neighbor.

All our needs and our priorities are included in this perfect prayer. Placing ourselves in the hands of our loving Father, we confidently pray the Our Father together with our brothers and sisters in Christ.

RESPONDING

Having been nourished by God's Word, we are able to respond to God's great love for us. In prayer, respond to God's call to you to share his word with others. You may also wish to respond in your prayer journal.

- How has your image of God the Father been shaped by your experiences?
- In what ways have you experienced God as loving, caring, and forgiving?

Loving God, may I, together with the children, grow in love and trust of you.

T78 UNIT 2 Growing In God's Love

Catechism of the Catholic Church
The themes of this lesson correspond to the following paragraphs: 239–240, 1655, 1931, 2780, 2790, 2794–2796, 2807.

THE FAITH EXPERIENCE

DAY ONE
We Belong to Families

DAY TWO
Family Members Love One Another

DAY THREE
We Belong to God's Family

DAY FOUR
God Is Our Loving Father

Scripture in This Chapter
- *Psalm 103 God treats those who revere him as tenderly as a father treats his children.*
- *Matthew 23:9 Jesus teaches us to pray to God our Father in heaven.*

Church Documents
General Directory for Catechesis #86.
Catechesis prepares the Christian to live in community and to participate in the life of the Church.

The Family and Human Rights #16.
The family is the basic element of human society and the most necessary force in the full development of the human person.

Dogmatic Constitution on the Church #11.
The family is the domestic church in which parents are the first preachers of the faith to their children.

Bulletin Board At the left is a suggestion for a bulletin-board design. Refer to BLM 9 Holy Family if you wish to make a photocopy or transparency. Display the picture of the Holy Family in the center of the board. Add the pictures that the children will draw of their own families on Day One. • *BLM 9 Holy Family*

For a list of children's literature suggestions, please see **page OV-47.**

Families Are Good CHAPTER 7 T79

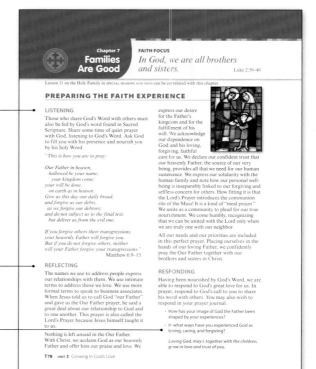

Multiple references to Scripture, the *Catechism*, and other resources provide background reading recommendations

The Faith Experience provides an overview of the week and the themes for each day

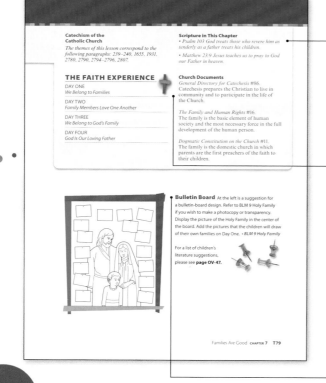

Bulletin-Board ideas and images are suggested for each chapter

Three-Step Teaching Method

A three-step teaching method—**Centering, Sharing, Acting**—provides children with routine and repetition to aid in understanding the content and learning to pray.

Step-by-step directions clearly show the progression of each step in the lesson. These numbered steps guide new and experienced catechists through the lesson.

Learning Outcomes identify clear focus for the lesson

Comments feature gives helpful teaching tips and additional background information

Clear step-by-step numbered directions

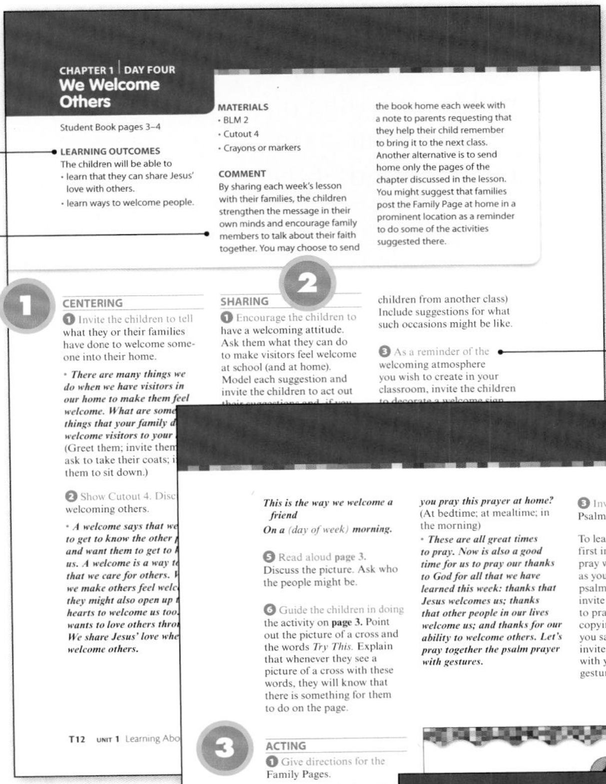
CHAPTER 1 | DAY FOUR
We Welcome Others

Student Book pages 3–4

LEARNING OUTCOMES
The children will be able to
• learn that they can share Jesus' love with others.
• learn ways to welcome people.

MATERIALS
• BLM 2
• Cutout 4
• Crayons or markers

COMMENT
By sharing each week's lesson with their families, the children strengthen the message in their own minds and encourage family members to talk about their faith together. You may choose to send the book home each week with a note to parents requesting that they help their child remember to bring it to the next class. Another alternative is to send home only the pages of the chapter discussed in the lesson. You might suggest that families post the Family Page at home in a prominent location as a reminder to do some of the activities suggested there.

1 CENTERING
1 Invite the children to tell what they or their families have done to welcome someone into their home.
• *There are many things we do when we have visitors in our home to make them feel welcome. What are some things that your family d... welcome visitors to your ...* (Greet them; invite them... ask to take their coats; ... them to sit down.)

2 Show Cutout 4. Disc... welcoming others.
• *A welcome says that we... to get to know the other ... and want them to get to ... us. A welcome is a way t... that we care for others. ... we make others feel welc... they might also open up ... hearts to welcome us too... wants to love others thro... We share Jesus' love whe... welcome others.*

2 SHARING
1 Encourage the children to have a welcoming attitude. Ask them what they can do to make visitors feel welcome at school (and at home). Model each suggestion and invite the children to act out ...
children from another class) Include suggestions for what such occasions might be like.

3 As a reminder of the welcoming atmosphere you wish to create in your classroom, invite the children ...

T12 UNIT 1 Learning Abo...

Checkpoint questions help teachers assess the outcome of the lesson.

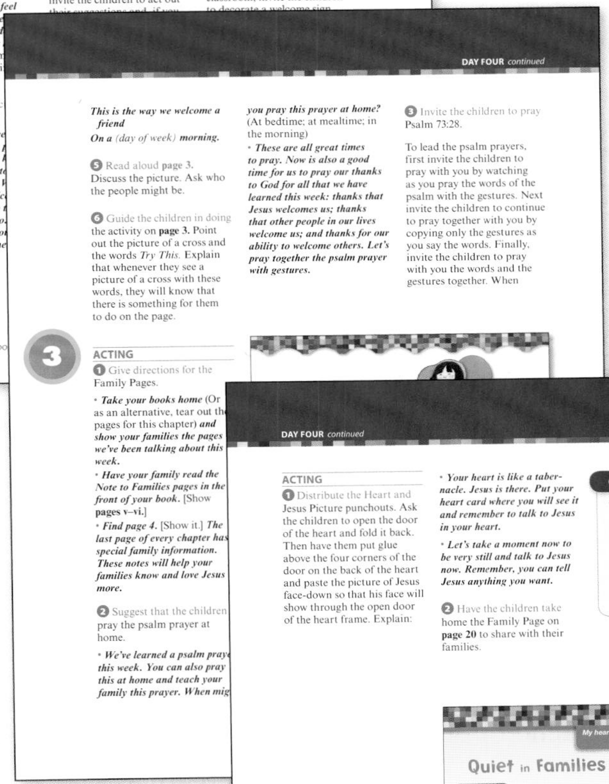
DAY FOUR *continued*

This is the way we welcome a friend
On a (day of week) morning.

5 Read aloud **page 3**. Discuss the picture. Ask who the people might be.

6 Guide the children in doing the activity on **page 3**. Point out the picture of a cross and the words *Try This*. Explain that whenever they see a picture of a cross with these words, they will know that there is something for them to do on the page.

you pray this prayer at home? (At bedtime; at mealtime; in the morning)
• *These are all great times to pray. Now is also a good time for us to pray our thanks to God for all that we have learned this week: thanks that Jesus welcomes us; thanks that other people in our lives welcome us; and thanks for our ability to welcome others. Let's pray together the psalm prayer with gestures.*

3 Invite the children to pray Psalm 73:28.

To lead the psalm prayers, first invite the children to pray with you by watching as you pray the words of the psalm with the gestures. Next invite the children to continue to pray together with you by copying only the gestures as you say the words. Finally, invite the children to pray with you the words and the gestures together. When

3 ACTING
1 Give directions for the Family Pages.
• *Take your books home* (Or as an alternative, tear out th... pages for this chapter) *and show your families the pages we've been talking about this week.*
• *Have your family read the Note to Families pages in the front of your book.* [Show **pages v–vi**.]
• *Find page 4.* [Show it.] *The last page of every chapter has special family information. These notes will help your families know and love Jesus more.*

2 Suggest that the children pray the psalm prayer at home.
• *We've learned a psalm pray... this week. You can also pray this at home and teach your family this prayer. When mig...*

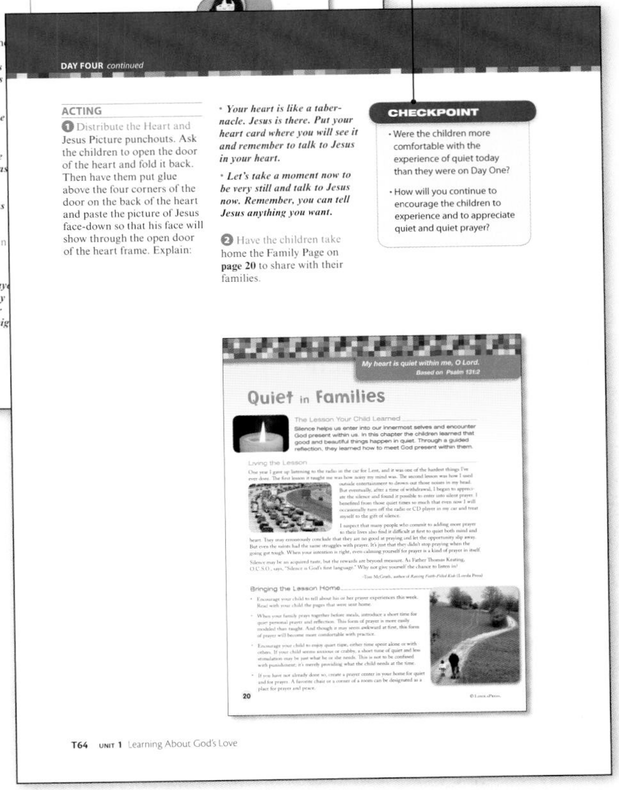
DAY FOUR *continued*

ACTING
1 Distribute the Heart and Jesus Picture punchouts. Ask the children to open the door of the heart and fold it back. Then have them put glue above the four corners of the door on the back of the heart and paste the picture of Jesus face-down so that his face will show through the open door of the heart frame. Explain:

• *Your heart is like a tabernacle. Jesus is there. Put your heart card where you will see it and remember to talk to Jesus in your heart.*
• *Let's take a moment now to be very still and talk to Jesus now. Remember, you can tell Jesus anything you want.*

2 Have the children take home the Family Page on **page 20** to share with their families.

CHECKPOINT
• Were the children more comfortable with the experience of quiet today than they were on Day One?
• How will you continue to encourage the children to experience and to appreciate quiet and quiet prayer?

My heart is quiet within me, O Lord. Based on Psalm 131:2

Quiet in Families

T64 UNIT 1 Learning About God's Love

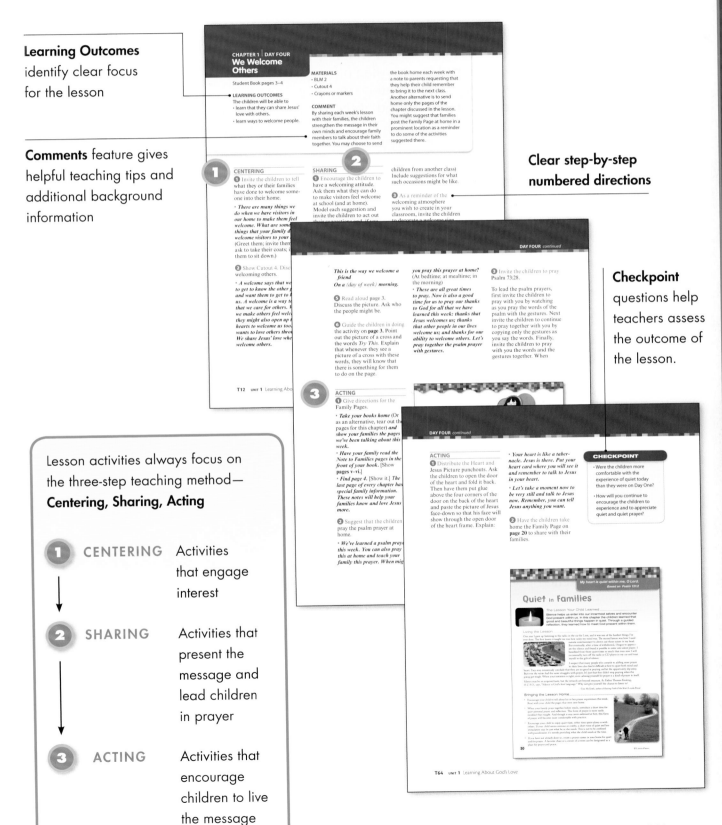

Lesson activities always focus on the three-step teaching method—**Centering, Sharing, Acting**

1 **CENTERING** Activities that engage interest

2 **SHARING** Activities that present the message and lead children in prayer

3 **ACTING** Activities that encourage children to live the message

The Program Structure

The *God Loves Us* program uses a holistic approach to faith formation. A variety of methods and techniques ensure that the Good News is conveyed in ways suited to various learning and teaching styles.

Each chapter is taught in four lessons that are 15–20 minutes long. Lessons for a fifth day can be developed by choosing one or more activities from the ENRICHING THE FAITH EXPERIENCE section at the end of the Day Four lesson.

Because young children need structure and delight in predictability, the weekly lessons have a similar pattern:

- **experiences** leading to a faith message
- **faith message**, usually from the Bible
- **creative activities** to internalize the faith message and relate it to everyday life
- **psalm refrain**—taught with gestures—that responds to the faith message
- age-appropriate variety of **prayer experiences**
- **application** of the faith message to everyday life
- **punchouts** from the back of the book, which the children take home as reminders to live and share the faith message

The format for each chapter is generally the same. The first two lessons introduce the experiences from which the theme is drawn. The third and fourth lessons share the faith message and extend or deepen it through activities. Children are led in prayer at various times throughout the week.

"... young children are active learners who need to learn through a variety of hands-on activities."

"Preschool for All: A First-Class Learning Intitiative."

California Department of Education, January 2005.

Preparing for the Year

1. Use the **Planning Calendar** on **pages OV-16–OV-18** to develop plans based on your school calendar and the year's activities, liturgical seasons, and feasts.
2. In the column on the right, note activities that will influence class time and content, such as dates of the movable **seasons and days of the Church's liturgical year**, holidays, celebrations in honor of Mary, such as a May crowning and holidays.
3. Use the **Table of Contents** and your goals for the year to determine which chapters you will teach. Note these chapters on the Planning Calendar.
4. To meet the needs of your children and **to adapt** to your local circumstances, you might combine or extend some chapters. See Suggestions for Pacing below.
5. Separate the **Cutouts** at the back of this manual and keep them in order in envelopes.
6. Write the **adapted Scripture verses** used in each lesson on note cards and keep them in order in an envelope. When these adapted Scripture verses are read during class, place the appropriate card in the Bible. Reading in this way will reinforce the children's reverence for and understanding of the Bible as God's Word.
7. If you wish, remove the **Punchouts** from the back of the Student Books and plan to distribute them when needed.
8. Print the children's **names in their books** and their copies of *A Child's Bible.*

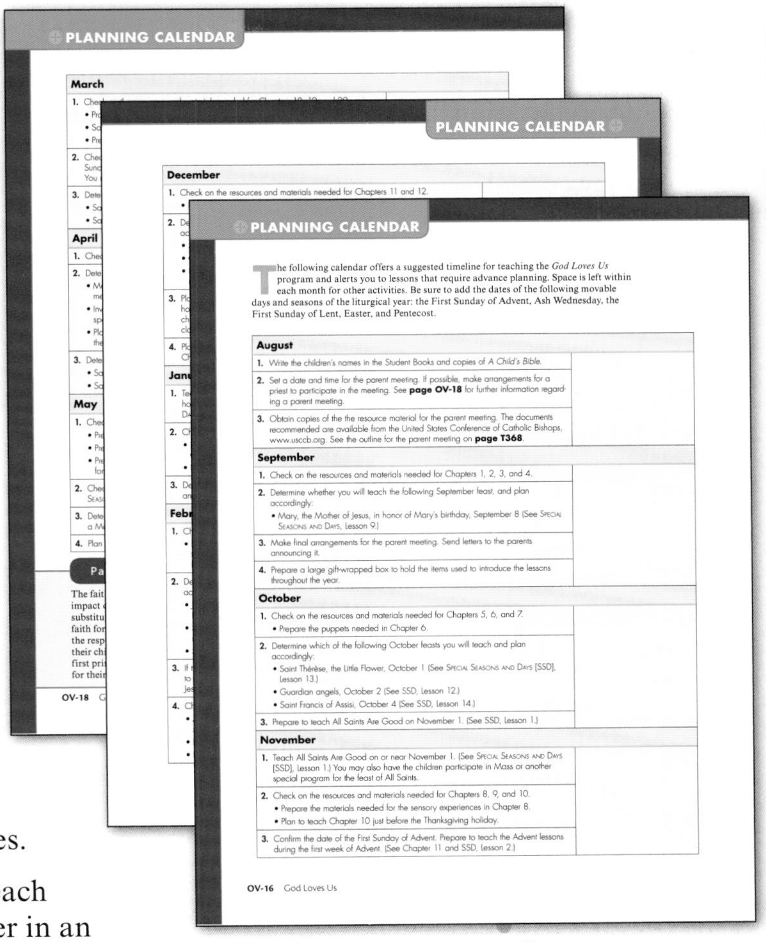

PLANNING CALENDAR

The following calendar offers a suggested timeline for teaching the *God Loves Us* program and alerts you to lessons that require advance planning. Space is left within each month for other activities. Be sure to add the dates of the following movable days and seasons of the liturgical year: the First Sunday of Advent, Ash Wednesday, the First Sunday of Lent, Easter, and Pentecost.

August	
1. Write the children's names in the Student Books and copies of *A Child's Bible.*	
2. Set a date and time for the parent meeting. If possible, make arrangements for a priest to participate in the meeting. See **page OV-18** for further information regarding a parent meeting.	
3. Obtain copies of the the resource material for the parent meeting. The documents recommended are available from the United States Conference of Catholic Bishops, www.usccb.org. See the outline for the parent meeting on **page T368**.	
September	
1. Check on the resources and materials needed for Chapters 1, 2, 3, and 4.	
2. Determine whether you will teach the following September feast, and plan accordingly: • Mary, the Mother of Jesus, in honor of Mary's birthday, September 8 (See Special Seasons and Days, Lesson 9.)	
3. Make final arrangements for the parent meeting. Send letters to the parents announcing it.	
4. Prepare a large gift-wrapped box to hold the items used to introduce the lessons throughout the year.	
October	
1. Check on the resources and materials needed for Chapters 5, 6, and 7. • Prepare the puppets needed in Chapter 6.	
2. Determine which of the following October feasts you will teach and plan accordingly: • Saint Thérèse, the Little Flower, October 1 (See Special Seasons and Days [SSD], Lesson 13.) • Guardian angels, October 2 (See SSD, Lesson 12.) • Saint Francis of Assisi, October 4 (See SSD, Lesson 14.)	
3. Prepare to teach All Saints Are Good on November 1. (See SSD, Lesson 1.)	
November	
1. Teach All Saints Are Good on or near November 1. (See Special Seasons and Days [SSD], Lesson 1.) You may also have the children participate in Mass or another special program for the feast of All Saints.	
2. Check on the resources and materials needed for Chapters 8, 9, and 10. • Prepare the materials needed for the sensory experiences in Chapter 8. • Plan to teach Chapter 10 just before the Thanksgiving holiday.	
3. Confirm the date of the First Sunday of Advent. Prepare to teach the Advent lessons during the first week of Advent. (See Chapter 11 and SSD, Lesson 2.)	

OV-16 God Loves Us

Suggestions for Pacing

Your class may not meet enough times to cover all the chapters in this program. If so, some chapters can be combined so that you can focus on the most important material.

The following chapters are closely related in content and can be combined if necessary:

- 1 & 2
- 5 & 6
- 8 & 9
- 14 & 15
- 20 & 21
- 23 & 25

In addition, there are lessons in Special Seasons and Days that teach the Church's liturgical season and saints' feast days. These are one-day lessons that can be taught on or near the appropriate date. All seven of the Special Seasons lessons should be taught. The Special Days lessons are optional.

Preparing for the Week

For each chapter, your manual presents material for preparation and personal reflection called PREPARING THE FAITH EXPERIENCE. This section is followed by lesson plans.

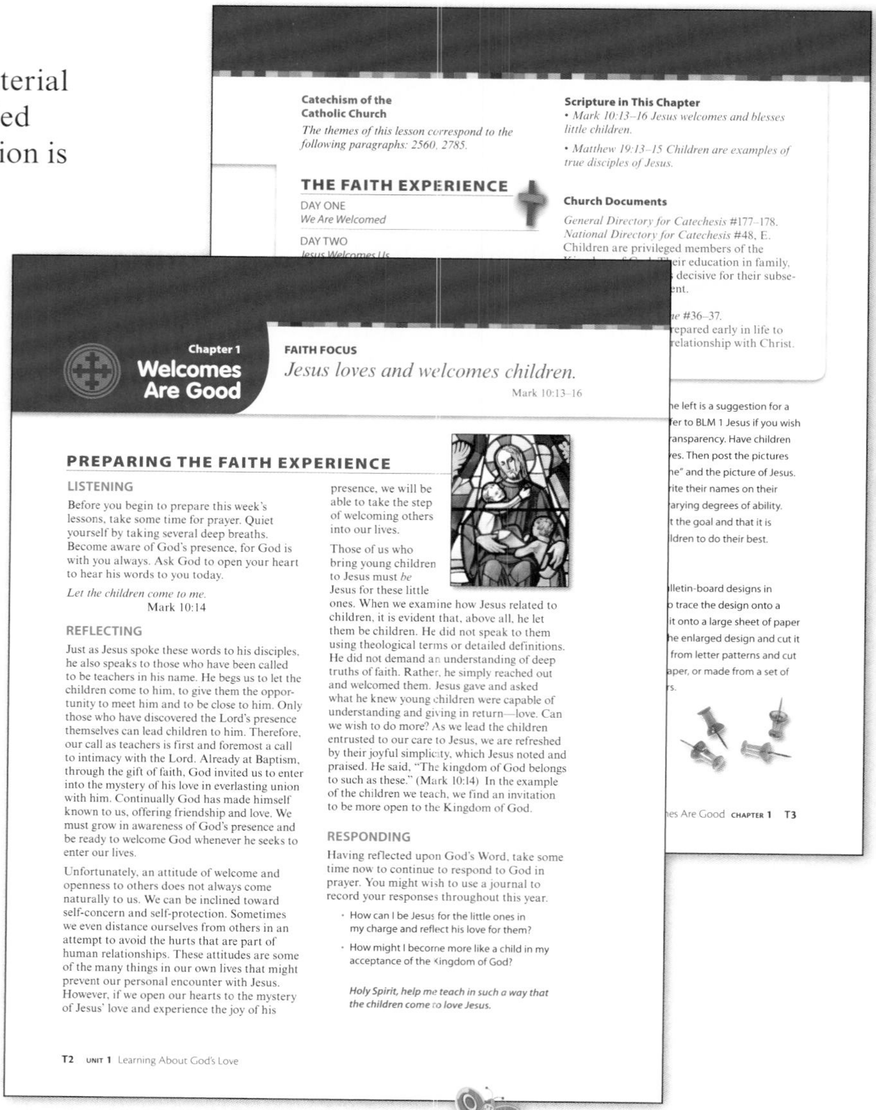

Catechism of the Catholic Church

The themes of this lesson correspond to the following paragraphs: 2560, 2785.

THE FAITH EXPERIENCE

DAY ONE
We Are Welcomed

DAY TWO

Scripture in This Chapter

- *Mark 10:13–16 Jesus welcomes and blesses little children.*
- *Matthew 19:13–15 Children are examples of true disciples of Jesus.*

Church Documents

General Directory for Catechesis #177–178. *National Directory for Catechesis* #48, E. Children are privileged members of the

Chapter 1
Welcomes Are Good

FAITH FOCUS
Jesus loves and welcomes children.
Mark 10:13–16

PREPARING THE FAITH EXPERIENCE

LISTENING

Before you begin to prepare this week's lessons, take some time for prayer. Quiet yourself by taking several deep breaths. Become aware of God's presence, for God is with you always. Ask God to open your heart to hear his words to you today.

Let the children come to me.
Mark 10:14

REFLECTING

Just as Jesus spoke these words to his disciples, he also speaks to those who have been called to be teachers in his name. He begs us to let the children come to him, to give them the opportunity to meet him and to be close to him. Only those who have discovered the Lord's presence themselves can lead children to him. Therefore, our call as teachers is first and foremost a call to intimacy with the Lord. Already at Baptism, through the gift of faith, God invited us to enter into the mystery of his love in everlasting union with him. Continually God has made himself known to us, offering friendship and love. We must grow in awareness of God's presence and be ready to welcome God whenever he seeks to enter our lives.

Unfortunately, an attitude of welcome and openness to others does not always come naturally to us. We can be inclined toward self-concern and self-protection. Sometimes we even distance ourselves from others in an attempt to avoid the hurts that are part of human relationships. These attitudes are some of the many things in our own lives that might prevent our personal encounter with Jesus. However, if we open our hearts to the mystery of Jesus' love and experience the joy of his presence, we will be able to take the step of welcoming others into our lives.

Those of us who bring young children to Jesus must *be* Jesus for these little ones. When we examine how Jesus related to children, it is evident that, above all, he let them be children. He did not speak to them using theological terms or detailed definitions. He did not demand an understanding of deep truths of faith. Rather, he simply reached out and welcomed them. Jesus gave and asked what he knew young children were capable of understanding and giving in return—love. Can we wish to do more? As we lead the children entrusted to our care to Jesus, we are refreshed by their joyful simplicity, which Jesus noted and praised. He said, "The kingdom of God belongs to such as these." (Mark 10:14) In the example of the children we teach, we find an invitation to be more open to the Kingdom of God.

RESPONDING

Having reflected upon God's Word, take some time now to continue to respond to God in prayer. You might wish to use a journal to record your responses throughout this year.

- How can I be Jesus for the little ones in my charge and reflect his love for them?
- How might I become more like a child in my acceptance of the Kingdom of God?

Holy Spirit, help me teach in such a way that the children come to love Jesus.

T2 UNIT 1 Learning About God's Love

T3

Background for the Lesson

1. Prayerfully read the LISTENING and REFLECTING sections.
2. Answer the personal questions found in the RESPONDING section, perhaps writing the answers in a prayer journal. Conclude your preparation in prayer, using your own words or the suggested prayer.
3. Use the suggested Scripture, *Catechism*, and Church documents references for further insights or clarification.
4. Read the LEARNING OUTCOMES for each of the four lessons.
5. Read the chapter in the Student Book.

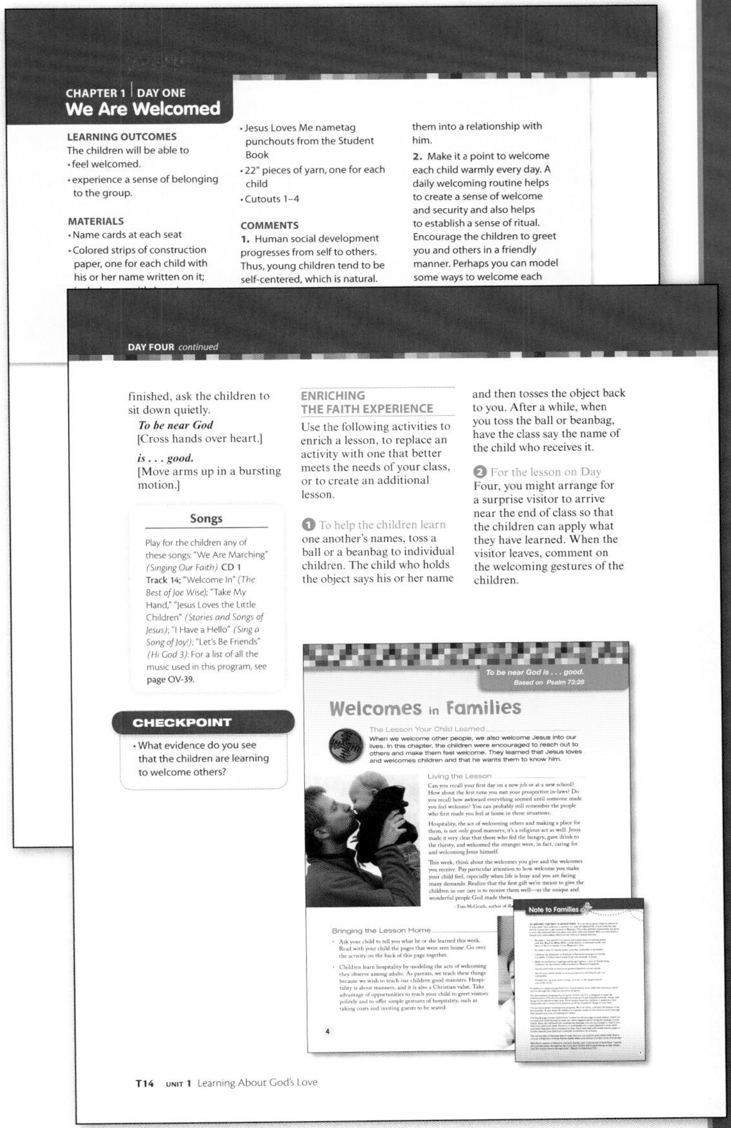
CHAPTER 1 | DAY ONE
We Are Welcomed

LEARNING OUTCOMES
The children will be able to
• feel welcomed.
• experience a sense of belonging to the group.

MATERIALS
• Name cards at each seat
• Colored strips of construction paper, one for each child with his or her name written on it;
• Jesus Loves Me nametag punchouts from the Student Book
• 22" pieces of yarn, one for each child
• Cutouts 1–4

COMMENTS
1. Human social development progresses from self to others. Thus, young children tend to be self-centered, which is natural.

them into a relationship with him.
2. Make it a point to welcome each child warmly every day. A daily welcoming routine helps to create a sense of welcome and security and also helps to establish a sense of ritual. Encourage the children to greet you and others in a friendly manner. Perhaps you can model some ways to welcome each

DAY FOUR *continued*

finished, ask the children to sit down quietly.
To be near God
[Cross hands over heart.]
is . . . good.
[Move arms up in a bursting motion.]

Songs
Play for the children any of these songs: "We Are Marching" (*Singing Our Faith*) CD 1 Track 14; "Welcome In" (*The Best of Joe Wise*); "Take My Hand," "Jesus Loves the Little Children" (*Stories and Songs of Jesus*); "I Have a Hello" (*Sing a Song of Joy!*); "Let's Be Friends" (*Hi God 3*). For a list of all the music used in this program, see page OV-39.

CHECKPOINT
• What evidence do you see that the children are learning to welcome others?

ENRICHING THE FAITH EXPERIENCE
Use the following activities to enrich a lesson, to replace an activity with one that better meets the needs of your class, or to create an additional lesson.

1 To help the children learn one another's names, toss a ball or a beanbag to individual children. The child who holds the object says his or her name and then tosses the object back to you. After a while, when you toss the ball or beanbag, have the class say the name of the child who receives it.

2 For the lesson on Day Four, you might arrange for a surprise visitor to arrive near the end of class so that the children can apply what they have learned. When the visitor leaves, comment on the welcoming gestures of the children.

To be near God is . . . good.
Based on Psalm 73:28

Welcomes in Families

The Lesson Your Child Learned
When we welcome other people, we also welcome Jesus into our lives. In this chapter, the children were encouraged to reach out to others and make them feel welcome. They learned that Jesus loves and welcomes children and that he wants them to know him.

Living the Lesson

Bringing the Lesson Home

Note to Families

T14 UNIT 1 Learning About God's Love

Immediate Preparation

1. Read the LEARNING OUTCOMES and lesson plans, including the COMMENTS, which provide important background information on the content to be taught as well as helpful teaching tips.
2. Read ENRICHING THE FAITH EXPERIENCE at the end of the Day Four lesson. Activities from this section can substitute for activities found in the lesson or can be used to extend the lesson. Decide which options best meet the needs of the children.
3. Annotate your manual. Make notes that will help the flow of the lesson. Use a highlighter to set off sections you plan to use.
4. Familiarize yourself with the scripted teacher-talk in boldface print so that you can present the lesson in your own words as you teach. Avoid reading from the teacher's manual.
5. Gather necessary MATERIALS for the lesson.

After the Lesson

1. Evaluate your lesson using the CHECKPOINT at the end of the lesson plan to assess whether the outcomes of the lesson have been met.
2. Write follow-up comments on the lesson plan in your manual. Record ideas for improvement. Consult helpers, parents, and the children who participated in the class to help determine the activities that worked well and those that could be improved.

Hints

- **Prepare for each class as soon as possible** after the previous class while the lesson is still fresh in your mind. Allow plenty of time to shape the lesson and make its message your own
- **Pray frequently to the Holy Spirit**, your partner and guide in the classroom.
- **Copy the FAITH FOCUS** or another key thought from the lesson and put it on your refrigerator, medicine cabinet, or another place where you will see it often during the week.
- **Write an outline of your plan** on a note card for easy reference.

The following calendar offers a suggested timeline for teaching the *God Loves Us* program and alerts you to lessons that require advance planning. Space is left within each month for other activities. Be sure to add the dates of the following movable days and seasons of the liturgical year: the First Sunday of Advent, Ash Wednesday, the First Sunday of Lent, Easter, and Pentecost.

August	
1. Write the children's names in the Student Books and copies of *A Child's Bible*.	
2. Set a date and time for the parent meeting. If possible, make arrangements for a priest to participate in the meeting. See **page OV-18** for further information regarding a parent meeting.	
3. Obtain copies of the the resource material for the parent meeting. The documents recommended are available from the United States Conference of Catholic Bishops, www.usccb.org. See the outline for the parent meeting on **page T368**.	
September	
1. Check on the resources and materials needed for Chapters 1, 2, 3, and 4.	
2. Determine whether you will teach the following September feast, and plan accordingly: • Mary, the Mother of Jesus, in honor of Mary's birthday, September 8 (See Special Seasons and Days, Lesson 9.)	
3. Make final arrangements for the parent meeting. Send letters to the parents announcing it.	
4. Prepare a large gift-wrapped box to hold the items used to introduce the lessons throughout the year.	
October	
1. Check on the resources and materials needed for Chapters 5, 6, and 7. • Prepare the puppets needed in Chapter 6.	
2. Determine which of the following October feasts you will teach and plan accordingly: • Saint Thérèse, the Little Flower, October 1 (See Special Seasons and Days [SSD], Lesson 13.) • Guardian angels, October 2 (See SSD, Lesson 12.) • Saint Francis of Assisi, October 4 (See SSD, Lesson 14.)	
3. Prepare to teach All Saints Are Good on November 1. (See SSD, Lesson 1.)	
November	
1. Teach All Saints Are Good on or near November 1. (See Special Seasons and Days [SSD], Lesson 1.) You may also have the children participate in Mass or another special program for the feast of All Saints.	
2. Check on the resources and materials needed for Chapters 8, 9, and 10. • Prepare the materials needed for the sensory experiences in Chapter 8. • Plan to teach Chapter 10 just before the Thanksgiving holiday.	
3. Confirm the date of the First Sunday of Advent. Prepare to teach the Advent lessons during the first week of Advent. (See Chapter 11 and SSD, Lesson 2.)	

December

1. Check on the resources and materials needed for Chapters 11 and 12.
   - Prepare the gift-wrapped box and sample manger craft needed in Chapter 11.
2. Determine which of the following December feasts you will teach, and plan accordingly:
   - Saint Nicholas, December 6 (See Special Seasons and Days [SSD], Lesson 16.)
   - Our Lady of Guadalupe, December 12 (See SSD, Lesson 21.)
   - Holy Family, the Sunday between December 25 and January 1, or December 30 (See SSD, Lesson 11.)
3. Plan to teach Christmas Is Good during the final week of school before the Christmas holiday. Make arrangements for the dramatization of the Christmas story if you choose to have the children present their Nativity play for their parents or another class. (See SSD, Lesson 3.)
4. Plan to teach The Wise Men Are Good during the first week of school after the Christmas holiday, on or near January 6, the feast of the Epiphany. (See SSD, Lesson 4.)

January

1. Teach The Wise Men Are Good during the first week of school after the Christmas holiday, on or near January 6, the feast of the Epiphany. (See Special Seasons and Days [SSD], Lesson 4.)
2. Check on the resources and materials needed for Chapters 13, 14, and 15.
   - Prepare the sample sheep craft and Good Shepherd picture needed in Chapter 13.
   - Prepare the sample heart basket needed in Chapter 14.
3. Determine whether you will teach the feast of Saint Elizabeth Ann Seton, January 4, and plan accordingly. (See SSD, Lesson 15.)

February

1. Check on the resources and materials needed for Chapters 16 and 17.
   - Prepare the sample of the church-triptych craft and make arrangements for the visit to church in Chapter 17. You might choose to arrange for a priest or the parish liturgist to lead the tour of the church during your visit.
2. Determine which of the following February feasts you will teach, and plan accordingly:
   - Jesus Our Light Is Good, February 2 (See Special Seasons and Days [SSD], Lesson 8.)
   - Saint Bernadette (Our Lady of Lourdes), February 11 (See SSD, Lesson 17; you may also choose to teach this lesson in April.)
   - Saint Valentine, February 14 (See SSD, Lesson 18.)
3. If the blessing of the throats is planned on the feast of Saint Blase, February 3, plan to teach the activity about this found in the Enriching the Faith Experience section of Jesus Our Light Is Good. (See SSD, Lesson 8.)
4. Check the date of Ash Wednesday and the First Sunday of Lent.
   - Activities for Ash Wednesday are included in the Enriching the Faith Experience section of Chapter 19.
   - Prepare to teach Lent Is Good during the first week of Lent. (See SSD, Lesson 5.)
   - Plan to teach Chapter 19 during Lent.

March	
1. Check on the resources and materials needed for Chapters 18, 19, and 20. • Practice telling the story of the Last Supper for Chapter 18. • Soak lima beans overnight for Chapter 19. Plan to teach Chapter 19 during Lent. • Prepare the sample Good News banner and butterfly craft needed in Chapter 20.	
2. Check the date of Easter. Prepare to teach the Easter lesson as close to Easter Sunday as your schedule allows. (See SPECIAL SEASONS AND DAYS [SSD], Lesson 6.) You may also wish to teach Chapter 20 close to Easter Sunday.	
3. Determine which of the following March feasts you will teach, and plan accordingly: • Saint Patrick, March 17 (See SSD, Lesson 19.) • Saint Joseph, March 19 (See SSD, Lesson 10.)	
April	
1. Check on the resources and materials needed for Chapters 21 and 22.	
2. Determine which of the following activities you will include in Chapter 22: • Make arrangements with a priest or deacon to show and explain the Mass vestments and sacred vessels to the children. • Invite a priest, a deacon, and lay persons involved in the liturgy to explain their special roles in the celebration of Mass. • Plan with a priest for the children's celebration of the Mass. Send him a copy of the plan a week before the date of the celebration.	
3. Determine which of the following April feasts you will teach, and plan accordingly: • Saint Julie Billiart, April 8 (See SPECIAL SEASONS AND DAYS [SSD], Lesson 20.) • Saint Bernadette, April 16 (See SSD, Lesson 17.)	
May	
1. Check on the resources and materials needed for Chapters 23, 24, and 25. • Prepare the sample pinwheel craft for Chapter 23. • Prepare the sample New Year cracker for Chapter 24. • Prepare two boxes, one attractive and one plain, and the sample blessings banner for Chapter 25.	
2. Check the date of Pentecost and teach Pentecost Is Good near this day. (See SPECIAL SEASONS AND DAYS [SSD], Lesson 7.)	
3. Determine if you will teach Our Mother in Heaven Is Good. (See SSD, Lesson 22.) If a May crowning of Mary is planned, prepare the children for this celebration.	
4. Plan a special treat after the closing celebration of the year.	

Parent-Catechist Meeting

The faith of parents makes such a profound impact on children that there is no adequate substitute for the parents' role in their children's faith formation. Parents have the privilege and the responsibility to nurture the life of faith their child received at Baptism. They are the first primary teachers in the ways of the faith for their children.

The *God Loves Us* program encourages parents to share their own faith with their child.

It is recommended that a parent meeting be held early in the school year to support parents as they guide their children in living the Catholic faith. See the guidelines for a parent meeting and a sample meeting outline beginning on **page T368**.

Sharing the Good News

Effective catechists are people who live their faith and share the Good News of Jesus with others, inviting them to develop and deepen their relationship with Christ. Catechists attend to their own faith and spiritual growth. In addition, catechists seek to increase their knowledge and skills in a variety of areas.

Effective catechists are

- sensitive to the developmental characteristics of those they will teach.
- aware of the process of faith and spiritual growth.
- knowledgeable about the role of the catechist in faith formation.
- grounded in the Church's faith tradition, including the *Catechism of the Catholic Church.*
- familiar with a variety of effective teaching methods, tools, and techniques.

This Catechist's Handbook provides essential information to help catechists craft their lessons with confidence and skill.

God made and loves me.

Kindergartners

• *are active* • *need affirmation* • *are literal-minded* • *develop their own identities*

Physical Characteristics

- are very active in play; can hop, skip, and run with more poise
- can cut and draw, copy patterns, and print some letters (usually with hand preference)
- are increasingly competent in caring for themselves: dressing, washing, picking up objects, taking care of belongings
- can follow musical contrasts: loud and soft, high and low
- love to play; can sit still for about 10 minutes

Socioemotional Characteristics

- need individual attention and affirmation; are shy in approaching others
- are self-sufficient and self-motivated; do not see effects of their actions on others
- are friendly; like to talk and tell stories; seek affection from adults and other children
- may become stubborn, blame others for their own wrongdoing, or use name-calling when angry
- need protective environment to choose friends and develop social relationships

Intellectual Characteristics

- learn well through experience and activity; enjoy dramatic storytelling
- have attention span of about 10 minutes; can listen and follow directions; can work energetically for short periods
- can express thoughts through drawing; enjoy coloring, cutting, and pasting
- are literal-minded
- focus on detail or on one aspect of a situation
- like stories and activities with exchange of ideas among children

Religious Characteristics

- Have growing sense of identity and self-worth
- need assurance of God's love through adult concern and care
- can understand that God desires their response of love for him and others
- need to associate God and religion with positive, happy experiences and to learn faith concepts in a warm, secure environment
- can express simple prayers

Faith

God Loves Us gradually introduces the children to the simple truths of faith in the Apostles' Creed at their level of experience and understanding. The program recognizes that young children possess the gift of faith implanted in them at Baptism and, therefore, have a readiness to learn about things of God. It engages them in experiences that prepare them for his message and help them respond to it in their lives. Kindergartners already possess a wealth of human experiences. The *God Loves Us* program helps them see the religious dimension of what they experience every day—to see life and religion as an integrated whole. It also invites them to experience the rich variety of Catholic traditions.

Prayer

The ultimate purpose of catechesis is to enable the children to sense God's presence, to encounter him, and to enter into communion with him. In the *God Loves Us* program, the children take part in a variety of prayer experiences to help them respond to God in ways appropriate to their stage of spiritual development. Some of these are simple vocal prayers, spontaneous prayers, dance prayers, psalm responses with gestures, prayers of the heart, and celebrations. The children are introduced in a meaningful way to a few prayer formulas that are part of our Catholic heritage and the worship of the Church. They learn to appreciate silence and to become attentive to God.

Liturgical Life

The *God Loves Us* program invites the children to participate more fully in liturgy by practicing the following everyday activities

- exchanging greetings
- using symbols, gestures, and rituals
- listening and responding to others
- asking and receiving forgiveness
- expressing gratitude
- using silence to enter within themselves
- participating actively in celebration
- sharing food with others

The program provides experiences that introduce the children to the liturgy. These include

- listening to Scripture verses and learning psalm refrains used in Sunday responsorial psalms
- taking part in simple intercessory prayer
- participating in processions
- being encouraged to participate more fully at Sunday Eucharist
- experiencing a sense of mystery and of the sacred
- learning reverent church behavior
- being introduced to the seasons of the liturgical year, the feasts of Mary, the saints, and other special feasts

The children also become acquainted with a number of sacramentals during the year.

Morality

The years of early childhood are crucial for building attitudes and dispositions upon which a good Christian moral life can develop. The foundation for good decision making is also laid in the early years. The *God Loves Us* program fosters the awakening of a Christian conscience in the children by leading them to

- appreciate God's goodness and personal love for them
- sense that they are loved by important people in their lives
- realize that there are good and bad choices
- learn to think before choosing
- know that they are responsible for their decisions
- understand that choosing what God wants is good and brings them happiness
- be aware that evil exists in our world
- realize that it is not always easy to do what is right
- know how to express penitence
- respect all people and all forms of life
- value God's world and care for it
- develop self-discipline and form good habits
- sense solidarity with people everywhere
- desire to share with those in need

Social Justice and Service

Catechists must assume the responsibility for raising the children's awareness of the needs and feelings of the people in their families, their community, and the world. In *God Loves Us,* the children engage in activities that nurture kindness, honesty, forgiveness, and concern for others, especially for older persons, people with special needs, people who are poor, and people who are lonely. Some of these activities are

- discussing and role-playing how kindness, honesty, forgiveness, and concern for others can be shown in their everyday lives
- sharing with one another their experiences of meeting the needs of other people
- listening to stories of saints who have shown concern for others
- engaging in music and art activities that promote a spirit of sharing and caring for others

The effectiveness of religious instruction is closely tied to the personal witness given by the teacher; this witness is what brings the content of the lessons to life. . . . A teacher who has a clear vision of the Christian milieu and lives in accord with it will be able to help young people develop a similar vision, and will give them the inspiration they need to put it into practice.

Congregation for Catholic Education,
The Religious Dimension of Education in a Catholic School, 96 (April 7, 1988)

Spiritual and Professional Growth as a Catechist

The National Directory for Catechesis names six tasks in catechesis:

- To promote knowledge of the faith.
- To promote knowledge of the meaning of the Liturgy and the sacraments.
- To promote moral formation in Christ.
- To teach the Christian how to pray with Christ.
- To prepare the Christian to live in community and to participate actively in the life and mission of the Church.
- To promote a missionary spirit that prepares the faithful to be present as Christians in society. (*NDC*, 20)

In accomplishing this sixfold task, catechists are aided by the Holy Spirit. However, to reflect effectively the teaching and the life of Jesus in their words and behavior, catechists need to grow continually in their faith. They should

- know and study further the teaching of the Church's Magisterium through lectures, courses, and Catholic publications
- become imbued with the thought and spirit of the Bible through prayerful reflection
- have a profound spirit of prayer and a deep sacramental life, for only union with Christ gives the light and strength needed for authentic catechesis
- give service to others and encourage the children to serve
- become more aware of the missionary nature of the Church and educate the children in global problems and needs
- become better trained for the task of catechizing by always seeking better methods

Ways to Build a Faith Community as a Catechist

- Communicate with parents, and value their primary role in their children's faith formation.
- Share goals, values, projects, and ideas with fellow catechists and parish leaders.
- Be familiar with guidelines for parish and diocesan catechetical programs.
- Cooperate with others in making the parish a focal point of the community, especially in grade-level planning and projects.
- Participate in meetings and prayer services for catechists.
- Seek out opportunities for spiritual enrichment.
- Accept the strengths and weaknesses of the faith community and strive together to witness the Gospel.

A Catechist Is

confident, but dependent on God

knowledgeable, but open to children's ideas

efficient, but relaxed

spiritual, but practical

professional, but caring

enthusiastic, but calm

Professional Ethics for Catechists

- Keep comments about the children and their families on a professional level.
- Use information about the children and their families prudently and discreetly. Observe professional confidentiality.
- Hold conferences with or about the children at appropriate times and places.
- Inform the coordinator, a priest, or other appropriate persons when you discern unusual needs or problems of the children.
- Strive to make your daily living reflect your faith.
- Prepare thoroughly for each lesson.

A Guide for Self-Improvement

As a catechist, you are a minister of the Word of God. Every child hopes to see and hear the kindness, the warmth, and the love of Jesus reflected in your facial expressions, your voice, and your very life. If you are receptive to God each day, if you take time to ponder his Word and deepen your relationship with God, if you are convinced of the power of the gospel message, then the children in your class will hear the Lord reveal the mystery of his love through you. You will discover that as you share your faith, you are personally enriched. Reflect on the following questions periodically to examine your effectiveness as a catechist and to determine areas for improvement.

- Do I present the message with the conviction, joy, love, enthusiasm, and hope that come from a commitment to Christ?
- Do I pray for light to understand what I am teaching and to know how to present God's Word persuasively?
- Do I reflect on Scripture as part of my preparation for each lesson?
- Do I have all materials ready before class?
- Do I share my heart, my spirit, and my personal faith story as I convey the Christian message?
- Do I lead the children in prayer during class? Do I use a variety of prayer forms?
- How sensitive am I to the individual needs of the children?
- Have I communicated with the parents?
- Do I make an evaluation after each lesson and use it in future planning?
- Am I willing to spend time to promote my own growth in faith and understanding?

Catechists are to identify and create "suitable conditions which are necessary for the Christian message to be sought, accepted, and more profoundly investigated" for each of the various groups they serve.

(National Directory for Catechesis, 54.B.8)

Prepare the Learning Space

- Arrange an attractive prayer corner with a Bible, flowers, a candle, and other religious symbols. (Remember to check with the proper authority regarding local regulations for using candles in a classroom setting.)
- Post pictures related to the message of the day.
- Have recorded music playing as the children enter or as you begin the lesson.
- Display all the children's drawings or projects.
- Arrange seats so that each child feels comfortable.
- Note whether light, heat, and ventilation are adequate.

Establish a Climate for Growth

- Address the children by name. Be sure to pronounce and spell their names correctly.
- Be calm in your manner, reverent in your gestures, and joyful in your presentation.
- Question the children about their families, hobbies, sports, and interests.
- Listen to what the children are saying verbally and nonverbally. Be eager to understand their fears, worries, plans, stories—even their complaints.
- Speak in a well-modulated voice, loud enough for everyone to hear, but soft enough to convey the wonder of the message you share.
- Write short positive notes of encouragement on their papers like "Sounds good," "I agree," and "I'd like to hear more about your idea," or just "Yes."
- See the children as individuals. Try not to generalize, but see each child as gifted by God. Make allowances for individual circumstances.
- Use frequent eye contact so each child feels you are speaking personally to him or her.
- Be sensitive to the children's responses during a presentation.
- Ask to keep the children's work. This is the greatest compliment you can pay a child.
- Ask for the children's help. Everyone likes to be needed.
- Love your work. Teaching is hard work, but it is also a privilege. Show the children you like teaching because you like them. More importantly, love your work as a person who shares the work of Jesus the Teacher.

Maintain a Healthy Classroom Discipline

- Aim for "comfortable order."
- Establish procedures and policies on the first day so that the children know exactly what behavior is expected.
- Have only a few rules, but enforce them.
- In order to prevent discipline problems, rely on thorough preparation for lessons, not on spontaneous inspiration.
- Speak and act with confidence.
- Have the children keep their books closed and materials away until they need them.
- Phrase directions and corrections positively. For example, instead of saying, "Don't mark up your book," say, "Keep your book clean and neat."
- Have all class materials and audiovisuals ready for use before class.
- Vary activities to hold the children's attention and to meet different learning styles.
- Involve the children in the lesson. Don't do for them what they can do for themselves.
- Be observant while you are teaching.
- Expect good behavior. Don't tolerate misbehavior.
- When a problem arises, use a pleasant but firm tone of voice. Keep calm and avoid becoming angry. This will help you win over rather than antagonize the child.
- Help the children want to do what they ought to do. Motivate them. Offer incentives and rewards.
- Avoid letting one child prevent others from learning and cooperating. Speak with him or her after class.
- Enlist the aid of parents and other people.
- Be consistent in your reactions.
- Pray for the children daily.

The *Catechism of the Catholic Church* is a marvelous tool for catechists. It provides information that can be useful in preparing lesson plans, and it also serves as a reference book. Each chapter in *God Loves Us* includes references to paragraphs in the *Catechism* that are related to it.

Catechists are cautioned, however, that the *Catechism* is not intended to be used as a student textbook.

In addition to being a source of background material, the *Catechism* contains messages specifically for catechists. Paragraphs 426 through 429 are the centerpiece of what it says to us. They contain our mission statement, our goal, and our job description. The boldface title for this passage says it all—"At the heart of catechesis: Christ." Paragraph 426 states, "'At the heart of catechesis we find, in essence, a Person, the Person of Jesus of Nazareth, the only Son from the Father . . . who suffered and died for us and who now, after rising, is living with us forever.' To catechize is to reveal in the Person of Christ the whole of God's eternal design reaching fulfillment in that Person. It is to seek to understand the meaning of Christ's actions and words and of the signs worked by him.'" Only Christ "'can lead us to the love of the Father in the Spirit and make us share in the life of the Holy Trinity.'"

Our call is to bring people to the person of Jesus Christ, who lives and who is with us and who loves us. Religion class is a community of people who are journeying together, sharing faith in Jesus Christ, and growing in it. Religion class is a matter of formation—changing lives to be more Christlike. The room where it is held is sacred space, as holy as the catacombs where the first Christians gathered to deepen their relationship with Christ and their commitment to him.

We can't give what we don't have. It was only after Paul encountered the risen Lord for himself that he was enflamed with a passion for teaching the world about him. The more we ourselves come to know Jesus Christ, the more zealous and convincing we will be in persuading others to live for him. The more we enter into the mystery of Christ's death and Resurrection in our daily lives, the more we will be able to persuade others to live like him.

We can take heart that when we teach in the name of Jesus, he teaches through us, because we have been mandated and commissioned by him. Through his Spirit he is our invisible partner.

Seven essential messages from the *Catechism* are listed here, along with with their paragraph numbers for reading and reflection:

131–133 **Teach Scripture.**
By reading it we learn "'the surpassing knowledge of Jesus Christ.'"

282 **Teach Creation.**
It is of major importance because it concerns the very foundations of human and Christian life.

426–429 **Teach Christ.**
Put people in communion with him.

1072 **Teach Liturgy.**
In the sacraments, especially in the Eucharist, Christ Jesus works in fullness for our transformation.

1697 **Teach the Way of Christ.**
Reveal the joy and the demands of the way of Christ.

1917 **Teach Hope.**
"[T]he future of humanity is in the hands of those who are capable of providing the generations to come with reasons for life and optimism."

2663 **Teach Prayer.**
Explain its meaning, always in relation to Jesus Christ.

Art

Throughout history, faith has been expressed in painting and sculpture. Art is a concrete expression of a person's thoughts and feelings. When children see their inner religious thoughts and feelings expressed visually, they can grow spiritually. Art helps them become more aware of religious concepts and relates the messages they have heard to their own lives.

- Give clear directions. Provide a sample.
- Create a quiet, reflective atmosphere by playing appropriate background music as the children work. Encourage them to think about what they have just experienced or learned.
- Give the children who wish to do so an opportunity to talk about their work.
- Display the work at the children's eye level so that it can be appreciated.
- Be aware that coloring books and patterns do not stimulate creativity.

Audiovisuals

Audiovisuals (movies, videotapes, DVDs, slides, audio CDs, and audiotapes) can lead the children to a deeper appreciation of the message in each chapter.

- Preview the entire audiovisual and read the guide that comes with it. Determine whether it is appropriate for your lesson and your class. Decide how you will use it—to introduce a subject or to review it.
- Prepare to introduce audiovisual presentations. Give adequate background information to the children. Tell them what to look for, focusing attention on the main purpose for listening or viewing.
- Plan discussion questions and/or activities to follow the presentation.
- Introduce new vocabulary and concepts before showing the audiovisual.
- After the presentation, provide time for quiet reflection and/or written response.

Bulletin Boards

An effective bulletin-board display is simple, timely, and catches people's attention. Its unity, with emphasis on the more important elements, and its balanced arrangement, with movement (or flow), make it educational as well as attractive. It is an easily understood teaching aid.

- Think of a caption that draws attention, such as a question, a three-dimensional device, current idiom, "big," or stylized words.
- Create an overall effect to hold interest.
- Plan the movement of the board. Displays are usually viewed left to right, top to bottom. Figures of people and animals draw attention. Repeat shapes, textures, and colors—or related variations—for unity.
- Achieve balance, which can be symmetrical or asymmetrical. For informal balance, use two or more small shapes with a larger one, a small colorful shape with a larger dull one, a small shape near the bottom with a larger shape near the top, a small eye-catching shape with a larger common shape.
- Make objects touch one another, or connect them with yarn, paper, or colored lines. An odd number of items is better than an even number.
- Use wallpaper, wrapping paper, construction paper, shelf paper, velour, felt, or burlap as a background for letters and pictures.
- Arrange the children's papers so that they can be easily seen; never place one on top of another.

Celebrations

Celebrations can be powerful learning experiences. Song, prayer, Scripture, ritual, and symbol draw the children more deeply into the message of the lesson. Through the communal prayers and private reflections in the celebrations, the children are imbued with the mystery of faith celebrated. They also come to appreciate liturgical elements. The impressions that celebrations make on the children justify the time, preparation, and practice they entail.

- Create an atmosphere of beauty, peace, and prayer through the use of candles, flowers or plants, cloth, religious art, music, and symbols. (Remember to check with the proper authority regarding local regulations for using candles in a classroom setting.)
- Make sure all the children know what to do and say.
- Practice the songs used.
- Encourage the children to make the celebration a prayer. Suggest that they offer it for an intention.

Children's Literature

Books are one of the most effective tools for shaping attitudes and imparting values. They help children discover meaning in life. Through stories the children come to understand themselves and others, and they learn to relate to others and to their world in a better way. Good literature confronts readers with basic human problems and helps them deal with them. It reinforces the Christian message presented in class and helps children apply Christian principles to their lives. Jesus was conscious of the power of stories and used them in his teaching. Encourage the children to read supplementary books such as those recommended for each chapter in the Literature List on **page OV-47.**

- Describe a book in class.
- Incorporate an incident from a book into a lesson.
- Hold a copy of the book in your hand when you talk about it.

Dramatization

Dramatization effectively reinforces the Christian message and helps children internalize it. The *God Loves Us* program contains plays and role-playing situations that enable children to apply religious truths to daily life.

- Maintain an atmosphere of security and seriousness needed to give the children self-confidence. Use role-playing only when the children are comfortable with one another.
- Ignore giggles and awkwardness.
- Allow the children to choose their roles. Have them take turns.
- Use simple props and costumes.
- Prepare the performers sufficiently.
- Put signs on the participants for identification, if necessary. Children like to wear sandwich boards to identify who they are.
- Accept the children's interpretations and praise their efforts. However, if their interpretations lack insight, guide them to understand the feelings of the people in the situations.
- Discuss the activity with the children in the light of Christian values.

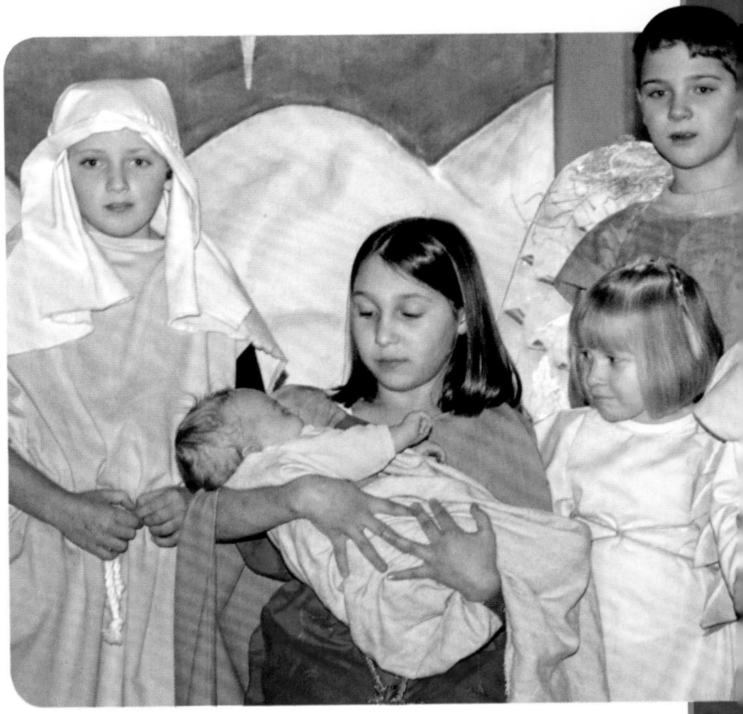

Flannel Board

Flannel-board figures add another dimension to storytelling. Sets of flannel figures can be purchased, or you can make your own. Glue small pieces of flannel or velour paper to the back of paper figures, or use flannel to make the figures.

- Arrange the figures in order of use.
- Practice telling your story until you feel at ease with the story and the movement of the figures.
- Use the figures for review. For instance, distribute them to the children and have them tell the story, or have them give a clue about their figure and ask the class to guess which one they have.

Group Projects

As the children work together to reach a common goal, qualities needed in community are fostered: consideration, understanding, cooperation, patience, initiative, and responsibility. Small-group activities afford the children an experience of interdependence and provide a welcome change from the classroom routine.

- Explain the directions clearly and write them on the board.
- Show interest in the groups' work by encouraging them, offering suggestions, and asking questions.
- Make sure that all the children are participating.

Games

Playing games not only is fun for children but also contributes to their development in many ways. Games provide children with practice in mental, physical, and social skills; offer opportunities for problem solving and creativity; stimulate imagination; and increase attention spans.

- Explain the game clearly and simply. Establish ground rules.
- Have several groups play a game to allow the children to have more turns.
- Replay the children's favorite games.

Memorization

Knowledge of certain elements of Catholic belief is best acquired by memorizing them. Pope John Paul II pointed out that "the blossoms . . . of faith and piety do not grow in the desert places of a memoryless catechesis. What is essential is that the texts that are memorized must at the same time be taken in and gradually understood in depth, in order to become a source of Christian life on the personal level and the community level." (*On Catechesis in Our Time,* 55)

- The children should understand the material they are memorizing.
- Acknowledge the children's success by charting their progress.
- Integrate memorized material into the lesson in a meaningful way.
- Lead the way by memorizing the material first.

Music

Music can set the mood for the lesson and predispose the children to receive God's message. Besides introducing the lesson, music can be used to review and reinforce the message. It can serve as a prayer before or after class. Music unites the group, provides an enjoyable opportunity for self-expression, and stirs up feelings of love and loyalty to Christ and his Church. Both singing and listening to music have the power to open hearts to the Lord.

- As you teach a song, consider the following steps:
  1. Give a general introduction and ask the children to listen to the song.
  2. Have them listen again for specific ideas. Discuss difficult lyrics.
  3. Have them sing the song softly or hum along as you sing or play it.
- Ask the children to sing with enthusiasm and make the song a prayer. Suggest that they think about the meaning of the song and sing with all their hearts.
- Invite the children to add gestures or interpretive dance steps.
- If you lack musical talent, find ways to compensate. For example, use recorded music provided for the program or invite assistance from other members of the community.
- Encourage the children to sing spontaneous original songs and create your own.

Overhead Projectors

The overhead projector can be used creatively.

- Tell or have the children tell stories with cutout shapes. When placed on the glass top of the projector, the cutouts cast shadows on the screen.
- Project a transparency with questions or a puzzle onto the board or a large sheet of paper. Have the children write the answers on the board or on paper, and the transparency can be used again.
- Make an outline of the lesson on a transparency and reveal it part by part during class.
- Let the children write answers on a transparency of review activities.
- Use the overhead to enlarge maps or pictures. Trace or photocopy the image onto a transparency and post a large sheet of paper onto the wall. Project the image in its desired size onto the paper and trace it.
- Experiment with different effects: add oil or food coloring to water in a glass baking dish; rotate a cut glass or plastic bowl above the glass top of the projector.

Pictures and Visuals

The icons of the Eastern Churches are treasured because of their power to sweep us up to God. Stained-glass windows have been a medium of religious instruction for centuries. Similarly, pictures such as art masterpieces and the photos and illustrations in the Student Book can influence the children's response to the catechesis. They can stimulate learning, awaken an appreciation of the message, and lead to prayer.

- Use visuals to arouse interest, to raise questions, and to clarify concepts.
- Choose visuals that are artistically good, convey an accurate religious message, and are large enough to be seen by all.
- Use questions or comments to lead the children to share insights. Ask them how the picture makes them feel and how it relates to the lesson. Have them create a story based on the picture or role-play the situation depicted.

Prayer

Prayer opens children's hearts to God's message. It gives them the time and space they need to reflect on God's words and the meaning the words have for their lives. Most important, it provides an avenue for God to touch the children and to change them by his love.

- Be a person of prayer yourself, and share your own prayer life with the children as appropriate.
- Respect each child's needs. Some will feel comfortable praying aloud and spontaneously. Others will prefer to pray silently. Show respect and appreciation for the various types of prayer.
- Prepare the children for prayer. Provide time for them to settle down and focus on God. Teach them to adopt a posture that is conducive to prayer.
- Give the children opportunities to lead the class in prayer.
- Create an attractive Prayer Center. Place there a Bible, a crucifix, a banner, a candle, religious statues, or pictures related to the feast, season, or topic of study.

Regularly gather the group in the Prayer Center for prayer experiences. Encourage the children to use the area for personal prayer. Suggest that they have their families arrange similar Prayer Centers at home.

Puppets

Puppets are a valuable teaching aid, especially for young or shy children. Since puppets are merely toys, they should not pray or speak the religious message. The faith message should be grounded in reality.

Puppets can be made in the following ways.

- Lunch bags—Draw, paint, or glue on features. The bags may be stuffed and tied or left open so that a hand can be inserted.
- Paper—Mount paper cutouts on pencils, rulers, craft sticks, kitchen utensils (like spoons and spatulas), or even brooms. Paper plates make good puppet faces.
- Socks and mittens—Fabric scraps and other decorations can be sewed or glued to them to make faces and clothing.
- Finger puppets—These can be cut from paper and taped together to fit a finger, or they can be made from old gloves.
- Puppets with arms—Use a paper cup or a card-board tube, cutting holes on the sides for a thumb or finger.
- Wooden clothespins—Decorate them with felt-tipped pens, yarn, and fabric.

Questions

Posing questions is a time-honored technique for leading children to the truth. Both Socrates and Jesus relied heavily on questions when they taught. Asking questions keeps the children's attention.

- Address questions to the entire class before calling on a child to answer.
- Be comfortable with the silence as the children reflect on the question.
- Call on every child in the class, not just the same ones over and over again. To encourage children to give more thoughtful responses, avoid calling on the first child who raises his or her hand.
- Vary the types of questions you ask, from simple recall questions to those that require some explanation.

Storytelling

Through Bible stories and stories from the lives of Christians past and present, we share the heritage of our faith. Storytelling can also be used to share one's personal faith. Sharing one's faith journey gives witness to the faith. Both forms of storytelling deepen the children's understanding of Jesus and their relationship with him.

- Make a story your own by adapting it to the children and to your message.
- Practice telling the story using facial expressions, animated gestures, and expression in your voice for effect and emphasis.
- Use visuals to enhance the telling: pictures, pup-pets, chalkboard, flannel board, etc.
- Relate personally to each child during the telling of the story. Establish eye contact with individuals and be sensitive to how each is responding to the story.
- Let the story speak for itself. Its message may be less effective if you moralize.

Art

Banners

Book jackets

Booklets (bound with yarn or staples, accordion-type)

Bookmarks

Boxes (joy, glory, acts of mercy, for art projects, for collections)

Bulletin boards

Bumper stickers

Buttons

Cartoons

CD covers

Children's storybooks

Christmas tree

Coats of arms

Collages (magazine pictures or odds and ends)

Comic books

Commemorative stamps

Dioramas in boxes

Displays

Doorknob hangers

Dot pictures

Finger paintings

Fingerprint pictures from ink pads (details with felt-tipped pens)

Flyers

Friezes

Greeting cards

Holy cards

Jesse tree

Mobiles

Models from clay or dough

Mosaics (construction paper, colored magazine pages, paper-punch holes, Easter-egg shells, seeds)

Movies

Murals

Paper dolls

Paperweights from rocks

Pennants

Photo albums with illustrations and captions

Photo essays (magazine pictures or photos)

Place mats

Plaques (coated with shellac)

Portraits

Posters

Puppets (sock, balloon, clothespin, mitten, paper bag, paper plate, paper pasted on a pencil, finger)

Sculpture (wire, paper, aluminum foil, clay, papier-mâché)

Sidewalk art with chalk

Silhouettes

Sponge paintings

Stabiles (stationary sculptures)

Stained-glass windows

Torn-paper pictures

T-shirts

Water pictures on the blackboard

Yarn-and-cloth pictures

Writing

Acrostics

Conversations

Crossword puzzles

Interviews

Letters

Litanies

Logs

Newscaps

Paraphrases of Bible passages

Prayers

Raps

Riddles

Skits

Songs

Speeches

Summaries

Telegrams

Audiovisuals

Chalktalk (colored chalk)

Charts

Computer

Concrete aids

DVDs

Flannel board

Maps

Models

Movies

Multimedia shows

Opaque projector

Pictures

PowerPoint presentations

Scrapbooks

Slides

Songs

Audio CDs and tapes

Transparencies

Videocassettes

Drama

Charades

Choral reading

Cutouts on overhead

Dance

Dramatic reading

Gestures to songs

Mime

Pageants

Plays

Puppet shows

Role-play

Shadow play

Each person is created in God's image, yet there are variations in individual abilities. Positive recognition of these differences discourages discrimination and enchances the unity of the Body of Christ.

Statement of the U.S. Bishops:
Welcome and Justice for Persons with Disabilities (1998)

The catechist should choose teaching techniques that meet the needs of children with special needs and make use of their strengths. These children can include both those with some form of learning challenge, as well as those who are considered gifted. Efforts made in this area enhance the learning experience for everyone in class.

Use of Scripture Stories

- Tell some stories as an eyewitness, using direct address. Be dramatic.
- Use the Bible and pictures during storytelling.
- After the story is read, have children dramatize it, perhaps by using pantomime.

Use of Music and Gesture

- Provide silent, reflective time to draw children into a sense of the sacred.
- Peaceful, calming music is helpful for centering.
- Echo-type songs and prayers are very effective.
- Songs with direct, simple messages of the faith help retention of basic truths.
- Simple gestures for refrains promote participation of children with verbal differences.
- Limit gestures to two or three for each song, selected from signs used by those who are hearing impaired.

Questioning Techniques

- State questions in their entirety, and then break them down into basic components.
- Use simple questions to increase class participation. These include repeat-after-me questions or statements and simple completion questions.
- Ask questions immediately after presenting material.
- Use critical-thinking questions for those children who can handle them.

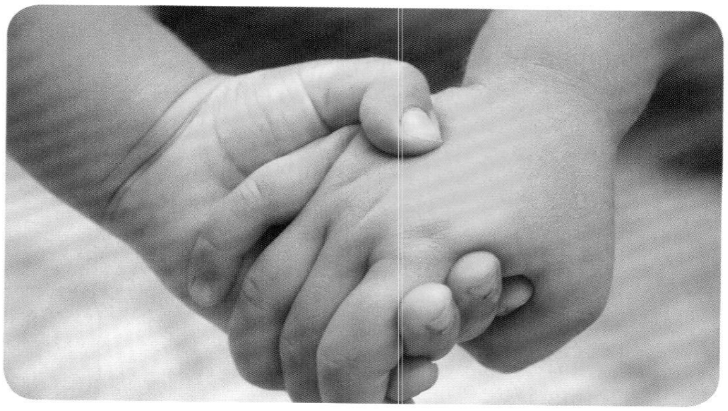

Physical Challenges

- Adapt your program to fit the needs of children with a physical impairment by using individualized instruction.
- Consult special education professionals.
- Develop strategies, such as a buddy system, to help children with materials and class activities.
- If a child has symptoms that at times might be disruptive to the class, deal with the situation calmly and quietly to minimize embarrassment.
- Encourage social interaction through verbal activities and other opportunities.

Visual Challenges

- Consider range of vision and lighting needs. For example, be sure the light source isn't shining in a child's eyes.
- Permit children to move for closer views of charts or demonstrations.
- Provide large-print books, audio materials, and tangible materials.
- Plan lessons that use senses other than sight.
- Allow children to do assignments and tests orally or to record them.
- Assign a partner for visual activities.
- Keep the learning area clear of hazards.

Hearing Impairment

- Directly face children when you talk to them.
- Seat children near the front of the room or close to audio equipment.
- If children have hearing loss in one ear, seat them so that the impaired ear faces the wall.
- Avoid standing where glare from light inhibits children's ability to read your lips.
- Speak clearly, using a normal tone and pace.
- Write difficult or unfamiliar words and key words and phrases on the board.
- Make copies of class notes for children.
- Write directions on the board or reword them. Some sounds are heard better than others.
- Encourage verbal interaction.
- For those children with complete hearing loss, provide an American Sign Language (ASL) translator to communicate what you say.

Speech Delay or Impairment

- Speak distinctly and in short phrases.
- Use visual and written instruction.
- Work separately with children whose oral communication needs attention.
- Allow extra time for children to respond to your questions and comments.

Social and Behavioral Challenges

- Arrange the room to minimize distractions. Carpeting, sound-absorbing materials, and room dividers can help.
- Structure the schedule to avoid last-minute changes and to allow mastery of content within children's attention span.
- Help children develop routines.
- Prepare change-of-pace activities that give children opportunities to move.
- Give children specific tasks they find interesting.
- Plan stimulating activities for after—not before—periods of concentration.
- Explain the rationale for what children are learning.
- Establish a plan of action for completing work.
- Reward children for demonstrating self-control and responsibility and for completing a task in an appropriate length of time.
- Use strategies that provide immediate feedback, such as hand raising and flash cards.
- Provide clear transitions between activities.

Learning Disabilities

- Provide routine and orderly procedures. Avoid distractions.
- Keep lessons short and varied. Introduce skills one at a time and review often. Allow extra learning time.
- Use books and materials with large print and simple setup.
- Reinforce verbalized concepts with visual and kinesthetic cues.
- Grade for content rather than for spelling or reading comprehension.
- Set up situations in which children will experience success. Frequently praise children on their strengths.
- Review and clarify directions.
- Ask questions often to assess children's understanding of the lesson.

Cognitive Differences

- Adjust class work to children's attention span and gross motor and fine motor skill levels.
- Individualize learning, and use teacher assistants or volunteers.
- Simplify concepts, teaching in a concrete manner with a variety of approaches.
- Group children of varying levels.
- Consider writing narrative progress reports rather than using traditional grading scales.

Children Identified as Gifted

- Challenge children by suggesting independent study, small-group work, enrichment activities, out-of-school activities, and discovery learning that is related to their interests.
- Provide supplementary resources and direct children to pursue interesting topics.
- Capture children's interest with puzzles, games, and technology.
- Ask children to help prepare class materials and demonstrations.
- Encourage higher-level thinking skills and persistence in difficult learning.

The cultural and racial diversity of the Body of Christ witnesses to the creativity of God and to the universality of the Church. The life conditions of people affect how they hear and respond to the Word of God.

Convinced of these two truths, the Church urges its catechists to

- incorporate the cultures of the people in their catechesis
- address the needs of various groups of people
- respect and cherish the uniqueness of different groups
- lead others to know and respect cultures different from their own

The following suggestions can help catechists teach more effectively as they promote multicultural awareness and respect.

Responding to the Needs of Other Cultures

- Understand and be sensitive to both the home and the community that are each child's world.
- Learn about the history, traditions, values, and customs of the ethnic groups to which the children belong.
- Make sure that your teaching takes into account the life experiences of the children.
- Make the effort to have all written communications to parents or guardians translated into the language spoken at home.
- Be aware that there are subgroups within larger groups. For example, Spanish-speaking people come from Mexico, Puerto Rico, Cuba, and other countries. Each of these peoples has a distinct culture. The same is true for people of Native American, African American, Asian, and other ancestries.
- Take into account the educational and economic circumstances of the children and their families, avoiding unrealistic demands on their time, physical resources, and finances.
- Consider your class's special needs in relation to justice and peace. Prepare the children to assume responsibility for achievement of their goals.
- Enter into the spirit of popular religiosity, be sympathetic to the needs it meets, and direct its expression in line with sound theological and liturgical teaching.
- Read books with positive reflections of multicultural diversity to the children.

Incorporating the Gifts of Other Cultures

- Encourage the children to share their customs and family celebrations with the class.
- Integrate cultural holidays and feasts, special events, and neighborhood celebrations into the life examples you use in your teaching.
- In liturgical and social celebrations, especially on important occasions, incorporate the language and symbols of the groups that make up your learning community.
- Encourage liturgical and social celebrations that express the spirit, history, and traditions of the cultural groups in your learning community.

Educating Children to Know and Respect Other Cultures

- Watch for unjust or stereotypical treatment of sexes, races, and cultures in the materials you use and in your own words as you teach. Raise the consciousness of those around you.
- Do not use racial, ethnic, or cultural nicknames or make jokes that label or stereotype.
- Be alert to ways of acknowledging contributions made by various cultural groups to the rich traditions of the Catholic Church.
- Share stories about saints from a variety of cultures and social conditions.
- Mindful of the struggles of our forebears in attaining freedom, be understanding of the present struggle of other cultural groups in finding their place in U.S. society and in the Church.

Recent Church Documents for Catechesis

1979 *Catechesis in Our Time*

1997 *General Directory for Catechesis*

2005 *National Directory for Catechesis*

Other Papal and Vatican Documents

1963 *Peace on Earth* (Pope John XXIII)

1963–1965 *Documents of the Second Vatican Council*

1987 *On Social Concern* (Pope John Paul II)

1994 *Letter to Families* (Pope John Paul II)

1998 *Towards a Better Distribution of Land*

1998 *The Day of the Lord* (Pope John Paul II)

1998 *The Dignity of Older People and their Mission in the Church and in the World*

1999 *The Family and Human Rights*

1999 *Memory and Reconciliation: The Church and the Faults of the Past*

2001 *Directory on Popular Piety and the Liturgy*

2006 *God Is Love* (Pope Benedict XVI)

Other Documents of the United States Conference of Catholic Bishops

1991 *Putting Children and Families First: A Challenge for Our Church, Nation, and World*

1995 *Called and Gifted for the Third Millennium*

1998 *Sharing Catholic Social Teaching: Challenges and Directions*

1999 *In All Things Charity: A Pastoral Challenge for the New Millennium*

Most of these documents are available from Publishing Services, USCCB, 3211 Fourth Street, N.E., Washington, DC 20017.

For reflective music recommendations, please see page OV-46.

Song	Publisher	Collection	CD	Track
Chapter 1				
We Are Marching	GIA	*Singing Our Faith*	1	14
Welcome In	GIA	*The Best of Joe Wise*		
Jesus Loves the Little Children	OCP	*Stories and Songs of Jesus*		
Let's Be Friends	OCP	*Hi God 3*		
Take My Hand	OCP	*Stories and Songs of Jesus*		
I Have a Hello	WLP	*Sing a Song of Joy*		
Chapter 2				
Jesus in the Morning	GIA	*Singing Our Faith*	1	4
By Name I Have Called You	OCP	*By Name I Have Called You*		
God Is So Good	OCP	*Color the World with Song*		
Jesus, Jesus	OCP	*Hi God 2*		
Oh, How I Love Jesus	OCP	*Hi God!*		
Thank You, Lord	OCP	*Hi God!*		
Chapter 3				
I Have Loved You	OCP	*On Eagle's Wings*		
I Like God's Love	OCP	*Hi God!*		
Our God Is a God of Love	OCP	*Hi God 2*		
God Loves Little People	WLP	*Sing a Song of Joy*	2	8
Chapter 4				
All You Works of God	GIA	*Singing Our Faith*		
I Wonder	MLW	*Peaceable Kingdom*		
Happy the Heart	OCP	*Hi God!*		
Hip Hip Hooray	Pauline	*Fingerprints*		
Greatest Show on Earth	WLP	*I See a New World*	2	1
Chapter 5				
Go Now in Peace	GIA	*Singing Our Faith*		
Jesus, Remember Me	GIA	*Singing Our Faith*		
My Soul in Stillness Waits	GIA	*Singing Our Faith*		
General Intercessions	GIA	*Singing Our Faith*		
Over My Head	GIA	*Singing Our Faith*	1	8
Prayer of Peace	GIA	*Singing Our Faith*		
Take, O Take Me As I Am	GIA	*Singing Our Faith*		
Come to the Father	MLW	*Songs for Young Children*		
Psalm of Trust	OCP	*Color the World with Song*		
Color the World with Song	OCP	*Color the World with Song*		
Jesus, Jesus	OCP	*Hi God 2*		
Chapter 6				
All Night, All Day	GIA	*Singing Our Faith*	1	7
Good Morning, God	GIA	*Singing Our Faith*		
Sing, Sing, Praise and Sing!	GIA	*Singing Our Faith*	1	12
Somebody's Knockin' at Your Door	GIA	*Singing Our Faith*		

For music publisher contact information, see **page T375.**

For reflective music recommendations, please see page OV-46.

Song	Publisher	Collection	CD	Track
Sing Praise	MLW	*Songs for Young Children*		
Sing-a-Prayer	MLW	*Songs for Young Children*		
If I Were a Butterfly	OCP	*Hi God 2*		
Make a Joyful Noise	OCP	*Color the World with Song*		
Talk to You	Pauline	*Come Meet Jesus! (MRH)*		
Fly	WLP	*Even a Worm (NA)*		
Make a Wonderful Noise	WLP	*Sing a Song of Joy!*	2	16
Glory in the Light	WLP	*I See a New World*	2	11
Chapter 7				
All Grownups, All Children	GIA	*Singing Our Faith*		
Caring	MLW	*Peaceable Kingdom*		
Child in the House	MLW	*Peaceable Kingdom*		
Families Are Fun	MLW	*Peaceable Kingdom*		
Family	MLW	*Peaceable Kingdom*		
Family Thank You	MLW	*Peaceable Kingdom*		
God Is Our Father	OCP	*Color the World with Song*		
What God Is Like	OCP	*Color the World with Song*		
What God Is Like	OCP	*Hi God 2*		
God Loves Little People	WLP	*Sing a Song of Joy!*		
In The Presence of the Angels	WLP	*I See a New World*	2	13
Chapter 8				
Behold I Make All Things New	GIA	*Singing Our Faith*		
God Is So Good	OCP	*Color the World with Song*		
God's Circle of Love	OCP	*Hi God 3*		
If I Were a Butterfly	OCP	*Hi God 2*		
Here I Am, God	WLP	*I See a New World*	2	5
Rainbow Children	WLP	*Sing a Song of Joy!*		
Chapter 9				
Guide My Feet	GIA	*Singing Our Faith*		
You Have Put on Christ	GIA	*Singing Our Faith*	1	5
Giant Love Ball Song	OCP	*Hi God!*		
I Like God's Love	OCP	*Hi God!*		
Living and Loving and Learning	OCP	*Hi God 3*		
Thank You, Lord	OCP	*Hi God!*		
What Makes Love Grow?	OCP	*Hi God!*		
You Have Been Baptized in Christ	OCP	*Abba, Father*		
Chapter 10				
Family Thank You	MLW	*Peaceable Kingdom*		
Thanksgiving Blessing	MLW	*Peaceable Kingdom*		
I Like God's Love	OCP	*Hi God!*		
Receive Our Prayer	OCP	*Hi God 3*		
Thank You, Lord	OCP	*Hi God!*		
Thank You, Lord	OCP	*Stories and Songs of Jesus*		

Song	Publisher	Collection	CD	Track
Say Thank You	Pauline	*Miracle Mud*		
To Give Thanks	WLP	*Sing a Song of Joy!*	2	2
Chapter 11				
O Come, O Come, Emmanuel	GIA	*Singing Our Faith*		
Stay Awake, Be Ready	GIA	*Singing Our Faith*		
Advent Song	MLW	*Dandelions*		
Come, Lord Jesus	OCP	*Hi God 2*		
Advent Song	Paulist	*Best of Mary Lu Walker*		
Come, Lord Jesus	WLP	*Sing a Song of Joy!*		
Mary's Cradle Song	WLP	*Sing a Song of Joy!*	2	12
O Antiphons	WLP	*Sing a Song of Joy!*		
We Are Little Gifts	WLP	*Sing a Song of Joy!*		
Chapter 12				
I Say "Yes," My Lord/Digo "Si," Senor	GIA	*Singing Our Faith*		
Immaculate Mary	GIA	*Singing Our Faith*	1	9
Hail Mary	MLW	*Dandelions*		
Yes, We Will Do What Jesus Says	OCP	*Stories and Songs of Jesus*		
Chapter 13				
Lead Me, Guide Me	GIA	*Singing Our Faith*		
The Lord, the Lord, the Lord Is My Shepherd	GIA	*Singing Our Faith*	1	11
You Are My Shepherd	GIA	*Singing Our Faith*		
Caring	MLW	*Peaceable Kingdom*		
I Wonder	MLW	*Peaceable Kingdom*		
Lead Me, Shepherd, Lead Me	MLW	*Dandelions*		
Psalm of the Good Shepherd	OCP	*Color the World with Song*		
The Good Shepherd	OCP	*Stories and Songs of Jesus*		
Chapter 14				
Love One Another	GIA	*Singing Our Faith*	1	6
This Is My Commandment	GIA	*Singing Our Faith*		
Handle with Care	MLW	*Peaceable Kingdom*		
Put on Love	MLW	*Songs for Young Children*		
Things That Money Can't Buy	MLW	*Songs for Young Children*		
God's Circle of Love	OCP	*Hi God 3*		
Happy the Heart	OCP	*Hi God!*		
How Much God Loves Us	OCP	*Stories and Songs of Jesus*		
I Like God's Love	OCP	*Hi God!*		
If I Were a Butterfly	OCP	*Hi God 2*		
Jesus and His Friends Have Breakfast on the Beach	OCP	*More Stories and Songs of Jesus*		
Jesus, You Love Us	OCP	*Calling the Children*		
Love That Is Kept Inside	OCP	*Hi God!*		
Thank You, Lord	OCP	*Hi God!*		
This Is My Commandment	OCP	*Hi God 2*		
Together We'll Share	OCP	*More Stories and Songs of Jesus*		

For music publisher contact information, see **page T375**.

For reflective music recommendations, please see page OV-46.

Song	Publisher	Collection	CD	Track
God's Love	Pauline	*Big Steps for Little Feet*		
Put on Love	Paulist	*Best of Mary Lu Walker*		
Things That Money Can't Buy	Paulist	*Best of Mary Lu Walker*		
God Is Love	WLP	*Sing a Song of Joy!*		
God Loves Little People	WLP	*Sing a Song of Joy!*	2	8
God's Love	WLP	*Sing a Song of Joy!*	2	14
Love One Another	WLP	*Sing a Song of Joy!*	2	4
We Are Little Gifts	WLP	*Sing a Song of Joy!*	2	6
Chapter 15				
A Little Peace Song	MLW	*Dandelions*		
Make a Joyful Noise	OCP	*Color the World with Song*		
Peace to You and Me	OCP	*Hi God 3*		
Yes, We Will Do What Jesus Says	OCP	*Stories and Songs of Jesus*		
Fingerprints	Pauline	*Fingerprints*		
A Little Peace Song	Paulist	*Best of Mary Lu Walker*		
Bless Our Hands	WLP	*Sing a Song of Joy!*	2	10
I Am Wonderfully Made	WLP	*Sing a Song of Joy!*		
Chapter 16				
Hold Us in Your Mercy	GIA	*Singing Our Faith*		
A Little Peace Song	MLW	*Dandelions*		
I Am Sorry	MLW	*Songs for Young Children*		
I Forgive, You Forgive	MLW	*Songs for Young Children*		
God Is Our Father	OCP	*Hi God!*		
Got to Get in Touch	OCP	*Hi God!*		
I Forgive You	OCP	*Hi God 5*		
I'm Sorry	OCP	*Stories and Songs of Jesus*		
Jesus, You Love Us	OCP	*Calling the Children*		
Peace Time	OCP	*Hi God!*		
Zacchaeus	OCP	*Stories and Songs of Jesus*		
A Little Peace Song	Paulist	*Best of Mary Lu Walker*		
Zacchaeus	PSS	*Wee Sing Bible Songs*		
Love One Another	WLP	*Sing a Song of Joy!*	2	4
Chapter 17				
A Place in the Choir	GIA	*The Best of Joe Wise 2*	1	1
Spirit-Friend	GIA	*Singing Our Faith*		
We Are the Church	GIA	*Singing Our Faith*		
Where I Am, God Is!	MLW	*Songs for Young Children*		
Come and Go with Me	OCP	*Hi God 2*		
God Has Made Us a Family	OCP	*Hi God 3*		
God Is Building a House	OCP	*Hi God 2*		
Let Everyone Be Happy	OCP	*Color the World with Song*		
Holy House	WLP	*Sing a Song of Joy!*		

Song	Publisher	Collection	CD	Track
Chapter 18				
Friends All Gather 'Round	GIA	*Singing Our Faith*		
Gathered Together	MLW	*Songs for Young Children*		
God Is So Good	OCP	*Color the World with Song*		
His Banner Over Me Is Love	OCP	*Hi God!*		
Tell Them, Feed Them Well	OCP	*Stories and Songs of Jesus*		
Plant Love	WLP	*I See a New World*	2	7
We Come to Your Table	OCP	*Hi God 2*		
Chapter 19				
Mem Accl./Mass of Plenty	GIA	*Singing Our Faith*		
O How Good Is Christ the Lord	GIA	*Singing Our Faith*	1	10
The Seed	GIA	*The Best of Joe Wise*		
The Flower Song	MLW	*Songs for Young Children*		
Bloom Where You're Planted	OCP	*Bloom Where You're Planted*		
Chapter 20				
Alleluia, Alleuia, Give Thanks	GIA	*Singing Our Faith*		
Easter Alleluia	GIA	*Singing Our Faith*		
People of God/Alleluia	GIA	*Singing Our Faith*	1	13
A Celebration of Sunshine	MLW	*Dandelions*		
All Men on Earth Rejoice and Sing	MLW	*Songs for Young Children*		
God Loves the Animals	WLP	*I See a New World*	2	15
Jesus Lives	OCP	*Stories and Songs of Jesus*		
New Hope	OCP	*Hi God 2*		
O Yes! Lord Jesus Lives	OCP	*Hi God 2*		
Signs of New Life	OCP	*Bloom Where You're Planted*		
Take My Hand	OCP	*Stories and Songs of Jesus*		
We Believe	OCP	*Stories and Songs of Jesus*		
The Butterfly Song	Paulist	*Best of Mary Lu Walker*		
Chapter 21				
Bring Forth the Kingdom	GIA	*Singing Our Faith*		
Walk, Walk in the Light	GIA	*Singing Our Faith*		
We Are Marching	GIA	*Singing Our Faith*	1	14
We Are Walking in the Light	GIA	*Singing Our Faith*	1	2
A Celebration of Sunshine	MLW	*Dandelions*		
Light	MLW	*Songs for Young Children*		
Lightning Bug	MLW	*Songs for Young Children*		
How Much God Loves Us	OCP	*Stories and Songs of Jesus*		
Chapter 22				
All You Works of God	GIA	*Singing Our Faith*		
Glory and Gratitude and Praise	GIA	*Singing Our Faith*		
Jesus in the Morning	GIA	*Singing Our Faith*	1	4
Rejoice in the Lord Always	GIA	*Singing Our Faith*		

For music publisher contact information, see **page T375**.

For reflective music recommendations, please see page OV-46.

Song	Publisher	Collection	CD	Track
Sing, Sing, Praise and Sing!	GIA	*Singing Our Faith*	1	12
Uyai Mose/Come All You People	GIA	*Singing Our Faith*		
We Are the Church	GIA	*Singing Our Faith*		
Purim Song	MLW	*Dandelions*		
Celebrate God	OCP	*Hi God!*		
His Banner over Me Is Love	OCP	*Hi God!*		
Into the House of God	OCP	*Young People's Glory and Praise*		
Thank You, Lord	OCP	*Hi God!*		
Make a Wonderful Noise	WLP	*Sing a Song of Joy*	2	16
Chapter 23				
If You Believe and I Believe	GIA	*Singing Our Faith*		
Spirit-Friend	GIA	*Singing Our Faith*		
Kathy's Special Day	MLW	*Dandelions*		
Sing Praise	MLW	*Songs for Young Children*		
The Wind Song	MLW	*Songs for Young Children*		
A Psalm for All Seasons	OCP	*Color the World with Song*		
Alleluia Round	OCP	*Color the World with Song*		
Jesus Always Helps Us	OCP	*Stories and Songs of Jesus*		
Our God Is a God of Love	OCP	*Hi God 2*		
Hold My Hand	WLP	*I See a New World*	2	9
Chapter 24				
Shout for Joy	GIA	*Singing Our Faith*		
Sing, Sing, Praise and Sing!	GIA	*Singing Our Faith*	1	12
Color the World with Song	OCP	*Color the World with Song*		
Come and Go with Me	OCP	*Hi God 2*		
Joy, Joy, Joy	OCP	*Hi God!*		
Let Everyone Be Happy	OCP	*Color the World with Song*		
Our God Is a God of Love	OCP	*Hi God 2*		
Rejoice in the Lord Always	OCP	*Hi God!*		
Thank You, Lord	OCP	*Hi God!*		
The Joy of the Lord	OCP	*Hi God!*		
Give It Away	Pauline	*Fingerprints*		
Make a Wonderful Noise	WLP	*Sing a Song of Joy!*	2	16
This Is the Day	WLP	*Sing a Song of Joy!*		
Chapter 25				
All Night, All Day	GIA	*Singing Our Faith*	1	7
Behold I Make All Things New	GIA	*Singing Our Faith*		
Blest Are They	GIA	*Singing Our Faith*		
Circle Round for Freedom	GIA	*Singing Our Faith*		
On Holy Ground	GIA	*When Children Gather*		
Over My Head	GIA	*Singing Our Faith*		
Soon and Very Soon	GIA	*Singing Our Faith*		
All Your Gifts of Life	OCP	*Hi God 2*		

Song	Publisher	Collection	CD	Track
Father, We Adore You	OCP	*Hi God!*		
If I Were a Butterfly	OCP	*Hi God 2*		
Lesson 1				
All Night, All Day	GIA	*Singing Our Faith*	1	7
Lesson 2				
Advent Song	MLW	*Dandelions*		
Come, Lord Jesus	OCP	*Hi God 2*		
Advent Song	Paulist	*Best of Mary Lu Walker)*		
Come, Lord Jesus	WLP	*Sing a Song of Joy!*		
Mary's Cradle Song	WLP	*Sing a Song of Joy!*		
O Antiphons	WLP	*Sing a Song of Joy!*		
Leap Like a Deer	WLP	*I See a New World*	2	3
Lesson 3				
Glory to God	OCP	*Stories and Songs of Jesus*		
We Are Little Gifts	WLP	*I See a New World*	2	6
Mary's Cradle Song	WLP	*Sing a Song of Joy*	2	12
Lesson 4				
We Are Little Gifts	WLP	*I See a New World*	2	6
Lesson 5				
God's Love	WLP	*Sing a Song of Joy!*	2	14
Lesson 6				
Halle, Halle (Haugen)	GIA	*Singing Our Faith*	1	3
Alleluia, Alleuia, Give Thanks	GIA	*Singing Our Faith*		
Easter Alleluia	GIA	*Singing Our Faith*		
People of God/Alleluia	GIA	*Singing Our Faith*	1	13
A Celebration of Sunshine	MLW	*Dandelions*		
All Men on Earth Rejoice and Sing	MLW	*Songs for Young Children*		
The Butterfly Song	MLW	*Songs for Young Children*		
Jesus Lives	OCP	*Stories and Songs of Jesus*		
New Hope	OCP	*Hi God 2*		
O Yes, Lord Jesus Lives	OCP	*Hi God 2*		
Signs of New Life	OCP	*Bloom Where You're Planted*		
Take My Hand	OCP	*Stories and Songs of Jesus*		
We Believe	OCP	*Stories and Songs of Jesus*		
The Butterfly Song	Paulist	*Best of Mary Lu Walker*		
Lesson 7				
Go Now in Peace	GIA	*Singing Our Faith*		
Peace of the Lord	GIA	*Child of God*		
Prayer of Peace	GIA	*Singing Our Faith*		
We Will Bring Your Peace	GIA	*Great Stories and Songs*		
Peace Is Flowing Like a River	OCP	*Hi God 2*		
Peace to You and Me	OCP	*Hi God Gesture Book Recording*		

For music publisher contact information, see **page T375**.

For reflective music recommendations, please see below.

Song	Publisher	Collection	CD	Track
Peace Chant	WLP	*Sing a Song of Joy!*		
Peaceable People	WLP	*Sing a Song of Joy!*		
Lesson 8				
Walk, Walk in the Light	GIA	*Singing Our Faith*		
We Are Marching	GIA	*Singing Our Faith*	1	14
We Are Walking in the Light	GIA	*Singing Our Faith*	1	2
Lesson 9				
Immaculate Mary	GIA	*Singing Our Faith*	1	9
Jesus, I Will Stay with You	OCP	*Stories and Songs of Jesus*		
Lesson 12				
All Night, All Day	GIA	*Singing Our Faith*	1	7
Lesson 14				
A Means of Your Peace	GIA	*Singing Our Faith*		
All You Works of God	GIA	*Singing Our Faith*		
Canticle of the Sun	GIA	*Singing Our Faith*	1	15
Lesson 15				
Bless Our Hands	WLP	*Sing a Song of Joy!*	2	10
Jesus' Hands Were Kind Hands	GIA	*Singing Our Faith*		
Love One Another	GIA	*Singing Our Faith*	1	6
This Is My Commandment	GIA	*Singing Our Faith*		
Love One Another	WLP	*Sing a New Song*	2	4
Lesson 18				
God's Circle of Love	OCP	*Hi God 3*		
Happy the Heart	OCP	*Hi God!*		
I Like God's Love	OCP	*Hi God!*		
If I Were a Butterfly	OCP	*Hi God 2*		
Love That Is Kept Inside	OCP	*Hi God!*		
This Is My Commandment	OCP	*Hi God 2*		
God Is Love	WLP	*Sing a Song of Joy!*		
God's Love	WLP	*Sing a Song of Joy!*	2	14
Love One Another	WLP	*Sing a Song of Joy!*	2	4
We Are Little Gifts	WLP	*Sing a Song of Joy!*	2	6
Song of St. Patrick	GIA	*Singing Our Faith*		
All the Time	OCP	*Bloom Where You're Planted*		
Lesson 19				
Father We Adore You	OCP	*Hi God 2*		
Lesson 21				
Holy Is Your Name	GIA	*Singing Our Faith*		
Magnificat/Sing Out, My Soul	GIA	*Singing Our Faith*		
Lesson 22				
Yes, We Will Do What Jesus Says	OCP	*Stories and Songs of Jesus*		

Available from www.giamusic.com
Water, Wind & Soul by Jeanne Cotter CD-374
Wellspring Sampler (Various Artists) CD-261

Available from www.wlpmusic.com
For the Beauty of the Earth by Laura Kutscher CD-2536
Blessed Assurance by Malcolm Kogut/Les Stahl CD-2530

	Title	Author	Publisher	© Date	ISBN
Chapter 1	*If You Give a Mouse a Cookie*	Numeroff, Laura Joffe	Laura Geringer/ HarperCollins	1994	0060245867
	Ira Sleeps Over	Waber, Bernard	Houghton Mifflin	1993	0395205034
	It's So Nice to Have a Wolf Around the House	Allard, Harry	Yearling	1997	0440413532
	Miss Spider's Tea Party	Kirk, David	Scholastic Press	1994	0590477242
	Weekend with Wendell, A	Henkes, Kevin	HarperTrophy	1995	0688140246
Chapter 2	*Andy, That's My Name*	dePaola, Tomie	Aladdin	1999	0689826974
	God Lives in Glass: Reflections on God Through the Eyes of Children	Landy, Robert J.	Skylight Paths Publishing	2001	1893361306
	In God's Name	Sasso, Sandy Eisenberg	Jewish Lights Publishing	1994	1879045265
	Old Turtle	Wood, Douglas	Scholastic Press	1992	0439309085
	Oliver Button Is a Sissy	dePaola, Tomie	Voyager Books	1990	0156681404
Chapter 3	*Aunt Isabel Tells a Good One*	Duke, Kate	Puffin	1994	0140505342
	Miss Smith's Incredible Storybook	Garland, Michael	Dutton Children's Books	2003	0525471332
	Noah's Ark	Spier, Peter	Doubleday	1992	0385094736
	Once Upon a Golden Apple	Little, Jean	Puffin	1994	0140541640
	Small Gifts in God's Hands	Lucado, Max	Tommy Nelson, Inc.	2000	0849958423
Chapter 4	*At Mary Bloom's*	Aliki	HarperCollins Publishers	1998	0688024815
	Cain and Abel: Finding the Fruits of Peace	Sasso, Sandy Eisenberg	Jewish Lights Publishing	2001	1580231232
	God in Between	Sasso, Sandy Eisenberg	Jewish Lights Publishing	1998	1879045869
	Good-Night, Owl!	Hutchins, Pat	Simon & Schuster	1990	0027459004
	On the Day You Were Born	Frasier, Debra	Harcourt Children's Books	1997	0152579958
Chapter 5	*A Quiet Place*	Wood, Douglas	Simon & Schuster	2002	0689815115
	All I See	Rylant, Cynthia	Scholastic Press	1994	0531070484
	God's Quiet Things	Sweetland, Nancy	Eerdmans Books for Young Readers	1998	0802851673
	Quiet Noisy Book, The	Brown, Margaret Wise	HarperTrophy	1993	0064432157
	Where Does God Live?	Gold, August and Perlman, Matthew J.	Skylights Paths Publishing	2001	189336139X
Chapter 6	*Child's Book of Celtic Prayers, A*	Denham, Joyce	Loyola Press	1998	0745948804
	God in Between	Sasso, Sandy Eisenberg	Jewish Lights Publishing	1998	1879045869
	Grandad's Prayers of the Earth	Wood, Douglas	Candlewick Press	1999	076360660X
	I Can Pray About Anything	Donze, Mary Terese	Liguori Publications	1994	0892436336
	Just the Way You Are	Lucado, Max	Scholastic Press	1992	0439210674

	Title	Author	Publisher	© Date	ISBN
Chapter 7	*Grandma and Grandpa*	Oxenbury, Helen	Puffin	1993	0140549781
	Great Fuzz Frenzy, The	Stevens, Janet and Crummel, Susan Stevens	Harcourt	2005	0152046267
	Tenth Good Thing About Barney, The	Viorst, Judith	Aladdin	1976	0689712030
	What Daddies Do Best	Numeroff, Laura	Simon & Schuster	1998	0439186927
	What Mommies Do Best	Numeroff, Laura	Simon & Schuster	1998	0439186927
Chapter 8	*Hermie: A Common Caterpillar*	Lucado, Max	Tommy Nelson, Inc.	2002	1400301173
	How Does God Listen?	Lindahl, Kay	Skylight Paths Publishing	2005	1594730849
	Just the Way You Are	Lucado, Max	Scholastic Press	1992	0439210674
	Little Rabbit Who Wanted Red Wings, The	Bailey, Carolyn Sherwin	Penguin Putnam	1988	0448190893
	Playing Right Field	Welch, Willy	Scholastic Press	1995	0439139945
	You Are Special	Lucado, Max	Crossway Books	1997	0891079319
Chapter 9	*Have You Seen My Duckling?*	Tafuri, Nancy	Mulberry	1991	0688109942
	Now One Foot, Now the Other	dePaola, Tomie	Putnam	1988	0399242597
	How the Children Became Stars	Zerah, Aaron	Sorin Books	2000	1893732177
	Peter's Chair	Keats, Ezra Jack	Puffin	1998	0140564411
Chapter 10	*He Remembered to Say Thank You*	Mann, Victor	Concordia Publishing	1976	0570061032
	Child's World of Thankfulness, The	McDonnell, Janet	Child's World	1996	01567662951
	Magic Fish, The	Littledale, Freya	Scholastic Press	1966	0590411004
	Story of Johnny Appleseed, The	Aliki	Aladdin	1987	0671667467
	Tico and the Golden Wings	Lionni, Leo	Knopf	1987	0394830784
Chapter 11	*Baby Born in a Stable, The*	Kramer-Lampher, A. H.	Arch Books	1990	0570060133
	Fourth Wise Man, The	Holder, Mig	Augsburg Fortress	1995	0806627131
	Legend of Old Befana, The	dePaola, Tomie	Voyager Books	1989	0152438173
	Once Upon a Pony: A Mountain Christmas	Balderose, Nancy Ward	Morehouse	1994	0819270016
	Saint Francis Celebrates Christmas	Walsh, Mary Caswell	Loyola Press	1998	0829411127
Chapter 12	*Are You My Mother?*	Eastman, P. D.	Random House	1988	0394800184
	I Love You as Much…	Melmed, Laura Krauss	Lothrop	1993	0688159788
	Milo and the Magical Stones	Pfister, Marcus	North-South Books	1997	1558586822
	Most Wonderful Egg in the World, The	Heine, Helme	Aladdin	1987	0689711174
	Way Mothers Are, The	Schlein, Miriam	Albert Whitman	2000	0807586900

	Title	Author	Publisher	© Date	ISBN
Chapter 13	*Charlie Needs a Cloak*	dePaola, Tomie	Aladdin	1988	0671664670
	Jim's Lion	Hoban, Russell	Walker Books Ltd.	2001	0744594065
	Little Lost Lamb, The	Haines, Geri Berger	Pauline Books	1981	0819844896
	Shepherd Boy, The	Lewis, Kim	Four Winds	1990	0744517621
	Stray, The	Pottebaum, Gerard A.	Treehaus	2001	1886510547
Chapter 14	*ABC's Lessons of Love, The: Sermon on the Mount for Children*	O'Connor, Francine M.	Liguori Publications	1991	0892433450
	Big Sister and Little Sister	Zolotow, Charlotte	HarperTrophy	1990	0064432173
	Child of the Moon	Cotter, Jeanne	Mythic Rain, Inc.	2001	0967298229
	New Friends, True Friends, Stuck-Like-Glue Friends	Kroll, Virginia	Eerdmans	2000	0802852025
	When the New Baby Comes, I'm Moving Out	Alexander, Martha G.	Dial	1992	01570916780
Chapter 15	*Just For You*	Mayer, Mercer	Golden	1982	030711838X
	Lion and the Mouse, The : A Fable by Aesop	Watts, Bernadette	North-South Books	2000	0735812209
	Mother's Helper	Oxenbury, Helen	Dial	1991	0803754256
	Shoemaker Martin	Watts, Bernadette	North-South Books	1986	1558580441
Chapter 16	*A Bargain For Frances*	Hoban, Russell	HarperTrophy	1999	006444001X
	Best Friends	Cohen, Miriam	Aladdin	1989	0689713347
	Broken Promise, The	Zacharias, Ravi	Faith Kidz	2000	0781434513
	Peter's Angry Toys	Plum, Carol Therese	Our Sunday Visitor	1989	0879730129
	Way I Feel, The	Cain, Janan	Parenting Press	2000	1884734715
Chapter 17	*ABC's of the Mass for Children, The*	O'Connor, Francine M.	Liguori Publications	1988	0892432918
	Caterpillar That Came to Church, The : A Story of the Eucharist	Brindle, Susan Andrews; Hooker, Irene H.; Lademan, Miriam Andrews	Our Sunday Visitor	1993	0879738758
	My Big Family at Church	Caswell, Helen Rayburn	Abingdon Press	1989	0687275334
	Our Church	English, Graham	Liturgical Press	1995	0814620612
	This Is My House	Dorros, Arthur	EconoClad	1999	0785756310
Chapter 18	*Bread and Jam for Frances*	Hoban, Russell	HarperTrophy	1993	0064430960
	Cloudy with a Chance of Meatballs	Barrett, Judi	Aladdin	1982	0689707495
	Gregory the Terrible Eater	Sharmat, Mitchell	Scholastic Press	1989	0590433504
	Hunky Dory Ate It	Evans, Katie	Puffin	1996	014055856X
	Stone Soup	Brown, Marcia	Aladdin	1987	0689878362

	Title	Author	Publisher	© Date	ISBN
Chapter 19	*Carrot Seed, The*	Krauss, Ruth	HarperCollins Publishers	1989	0694004928
	Tiny Seed, The	Carle, Eric	Simon & Schuster	1987	0689842449
	Titch	Hutchins, Pat	Aladdin	1993	0689716885
Chapter 20	*Butterfly Secret, The*	Plum, Carol Therese	Our Sunday Visitor	1989	0879730145
	Charles Caterpillar	Haas, James	Twenty-Third Publications	1992	0896225305
	Hermie: A Common Caterpillar	Lucado, Max	Tommy Nelson, Inc.	2002	1400301173
	I Wish I Were a Butterfly	Howe, James	Voyager Books	1994	0152380132
	Very Hungry Caterpillar, The	Carle, Eric	Putnam	1986	0399208534
Chapter 21	*Frog and Toad Are Friends*	Lobel, Arnold	HarperTrophy	1990	0064440206
	God Is Like...: Three Parables for Children	Walters, Julie	WaterBrook	2000	0877930732
	Sun Song	Marzollo, Jean	HarperTrophy	1995	0064434761
	Wake Up, Sun!	Harrison, David L.	Random House	1986	0394882563
Chapter 22	*Chato's Kitchen*	Soto, Gary	Putnam	1995	0698116003
	I'm in Charge of Celebrations	Baylor, Byrd	Aladdin	1995	0689806205
	God's Paintbrush	Sasso, Sandy Eisenberg	Jewish Lights Publishing	1992	1879045222
	Velveteen Rabbit, The	Williams, Margery	Holt	1999	0385077254
Chapter 23	*Have You Seen the Wind?*	Crawford, Kathleen	Chariot Victor	1995	1564764737
	Letter to Amy, A	Keats, Ezra Jack	Puffin	1998	014056442X
	Place for Ben, A	Titherington, Jeanne	Greenwillow	1999	0688170641
	Swinging Tree, The	Plum, Carol Therese	Our Sunday Visitor	1989	0879730161
	When the Wind Stops	Zolotow, Charlotte	HarperCollins Publishers	1962, 1995	0060254262
Chapter 24	*Frog and Toad Together*	Lobel, Arnold	HarperTrophy	1990	0064440214
	God Said Amen	Sasso, Sandy Eisenberg	Jewish Lights Publishing	2000	1580230806
	Peace Book, The	Parr, Todd	Little, Brown and Company	2004	0316835315
	Selfish Giant, The	Wilde, Oscar	Derrydale	2001	0517220091
	Unlovable	Yaccarino, Dan	Scholastic Press	2001	0439411165
	Will I Have a Friend?	Cohen, Miriam	Aladdin	1989	0689713339
Chapter 25	*Dead Bird, The*	Brown, Margaret Wise	Dell	1995	0064436683
	God's Easter Plan	Greene, Carol	Concordia	1994	0570090385
	Grandad's Prayers of the Earth	Wood, Douglas	Candlewick Press	1999	076360660X
	Tenth Good Thing About Barney, The	Viorst, Judith	Aladdin	1976	0689712030

God Loves Us

This kindergarten program is designed to invite the children to discover God's great love shown through the many good things God has placed in their world. *God Loves Us* utilizes the children's natural characteristics and human experiences to lead them to an awareness of God's goodness and presence in their everyday lives. They reflect on God's goodness in creation, in the wonder of their unique selves, and in the love of the people around them.

A simple introduction to the mysteries of the faith as expressed in the Apostles' Creed is presented to help the children grow in understanding and appreciation of God's love for them. They are helped to see themselves as belonging to the Catholic community and are encouraged to make Catholic beliefs and traditions their own. They are led to respond spontaneously and intimately to God in personal prayer and in celebration with others. They are also inspired to express love for God and one another.

In the first unit the children are invited to respond to God's goodness with a sense of wonder, reverence, and gratitude. After learning about the holiness of God's name, the holy Bible, and the marvels of creation, the children are led to respond to God's love through prayer. As they learn how to pray with quiet hearts, they discover that prayer includes both talking and listening to God.

In the second unit the children consider their uniqueness as a gift from God and are led to respond with gratitude. They learn that God gave them a family and, through Baptism, made them members of God's family, the Church. They are encouraged to have a listening attitude toward God and a desire to choose what God wants for them. As they learn about Advent and Christmas, they meet Mary as someone who always said yes to God.

In the third unit the children deepen their awareness of God's love for them and their appreciation of their uniqueness. They are drawn to love God in return by praying and asking forgiveness. They discover that their love for God is also shown through their acts of kindness for others. They learn about God's people and the Mass they celebrate together.

In the fourth unit the children continue to celebrate God's love for them, especially as they learn about Jesus' gift of new life and about Easter. They learn that they received a share in Jesus' new life through their Baptism and are called to share Jesus' love with others. The children are introduced to the Holy Spirit, who helps them live as Jesus did so that they can have joy and life forever with God.

unit one

Learning About God's Love

In this unit the children will learn to be aware of God's love shown to them through the good persons, events, and things in their lives.

1 WELCOMES ARE GOOD

The children are made to feel welcome in the class and are invited to welcome others. They come to understand that Jesus welcomes children and that he loves them through others.

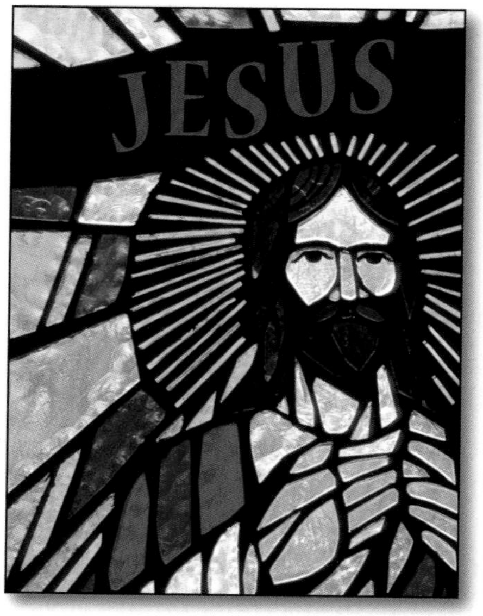

2 NAMES ARE GOOD

A sense of the sacred is fostered in the children. They learn that names are important and become aware that Jesus' name is holy. They practice genuflecting.

3 STORIES ARE GOOD

The children are introduced to the Bible as God's holy book. They learn that during Mass they hear God's story and God's Word. They listen to the story of Jonah.

4 GOD'S WORLD IS GOOD

Through a nature walk, the children are led to see creation as a gift of God's love. They praise God for the goodness and love manifested in creation.

5 QUIET IS GOOD

Through the experience of blowing bubbles, the children come to realize the value of silence. They learn how to quiet themselves. They visit the church, where they practice praying with a quiet heart.

6 TALKING TO GOD IS GOOD

The children reflect on verbal and nonverbal communication. They come to see prayer as talking with God. They experience praying with words as well as with their bodies.

Chapter 1
Welcomes Are Good

FAITH FOCUS

Jesus loves and welcomes children.

Mark 10:13–16

PREPARING THE FAITH EXPERIENCE

LISTENING

Before you begin to prepare this week's lessons, take some time for prayer. Quiet yourself by taking several deep breaths. Become aware of God's presence, for God is with you always. Ask God to open your heart to hear his words to you today.

Let the children come to me.
Mark 10:14

REFLECTING

Just as Jesus spoke these words to his disciples, he also speaks to those who have been called to be teachers in his name. He begs us to let the children come to him, to give them the opportunity to meet him and to be close to him. Only those who have discovered the Lord's presence themselves can lead children to him. Therefore, our call as teachers is first and foremost a call to intimacy with the Lord. Already at Baptism, through the gift of faith, God invited us to enter into the mystery of his love in everlasting union with him. Continually God has made himself known to us, offering friendship and love. We must grow in awareness of God's presence and be ready to welcome God whenever he seeks to enter our lives.

Unfortunately, an attitude of welcome and openness to others does not always come naturally to us. We can be inclined toward self-concern and self-protection. Sometimes we even distance ourselves from others in an attempt to avoid the hurts that are part of human relationships. These attitudes are some of the many things in our own lives that might prevent our personal encounter with Jesus. However, if we open our hearts to the mystery of Jesus' love and experience the joy of his presence, we will be able to take the step of welcoming others into our lives.

Those of us who bring young children to Jesus must *be* Jesus for these little ones. When we examine how Jesus related to children, it is evident that, above all, he let them be children. He did not speak to them using theological terms or detailed definitions. He did not demand an understanding of deep truths of faith. Rather, he simply reached out and welcomed them. Jesus gave and asked what he knew young children were capable of understanding and giving in return—love. Can we wish to do more? As we lead the children entrusted to our care to Jesus, we are refreshed by their joyful simplicity, which Jesus noted and praised. He said, "The kingdom of God belongs to such as these." (Mark 10:14) In the example of the children we teach, we find an invitation to be more open to the Kingdom of God.

RESPONDING

Having reflected upon God's Word, take some time now to continue to respond to God in prayer. You might wish to use a journal to record your responses throughout this year.

- How can I be Jesus for the little ones in my charge and reflect his love for them?
- How might I become more like a child in my acceptance of the Kingdom of God?

Holy Spirit, help me teach in such a way that the children come to love Jesus.

Catechism of the Catholic Church

The themes of this lesson correspond to the following paragraphs: 2560, 2785.

THE FAITH EXPERIENCE

DAY ONE
We Are Welcomed

DAY TWO
Jesus Welcomes Us

DAY THREE
Jesus Welcomes Us Through Others

DAY FOUR
We Welcome Others

Scripture in This Chapter

- *Mark 10:13–16 Jesus welcomes and blesses little children.*
- *Matthew 19:13–15 Children are examples of true disciples of Jesus.*

Church Documents

General Directory for Catechesis #177–178. *National Directory for Catechesis* #48, E. Children are privileged members of the Kingdom of God. Their education in family, school, and Church is decisive for their subsequent faith development.

Catechesis in Our Time #36–37. Children should be prepared early in life to enter into a personal relationship with Christ.

Bulletin Board At the left is a suggestion for a bulletin-board design. Refer to BLM 1 Jesus if you wish to make a photocopy or transparency. Have children draw pictures of themselves. Then post the pictures around the word "Welcome" and the picture of Jesus. Remind the children to write their names on their drawings. Children have varying degrees of ability. Note that perfection is not the goal and that it is important only for the children to do their best.

- ***BLM 1 Jesus***

To make the individual bulletin-board designs in this book, you may wish to trace the design onto a transparency and project it onto a large sheet of paper attached to a wall. Trace the enlarged design and cut it out. Words may be traced from letter patterns and cut out, printed on strips of paper, or made from a set of purchased, reusable letters.

For a list of children's literature suggestions, please see **page OV-47.**

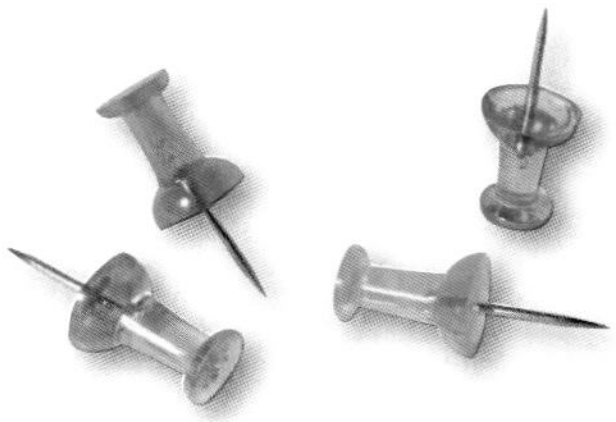

CHAPTER 1 | DAY ONE

We Are Welcomed

LEARNING OUTCOMES

The children will be able to
- feel welcomed.
- experience a sense of belonging to the group.

MATERIALS

- Name cards at each seat
- Colored strips of construction paper, one for each child with his or her name written on it; include one with Jesus' name
- Crayons
- Glue sticks or tape
- Poster 1
- Jesus Loves Me nametag punchouts from the Student Book
- 22″ pieces of yarn, one for each child
- Cutouts 1–4

COMMENTS

1. Human social development progresses from self to others. Thus, young children tend to be self-centered, which is natural. However, young children respond positively when encouraged to reach out to others. Openness to others disposes the children to welcome the Lord, who invites them into a relationship with him.

2. Make it a point to welcome each child warmly every day. A daily welcoming routine helps to create a sense of welcome and security and also helps to establish a sense of ritual. Encourage the children to greet you and others in a friendly manner. Perhaps you can model some ways to welcome each child. Invite the children to welcome one another in similar ways as they arrive.

CENTERING

1 Warmly welcome each child and pass out the Jesus Loves Me nametag punchouts. Guide the children to write their names on the line under the words "My name is." Punch out the perforated hole in each nametag and string it with a loop of yarn to make a pendant. Invite a volunteer to show his or her completed pendant. Read aloud the phrases on each side of the pendant. Have the children wear their nametags during the first week of school so that they can learn one another's names.

2 Ask the children to notice the name card at each place, explaining that the card lets everyone know whose place it is. Invite all the children to find the place with their name card and take their seats.

3 Sing or recite "Welcome Friends."

- ***We can show how glad we are to have everyone here by welcoming one another with a song. Listen as I sing it for you. If you wish, sing the lines "Welcome here today, friends" along with me. When I say your name, please stand and join our circle.***

Ask the children to form a circle as they each sit down at the end of the song verse (so that at the conclusion of the song all should be seated in a circle around you).

Welcome Friends
(Melody: "Where Is Thumbkin?")

Where is (*Name*)?
Where is (*Name*)?
Here (he/she) is.
Here (he/she) is.
[Take hand of each one.]
Welcome here today, friends.
Welcome here today, friends.
[Children join in.]
Please sit down.
Please sit down.

4 After all the children are seated in a circle, model the way in which you would like the children to greet you and one another each day. (Examples: shaking hands, high-fiving each other) Model the greeting first and then invite the children to send the greeting around the circle.

SHARING

1 Guide the children to reflect on how being welcomed made them feel.

- ***Welcomes are good. What did you do when we sang the welcome song to you?***
- ***What were we telling one another when we sang, "Welcome here today, friends"?*** (We're glad you're here. We like you.)

2 Give three children Cutouts 2 Sun, 3 Smiling Face, and 4 Heart to hold as they stand in front of the group.

- ***Welcomes are like warm*** **sunshine** [Invite child with Cutout 2 to show the sun.],

  spreading **smiles** ***everywhere*** [Invite child with Cutout 3 to show the smiling face.], ***and***

  opening **hearts.** [Invite child with Cutout 4 to show the heart.]

Invite the group to repeat this verse with you.

3 Tell the children we hope that we will become a community of friends and we want each person to feel welcome here. To show this, make a friendship chain. Distribute the strips of construction paper with the children's names on them. Help them glue or tape the strips together to form a chain. When the chain is finished, gather the children in a circle.

4 Discuss with the children why they come to school.

- ***Why do you come to*** *(Name of school)****?*** (To learn many things, but especially to learn about God; to make friends; to learn how our Church community shows love for God)
- [Show Cutout 1 Jesus.] ***Do you know who this is?*** (Jesus)
- ***A long, long time ago God the Father sent Jesus, his Son, into our world, which shows us how much God loves us.***
- ***Jesus is an important part of our classroom community.***

Add a link for Jesus to your friendship chain.

ACTING

1 Point to Poster 1 Welcome, Children. Ask how the children think the children pictured on the poster feel. Tell the children that they will have many happy times as they come together during the year to learn about Jesus and his love for them.

2 Throughout this year, you will be sharing psalm prayers. If possible, share this time of prayer in an area of your classroom designated as the Prayer Center. After everyone gathers in this area and before you begin to teach the psalm, invite the children to be quiet and still so that they can be more attentive to God. Ask the children to stand while you pray so that they are better able to participate in the prayer gestures.

3 Teach Psalm 73:28 with gestures:

To lead the psalm prayers, first invite the children to pray with you by watching as you pray the words of the psalm with the gestures. Next invite the children to continue to pray together with you by copying only the gestures as you say the words. Finally, invite the children to pray with you the words and the gestures together. When finished, ask the children to return to their seats quietly.

> ***To be near God***
> [Cross hands over heart.]
>
> ***is . . . good.***
> [Move arms up in a bursting motion.]

CHECKPOINT

- What did you observe that showed that the children feel welcome and comfortable? What will you do to continue and extend this welcoming atmosphere? If any child seems uncomfortable, how will you help this child to feel more at ease?
- What did the children say or do to indicate their eagerness to learn more about Jesus?

CHAPTER 1 | DAY TWO

Jesus Welcomes Us

Student Book pages 1–2

LEARNING OUTCOMES

The children will be able to

- know that Jesus loves them and invites them to be close to him.

MATERIALS

- Posters 1–2
- Cutout 1
- Copies of the Student Book on which you have written the children's names in large letters, tied up with ribbon
- Gift-wrapped box containing the copies of the Student Book (prepared as noted above)
- Bible enthroned with note card on which you have written the adapted Scripture reading for SHARING #5, Mark 10:13–16

COMMENTS

1. Plan a Prayer Center for your room. Use a table covered with a colored cloth that corresponds to the liturgical season. Green is the liturgical color for Ordinary Time. Place a thick candle on the table to light on special occasions. Remember to check with the proper authority regarding local regulations for using candles in a classroom setting.

Each week you might place a symbol of the week's lesson in the Prayer Center. Gather the children in the Prayer Center for prayer. Enthrone the Bible in this worship space during your prayer. To enthrone the Bible is to show reverence for God's Word by setting it in a place of honor in your Prayer Center. Keep the Bible enthroned in this worship space throughout the year.
Read from this Bible whenever Scripture is proclaimed in the lesson or the Student Book. Explain to the children that the Prayer Center is special. They will go there to talk to God. You might have them practice moving there quietly.

2. When sharing Gospel stories with children, relate these stories simply and vividly. Strive to know these stories well so that you can tell them rather than read them. Pause now and then to give the children time to absorb the message and reflect on it. In order to help establish a sense of reverence for God's Word in the Bible, present these stories with the Bible open whenever feasible.

3. In this lesson and throughout the year, you will have the opportunity to lead the children in experiences of reflective prayer. While this experience may be new to them, most young children are quite capable of this form of prayer. Introduce reflective prayer by explaining that Jesus is always present with us and that we can talk to Jesus in our hearts. To do this, we must learn to be quiet and still. Because we are praying this way with others, we also must be careful not to disturb others who are talking with Jesus. With practice, children can become quite adept at this style of prayer and will welcome the opportunity to speak to Jesus in their hearts.

CENTERING

1 Recall the last lesson. Hold up Poster 1. Ask the children how this person is welcoming the children and how they think the children feel.

2 Talk about things that have created feelings of welcome in the classroom. Show the friendship chain made on Day One. Say that we hope that we will become a community of friends who will learn about Jesus together. Explain that Jesus is already a special part of our classroom community.

3 Show Cutout 1. Remind the children that in the last lesson we learned that God sent his Son, Jesus, into our world, which shows us how much God loves us. Talk about how learning about Jesus and knowing him better will be important in our year together. Ask the children what they already know about Jesus. Invite a few volunteers to share.

SHARING

1 Present the Student Book to the children. Show them the gift-wrapped box containing the student textbooks. Explain:

• ***This gift box contains something special for each one of you. It will help you know even more about Jesus. Let's work together to see what is inside this box.*** [Help the children as necessary.]

• *(Name of child),* ***would you like to take the bow off the gift? Please do that now.***

• *(Name),* ***would you like to remove the ribbon?***

• *(Name),* ***would you like to take the paper off the box?***

• *(Name),* ***would you like to open the box now?***

• [Read the title of the book aloud.] ***This book will help you know about all the good things God has given us because God loves us. You will learn how to use these good things to show that you love God.***

• ***The books have your names on them. Please come forward to receive your special book when I call your name. When you return to your seat, you may begin looking at your book.***

2 Call the children to receive their books. As you reverently give each child a book, make a comment such as, "Maria, this is your very own book about God's love for you" or "Christopher, this beautiful book about God is yours."

• ***You will want to take good care of your religion books. They are special.***

3 Allow time for the children look through their books. Then show them how to find the page numbers at the bottom of each page.

4 Help each child to find **page 1.** Read it aloud. Ask them to describe the picture that they see there. (Children saying hello in Chinese, English, Spanish, French, and Swahili.) Tell the children that throughout our year together we will be learning stories about Jesus. Talk about how we find these stories in a very special book called the Bible. Then say that you would like to share a story with everyone now.

5 Ask the children to put their books aside and invite them to form a semicircle in the Prayer Center. Show the

UNIT ONE
CHAPTER 1
Welcomes Are Good
Jesus welcomed little children.
Ni hao
Hello
Buenos Días
Bonjour
Jambo
Scripture
He said, "Let the children come to me."
Based on Mark 10:14
1

children the Bible and open it to the Gospel according to Mark, Mark 10:13–16. Ask them to listen quietly as you tell the story of Jesus welcoming the children. Note: Whenever you read Scripture to the children, find and read the Scripture verse from the Bible. Or write the adapted version on a card and place it in the Bible.

Jesus Welcomes the Children

One day, a long, long time ago when Jesus walked on the earth, some people brought little children to him. They wanted Jesus to bless their children and to pray for them. Some of Jesus' friends thought that Jesus was too tired. They told the parents and their children to go away and leave Jesus alone. But Jesus called out to the children and welcomed them. "Let the little children come to me," he said. "Do not send them away." Then Jesus welcomed the children and blessed them.
(Based on Mark 10:13–16)

6 Guide the children to reflect on the story. Show Poster 2 Jesus and the Children. Ask:

- ***What did Jesus say to welcome the children?*** ("Let the little children come to me.")
- ***Why do you think Jesus wanted the children to come to him?*** (He wanted them to know him. He loved the children and wanted to be with them.)
- ***How did Jesus show that he loved the children?*** (He wanted them to be with him. He blessed them.)
- ***How do you think the children felt when Jesus loved and blessed them?*** (happy)
- ***What would you have said to Jesus if you were one of these children?***

7 Show Cutout 1 as you guide the children to realize that Jesus welcomes them.

- ***Jesus is with us even though we can't see him in the same way the children did long ago. Jesus knows you. He knows everyone's name. He knows your name, and he loves you very, very much, and he will love you forever and ever. Jesus welcomes you today.***
- ***Our hearts are happy because we know Jesus loves us and wants us near him.***

8 Lead the children in reflective prayer.

- ***Jesus wants you to talk to him too. Because Jesus is with us always, you can speak to him now. To do this, we all must be quiet and still so that we can help one another focus on our prayer time with Jesus.*** [Pause.]
- ***To become even more quiet, it helps to close our eyes. So, close your eyes now if you want or look down at your hands resting in your lap.***
- ***Picture Jesus in your mind.*** [Pause.] ***See that Jesus is welcoming you.*** [Pause for several seconds to allow the children time to picture this.]
- ***Deep down in your heart, without saying anything out loud, quietly tell Jesus about how you feel, knowing that Jesus welcomes you.*** [Pause for several seconds to allow time for the children to do this.] ***Perhaps there is something else you would like to say to Jesus. If so, you may do that now.*** [Pause for several seconds.]
- ***When you have finished speaking with Jesus in your heart, open your eyes so that I know when everyone has finished the prayer.***

9 When all have finished their prayer, have the children return to their seats and turn to **page 2** of their books. Ask them to tell what the picture shows. Read aloud the first three sentences. Then read the following together as a class:

- ***Jesus loves us.***

ACTING

Invite the children to stand to pray Psalm 73:28 as taught in the first lesson with gestures:

To lead the psalm prayers, first invite the children to pray with you by watching as you pray the words of the psalm with the gestures. Next invite the children to continue to pray together with you by copying only the gestures as you say the words. Finally, invite the children to pray with you the words and the gestures together. When finished, ask the children to sit down quietly.

To be near God
[Cross hands over heart.]

is . . . good.
[Move arms up in a bursting motion.]

CHECKPOINT

- Were the children attentive to the Gospel story about Jesus welcoming the children? How will you strive to be Jesus' welcoming presence for these children?

Jesus loves children.

Jesus welcomes us.

He wants us to know him.

Jesus loves us.

2

CHAPTER 1 | DAY THREE

Jesus Welcomes Us Through Others

LEARNING OUTCOMES

The children will be able to
- be aware that they experience Jesus' love through others.

MATERIALS

- Posters 1–2
- Magazine pictures that show people who give Jesus' love to children
- A poster with the title, "Welcomes are like warm sunshine," showing a large yellow circle as the sun
- Yellow construction paper cut to look like rays of sunshine, one for each child
- Tape or glue sticks

CENTERING

1 Show Poster 2 and have the children tell the story of Jesus welcoming the children.

2 Teach a song to the melody of "God Is So Good." (Or another simple song about the Bible story of Jesus and the children, such as "Let the Children Come to Me.")

Welcomes are good.
(Three times)
Jesus welcomes me.

God loves me so.
(Three times)
God's so good to me.

SHARING

1 Guide the children to understand that Jesus loves them through others. Display Poster 1.

- ***Jesus welcomes you and the little children all over the world today through other people. Through whose love is Jesus welcoming the little children in this picture?*** (The teacher's)
- ***The welcome of others helps us to experience Jesus' love.*** Show magazine pictures of people who give Jesus' love to children. Invite the children to identify how each person is showing a welcome.
- ***Even though you do not see Jesus in the same way the children in the Gospel story did, he is with you. He welcomes and loves you through the love of the people you know.***

2 Lead the children in the following activity to help them see how they experience Jesus' love through the love of others. Remind the children that they learned that "Welcomes are like warm sunshine." Show the children the poster that you prepared showing a large yellow circle representing the sun with the title, "Welcomes are like warm sunshine." Distribute to each child one yellow construction paper "ray" of sunshine. Ask the children to think about a person who shows them love and what this person does to show them love. Invite each child to name one person who shows them love and to say what this person does. As they make their contributions, help them to glue or tape their "ray of sunshine" to the poster. Ask:

- ***Who also loves you when*** *(Name)* ***loves you?*** [Help the children to respond, "Jesus loves me."] When finished, guide the children to notice all the rays of sunshine on the poster.

ACTING

❶ Remind the children that even though they do not see Jesus in the same way the children in the story did, Jesus is with them. He welcomes and loves them through the love of the people they know. Have the children sit quietly, gently close their eyes if they are comfortable doing so, and deep within their hearts tell Jesus how much they love him. Suggest that they say thank you to Jesus for the people in their lives who love them.

❷ Invite the children to pray Psalm 73:28:

To lead the psalm prayers, first invite the children to pray with you by watching as you pray the words of the psalm with the gestures. Next invite the children to continue to pray together with you by copying only the gestures as you say the words. Finally, invite the children to pray with you the words and the gestures together. When finished, ask the children to sit down quietly.

To be near God
[Cross hands over heart.]

is . . . good.
[Move arms up in a bursting motion.]

CHECKPOINT

- Were the children able to identify ways in which family and friends show Jesus' love to them?

CHAPTER 1 | DAY FOUR

We Welcome Others

Student Book pages 3–4

LEARNING OUTCOMES

The children will be able to

- learn that they can share Jesus' love with others.
- learn ways to welcome people.

MATERIALS

- BLM 2
- Cutout 4
- Crayons or markers

COMMENT

By sharing each week's lesson with their families, the children strengthen the message in their own minds and encourage family members to talk about their faith together. You may choose to send the book home each week with a note to parents requesting that they help their child remember to bring it to the next class. Another alternative is to send home only the pages of the chapter discussed in the lesson. You might suggest that families post the Family Page at home in a prominent location as a reminder to do some of the activities suggested there.

CENTERING

1 Invite the children to tell what they or their families have done to welcome someone into their home.

• ***There are many things we do when we have visitors in our home to make them feel welcome. What are some things that your family does to welcome visitors to your home?*** (Greet them; invite them in; ask to take their coats; invite them to sit down.)

2 Show Cutout 4. Discuss welcoming others.

• ***A welcome says that we want to get to know the other person and want them to get to know us. A welcome is a way to show that we care for others. When we make others feel welcome, they might also open up their hearts to welcome us too. Jesus wants to love others through us. We share Jesus' love when we welcome others.***

SHARING

1 Encourage the children to have a welcoming attitude. Ask them what they can do to make visitors feel welcome at school (and at home). Model each suggestion and invite the children to act out their suggestions and, if you wish, some of the following suggestions.

- Greet visitors with a smile.
- Open and close doors courteously.
- Place a welcome sign on the door.
- Offer visitors a chair.
- Listen politely.
- Be friendly.
- Show visitors around.
- Ask visitors to join activities.
- Invite other students to share your toys or to join your game.

2 Let the children dramatize how they will greet visitors to the classroom throughout the year. (Examples: a guest speaker, the principal, or children from another class) Include suggestions for what such occasions might be like.

3 As a reminder of the welcoming atmosphere you wish to create in your classroom, invite the children to decorate a welcome sign for the classroom door. Use a large poster and allow each child to contribute to the welcome sign. If time allows, each child can also decorate a welcome sign from BLM 2 Welcome Sign for the door of his or her room at home.

• ***BLM 2 Welcome Sign***

4 Create with the children a welcome song to a familiar melody, such as the following example sung to the melody of "Here We Go 'Round the Mulberry Bush."

This is the way we welcome a friend,
[Children smile and wave at one another.]
Welcome a friend, welcome a friend.

This is the way we welcome a friend
On a** (day of week) **morning.

5 Read aloud **page 3.** Discuss the picture. Ask who the people might be.

6 Guide the children in doing the activity on **page 3.** Point out the picture of a cross and the words *Try This.* Explain that whenever they see a picture of a cross with these words, they will know that there is something for them to do on the page.

ACTING

1 Give directions for the Family Pages.

- ***Take your books home*** (Or as an alternative, tear out the pages for this chapter) ***and show your families the pages we've been talking about this week.***
- ***Have your family read the Note to Families pages in the front of your book.*** [Show **pages v–vi.**]
- ***Find page 4.*** [Show it.] ***The last page of every chapter has special family information. These notes will help your families know and love Jesus more.***

2 Suggest that the children pray the psalm prayer at home.

- ***We've learned a psalm prayer this week. You can also pray this at home and teach your family this prayer. When might you pray this prayer at home?*** (At bedtime; at mealtime; in the morning)
- ***These are all great times to pray. Now is also a good time for us to pray our thanks to God for all that we have learned this week: thanks that Jesus welcomes us; thanks that other people in our lives welcome us; and thanks for our ability to welcome others. Let's pray together the psalm prayer with gestures.***

3 Invite the children to pray Psalm 73:28.

To lead the psalm prayers, first invite the children to pray with you by watching as you pray the words of the psalm with the gestures. Next invite the children to continue to pray together with you by copying only the gestures as you say the words. Finally, invite the children to pray with you the words and the gestures together. When

Others welcome us.
We welcome others.

Try This

Look at the pictures of people showing welcome.

Circle them.

Think about how you might welcome others today.

3

finished, ask the children to sit down quietly.

To be near God
[Cross hands over heart.]

is . . . good.
[Move arms up in a bursting motion.]

Songs

Play for the children any of these songs: "We Are Marching" *(Singing Our Faith)* CD 1 Track 14; "Welcome In" *(The Best of Joe Wise)*; "Take My Hand," "Jesus Loves the Little Children" *(Stories and Songs of Jesus)*; "I Have a Hello" *(Sing a Song of Joy!)*; "Let's Be Friends" *(Hi God 3)*. For a list of all the music used in this program, see page OV-39.

CHECKPOINT

- What evidence do you see that the children are learning to welcome others?

ENRICHING THE FAITH EXPERIENCE

Use the following activities to enrich a lesson, to replace an activity with one that better meets the needs of your class, or to create an additional lesson.

1 To help the children learn one another's names, toss a ball or a beanbag to individual children. The child who holds the object says his or her name and then tosses the object back to you. After a while, when you toss the ball or beanbag, have the class say the name of the child who receives it.

2 For the lesson on Day Four, you might arrange for a surprise visitor to arrive near the end of class so that the children can apply what they have learned. When the visitor leaves, comment on the welcoming gestures of the children.

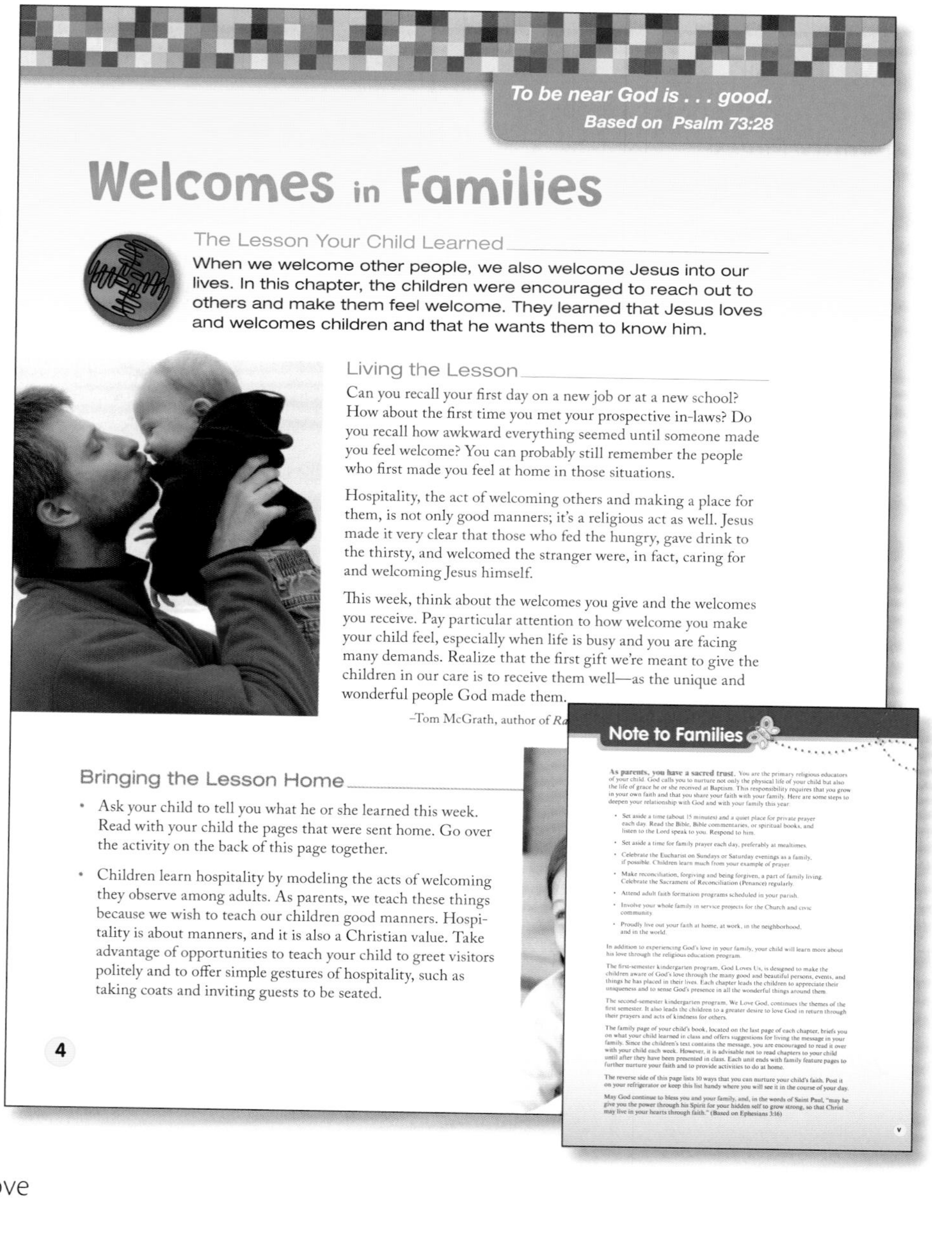

To be near God is . . . good.
Based on Psalm 73:28

Welcomes in Families

The Lesson Your Child Learned

When we welcome other people, we also welcome Jesus into our lives. In this chapter, the children were encouraged to reach out to others and make them feel welcome. They learned that Jesus loves and welcomes children and that he wants them to know him.

Living the Lesson

Can you recall your first day on a new job or at a new school? How about the first time you met your prospective in-laws? Do you recall how awkward everything seemed until someone made you feel welcome? You can probably still remember the people who first made you feel at home in those situations.

Hospitality, the act of welcoming others and making a place for them, is not only good manners; it's a religious act as well. Jesus made it very clear that those who fed the hungry, gave drink to the thirsty, and welcomed the stranger were, in fact, caring for and welcoming Jesus himself.

This week, think about the welcomes you give and the welcomes you receive. Pay particular attention to how welcome you make your child feel, especially when life is busy and you are facing many demands. Realize that the first gift we're meant to give the children in our care is to receive them well—as the unique and wonderful people God made them.

–Tom McGrath, author of *Ra*

Bringing the Lesson Home

- Ask your child to tell you what he or she learned this week. Read with your child the pages that were sent home. Go over the activity on the back of this page together.
- Children learn hospitality by modeling the acts of welcoming they observe among adults. As parents, we teach these things because we wish to teach our children good manners. Hospitality is about manners, and it is also a Christian value. Take advantage of opportunities to teach your child to greet visitors politely and to offer simple gestures of hospitality, such as taking coats and inviting guests to be seated.

4

Note to Families

As parents, you have a sacred trust. You are the primary religious educators of your child. God calls you to nurture not only the physical life of your child but also the life of grace he or she received at Baptism. This responsibility requires that you grow in your own faith and that you share your faith with your family. Here are some steps to deepen your relationship with God and with your family this year:

- Set aside a time (about 15 minutes) and a quiet place for private prayer each day. Read the Bible, Bible commentaries, or spiritual books, and listen to the Lord speak to you. Respond to him.
- Set aside a time for family prayer each day, preferably at mealtimes.
- Celebrate the Eucharist on Sundays or Saturday evenings as a family, if possible. Children learn much from your example of prayer.
- Make reconciliation, forgiving and being forgiven, a part of family living. Celebrate the Sacrament of Reconciliation (Penance) regularly.
- Attend adult faith formation programs scheduled in your parish.
- Involve your whole family in service projects for the Church and civic community.
- Proudly live out your faith at home, at work, in the neighborhood, and in the world.

In addition to experiencing God's love in your family, your child will learn more about his love through the religious education program.

The first-semester kindergarten program, God Loves Us, is designed to make the children aware of God's love through the many good and beautiful persons, events, and things he has placed in their lives. Each chapter leads the children to appreciate their uniqueness and to sense God's presence in all the wonderful things around them.

The second-semester kindergarten program, We Love God, continues the themes of the first semester. It also leads the children to a greater desire to love God in return through their prayers and acts of kindness for others.

The family page of your child's book, located on the last page of each chapter, briefs you on what your child learned in class and offers suggestions for living the message in your family. Since the children's text contains the message, you are encouraged to read it over with your child each week. However, it is advisable not to read chapters to your child until after they have been presented in class. Each unit ends with family feature pages to further nurture your faith and to provide activities to do at home.

The reverse side of this page lists 10 ways that you can nurture your child's faith. Post it on your refrigerator or keep this list handy where you will see it in the course of your day.

May God continue to bless you and your family, and, in the words of Saint Paul, "may he give you the power through his Spirit for your hidden self to grow strong, so that Christ may live in your hearts through faith." (Based on Ephesians 3:16)

v

3 Teach the children the poem "Welcomes" and have them make up gestures.

Welcomes

"Hello," "Hi," and "How [are]
you doing?"
Let Jesus' love shine through.
So I welcome everyone—
You and you and you!

M. Kathleen Glavich, S.N.D.

4 Practice ways in which children might welcome others to share in their play activities. Role-play such situations and model invitations or requests such as "Would you like to join our game?" "I'm building a castle with these blocks. Would you like to help?" "May I sit next to you so I can share your crayons?"

5 Make heart-shaped cookies for the children to eat during snack time. Before serving the cookies, remind the children that welcomes tell others that we love them. If you choose this option, be sure to find out if any children have food allergies and take these into consideration when planning snacks.

Chapter 2

Names Are Good

FAITH FOCUS

Because Jesus is God, his name is holy.

Psalm 8:2; Philippians 2:9–10

PREPARING THE FAITH EXPERIENCE

LISTENING

As you prepare to share God's Word of love with the children, spend some quiet time with God in prayer. Relax your body, quiet your mind, and let yourself be aware that you are filled with God's love. Ask God to speak to you his Word of love.

God greatly exalted him
and bestowed on him the name
that is above every name,
that at the name of Jesus
every knee should bend,
of those in heaven and on
earth and under the earth.
Philippians 2:9–10

REFLECTING

Since ancient times, a person's name has been thought to have great significance and is chosen with great care. Historically, names often expressed one's role in life and might be changed as the individual's personality or position in the community changed. In biblical times the name embodied the very mystery of the person. In the early Church, adult converts often took new names at Baptism to signify their new identity in Christ. Calling someone by his or her first name has long been considered a sign of a certain degree of intimacy.

The word *God* is not actually a name, but a word that designates the supreme being. When God revealed himself to Moses, he revealed his name. *Yahweh*, or "I Am Who Am," is a name that designates God as creator and signifies his presence with us. However, out of reverence and awe, the Jewish people do not pronounce it. Instead they use the word *Lord* (*Adonai*), which consequently bears all the mystery and holiness of the name Yahweh.

God the Father bestowed upon his Son "a name above every name," Jesus. *Jesus* means "Yahweh saves." Jesus is the Lord, the Most High God. He is the Savior. Only after his death and Resurrection did his followers understand that Jesus' name expresses who he is. On Easter night, the disciples told the missing Thomas, "We have seen the Lord." (John 20:25) When Thomas knew Jesus for who he was, he uttered, "My Lord and my God." (John 20:28) John recognized the risen Jesus on the shores of Tiberias and said to Peter, "It is the Lord." (John 21:7) After experiencing Jesus' presence in the breaking of the bread at Emmaus, the disciples rushed back to the others in Jerusalem, who agreed that "the Lord has truly been raised." (Luke 24:34)

Now all creatures in heaven and on earth bow their heads at the name of Jesus. Reverently repeating the holy name of Jesus is a testimony of our love and faith in his divinity and brings us into his presence. This form of prayer, sometimes called the Jesus Prayer, has long been a part of the Christian tradition. *Jesus . . . Jesus . . . Jesus* . . . "O LORD, our Lord, how awesome is your name through all the earth!" (Psalm 8:2)

RESPONDING

God's Word calls us to respond in love. Respond to God now in the quiet of your heart, and perhaps through a journal that you are keeping this year.

- How do I convey my reverence for God's name through my voice, my actions, and my posture?

Jesus, instill in me and in these children a great love for your name.

Catechism of the Catholic Church

The themes of this lesson correspond to the following paragraphs: 203, 2143, 2158, 2666.

THE FAITH EXPERIENCE

DAY ONE
Names Are Important

DAY TWO
My Name and God's

DAY THREE
Jesus Is God

DAY FOUR
Honoring Jesus' Name

Scripture in This Chapter

- *Exodus 20:7 God commands the Israelites to respect his name.*
- *Isaiah 43:1–4 God has called us by name. We are precious in his sight.*
- *Acts 4:12 Jesus is Lord. We are saved in his name.*

Church Documents

General Directory for Catechesis #41.
National Directory for Catechesis #25, A.
The job of the teacher is to present the faith as a following of the person of Jesus.

God Is Love #1.
God lavishes his love on us, and we in turn must share it with others.

Bulletin Board At the left is a suggestion for a bulletin-board design. You might make more stars out of aluminum or gold foil.

- *BLM 1 Jesus*

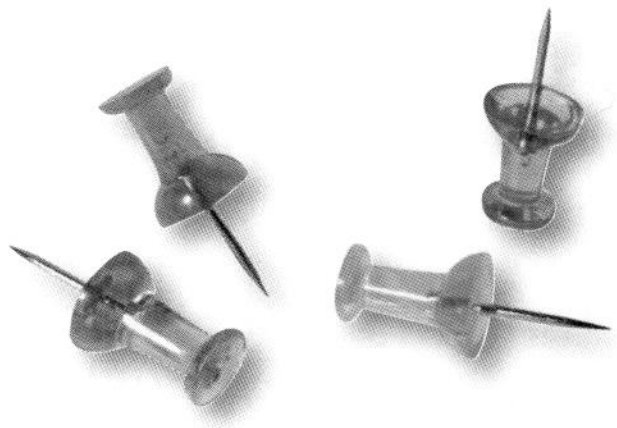

For a list of children's literature suggestions, please see **page OV-47.**

CHAPTER 2 | DAY ONE

Names Are Important

LEARNING OUTCOMES

The children will be able to

- know why names are important.
- experience silence as a way to show reverence.

MATERIALS

- Name card for each child
- Poster 2

COMMENTS

1. Children have a natural capacity for wonder, which makes them open to experiencing the sacred. We can help to develop this sense of the sacred in children. Learning to appreciate and practice silence is a step in this development.

2. Even before cognitive understanding, children recognize and respond to the attitudes behind our words. Children will sense from our reverent tone of voice and respectful manner our beliefs about the transcendence of God, even if they do not fully comprehend this.

CENTERING

1 Introduce the topic of names by playing a name game. Sing the children's names one by one on two notes (G and E) and have each child sing the response "I'm here" on the same two notes. Invite the children to hold up a card with their name on it as their name is called.

2 Ask:

- ***How do you know when your mother wants you?*** (She calls your name.)
- ***How do you know when your friends want you?*** (They call you by name.)
- ***How do you know which seat is yours?*** (It has your name on it.)
- ***How do you know which book is yours?*** (It has your name written on it.)

3 Recall the last class. Display Poster 2 Jesus and the Children.

- ***How do we make people feel welcome?*** (We greet them. We smile at them.)
- ***Another way we make people feel welcome is by calling them by name when we speak to them.***

SHARING

1 Discuss the purpose of names.

- ***Names are good because they let people know who we are. People who know and love us call us by name. Names tell us who other people are.***

2 Have the children play "Nametown" to help them learn one another's names.

- Designate a far section of the room as Nametown. Place a chair near this section and call it the namechair.
- Have the children sit in a semicircle with their backs to Nametown and their eyes closed. Tell them it is important to be very quiet during the game.
- Tap a child, who then tiptoes to the namechair and sits there quietly.
- Tell the children to open their eyes. Without looking at the namechair, they guess who is missing from the circle by asking a question, such as "Peter, are you on the namechair?" The missing child does not answer unless his or her name is guessed. When the child's name is guessed, he or she answers yes and then quietly sits down in Nametown.
- When all the children have moved to Nametown, invite them back to their original places by whispering each of their names. When a child hears his or her name, he or she returns quietly.
- After all of them have returned, let them clap for being good listeners. (Alternatively, another name game could be played, such as the beanbag toss in Chapter 1, ENRICHING THE FAITH EXPERIENCE #1.)

3 Guide the children to understand the origin of some names.

- ***Long ago people's last names told something about them. Perhaps Mr. Hill lived on a hill. Mr. Carpenter was a carpenter who made things out of wood. What might Mr. Baker do? Why might a man be called Mr. Little?***
- ***Sometimes we know why we were given our name.*** [Invite volunteers to share.]

4 Ask the children:

- ***How would you feel if someone called you by saying, "Hey, you"?***
- ***How would you feel if someone made fun of your name? Why would you feel this way?***

Encourage the children to call others politely by name during class and at other times.

- ***Because we want to help others to feel welcome in our class, we will not make fun of other people's names.***
- ***God calls us by our name and also invites us to know his name. We use God's name respectfully. We use God's name when we pray. Whenever we say God's name, we say it like a prayer because God's name is special and important to us.***

ACTING

1 Introduce the closing prayer:

- ***We can call God by name when we pray. We can also show respect for God through our silence. We will do both in our prayer today.***

2 Invite the children to pray the following adaptation of Psalm 8:2 with gestures.

To lead the psalm prayers, first invite the children to pray with you by watching as you pray the words of the psalm with the gestures. Next invite the children to continue to pray together with you by copying only the gestures as you say the words. Finally, invite the children to pray with you the words and the gestures together. When finished, ask the children to sit down quietly.

O Lord,
[Raise extended arms.]

how great is your name
[Extend arms from sides.]

over all the earth.
[Bring hands down together to form a circle.]

You can also pray this psalm silently. Invite the children to pray with you only the gestures silently and reverently.

CHECKPOINT

- Do the children call one another by name?
- How did the children react to being silent?

CHAPTER 2 | DAY TWO

My Name and God's

Student Book page 5

LEARNING OUTCOMES

The children will be able to
- know that God calls them by name.
- regard God and the things that belong to God with reverence.

KEY TERM

God—the wonderful, all-powerful one who made everything and who loves us

MATERIALS
- Name card for each child
- Large poster with a large heart drawn on it
- Second set of decorated name cards or a set of letters for each child to spell his or her name
- Crayons or markers
- Glue sticks or transparent tape
- Scrap paper

COMMENT

Young children know with their bodies before they know with their minds. Therefore, gestures accompanying songs and prayers are an important part of children's prayer and catechesis. Practice before you present gestures to the children. Refer to page T21 for reminders on how to teach the psalm prayers. By the fourth day, this repetition may no longer be necessary. Occasionally, pray using only gestures to encourage the practice of showing reverence for God through silence.

CENTERING

1 Have the children open their books to **page 5**. Show the picture.

- ***The child in the picture is saying her name is Anna. How do you think she feels?*** (Happy, proud) ***The words above the picture ask, "Who are you?"***

2 Comment:

- ***Just as we see Anna's name on this page, your names are found in many places around our classroom. Listen for your own name as I read them.*** [Read each child's name at least once from nametags on desks, cubbies, books, bulletin-board displays.]

Allow time for the children to walk around the room to find their names in at least two different places (done as a "Read Around the Classroom" activity; name game/word find). Then have the children return to their seats.

3 Invite the children to notice the message in the box.

- ***In the box it says, "When our friends call us by name, we feel good."***

4 Invite the children to write their names on **page 5**. Distribute paper and crayons or markers and let the children practice writing their names using their name cards as a pattern. Circulate and assist them as needed. Children have varying degrees of ability. Note that perfection is not the goal and that it is important only for the children to do their best.

SHARING

1 Invite the children to join you in a circle around the poster with a large heart drawn on it. Give each child a decorated card with his or her name printed on it (or letter cutouts to spell his or her name). Invite each child to glue his or her name card (or the letters) inside the heart. Tell them that God loves each of them and calls them by name. Display the large heart in the classroom.

2 Introduce God's name.

- ***What do you think is the greatest name in the whole world?*** (God)
- ***Everyone's name is important because every person is important. However, God's name is the greatest name throughout the whole earth because God is so wonderful. God is Lord over all the earth. God made everything.***

- ***God told us his name. God wants us to know him.***
- ***Just as we like it when people we know say our names with love, God also wants us to show our love for him by the way we speak God's name. Whenever we speak about God or say God's name, we speak our words with care so we show our respect for God.***

ACTING

1 Invite the children to thank God in their hearts for telling us his name and letting us know him.

2 Encourage the children always to say God's name with love.

3 Invite the children to pray the adaptation of Psalm 8:2.

To lead the psalm prayers, first invite the children to pray with you by watching as you pray the words of the psalm with the gestures. Next invite the children to continue to pray together with you by copying only the gestures as you say the words. Finally, invite the children to pray with you the words and the gestures together. When finished, ask the children to sit down quietly.

O Lord,
[Raise extended arms.]

how great is your name
[Extend arms from sides.]

over all the earth.
[Bring hands down together to form a circle.]

CHECKPOINT

- Are the children using others' names respectfully? Do the children say God's name with respect?

CHAPTER 2
Names Are Good
Who Are You?
I'm Anna!
When our friends call us by name, we feel good.
My name is
5

Jesus Is God

Student Book pages 6–7

LEARNING OUTCOMES

The children will be able to
- know that Jesus is God.
- reverence the name of Jesus.

KEY TERMS

genuflect—to show respect in church by touching a knee to the ground

holy—relating to God or things of God

MATERIALS

- Cutout 1
- Flashcard 1
- Bible enthroned, with note card on which you have written the adapted Scripture reading for SHARING #2, Philippians 2:9–10
- Sample holy cards, icons, or pictures of stained glass windows (optional)
- Crayons or markers

COMMENT

Gestures and posture are important parts of our liturgical prayer as Catholics. When we gather for Mass, we stand, kneel, genuflect, and bow, expressing with our bodies our reverence for God. Performing these gestures with reverence and care helps to raise our hearts and minds to God.

Game showing respect for God & Jesus
- kneel
- silence
- bow
- stand
- sit
- close eyes
- put hand together

CENTERING

1 Remind the children that names are important.

- ***We show respect for people when we respect their names. God told us his name. We show our love for God by respecting his name.*** Ask the children how we show our respect, or reverence, for God's name. (We say God's name with care and love; We use God's name only in prayer; We show our respect through silence.)

2 Sing a song to praise God's name. (Examples: teach a song to the melody of "God Is So Good" or choose a song from the song list on **page T24**)

Names are so good.
(Three times)
Jesus' name is good.

God's name is good.
(Three times)
Holy is God's name.

SHARING

1 Remind the children who Jesus is.

- ***God our Father loves us very much. God our Father sent his Son into our world. His name is Jesus.*** [Show Flashcard 1 *Jesus.* Pause.] ***We say Jesus' name with love.*** [Pause.]

2 Explain why and how we should honor the name of Jesus. Show Cutout 1 Jesus.

- ***What is this man's name?*** (Jesus)
- ***Who is Jesus?*** (God)
- ***God our Father is holy. Jesus is God's Son, and he is holy. So his name is very special. His name is holy. We should say the name "Jesus" with love.***
- ***One of God's special friends, Saint Paul, wrote about Jesus' name. His words are in the Bible. Here is what he wrote:*** [Read from the Bible, Philippians 2:9–10.] ***He wrote that when Jesus' name is said, everyone in heaven, on earth, and under the earth should kneel.*** [Genuflect.] ***This is because Jesus is God's Son.***

3 Explain genuflecting to the children.

- ***Just as we can say God's name with respect and love, we have other special ways of showing our respect for God. One way is by kneeling in a special way, called genuflecting.*** [Demonstrate how we genuflect and have the children practice genuflecting on the right knee. Gestures can and should be adapted when necessary to accommodate different needs, such as bowing instead of genuflecting.]

4 Show Flashcard 1 again and ask why we should always say the name of Jesus with love. (Jesus is God.)

- ***There is a special prayer through which we show our love for God by quietly praying Jesus' name.*** Invite the children to pray this quiet prayer.
- ***Please close your eyes and sit very still.*** [Pause.] ***Remember that Jesus is with us always.*** [Pause.] ***As I say Jesus' name, in your heart quietly tell Jesus how much you love him.*** Pray the Jesus Prayer by repeating the name "Jesus" silently and reverently.
- ***Jesus.*** [Pause.]
- ***Jesus.*** [Pause.]
- ***Jesus.*** [Pause.]
- ***When you have finished your prayer, open your eyes so I know that you are finished.***

5 When everyone has finished their quiet prayer, ask the children to open their books to **page 6.** Read aloud the text, pausing before the last word in each sentence and allowing the children to say the last words with you.

- ***Jesus is (***God).
- ***His name is*** (holy).
- ***We say Jesus' name with*** (love).
- ***God tells us his*** (name).
- ***He loves*** (us).

ACTING

1 Guide the children to do the activity on **page 7.** Comment:

- ***We can also draw and color pictures in a special way when we want to show that something or someone is holy.***
- ***Look at the picture of Jesus on page 6. What do you notice about this picture?*** You might also show examples of holy cards, an icon, or a stained-glass window. Continue to note with the children what makes these pictures different from other pictures.
- ***Color and decorate the name "Jesus" found on page 7 to show that it is holy.***
- ***Work carefully because you want to show that Jesus' name is holy. When you are finished, look at Jesus' name and say it softly with love.***
- ***Jesus' name is a prayer.***

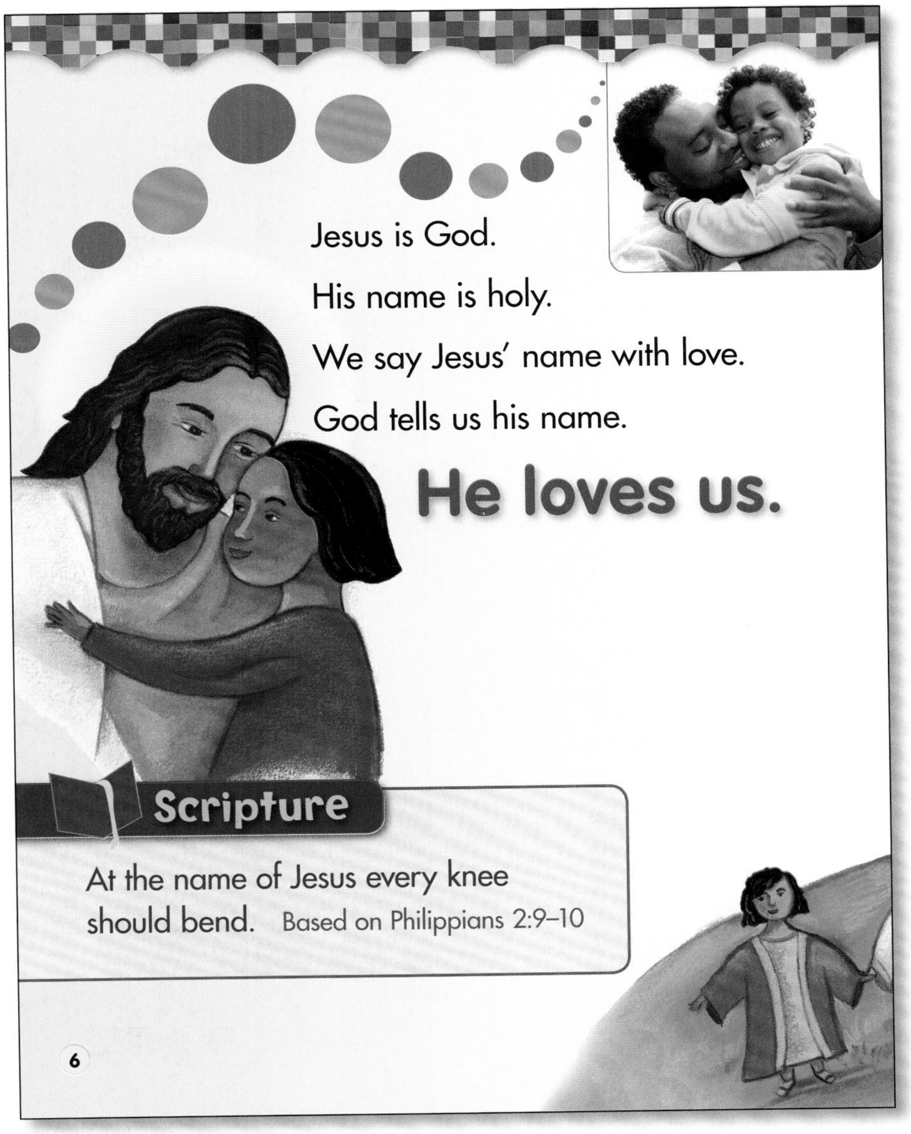
Jesus is God.

His name is holy.

We say Jesus' name with love.

God tells us his name.

He loves us.

Scripture

At the name of Jesus every knee should bend. Based on Philippians 2:9–10

6

2 Pray Psalm 8:2 with gestures, incorporating Jesus' name: "Jesus, how great is your name over all the earth." When finished, invite the children to show their love for Jesus' name by genuflecting.

To lead the psalm prayers, first invite the children to pray with you by watching as you pray the words of the psalm with the gestures. Next invite the children to continue to pray together with you by copying only the gestures as you say the words. Finally, invite the children to pray with you the words and the gestures together. When finished, ask the children to sit down quietly.

> **O Lord,**
> [Raise extended arms.]
>
> **how great is your name**
> [Extend arms from sides.]
>
> **over all the earth.**
> [Bring hands down together to form a circle.]

Songs

Play for the children any of these songs: "Jesus in the Morning" (*Singing Our Faith*) **CD 1 Track 4;** "By Name I Have Called You" (*By Name I Have Called You*); "God Is So Good" (*Color the World with Song*); "O, How I Love Jesus," "Thank You, Lord" (*Hi God!*); "Jesus, Jesus" (*Hi God 2*). For a list of all the music used in this program, see **page OV-39**.

CHECKPOINT

- Do the children show reverence for Jesus' name?

Try This

Jesus' name is holy.
Color the letters in Jesus' name.

Honoring Jesus' Name

Student Book page 8

LEARNING OUTCOMES

The children will be able to
- give honor to Jesus' name through art and prayer.

MATERIALS

- Sample holy cards, icons, or pictures of stained-glass windows (optional)
- Jesus Name Card punchouts from the Student Book
- Cutout 1
- Crayons or markers
- Glue sticks
- Colored cellophane

COMMENTS

Prepare samples of decorated Jesus Name Cards for use in SHARING #2–3. These might also be drawn on the board or on a large sheet of paper.

CENTERING

Ask the children why Saint Paul said that all people should kneel when they hear the name of Jesus. (Jesus is God. He is holy.)

- ***Let's practice our special way of kneeling, called genuflecting.*** Invite the class to genuflect with you. Tell the children that we genuflect at church. Suggest that they watch for this the next time they are at Mass. For example, we genuflect when we enter and leave church. The priest genuflects before the Eucharist.

SHARING

1 If you have prepared the bulletin board or have other classroom displays that show Jesus' name, invite the children to look for these in your classroom.

2 Show examples of a holy card, an icon, or a stained-glass window. Remind the children how we can color and draw in ways that show something to be holy. Distribute the Jesus Name Card punchouts. Have the children decorate them on the front and the back. Show the children how to fold the cards so they stand.

3 Alternatively, cut out the letters of Jesus' name from the Jesus Name Card punchouts. Distribute these precut Jesus name cards. Help the children glue pieces of colored cellophane to make "stained-glass" pictures of Jesus' name.

4 Tell the children that they should say God's name only for prayer and for talking about God. Suggest that they put their Jesus Name Cards (or the "stained-glass" pictures) where they will remember to pray "Jesus."

ACTING

1 Hold up Cutout 1. Have the children hold their Jesus name cards in their hands and pray with you. Tell them that you will say the first part of the prayer and invite them to respond by saying "Jesus."

- ***You welcome us . . .*** (Jesus.)
- ***You are God . . .*** (Jesus.)
- ***You love us . . .*** (Jesus.)
- ***Your name is holy . . .*** (Jesus.)
- ***We love you . . .*** (Jesus.)

2 Invite the children to thank Jesus for all that we have learned this week about God's name. Have them pray the adapted psalm verse Psalm 8:2.

To lead the psalm prayers, first invite the children to pray with you by watching as you pray the words of the psalm with the gestures. Next invite the children to continue to pray together with you by copying only the gestures as you say the words. Finally, invite the children to pray with you the words and the gestures together. When finished, ask the children to sit down quietly.

O Lord,
[Raise extended arms.]

how great is your name
[Extend arms from sides.]

over all the earth.
[Bring hands down together to form a circle.]

3 Have the children take home the Family Page on **page 8** to share with their families.

CHECKPOINT

- How will you continue to invite the children to honor Jesus' name?

ENRICHING THE FAITH EXPERIENCE

Use the following activities to enrich a lesson, to replace an activity with one that better meets the needs of your class, or to create an additional lesson.

1 Have the children trace around their own names with three different colors of crayons to make a special name card.

2 Let the children listen to a song about being called by name or a song about Jesus' name. Possible choices are "Jesus, Jesus" (*Hi God 2*) or "How Much God Loves Us" (*Stories and Songs of Jesus*). Ask the children to sit quietly with their hands in their laps so that they can listen carefully to the song. Teach this song to the children.

O Lord, how great is your name, over all the earth.
Based on Psalm 8:2

Names in Families

The Lesson Your Child Learned

To pronounce the name of Jesus reverently is to show respect for him. In this chapter the children talked about the importance of names. They were led to experience the mystery of God by becoming aware that Jesus' name is holy.

Living the Lesson

You may have seen that running gag on the TV show *Seinfeld*. Every time Jerry ran into the irritating neighbor who lived upstairs, he would sneer his name, "Newman," in the same way you might talk about a dreaded disease. That one word spoke volumes about Jerry's negative feelings. It was a recurring example of how the way we use names reveals what's in our hearts.

We should be careful with the names we use and how we use them. Every one of us longs for respect. We can offer that respect to those in our family as a way of recognizing that we are all made in the image of God. One of the surest ways to show respect is to say one another's names with kindness and care—even when we are angry!

There was an e-mail going around the Internet a few years ago listing the responses of young children to the question, "How would you define the word love?" One five-year-old reportedly said, "When somebody loves you, your name is safe in their mouth." To take this week's lesson to heart, make sure the names of your family members are "safe in your mouth" and show the same care for the names we use for God.

–Tom McGrath, author of *Raising Faith-Filled Kids* (Loyola Press)

Bringing the Lesson Home

- Read with your child the pages that were sent home.
- Share with your child the significance of his or her name—its meaning and why it was chosen. If the name was given to honor a family member or friend, tell about the qualities of that person that you admire. Encourage your child to greet by name the people he or she meets.
- Talk with your child about nicknames. Tell your child that nicknames are welcome and fun only if the person likes the name he or she is being called. Explain that one of the first things bullies usually do is give mean names to the kids they want to bully—and that is wrong.
- Some families make a practice of bowing their head slightly whenever they use the name of Jesus. This is something your family might like to do as a sign of respect for our Lord.
- Pray Psalm 8:2 as part of your family prayers this week. Ask your child to teach you and other family members the gestures for this psalm and pray it together as a family.

8

3 Make a "Name Tree." Find a large, leafless tree branch, paint it white or green, and place it in a coffee can. Anchor it with sand or plaster of Paris. Give each child a pink heart with his or her name on it. (String yarn through holes in the top so that the hearts are ready to hang.) The children may put the hearts on the tree to show that their names are good and that people who love them call them by name. Each child may say his or her name when placing the heart on the tree.

4 Prepare a heart name card for Jesus, which will be placed on the "Name Tree" in #3. Make it a little larger than the others and sprinkle it with glitter. Let a child hang the heart in a special place on the tree as he or she says, "Jesus is God" or "We love the name of Jesus."

5 Have the children sing "Thank You, Lord" from *Hi God!* and insert the names of the children to whom you point. If the class is too large to sing to everyone, sing the song each lesson until you have thanked God for each child. Examples:

Thank you, Lord, for giving us José.

Thank you, Lord, for giving us Evan.

Thank you, Lord, for giving us Min.

Right where we are.

6 To help the children learn one another's names, have them play a variation of Duck—Duck—Goose! All the children sit in a circle. One child who is "It" walks around the outside of the circle, tapping each child's head while saying "duck." When the child who is "It" comes to the one he or she wants to be "It" next, he or she says the child's name instead of "duck." That child jumps up quickly and chases the first child back to his or her place, trying to tag him or her before reaching it. The second child becomes "It" if the first child is not caught; otherwise, the first child must be "It" again. Other games might be similarly adapted.

7 Encourage the children to ask their parents about their names: why they were given them and what they mean. Let the children informally tell about their names.

Chapter 3

Stories Are Good

FAITH FOCUS

God tells us in the Bible that he loves us.

Jeremiah 31:3; Book of Jonah

PREPARING THE FAITH EXPERIENCE

LISTENING

Those who share God's Word with others must be nourished themselves by God's Word found in Sacred Scripture. Share some time of quiet prayer with God, listening to his Word. Ask God to fill you with his presence and nourish you by his holy Word.

With age-old love I have loved you.
Jeremiah 31:3

You might also wish to read the Book of Jonah.

REFLECTING

Since the beginning of time, storytellers have had an important role in preserving and transmitting the cultural heritage of peoples from one generation to the next. The Church has a similar heritage—a tradition that is preserved in the Bible and passed on to each generation and continues to be passed on to us today. The Bible is the unique story of a people's struggle to respond to their God. Through the Bible, we learn that God continued to love and care for his people as they tried to live up to the ideal of life he set before them. The story of the Bible is our story. The Bible is unique because God speaks to us through its sacred words and is continually revealed anew to us.

Just as ancient people learned who they were by listening to the storyteller's song or chant, we find meaning for our lives in the Christian story. Therefore, as we gather each Sunday as a people of faith, we hear our faith story related through the readings of Sacred Scripture and discover and reflect upon God's presence and action in our lives. As we listen to the account of our biblical ancestors' failings and victories, hopes and fears, we come to realize that the Bible, God's story of love for his people, is the story of our lives and of God's love for us. God speaks to us from burning bushes, calls us by name in the stillness of night, bids us go to foreign lands to speak his name, and leads us through a parted Red Sea if we trust and follow him.

In the stories of the Bible, we see how God leads each of us on a pilgrimage to him. We hear God speak his Word of love.

RESPONDING

Having been nourished by God's Word, we are able to respond to God's great love for us. In prayer, respond to God's call to you to share his Word with others. You may also wish to respond in your prayer journal.

- What am I doing to grow in my own understanding and appreciation of the Bible?
- How might I practice and improve my storytelling skills so that I can better present God's Word to the children?

Father, open our hearts to respond with love to your Word.

Catechism of the Catholic Church

The themes of this lesson correspond to the following paragraphs: 97, 104, 131, 1190.

THE FAITH EXPERIENCE

DAY ONE
Books Tell Stories

DAY TWO
The Bible Is Holy

DAY THREE
Jonah: A Bible Story

DAY FOUR
Celebrating the Bible

Scripture in this chapter

- *John 20:30–31 Events of Jesus' life are recorded to enable us to believe in him.*
- *Timothy 3:14–17 In Sacred Scripture, we find wisdom about salvation in Jesus Christ.*

Church Documents

General Directory for Catechesis #127.
National Directory for Catechesis #24, B.
Those who teach the faith to others should be filled with biblical thought, spirit, and attitudes.

Dogmatic Constitution on Divine Revelation #23.
God's Word enlightens our minds, strengthens our wills, and sets our hearts on fire with love.

Bulletin Board At the left is a suggestion for a bulletin-board design. Refer to BLM 3 Bible Coloring Activity if you wish to make a photocopy or transparency. You might invite the children to make their own drawings of the Bible, or distribute copies of BLM 3 and have each child decorate his or her copy of the Bible to post on the bulletin board. Remind the children to write their names on their drawings. Children have varying degrees of ability. Note that perfection is not the goal and that it is important only for the children to do their best.

- *BLM 3 Bible Coloring Activity*

For a list of children's literature suggestions, please see **page OV-47.**

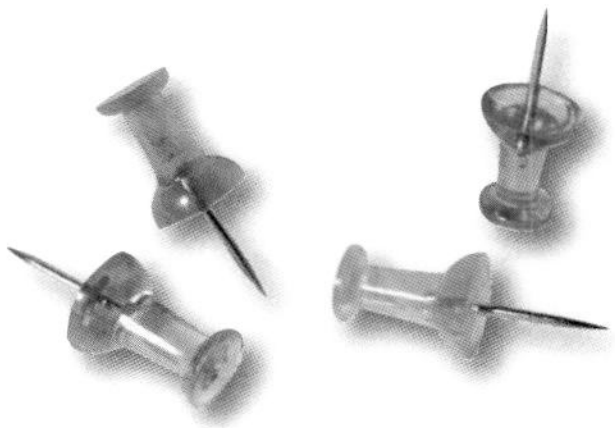

CHAPTER 3 | DAY ONE

Books Tell Stories

Student Book page 9

LEARNING OUTCOMES

The children will be able to

- practice good listening skills.
- realize that they have a story to tell and learn how to share it.

MATERIALS

- Storybooks containing familiar stories
- Stuffed animal or beanbag

COMMENTS

1. A child's sense of wonder is the beginning of worship. Some stories, such as fairy tales, call forth wonder and invite us to look at our world with eyes that see mystery behind what is commonplace, beauty hidden in ugliness, hope issuing from the impossible, and joy bursting forth from sorrow. These stories can help prepare children to recognize the wonder of God at work in our lives.

2. By the age of five, most young children are able to distinguish between fact and fantasy. They somehow perceive that fairy tales speak to them of reality through the medium of symbol. Our Catholic tradition is full of symbols. In our sacramental system, God is mediated to us through sign and symbol. Therefore, leading the children to look upon their world and their lives as containing mystery and wonder prepares them to participate more fully as a member of our worshiping community.

3. The Church has shown special concern for the instruction and participation of children in the Eucharist through the publication of the document *Directory for Masses with Children* in 1973 by the Sacred Congregation for Divine Worship. The *Directory* points out that, by reason of their baptism, children have both the right and the duty to participate in the Church's liturgy. It is the hope of the Church that young Christians who participate in the eucharistic sacrifice will learn to proclaim Christ by expressing love for others. (#55) The *Directory* recommends that from their early years children take part in the Mass with their families.

CENTERING

Recall the last chapter. Comment:

- ***The last time we met, we talked about names. Whose name is the greatest and holiest?*** (God's, Jesus') ***God told us his name because God loves us.***
- ***How might we honor God's name?*** (By genuflecting; with silence)
- ***In the next lessons you will learn more about God's love for you.***

SHARING

1 Show the storybooks and comment that many books tell us stories. Read the titles and ask the children whose story is told. Tell or have the children tell each character's story. (Example: "The Gingerbread Man." A gingerbread man runs away from many others, but gets eaten by a clever fox.) Ask if they have any favorite stories and invite them to share details from these stories.

2 Lead the children to tell their stories.

- ***People have been telling stories for a long, long time. Before stories were printed in books, people told stories to one another. Each of us can tell a story about ourselves. Would you like to hear my story?*** Tell your own story. (Examples: I live with my husband, my little boy, Michael, and my little girl, Anita. I love them very much. We have fun together. I like to take care of my cat, Miles. God is very good to me.)
- ***Each of you has a story too. If you wish, I will help you tell your story.*** Pass a stuffed animal or beanbag around the circle to help the children take turns answering simple questions. Some questions might include Who are the people in your family? What do you like to do? What is your favorite toy?

All children have different personalities and learning styles. Some will be eager to speak in front of groups. How will you invite others to share their stories? You might encourage children to participate by responding to other people's stories or through drawing.

3 Ask the children to turn to **page 9** in their books. Read aloud the text and have them follow along.

4 Read aloud **page 9** again, letting the children fill in the missing words:

- ***Books are full of*** (stories). ***Stories can make us*** (laugh) ***or*** (cry), ***open wide our*** (eyes) ***with wonder, or even shout with*** (joy).

ACTING

Teach the following adaptation of Psalm 78:4.

- ***This year I have many good stories to tell you of the wonderful things God has done. Let's pray our prayer for this week:***

To lead the psalm prayers, first invite the children to pray with you by watching as you pray the words of the psalm with the gestures. Next invite the children to continue to pray together with you by copying only the gestures as you say the words. Finally, invite the children to pray with you the words and the gestures together. When finished, ask the children to sit down quietly.

We will tell
[Touch your lips.]

the wonderful things
[Raise your hands above your head to form a large circle.]

the LORD has done.
[Bring your arms down, hands open with palms up in front of you.]

CHECKPOINT

- Did the children listen attentively as others told their stories? How might you help them learn to listen well to others?
- How many children participated in the storytelling? How will you invite others who were not comfortable with this exercise to share their stories?

CHAPTER 3

Stories Are Good

Books are full of stories.
Stories can make us laugh or cry,
open wide our eyes with wonder,
or even shout with joy.

9

The Bible Is Holy

Student Book page 10

LEARNING OUTCOMES

The children will be able to

- learn to reverence the Bible as God's Word.
- know that we hear the Bible read at Mass.

MATERIALS

- Bible enthroned, with note card on which you have written the adapted Scripture reading for SHARING #3, Jeremiah 31:3
- BLM 4
- Flashcard 2
- Crayons or markers
- Candle and matches

Remember to check with the proper authority regarding local regulations for using candles in a classroom setting. If candles are not permitted, you might consider using an electric candle or moving the activity to the church or chapel where candles are permitted.

COMMENT

Children may be more affected by nonverbal signs than by words. A beautifully bound Bible enthroned on a table communicates immediately that this book deserves special respect. Keep the Bible enthroned in the Prayer Center throughout the year. Reinforce reverence for the Bible by reading directly from this Bible whenever a Scripture story is told and when Scripture is prayed or proclaimed in the lesson or in the Student Book.

CENTERING

Invite the children to pray the psalm verse with gestures learned in the last lesson for Psalm 78:4.

To lead the psalm prayers, first invite the children to pray with you by watching as you pray the words of the psalm with the gestures. Next invite the children to continue to pray together with you by copying only the gestures as you say the words. Finally, invite the children to pray with you the words and the gestures together. When finished, ask the children to sit down quietly.

We will tell
[Touch your lips.]
the wonderful things
[Raise your hands above your head to form a large circle.]
the LORD has done.
[Bring your arms down, hands open with palms up in front of you.]

SHARING

1 Introduce the Bible. Show Flashcard 2 *good* as you say the word "good." Show the storybooks again. Comment:

- ***These are all good books. Which of these books did you like best? Why?***
- ***There is one book that is different from all others. It is the best book of all. It is God's book. The story of Jesus is in it. Do you know what it is called?*** (The Bible) Bring the Bible from the Prayer Center and show it to the children.
- ***Because God is holy, God's words are holy. Because God's words are in the Bible, it is a holy book. How should we treat it?*** (Carefully, reverently, respectfully)
- ***We will keep the Bible in a special place, our Prayer Center. We honor it. When we are reading from the Bible in church, we sometimes light a candle or use incense near the Bible.***
- ***What are some other things you have seen people do to honor the Bible in church?*** (Bow, carry it in procession, trace the cross on the Bible)
- ***Do you have a Bible at home? You might ask your parents to let you look at it.*** This might also be done in class. Look for moments in your day to allow children to handle the Bible and to look through it.

2 Direct the children to **page 10.** Read it to them.

- ***God's people come together every week to pray to God. At church during Mass we listen to God's story in the Bible. We listen to God speak to us.***
- ***Have you ever gone to church with your family and heard a priest or reader read from the Bible?*** Invite the children to talk about what they noticed

when the Bible was read in church (It was read from a special place, the lectern, or ambo.)

- ***Even though you may not understand everything you hear, you can listen quietly when the Bible is read aloud to show God that you know that God's Word is holy. Listening to God's Word is important. We show respect for God when we listen carefully to his words to us in the Bible.***

3 Prepare to read Jeremiah 31:3 from the Bible.

- ***I would like you to hear something from God's special book, the Bible. Listen carefully to what God says to you: "I have loved you with an everlasting love."*** (Jeremiah 31:3)
- ***Listen to these words again.*** [Reverently reread the verse.]
- ***Who spoke to you from the Bible?*** (God)
- ***What did God tell you?*** (He loves us.)
- ***What do you think the words "everlasting love" mean?*** (God's love for us goes on and on and will never stop.)
- ***God wants all people to read his book. We will read from the Bible often this year. Reading the Bible helps us to learn more about God's love and about Jesus.***

Take pictures c̄ Bible + children

ACTING

1 Distribute copies of BLM 4 Passage from Jeremiah and have the children color and decorate it. • ***BLM 4 Passage from Jeremiah***

2 Explain that we mark holy things with a cross. Teach the children to trace a cross slowly and reverently on their forehead, their lips, and their heart. Note that we can do this at Mass before we listen to the reading from the Bible called the Gospel.

3 Gather in the Prayer Center where the Bible is enthroned. Guide the children in making the Sign of the Cross before sitting in the Prayer Center.

4 Invite the children to pray together Psalm 78:4 as they did at the beginning of class.

CHECKPOINT

- Did the children listen attentively when the Bible verse was read to them?
- Are the children familiar with the Bible? Do they know that the Bible is a special book because it is God's Word?

The Bible is a holy book.

It tells the story of God's love for us.

The Bible tells the story of Jesus.

He came to show us God's love.

God's people listen to his story.

Scripture

We will tell the wonderful things the Lord has done.

Based on Psalm 78:4

10

CHAPTER 3 | DAY THREE

Jonah: A Bible Story

Student Book page 11

LEARNING OUTCOMES

The children will be able to

- practice listening to God's Word to us in the Bible.
- become familiar with the story of Jonah.

COMMENTS

In sharing Bible stories with our children, we share our faith community's experiences of God's action in our lives and in the world. Scripture stories can speak to us on many levels. Naturally, the children are not ready to analyze the Bible stories. However, they can be quite insightful in their reflections and observations. Their understanding will grow as they hear these stories again and again.

CENTERING

Recall the last lesson.

- ***What is God's special book called?*** (The Bible)
- ***What do the stories in the Bible tell us?*** (God loves us.)

SHARING

1 Invite the children to be good listeners.

- ***Today I have a good story to tell you from the Bible. First I will tell you an easy way to be good listeners. Besides having listening ears, you must have listening eyes, listening hands, listening feet, and listening hearts.***
- ***Listening eyes are on the storyteller.*** [Pause until all the children are looking at you.] ***Listening hands are quietly in your lap.*** [Pause until all the children have put their hands in their lap.] ***Listening feet are comfortable and quiet.*** [Pause until all the children's feet are still.] ***Listening hearts are ready to hear God's Word.*** [Pause.]
- ***This is a way we can prepare to listen well to all stories. We want to do this especially when we prepare to listen to God's Word to us in the Bible.***

2 Show **page 11**. Tell God's story of Jonah. Refer to the pictures as you tell the story.

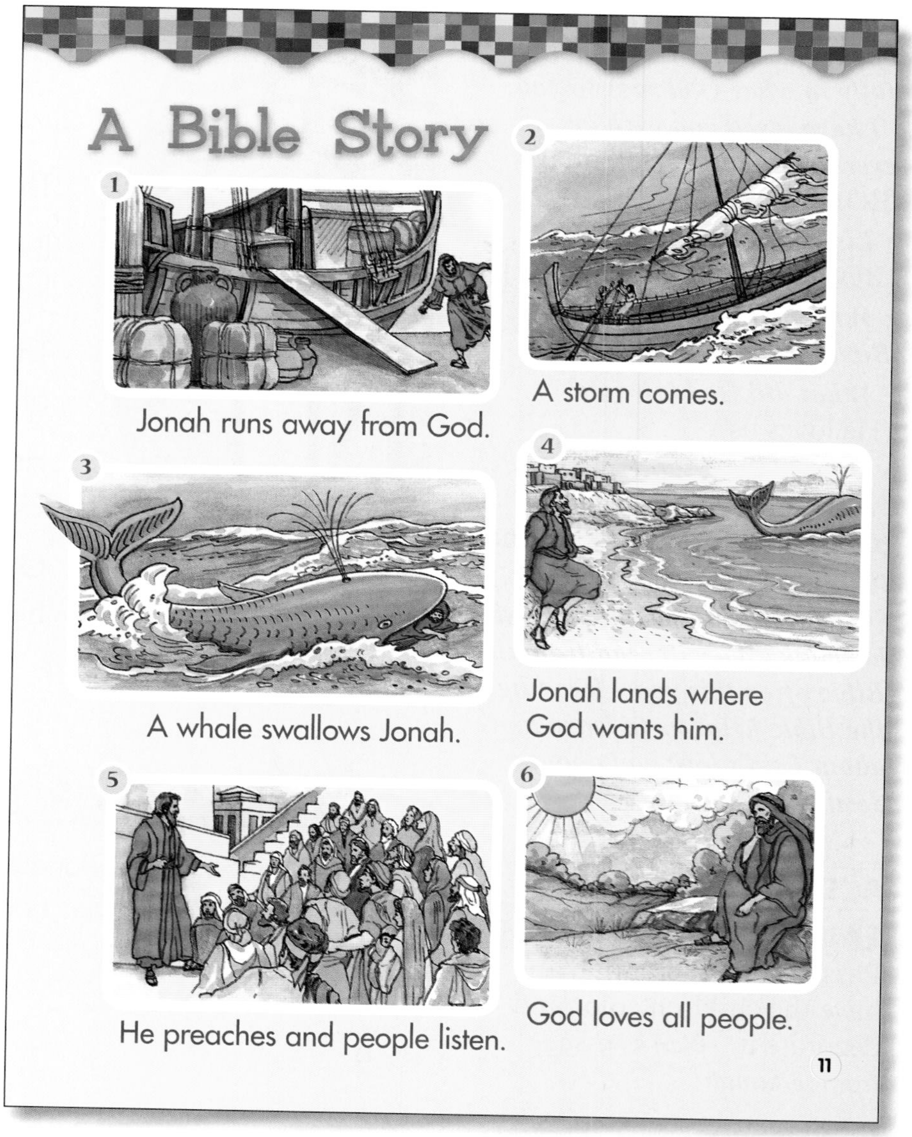

A Bible Story
1
Jonah runs away from God.
2
A storm comes.
3
A whale swallows Jonah.
4
Jonah lands where God wants him.
5
He preaches and people listen.
6
God loves all people.
11

Jonah and the Whale

Jonah was a good man. One day God told him to go to an enemy land. When he got there, God told Jonah to tell the people to change their evil ways and be good. Jonah was afraid to do this. He got on a boat and sailed away from the enemy country.

While Jonah was on the boat, a terrific storm came up. Thunder crashed and lightning flashed. The sailors thought the boat was going to sink. Jonah knew that he was running away from doing what God wanted. So he thought that the storm was his fault. He told the sailors to toss him into the sea.

Jonah was thrown overboard and the storm stopped. The sun came out. Jonah did not drown. God sent a whale to save him. The whale came and swallowed Jonah. Jonah lived inside the whale and prayed to God.

After three days the whale spat Jonah out onto a beach. Jonah looked around. He was in the enemy country, the country that he had been running away from.

Jonah decided to do what God had told him to do. He walked into the town and told the people to be good. Everyone listened to Jonah—even the king and the animals. They all felt sorry for the wrong things they had done. They made up for it and promised to be good.

But Jonah was not happy. He had hoped that God would punish the enemy. Jonah sat and pouted. A plant grew up over Jonah and shaded him from the sun. Jonah was happy to have the plant. But the next morning a worm bit into the plant and killed it. Jonah missed the plant.

God spoke to Jonah. "See how sad you are about the plant. Don't you think I care about the thousands of people in this country, not to mention the cattle?"

Then Jonah understood how much God loves us all.

3 Talk about the story.

- ***I was happy to see so many good listeners. There are many more stories from God's book that I will tell you this year.***
- ***What did you like about this story? What was your favorite part?***

4 Remind the children that the Bible tells of God's love.

- ***What did Jonah learn about God?*** (God loves all people)
- ***The Bible stories tell about God's people. Most of all, they tell how God loves his people. Each of you is one of God's people.***

Songs

Play for the children any of these songs: "God Loves Little People" (*Sing a Song of Joy!*) CD 2 Track 8; "I Like God's Love" (*Hi God!*); "Our God Is a God of Love" (*Hi God 2*); "I Have Loved You" (*On Eagle's Wings*). For a list of all the music used in this program, see page OV-39.

ACTING

Invite the children to pray Psalm 78:4 with gestures.

To lead the psalm prayers, first invite the children to pray with you by watching as you pray the words of the psalm with the gestures. Next invite the children to continue to pray together with you by copying only the gestures as you say the words. Finally, invite the children to pray with you the words and the gestures together. When finished, ask the children to sit down quietly.

We will tell
[Touch your lips.]

the wonderful things
[Raise your hands above your head to form a large circle.]

the LORD has done.
[Bring your arms down, hands open with palms up in front of you.]

CHECKPOINT

- Did the children listen attentively to the Bible story?

CHAPTER 3 | DAY FOUR

Celebrating the Bible

Student Book page 12

LEARNING OUTCOMES

The children will be able to

- show their reverence for the Bible.

MATERIALS

- Bible enthroned, with note card from Day Two, as center of the celebration
- Song for the celebration (optional)
- *A Child's Bible*, one copy for each child
- Jeremiah Bookmark punchouts from the Student Book

COMMENTS

Copies of *A Child's Bible* were provided with the Student Book. Additional copies are available from Loyola Press.

CENTERING

1 Introduce the celebration. Tell the children that they have been learning about God's wonderful book, the Bible. Today we will celebrate the Bible.

2 Explain what a great honor it is to read from the Bible or to hold it. Demonstrate how we handle and hold the Bible with reverence.

Also talk about how the Bible is raised and reverenced, as in procession at Mass. Invite the children to practice this.

3 There is another special way we honor God's Word to us when we read the Bible. Introduce the children to the response we say at Mass after we hear a reading from the Bible. The reader says, "The Word of the Lord." All respond, "Thanks be to God." Practice this with the children and tell them that we can use this response throughout the year when we read from the Bible.

4 Lead the children in a procession with the Bible to honor it as God's Word. Raise the Bible high at the head of the line. Let the children follow reverently while a song about God's Word or God's love is played. For suggestions, see the song list on **page T35.** End by setting the Bible on the place where it will remain enthroned in your Prayer Center. Invite the children to sit in the Prayer Center. Ask for a volunteer to hold the Bible while you read from it during the celebration.

SHARING

1 Recall that we mark holy things with a cross. Review with the children how to trace a cross on their forehead, their lips, and their heart. Note that we can do this at Mass before we listen to the reading from the Bible called the Gospel.

2 Read from the Bible, Jeremiah 31:3.

- ***Boys and girls, let us listen to God speak to us through the words of the holy Bible. God says, "I have loved you with an everlasting love."*** [Pause.] The Word of the Lord. ***Let us thank God for speaking to us. Say after me: "Thanks be to God."***

3 Sing "God Is So Good" with the children or play an appropriate song such as "I Like God's Love" from *Hi God!*

4 Present *A Child's Bible* to the children. Say:

- ***Today I have a special surprise for you. You will receive your very own Bible. It has some of the same stories that the class Bible has, but in words that are easier to understand.***
- ***When I give you your Bible, come to the large class Bible and place your Bible on it for a moment. Trace a cross on your forehead, lips, and heart as we practiced.*** [Demonstrate this for the children.] ***Then return to your seats. Do not open your books until I tell you to do so.***

• ***Your Bibles have God's holy words in them. They are special. This year we will be reading the stories in them. You may look through your Bibles now.*** [Allow time for the children to do this.]

ACTING

1 Distribute the Jeremiah Bookmark punchouts. Read the text to them. Tell the children that they can use it in their family Bible at home or keep it in their *Child's Bible*. Invite the children to write their names on the back of their bookmarks.

2 Invite the children to pray together Psalm 78:4 with gestures.

To lead the psalm prayers, first invite the children to pray with you by watching as you pray the words of the psalm with the gestures. Next invite the children to continue to pray together with you by copying only the gestures as you say the words. Finally, invite the children to pray with you the words and the gestures together. When finished, ask the children to sit down quietly.

We will tell
[Touch your lips.]

the wonderful things
[Raise your hands above your head to form a large circle.]

the LORD has done.
[Bring your arms down, hands open with palms up in front of you.]

3 Have the children take home the Family Page on **page 12** to share with their families.

CHECKPOINT

- How reverent were the children during the prayer celebration? How will you continue this spirit of reverence in future lessons?

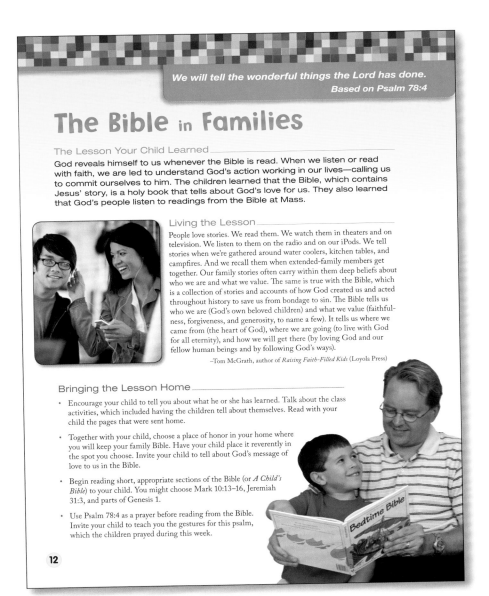

We will tell the wonderful things the Lord has done.
Based on Psalm 78:4

The Bible in Families

The Lesson Your Child Learned

God reveals himself to us whenever the Bible is read. When we listen or read with faith, we are led to understand God's action working in our lives—calling us to commit ourselves to him. The children learned that the Bible, which contains Jesus' story, is a holy book that tells about God's love for us. They also learned that God's people listen to readings from the Bible at Mass.

Living the Lesson

People love stories. We read them. We watch them in theaters and on television. We listen to them on the radio and on our iPods. We tell stories when we're gathered around water coolers, kitchen tables, and campfires. And we recall them when extended-family members get together. Our family stories often carry within them deep beliefs about who we are and what we value. The same is true with the Bible, which is a collection of stories and accounts of how God created us and acted throughout history to save us from bondage to sin. The Bible tells us who we are (God's own beloved children) and what we value (faithfulness, forgiveness, and generosity, to name a few). It tells us where we came from (the heart of God), where we are going (to live with God for all eternity), and how we will get there (by loving God and our fellow human beings and by following God's ways).

–Tom McGrath, author of *Raising Faith-Filled Kids* (Loyola Press)

Bringing the Lesson Home

- Encourage your child to tell you about what he or she has learned. Talk about the class activities, which included having the children tell about themselves. Read with your child the pages that were sent home.
- Together with your child, choose a place of honor in your home where you will keep your family Bible. Have your child place it reverently in the spot you choose. Invite your child to tell about God's message of love to us in the Bible.
- Begin reading short, appropriate sections of the Bible (or *A Child's Bible*) to your child. You might choose Mark 10:13–16, Jeremiah 31:3, and parts of Genesis 1.
- Use Psalm 78:4 as a prayer before reading from the Bible. Invite your child to teach you the gestures for this psalm, which the children prayed during this week.

12

ENRICHING THE FAITH EXPERIENCE

Use the following activities to enrich a lesson, to replace an activity with one that better meets the needs of your class, or to create an additional lesson.

1 Read the poem "Jonah's Journey" to the children. Have them stand and say the repeated words. Teach the gestures.

2 Teach the children a song to the melody of "God Is So Good."

Stories are good.
(Three times)
God has stories too.

God loves us all.
(Two times)
Bible stories tell

That God loves us all.

Jonah's Journey

God said to Jonah,
"Go, go, go." [Point finger.]
But Jonah thought,
"No, no, no." [Shake head.]

He hid on a ship.
Row, row, row. [Make rowing motions.]
And winds began to
Blow, blow, blow. [Cup hands at mouth.]

"It's my fault," said Jonah.
"Oh, oh, oh. [Throw up arms.]
Throw me over.
Woe, woe, woe." [Put hands to head. Shake head.]

A whale ate him.
Yum, yum, yummy. [Lick lips.]
Jonah lived three days in his
Tum, tum, tummy. [Pat stomach.]

To the enemy land Jonah
Came, came, came. [March in place.]

He preached to the people
Shame, shame, shame. [Shake forefinger.]

The people turned good.
Yea, yea, yea. [Wave fists in air.]
And Jonah was surprised
Hey, hey, hey. [Raise hands, palms upturned.]

God sent a plant to
Grow, grow, grow. [Stoop and rise.]
Jonah was happy.
Ho, ho, ho. [Rock back and forth.]

A worm ate the plant.
Chomp, chomp, chomp. [Chew.]
And Jonah was angry.
Stomp, stomp, stomp. [Stomp.]

"See," said God, "You loved
One, one, one. [Hold up one finger.]
I love everyone
Under the sun!" [Extend arms wide.]

M. Kathleen Glavich, S.N.D.

3 Tell the children that many of the prayers with gestures that they are learning come from a section of the Bible called Psalms. Show where to find the Book of Psalms in the Bible. Tell them that a long time ago people celebrated God's feasts with singing and dancing. The psalms are prayers that we sing to praise God.

4 Let the children act out the story of Jonah. Assign roles so that all the children can participate.

5 Read a fairy tale, a folktale, or a good children's book to the children each week, if possible.

6 Encourage the children to ask their parents to take them to the library to get picture books and storybooks to read to them. Tell the children that they might also ask for stories to be read to them from the Bible.

7 Help the children to make their own books to tell their own stories (four pages long). Include prompts to which the children can add their own illustrations.

8 Show samples of children's Bible storybooks. Include these in your classroom library collection. Read these as part of your shared reading time in class.

9 Show many different kinds of Bibles. Invite children to look through them and to talk about how they look different. Emphasize that all contain God's Word.

10 Teach the children to trace a cross on the Bible as part of prayer.

Chapter 4

God's World Is Good

FAITH FOCUS

God made the world.

Genesis 1:1—2:3; 6:5—9:17

PREPARING THE FAITH EXPERIENCE

LISTENING

The vocation of a teacher is to communicate with joy the good news of God's love. Take some time to let yourself be refreshed by the good news found in the Bible. As you pray, hear God speak to you his good news of love and salvation.

Read the Creation story found in Genesis 1:1—2:3. You might also wish to read the story of Noah and the Flood, Genesis 6:5—9:17

God looked at everything he had made, and he found it very good.

Genesis 1:31

REFLECTING

Indeed, creation is very good—so good that we, in looking at the things God has made, are able to perceive his very presence. If a work of art reveals the artist, should not the works of creation show forth their Creator? To immerse ourselves in the beauties of creation and to allow ourselves to be awed by them is a simple way of coming to know the Creator. The magnificence of a snow-capped mountain range proclaims God's majesty, a flaming sunset his beauty. We know God's power in the ocean's roar, his tenderness in a parent's love, and his gentleness in a tiny flower or a soft breeze. The winter's dying and the spring's new budding repeat his mystery—the Paschal Mystery—of Jesus' dying and rising for our salvation. Our wonder and awe flow spontaneously into prayer.

RESPONDING

God's Word moves us to respond in word and action. Let the Holy Spirit work within you as you prayerfully consider how you are being called to respond to God's message to you today.

- What in creation particularly speaks to me of God's goodness?
- How do I care for God's creation?

Holy Spirit, help me to reveal your goodness and the goodness of creation to the children.

Catechism of the Catholic Church

The themes of this lesson correspond to the following paragraphs: 290, 293, 295–301.

THE FAITH EXPERIENCE

DAY ONE
We Look at God's World

DAY TWO
We Care for the World God Made

DAY THREE
God Loves the World

DAY FOUR
Celebrating God's World

Scripture in This Chapter

- *Psalm 148 All the universe is a hymn of praise to God.*
- *Romans 1:20 The created world reveals God's power and divinity.*

Church Documents

Sharing Catholic Social Teaching: Challenges and Directions.
Catholic Tradition teaches us to show respect for the Creator by caring for his creation.

Pastoral Constitution on the Church in the Modern World #34.
The purpose of human activity and all of creation is to glorify God and make his name known throughout the earth.

Towards a Better Distribution of Land #22–23.
Human beings, created in the image of God, are responsible for the care of creation, which is God's gift to each and every one of them.

Bulletin Board At the left is a suggestion for a bulletin-board design. Refer to BLM 5 God's Gifts if you wish to make a photocopy or transparency. Distribute copies of BLM 5 and have each child color his or her copy to post on the bulletin board. Remind the children to write their names on their drawings. Children have varying degrees of ability. Note that perfection is not the goal and that it is important only for the children to do their best. You might include a banner with the words, "God's Gifts."

- ***BLM 5 God's Gifts***

For a list of children's literature suggestions, please see **page OV-47.**

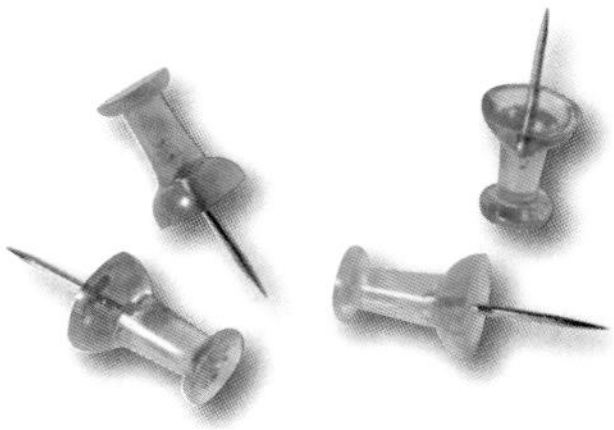

CHAPTER 4 | DAY ONE

We Look at God's World

Student Book page 13

LEARNING OUTCOMES

The children will be able to

- know that God made the world.
- know that everything God made is good.
- respond in prayer to the signs of God's love in creation.

MATERIALS

- A Bible
- *A Child's Bible*
- Table on which the children may place the objects they collect

COMMENTS

1. Many young children show great interest in nature. Young children are stimulated by natural beauty and wonder to a sense of reverence and awe. Putting children in touch with creation is a natural means of putting them in touch with God.

2. If it is not possible to take a walk for SHARING #1, have pictures or photographs of creation posted around the room and take the children for an indoor walk. Put magazine pictures of animals, trees, flowers, sky, fruits, vegetables, and people in places where the children may select one as they go on their walk. Also include objects from nature (at least one for each child) that you have collected. Place these where the children will find them.

CENTERING

1 Remind the children that in the last chapter they learned about the Bible.

- ***What is the Bible?*** (A holy book, God's Word) [Show a Bible and a copy of *A Child's Bible*.]
- ***What do the stories in the Bible tell us?*** (God loves us.)
- ***You will be hearing more stories from the Bible about God's love for us.***

If *A Child's Bible* has been sent home, tell the children to ask their parents to read the stories to them.

2 Read **page 13** to the children. Guide the children to read the following text together:

- ***God made this wonderful world!***

Tell the children that they will be learning more about the wonderful world that God made.

SHARING

1 Prepare to take the children outside for a walk to look at the wonderful world and the many good things in it. (If a walk outdoors is not possible, prepare this activity as suggested in COMMENT #2). While on your walk, encourage the children to comment on what they see, pointing out things that may escape their notice. Allow time for them to examine whatever captures their attention. Tell the children that each thing they see is a gift God has placed in the world for us to enjoy. Let each child take back to the room one object from nature he or she found, such as a stone or a leaf.

2 Invite the children to show their objects, to tell why they are good, and to set them on a display table. These objects can be saved to use again in lessons this week. They might also remain displayed in the Prayer Center throughout the week. Ask:

- ***Who made this wonderful world?*** (God made this wonderful world.) ***God made everything in our world. Everything that God made is good.***

ACTING

Lead the children in praying an adaptation of Psalm 33:5 with gestures.

To lead the psalm prayers, first invite the children to pray with you by watching as you pray the words of the psalm with the gestures. Next invite the children to continue to pray together with you by copying only the gestures as you say the words. Finally, invite the children to pray with you the words and the gestures together. When finished, ask the children to sit down quietly.

- ***Look at all the good things we found on our walk. God made all these things. We can pray, "The earth is full of the goodness of the LORD."***

The earth
[Hands opened, extended in front.]

is full
[Slowly move hands outward.]

of the goodness of the LORD.
[Raise arms and eyes.]

CHECKPOINT

- What have the children said or done that shows they take delight in the many gifts of creation?
- How will you continue to invite the children to experience creation as a sign of God's goodness and love?

CHAPTER 4

God's World Is Good

Blue skies
Spotted giraffes
Hoppity rabbits
Puddles to splash.

Red-ripe apples
Trees to climb
Sandy beaches
Shells to find.

Green grass
Tickling my toes
People with hugs
A baby that grows.

God made this wonderful world!

13

CHAPTER 4 | DAY TWO

We Care for the World God Made

Student Book page 14

LEARNING OUTCOMES

The children will be able to

- see God's love and goodness in the world.
- desire to take care of the world.

KEY TERMS

create—to make out of nothing
creation—all that God made; everything that exists

MATERIALS

- Objects from nature collected on Day One
- Bible enthroned, with note card on which you have written the adapted Scripture reading for SHARING #3, Genesis 1:31
- Cutouts 2, 5–20, 22–28
- Flashcard 2
- Construction paper: one sheet each of black, yellow, blue, brown

COMMENT

Decide how you will display the Cutouts as you tell the story of Creation in SHARING #1 (Examples: on a felt board, a bulletin board, or a magnetic board) and prepare the Cutouts accordingly. Be sure to have the Cutouts in sequential order before you begin your lesson. You may wish to practice the telling of the story to ensure a smooth, reverent narration. Plan to invite the children to help you tell the story by taking turns placing the Cutouts on the display board.

CENTERING

Invite the children to talk about some wonderful things in nature that they have seen or experienced (The changing colors of the leaves in autumn, the power of a waterfall, the view from a mountaintop, the peace of a white, fluffy cloud). Show some of the objects saved from Day One and continue to display these objects in the Prayer Center.

SHARING

1 Introduce the Creation story.

- ***A very important story in the Bible tells us about how God created the world.***

Show the children a Bible and open the Bible to the Book of Genesis. Enthrone the Bible on a table next to the display board.

Say that you would like to tell this story about God and the world. Invite some children to help you tell the story by placing the colored construction paper and Cutouts on the display board. Other children can help to tell the story by holding up Flashcard 2 *good* each time you say, "God saw that it was . . . " All the children can participate by completing the sentence, saying "good" whenever you say, "God saw that it was . . . "

2 Invite the children to remember what they learned about how to be good listeners.

- ***Let's prepare ourselves to listen well to today's Bible story.***
- ***Listening eyes are on the storyteller.*** [Pause until all the children are looking at you.] ***Listening hands are quietly in your lap.*** [Pause until all the children have put their hands in their lap.] ***Listening feet are comfortable and quiet.*** [Pause until all the children's feet are still.] ***Listening hearts are ready to hear God's Word.*** [Pause.]

3 Tell the story of Creation using the Cutouts and guide the children to help.

- ***A very long time ago, there was only God. There wasn't any world. There weren't any people or planets. There wasn't anything anywhere.*** [Invite a child to place the black paper on the display board.]
- ***God was filled with love. God wanted to share his love, but there was no one around anywhere. So God made the world and everything in it. We say God created the world.***

• ***God made light and called it day.*** [Ask a child to place the yellow paper on the display board.] ***The darkness he called night.*** [Point to the black paper on the display board.] ***God made the blue sky and the deep blue seas.*** [Invite two children to place the blue paper and Cutout 5 Seas and rivers on the display board.] ***He made the waters come together in places so that land would appear. He called the land earth.*** [Invite two children to place the brown paper and Cutout 6 Mountains and hills on the display board.] [Pause.] ***God saw that it was . . .*** (good).

• ***God commanded the earth to bring forth all kinds of plants. And it did.*** [Invite children to place Cutouts 7–10, Apple tree, Fir tree, Flowers, and Pumpkin on the display board.] ***This is why we have trees to climb, beautiful flowers to make us happy, and good things to eat such as apples, bananas, cherries, and pumpkin pies. What are some other plants that you know that God has made?*** [Allow children to offer examples of plants.]

• ***Then God made the sun, the moon, and the stars in the sky.*** [Invite two children to place Cutouts 2 Sun and 11 Moon and stars on the display board.] [Pause.] ***God saw that it was . . .*** (good).

• ***God still wasn't finished with his world. He commanded that the water be filled with many kinds of fish and sea creatures, and that the sky be filled with all kinds of flying birds. And it happened.*** [Invite children to place Cutouts 12 Dolphins and other water creatures and 17 Birds on the display board.] [Pause.] ***God saw that it was . . .*** (good).

• ***Then God commanded the earth to bring forth all kinds of animals, big and small—and it did. Diving dolphins, wondrous whales, mischievous monkeys, active ants, loud lions, wild wolves, lively lambs, cute kittens, playful puppies, beautiful birds, and brightly colored butterflies all appeared on the earth.*** [Invite children to place Cutouts 12–18 on the display board.] [Pause.] ***God saw that it was . . .*** (good).

God gave the world to us.

God wants us to care for it.

The Bible tells us so.

All the good things in the world tell us about God.

They tell us that God loves us.

Scripture

The earth is full of the goodness of the Lord. Based on Psalm 33:5

14

• ***Last of all, God made human beings. God told them to take care of the world he made. We call the first man Adam and the first woman Eve.*** [Invite a child to place Cutout 20 Adam and Eve on the display board.] Pick up the Bible that has been enthroned next to the display board and read aloud the conclusion of the Creation story, Genesis 1:31: "God looked at everything he had made, and he found it very good."

4 Invite the children to look at all the wonderful things that God has made. Point out that God gave the world to us and that God told us to care for the world he made.

• ***Have you ever made something for someone?*** (A gift) ***Why?*** (To show love for this person.)

• ***Who did God make the world for?*** (Us) ***Why did God give us such a beautiful world?*** (God loves us.)

• ***When you give someone a gift, how do you hope the gift will be treated?*** (With care) ***God also wants us to care for the world he gave to us.***

5 Have the children turn to **page 14.** Read it aloud. Ask:

• ***What are the people doing?*** (Planting a tree; playing with animals; enjoying the outdoors)

• ***Who made the tree for them to plant?*** (God)

• ***Who made the cute little puppy?*** (God)

• ***What do all the good things God made tell us?*** (God loves us.)

• ***How does God want us to treat the world he gave to us?*** (God wants us to care for the world he made.)

ACTING

1 Discuss caring for the world.

• ***How can we take good care of things in the world?*** (Help keep places neat and clean. Take care of plants and animals so they can have healthy lives. Care for all people.) ***We show our love for God when we take good care of the world he made.***

2 Invite the children to pray the adaptation of Psalm 33:5 with gestures.

To lead the psalm prayers, first invite the children to pray with you by watching as you pray the words of the psalm with the gestures. Next invite the children to continue to pray together with you by copying only the gestures as you say the words. Finally, invite the children to pray with you the words and the gestures together. When finished, ask the children to sit down quietly.

The earth
[Hands opened, extended in front.]

is full
[Slowly move hands outward.]

of the goodness of the LORD.
[Raise arms and eyes.]

CHECKPOINT

- How do the children show that they recognize that the world is a gift from God?
- How will you help the children learn ways to care for God's creation?

CHAPTER 4 | DAY THREE

God Loves the World

Student Book page 15

LEARNING OUTCOMES

The children will be able to
- be familiar with the story of Noah.
- know that God's love is everlasting.

MATERIALS

- Cutouts 2, 5–20
- *A Child's Bible*, pages 1–4
- Poster 3
- Picture of a rainbow
- Crayons or markers

COMMENT

Many children might enjoy acting out the story of Noah. You might choose to invite the children to do this after you read the story of Noah in SHARING #6.

CENTERING

1 Show the cutouts from the Creation story and the objects from nature displayed in the Prayer Center from Day One. Ask:

- ***What are these examples of?*** (God's world, God's creation) ***Who made these things?*** (God) ***Why?*** (To show his love for us) ***What does God want us to do with the world he gave to us?*** (Care for it)

2 Invite the children to thank God for the gifts of creation by praying the adaptation of Psalm 33:5 with gestures.

To lead the psalm prayers, first invite the children to pray with you by watching as you pray the words of the psalm with the gestures. Next invite the children to continue to pray together with you by copying only the gestures as you say the words. Finally, invite the children to pray with you the words and the gestures together. When finished, ask the children to sit down quietly.

The earth
[Hands opened, extended in front.]

is full
[Slowly move hands outward.]

of the goodness of the LORD.
[Raise arms and eyes.]

SHARING

1 Introduce the story "Noah, the Flood, and the Rainbow" from *A Child's Bible.*

- ***People have not always taken care of the world and one another. They damaged the earth, and they hurt one another. A story in the Bible tells us that people acted so badly that God was sorry he made the world. One day God decided to make the world over. Let's listen to the story of Noah.***

2 Invite the children to remember what they learned about how to be good listeners.

- ***Let's prepare ourselves to listen well to this Bible story.***
- ***Listening eyes are on the storyteller.*** [Pause until all the children are looking at you.] ***Listening hands are quietly in your lap.*** [Pause until all the children have put their hands in their lap.] ***Listening feet are comfortable and quiet.*** [Pause until all the children's feet are still.] ***Listening hearts are ready to hear God's Word.*** [Pause.]

3 Read the story from *A Child's Bible*, **pages 1–4.** Refer to Poster 3 The Story of Noah as you read.

4 Discuss the story.

- ***Why did God save Noah and his family?*** (They lived the way God had asked.)
- ***What did Noah take on the ark with him?*** (Two of every animal)
- ***After Noah and his family were able to leave the ark, what did Noah do?*** (He thanked God.)

• ***What did God give as a sign of his promise to love the world forever?*** (A rainbow)

5 Talk about rainbows. Show a picture of one.

• ***Have you ever seen a rainbow? When? What did it look like?***

• ***What will rainbows remind you of from now on?*** (God's love)

6 Ask the children to turn to **page 15.** Have them do the activity. If time allows, invite the children to dramatize the story of Noah and the flood.

Songs

Play for the children any of these songs: "Greatest Show on Earth" (*I See a New World*) **CD 2 Track 1;** "Hip Hip Hooray" (*Fingerprints*); "I Wonder" (*Peaceable Kingdom*); "Happy the Heart" (*Hi God!*); "All You Works of God" (*Singing Our Faith*). For a list of all the music used in this program, see **page OV-39.**

CHECKPOINT

- How did the children respond to the story of Noah?
- How will you help the children to remember that God loves all creation?

ACTING

1 Teach the "Rainbow Song," encouraging the children to join in and clap along.

Rainbow Song

(Melody: "The Farmer in the Dell.")

A rainbow in the sky,
A rainbow in the sky,
A rainbow tells us of God's love,
A rainbow in the sky.

2 Invite the children to pray the adaptation of Psalm 33:5 with gestures as on **page T47.**

• ***Let's thank God for all the wonderful things he has made.***

The earth
[Hands opened, extended in front.]

is full
[Slowly move hands outward.]

of the goodness of the Lord.
[Raise arms and eyes.]

In the Bible God made a promise to Noah. God promised to always love everything on earth. The rainbow is a sign of God's love.

Try This

1. Find the animals in the clouds. Circle them.

2. Say thank you to God for the beautiful things he made.

15

CHAPTER 4 | DAY FOUR

Celebrating God's World

Student Book page 16

LEARNING OUTCOMES

The children will be able to

- learn to give thanks and praise to God for the gifts of creation.
- participate joyfully and reverently in a prayer experience.

MATERIALS

- Bible enthroned, with note card from Day Two for SHARING #2, Genesis 1:31
- Cutouts 2, 5–20
- Holy water in a small bowl and a small evergreen branch to use in the sprinkling rite
- Paper and crayons or markers if the additional activity in ACTING #2 is chosen

COMMENTS

1. To appreciate and enter into the spirit of our Catholic liturgy, we must appreciate the richness of its symbols. Symbols are actions, sounds, or objects that express meaning and beliefs. They reveal mystery by concretely expressing invisible realities. Symbols speak to us on many levels. While children will not yet be able to articulate the layers of meaning that symbols express, using symbols in our celebration will enhance their familiarity with them and will help the children to grow in their appreciation of symbols.

2. Let every child who wishes have a special part in the celebration. If your class is small, you may shorten the litany of praise or let each child select two symbols. If your class is large, add more objects to the litany of praise, perhaps choosing objects that were collected on Day One and displayed in your Prayer Center.

CENTERING

1 Prepare for today's prayer celebration. Ask a child to hold the Bible during the reading in SHARING #2. Invite each child to select a symbol from the cutouts from the Creation story or an object from nature collected on Day One.

2 Call the children to prayer.

- ***God made the world good for us. God loves us very much. Today we will show God our love by celebrating and praising him for our good world.***

3 Invite the children to move quietly to the Prayer Center and to put their chosen cutouts and objects in the center of the circle.

SHARING

1 Lead the children in singing "God Is So Good" on **page T10** or another song about God's world. See the song list on **page T48.**

2 Invite the children to be good listeners.

- ***Let's prepare ourselves to listen well to today's Bible story.***
- ***Listening eyes are on the storyteller.*** [Pause until all the children are looking at you.] ***Listening hands are quietly in your lap.*** [Pause until all the children have put their hands in their lap.] ***Listening feet are comfortable and quiet.*** [Pause until all the children's feet are still.] ***Listening hearts are ready to hear God's Word.*** [Pause.] Read Genesis 1:31 from the Bible held by a child.
- ***A reading from the Book of Genesis: "God looked at everything he had made, and he found it very good."*** [Pause.] ***The Word of the Lord.*** Invite the children to respond by repeating after you "Thanks be to God."

3 Guide the children in a litany of praise using the cutouts from the Creation Story and the objects collected on Day One. Modify the litany to include any additional objects from nature or to combine/delete items as needed to accommodate the size of your class.

- ***God has created many wonderful things. We show our love for God when we care for God's creation. When I name one of the creatures God has made, say, "Bless the Lord." Whoever has the symbol or picture for the creature I name may hold it up for us to see.***

  Sun . . .
  (Children respond, "Bless the Lord.")

  Moon and twinkling stars . . .

  Dew and rain . . .

  Red apples and orange pumpkins . . .

  Mountains and hills . . .

  Dolphins and all other water creatures . . .

  Wolves . . .

  Lambs . . .

  Kittens . . .

  Puppies . . .

  Mothers and fathers . . .

  Grandmothers and grandfathers . . .

  Little babies . . .

  Children everywhere . . .

  Everything the Lord has made . . .

4 Invite the children to pray the adaptation of Psalm 33:5 with gestures.

The earth
[Hands opened, extended in front.]

is full
[Slowly move hands outward.]

of the goodness of the LORD.
[Raise arms and eyes.]

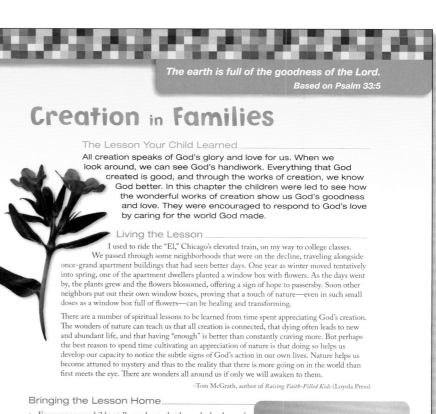

The earth is full of the goodness of the Lord.
Based on Psalm 33:5

Creation in Families

The Lesson Your Child Learned

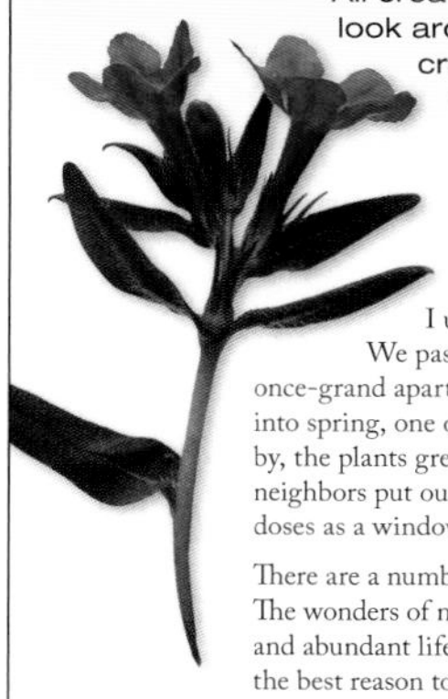

All creation speaks of God's glory and love for us. When we look around, we can see God's handiwork. Everything that God created is good, and through the works of creation, we know God better. In this chapter the children were led to see how the wonderful works of creation show us God's goodness and love. They were encouraged to respond to God's love by caring for the world God made.

Living the Lesson

I used to ride the "El," Chicago's elevated train, on my way to college classes. We passed through some neighborhoods that were on the decline, traveling alongside once-grand apartment buildings that had seen better days. One year as winter moved tentatively into spring, one of the apartment dwellers planted a window box with flowers. As the days went by, the plants grew and the flowers blossomed, offering a sign of hope to passersby. Soon other neighbors put out their own window boxes, proving that a touch of nature—even in such small doses as a window box full of flowers—can be healing and transforming.

There are a number of spiritual lessons to be learned from time spent appreciating God's creation. The wonders of nature can teach us that all creation is connected, that dying often leads to new and abundant life, and that having "enough" is better than constantly craving more. But perhaps the best reason to spend time cultivating an appreciation of nature is that doing so helps us develop our capacity to notice the subtle signs of God's action in our own lives. Nature helps us become attuned to mystery and thus to the reality that there is more going on in the world than first meets the eye. There are wonders all around us if only we will awaken to them.

–Tom McGrath, author of *Raising Faith-Filled Kids* (Loyola Press)

Bringing the Lesson Home

- Encourage your child to tell you about what he or she has learned this week. Read with your child the pages that were sent home.
- To help your family stay more attuned to your surroundings, create your own litany. Have each of your family members pick out something they observe and say, for example, "For that tall tree," to which everyone else responds, "Praise the Lord."
- Let your child participate in a recycling program in your area or work in your garden. Your child will learn responsibility and various ways to respond to God's call to care for the earth.
- Pray Psalm 33:5 as part of your family prayers this week. Invite your child to lead your family as you pray this together.
- Read aloud Genesis 1:31 and appropriate sections from Psalms 65, 66, and 104.

16

ACTING

1 Encourage the children to thank God for his gifts.

• ***Each good thing in the world is a gift that tells of God's love for us. What might you say to God when you see one of his gifts?*** (Thank you, God. I love you, God. Your world is pretty, dear God. Your world makes me happy, God.)

2 If time allows, you might ask each child to draw a picture of something in creation that they want to thank God for. These pictures could be combined to create a class collage, showing our gratitude to God for the gifts of his world. Another option is to help the children make a collage using natural objects (seeds, branches, leaves).

3 Have the children take home the Family Page on **page 16** to share with their families.

CHECKPOINT

• How reverently and joyfully did the children enter into the prayer experience?

ENRICHING THE FAITH EXPERIENCE

Use the following activities to enrich a lesson, to replace an activity with one that better meets the needs of your class, or to create an additional lesson.

1 Teach a song to the melody of "God Is So Good."

God's world is good.
(Three times)
God made it so good.

God loves us so. (Two times)
God made the world
To show us great love.

2 Distribute copies of BLM 6 Creation (a cut-and-paste activity). Invite the children to color the picture of God's world. Assist them in cutting out the pieces at the bottom and gluing them to the picture. Remind the children to write their names on their work. • ***BLM 6 Creation***

3 Teach the children a song about creation. Choose one from the list on **page T48.**

4 Make a "Creation Tree." Paint a large, leafless tree branch with white or green paint and place it in a coffee can. Anchor it with sand or plaster of Paris. (You might use the tree you made in ENRICHING THE FAITH EXPERIENCE, Chapter 2.) Punch holes in the cutout creation symbols and string them with yarn so they can be hung on the tree. As the children place the symbols on the tree, they may thank God for the gift each symbol represents, saying for example, "Thank you, God, for the warm sun and the bright moon."

5 Let the children take turns pretending to be one of God's gifts in the world. Invite the group to guess which gift they are imitating.

6 Have the children draw or paint something that tells them of God's goodness and love. Invite them to show their pictures to the group and tell about them.

7 Teach the children the following finger play.

What God Made

God made the sun and the
great blue sky.
[Make a circle with arms; open
and raise hands.]
God made the stars and the
moon.
[Open and close fingers.]
God made lakes and birds that
fly.
[Flap arms.]
God made the little raccoon.
[Make circles with fingers
around eyes.]
God made mountains and
green, grassy hills.
[Make a peak with hands.]
God made the fish in the sea.
[Put palms together and wiggle
hands forward.]
God made flowers like
daffodils.
[Pretend to smell flower.]
But best of all, God made me!
[Point to self.]

M. Kathleen Glavich, S.N.D..

Chapter 5

Quiet Is Good

FAITH FOCUS

God speaks to us in quiet.

Psalm 131:2

PREPARING THE FAITH EXPERIENCE

LISTENING

Before you begin to prepare this week's lessons, take some time for prayer. Quiet yourself by taking several deep breaths. Become aware of God's presence, for God is with you always. Ask God to open your heart to hear his words to you today.

"And behold, I am with you always, until the end of the age."

Matthew 28:20

REFLECTING

"Where are you?" called God, seeking Adam and Eve in the cool of the evening. However, they were ashamed of their sin and hid. Today we sometimes use the activity and noise of our world to conceal ourselves from God. But God knows that only in him will we find fulfillment and perfect peace. God seeks us out and calls us to be present with him.

Again and again Sacred Scripture depicts God's yearning to be with us. God reveals himself as Yahweh, or "I am who am." God wishes us to experience his presence. Through the mystery of the Incarnation, God became visible in the person of Jesus. Now Jesus promises that he and his Father will come to those who keep his word and will make their dwelling place with them.

At Baptism, we became the dwelling place of the blessed Trinity. The Kingdom of God is indeed within us. To grow spiritually, we are called to become aware of God's presence. Our spiritual life is strengthened when we withdraw from the busy, anxious world around us to seek God within. Although silence is not popular in today's noisy, bustling, clamoring world, never has there been such a need for us to enter into stillness. To become a whole person demands a solitude in which we discover God's presence, ourselves, and the gifts we have to offer.

Dag Hammarskjöld, former secretary-general of the United Nations, understood the value of silence. In 1957, the Meditation Room was set aside at the United Nations. Hammarskjöld planned and supervised the details for this room and composed the text for the leaflet that is distributed to visitors:

"We all have within us a center of stillness surrounded by silence." Then, calling attention to the symbols employed—"the shaft of light striking the shimmering surface of solid rock"—he explains that the light suggests "how the light of the spirit gives life to matter" while "the stone in the middle of the room" may be seen "as an altar . . . There are no other symbols, there is nothing to distract our attention or to break in on the stillness within ourselves. . . . It is for those who come here to fill the void with what they find in their center of stillness."

From deep within our being, God calls to each of us. Those who withdraw from the noise of the world hear God's voice.

RESPONDING

Having reflected upon God's Word, take some time now to continue to respond to God in prayer. You might wish to use a journal to record your responses throughout this year.

- How comfortable am I with quiet?
- How often do I spend time with God by finding the center of stillness within me?

Gentle Spirit, quiet the children and me so that we may hear your voice.

Catechism of the Catholic Church

The themes of this lesson correspond to the following paragraphs: 2562–2563, 2691.

THE FAITH EXPERIENCE

DAY ONE
Good Things Happen in Quiet

DAY TWO
We Listen

DAY THREE
We Meet God in Church

DAY FOUR
We Meet God in Quiet

Scripture in This Chapter

- *Romans 5:5 Christians share in the life of the Trinity through sanctifying grace.*
- *John 14:23–24 Those who keep the Father's word will experience Jesus' presence.*

Church Documents

General Directory for Catechesis #85.
National Directory for Catechesis #20.
Catechesis should be permeated by a climate of prayer, especially the sentiments reflected in the Lord's Prayer.

Constitution on the Sacred Liturgy #12.
In addition to joining in liturgical prayer, Christians must pray in solitude.

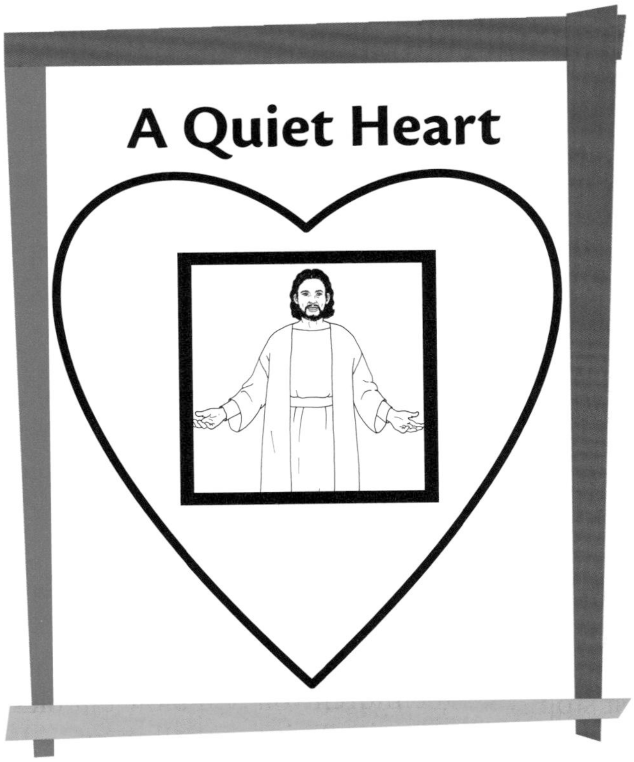

Bulletin Board At the left is a suggestion for a bulletin-board design. Refer to BLM 1 Jesus if you wish to make a photocopy or transparency. Post the picture of Jesus in the heart with the words, "A Quiet Heart."

- ***BLM 1 Jesus***

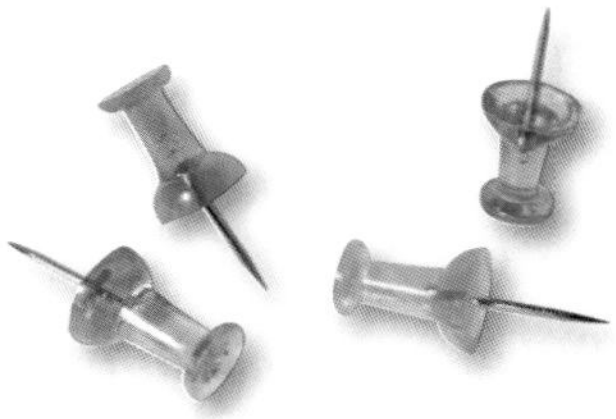

For a list of children's literature suggestions, please see **page OV-47.**

CHAPTER 5 | DAY ONE

Good Things Happen in Quiet

Student Book page 17

LEARNING OUTCOMES

The children will be able to

- experience inner peace and calm through silence.
- suggest good things that happen in silence.

MATERIALS

- Cutouts 2, 7, 9
- Flashcard 2
- Bubble solution, either purchased or homemade. For a homemade solution, mix 1/3 cup dishwashing liquid and 1 tablespoon sugar.
- Bubble wand

COMMENTS

1. Silence helps us discover our inner selves. Through silence and recollection, we invite children to sense the presence of God. The ability to quiet ourselves requires a certain amount of self-control. The order and routine of the classroom can help promote this self-control. You can also establish quieting rituals and signals with the children. Experiment and determine which ones work well for you and for each class. This lesson presents an opportunity to introduce and reinforce the strategies that you will use throughout the year.

2. All prayer can begin with a quieting exercise. You might invite the children into an experience of quiet prayer by suggesting that they take several deep breaths, then gently close their eyes or look down at their hands resting in their laps. Make suggestions that will help the children to relax their bodies and to focus on a single quiet sound, such as their own breathing. When we lead prayer, we strive to carry out every religious act and ritual with reverence and recollection. When we do so, the children will sense that worship is being rendered to someone much greater than themselves.

CENTERING

Recall the last chapter.

- ***In the last chapter you learned where everything in the world came from. Who made the world?*** (God) ***Why did God make the world?*** (Because God loves us)
- ***Today one beautiful thing that God made will teach us a lesson.***

SHARING

1 Introduce the bubble activity.

- ***Sometimes we do loud and noisy activities. What are some loud and noisy activities we might do outdoors?*** (Play games, play on playground equipment) ***But we can also enjoy doing the same or similar activities quietly. For example, we can use chalk to play hopscotch with friends, or we can draw quietly by ourselves. Both experiences can make us feel happy, but each in its own way. Today we are going to see how this is true by using bubbles.***
- ***Before I bring out the bubbles, I want to teach you a signal that will help us all year when we need to quiet ourselves so we can hear one another better.*** [Teach the children a signal to be quiet, such as a hand raised in the air.] Tell them that when they see this signal, they can raise their hands, but they must stop talking and making noise. Practice this a few times until the children are able to quiet themselves quickly when you give them the signal.

2 Lead the bubble activity.

- ***Now we can enjoy our bubble activity.*** [Bring out the bubbles and blow some bubbles into the air.] Let the children exclaim with delight at the wonder of the bubbles. Allow this to continue for a reasonable amount of time and then stop blowing bubbles and give the quiet signal. Wait patiently until all have quieted down.
- ***Blowing bubbles can be a noisy activity. But we can also enjoy bubbles as a quiet activity.*** In a soft voice tell the children you will blow bubbles again. This time tell them to listen for the sound of the bubbles floating in the air, the sound they make when they land, and the sound when they break. Tell the children

that they will need to be very quiet to hear these things. They may watch and listen, but they may not touch the bubbles. Blow some bubbles into the air and remind the children to stay quiet by gently putting your finger to your lips. When the bubbles are gone, ask what sound they made. Encourage the children to respond quietly as they describe the sounds.

3 Lead the children to discover that many good things happen in quiet. Show Flashcard 2 *good.*

• ***Quiet is good. Many good things happen in quiet. Our book tells us about some of these good things. Listen quietly.*** Read aloud **page 17,** showing it as you read. Reread the page, pausing after each phrase to allow the children to put their fingers to their lips, as if to say "Shh-shh-shh." [Allow the children to say "Shh-shh-shh" spontaneously, but don't encourage this.] As you read the page again, let the children perform actions such as those suggested here.

Clouds moving across the sky,
[Make waves with hands.]

a loving hug and a friendly smile,
[Gently hug yourself and smile.]

yellow butterflies dancing in the sun,
[Cross wrists and join thumbs together. Flap fingers to represent butterflies flying.]

green grass growing in the yard,
[Have closed fists facing you. Open fingers one by one to show grass sprouting.]

a warm and happy feeling deep inside,
[Smile. Cross hands over chest.]
SHH-SHH-SHH
[Put one finger to lips.]

4 Let the children name other good and beautiful things that are quiet. Invite them to thank God for these quiet things.

CHAPTER 5

Quiet Is Good

Quiet is clouds moving across the sky,
a loving hug and a friendly smile,
yellow butterflies dancing in the sun,
green grass growing in the yard,
a warm and happy feeling deep inside,
SHH-SHH-SHH.

Scripture

Be still and know that I am God.
Based on Psalm 46:11

ACTING

1 Have the children reflect on more wonders that happen in silence.

• ***Do you ever hear the sun shining? Does it go "sizzle, sizzle"?*** [Show Cutout 2 Sun.] ***What good things happen when the sun shines?*** (Warmth, plants grow)

• ***What sounds do apples make when they grow? Do they go "crash, bang"?*** [Show Cutout 7 Apple tree.] ***They grow from pretty blossoms into delicious apples without making even a tiny sound. Good things happen in quiet.***

• ***Have you ever heard a bud open up into a beautiful flower?*** [Show Cutout 9 Flowers.] ***Flowers open quietly, so you can't hear them. A scientist discovered that some plants did not grow well when there was loud noise around them. They grew better with soft, quiet music.***

2 Introduce the closing quiet prayer. Say:

• ***Sometimes we pray with words. Sometimes we pray quietly, without any words at all. All week we are going to be learning about how we meet God in the quiet of our hearts. We will need to practice quieting ourselves. Remember how quiet and focused you were when you listened for the sounds of the bubbles? We can quiet ourselves for prayer by listening for the sound of our heartbeat. Let's do this together now.***

3 Encourage the children to sit quietly and still. Suggest that they may want to close their eyes. They may also wish to place their hands over their hearts [Model this for the children.] Then invite them to listen quietly to the sound of their heartbeat. [Pause.] Suggest that they quietly thank God for being with them in this quiet moment. [Pause.] Invite them to open their eyes when they have finished their prayer.

4 Invite the children to talk about this experience. Reassure them if they found this quiet prayer exercise difficult. Tell them that we can get better through practice.

CHECKPOINT

- Which strategies will you use to help the children quiet themselves?
- How did the children respond to the experience of quiet introduced in today's lesson?

We Listen

LEARNING OUTCOMES

The children will be able to
- become aware of God's presence as they discover the world within themselves.
- pray a simple reflection with guidance.

MATERIALS
- Cutout 32 or a doll
- BLM 7
- Bell

COMMENTS

Some young children seem to be bundles of energy and constant movement. As we teach them to be attentive to their bodies' posture in prayer, we can encourage them to channel this energy to create moments of stillness, quiet, and peace. However, we can only invite children to experience stillness and quiet; we cannot force these upon them.

CENTERING

1 Remind the children that they learned about many wonderful things that take place in quiet. Ask them to name a few.

2 Encourage the children to practice being still.

- ***If you wish to discover some of the good and beautiful things that happen in quiet, you must learn to be still and to have quiet hearts. Today we will practice a special way of helping ourselves become quiet and still. But first, let's play a listening game.***

Tell the children to find a place in the room to stand quietly, without touching anyone or anything. When you ring a bell, tell the children to move silently around the room without touching anyone or anything. Then ring the bell again and tell them to stop and wait quietly for you to ring the bell to signal that they may move. Continue in this way for a few minutes until the children no longer require verbal directions. Then change the game slightly as follows.

Continue as above, but this time when the children stop, tell them to quietly listen for a sound that you designate, such as someone walking in the hall, a bird singing, a passing car, an airplane, or a dog barking. Tell them to raise their hands when they hear the sound that you identified. When everyone's hand is raised, continue the game. When you have practiced listening for four or five different sounds, ask the children to quietly return to their seats.

SHARING

1 Introduce the next activity.

- ***Now that we have practiced listening for quiet sounds, let's practice quieting our hearts so we can hear the quiet sounds within us.***

2 Teach the posture for a quiet heart.

- ***Sitting correctly helps us to quiet our hearts so we can listen well.***
- ***Sit back in your chair, with your back straight.*** [Show Cutout 32 Prayer posture or use a doll to demonstrate. You may also wish to demonstrate this posture yourself.]

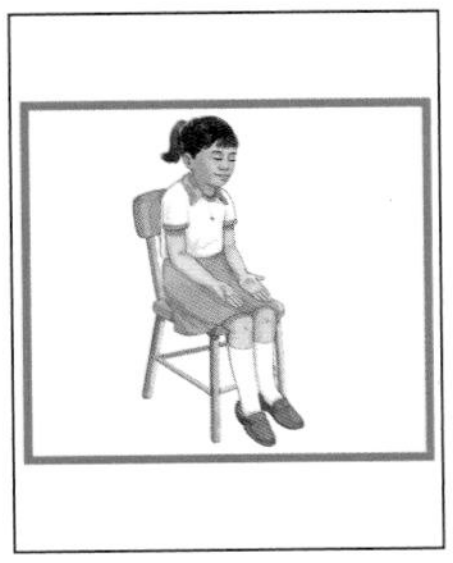

- ***Keep your feet flat on the floor.***
- ***Have your hands resting in your lap and open.***
- ***To become even more quiet when we talk to God in prayer, it helps to close our eyes. So close your eyes now if you want, or look down at your hands resting in your lap.***

3 Invite the children to listen for sounds inside themselves. Direct them to listen for their breathing, swallowing, and heartbeat. (You may need to remind them to breathe and swallow normally.) Have them raise their hands when they hear what they are listening for.

❹ Invite the children to be aware of their thoughts in quiet.

- ***You have a wonderful world inside of you that you come to know when you are quiet. Your thoughts are part of this world. We don't hear thoughts, but when we are very quiet, we become aware of them. Knowing our thoughts is like hearing them inside us.***

- ***Continue to sit quietly now and listen to your thoughts.***

After a sufficient amount of time, invite the children to open their eyes when they are finished listening to their thoughts. Continue when everyone's eyes are open.

- ***Does anyone wish to share any thoughts that came into his or her mind?*** If time allows, invite the children to draw a picture of any thoughts they had, or to draw a picture of themselves practicing how to listen to the quiet of their hearts. Alternatively, you might give the children copies of BLM 7 Bubbles and have them draw themselves praying and color the bubbles.
  - *BLM 7 Bubbles*

ACTING

❶ Discuss the idea that God meets us in quiet.

- ***We cannot see or hear God, but God is always with us. God meets us in the quiet of our hearts. When we know how to quiet ourselves, it helps us to meet God in our hearts. We can also ask God to help us with this way to pray.***

❷ Invite the children to pray together this prayer based on Psalm 131:2 with gestures.

To lead the psalm prayers, first invite the children to pray with you by watching as you pray the words of the psalm with the gestures. Next invite the children to continue to pray together with you by copying only the gestures as you say the words. Finally, invite the children to pray with you the words and the gestures together. When finished, ask the children to sit down quietly.

My heart is quiet
[Cross hands over heart.]

within me,
[Cross arms over chest.]

O LORD.
[Unfold arms in an outward movement.]

CHECKPOINT

- How did the children respond to the experience of quiet in church?

CHAPTER 5 | DAY THREE

We Meet God in Church

Student Book page 18

LEARNING OUTCOMES

The children will be able to

- identify church as a holy place where God is present.

KEY TERMS

church—the building where God is present in a special way and where God's people gather together to worship

pew—seat in church where the people pray

tabernacle—place in church where Jesus is present in a special way, in the Blessed Sacrament

COMMENTS

1. Young children are awed by the silence of a church, which speaks to them of mystery. Let your every word and action during the church visit contribute to their reverence and awe. However, avoid giving the notion that talking in church is inappropriate. Rather, convey the idea that we don't talk as freely in church as we do in other places because we want to respect others who wish to pray quietly.

2. Prepare to lead the prayer experience in church so that you can do so without shuffling too many papers. In particular, practice the psalm prayer so that you can lead this without the book. You might also consider singing a hymn with the children as part of the prayer experience in church. If you choose to do this, practice with the children in your classroom before going to church.

3. As you name the sacred objects found in church, be aware that many of these words will be new to the children in your group. Young children can easily mishear these new vocabulary words. Be sure that you are pronouncing these words clearly and distinctly. You may even choose to have the children repeat these words to confirm their understanding.

CENTERING

Recall the prayer experience of the last class.

- ***Quiet places are good because they help us enter into our quiet hearts, where we can always meet God. God speaks to us in the quiet of our hearts.***

SHARING

If a visit to church is not possible, the activities indicated in SHARING #1–5 can be modified and shared in your classroom.

1 Explain how the church is a place where the children can meet Jesus.

- ***There is a holy, quiet place where we can meet Jesus in a special way. When we are there, we might find it easier to enter into our quiet hearts and be with God.***

- ***Today we will go to church so that we can meet Jesus in the holy quiet that is there. To show that we know Jesus is present in church, we genuflect before we go into the benches or seats, which are called pews.*** Have the children practice genuflecting on their right knees. Gestures can and should be adapted when necessary to accommodate different needs, such as bowing instead of genuflecting.

- ***Sometimes people talk in church. But when we talk, we talk quietly. The quiet of church helps us prepare our hearts for God. Walk quietly, move into your places quietly, and be very quiet so you can experience God's special presence in church.***

2 Walk the children to church in a quiet, orderly manner. Do not enter until the children are quiet. Use the quiet signal taught on Day One. If some continue to be noisy or restless, gently tell them that you will lead them into church when you see that they are quiet and ready to pray to Jesus.

3 Inside the church, genuflect facing the tabernacle. [Model this for the children.] Then quietly direct the children into the pews or around the tabernacle. They should sense your reverence and joy at being in God's presence. Tell them in a soft voice that the tabernacle is the place where Jesus is present in a special way.

4 Have the children stand quietly for a moment, looking at the tabernacle. Invite them to pray the adaptation of Psalm 131:2 with gestures.

To lead the psalm prayers, first invite the children to pray with you by watching as you pray the words of the psalm with the gestures. Next invite the children to continue to pray together with you by copying only the gestures as you say the words. Finally, invite the children to pray with you the words and the gestures together. When finished, ask the children to sit down quietly.

My heart is quiet
[Cross hands over heart.]

within me,
[Cross arms over chest.]

O Lord.
[Unfold arms in an outward movement.]

5 Ask the children to be seated. Guide them to take the posture for a quiet heart.

- ***Sit back in the pew.*** [Pause; if the children are sitting on the floor, have them sit with their backs straight.]
- ***Rest your arms on your lap, hands open in front of you.*** [Pause.]
- ***You may gently close your eyes if you want to. Pretend that you are outside, sitting against a big tree. The sun warms your face and arms. You are breathing very gently, in and out, in and out.*** [Pause.]
- ***Now you have entered deep within your quiet heart. You see Jesus. Softly he calls your name and smiles at you.*** [Pause.] ***You smile at him.*** [Pause.] ***Jesus holds out his hand for you. He holds your hand tightly and whispers, "I am with you always.*** [Pause.] ***I am always deep in your quiet heart."*** [Pause.] (Based on Matthew 28:20)
- ***Be very still. Jesus may wish to let you know something else.*** [Pause.]
- ***You may wish to say something more to Jesus, or you may wish to enjoy just being with him without saying anything at all.*** [Pause.]
- ***When you have finished your prayer, open your eyes and look up at me. Then I will know when everyone's ready. Remember to stay quiet even if you have finished your prayer so that others can finish praying too.***

As the children leave the pews, model for them how to genuflect before the tabernacle and help them to line up quietly at the door. Encourage the children to return to the classroom still observing the spirit of quiet they have just shared.

ACTING

1 After you have returned to your classroom, let the children talk about the experience of meeting Jesus in the quiet of the church.

2 Have the children turn to **page 18.** Read it aloud and guide the children to read the following together:

- ***God loves us.***

3 Ask the children how they should act when they go to church with their parents or with others.

Songs

Play for the children any of these songs: "Over My Head" (*Singing Our Faith*) CD 1 Track 8; "Color the World with Song," "Psalm of Trust" (*Color the World with Song*); "Come to the Father" (*Songs for Young Children*); "Jesus, Jesus" (*Hi God 2*); "Go Now in Peace," "Jesus, Remember Me," General Intercessions," "My Soul in Stillness Waits," "Prayer of Peace," "Take, O Take Me As I Am" (*Singing Our Faith*). For a list of all the music used in this program, see **page OV-39.**

CHECKPOINT

- How did the children respond to the invitation to sit quietly?
- How will you continue to help the children to become comfortable with quiet?

Quiet helps us enter into our hearts.
We meet God there.
God is also with us
in a special way in church.
God loves us.
18

We Meet God in Quiet

Student Book pages 19–20

LEARNING OUTCOMES

The children will be able to
- begin to appreciate quiet.
- experience quiet prayer.

MATERIALS
- Enthroned Bible
- Heart and Jesus Picture punchouts from the Student Book
- Cutouts 2–3, 18
- Flashcard 2
- Three clouds cut from white paper
- Three large strips of grass cut from green paper
- A bubble wand for each child
- Bubble solution (see Day One materials)
- Attractive bowl
- Song for SHARING #4 (optional)
- Glue sticks
- Crayons or markers

COMMENTS

1. For the celebration, place the bubble solution in an attractive bowl on the table in the Prayer Center near the Bible.

2. Prepare the Heart and Jesus Picture punchouts. Punch out the door of the heart and fold it back to set up this activity for the children.

CENTERING

1 Before the celebration, ask children to volunteer for the following parts and practice with them. Give them their respective cutouts to hold.

- Flashcard 2
- Clouds (three children)
- Grass (three children)
- Cutout 2 Sun (one child)
- Cutout 18 Butterflies (one child)
- Cutout 3 Smiling face (one child)

Then have them line up in order before the celebration begins.

2 Prepare the children for the celebration.

- ***Boys and girls, today we will celebrate how good it is to meet God in the quiet of our hearts.***

3 Invite the children to move quietly to the Prayer Center.

SHARING

1 Help the children to dramatize quiet.

- ***Quiet is . . .*** [Have the child with the flashcard show it. Let all the children finish the statement by saying "good."]

- ***Quiet is . . . clouds moving across the sky.*** [Children with clouds tiptoe across the front.]

. . . a loving hug and a friendly smile. [Have all the children hug themselves and smile.]

. . . yellow butterflies dancing in the sun. [Child with sun holds it high. Child with butterflies dances quietly about on tiptoe.]

. . . green grass growing in the yard. [Children with grass sit cross-legged, heads bowed in lap. On the word "growing," they sit up, holding the strips of grass.]

. . . a warm and happy feeling deep inside. [Child with smiling face shows it.] Have all the children in the Prayer Center smile and cross their hands over their chests to show the warm feeling inside.

- ***SHH-SHH-SHH*** [Have all the children put a finger to their lips.]

2 Guide the children to pray.

- ***We can meet God in quiet. We can meet God deep within our quiet hearts. Let us prepare ourselves to meet God.***

- ***Straighten your back.*** [Pause.]

- ***Rest your arms on your lap, hands open in front of you.*** [Pause.]

- ***You may gently close your eyes if you want to.*** [Pause.]

- ***Slowly breathe in and out, in and out, in and out.*** [Pause.]

- ***Deep within you, see Jesus holding out his hand to you.*** [Pause.]

- ***He whispers, "I am with you always."*** (Matthew 28:20)

[Pause.] ***You sit quietly with Jesus. You feel so happy inside your quiet heart. You tell Jesus that you love him.*** [Pause.] ***You smile at Jesus and he smiles back at you.*** [Pause.]

• ***When you are finished praying, open your eyes.***

3 Invite the children to blow bubbles of praise. Give each child a bubble wand that has been dipped in the bubble solution. As you do this, tell them to wait for the signal before they begin to blow bubbles. Tell them that the signal to begin is when they see you start blowing bubbles. Pray:

• ***Dear God, we wish to praise you with our beautiful bubbles. Each bubble will tell you we love you.*** Begin to blow bubbles. Quietly watch the bubbles until they disappear. When finished, have the children place the bubble wands in the bowl of bubble solution.

4 Invite the children to pray the adaptation of Psalm 131:2 with gestures or sing an appropriate song.

To lead the psalm prayers, first invite the children to pray with you by watching as you pray the words of the psalm with the gestures. Next invite the children to continue to pray together with you by copying only the gestures as you say the words. Finally, invite the children to pray with you the words and the gestures together. When finished, ask the children to sit down quietly.

My heart is quiet
[Cross hands over heart.]

within me,
[Cross arms over chest.]

O Lord.
[Unfold arms in an outward movement.]

5 Invite the children to return to their seats and to open their books to **page 19.** Read aloud the text and have the children do the activity.

Quiet helps us think of God.
It helps us love God.

Try This

Look at the pictures showing quiet times that help you think of God.

Circle them.

Think of God. Remember how much God loves you.

19

ACTING

1 Distribute the Heart and Jesus Picture punchouts. Ask the children to open the door of the heart and fold it back. Then have them put glue above the four corners of the door on the back of the heart and paste the picture of Jesus face-down so that his face will show through the open door of the heart frame. Explain:

- ***Your heart is like a tabernacle. Jesus is there. Put your heart card where you will see it and remember to talk to Jesus in your heart.***
- ***Let's take a moment now to be very still and talk to Jesus now. Remember, you can tell Jesus anything you want.***

2 Have the children take home the Family Page on **page 20** to share with their families.

CHECKPOINT

- Were the children more comfortable with the experience of quiet today than they were on Day One?
- How will you continue to encourage the children to experience and to appreciate quiet and quiet prayer?

My heart is quiet within me, O Lord.
Based on Psalm 131:2

Quiet in Families

The Lesson Your Child Learned

Silence helps us enter into our innermost selves and encounter God present within us. In this chapter the children learned that good and beautiful things happen in quiet. Through a guided reflection, they learned how to meet God present within them.

Living the Lesson

One year I gave up listening to the radio in the car for Lent, and it was one of the hardest things I've ever done. The first lesson it taught me was how noisy my mind was. The second lesson was how I used outside entertainment to drown out those noises in my head. But eventually, after a time of withdrawal, I began to appreciate the silence and found it possible to enter into silent prayer. I benefited from those quiet times so much that even now I will occasionally turn off the radio or CD player in my car and treat myself to the gift of silence.

I suspect that many people who commit to adding more prayer to their lives also find it difficult at first to quiet both mind and heart. They may erroneously conclude that they are no good at praying and let the opportunity slip away. But even the saints had the same struggles with prayer. It's just that they didn't stop praying when the going got tough. When your intention is right, even calming yourself for prayer is a kind of prayer in itself.

Silence may be an acquired taste, but the rewards are beyond measure. As Father Thomas Keating, O.C.S.O., says, "Silence is God's first language." Why not give yourself the chance to listen in?

–Tom McGrath, author of *Raising Faith-Filled Kids* (Loyola Press)

Bringing the Lesson Home

- Encourage your child to tell about his or her prayer experiences this week. Read with your child the pages that were sent home.
- When your family prays together before meals, introduce a short time for quiet personal prayer and reflection. This form of prayer is more easily modeled than taught. And though it may seem awkward at first, this form of prayer will become more comfortable with practice.
- Encourage your child to enjoy quiet time, either time spent alone or with others. If your child seems anxious or crabby, a short time of quiet and less stimulation may be just what he or she needs. This is not to be confused with punishment; it's merely providing what the child needs at the time.
- If you have not already done so, create a prayer center in your home for quiet and for prayer. A favorite chair or a corner of a room can be designated as a place for prayer and peace.

20

ENRICHING THE FAITH EXPERIENCE

Use the following activities to enrich a lesson, to replace an activity with one that better meets the needs of your class, or to create an additional lesson.

1 Teach a song to the melody of "God Is So Good."

Quiet is good. (Two times)
We can meet God
in our quiet hearts.

God loves us so. (Two times)
God meets with us
in our quiet hearts.

2 If you haven't already done so, distribute copies of BLM 7 Bubbles. Have the children draw themselves praying and color the bubbles.

3 Have the children draw pictures of themselves in church.

4 Ask the children to listen for sounds. Perform some of the following actions and have the children tell what they heard.

- Open and close a door.
- Write with chalk on the board.
- Cut paper with scissors.

5 Meditative songs, while not a substitute for quiet prayer, can help children who may need more time to quiet themselves so that they can meet God in their hearts. Teach some of these meditative songs and use them occasionally to begin experiences of quiet prayer. Some examples of meditative songs include "Jesus, Jesus" (Carey Landry), "Jesus, Remember Me," "Take, O Take Me as I Am," "Prayer of Peace," and "O Lord, Hear My Prayer" (*Singing Our Faith*).

Chapter 6

Talking to God Is Good

FAITH FOCUS

In prayer we talk to God.

1 Samuel 3:2–12

PREPARING THE FAITH EXPERIENCE

LISTENING

As you prepare to share God's Word of love with the children, spend some quiet time with God in prayer. Relax your body, quiet your mind, and let yourself be aware that you are filled with God's love. Ask God to speak to you his Word of love.

[T]he love of God has been poured out into our hearts through the holy Spirit that has been given to us.

Romans 5:5

REFLECTING

Whenever we are really present to people, we respond to them—even though the response may be nonverbal. Prayer is our voluntary response to an awareness of God's presence. It is a conversation with the Lord—listening and responding to God. Scripture helps us in our prayer, for in it we hear God speak. It also shows us how God's people have responded before.

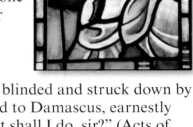

- *Adoration.* Moses divined God's presence in a burning bush, took off his shoes, covered his face, and bowed low. (Exodus 3:2–6)
- *Openness and readiness to obey.* The boy Samuel called out, "Here I am. Speak, for your servant is listening." (1 Samuel 3:8–11)
- *Praise.* Mary, so conscious of God's presence in her life, sang out joyfully, "My soul proclaims the greatness of the Lord!" (Luke 1:46)
- *Petition.* The blind man of Jericho jumped up at Jesus' call and humbly pleaded, "Master, I want to see." (Mark 10:50–51)
- *Contrition, conversion.* Zacchaeus, overwhelmed by the graciousness of Jesus, stood up to those murmuring against him and said to the Lord, "Behold, half of my possessions, Lord, I shall give to the poor, and if I have extorted anything from anyone I shall repay it four times over." (Luke 19:8)
- *Conversion, commitment.* Saul, blinded and struck down by a vision on the road to Damascus, earnestly asked Jesus, "What shall I do, sir?" (Acts of the Apostles 22:10)

Prayerful people are alert to the presence of the Lord at all times and in all places. In one of her poems, Elizabeth Barrett Browning spoke of this presence:

Earth's crammed with heaven,
And every common bush afire with God;
But only he who sees, takes off his shoes—
The rest sit round it and pluck blackberries.

"Aurora Leigh"

Truly, God is present in the breathless beauty and wonders of creation, and even more so in the selfless love and deep sensitivity of people. And yes, God dwells within our very selves, "but only he who sees," only the one who perceives, responds.

RESPONDING

God's Word calls us to respond in love. Respond to God now in the quiet of your heart and perhaps through a journal that you are keeping this year.

- How have I responded to God when I have been aware of his presence?

Jesus, teach me and the children to pray.

Catechism of the Catholic Church

The themes of this lesson correspond to the following paragraphs: 1156, 2565, 2663, 2701.

THE FAITH EXPERIENCE

DAY ONE
We Talk to Those We Love

DAY TWO
We Talk to God

DAY THREE
We Pray in Different Ways

DAY FOUR
Listening to God Is Praying

Scripture in This Chapter

- *Exodus 33:7–10 Moses prepared a meeting tent where he consulted Yahweh. The people stood at the doors of their tents when Moses went there to pray, and they bowed their heads when the pillar of cloud covered the door of the meeting tent.*
- *Luke 5:16 Jesus would withdraw to deserted places to pray.*
- *Luke 6:12 According to his custom, Jesus spent a night in prayer before choosing his apostles.*

Church Documents

General Directory for Catechesis #145. Catechesis should encourage a climate of listening, thanksgiving, and prayer.

National Directory for Catechesis #34. Catechesis for prayer includes communal prayer, private prayer, traditional prayer, spontaneous prayer, gesture, song, meditation, and contemplation.

Directory on Popular Piety and the Liturgy #78. We are guided by the Spirit, who is given to us to sustain, nourish, and direct our prayer.

Bulletin Board At the left is a suggestion for a bulletin-board design. Refer to BLM 8 Praying Hands if you wish to make a photocopy or transparency. Distribute copies of BLM 8 and have the children color and decorate them. Post the completed drawings on the bulletin board. Children have varying degrees of ability. Note that perfection is not the goal and that it is important only for the children to do their best.

- ***BLM 8 Praying Hands***

For a list of children's literature suggestions, please see **page OV-47.**

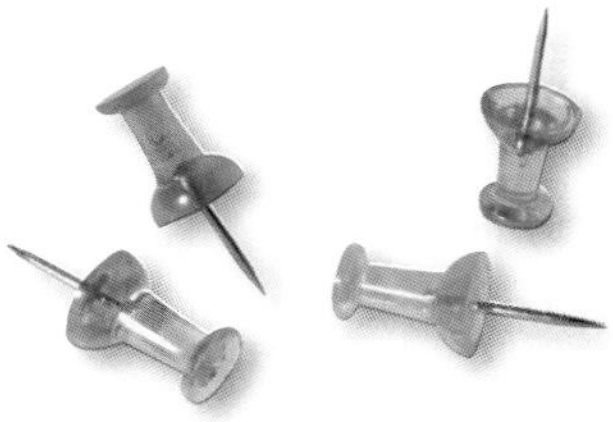

CHAPTER 6 | DAY ONE

We Talk to Those We Love

Student Book page 21

LEARNING OUTCOMES

The children will be able to

- know that prayer includes both listening and responding to God.
- realize that communication can be nonverbal.

MATERIALS

- Cutouts 34–40
- 7 craft sticks

COMMENT

Puppets capture the attention of the children and help shy children share comfortably with a group. Tape or glue a craft stick to the back of Cutouts 34–40 to make puppets.

CENTERING

1 Recall the previous chapters.

- ***Where did you meet God in our last lessons?*** (In church, in our hearts)
- ***How did you behave so that you could meet God in your heart?*** (Quietly)

2 Have the children turn to **page 21** and look at the picture.

- ***Whom do you talk to first thing in the morning?***
- ***How do you feel when you talk to someone you love?***
- ***Today you will learn how you can also talk to Jesus, God's Son.***

SHARING

1 Introduce the puppets: Mr. Garcia, Mrs. Garcia, Carlos, Ana, Baby Raul, Dog, and Cat.

Comment:

- ***Carlos and Ana don't see their mother and father during the day because Carlos and Ana go to school and their parents go to work.***

So the children have many things to tell their parents when they see them. They might say some things like those in your book.

CHAPTER 6

Talking to God Is Good

We like to talk to those we love:

"Dad, I love you very much."

"Look at the pretty butterflies."

"Thank you for letting me play."

"I'll try to do my best today."

21

2 Read the first line on **page 21.** Then use the puppets to dramatize the remaining lines. You may use different puppets for each line.

3 Let the children take turns using the puppets.

- ***How many of you talked to someone in your family before you came to school? You may use the puppets to act out what you and your family member said. Begin by telling us who the puppets are.***

Continue letting the children take turns until all who wish have had a turn with the puppets.

4 Discuss talking.

- ***Talking is a way of showing a person that we know he or she is with us. Unless we use a telephone, we don't talk to people who are not near us. Why not?*** (The person would not hear us and could not answer.)

5 Discuss talking without words.

- ***Have you ever told a family member that you love them? What are some things that you have done to show someone that you love him or her?*** (A hug or kiss, offering to help, making a card, giving a gift)
- ***We can also talk to people without using words. I will ask you to say something without using any words. Show me how you could say each of these things without words.*** Say:

"Good-bye."
"Hello."
"I'm happy."
"Yum-yum."
"Be quiet."
"I'm sad."

6 Talk about the importance of both talking and listening in conversations.

- ***When we talk with someone, do we do all the talking?*** (No) ***When we talk, we also want someone to be listening. Talking and listening are both important. Let's practice talking and listening to one another now.*** Have the children form small groups of two or three so that they can experience talking and listening to one another. Make suggestions about what they might talk about. (Examples: their pets, favorite toys, games, or anything else that interests them)

ACTING

Introduce the following adaptation of Psalm 90:14 with gestures.

- ***There is someone who is with us always, even though we do not see him. Who is that someone?*** (God) ***God is with us when we go to bed at night. God is with us early in the morning. We can talk to God anytime. Using the words of this psalm, let's talk to God now.***

To lead the psalm prayers, first invite the children to pray with you by watching as you pray the words of the psalm with the gestures. Next invite the children to continue to pray together with you by copying only the gestures as you say the words. Finally, invite the children to pray with you the words and the gestures together. When finished, ask the children to sit down quietly.

Fill us
[Draw up hands from knees to head.]

in the morning
[Stretch out arms.]

with your love.
[Cross hands over heart.]

CHECKPOINT

- Are the children becoming more confident and at ease in sharing with the group?
- Were the children able to take turns talking and listening in SHARING #6? How will you continue to encourage this?

We Talk to God

Student Book page 22

LEARNING OUTCOMES

The children will be able to

- join in spontaneous prayer as a response to God's presence.
- know the meaning of *amen*.

KEY TERMS

amen—a prayer word that means "yes"
prayer—talking with God

MATERIALS

- Cutouts 2, 7, 9, 15–17, 22–25, 34–40
- Flashcard 3

COMMENT

Throughout this year, the children will be invited to pray with you using words found in the Book of Psalms. You will also begin sharing the prayers of our Catholic tradition. Also, the children will learn to pray in their own words by offering spontaneous prayer. This form of prayer will be introduced in this lesson. To help the children pray in their own words, you can ask them questions. When you share this prayer, be sure to give the children time to think as they formulate their words of prayer. However, because some may be uncomfortable with this form of prayer, never force or cajole a child to respond. Simply extend the invitation and move on if a child would rather not participate.

CENTERING

Lead the children to discuss prayer.

- ***Can we talk to God? Why?*** (God is with us always.)
- ***Where can we talk to God?*** (Anywhere, in church)
- ***When can we talk to God?*** (In the morning, at night, anytime)
- ***God always listens to us. Talking to God is so special that we have a special name for it. We call talking to God* prayer.**

SHARING

1. Let the children use the puppets to create an ending for each situation here. Then read a parallel situation that can elicit a prayer. Call upon the children to dramatize possible responses, allowing them to create different endings to the same situation so that all who wish get a turn.

- ***Carlos sees his father, Mr. Garcia, wearing a new tie. He thinks his dad looks great, so he says . . .***

  You go outside and see some beautiful birds. [Show Cutout 17 Birds.] ***You say to God. . .*** ("Your birds are very beautiful, God." "Thank you for the beautiful birds, God.")

- ***When Carlos wakes up in the morning, his mother is in his room, turning on the light. Because it's morning, Carlos says . . .***

  You wake in the morning filled with God's love. God has been taking care of you all night. You say . . . ("Good morning, God." "I love you, God." "Thank you, God, for taking care of me all night.")

- ***It is time for bed. Ana goes to her father, Mr. Garcia. She says . . .***

  It is time for you to go to bed. You think of God, who is with you always. You say . . .

2. Talk more about ideas for night prayers.

- ***Just before going to bed is a great time for prayer. There are many things we might say to God when we pray before going to sleep.*** Suggest the ideas below for night prayers. Invite volunteers to respond.
- ***We can thank God for our day. How might you thank God for any gifts you saw or used today?***
- ***We can ask God for help. What might you say if you want to ask God to help someone who needs special help?***
- ***We can ask God to bless people that we love. How can you ask God to bless some of the people you love?***
- ***We can also ask God to watch over us while we sleep. How might you ask God to bless you and watch over you?***

3 Teach the children to pray *amen.* Show Flashcard 3 *amen.* You might have the children sing it.

- ***Have you heard people say "amen" in church or while praying?***
- ***Amen is a prayer word. It means "Yes, Lord." When we answer amen after a prayer said by another person, we make the prayer our own.***
- ***I shall say a prayer. If you would like to make it your prayer, answer, "Amen."***

  God, you are so very good. (Amen.)

  God, you made the world beautiful. (Amen.)

  We love you, God. (Amen.)

4 Have the children turn to **page 22.** Read it aloud. Guide the children to read the following text together:

- ***God loves us.***

ACTING

Ask the children to move quietly to the Prayer Center. Say:

- ***Sometimes we want to pray to God using our own words. Let's do this now.***

Invite the children to pray to God using their own words. Place in front of them Cutouts (listed in MATERIALS) that will remind them of something they would like to tell God. Tell them that they can make each prayer their own by responding amen. Help the children pray spontaneously by asking questions:

- ***How does warm sunshine make you feel? What would you like to tell God about this?***
- ***Would you like to ask God to help someone you know? What help would you like to ask for from God?***

CHECKPOINT

- How did the children respond in the spontaneous prayer?

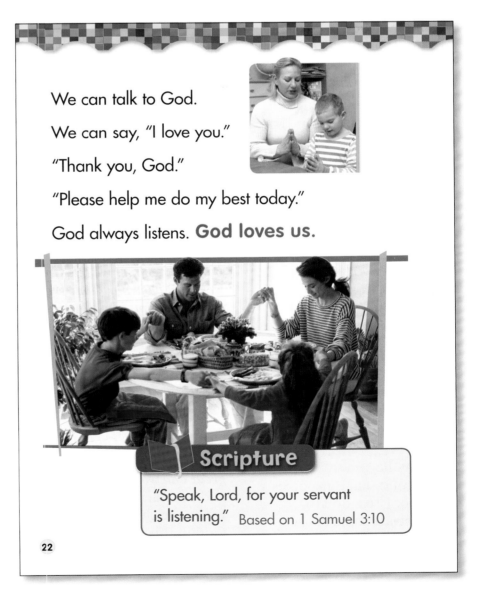

We can talk to God.

We can say, "I love you."

"Thank you, God."

"Please help me do my best today."

God always listens. **God loves us.**

Scripture

"Speak, Lord, for your servant is listening." Based on 1 Samuel 3:10

22

CHAPTER 6 | DAY THREE

We Pray in Different Ways

Student Book page 23

LEARNING OUTCOMES

The children will be able to

- experience singing, movement, and talking to God as prayer.

MATERIALS

- Doll
- A song of praise for SHARING #3, such as "If I Were a Butterfly" (*Hi God 2*) or "Make a Wonderful Noise" (*Sing a Song of Joy*)
- "David Dances" (*Peaceable Kingdom*) for SHARING #4 (optional)

COMMENT

Prayer is not limited to words. Young children, who have limited verbal skills but are active by nature, are able to express themselves more easily through bodily movements. This gives them an advantage in understanding nonverbal prayer and in praying with total involvement: emotions, body, and mind.

CENTERING

Teach the children a sung prayer, such as "Father, We Adore You." (Alternatively, you might teach "Glory and Gratitude and Praise," "Holy Is Your Name," "Alleluia, Alleluia, Give Thanks" (*Singing our Faith*) or "Kum Ba Yah.")

Then ask:

- ***Was singing this song praying?*** (Yes.) ***Why?*** (We were talking to God through the words of the song.)

SHARING

1 Expand the children's understanding of prayer.

- ***Do you remember when we met Jesus deep within our quiet hearts? We were praying then too. Whenever we are aware that Jesus is with us and we are with him, we are praying.***

2 Help the children understand that our bodies pray too. Use a doll to demonstrate some of the actions. Model these actions yourself.

- ***Our bodies help us to pray. When we sit quietly and close our eyes, it is easier for us to meet God deep within our quiet hearts.***
- ***We can speak to God through our bodies. Sometimes we stand to pray and fold our hands.*** [Demonstrate and have the children imitate your actions.]
- ***Sometimes we kneel and fold our hands when we pray. You may wish to kneel and pray when you wake in the morning or before you go to bed at night. Let us kneel down. By our kneeling, we tell God we know he is our God. We belong to him.*** [Demonstrate and have the children imitate your actions.] Gestures can and should be adapted when necessary to accommodate different needs, such as sitting instead of kneeling.
- ***We can praise God. That means telling God that he is great and wonderful.*** [Stand and raise arms and hands. Invite the children to praise God in this way.]
- ***Sometimes we ask God for things we need.*** [Raise arms to shoulder height, elbows bent, palms open. Have the children imitate you.]
- ***Some people tell God they adore him by bowing low.*** [Bow.] ***Sometimes they bow very low to tell God they are sorry for something they have done.*** [Have the children imitate you.]

3 Invite the children to think of dance as prayer.

- ***Music can help us think about and love God. Sometimes we may dance to tell God how much we love him.***
- ***Let your hands, arms, and feet tell God how much you love him. Listen to the music first so that you know what you wish to tell God through your dance prayer.***

Play a song that lends itself to creative dance, such as "If I Were a Butterfly" (*Hi God 2*) or "Make a Wonderful Noise" (*Sing a Song of Joy*).

• ***Let's all dance a prayer now. Keep a holy space around you so that you do not interrupt anyone else's prayer.***

Play the song. To help the children feel free, you might participate as well. However, do not force any child to participate.

4 Tell the children about King David from the Old Testament.

• ***Long ago, God had a special friend named David who became the king of his people. King David loved God very much. David liked to show his joy and love for God by dancing.*** You might have the children listen to the song "David Dances" (*Peaceable Kingdom*).

5 Ask the children to name different ways of praying.

ACTING

1 Have the children turn to **page 23.** Read it aloud and have the children do the activity.

2 Introduce the psalm prayer.

• ***Sometimes we pray using words that other people have prayed before us. Many of the psalm prayers we are learning this year were written by King David. The words of these prayers are found in the Bible. By praying these prayers with the gestures we are learning, we are praying like King David.***

Invite the children to pray the adaptation of Psalm 90:14 with gestures.

To lead the psalm prayers, first invite the children to pray with you by watching as you pray the words of the psalm with the gestures. Next invite the children to continue to pray together with you by copying only the gestures as you say the words. Finally, invite the children to pray with you the words and the gestures together. When finished, ask the children to sit down quietly.

Fill us
[Draw up hands from knees to head.]

in the morning
[Stretch out arms.]

with your love.
[Cross hands over heart.]

CHECKPOINT

• How freely did the children join in the dance?

When we talk to God, we pray. God bless . . .

Try This

Finish the prayer. Draw a circle around the people you want to pray for.

Remember that you can talk to God anytime.

You can pray to God in different ways.

23

CHAPTER 6 | DAY FOUR

Listening to God Is Praying

Student Book pages 24–26

LEARNING OUTCOMES

The children will be able to
- become acquainted with story of Samuel found in the Bible.
- know how to listen to God during prayer.

MATERIALS
- *A Child's Bible,* page 10

CENTERING

1 Ask the children to suggest a prayer to begin the lesson. Invite the children to pray together.

2 Explain that sometimes in prayer we do not need to sing or dance or even talk. We just have to listen.

SHARING

1 Help the children understand that conversing involves talking and listening.

- ***When you are with a friend, do you do all the talking? Why not?*** (Your friend wants to talk too. You want to listen to your friend.) ***Talking with someone means both speaking and listening.***

2 Invite the children to remember what they learned about how to be good listeners.

- ***Let's prepare ourselves to listen well to today's Bible story.***
- ***Listening eyes are on the storyteller.*** [Pause until all the children are looking at you.] ***Listening hands are quietly in your lap.*** [Pause until all the children have put their hands in their laps.] ***Listening feet are comfortable and quiet.*** [Pause until all the children's feet are still.] ***Listening hearts are ready to hear God's Word.*** [Pause.]

Read or tell the story "A Strange Night for Samuel" from *A Child's Bible*, **page 10.**

3 Discuss the story of Samuel.

- ***How did Samuel show he was ready to listen to God?*** (He said, "Speak, Lord, for your servant is listening.")
- ***What is a servant?*** (Someone whose job it is to serve another by doing what that person asks.)
- ***Why does Samuel call himself a servant?*** (He is ready to do whatever God asks.)
- ***How can we show God that we are ready to listen?*** (Be quiet. Give God some of our time. Think about God.)
- ***What did God ask Samuel to do?*** (Give a message to Eli.)
- ***Samuel showed that he really listened to God. He did what God told him.***
- ***When you are quiet and listening to God, you will know what God wants you to do too. You will come to know and love God more and more.***

4 Invite the children to act out the story of Samuel.

5 Help the children prepare for prayer by teaching them the following poem.

Prayer Time

One, two: Here's what I do.
Three, four: To love Jesus more.
Five, six: On him my heart fix.
Seven, eight: Sit still and wait.
Nine, ten: Talk to my Friend,
Jesus.

M. Kathleen Glavich, S.N.D.

ACTING

1 Encourage the children to talk to God many times each day to show their love. Tell them they can use Samuel's words as a prayer: "Speak, Lord, for your servant is listening." Prepare these words with gestures, just as the psalm prayers (cup mouth when saying, "Speak, Lord"; cup ears when saying, "for your servant is listening").

2 If *A Child's Bible* has been sent home, tell the children to ask their parents to read the stories to them.

3 Have the children take home the Family Page on **page 24** to share with their families.

CHECKPOINT

- Are the children learning the give-and-take of conversation?
- How will you continue to share prayer experiences that encourage both talking and listening to God?

FAMILY FEATURE

Help the children carefully tear out the Family Feature on **pages 25-26.** Ask them to take home the Family Feature to read and to work on with their families.

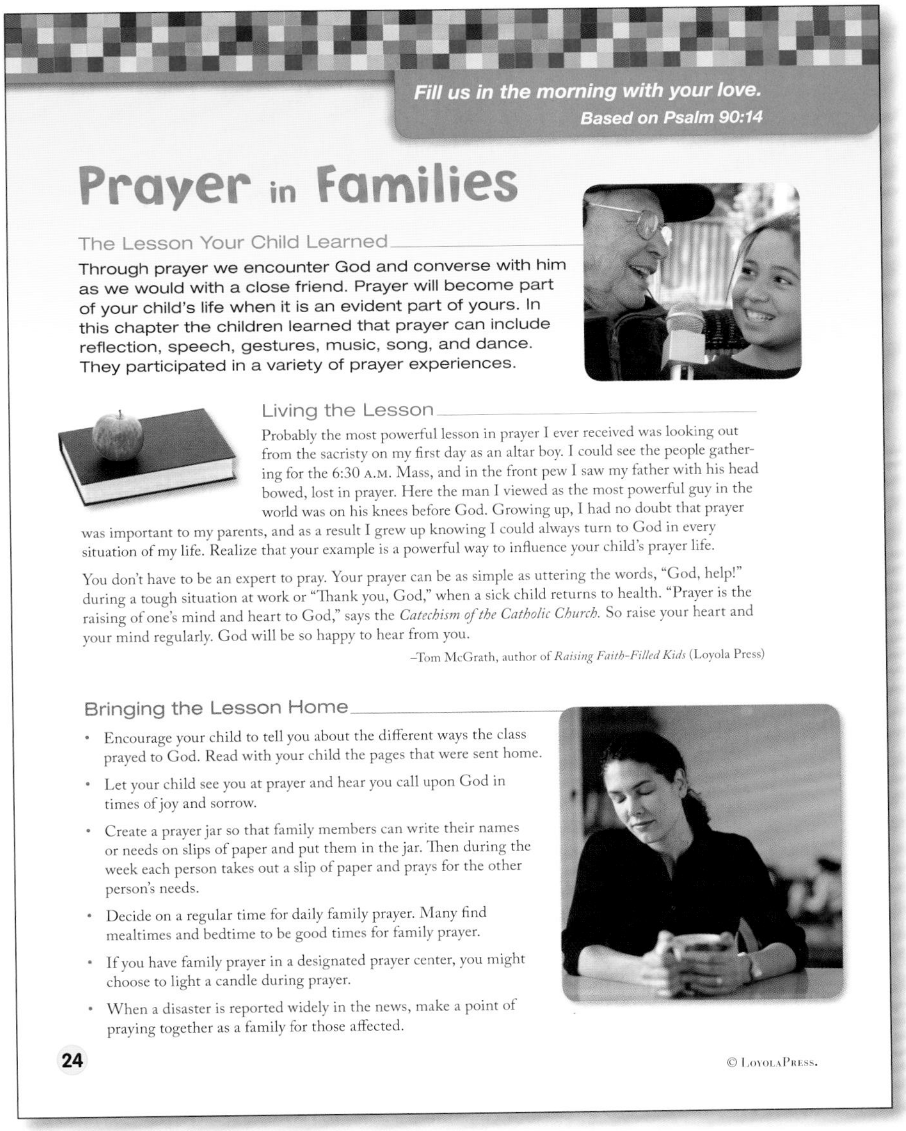

Fill us in the morning with your love.
Based on Psalm 90:14

Prayer in Families

The Lesson Your Child Learned

Through prayer we encounter God and converse with him as we would with a close friend. Prayer will become part of your child's life when it is an evident part of yours. In this chapter the children learned that prayer can include reflection, speech, gestures, music, song, and dance. They participated in a variety of prayer experiences.

Living the Lesson

Probably the most powerful lesson in prayer I ever received was looking out from the sacristy on my first day as an altar boy. I could see the people gathering for the 6:30 A.M. Mass, and in the front pew I saw my father with his head bowed, lost in prayer. Here the man I viewed as the most powerful guy in the world was on his knees before God. Growing up, I had no doubt that prayer was important to my parents, and as a result I grew up knowing I could always turn to God in every situation of my life. Realize that your example is a powerful way to influence your child's prayer life.

You don't have to be an expert to pray. Your prayer can be as simple as uttering the words, "God, help!" during a tough situation at work or "Thank you, God," when a sick child returns to health. "Prayer is the raising of one's mind and heart to God," says the *Catechism of the Catholic Church.* So raise your heart and your mind regularly. God will be so happy to hear from you.

–Tom McGrath, author of *Raising Faith-Filled Kids* (Loyola Press)

Bringing the Lesson Home

- Encourage your child to tell you about the different ways the class prayed to God. Read with your child the pages that were sent home.
- Let your child see you at prayer and hear you call upon God in times of joy and sorrow.
- Create a prayer jar so that family members can write their names or needs on slips of paper and put them in the jar. Then during the week each person takes out a slip of paper and prays for the other person's needs.
- Decide on a regular time for daily family prayer. Many find mealtimes and bedtime to be good times for family prayer.
- If you have family prayer in a designated prayer center, you might choose to light a candle during prayer.
- When a disaster is reported widely in the news, make a point of praying together as a family for those affected.

24

ENRICHING THE FAITH EXPERIENCE

Use the following activities to enrich a lesson, to replace an activity with one that better meets the needs of your class, or to create an additional lesson.

1 Teach a song to the melody of "God Is So Good."

> **Praying is good.**
> (Three times)
> **We can talk to God.**
>
> **God loves us so.**
> (Three times)
> **God hears when we pray.**

2 Play musical selections, such as "Morning" from *Peer Gynt* Suite No. 1, "Scherzo" and "Nocturne" from *A Midsummer Night's Dream*, "Clair de Lune" from *Suite Bergamasque*, and "Devil's Dance" from *A Soldier's Tale*, that depict different emotions. Ask the children what the composer might be saying through the music.

Be still and know that I am God.
Adapted from Psalm 46:11

Growing Family Faith

The Power of Prayer

Few things are as essential to our health and well-being, yet carry as vast an assortment of experience (and therefore baggage), as prayer. Some of us were never taught how to pray. For others, what was taught wasn't meaningful, so we have placed prayers and praying in a box on a shelf in the back of the closet, to be taken out only on special occasions—at funerals, for example, or when a loved one is ill.

Many of us do use prayer more or less regularly, but we aren't sure what we're doing is right. As one parent lamented, "I keep thinking there must be something like a 'secret handshake' that would make my prayers more effective, but I don't know what it is—or how to find out."

Whatever your experience of prayer is or has been, consider this: Prayer is, at its heart, a remembering. We pray in order to remember who we are. We pray to remember God who is both our source and the eternal essence within each of us that is whole, perfect, and unchanging.

Whether we have been praying all our lives or are just taking the first few tentative steps toward remembering who we are, let us take encouragement from the Trappist monk Thomas Merton, who observed, "We do not want to be beginners, but let us be convinced that we will never be anything else but beginners all our life."

If prayer is not yet a part of your daily life, the good news is that it's never too late to begin! Here are a few old and new ideas to try alone or with your family:

Putting More Prayer in Your Day

- Create a regular time and a place to pray. Plan to wake up 30 minutes earlier every morning, or take 20 minutes of your lunch hour, or commit to a prayer time before you go to sleep each night. Experiment until you find the time and place that you are least likely to be interrupted.
- Find a book of prayers that you like and use it daily. There are hundreds of them on the market, or you may already have one at home.
- If you prayed as a child, revisit some of the prayers you prayed then. You have a different perspective now that you are a parent, and these prayers may resonate in ways they did not when you were younger. For example, see **The Practicing Catholic** on page 26. Pray these prayers with your child and tell why they mean so much to you.
- Create a simple ritual that you and your child could perform at the beginning or end of each day.

25

3 Have the children make pretzels. Show them a pretzel and point out that it is made in the shape of crossed arms. Long ago, when pretzels were first made, people often crossed their arms over their chests while praying. Use the recipe below.

Soft Pretzel Recipe

1 cake yeast
1 1/2 cups water
4 cups flour
1 teaspoon salt
1 tablespoon sugar
1 egg
Coarse salt

- Dissolve 1 cake yeast in 1 1/2 cups warm water.
- Add 1 teaspoon salt and 1 tablespoon sugar. Blend in the flour.
- Knead dough until smooth and cut into small pieces.
- Give each child one piece of dough and explain how to roll the dough into ropes. Show the children how to twist the pretzels into shape, helping them if necessary.
- Place the pretzels on a lightly greased cookie sheet. Brush them with a beaten egg and sprinkle with coarse salt.
- Bake the pretzels immediately at 425° for 12 to 15 minutes.

(For hard pretzels, use only 1 1/4 cups water and add 1/4 cup melted butter. Make smaller pretzels and bake until brown.)

Songs

Play for the children any of these songs: "All Night, All Day," (*Singing Our Faith*) **CD 1 Track 7;** "Sing, Sing, Praise and Sing!" (*Singing Our Faith*) **CD 1 Track 12;** "Glory in the Light" (*I See a New World*) **CD 2 Track 11;** "Make a Wonderful Noise" (*Sing a Song of Joy!*) **CD 2 Track 16;** "If I Were a Butterfly" (*Hi God 2*); "Make a Joyful Noise" (*Color the World with Song*); "Talk to You" (*Come Meet Jesus*); "Fly" (*Even a Worm*); "Sing-a-Prayer," "Sing Praise" (*Songs for Young Children*); "Good Morning, God," "Somebody's Knockin' at Your Door" (*Singing Our Faith*). *For a list of all the music used in this program, see* **page OV-39.**

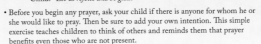

Putting More Prayer in Your Day *continued*

Try reading these two lines from Psalm 118:24 each morning:

Adult: *This is the day the Lord has made...*
Child: *Let us rejoice and be glad.*

- Before you begin any prayer, ask your child if there is anyone for whom he or she would like to pray. Then be sure to add your own intention. This simple exercise teaches children to think of others and reminds them that prayer benefits even those who are not present.

- Check out bookstores, the Internet, or your local library for a book of mealtime prayers to use each time you and your child share a meal together.
- Take your child to Mass with you each week. The Mass, of course, is *the* prayer, the great remembering of who we are and who we aspire to be. If your child reacts negatively, have your response ready: "This is who we are. This is what we do."
- Write your prayer in the form of a letter to God each prayer time. At first this might seem like an impossible undertaking, but the inspiration, peace, and comfort it provides make it an exercise that will become a joyful, life-giving habit. Try it, you'll like it!

The Practicing Catholic

During the Vietnam War, my father decided that our family would pray the Rosary together every night for three years while my brother was in the Marines. My brother came home safely, but by then I was pretty sure I never wanted to say another Rosary again! Recently though, I had the idea to time my morning stretching exercises by saying the Our Father and the Hail Mary instead of counting the seconds. After a week I realized I had an entire Rosary in my exercise routine. This simple change has transformed my experience of both prayer and exercise. It also connects me in a profound way to my father, who died over ten years ago.

—Ann O'Connor, author of *The Twelve Unbreakable Principles of Parenting* (ACTA Publications)

We cannot find God in noise or agitation. Nature: trees, flowers, and grass grow in silence. The stars, the moon, and the sun move in silence. —Mother Teresa

26

unit two

Growing In God's Love

In this unit the children will learn to appreciate their own uniqueness as a gift from God.

7 FAMILIES ARE GOOD

After a discussion of families, the children reflect on the Holy Family. They learn that they belong to the human family and to God's family, the Church. They are introduced to God as Father and to the first two lines of the Our Father.

8 I AM GOOD

The children come to an appreciation of themselves through reflection on their senses, their feelings, and the wonderful things they can do. They learn that God made them good and that they are precious to God.

9 GROWING IS GOOD

The children consider their natural growth and then become aware that they are to grow in Christ's love. They learn that at Baptism they became Christians and were anointed with oil. They are introduced to the next two lines of the Our Father.

10 THANKING IS GOOD

The children discuss when and why we say thank you and come to realize that we owe God much gratitude. They are introduced to the prayer before meals, and they learn the next line of the Our Father.

11 PREPARING IS GOOD

The children learn that Christmas is a celebration of Jesus' birthday. They learn how to prepare for the celebration by being more loving. They are introduced to the custom of the Advent wreath.

12 CHOOSING IS GOOD

The children learn about making good choices. They study Mary and hear about her choice to say yes to God, in particular at the Annunciation. They learn that Mary is their mother, who will help them make good choices. They learn the first words of the Hail Mary.

Chapter 7

Families Are Good

FAITH FOCUS

In God, we are all brothers and sisters.

Luke 2:39–40

Lesson 11 on the Holy Family in SPECIAL SEASONS AND DAYS can be correlated with this chapter.

PREPARING THE FAITH EXPERIENCE

LISTENING

Those who share God's Word with others must also be fed by God's word found in Sacred Scripture. Share some time of quiet prayer with God, listening to God's Word. Ask God to fill you with his presence and nourish you by his holy Word.

"This is how you are to pray:

Our Father in heaven,
hallowed be your name,
your kingdom come;
your will be done,
on earth as in heaven.
Give us this day our daily bread;
and forgive us our debts,
as we forgive our debtors;
and do not subject us to the final test,
but deliver us from the evil one.

If you forgive others their transgressions,
your heavenly Father will forgive you.
But if you do not forgive others, neither
will your Father forgive your transgressions."

Matthew 6:9–15

REFLECTING

The names we use to address people express our relationships with them. We use intimate terms to address those we love. We use more formal terms to speak to business associates. When Jesus told us to call God "our Father" and gave us the Our Father prayer, he said a great deal about our relationship to God and to one another. This prayer is also called the Lord's Prayer because Jesus himself taught it to us.

Nothing is left unsaid in the Our Father. With Christ, we acclaim God as our heavenly Father and offer him our praise and love. We express our desire for the Father's kingdom and for the fulfillment of his will. We acknowledge our dependence on God and his loving, forgiving, faithful care for us. We declare our confident trust that our heavenly Father, the source of our very being, provides all that we need for our human sustenance. We express our solidarity with the human family and note how our personal well-being is inseparably linked to our forgiving and selfless concern for others. How fitting it is that the Lord's Prayer introduces the communion rite of the Mass! It is a kind of "meal prayer." We unite as a community to plead for our true nourishment. We come humbly, recognizing that we can be united with the Lord only when we are truly one with our neighbor.

All our needs and our priorities are included in this perfect prayer. Placing ourselves in the hands of our loving Father, we confidently pray the Our Father together with our brothers and sisters in Christ.

RESPONDING

Having been nourished by God's Word, we are able to respond to God's great love for us. In prayer, respond to God's call to you to share his word with others. You may also wish to respond in your prayer journal.

- How has your image of God the Father been shaped by your experiences?
- In what ways have you experienced God as loving, caring, and forgiving?

Loving God, may I, together with the children, grow in love and trust of you.

Catechism of the Catholic Church

The themes of this lesson correspond to the following paragraphs: 239–240, 1655, 1931, 2780, 2790, 2794–2796, 2807.

THE FAITH EXPERIENCE

DAY ONE
We Belong to Families

DAY TWO
Family Members Love One Another

DAY THREE
We Belong to God's Family

DAY FOUR
God Is Our Loving Father

Scripture in This Chapter

- *Psalm 103 God treats those who revere him as tenderly as a father treats his children.*
- *Matthew 23:9 Jesus teaches us to pray to God our Father in heaven.*

Church Documents

General Directory for Catechesis #86.
Catechesis prepares the Christian to live in community and to participate in the life of the Church.

The Family and Human Rights #16.
The family is the basic element of human society and the most necessary force in the full development of the human person.

Dogmatic Constitution on the Church #11.
The family is the domestic church in which parents are the first preachers of the faith to their children.

Bulletin Board At the left is a suggestion for a bulletin-board design. Refer to BLM 9 Holy Family if you wish to make a photocopy or transparency. Display the picture of the Holy Family in the center of the board. Add the pictures that the children will draw of their own families on Day One. • ***BLM 9 Holy Family***

For a list of children's literature suggestions, please see **page OV-47.**

CHAPTER 7 | DAY ONE

We Belong to Families

Student Book page 27

LEARNING OUTCOMES

The children will be able to

- realize that they belong to a family.
- identify the Holy Family.

KEY TERMS

family—people who love and care for one another; a family includes parents, brothers and sisters, and sometimes others

Holy Family—the family made up of Jesus, his mother, Mary, and his foster father, Joseph

MATERIALS

- BLM 9
- Cutouts: 13–16, 22–28
- Drawing paper
- Crayons or markers
- Song about families (optional)

COMMENT

In presenting the concept of family, be aware of contemporary family structures and the changing roles of men and women. Pay close attention to the family portraits that the children draw at the beginning of today's lesson. Your familiarity with the family circumstances of the children in your class can help you present this chapter in a way that will make all the children feel comfortable about their families' circumstances.

CENTERING

1 Recall the last lesson.

- ***In the last lesson you learned the word for talking to God. What is it?*** (Prayer)
- ***When can we pray?*** (Anytime)
- ***This week you will learn a very special prayer that we can pray every day. It has to do with being a member of a family.***
- ***This week we will talk about our families and about God's special family, the Church.***

2 Have the children draw pictures of their families. Tell them to be sure to include every family member in their picture, including themselves. Tell them if you will be displaying these pictures on the bulletin board (as described on page **T79.**) As the children work, guide them to write titles, such as "Tamara's Family," on their pictures. Explain to the children that they will use these pictures soon to "introduce" their family members to the class.

SHARING

1 Show Cutouts 13 Wolves, 14 Lambs, 15 Kittens, and 16 Puppies. Show Cutout 13. Say:

- ***This looks like it might be a family of wolves. We can call this a wolf family.***
- [Show Cutout 14.] ***What do you see in this picture?*** (Lambs) ***Lambs belong to their lamb family.***
- [Show Cutouts 15 and 16.] ***What do you see in these pictures?*** (Kittens and puppies) ***Kittens belong to their cat family and puppies belong to their dog family.***

2 Show **page 27** to the children. Ask the children to look at the people in the picture. Ask:

- ***Do these people belong to a cat or a dog family? Of course not, they belong to a human family.***

Read aloud the chapter title and the first two sentences on **page 27.**

3 Tell the children that each one of them belongs to a family and that their family is special. Invite the children to show the family pictures they drew in CENTERING #2 and to tell the class who is shown in their drawings.

4 Use Cutouts 22–28 to show how the makeup of families differs. You can use the Cutouts to show examples of family configurations that the children shared. (Examples: one parent/one child, two parents/three children, two parents/one grandparent/two children) Explain:

- ***Although there are different kinds of families, God wants all families to love and care for one another.***
- ***When each person does his or her part to help, the family is happy.***

5 Discuss the Holy Family.

- ***Jesus belonged to a family too. Who was in his family?*** (Mary and Joseph) Read aloud the last two sentences on **page 27.**
- ***Jesus' family is called the Holy Family. Why do you think we call it that?*** (Jesus is God. Mary and Joseph were very good.)
- ***The members of the Holy Family loved one another. They took care of one another.***
- ***How do you think Jesus might have helped Mary and Joseph?*** (Doing chores, obeying his parents, cooperating) ***How do you think Mary helped Jesus and Joseph?*** (Teaching Jesus, cooking meals, going to the market, sewing clothes, being kind and loving) ***How do you think Joseph helped Jesus and Mary?*** (Teaching Jesus, doing chores, working as a carpenter, being kind and loving)

6 Invite the children to color and decorate the picture of the Holy Family on BLM 9 Holy Family.

- *BLM 9 Holy Family*

7 Introduce the poem "The Holy Family."

- ***Let's imagine what life was like for Jesus, Mary, and Joseph. Listen to this poem called "The Holy Family."***

Read the poem "The Holy Family" on **page T82.** Have the children discuss it.

(Alternatively, teach a song about families. See the song list on **page T89** for a list of possible songs.)

UNIT TWO
CHAPTER 7

Families Are Good

God made us to belong to families. Family members love and care for one another.

Jesus lived with Mary and Joseph. They are called the Holy Family.

27

The Holy Family

Jesus, Mary, and Joseph
Lived in Galilee.
They seemed to all the
neighbors
A normal family.
Mary, Jesus' mother,
Worked hard all day long:
Baked bread, sewed clothes,
fetched water.
She often sang a song.
Joseph, Mary's husband,
Loved her and her boy.
By working as a carpenter,
He cared for them with joy.
Jesus was a good son.
He did as he was told,
And helped his mom and dad
Until he was quite old.
Jesus, Mary, and Joseph,
They're a special three—
For Jesus was God's Son
In the Holy Family.

M. Kathleen Glavich, S.N.D

ACTING

Teach the children the prayer based on Psalm 22:11, using these gestures, and invite them to pray the psalm verse with you:

LORD, even before I was born
[Extend open hands in front at waist level.]

I was
[Raise arms slightly.]

in your care.
[Cross arms on chest.]

CHECKPOINT

- What did the children's family drawings tell about their experience of family?
- How will you continue to acknowledge the different family circumstances of the children in your class?

CHAPTER 7 | DAY TWO

Family Members Love One Another

LEARNING OUTCOMES

The children will be able to

- appreciate how family members help one another.
- desire to contribute to the family by acts of love and care.

MATERIALS

- BLM 11
- Cutouts: 22–28
- Song about families (optional)

COMMENT

As you talk about ways in which family members help one another, a child might talk about ways in which members of his or her family do not always show love and care. If this happens, it is important to acknowledge that no family is perfect and that God can help families to be more loving and caring. Tell the children that we can pray that God will help all families become more loving and caring. However, if a child shares a situation or incident that raises a serious concern for you, check with the proper authority regarding local and diocesan child-protection policies and follow up as necessary.

CENTERING

1 Have the children sing a song about families (from last lesson or from the song list on **page T89**) or pray the psalm verse based on Psalm 22:11.

Lord, even before I was born
[Extend open hands in front at waist level.]

I was
[Raise arms slightly.]

in your care.
[Cross arms on chest.]

2 Recall the last lesson. If the bulletin board suggested on **page T79** was prepared, show the children that the display now includes their family pictures. Say:

- ***In the last lesson, we talked about our families and about the people who make up our families.***

Ask:

- ***Who are the members of the Holy Family?*** (Jesus, Mary, Joseph)
- ***What do members of a family do for one another?*** (Love and care for one another)
- ***Today we will talk about some of the ways that family members show that they love and care for one another.***

SHARING

1 Show Cutouts 22–28 and have the children name the family member pictured. Say:

- ***Each family member is important to the whole family. Mothers, fathers, grandparents, brothers, sisters, even babies; each person in a family shows love and care for every other person in the family.***

2 Show Cutouts 22–28 again and this time, discuss some of the things that each family member might do to help other members of the family. If the children in your class enjoy role-playing, invite volunteers to demonstrate some of these activities as they are named.

- [Show Cutouts 22 and 23.] ***Parents do many things to show their love and care for their family. What are some things that your parents do to show their love and care for the people in your family?***
- [Show Cutouts 24 and 25.] ***Grandparents do many things to show their love and care for their family. What are some things that your grandparents do to show their love and care for the people in your family?***
- [Show Cutouts 26 and 27.] ***Children do many things to show their love and care for their family. What are some things that you and the children in your family do to show your love and care for the people in your family?***
- [Show Cutout 28.] ***Even babies and toddlers do things to show their love and care for their family. What are some***

things that the babies and toddlers in your family do to show their love and care for the people in your family?

3 Observe that the children have named many important ways in which families show their love and care for one another. Say:

- ***When family members show their love and care for one another, it helps everyone in the family feel happy.***

4 Encourage the children to add to the joy of family life through their love, helpfulness, and obedience. Ask:

- ***What is one thing that you can do this week to show the people in your family that you love and care about them?***

5 Distribute copies of BLM 11 Card for Family and have the children make cards for their mothers, fathers, or others who take care of them. Tell them to trace over the letters and print their names on the inside of the cards. Help them print *Mommy*, *Daddy*, or the names of others. Have them decorate the cards with things these people like or things they do for them.

• ***BLM 11 Card for Family***

ACTING

1 Introduce the closing prayer:

- ***You have learned that Jesus loves you. He loves your family too. We can ask Jesus to bless our families and to help them show our love and care for one another.***

2 Guide the children to pray this prayer to ask God to bless their families:

- ***Quiet helps us to pray. We can be with God deep within our quiet hearts. Let us prepare ourselves to spend time with God.***
- ***Straighten your back.*** [Pause.]
- ***Rest your arms on your lap, hands open in front of you.*** [Pause.]
- ***Gently close your eyes or look down at your hands resting in your lap.*** [Pause.]
- ***Slowly breathe in and out, in and out, in and out.*** [Pause.]
- ***Deep within you, see Jesus sitting next to you.*** [Pause.]
- ***In the quiet of your heart, tell Jesus about each person in your family. As you tell Jesus about each person in your family, ask Jesus to bless your family and to help you love and care for one another.*** [Pause.]
- ***When you are finished praying, open your eyes.***

CHECKPOINT

- Were the children aware of the importance of each family member?
- Were the children able to identify ways in which they contribute to their families' well-being?

CHAPTER 7 | DAY THREE

We Belong to God's Family

Student Book pages 28–29

LEARNING OUTCOMES

The children will be able to

- realize that they are brothers and sisters to people all over the world.
- learn that they are members of God's special family, the Church.
- regard God as their loving heavenly Father.

KEY TERMS

Baptism—the ceremony that joined us to the Church
Christian—a person who believes in Jesus and who loves and follows him
Church—God's special family who believes in Jesus and tries to love as he did
Father in heaven—God
Pope—the head of the Church who lives in Rome

MATERIALS

- BLM 10
- Birthday candles
- Crayons or markers
- Pictures of the pope and the Vatican

COMMENT

It is important to be aware that some of the children in your class may have been adopted. Therefore, in the CENTERING activity, you might adapt language about when a child was "born" into his or her family.

CENTERING

Show the birthday candles. Discuss:

- ***What are these candles used for?*** (Birthday cakes) ***Do you know that you have two birthdays? The first one is the day you were born and became a member of your family.***

Talk about how we become members of our family through our birth. Use the name of a child in your class to make the following message personal:

- ***When*** [Thomas] ***was born into the*** [Gibbons] ***family, he became a little*** [Gibbons] ***and shared in everything the family had. What did he share in?*** (Home, food, clothing, car, the life of the family—its celebrations and its happy and sad times) ***Each of you shares these things in your family because you belong to it.***
- ***Today you will learn about your other birthday and another family of which you are also a member.***

SHARING

1 Lead the children to know they belong to God's family.

- ***Your other birthday was the day you were born into God's special family, the Church. You became a member of the Church on the day you were baptized with water. Then you began to share in God's life, goodness, and love. You became a member of the Catholic Church. The pope who lives in Rome is the head of the Catholic Church. We are brothers and sisters to people all over the world.***

2 Read aloud **page 28** to the children.

3 Explain to the children that they are all brothers and sisters. Use the names of the children in your class.

- (Name) ***and*** (Name) ***are brothers in God's family.***
- (Name) ***and*** (Name) ***are sisters in God's family.***
- (Name) ***and*** (Name) ***are brother and sister in God's family.***
- ***In God's family we are brothers and sisters with people all over the world. We are all brothers and sisters in God's family.***
- ***Pope*** (Name) ***is the head of our family who lives in Rome.***
- ***All the people who are with God in heaven belong to God's family too. We call these people saints. The saints in heaven are also our brothers and sisters.***

4 Teach the children the following song. They might hold hands and walk in a circle while singing it, or they might add the gestures.

God's Family
(Melody:"Row, Row, Row Your Boat")

Women, men, girls, and boys,
[Point to several people.]
Mary, saints, and me—
[Point up and then to self.]
All are members of God's
Church.
[Extend arms wide.]
We're God's family.
[Clap twice at the end.]
M. Kathleen Glavich, S.N.D.

5 Distribute copies of BLM 10 Paper Doll Pattern and have the children make dolls that represent God's family. Have the figures already cut out, or guide the children to fold the papers and cut out two figures. Warn them not to cut apart the hands. Have the children color one doll to look like themselves and the other doll to look like another person in our Church family. Staple all the pairs of dolls together at the hands to form a chain or circle and display it. • ***BLM 10 Paper Doll Pattern***

6 Discuss our individual families and God, our Father. Ask:

• ***What are some things our families might do to show love?***

• ***Our very big family has a Father who loves and cares for us. Who is he?*** (God)

• ***God is the Father of all people all over the world. He is our Father in heaven. Jesus told us to call God our Father.***

In God, we are brothers and sisters to people all over the world.

When we were baptized we became part of God's special family, the Church.

The pope in Rome is the leader of the Church.

God is our Father.
He loves us and watches over us. We pray,

Scripture

"Our Father, who art in heaven, hallowed be thy name."
Based on Matthew 6:9

28

• ***Do you remember what we learned about what God tells us in the Bible? God loves us and people all over the world with an everlasting love. He loves each of us very, very much and will love us forever and ever.***

7 Lead the children to have confidence in God as a loving Father.

• ***God takes care of us all the time. God knows when things happen that hurt us, such as when we fall down and skin a knee or when someone we love gets sick. God helps us through these hard things.***

• ***God gives us everything we need—good food, water, and most especially, people who love and care for us.***

• ***God always loves us, even if we do something wrong. We can always tell God we are sorry, and God will forgive us.***

ACTING

1 Have the children turn to **page 29.** Read it aloud and guide the children in doing the activity.

2 Invite the children to pray the psalm verse based on Psalm 22:11:

Father, even before I was born
[Extend open hands in front at waist level.]

I was
[Raise arms slightly.]

in your care.
[Cross arms on chest.]

CHECKPOINT

• How interested were the children in the concept of being brothers and sisters with people everywhere?

We belong to God's family.
We are his children. **God is our Father.**

Try This

1. Draw lines to show to which family each one belongs.
2. Pray for people all over the world. They are your brothers and sisters.

29

God Is Our Loving Father

Student Book page 30

LEARNING OUTCOMES

The children will be able to

- pray the first two lines of the Our Father.

KEY TERMS

hallowed—holy

Our Father—the prayer Jesus taught us

MATERIALS

- Cutout 1
- Our Father Prayer Card punch-outs from the Student Book

COMMENTS

1. The Our Father prayer is also called the Lord's Prayer. In teaching the prayer, follow the local usage.

2. The other lines of the Our Father will be taught in appropriate lessons during the year.

CENTERING

Ask the children what prayer is. (Talking to God) Tell them that today they will begin to learn a special prayer to God our Father.

SHARING

1 Use Cutout 1 Jesus to introduce the Our Father.

- ***Jesus called God Father. He even called him* Abba*, which means "Daddy."***
- ***Jesus said God is our Father too. Because God is our Father, we can talk to him. Jesus told us what to say when we talk to God. He said, "You should pray like this: Our Father, who art in heaven."*** (Adapted from Matthew 6:9) ***This is the beginning of the Our Father prayer.***
- ***What did Jesus tell us to call God?*** (Our Father)

2 Explain the next part of the prayer.

- ***Jesus said that when we pray, "Our Father" we should say "who art in heaven." Jesus is telling us that God cares for us from his place in heaven. From heaven, God can love and care for everyone on earth.***
- ***Where do we say God is?*** (In heaven)
- ***Let's finish this line of the prayer: "Our Father, who art*** (in heaven)***."***
- ***Now say the line with me.***

3 Help the children understand the first petition of the Our Father.

- ***God's name is very good. It is holy. We pray that God's name will always be kept holy. We say: "Hallowed be thy name."***
- ***Which word sounded like the word holy?*** (Hallowed) ***The word* hallowed *means "holy." Say it after me: "hallowed." When we say the words "Hallowed be thy name," we are telling God, "Holy be your name" or "We want everyone to keep your name holy."***
- ***Listen carefully: "Hallowed be thy name." Now say the line with me.***

4 Invite the children to stand in a circle and pray the first two lines of the Our Father, using the gestures.

Our Father,
[All join hands.]

who art in heaven,
[Raise joined hands.]

hallowed
[Fold hands, fingers pointing up.]

be thy name.
[Bow head.]

ACTING

1 Show an Our Father Prayer Card punchout.

- ***On one side of the card is our yes word, amen. The other side says, "Our Father." The whole prayer is inside.***
- ***Today you will take home your prayer card. Put it where it will remind you to pray to God our Father in heaven.***

2 Call each child by name and hand him or her the prayer card. Say:

- (Name), ***God is your Father. He wants you to call him "Father." Here is your Our Father prayer card.***

3 Invite the children to stand in a circle and pray

the first two lines of the Our Father, using the gestures they learned today.

4 Have the children take home the Family Page on **page 30** to share with their families.

Songs

Play for the children any of these songs: "In The Presence of the Angels" (*I See a New World*) **CD 2 Track 13;** "Caring," "Child in the House," "Families Are Fun," "Family," "Family Thank You" (*Peaceable Kingdom*); "What God is Like," "God Is Our Father" (*Color the World with Song*); "What God Is Like" (*Hi God 2*); "God Loves Little People" (*Sing a Song of Joy!*); a simple version of the Lord's Prayer (traditional chant version or the version from Bloom Where You're Planted). For a list of all the music used in this program, see **page OV-39.**

CHECKPOINT

- Can the children pray the first two lines of the Our Father?

ENRICHING THE FAITH EXPERIENCE

Use the following activities to enrich a lesson, to replace an activity with one that better meets the needs of your class, or to create an additional lesson.

1 If you have not already done so, distribute copies of BLM 11. Have the children make cards for their mothers and fathers or others who take care of them. Tell them to trace over the letters and print their names on the inside of the cards. Help them print *Mother, Father,* or the names of others. Have them decorate the cards.

2 Read the children a book that presents family life in a positive way.

3 Have the children bring in their baptismal pictures and tell about them. You might display the pictures.

4 If you have not already done so, distribute copies of BLM 9 Holy Family. Have the children identify the people and color the picture.

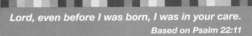

Lord, even before I was born, I was in your care.
Based on Psalm 22:11

God's Love in Families

The Lesson Your Child Learned

Jesus reveals that God is the Father of us all and that we are to be as brothers and sisters in his family. The children learned that all members contribute to making a happy family. They learned that in God, they are brothers and sisters to people all over the world. Through their Baptism, they are members of God's family, the Church, and call God "Father." They were introduced to the first two lines of the Our Father. Place the Our Father prayer card your child brought home in a special place of honor.

Living the Lesson

My most vivid image of family is when a dozen of my cousins and I crammed into a side bedroom at my grandparents' house on Thanksgiving. There wasn't enough room for all us kids at the big dining room table and so we had our own private dining room, where we laughed and told stories and got to know one another, even the cousins who lived far away.

Now whenever we gather, whether it's joyously at a wedding or solemnly at a funeral, we share memories of Thanksgiving dinners tucked away in one of Grandma's extra bedrooms. That's where we learned some fundamental life lessons we'll never forget: everyone belongs at the table; we'll always be family; we are loved; and it is gratitude that brings us together. Whether yours is a large, raucous family or just a few who gather around your table, families are meant to be gifts. When a family is healthy, loving, nurturing, and forgiving, it reflects the loving community of the Trinity.

–Tom McGrath, author of *Raising Faith-Filled Kids* (Loyola Press)

Bringing the Lesson Home

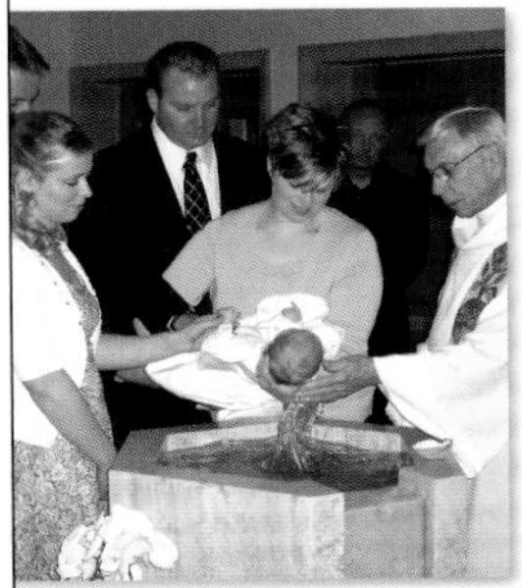

- Read with your child the pages that were sent home.
- Children grow physically, psychologically, and spiritually when they know that they are loved. The signs of affection that you share with your child and with other family members help to strengthen each one's sense of well-being. These also help to strengthen the bonds between all family members.
- Show your child pictures of his or her Baptism.
- Declare and celebrate a special Family Week. Select a different member to honor at the family meal each day. Take turns telling the honored member about what makes him or her special and about how important he or she is to your family.
- Pray the Our Father together each day as a family.

30

Chapter 8

I Am Good

FAITH FOCUS

God made me wonderful.

Psalm 139:13–14; Isaiah 43:1–4

PREPARING THE FAITH EXPERIENCE

LISTENING

The vocation of a teacher is to communicate with joy the good news of God's love. Take some time to let yourself be refreshed by the good news found in the Bible. As you pray, hear God speak to you his good news of love and salvation.

Thus says the LORD,
who created you and formed you:
Fear not.
I have called you by name:
you are mine.
You are precious in my eyes,
and I love you.
Based on Isaiah 43:1–4

REFLECTING

In giving us human life, God has shared something of himself with us. Each person is made in the image of God. God has not only loved us into life but continually invites us to love in return and to grow in our relationship with him and with others. We have freedom to believe and to love, to decide and to choose. We have the ability and the responsibility to give human expression to God's loving, forgiving care for each person.

When we are the best persons we can be, we are, as Saint Irenaeus put it, fully alive—the glory of God. To recognize with humble wonder the gifts the Lord has given us, to develop our abilities and share them with one another—these acts are, in themselves, praise and thanksgiving to the Father.

You formed my inmost being;
you knit me in my mother's womb.
I praise you, so wonderfully you made me;
wonderful are your works!
Psalm 139:13–14

During the preparation of the gifts at our Eucharistic celebration, the priest voices our recognition of the Lord's goodness in giving us the bread and wine that we offer. Then he asks the Lord, in the name of the community, to accept our gifts:

Lord God, we ask you to receive us and be pleased with the sacrifice we offer you with humble and contrite hearts.

As the family of God, we come to the Father with grateful and trusting hearts. We belong to God and are loved by him. God calls us to share his truth and love with one another as his children, and to work for the betterment of a world where many still hunger for respect of their human rights. God calls us especially to use our gifts and talents to bring all people to his kingdom. At each Mass we open ourselves to God's love and reach out to others, giving freely of all that we have received.

RESPONDING

God's Word moves us to respond in word and action. Let the Holy Spirit work within you as you prayerfully consider how you are being called to respond to God's message to you today.

- How do I try to imitate the love of God as I care for every child entrusted to me?

Lord, make your image apparent in me and in those in my care.

Catechism of the Catholic Church

The themes of this lesson correspond to the following paragraphs: 355–357, 2288.

THE FAITH EXPERIENCE

DAY ONE
I Am Wonderful

DAY TWO
I Can Do Wonderful Things

DAY THREE
God Made Me Wonderful

DAY FOUR
Thank God for Wonderful Me

Scripture in This Chapter

- *Genesis 1:26–28 God created us in his own image and likeness and made us stewards of creation.*
- *Matthew 7:7–11 God is our heavenly Father who gives good things to those who ask.*

Church Documents

National Directory for Catechesis #48, E, 2.
Children are important not just for what they will do in the future but also for who they are now.

Peace on Earth #9–10.
Every human being is a person, with intelligence, free will, and the dignity that comes from being created by God and redeemed by Jesus Christ.

Called and Gifted for the Third Millennium, section entitled "The Call to Mission and Ministry."
The gifts we receive from God should be shared in the family, the workplace, the civic community, and the parish or diocese.

Bulletin Board At the left is a suggestion for a bulletin-board design. Ask the children to draw a picture of something they can do well or something they particularly like about themselves. (Examples: playing baseball or their beautiful green eyes) Post their drawings around the words, "We Are Special." You might use this bulletin board in tandem with the lesson about gifts on Day One.

For a list of children's literature suggestions, please see **page OV-47.**

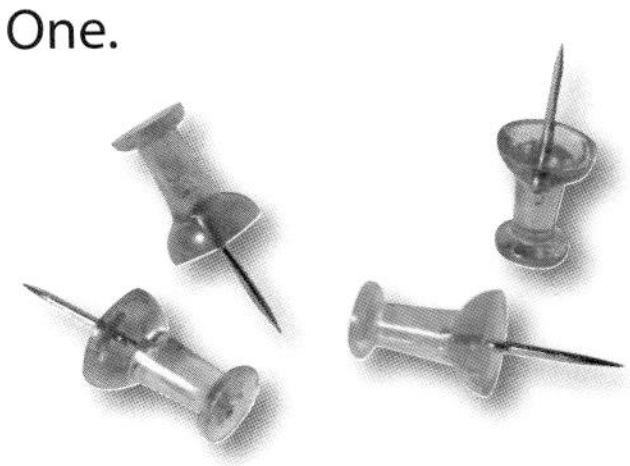

CHAPTER 8 | DAY ONE
I Am Wonderful

Student Book page 31

LEARNING OUTCOMES

The children will be able to
- begin to discover their own uniqueness.
- accept themselves as they are.

COMMENTS

1. God created the human person as a union of body and soul. In the mystery of God, the human person reflects the image of God. Through Jesus' Resurrection, the human person, body and soul, is destined to share eternal glory with him. When we show respect for our bodies, we honor our Creator.

2. A growing awareness and appreciation of themselves are conducive to the spiritual development of children. When they realize that God has gifted them with wonderful abilities, their hearts are moved with love for their Father in heaven.

CENTERING

Recall the last chapter.

- ***You have learned that you belong to families. What special family did you become part of when you were baptized?*** (God's special family, the Church) ***What do we call God, who is the head of this family?*** (Our Father)
- ***How does our prayer to God the Father start?*** (Our Father, who art in heaven, hallowed be thy name.)
- ***Today you will discover some great gifts that you received when God made you.***

SHARING

1 Invite the children to use some of the gifts that God gave them to play an action game. Tell the children that the purpose of the game is to have fun imagining what they can do with the gifts that God has given to them. Give these directions for the children to pantomime along with you:

- ***Walk like robots.***
- ***Pick flowers in a field.***
- ***Eat an ice-cream cone.***
- ***Wash dishes.***
- ***Climb stairs.***
- ***Melt like a snowman.***
- ***Drink a glass of water.***
- ***Throw a ball.***

Say:

- ***Each of us can do wonderful things. Let's learn about some more wonderful things that we can do by listening to a poem about a boy named Henry and some of the things he did one day.***

2 Read aloud the poem on **page 31.** Discuss:

- ***Why was Henry eager to wake up?*** (He wanted to go for a walk.)
- ***What were some things Henry did during the day?*** (Smelled a rose, played on a swing, ate peanut butter and jelly) ***Can you do any of these things?***
- ***Why do you think Henry wants his family to squeeze him and to hold him tight?*** (He loves them. He likes hugs.)
- ***What does Henry think about himself?*** (He is wonderful.) ***Do you think he is wonderful? Why?***

3 Guide the children to discover that they are wonderful.

- ***You are wonderful too! You also have ears and can hear wonderful and beautiful sounds. What do you like to listen to?***
- ***Henry likes to smell roses. What do you like to smell?***
- ***Henry has fun swinging. What do you have fun doing?***
- ***Henry likes peanut butter. What is your favorite food?***
- ***Henry likes it when his family hugs him. How do you feel when someone shares his or her love with you?***
- ***In this poem Henry feels happy. Do you think he always feels that way? How else do you sometimes feel?***
- ***Henry loves his family. They think Henry is wonderful, and they love him just because he is their Henry. You have***

people who think you are wonderful just because you are you. Who are they? (Parents, grandparents, aunts, uncles, brothers, sisters)

4 Help the children think about their uniqueness. Let them tell how they think they are special. Be ready to offer suggestions, such as having a happy smile, being a fast runner, being good at drawing, or being polite. Encourage the children to appreciate one another's uniqueness and avoid competition as much as possible.

5 Teach the song "God's Special Child" to the melody of "I'm a Little Teapot." At the conclusion of the song, let the children demonstrate a special skill or trait, such as whistling or sharing their special smile.

God's Special Child

I'm a child of God from head to toe.
[Gesture from head to toe.]
God made me special. This I do know.
[Point thumbs to shoulders.]
If you want to see what makes me so,
[Point to audience.]
Just watch. My special gift I will show.
[Move arms to the side with both hands open.]

M. Kathleen Glavich, S.N.D.

ACTING

Invite the children to pray the following adaptation of Psalm 139:14 with gestures:

I thank you,
[Raise arms to shoulder height, palms open.]

O Lord,
[Extend arms up.]

for the wonder
[Bring hands down in front.]

of myself.
[Cross arms on chest.]

CHECKPOINT

- Do the children know themselves to be unique and wonderful just as they are?
- Were the children able to recognize and to acknowledge their good qualities?

CHAPTER 8

I Am Good

Henry

Hey, wake me! Wake me!
Time to walk
Listening for the flowers' talk!
See me! See me!
Wrinkling my nose,
Smelling a rose.
Me! Me! Wrinkle-nose,
wonderful me!

Swing me! Push me!
Way up high.
I need to get me
a piece of sky.

Catch me! Catch me!
Here I come
Zooming right into
your open arms.

Feed me! Feed me!
I'm weak in the knees.
Some peanut butter
and jelly, please.

Hold me! Hold me!
Squeeze me tight.
Now's the time
to kiss good night.

Me! Me!
Sleepyhead,
wonderful
me!

31

I Can Do Wonderful Things

LEARNING OUTCOMES

The children will be able to

- appreciate the power of their five senses and their bodies.
- be aware of their responsibility to care for their gifts.

MATERIALS

- Materials for SHARING #1
- BLM 12
- Scissors
- Crayons or markers
- Stapler

COMMENTS

1. God has gifted us with our five senses. Through them, information about the world comes into our consciousness. The senses help us enjoy the world and protect us against some of its dangers. However, there is a great variety of abilities and preferences in the use of our senses. Be aware that some children will be more proficient and will have stronger natural preferences and abilities in some areas than others. For example, the noise threshold of each person is different. There will be varying abilities to smell things as well as strong preferences about scents.

2. Some of the activities listed in SHARING #1 can be used as break activities during later lessons.

CENTERING

1 Invite the children to pray Psalm 139:14 with gestures:

I thank you,
[Raise arms to shoulder height, palms open.]

O LORD,
[Extend arms up.]

for the wonder
[Bring hands down in front.]

of myself.
[Cross arms on chest.]

2 Tell the children that today they will learn even more about how wonderful they are.

SHARING

1 Prepare several of the following activities to help the children experience the joys of their bodies and their senses. If possible, prepare an activity for each of the five senses. Additional ideas can be found in the Enriching the Faith Experience section of this chapter (see **page T100**). You might design this lesson around centers or stations and have the children form small groups to rotate through the stations. If this option is chosen, engaging additional adult support for this lesson will be helpful.

- Show the children beautiful pictures or slides.
- Fill glasses with different levels of water and strike them to create sounds.
- Let the children play a "sniff-and-name" game. Place different foods and flavorings into paper cups covered with a piece of aluminum foil slit in the center. Let the children sniff and guess what is in each cup. (Possible foods: lemon slice, onion slice, coffee, drops of vanilla or almond extract, anise or licorice)
- Give the children refreshments, such as juice, crackers, or cookies. Be sure to find out in advance whether any children have food allergies and take these into consideration when planning snacks.
- Make a "feely" board. Staple or glue different-textured fabrics to a piece of poster board or heavy cardboard. Have the children feel the fabrics and discuss the differences. Use fabrics such as velvet, silk, lace, satin, corduroy, flannel, or terry cloth. Descriptive words include *smooth*, *fuzzy*, *spongy*, *stiff*, *rough*, *soft*, *stretchy*, and *furry*.

❷ Encourage the children to talk about the activities at the centers and their senses:

• ***You have five senses: you see with your eyes, you hear with your ears, you smell with your nose, you taste with your mouth, and you touch with your hands. Each activity center is focused on a different one of our five senses.***

• ***Which of the activity centers did you like the best? What sense did you use most at each center?***

❸ Have the children continue to reflect on their five senses by making a senses booklet. Use copies of BLM 12 Senses. Have them cut along the dotted lines. Staple each child's pages together to make a booklet. Have the children finish the sentences by drawing pictures. They might also glue seeds or other items to illustrate the sense of touch and use scented markers to illustrate the sense of smell.
• BLM 12 Senses

ACTING

❶ Invite the children to reflect on how God wants them to care for their bodies. Say:

• ***Our bodies are wonderful. Our bodies can do wonderful things. God gave us our bodies.***

• ***God wants us to take care of the bodies that he gave us so that we can continue to do wonderful things.***

Ask the children how they can take care of themselves (eating good foods, getting enough exercise, washing hands, brushing teeth).

❷ Invite the children to pray Psalm 139:14 with gestures:

I thank you,
[Raise arms to shoulder height, palms open.]

O Lord,
[Extend arms up.]

for the wonder
[Bring hands down in front.]

of myself.
[Cross arms on chest.]

CHECKPOINT

- What did the children like about this lesson?
- What different interests and abilities did you observe in your children as they used their various senses?

CHAPTER 8 | DAY THREE

God Made Me Wonderful

Student Book pages 32–33

LEARNING OUTCOMES

The children will be able to

- value themselves as individuals created by God and precious in God's eyes.
- be aware of their responsibility to use their gifts wisely.

KEY TERMS

precious—very dear to people; special, important, loved

soul—the part of us that is like God and lets us think, choose, and love

MATERIALS

- Bible enthroned, with note card on which you have written the adapted Scripture reading for SHARING #3, Isaiah 43:1–4
- Song for CENTERING
- Crayons or markers

CENTERING

Play for the children a song about themselves, such as "I Am Marvelous" (*Take Out Your Crayons*), "If I Were a Butterfly" (*Hi God 2*), or "Rainbow Children" (*Make a Wonderful Noise*) or sing "God's Special Child" on **page T93** to the melody of "I'm a Little Teapot." At the conclusion of the song, let the children demonstrate a special skill or trait, such as whistling or sharing their special smile.

SHARING

1 Ask the children who made them wonderful.

- ***Who made you so wonderful? Who gave you eyes so that you can see so many beautiful things? Who made ears for you so that you can hear all kinds of sounds? Who gave you a nose to smell with, and a nice pink tongue that can taste good things such as spaghetti, chocolate-chip cookies, and green beans?*** (God)

2 Have the children turn to **page 32.** Read it aloud and guide the children to read together the following text:

- ***God made me. God loves me.***

I can do all kinds of wonderful things.

I thank God for making wonderful ME.

God made me wonderful.

God made me.

God loves me.

Scripture

I thank you, O Lord, for the wonder of myself.

Based on Psalm 139:14

32

3 Reverently pick up the Bible and prepare to read the adaptation of Isaiah 43:1–4. Make the reading personal by making good eye contact with the children as you read. Pause two or three times during the reading.

- ***Today God, your heavenly Father, has something to tell you. We know that God speaks to us through the words in the Bible.***

- ***Let's prepare ourselves to listen well to God's words.***

- ***Listening eyes are on the storyteller.*** [Pause until all the children are looking at you.] ***Listening hands are quietly in your lap.*** [Pause until all the children have put their hands in their laps.] ***Listening feet are comfortable and quiet.*** [Pause until all the children's feet are still.] ***Listening hearts are ready to hear God's Word.*** [Pause.]

- ***The Lord God says, "I made you. You are mine. You are precious to me, and I love you." The Word of the Lord.*** Invite the children to respond, "Thanks be to God." Allow the children time to ponder God's Word.

- ***How good God is! God is the one who made each of us good and wonderful. Our heavenly Father tells us we are precious to him. Precious means we are very special and important. We are precious because God made us like himself. He wants us to live with him forever in heaven.***

4 Guide the children in doing the activity on **page 33.**

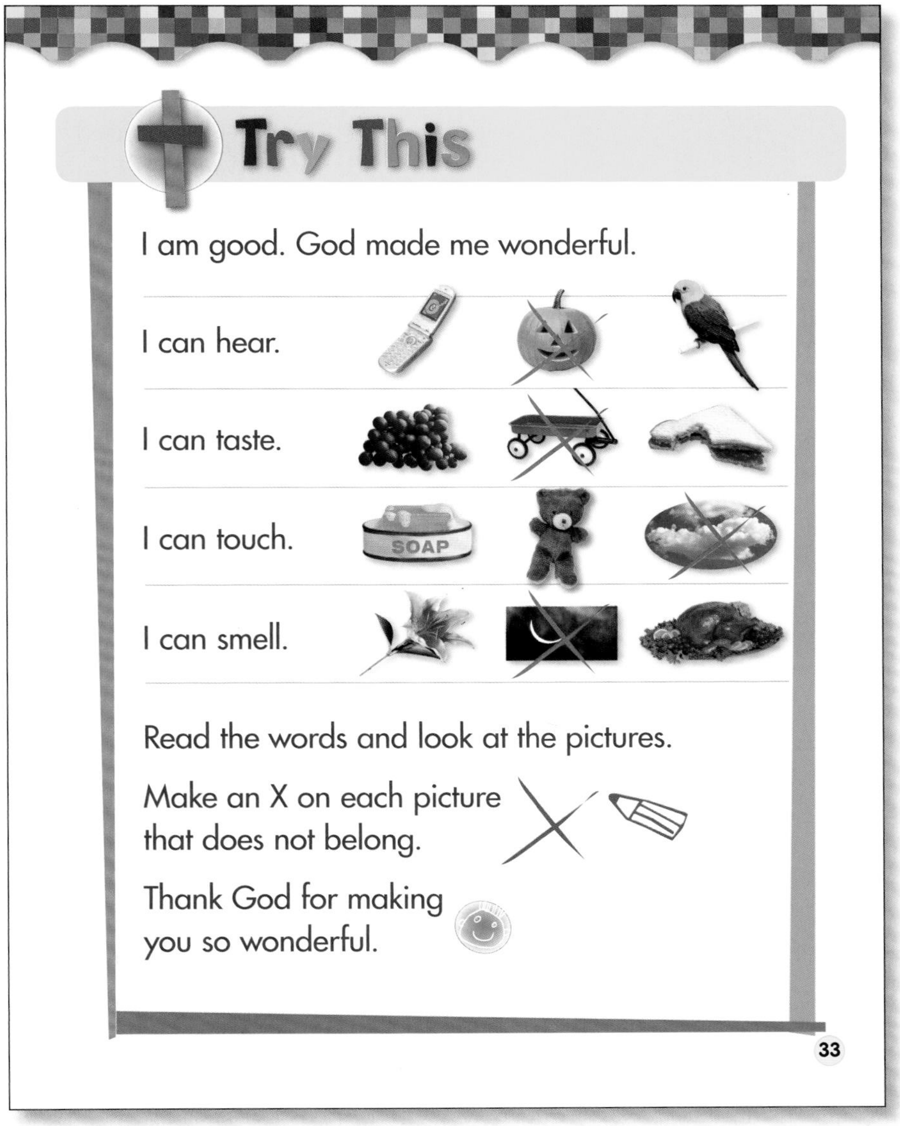

Try This

I am good. God made me wonderful.

I can hear.

I can taste.

I can touch.

I can smell.

Read the words and look at the pictures.

Make an X on each picture that does not belong.

Thank God for making you so wonderful.

33

ACTING

Teach the poem "All for Jesus" and the gestures. Explain the words *youth* (the period when we are children) and *obedient* (doing what God and those in charge of us tell us to do).

All for Jesus

Two little eyes to look to God.
[Point to eyes.]
Two little ears to hear his Word.
[Touch ears.]
One little tongue to speak the truth.
[Point to tongue.]
One little heart to give him all my youth.
[Cross hands on heart.]
Two little feet to walk his ways.
[Lift feet.]
Two little hands to work for him all my days.
[Extend opened hands.]
Take them, dear Jesus, and may they be
[Reverently raise arms up.]
Always obedient and true to thee.
[Bring hands down and look at them.]

Source Unknown

• ***We show our love for God when we use our wonderful bodies to do the things God made us to do. Jesus helps us to do this. Listen to the poem "All for Jesus." It tells how to use the gifts of our bodies to follow Jesus.***

Repeat the poem and invite the children to join in the gestures. After the children have learned the poem, invite them to use the poem as a prayer, asking Jesus to help them learn to use their bodies to follow him. Pray the poem and gestures together.

Songs

Play for the children any of these songs: "Here I Am, God" (*I See a New World*) **CD 2 Track 5**; "God Is So Good" (*Color the World with Song*); "God's Circle of Love" (*Hi God 3*); "Rainbow Children" (Sing a Song of Joy!); "If I Were a Butterfly" (*Hi God 2*); "Behold I Make All Things New," (*Singing Our Faith*). For a list of all the music used in this program, see **page OV-39**.

CHECKPOINT

• How are the children showing responsibility for caring for themselves and showing respect for others?

CHAPTER 8 | DAY FOUR

Thank God for Wonderful Me

Student Book page 34

LEARNING OUTCOMES

The children will be able to

- express gratitude to God for making them wonderful.

MATERIALS

- Bible with note card from Day Three
- I'm Wonderful pennant punchouts from the Student Book
- Straws for the pennants
- Sample pennant
- Crayons or markers
- Recording of a march, such as "March of the Toy Soldiers"
- Stapler

CENTERING

1 Play for the children a song about themselves, such as "I Am Marvelous" from *Take Out Your Crayons*, "If I Were a Butterfly" from *Kid's Praise!* or "Rainbow Children" from *Make a Wonderful Noise* or sing "God's Special Child" on **page T93** to the melody of "I'm a Little Teapot." At the conclusion of the song, let the children demonstrate a special skill or trait, such as whistling or sharing their special smile.

2 Tell the children that they will thank God for the gift of themselves through a special celebration.

SHARING

1 Help the children make their own I'm Wonderful pennants. Show the sample.

- ***A pennant is a special kind of flag that is used to show that someone or something is a champion. Can anyone read what is written on this pennant?*** (I'm wonderful.)
- ***Because God made you in such a special way, you will each make a pennant like this one.*** Distribute the pennant punchouts and help the children write their names on the back. Staple each pennant to a straw.

2 Share this celebration with the children. Ask for a volunteer to lead the parade. Tell him or her what to do.

- ***God made us good. Let's celebrate how wonderful we are. We'll begin with a parade. You may wave your pennants as you march.*** Have the children march to music (such as "March of the Toy Soldiers" or another marching song) as they process to the Prayer Center. Lead a prayer of thanks:
- ***Being able to see, hear, touch, smell, taste, and move is wonderful. Let us stand and pray our psalm prayer with gestures to thank God for these wonderful gifts:***

I thank you,
[Raise arms to shoulder height, palms open.]

O LORD,
[Extend arms up.]

for the wonder
[Bring hands down in front.]

of myself.
[Cross arms on chest.]

- ***Each of you is precious to God. God made each of you wonderful. I will tell something special about you. Then you may thank God for it. All of us will say yes to your being wonderful with our prayer word, amen. We shall say it twice: "Amen, amen." Say it with me now: "Amen, amen."***

Assist the children when necessary. Example:

Teacher: God gave Mario brown eyes.

Mario: Thank you, God, for my brown eyes.

All: Amen, amen.

3 Invite the children to pray the poem "All for Jesus" on **page T98** with gestures.

ACTING

1 Reverently open the Bible and read the adaptation of Isaiah 43:1–4. Tell the children to take their "quiet-heart" posture to ready themselves to hear God speak to them:

- ***Let's prepare ourselves to listen well to God's words.***

• ***Listening eyes are on the storyteller.*** [Pause until all the children are looking at you.] ***Listening hands are quietly in your lap.*** [Pause until all the children have put their hands in their laps.] ***Listening feet are comfortable and quiet.*** [Pause until all the children's feet are still.] ***Listening hearts are ready to hear God's Word.*** [Pause.]

• ***The Lord God says, "I made you. You are mine. You are precious to me, and I love you." The Word of the Lord.*** Have the children respond: "Thanks be to God."

2 Have the children take their pennants home and tell their families that God made them wonderful.

3 Have the children take home the Family Page on **page 34** to share with their families.

CHECKPOINT

- How will you help the children continue to show their appreciation to God for the gift of life?

ENRICHING THE FAITH EXPERIENCE

Use the following activities to enrich a lesson, to replace an activity with one that better meets the needs of your class, or to create an additional lesson.

1 Teach a song to the melody of "God Is So Good."

I am so good.
(Three times)
I am wonderful.

God loves me so.
(Three times)
God made me wonderful.

2 Help the children make self-portraits, using sheets of shelf paper as large as they are. Have them pair off, put their paper on the floor, and lie down on it while their partner traces around them. Additional adult help may be required for this activity.

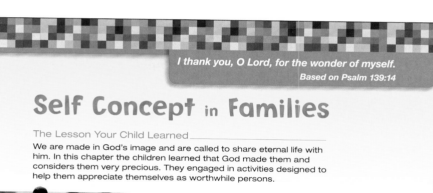

I thank you, O Lord, for the wonder of myself.
Based on Psalm 139:14

Self Concept in Families

The Lesson Your Child Learned

We are made in God's image and are called to share eternal life with him. In this chapter the children learned that God made them and considers them very precious. They engaged in activities designed to help them appreciate themselves as worthwhile persons.

Living the Lesson

Can you think of a significant person from your younger years who paid you a compliment that stuck with you? Someone you respected who told you something about yourself that gave you a sense of your self-worth? Maybe it was a boss on your first job, a coach who noticed your drive and commitment, or a favorite relative who saw something special in you.

We all need "mirrors" in our life, that is, people who can see us and reflect our goodness back to us. Our children need that positive mirroring from us as well as from others who care about them. They also need the opportunity to use their talents and skills, as well as to exercise their virtue. I'm not talking about giving manufactured compliments to artificially build up their self-esteem. The best way to gain self-esteem is to do "esteem-able" things.

So make a point of observing your child and mirroring back the good you see in him or her. And be sure to offer (and model) a variety of opportunities for your child to take virtuous and worthy action.

–Tom McGrath, author of *Raising Faith-Filled Kids* (Loyola Press)

Bringing the Lesson Home

- Read with your child the pages that were sent home.
- Encourage the members of your family to note and acknowledge one another's successes. Reinforce the importance of sending positive, encouraging messages.
- Children learn by doing. Refrain from helping your child before it is needed. This shows you have trust in your child's abilities and encourages his or her independence and development. Caregivers who rush in to do for their children what they can do for themselves or for others take away a golden opportunity for their children to learn independence as well as the value of contributing to the well-being of the family.
- Let family members make their own decisions whenever possible. Caregivers may worry about what decisions their child will make in the future. But if you give your child the gift of making small and relevant decisions now, your child will have the benefit of learning through consequences on small matters, such as what clothes to wear. As your child grows, the importance of the decisions will grow, and so will his or her ability to make wise choices.
- Show respect and appreciation for the work of each family member.

34

3 Read the following poem to the children.

My Nose

With my nose I smell things
like these:
Bacon, popcorn, and Christmas
trees,
Babies, roses, and apple pie;
And this is probably the reason
why
My nose has such an
important place—
Right in the middle of my face.

M. Kathleen Glavich, S.N.D.

4 Provide activities in which the children can delight in their senses.

Note: Be sure to find out if any children have food or fragrance allergies and take these into consideration when planning activities and snacks.

Sight

- Have the children play a visual memory game. On a tray, place a few items such as an eraser, a mitten, a crayon, and a paintbrush. Let the children look at the items for a short time, then cover the tray. Ask the children to name the items. Play again, using different items. Vary the game by removing one of the items while the children close their eyes. Ask them what is missing.

- Have the children use a magnifying glass to look more carefully at objects.

- Help the children make color boxes. Choose several colors of crayons. Have the children mark each side of a box with a different color. Allow them to cut out objects of each color from magazines and glue them to the side of the box marked with that color.

Hearing

- Let the children imitate clapping or rhythm patterns that you perform, such as clap-clap-clap—clap-clap. Vary the volume of these activities as well.

Touch

- Make "feely" bags. Place a variety of familiar objects, such as a marble, a comb, a spoon, a toy car, or a piece of clothing in a bag. Have the children identify the objects by feeling them.

- Have the children feel how their faces express emotions. Name an emotion, such as happy, sad, or angry, and have the children make their faces show it; then tell them to feel their faces.

- If you have not already done so, make a "feely" board. Staple or glue different-textured fabrics to a piece of poster board or heavy cardboard. Have the children feel the fabrics and discuss the differences. Use fabrics such as velvet, silk, lace, satin, corduroy, flannel, or terry cloth. Descriptive words include *smooth, fuzzy, spongy, stiff, rough, soft, stretchy*, and *furry*.

Taste

- Have a Taste Time. For each child, fill small plastic or paper cups with the following foods (in order): salt, syrup, and lemon juice. Give each child craft sticks. Guide them to dip one craft stick into a cup and then place a small amount of each food on their tongues. Have the children taste the same foods at the same time. Ask them to name the food and describe its taste. Introduce some of the following adjectives if the children do not: *salty, sweet*, and *sour*.

- Ask for volunteers to taste food while blindfolded and to guess what it is. Cover the eyes of a child with a blindfold. Show the class what food the child is tasting. Have the child describe the food as he or she is guessing. Some of the following foods may be used: potato slice, onion slice, apple slice, catsup, butter, cinnamon, sugar, pretzel, or potato chip.

Smell

- Spray perfume or a scented room deodorizer and have the children raise their hands when the scent reaches them.

5 Let the children play a game of skill, such as dropping clothespins into a jar or throwing beanbags into a wastebasket.

Chapter 9

Growing Is Good

FAITH FOCUS

We grow as Christians by showing love.

1 Samuel 16:1–13; Psalm 52:10

PREPARING THE FAITH EXPERIENCE

LISTENING

Before you begin to prepare this week's lessons, take some time for prayer. Quiet yourself by taking several deep breaths. Become aware of God's presence, for God is with you always. Ask God to open your heart to hear his words to you today.

[Y]ou are a "chosen race, a royal priesthood, a holy nation, a people of his own, so that you may announce the praises" of him who called you out of darkness into his wonderful light.

1 Peter 2:9

REFLECTING

God gifted us with life and called us to wholeness. Our growth as human beings is a lifelong process toward maturity that consists of never-ending struggles and new challenges. God has placed within us an impulse toward self-fulfillment. He supports our efforts to become fully human so that we may glorify him all the more through the full use of our gifts. God gifted us with Baptism and has called us to holiness. To be baptized is to become a new creation, a new person in Christ. Baptism is a once-and-for-all saving act of God's love through which we attain such a close union with Christ that we are clothed with him. (Galatians 3:27) Yet Baptism is only the beginning of a transformation that continues throughout our lives. As we grow into the likeness of the glorified Lord, we enter into a higher life, a life in which true freedom and human fulfillment are possible.

Saint Paul reminds us that Baptism has made us completely new people in Christ. We have "put on" the Lord Jesus. We are now risen with him and must live as God's children. (Ephesians 4:22–24) Through the grace of Baptism, it is possible for us to give generously of ourselves to others and to become loving children of God our Father. With the help of the Holy Spirit, we grow more and more each day into the likeness of Christ so that we may rightfully bear the exalted name of Christians. As we strive to become holy, we will be blessed by God.

RESPONDING

Having reflected upon God's Word, take some time now to continue to respond to God in prayer. You might wish to use a journal to record your responses throughout this year.

- What can I do to help the children recognize their God-given gifts?

Spirit of God, make the children and me grow as generous and loving children of God.

Catechism of the Catholic Church

The themes of this lesson correspond to the following paragraphs: 786, 908, 1698, 2816–2827.

THE FAITH EXPERIENCE

DAY ONE
Living Things Grow

DAY TWO
We Are Anointed to Grow as Christians

DAY THREE
We Grow by Loving

DAY FOUR
We Are Members of the Kingdom

Scripture in This Chapter

- *Ephesians 4:17–24 We must walk in the newness of life, day by day growing in the transformation begun in Baptism.*
- *1 Corinthians 12:12–26 Baptism effects a dynamic union with Christ and with all who have been baptized in him.*

Church Documents

General Directory for Catechesis #288.
National Directory for Catechesis #73.
All of our growth in the faith comes from the unseen action of the Holy Spirit.

Declaration on Christian Education #2.
Every Christian should be helped to grow daily in a consciousness of the gifts received at Baptism.

Bulletin Board At the left is a suggestion for a bulletin-board design. Draw and cut out a tree with branches from brown poster board or construction paper. Post the tree in the center of the bulletin board. Then draw and cut out leaves from green poster board or construction paper, one leaf for each child. Write the children's names on the leaves, one name per leaf. Post the leaves on the branches of the tree. You might add a banner with the words, "I am like a green olive tree growing before the Lord." (Based on Psalm 52:10)

For a list of children's literature suggestions, please see **page OV-47.**

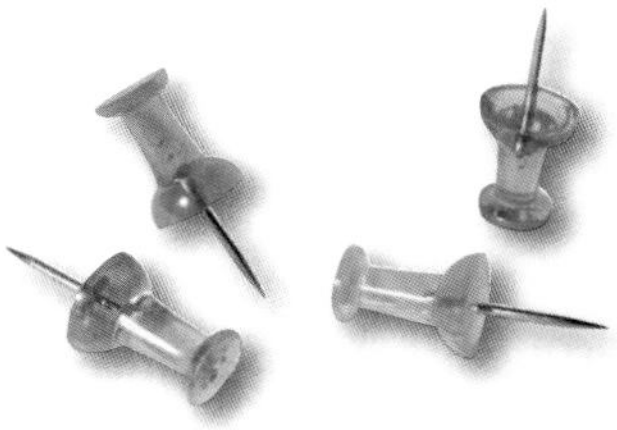

CHAPTER 9 | DAY ONE

Living Things Grow

Student Book pages 35–36

LEARNING OUTCOMES

The children will be able to

- realize that human growth is a lifelong process.
- know what chrism is.

KEY TERM

chrism—oil mixed with perfume and consecrated by the bishop for use in the Sacraments of Baptism, Confirmation, and Holy Orders

MATERIALS

- Cutouts 24–25, 28
- Jar of olives

COMMENTS

1. Chrism, a mixture of olive oil and aromatic balsam, has been used since Old Testament times for anointing. The rite of royal anointing in the Old Testament signified that those anointed had been elected by God, as in the case of David, and had become sharers in his Spirit. God commanded that Moses anoint Aaron to signify his consecrated priesthood. The word *Christ* means "anointed one." Jesus was anointed by the Holy Spirit. As priest, Jesus offered the sacrifice of himself for the redemption of sinners.

2. Invite the children bring in pictures of grandparents or great-grandparents to show to the class. Let them tell about their visits with these relatives. You may also wish to invite a grandparent or great-grandparent to visit with the class to talk about their life experiences and about how they have grown and changed throughout their lives.

CENTERING

1 Recall the last chapter.

- ***In our last lessons you learned that you were wonderful. Who made you wonderful?*** (God)
- ***Today you will learn another wonderful thing about yourself.***

2 Show Cutout 28 Baby. Discuss:

- ***Babies are special signs of love. They show the mother's and father's love. Babies show God's love.***
- ***Were you ever this small? What happened to you?*** (I grew.)
- ***Growing is good. All living things grow and change.***

SHARING

1 Read aloud **pages 35** and point out the pictures. Have the children follow along in their books. Pause after each sentence for the children to enjoy and to comment on the illustrations. Ask:

- ***What helped the pumpkin to grow?*** (Water, sunlight, warmth)
- ***What helped the bird to grow?*** (Food, rest, water)
- ***What helped the elephant to grow?*** (Food, rest, water)
- ***What helped the children to grow?*** (Food, rest, water, love)

2 Read aloud **page 36.** Direct the children to the picture of the boy in the middle of the page. Ask:

- ***Was the boy always this big?*** (No.) ***Will he get bigger?*** (Yes.) ***Why?*** (We continue to grow and change throughout our lives.)
- ***Our heavenly Father cares about us. He puts in the world everything that we need in order to grow. He watches over us as we grow up and throughout our entire lives.***

3 Recite the poem "Growing Up" with actions and have the children repeat each sentence and action after you.

Growing Up

When I was a baby
I was very, very small.
[Stoop down and be as small as possible.]
Today I am just this size.
[Stand and raise hand to top of head.]
And someday I'll be tall.
[Stretch hands high.]

M. Kathleen Glavich, S.N.D.

4 Lead the children to understand that they are growing up.

- ***You will not always be children. Each day you grow a little more. One day you will be grown up. You will keep on growing older.***
- [Show Cutouts 24 Grandmother and 25 Grandfather.] ***Do you know any older people? They are important. They have lived a long time and can teach us many things about loving God and other people. Even though they are grown up, they are still God's children. God loves and cares for them.***

If possible, arrange for a classroom visit from an older person, perhaps the grandparent of a child in the class. Invite him or her to talk about his or her life experience. Prepare the children to ask questions about how the visitor has changed and grown throughout his or her life.

5 Introduce the prayer based on Psalm 52:10.

- ***Our prayer for this week is "I am like a green olive tree growing before the LORD."***
- [Show a jar of olives.] ***Have you ever eaten olives? Long ago, when this prayer was written, olive trees were even more important than they are today. People got precious oil from the olives. This oil was used to cook food—just as it is now. It was put on wounds to***

CHAPTER 9

Growing Is Good

Birds grow. Pumpkins grow.
Elephants grow. Seeds grow. We grow.

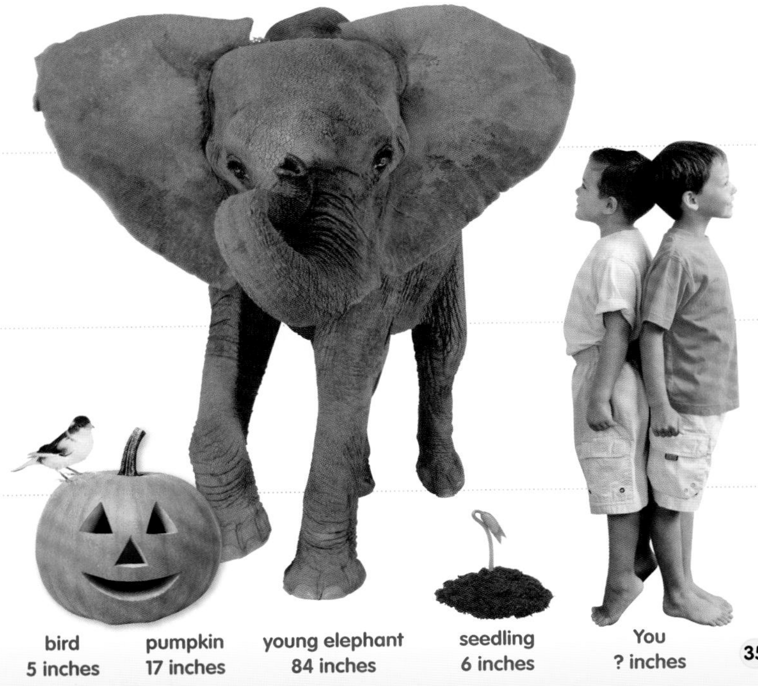

35

heal them. Oil was burned in lamps for light because there was no electricity in those times. Olive oil was also mixed with perfume to make special oil. We call this special oil **chrism.**

• ***What might you be telling God when you pray, "I am like a green olive tree growing before the Lord"?*** (I know I am precious. I am growing.)

I am
[Touch chest with both hands.]
like a green olive tree
[Stand straight with hands at sides.]
growing
[Raise hands, fingers reaching upward in growing gesture.]
before the Lord.

CHECKPOINT

• How have the children demonstrated that they understand growth is a lifelong process?

ACTING

Teach the children the gestures for the psalm prayer based on Psalm 52:10 and then pray it with them.

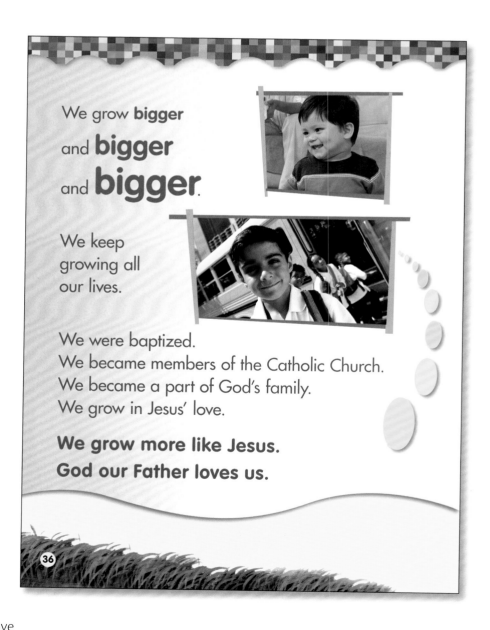

We grow **bigger**
and **bigger**
and **bigger**.

We keep growing all our lives.

We were baptized.
We became members of the Catholic Church.
We became a part of God's family.
We grow in Jesus' love.

We grow more like Jesus.
God our Father loves us.

36

CHAPTER 9 | DAY TWO

We Are Anointed to Grow as Christians

Student Book page 37

LEARNING OUTCOMES

The children will be able to

- know that they grow as Christians as well as human beings.
- become acquainted with the story of David's anointing as king.
- understand the meaning of their anointing at Baptism.

KEY TERMS

anoint—to pour oil over a person's head to make him or her holy; in the Bible, kings, priests, and prophets were anointed

Christians—people who believe in Jesus and who love and follow him

MATERIALS

- *A Child's Bible*, page 12
- Cutouts 1, 29
- Crown made of gold or yellow paper
- Chrism
- Crayons or markers

CENTERING

Be sure to find out if any children have fragrance allergies and take this into consideration when planning activities with chrism.

Invite the children to the Prayer Center and show them holy oil, or chrism. Let the children smell the chrism. Ask if anyone can recall what chrism is. (Perfumed olive oil) Tell them that today they will learn more about what chrism is used for.

SHARING

1 Explain anointing:

- ***Long ago, perfumed oil was very precious. It took a lot of olives and a lot of hard work to make just a little bit of oil. It was used to anoint kings.*** **Anoint** ***means "to pour oil on a person's head." Anointing showed that the kings were now holy.***

2 Introduce "David, the Shepherd-King" from *A Child's Bible*, **page 12.** Show the Bible and open it to First Samuel, Chapter 16. Enthrone the Bible. Say:

- ***David was a shepherd boy who wrote many of the prayers or psalms we pray each week. He was anointed king of God's people. Listen to his story from the Bible.***

Invite the children to remember what they learned about how to be good listeners.

- ***Let's prepare ourselves to listen well to today's Bible story.***
- ***Listening eyes are on the storyteller.*** [Pause until all the children are looking at you.] ***Listening hands are quietly in your lap.*** [Pause until all the children have put their hands in their laps.] ***Listening feet are comfortable and quiet.*** [Pause until all the children's feet are still.] ***Listening hearts are ready to hear God's Word.*** [Pause.]

3 Read the story from *A Child's Bible*, **page 12.** Conclude:

- ***David grew up to be a good king. He was a great-great-great-great grandfather of Jesus.*** [No one knows how many "greats."]

4 Tell the children that they were anointed with chrism at Baptism when they became Christians. Show Cutout 1 Jesus.

- ***Jesus is called Jesus Christ.*** **Christ** ***means "the anointed one."*** [Show the crown.] ***Jesus is king of heaven and earth.***
- ***After you were baptized with water, you were anointed with chrism. The priest or deacon put holy oil on the top, or crown, of your head. The anointing showed you belong to***

Jesus' kingdom, to his priesthood, [Show Cutout 29 Priest.] ***and to his family, the Church.***

You belong to a royal family.

- ***You are a Christian. Say the word* Christian. *As Christians, we try to grow more like Jesus Christ. Christians try to spread Jesus' love everywhere.***

5 Have the children open their books to **page 37.**

- ***You know that you grow by eating good food. Your body grows. Your mind grows. You grow as a Christian too. All your life you keep growing in Jesus' love. Let's read page 37 together.***

6 Guide the children in doing the activity on **page 37**.

ACTING

Invite the children to pray the psalm verse with gestures:

I am
[Touch chest with both hands.]
like a green olive tree
[Stand straight with hands at sides.]
growing
[Raise hands, fingers reaching upward in growing gesture.]
before the LORD.

Songs

Play for the children any of these songs: "You Have Put on Christ," (*Singing Our Faith*) **CD 1 Track 5**; "Giant Love Ball Song," "I Like God's Love," "Thank You, Lord," "What Makes Love Grow?" (*Hi God!*); "Living and Loving and Learning" (*Hi God 3*); "You Have Been Baptized in Christ" (*Abba! Father!*); "Guide My Feet" (*Singing Our Faith*). For a list of all the music used in this program, see **page OV–39**.

CHECKPOINT

- How have the children shown that they understand that we can grow to be more like Jesus?

Try This

Draw more branches, leaves, and flowers on the tree to show that it is growing.

Tell God you want to grow to be more like Jesus.

Tell Jesus you will spread his love everywhere.

Scripture

I am like a green olive tree growing before the Lord. Based on Psalm 52:10

37

CHAPTER 9 | DAY THREE

We Grow by Loving

LEARNING OUTCOMES

The children will be able to

- know the significance of the baptismal gown.
- know that they can grow to be more like Jesus.

MATERIALS

- Sample puppet
- BLM 13
- Craft sticks
- Scissors
- Glue
- Crayons

COMMENT

The puppets the children make in this lesson can be used to role-play other stories. Make a sample puppet prior to the lesson, using BLM 13 Baptism Puppets.

- BLM 13 Baptism Puppets

CENTERING

Recall the last lesson. Ask:

- ***What happened to you at Baptism after water was poured on you?*** (I was anointed with chrism on the crown of my head.)
- ***What does anointing with chrism mean?*** (I am a Christian. I belong to God's royal family. I try to grow in Christ's love.)
- ***Today you will find out more about what Baptism means.***

SHARING

1 Tell the children about their baptismal robes.

- ***Long ago, after people were baptized and became Christians, they were given robes of pure white to put on. The white robes reminded them that when they were baptized, they were born into God's special family.***
- ***As the new Christians walked into church wearing their shining white robes, all the other Christians greeted them with a song. They wore their white garments every day for an entire week when they went to celebrate Mass.***
- ***We still do this today. When you were baptized, you probably wore a white garment, or baptismal robe. Ask your parents to show you what you wore at your Baptism.***

2 Have the children make puppets of themselves in baptismal robes using copies of BLM 13. Display a sample puppet that you have made of yourself. Have the children draw hair and their faces on the heads. Then have them color and cut out the puppet figures. Help the children glue a craft stick to the back of the figure.

3 Let the children use their puppets to act out endings to some of these stories to show how to love like Jesus.

- ***Your mother is tired after working hard all day. You have finished playing with your toys. They are on the floor in the living room. To show that you love her, what will you tell your mother?***
- ***Your little brother wants someone to play with him. You are already playing something by yourself. To show that you love him, what will you say to your little brother?***
- ***You want your father to go outside and play with you. He is tired from working hard all day and wants to read the paper. To show that you love him, what will you say to your father?***
- ***Your grandmother has cooked a good meal for you. You are watching TV when she calls you to come and eat. To show that you love her, what will you say to your grandma?***
- ***Your friend wants to play with your new ball. To show that you love your friend, what will you say?***

ACTING

1 Have the children use their puppets to tell how they will bring Jesus' love to others.

2 Ask the children to put down their puppets and invite them to join you in the Prayer Center for prayer.

Introduce the prayer:

• ***Because it is not always easy to love the way Jesus does, we can ask Jesus to help us grow to be more like him.***

Guide the children to pray this prayer, asking God to help them grow to be more like Jesus:

• ***Quiet helps us to pray. We can meet God deep within our quiet hearts. Let us prepare ourselves to spend some time with God.***

• ***Straighten your back.*** [Pause.]

• ***Rest your arms on your lap, hands open in front of you.*** [Pause.]

• ***Gently close your eyes if you want or look down at your hands resting in your lap.*** [Pause.]

• ***Slowly breathe in and out, in and out, in and out.*** [Pause.]

• ***Deep within you, imagine Jesus sitting next to you.*** [Pause.]

• ***In the quiet of your heart, tell Jesus one thing you want to do in order to bring his love to others. Ask Jesus to help you do this.*** [Pause.]

• ***When you are finished praying, open your eyes.***

Invite the children to pray the psalm verse with gestures:

I am
[Touch chest with both hands.]
like a green olive tree
[Stand straight with hands at sides.]
growing
[Raise hands, fingers reaching upward in growing gesture.]
before the LORD.

CHECKPOINT

• How easily did the children determine loving responses to the situations in SHARING #3?

CHAPTER 9 | DAY FOUR

We Are Members of the Kingdom

Student Book page 38

LEARNING OUTCOME

The children will be able to

- grow in their ability and willingness to show love for others.

MATERIALS

- Bible enthroned, with note card on which you have written the adapted Scripture reading for ACTING #1, 1 Peter 2:9
- Flashcard 3
- I Am A Christian crown punchouts from the Student Book
- Sample crown
- Stars, sequins, foam shapes, pompoms, buttons, stickers, toothpicks, or other materials for decorating crowns (optional)
- Crayons or markers
- Glue
- Stapler

COMMENTS

1. The children could also make and/or wear the crowns in the lesson about All Saints' Day.

2. The Our Father prayer is also called the Lord's Prayer. In teaching the prayer, follow the local usage.

CENTERING

Show the children a finished I Am A Christian crown punchout. Discuss:

- ***Today you will make crowns. Can you guess why?*** (Because we were anointed at our baptism)
- ***Notice the cross on the crown. A cross is a special sign of Christians. Do you know why?*** (Jesus died on the cross.)
- ***The words on the crown say, "I am a Christian." When did you become a Christian?*** (At Baptism)

SHARING

1 Show the children how to make their own I Am A Christian crowns.

Have the children write their names on their crowns. Suggest different ways of decorating the crowns: Put a large sequin, a star, or other decoration on each tip, put a row along the bottom edge, or put them around the words. Finally, staple the crowns to fit the children's heads.

2 Explain:

- ***Your crowns tell you that you belong to Jesus' special royal family, the Church. One day, we hope to live with Jesus forever in his beautiful, heavenly kingdom.***

3 Teach the next two lines of the Our Father: "Thy kingdom come, thy will be done on earth as it is in heaven." Explain:

- ***We pray in the Our Father that all people will belong to God's kingdom and will help make it happen on earth by loving like Jesus. We pray that everyone in the whole world will love God and other people the way Jesus tells us.***
- ***Listen carefully: "Thy kingdom come." Now say the line with me.***

Explain the next line of the Our Father:

- ***God's will is done in heaven, and everyone is happy. We pray that it will be done on earth too.***
- ***Listen carefully: "Thy will be done on earth as it is in heaven." Now say the line with me.***

Invite the children to pray these two lines of the Our Father with you:

- ***"Thy kingdom come; thy will be done on earth as it is in heaven."***

ACTING

1 Ask the children to join you in the Prayer Center for prayer. Invite the children to get ready to listen to God's words in the Bible:

- ***Let's prepare ourselves to listen well to today's Bible reading.***

• ***Listening eyes are on the storyteller.*** [Pause until all the children are looking at you.] ***Listening hands are quietly in your lap.*** [Pause until all the children have put their hands in their laps.] ***Listening feet are comfortable and quiet.*** [Pause until all the children's feet are still.] ***Listening hearts are ready to hear God's Word.*** [Pause.]

Open the Bible to 1 Peter 2:9. Hold the Bible with reverence and read:

• ***A reading from the first letter of Saint Peter: "You are royal people. You are anointed. You have been chosen to praise God. Spread Jesus' love everywhere you go." The Word of the Lord.*** Invite the children to respond, "Thanks be to God."

• ***Let us praise God by saying yes to his words. What is our yes prayer word?*** (Amen) [Show Flashcard 3 *amen.*] ***Think about what I say. If you wish to say yes to it, say "Amen" when I show the card.***

We are Christians. (Amen.)
We belong to Jesus' kingdom. (Amen.)
We were anointed with perfumed holy oil at Baptism. (Amen.)
We want to spread Jesus' love. (Amen.)

Let us now pray the part of the Our Father that you know.
Our Father, who art in heaven,
hallowed be thy name;
thy kingdom come;
thy will be done on earth as it is in heaven.

2 Tell the children to take their crowns home to remind them to bring Jesus' love to everyone in their families.

3 Have the children take home the Family Page on **page 38** to share with their families.

CHECKPOINT

- Are the children open and willing to bringing Jesus' love to others?
- Do the children enter more readily into the quiet of prayer time?

I am like a green olive tree growing before the Lord.
Based on Psalm 52:10

Growing in Families

The Lesson Your Child Learned

Our growth is a lifelong process consisting of never-ending struggles, achievements, and new challenges. Baptism is the beginning of a new way of life, and with the help of the Holy Spirit we can grow into the likeness of Christ. Choosing Baptism for your child indicated your commitment to fostering his or her Christian growth. In this chapter the children learned that at Baptism they became members of the Church.

Living the Lesson

In the house where I grew up, we had a spot alongside our back doorway where Mom and Dad would measure the height of my brother and me every year on our birthdays. When Dad would paint that room, he'd always leave that strip unpainted so the record of our growth would remain visible. The day we moved from that house, I took one last look at all the empty rooms. I recall seeing those penciled lines, with our initials and the dates next to them, and they represented all the good times we'd had together in that home, as well as all the things my brother and I had learned about life, about family, and about ourselves.

Growth means life. Jesus said, "I came so that they might have life and have it more abundantly." (John 10:10) Your child is at a wondrous moment in his or her growth, and you get the privilege of witnessing this miracle as it unfolds. Make sure to stop once in a while and pay attention to how far your child has come and how many wondrous opportunities lie ahead. And don't forget to mark your own growth now and again. Take stock of how you measure up physically, intellectually, emotionally, and spiritually. Are you taking Jesus up on his offer of having life more abundantly?

–Tom McGrath, author of *Raising Faith-Filled Kids* (Loyola Press)

Bringing the Lesson Home

- Read with your child the pages that were sent home.
- Take out your child's baby book and recall some growing-up stories with your child.
- Look at old family pictures so that your child learns that everyone grows and changes—even mommies, daddies, and grandparents.
- Tell your child why you decided to have him or her baptized. Share memories of this day.
- Spend a moment in prayer together, inviting your child to feel God's love. Talk about ways your child can share that good feeling by showing love and kindness to others.

38

ENRICHING THE FAITH EXPERIENCE

Use the following activities to enrich a lesson, to replace an activity with one that better meets the needs of your class, or to create an additional lesson.

1 Teach a song to the melody of "God Is So Good."

> **Growing is good.**
> (Three times)
> **I grow as God's child.**
>
> **Christians are good.**
> (Three times)
> **They love like Jesus.**

2 Have the children sing a song about Baptism and discuss the words.

3 Ask families to share with you the date of their children's Baptisms and celebrate each child's baptismal day. Let him or her wear a crown while everyone sings "Happy Baptismal Day" to the tune of "Happy Birthday." Serve a small treat and let the honored child distribute it. Be sure to find out if any children have food allergies and take these into consideration when planning snacks.

4 Bring a small seedling to the classroom and, with the children's help, place it in a pot of good, rich soil in the sunlight. Discuss all the things the seedling will need to grow. Have the children care for it and watch it grow. At the end of the school year, let the children find a place to plant it so that it can continue growing outdoors. Tell the children that they are helping God's creation when they care for nature.

5 Have the children bring in pictures of themselves to talk about during a show-and-tell time.

6 Create an awareness of environmental problems. Show the children some magazine pictures of polluted water, land, and air. Ask why these wonderful gifts of God are so ugly now. Allow them to express their ideas of the causes of pollution. Explain that many problems have come from people who do not care about what happens to the water and air when they throw away waste. People who pollute water and air do not seem to value God's gifts the way they should. You might ask the children to think about the way they care for the gifts of nature that God has given our world.

7 Read the poem "I'm Growing" to the children.

I'm Growing

I am growing older,
And this is how I know.
Each year upon my birthday
Another candle glows.

I am growing taller,
Not as tall as trees.
But now I come up higher
Than my father's knees.

I am growing wider.
For I no longer fit
In the baby's highchair
Where I used to sit.

I am growing heavy.
That's what my mother said
Last evening when she picked
me up
To carry me to bed.

I am growing smarter.
I can count to three,
And sometimes I can even
Say my ABCs.

I am growing stronger,
Stronger day by day.
I can help clean up our house
And put my things away.

I am growing bigger,
Bigger than my clothes.
At least my skin still stretches
From my fingers to my toes!
M. Kathleen Glavich, S.N.D.

Chapter 10

Thanking Is Good

FAITH FOCUS

We thank God for giving us every good thing. Psalm 136:1; Luke 17:11–19; Colossians 3:16–17

PREPARING THE FAITH EXPERIENCE

LISTENING

As you prepare to share God's Word of love with the children, spend some quiet time with God in prayer. Relax your body, quiet your mind, and let yourself be aware that you are filled with God's love. Ask God to speak to you his Word of love.

Let the word of Christ dwell in you richly, as in all wisdom you teach and admonish one another, singing psalms, hymns, and spiritual songs with gratitude in your hearts to God. And whatever you do, in word or in deed, do everything in the name of the Lord Jesus, giving thanks to God the Father through him.

Colossians 3:16–17

REFLECTING

In giving thanks to God, we acknowledge that all things have been created by God, belong to him, and come to us through God's goodness.

Thanksgiving is the heart of our Christian life. Jesus has given the Church the perfect expression of thanksgiving in the gift of the Eucharist. Each Mass is our thanksgiving for the Father's great love. We address our thanksgiving to the Father who created us and redeemed us through his Son. Jesus gives thanks to the Father, and we offer our thanks in him and through him. The word *Eucharist* itself means "thanksgiving."

At Mass, when we offer thanksgiving to the Father through Christ, our daily joys and sorrows are transformed into our personal "eucharist." We give thanks for the food of salvation—the bread and wine that have become Christ—given to us so that we may abide in him.

Thus, the Church prays in the Memorial Prayer of Eucharistic Prayer III:

Therefore, O Lord,
as we celebrate
the memorial
of the saving
Passion of your Son,
his wondrous Resurrection
and Ascension into heaven,
and as we look forward to his second
coming,
we offer you in thanksgiving
this holy and living sacrifice.

Look, we pray, upon the oblation of your
Church
and, recognizing the sacrificial Victim by
whose death
you willed to reconcile us to yourself,
grant that we, who are nourished
by the Body and Blood of your Son
and filled with his Holy Spirit,
may become one body, one spirit in Christ.

RESPONDING

God's Word calls us to respond in love. Respond to God now in the quiet of your heart and perhaps through a journal that you are keeping this year.

- How do I thank God for the goodness he has shown to me?
- How do I invite these children to show gratitude to God for his gifts?

Thanks and praise to you, Lord, for each of the children in my care.

Catechism of the Catholic Church

The themes of this lesson correspond to the following paragraphs: 224, 2637–2638, 2828, 2837.

THE FAITH EXPERIENCE

DAY ONE
Every Day Is a Thank-You Day

DAY TWO
We Give Thanks to God

DAY THREE
We Give Thanks at Mealtime

DAY FOUR
We Thank God for Everything

Scripture in This Chapter

- *Psalm 106:1 God's infinite goodness leads us to respond with gratitude and praise.*
- *John 17:19 The sacrifice Jesus made in the gift of his life for us is the supreme act of thanksgiving—our Eucharist.*

Church Documents

National Directory for Catechesis #61, A, 2. Catechesis takes place within the family through prayerful celebrations.

Directory on Popular Piety and the Liturgy #23. Inspired by the Jewish tradition, the early Christians began and ended everything with an act of thanksgiving.

Putting Children and Families First #III, B. Parents have a responsibility to help make prayer an integral part of their children's lives.

The theme of this chapter corresponds well to Thanksgiving Day. This chapter can be taught during the week or two before the Thanksgiving holiday.

Bulletin Board At the left is a suggestion for a bulletin-board design. Distribute magazines to the children and ask them to cut out pictures of things they are thankful for. Invite the children to glue the pictures they have collected onto one large poster board. Then attach the poster board to the bulletin board. You might include a banner with the words, "We Give Thanks."

For a list of children's literature suggestions, please see **page OV-47.**

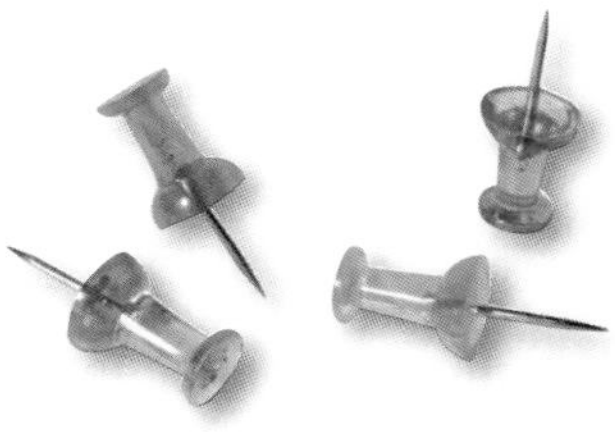

CHAPTER 10 | DAY ONE

Every Day Is a Thank-You Day

Student Book page 39

LEARNING OUTCOMES

The children will be able to

- offer thanks to God every day for his many blessings.
- learn a pattern of saying thank you for kindnesses and favors received.

MATERIALS

- Cutouts: 36–39
- Flashcard 4
- Globe or map (optional)
- Pencils, crayons, or markers
- Apple
- Flower
- Book

COMMENT

Days of thanks, such as the celebration of Thanksgiving Day in the United States, offer occasions for young children to experience many important human values found in the eucharistic celebration. On such festive days, family and friends gather in a spirit of joy to share a meal and to give thanks to God for his blessings. Experiencing a spirit of celebration is in itself a preparation for celebrating the Eucharist.

CENTERING

1 Recall the last chapter.

• ***Last time, we talked about growing as Christians. How do we want to grow as Christians?*** (In Jesus' love; more like Jesus)

• ***There is an important way that we can show that we are growing more like Jesus. It is a way that we can show love to other people every day just by saying two simple words. Let's imagine some everyday conversations using these puppets.*** [Show Cutouts 36–39 Mrs. Garcia, Mr. Garcia, Carlos, and Ana.] ***See if you can figure out what these two words are.***

2 Use Cutouts 36–39 for the following dialogs, asking for volunteers to help you present each dialog by holding the appropriate Cutouts. Present the first part of each dialog and ask the children to predict a response:

• ***Mom says, "Here is your lunch, Carlos."***

• ***What do you think Carlos will say?*** (Thank you, Mom.)

[Invite two volunteers to hold the Cutouts of "Mr. Garcia" and "Ana."]

• ***Ana asks, "Dad, will you please help me tie my shoes?"***

• ***What do you think Mr. Garcia will say?*** (Yes.)

• ***What do you think Ana will say next?*** (Thank you, Dad.)

• ***What did Carlos thank his mom for?*** (His lunch)

• ***What did Ana thank her dad for?*** (Helping her tie her shoes)

• ***How were these children showing love?*** (By saying thank you)

• ***What is something that we can do every day to be more like Jesus?*** (Say thank you.)

SHARING

1 Let the children talk about expressing thanks.

• [Show Flashcard 4 *Thank you.*] ***Why do we say thank you to people?*** (To show that they help us feel happy; to be polite; to show our love)

• ***Do you ever say thank you to other people? Let's share some examples of times when you said thank you to someone.*** [Invite the children to share their experiences.]

• ***Do other people say thank you to you? Let's share some examples of times when others said thank you to you.*** [Invite the children to share their experiences.]

• ***How do you feel when someone says thank you to you?*** (Happy, proud)

2 Ask the children to open their books to **page 39.** Ask:

• ***What is the family in the picture doing?*** (Celebrating Thanksgiving)

The Story of Thanksgiving

The Pilgrims decided to sail across the big Atlantic Ocean to America. [Point to the ocean on a globe or map.] Their ship was called the *Mayflower.* After two months at sea, they reached land and built their homes in a place called Plymouth. The first winter in America was very hard. The Pilgrims were often cold and hungry. Many became sick and died.

In the spring, two friendly Native Americans named Samoset and Squanto told the Pilgrims where to hunt and fish and how to plant.

In the fall when the crops were ready, the Pilgrims were filled with joy and thanksgiving. They had been in America for a whole year. The Pilgrims decided to celebrate with a big feast to thank God for all they had. They invited their friends, the Native Americans, to the feast.

Four Pilgrims went out to the woods and hunted wild turkeys and ducks for the feast. The Native Americans brought deer. They roasted the turkeys and deer outside over open fires. The Pilgrim women made pumpkin pies and pumpkin bread, cranberry sauce and cranberry tarts. They may have cooked corn, beans, and squash too. The children probably helped by gathering nuts and berries.

This first American thanksgiving celebration lasted for three days! It was a happy feast.

• ***People in the United States have Thanksgiving Day once a year. On this day, people share a special meal and remember the story of the first Thanksgiving Day. Let's listen to that story now.***

3 Read aloud "The Story of Thanksgiving."

4 Discuss the story:

• ***Who celebrated the first Thanksgiving Day?*** (The Pilgrims and the Native Americans)

• ***What were they giving thanks for?*** (The harvest, the good things they had)

• ***To whom were they giving thanks?*** (God)

• ***How long did the feast last?*** (Three days)

• ***Our celebration of Thanksgiving Day lasts just one day. But, as Christians, we believe that every day is really a***

CHAPTER 10

Thanking Is Good

On Thanksgiving Day, we say thank you with a special meal.

We hear and say the words thank you every day.

The words thank you tell people how we feel.

Saying thank you makes people happy.

39

thank-you day. Why? (There are reasons to say thank you every day.)

- ***Every day we can show our love for others by saying thank you.***
- ***There is someone who is good to us all the time, who has given us many good things or blessings. We can always say thank you to this person. Who is it?*** (God)
- ***Let's learn a psalm prayer that we can pray to say thank you to God. If you like this prayer, you might want to pray it every day.***

5 Teach the adaptation of Psalm 136:1.

> **We give you thanks, Lord,**
> [Fold hands together.]
> **for you are good.**
> [Raise hands and spread arms up and out.]

ACTING

1 Invite the children to practice saying thank you. Ask for volunteers to come to the front for each skit. Answer each child's "Thank you" with a "You're welcome," adding the child's name.

- ***We will have little plays to help you know when to say the words* thank you. *What do you say when someone gives you something?*** (Thank you.) [Hand an apple, a flower, or a book to different children and encourage each one to respond.]
- ***What do you say when someone helps you in some way?*** (Thank you.)

Ask a child to share a crayon or pencil with another child. Ask another child to give a book to another child. Ask a child to find a page in a book. Encourage each child to respond appropriately as they do so.

- ***What do you say when someone says something nice about you?*** (Thank you.)

Tell one child that he or she has a pleasant smile, another that you like the way he or she works hard, and another that he or she is listening carefully. Encourage the children to respond appropriately.

- ***What do we say to God for his goodness to us?*** (Thank you.)
- ***God is very good to us. Let's pray together the psalm prayer that we learned to say thank you to God.***

2 Pray the adaptation of Psalm 136:1.

> **We give you thanks, Lord,**
> [Fold hands together.]
> **for you are good.**
> [Raise hands and spread arms up and out.]

CHECKPOINT

- Are the children developing the habit of saying thank you?
- How will you encourage this habit?

CHAPTER 10 | DAY TWO

We Give Thanks to God

Student Book page 40

LEARNING OUTCOMES

The children will be able to

- realize that God wants their thanks.
- pray the next line of the Our Father.
- become familiar with the Bible story of the 10 lepers healed by Jesus.

MATERIALS

- *A Child's Bible*, page 17
- Bible enthroned, with note card on which you have written the adapted Scripture reading for SHARING #1, Colossians 3:16–17

COMMENT

The theme of giving thanks is particularly appropriate for children of kindergarten age. At this age, children tend to experience God as the satisfier of all their needs, great and small. We encourage their spiritual development when we invite them to recognize God's goodness to them and to respond with gratitude.

CENTERING

Invite the children to pray the adaptation of Psalm 136:1.

> **We give you thanks, LORD,**
> [Fold hands together.]
> **for you are good.**
> [Raise hands and spread arms up and out.]

SHARING

1 Introduce the children to the idea that God wants to hear our thanks. Reverently take the Bible.

• ***What is this book called?*** (The Bible)

• ***Who speaks to us through the words of the Bible?*** (God)

Open the Bible to Colossians 3:16–17:

• ***Let's prepare ourselves to listen well to today's Bible reading.***

Hold the Bible with reverence and read:

• ***A reading from the Letter of Saint Paul to the Colossians: "Always be thankful. Sing to God with thanksgiving in your hearts. Do everything in the name of the Lord Jesus, giving thanks to God the Father through him."*** (Based on Colossians 3:16–17). ***The Word of the Lord.***

Invite the children to respond, "Thanks be to God."

• ***How does Saint Paul say we should always be?*** (Thankful)

• ***What should be in our hearts?*** (Songs of thanksgiving)

• ***In whose name do we give thanks to God our heavenly Father?*** (In Jesus' name) ***Christians thank God in Jesus' name.***

2 Invite the children to sing their thanks to God by teaching this song to the melody of "God Is So Good," or by teaching another song of thanks to God (A suggested list of songs is found on **page T125**).

> **God gives us food.**
> **God gives us care.**
> **God gives us love.**
> **These are gifts to us.**
>
> **Thanking is good.**
> (Three times)
> **Thank God for all good gifts.**

3 Introduce the story "The Thankful Man" from *A Child's Bible*, **page 17.** Introduce this Bible story by showing the Bible and opening it to the Gospel according to Luke, Luke 17:11–19. Enthrone the Bible. Say:

• ***In the Bible, there is a story about someone who made Jesus happy because he took the time to say thank you. I would like to share this story with you now.***

Invite the children to remember what they learned about how to be good listeners.

• ***Let's prepare ourselves to listen well to this Bible story.***

4 Read the story from *A Child's Bible*, **page 17.** Conclude:

• ***What did Jesus do for the 10 sick men?*** (He healed them.)

• ***How many of the men who were healed returned to thank Jesus?*** (Only one)

• ***How do you think Jesus felt when this man returned to say thank you?*** (Jesus was happy.)

5 Observe that Jesus was happy when the one man returned to him to say thank you, but that Jesus was probably surprised that the other nine did not return to say thank you. Say:

- ***We can make Jesus happy by saying thank you for the good things in our world and in our lives.***

If time allows, take the children on a "thank-you walk" around the classroom, the school, or outdoors. As they walk, let them spontaneously thank God for the things they see.

6 Teach the children the next line of the Our Father: "Give us this day our daily bread."

- ***We ask God our heavenly Father for what we need, just as we ask our families for the things we need. In one part of the Our Father, we pray, "Give us this day our daily bread." Let's say this together.***
- ***When we say these words, we ask God for food and for all the things we need. God puts enough food in the world for everyone. He wants his children to share with one another so that every person has enough food to eat. Let's say the words again, with our hands held open to show God we are asking for something: "Give us this day our daily bread."***

ACTING

Lead the prayer on **page 40.**

- ***We ask God for many things, and God, in his goodness, gives us many good things. There is a beautiful poem in your books that is also a prayer. It is a prayer that thanks God for his many gifts to us. Let us pray this prayer together.***

CHECKPOINT

- Do the children know that they should thank God for his blessings every day?
- How will you encourage them to make this a daily habit?

Father, We Thank You

For flowers that bloom about our feet,
Father, we thank you.
For tender grass so fresh and sweet,
Father, we thank you.
For songs of birds and humming of bees,
For all things fair we hear or see,
Father in heaven, we thank you.

Author Unknown

We thank God for many gifts. Thank you, God.

40

CHAPTER 10 | DAY THREE

We Give Thanks at Mealtime

Student Book pages 39, 41

LEARNING OUTCOMES

The children will be able to

- offer thanks to God at mealtime.
- pray grace.
- recognize gifts for which they can be grateful to God.

KEY TERMS

grace—prayer through which we offer thanks to God at meals

MATERIALS

- Grace Before Meals Prayer Card punchouts from the Student Book
- Crayons or markers

COMMENT

Among the children in your classroom, there is likely to be a wide variety of experience with regard to the practice of praying grace at mealtimes. Some families pray grace daily, others occasionally, some only on special occasions, and some not at all. Encourage families to make saying grace before meals a frequent family practice. You can also help children become more familiar with this prayer tradition by praying grace with the children each day before their snack or before lunchtime.

CENTERING

Invite the children to pray the Our Father up to and including the line they last learned: "Give us this day our daily bread." Then comment:

- ***Today you will find out how we can thank God at mealtimes.***

SHARING

1 Ask the children to open their books to **page 39.** Invite them to look at the picture on the page. Ask:

- ***Why might people pray at the table when it is time to eat?*** (Food is a gift from God; God wants us to say thank you for the gifts he gives to us.)
- ***What might they say to God?***
- ***Do any of you pray with your family before you eat? What do you say when you pray? Do you ever lead the prayer?***

2 Explain the Grace Before Meals prayer.

- ***God gives us food to eat and other things we need to stay alive. God cares for us every day. What do you think we should do every day?*** (Pray our thanks to God.)
- [Show the Grace Before Meals Prayer Card punchout.] ***As Christians, we can thank God for our food every day before we eat it. This thank-you prayer is called*** **grace. *Listen as I pray grace.***

Bless us, O Lord,
and these your gifts
which we are about to receive
from your goodness.
Through Christ our Lord.
Amen.

- ***What do we ask God to bless?*** (Us and the gifts from God)
- ***What are the gifts that we are about to receive when we are at the table?*** (Food)
- ***When we say "from your goodness," we mean that the food comes from God who is all good and generous.***
- ***Christians always pray in the name of Jesus Christ our Lord, so we end grace by saying, "through Christ our Lord" and the yes word, "amen."***

3 Distribute the Grace Before Meals Prayer Card punchouts. Help the children pray the prayer with you by following along as you read the words.

- ***Now I will say part of the prayer and let you add the missing words.***

Bless (us), **O Lord,**
and these your (gifts)
which we are about to
(receive)
from your (goodness).
Through Christ our (Lord).
Amen.

• ***This is an important prayer for us to know so that we can say thank you to God for the food we eat. If you pray this prayer often, you will soon know it by heart.***

Show the children that this prayer is also printed on the inside back cover of their books. Tell the children that when they have memorized this prayer, they can color the cross next to it.

4 Invite the children to decorate their Grace Before Meals Prayer Cards for their tables at home to remind their families to thank God every day for their food. Invite the children to learn at home the Grace After Meals prayer, which is on the inside back cover of their books.

ACTING

1 Ask the children to turn to **page 41.**

• ***When we pray grace before meals, we thank God for our food. We can also thank God for the many other good gifts that he gives to us.***

Read aloud **page 41** and help the children do the activity.

2 When the children have finished the activity on **page 41,** invite the children to pray together their thanks to God by praying the adaptation of Psalm 136:1:

> **We give you thanks, LORD,**
> [Fold hands together.]
> **for you are good.**
> [Raise hands and spread arms up and out.]

Alternatively, sing together the song of thanks taught in SHARING #2 of Day Two.

CHECKPOINT

• How will you model praying grace before meals in your classroom?

• What else might you do to help the children express their gratitude to God for his goodness?

Try This

Think about the gifts that God gives you.

Draw a circle around the pictures of God's gifts.

Thank God for these wonderful gifts.

Scripture

Always be thankful.

Based on Colossians 3:15–17

CHAPTER 10 | DAY FOUR

We Thank God for Everything

Student Book page 42

LEARNING OUTCOME

The children will be able to

- offer thanks to God for a particular gift.

KEY TERM

horn of plenty—a kind of basket usually filled with fruits, grains, and nuts, used to represent God's blessings

MATERIALS

- Bible enthroned, with note card on which you have written the adapted Scripture reading for SHARING #1 from Day Two, Colossians 3:16–17
- Table or teacher's desk
- Tablecloth
- Horn of plenty (If you wish, make one out of 18-inch by 24-inch construction paper, twisted and stapled.)
- Drawing paper
- Crayons or markers
- Scissors
- Basket of turkey cookies or pumpkin bread as a treat (Be sure to find out if any children have food allergies and take these into consideration when planning snacks.)

CENTERING

Show the horn of plenty. Explain:

- ***This special basket is usually filled with fruits, grains, and nuts to show God's blessings. It is often seen at Thanksgiving. It is called the "horn of plenty."***
- ***Today we will celebrate and thank God for his gifts or blessings. Think of a gift or blessing from God for which you are especially grateful—parents, brothers, sisters, new baby, grandmother, grandfather, yourself, pets, certain foods, favorite animals, plants, or trees.***

SHARING

1 Invite the children to draw a picture of the gift they thought of. Tell them to make the picture large, color it, and cut it out. These pictures will be used in the prayer.

2 Ask for volunteers to help prepare the Prayer Center:

- Two children can lay the tablecloth on the desk or table during the opening song.
- One child can put the horn of plenty on the table after the tablecloth is laid.
- One child can place the treat on the table.

3 Invite the children to gather in the Prayer Center. You might choose to do this as a procession, inviting the children to carry their pictures and to raise them high as they walk reverently to the Prayer Center. You can play a song of thanks as they process. When all have gathered in the Prayer Center, continue the celebration with a song of thanks, using the song on this page or the song taught in SHARING #2 of Day Two.

It's Good to Give Thanks to the Lord

4 Take the Bible and open it to Colossians 3:16–17:

- ***Let's prepare ourselves to listen well to today's Bible reading.***

Hold the Bible with reverence and read:

- ***A reading from the Letter of Saint Paul to the Colossians: "Always be thankful. Sing to God with thanksgiving in your hearts. Do everything in the name of the Lord Jesus, giving thanks to God the Father through him." The Word of the Lord.***

Invite the children to respond, "Thanks be to God."

5 Invite the children to present their pictures as they pray their thanks to God.

• ***God spoke to us in the Bible and told us to be thankful always. Let us thank God for his blessings.***

Encourage the children to take turns bringing their pictures to the horn of plenty. Each child stands in front of the table and holds up his or her picture. The child says, "For (*name of gift*)." All answer, "We thank you, God." Then the child places the picture in the horn of plenty. Help the children as needed.

6 When all have offered a prayer of thanks, pray grace before sharing the treat that has been prepared.

• ***God has given us many blessings. We shall now enjoy a treat made with some of God's gifts. Let us pray grace together.***

Bless us, O Lord,
and these your gifts
which we are about to receive
from your goodness.
Through Christ our Lord.
Amen.

7 Invite the children to return to their seats and then pass around the treats. Gently remind the children to say thank you if they forget. As they eat, talk about the people they have thanked recently.

ACTING

1 After the children have eaten their snack, tell them that we can also offer our thanks to God by praying after our meal.

Invite the children to do this by praying the adaptation of Psalm 136:1:

We give you thanks, LORD,
[Fold hands together.]
for you are good.
[Raise hands and spread arms up and out.]

2 Have the children take home the Family Page on **page 42** to share with their families.

We give you thanks, Lord, for you are good.
Based on Psalm 136:1

Thanksgiving in Families

The Lesson Your Child Learned

In giving thanks to God, we acknowledge that all things have been created by him, belong to him, and come to us through his goodness. Thanksgiving provides an occasion for families to reflect and to express gratitude.

Mealtime is a daily opportunity to pray together. In this chapter the children talked about special times when we thank God. They discovered that thank-yous are for every day. They began to memorize the traditional grace before meals and colored a prayer card for their tables at home as a reminder to pray grace. In a prayer celebration they thanked God for their blessings.

Living the Lesson

In Moline, Illinois, Deacon Tom Vogelbaugh is known as "Mr. Thanksgiving." Years ago he owned a small grocery store in town, and he was moved by the fact that many of his regular customers had no one with whom to celebrate Thanksgiving. So he hosted a dinner for about a dozen such people that year. The idea took off, and the feast grew year after year. Recently, with the help of more than four hundred volunteers, Vogelbaugh served two thousand guests. Over the years he's served up more than 40,000 Thanksgiving meals. When asked why he does this, Vogelbaugh points to his own sense of gratitude for all that people—and God—have done for him through the years.

Gratitude is a fundamental building block of all spirituality. Cultivate an attitude of gratitude, and you will have the eyes to see God's gifts all around you. One of the best gifts we can give our children is the habit of being thankful for the life that we share as a family. And the first step in teaching that is to model the attitude we hope they will assume. If they see us being thankful, they will learn to be thankful.

–Tom McGrath, author of *Raising Faith-Filled Kids* (Loyola Press)

Bringing the Lesson Home

- Read with your child the pages that were sent home.
- Share a family thank-you meal. Take turns thanking each person for his or her special contribution to the family.

- Place the Grace at Meals prayer card by a different person each day, indicating whose turn it is to lead the meal prayer.
- Make a renewed effort to encourage all members of the family to use the words *please* and *thank you*.
- Before your family's Thanksgiving meal, let each person thank God for a blessing received.
- Make it a family habit to thank God daily for blessings received, perhaps at mealtime or bedtime.

42

Songs

Play for the children any of these songs: "To Give Thanks" (*Sing a Song of Joy!*) CD 2 Track 2; "Family Thank You," "Thanksgiving Blessing" (*Peaceable Kingdom*); "I Like God's Love," "Thank You, Lord" (*Hi God!*); "Thank You, Lord" (Stories and Songs of Jesus); "Receive Our Prayer" (*Hi God 3*); "Say Thank You" (*Miracle Mud*). For a list of all the music used in this program, see page OV–39.

CHECKPOINT

- How have the children shown that they are grateful to God for his many gifts?

ENRICHING THE FAITH EXPERIENCE

Use the following activities to enrich a lesson, to replace an activity with one that better meets the needs of your class, or to create an additional lesson.

1. Have the children make up riddles about God's gifts. Examples:

- ***I am soft and furry. I go hop, hop, hop. My tail is round. What am I?*** (A bunny)
- ***I am round and yellow. I live in the sky. God made me to keep the world bright and warm. What am I?*** (The sun)

2. Have the children make Thanksgiving plates. Supply paper plates and construction paper in a variety of colors. Distribute one paper plate and one large sheet of construction paper to each child. Ask them to glue the paper plate to the center of the sheet of construction paper. Then using the other sheets of construction paper, invite the children to draw and cut out shapes of their favorite foods. Have them glue the "food" to the paper plates. Guide the children to write their names and the phrase "Thank you, God" on their work.

3. Suggest that the children ask their parents to take them to the Thanksgiving Mass so that they can thank God for his blessings and bring food to share with others who have less than they do. If it is customary to bring food offerings for families in need to the parish Thanksgiving Day liturgy, tell the children about it.

4. Let the children thank God with "moving prayers." Direct them to take a standing, squatting, or kneeling position to begin the prayer. As you read the following prayers, have the children imitate each gift. After each prayer, they return to their beginning places.

- ***All the creatures that God has made praise and thank him by being and doing what he made them to be and do. We can praise and thank God for some of his gifts with special "moving prayers." You may pretend to be each gift as I tell about it.***
- ***Turkeys are a gift from God. They praise God when they open up their tails and spread wide their pretty feathers. They strut about and sometimes say, "gobble, gobble." They thank God by being turkeys.***
- ***Corn is a gift from God. The kernels of corn are planted in the brown soil. With the help of the sun and the rain, the corn begins to grow. The tiny green leaves poke up out of the ground. The corn grows until it becomes a tall, slender stalk. When the wind blows, the stalk sways gently back and forth. A corncob with tiny kernels of corn grows on the stalk. The corn keeps growing until it is ripe and ready. Corn praises God by growing and being corn.***
- ***The sun is a gift from God. It brings the morning to our dark world each day with its rays of light. The sun shines on the world and warms it, helping plants to grow. The sun spreads sunshine, bringing joy everywhere.***
- ***Rain is a gift from God. It washes our world and makes it fresh and clean. It helps things grow. Think of rain falling softly and quietly on the ground. With your movements, thank God for soft, gentle rain.***

Chapter 11
Preparing Is Good

FAITH FOCUS

During Advent we prepare for the coming of Jesus at Christmas. Luke 2:1–7

PREPARING THE FAITH EXPERIENCE

LISTENING

Those who share God's Word with others must be fed themselves by God's Word found in Sacred Scripture. Share some time of quiet prayer with God, listening to God's word. Ask God to fill you with his presence and nourish you by his holy Word.

Prepare the way of the Lord,
make straight his paths.
Every valley shall be filled
and every mountain and hill shall be made low.
The winding roads shall be made straight,
and the rough way made smooth,
and all flesh shall see the salvation of God.

Luke 3:4–6

REFLECTING

During the season of Advent, we prepare to celebrate a great and wonderful mystery of our faith: God's Son, Jesus, was born among us as our Savior. The word Advent means "coming" or "arrival." During Advent we prepare to celebrate the fulfillment of God's promise of salvation in the birth of his Son, Jesus. At the same time, we yearn for the day when Christ will come in glory "as we await the blessed hope, the appearance of the glory of the great God and of our savior Jesus Christ." (Titus 2:13)

Meanwhile, we experience Christ's personal advent into each of our lives on Christmas Day, and every day in the Eucharist. He comes to us in grace through the sacraments and prayer; he comes to us through the people and events of our daily lives.

Christ comes to us in history, in grace, and in glory. These are related to one another as one great mystery of God's loving encounter with humanity and with each of us as individuals. Advent is the season of waiting and preparing for Jesus. We ready ourselves so that the wonderful event of God coming to dwell among us can effect in our hearts the peace and joy Jesus came to bring. The more our hearts are prepared to receive Jesus, the more we will recognize his presence in our lives and his coming to us in grace.

We still wait for what is to come: the fulfillment of the Kingdom of God, where all will walk in the way of truth, peace, and justice. We wait for his coming in majesty, resplendent with glory, when he will take us to the heavenly Jerusalem,

The city had no need of sun or moon to shine on it, for the glory of God gave it light, and its lamp was the Lamb.

Revelation 21:23

As we prepare for Jesus by clearing away whatever is blinding us to God's saving action in our lives, we pray, "Help us that we may one day see your glory, the glory that is yours as the only Son of the Father, full of grace and truth." (Based on John 1:14)

RESPONDING

Having been nourished by God's Word, we are able to respond to God's great love for us. In prayer, respond to God's call to you to share his word with others. You may also wish to respond in your prayer journal.

- How can I honor the season of Advent as a time of waiting and preparing for Jesus to dwell among us?

Spirit, move me and these children as we await Jesus in a spirit of love and prayer.

Catechism of the Catholic Church

The themes of this lesson correspond to the following paragraphs: 522–524, 1095.

THE FAITH EXPERIENCE

DAY ONE
Christmas Is Coming

DAY TWO
God's Family Prepared for Jesus

DAY THREE
We Prepare Our Hearts

DAY FOUR
We Prepare Through Prayer

Scripture in This Chapter

- *Matthew 3:1–12 John the Baptist prepares the way for Jesus.*
- *2 Peter 3:8–14 Each person must be holy and make every effort to live in faith and love while waiting for the coming of the Lord.*

Church Documents

General Directory for Catechesis #98.
National Directory for Catechesis #25, A.
Every Christian should be helped to grow daily in a consciousness of the gifts received at Baptism.

Constitution on the Liturgy #102.
Through the celebration of the liturgical year, the Church opens to us the riches of the mysteries of salvation.

The theme of this chapter corresponds to the season of Advent. This chapter is best taught after the first Sunday of Advent. Lesson 2 of SPECIAL SEASONS AND DAYS is an additional Advent lesson, about the Advent wreath. Refer to the ENRICHING THE FAITH EXPERIENCE section of this chapter and Lesson 2 of SPECIAL SEASONS AND DAYS for additional ideas to expand upon the themes of Advent.

Bulletin Board At the left is a suggestion for a bulletin-board design. Arrange artificial green garland into a wreath design. Secure it to the bulletin board. Draw and cut out four candles, three purple and one pink, from colored construction paper. On the outer edges of the wreath, attach to the bulletin board the four Advent candles. During each week of Advent, add a "flame" cut from yellow construction paper to its respective candle. You might post a banner with the words, "Come, Lord Jesus."

For a list of children's literature suggestions, please see **page OV-47.**

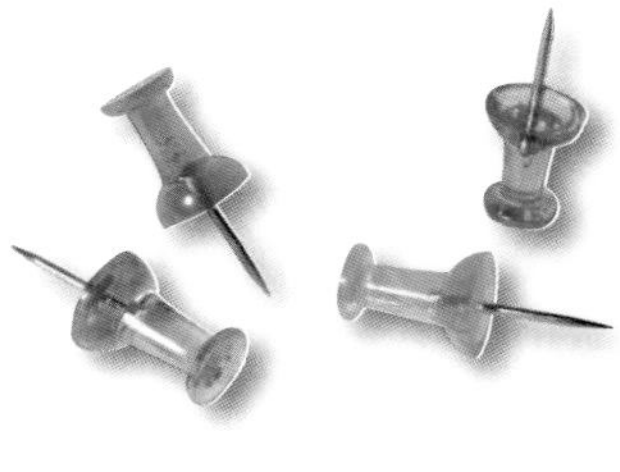

CHAPTER 11 | DAY ONE

Christmas Is Coming

Student Book page 43

LEARNING OUTCOMES

The children will be able to

- tell ways their families prepare for Christmas.
- know that Christmas is the celebration of Jesus' birthday.

KEY TERMS

Advent—the four weeks before Christmas, a time when we prepare our hearts for Jesus' coming

Advent wreath—an evergreen wreath, with four candles, that reminds us to prepare for Jesus' coming

Christmas—the celebration of Jesus' birthday

MATERIALS

- Items that might be used at a birthday party (Examples: paper plates, napkins, candles, cake, a gift, decorations, a goody bag)
- Advent wreath
- Christmas card
- Poster 4
- Cookie jar or decorative tin
- Crayons or markers

COMMENTS

1. Advent, the beginning of a new liturgical year, is the season of spiritual preparation for the coming of Christ at Christmas. Through this lesson, the children come to realize that the celebration of Jesus' birth is the focus of our Christmas activities. Advent and Christmas are related but distinct liturgical seasons. In your classroom activities, honor Advent's distinction from Christmas as a season of waiting and preparation so that the children will be ready to celebrate the Christmas season more fully.

2. When you attend Mass on the First Sunday of Advent, take note of the changes in the church environment and liturgical prayer for the Advent season. The color of the altar cloth and vestments has changed to purple. An Advent wreath may now be displayed and lit before Mass. There may be new banners displayed in the church. The Gloria is not prayed during the opening rite. During class this week, comment on these changes to the children. If time allows, you might tour the church with the children to observe the Advent symbols and colors now seen in church.

3. The Advent wreath, with its four candles are lit successively on the four Sundays of Advent, is a sign of preparation for Christmas, when Jesus, the Light of the World, was born. The lighting of candles is accompanied by Scripture readings, hymns, and prayers. Usually three of the candles are violet and one is pink. Violet is the color the Church often uses in preparation for a feast. Pink or rose is a symbol of joy. The pink candle is lighted on the third Sunday of Advent to tell us that the time of waiting is almost over and that Christmas is near.

4. Note that Lesson 2 of SPECIAL SEASONS AND DAYS is an additional Advent session that teaches the children about the Advent wreath. There is an Advent wreath in the Student Book. Lesson 3 of SPECIAL SEASONS AND DAYS is a Christmas session. There is a Nativity scene punchout in the Student Book.

CENTERING

Recall the last chapter.

- ***In the last chapter you thought about the many things God gave you. What do we say to God for his gifts?*** (Thank you)
- ***Today we'll talk about God's greatest gift. His name starts with a J. Who do you think this is?*** (Jesus)

SHARING

1 Tell the children to imagine that they have been asked to prepare for a birthday party. Ask them what might be needed to prepare for the party. As items are named, bring out the item if you have it. (Examples: paper plates, napkins, candles, cake, a gift, decorations, a goody bag) Make a list of additional items or things to do. When finished, say:

- ***There is a lot to do to get ready for a birthday party.***
- ***On Christmas we celebrate the birthday of someone very special. Christmas is the day Jesus was born.***

❷ Let the children talk about preparing for Christmas. Show Poster 4 Advent Wreath.

• ***We need to get ready, or prepare, for celebrations. The four weeks before Christmas are a special time. This season is called Advent. During Advent, we light an Advent wreath to remind us that we are preparing for Christmas.***

❸ Relate the preparation to the real meaning of Christmas.

• ***We do many things to get ready to celebrate Christmas. What do we celebrate on Christmas?*** (Jesus' birthday)

• ***Jesus is so wonderful because he is God. Christians all over the world celebrate his birthday. People everywhere are getting ready to celebrate Christmas.***

• [Show an Advent wreath.] ***We light the candles on an Advent wreath because Jesus brought us joy by being our light. We decorate a Christmas tree with lights because the light of Jesus is brighter than any darkness.***

• [Show a Christmas card.] ***We send cards to show our love for others because God our Father sent Jesus to show his love for us.***

• [Show a cookie jar or tin.] ***We make good things to eat to celebrate how good God is because God gave us Jesus.***

• ***We prepare to give gifts because God our Father gave us Jesus, the first and most wonderful Christmas gift.***

ACTING

❶ Teach and pray with the children the adaptation of Psalm 25:5 with gestures:

Oh, Lord,
[Extend hand up.]
I wait for you
[Cross hands over heart.]
all day long.
[Bring crossed hands out in front and over to the sides.]

❷ Read aloud **page 43.**

❸ Discuss with the children how their families prepare for Christmas.

CHECKPOINT

- Are the children aware of the real meaning of Christmas?
- How will you help the children honor Advent as a season of waiting and preparing for Christmas?

CHAPTER 11

Preparing Is Good

God promised to send his Son, Jesus.
God's people waited and prayed.
God prepared to send Jesus.

43

CHAPTER 11 | DAY TWO

God's Family Prepared for Jesus

Student Book page 44

LEARNING OUTCOME

The children will be able to
- tell how God prepared the world for Jesus' birth.

KEY TERMS

manger—feeding box for animals

stable—place where animals are kept

MATERIALS

- Wrapped present with sample empty-manger craft (see ACTING #1, Day Four) and copies of BLM 14 inside
- BLM 14
- BLM 15
- Cutout 1
- Advent wreath
- Materials for ornaments made in SHARING #5: Plastic lids prepared with a hole punched out and a loop of yarn tied through, crayons, scissors, glue, glitter
- Song for ACTING (optional)

COMMENTS

1. Prepare sample ornaments using BLM 15 Ornaments for SHARING #2. These can be made to stand by gluing a 1-inch strip of paper into a circle and then attaching the circle to the back of each ornament. Alternatively, magnets can be attached to the back of each picture to post on a magnetic display board. • ***BLM 15 Ornaments***

2. Young children live mainly in the present moment. Since their sense of time is not yet well developed, being asked to be patient and to wait for something or someone can be difficult. Patience cannot be taught; it can only be practiced. During the season of Advent, the community of the Church is invited to practice patience as we joyfully anticipate our celebration of Jesus' birth at Christmas. We model patience for children when we honor our Church's liturgical seasons.

CENTERING

1 Teach and pray with the children the adaptation of Psalm 25:5 with gestures:

> **Oh, Lord,**
> [Extend hand up.]
> **I wait for you**
> [Cross hands over heart.]
> **all day long.**
> [Bring crossed hands out in front and over to the sides.]

2 Show the children a wrapped present (inside are a sample empty manger craft to be made on Day Four and copies of BLM 14 Advent Calendar). Tell the children that the present cannot be opened until the next lesson. Acknowledge their curiosity about what the present contains, but tell them that they must wait to find out.
• ***BLM 14 Advent Calendar***

- ***Waiting can be very difficult.***
- ***What holiday are we waiting for and preparing to celebrate soon?*** (Christmas)
- ***What do we call the weeks before Christmas when we wait and prepare for Jesus' birthday?*** (Advent)
- ***During Advent, we remember how God's people waited for Jesus.***

SHARING

1 Show the children the Bible. Ask:

- ***What does God tell us in the Bible?*** (He loves us.) Explain that the Bible also tells us stories about how God helped the world prepare for Jesus' birth:
- ***The Bible tells us many wonderful stories. What stories from the Bible do you remember?*** (The story of Creation, the story of Noah and the Flood, how God chose David to be king, the story of Samuel)
- ***In these and many other wonderful stories found in the Bible, we learn that God helped the world prepare for Jesus' birth.***

2 Tell the children how God helped the world prepare for

Jesus' birth by telling the story "God Promised to Send his Son, Jesus" on **page T132.** At the end of each section of the story, let the children put the respective ornaments from BLM 15 that you have prepared in advance around the Advent wreath or on a magnetic display board. Let the children sense your awe and anticipation as you share the story of how God prepared the world for Jesus' birth.

3 Ask:

- ***Do you think it was easy for God's people to wait for God to keep his promise? Is it easy for you when people tell you that you have to wait your turn or wait to open a present?***
- ***Waiting can be very difficult. We are still waiting to find out what is in this present.***

4 Read aloud the text on **page 44**. Have the children do the activity.

5 Help the children make Christmas ornaments. Distribute plastic lids with a hole punched in each and a loop of yarn tied through the hole and copies of BLM 15. Have the children color one or more of the pictures. Help them cut out the pictures. Have them glue the pictures to the plastic lids. Decorate the ornaments with glitter and/or yarn. Invite the children to take the ornaments home to help them remember how God's people waited and prepared for Jesus.

ACTING

Teach the children an Advent song, such as "Come, Lord Jesus" from *Hi God 2*. Other options can be found on the song list on **page T137.**

- ***While we prepare to celebrate Jesus' birthday, we also pray and wait, just like God's people did before Jesus was born. We pray that God will send his Son, Jesus.***

Invite the children to sing the song as a prayer to prepare for Jesus' birthday.

Keep the wrapped present for Day Three.

CHECKPOINT

- How will you continue to help the children practice patience?
- How have the children shown that they understand that Advent is a time of waiting and preparing for Christmas?

Try This

At Christmas, we celebrate Jesus' birthday.
During Advent, we get ready for Christmas.
We light an Advent wreath.
Draw four candles on this Advent wreath.

We also make cookies and
other good things to eat.
Draw decorations on
each Christmas cookie.

44

God Promised to Send his Son, Jesus

A long, long time ago, God made the world and the first people. [Show the Adam-and-Eve ornament.] Everything God made was good. When God made people, he made them good too. God told his people what to do to be good. Adam and Eve did not obey God. That was not good. God was not pleased. God's people were very unhappy. They were sorry they had not obeyed God. They found it very hard to be good after that. They needed someone to help them.

God the Father promised to send someone to help them. He was going to send his own Son, Jesus. [Show Cutout 1 Jesus.] He did not send Jesus right away. He wanted his people to get ready first. So God's people waited and prayed.

Many, many years passed. It was not yet time for God to send his Son, Jesus. Do you remember the story of Noah and the Flood? [Show the Noah ornament.] The Bible tells us that the people did not always take care of the world and one another. So God decided to make the world over and sent a great flood. But God saved Noah and the animals. After the Flood, God promised never to flood the earth again. He gave the rainbow as a sign of his promise and his love.

Many, many more years passed. The people prayed some more. They waited for God to send his Son, Jesus. [Show the David ornament.] Remember the story of David, the Shepherd-King. God chose David to be the new king. David became a king, the greatest king Israel ever had. The shepherd-king David waited and prayed. The people prayed and waited. But still, it was not yet time for God to send his Son, Jesus. [Pause.]

[Show the Mary-and-Joseph ornament.] And then, a long time after the time of David, God prepared a young girl to be the mother of his Son, Jesus. Do you know her name? Mary was very good. She listened to God and did what he asked. Her heart was ready for Jesus. She was full of God's love.

Joseph was Mary's husband, although he was not the father of Jesus. God prepared him to take care of Mary and Jesus. Joseph's heart was full of love. He did what God told him to do. He was ready for Jesus.

What do you think happened next? (Jesus was born.) Yes, now Mary and Joseph were ready to welcome Jesus. And many other people were ready to welcome Jesus too. God knew that everything was now ready for his Son, Jesus. Soon Jesus would be born and Jesus, God's own Son, would show people how to love and obey God.

CHAPTER 11 | DAY THREE

We Prepare Our Hearts

Student Book page 45

LEARNING OUTCOME

The children will be able to

- prepare their hearts for the celebration of Christmas by performing loving acts.

MATERIALS

- Cutout 4
- Crayons or markers
- Background music (optional)

COMMENT

Encourage the children to perform at least one loving act at home and at school every day during Advent. The Advent calendars they receive today can help with this. Suggest that each day they show love to a different family member and to a different person at school. Periodically remind the children to ask themselves if their hearts are almost ready for Jesus because of the loving deeds they are performing. Let the children tell some loving things they have done.

CENTERING

Recall the last lesson.

- ***What do we celebrate at Christmas?*** (Jesus' birthday)
- ***Who are some of the people who prepared for the coming of Jesus?*** (Mary, Joseph, David, Noah, Adam and Eve)
- ***What do we do during the season of Advent?*** (We wait and prepare for Jesus' birthday.)

Show the wrapped present introduced on Day Two. Tell the children that they must wait just a little bit longer to learn what is inside this box. The present will be opened at the end of today's lesson.

SHARING

1 Encourage the children to prepare their hearts.

- ***As we wait for Jesus, we prepare one very important thing. We prepare our hearts.*** [Show Cutout 4 Heart.]
- ***God made our hearts to love. The best gift we can give Jesus on his birthday is the gift of our love. During Advent, we prepare our hearts for Jesus by being loving toward our families and others.***

2 Have the children role-play loving responses. Let them suggest ways of being loving at home and at school, or ask them what they will say and do to prepare their hearts with love for Christmas when the following things happen.

- Your father says you can't go to a friend's house after school.
- You hurt your little brother's feelings by not letting him play with you.
- The babysitter asks you to pick up your toys.
- Your little sister wants to play with you.
- A friend wants to play with one of your toys.
- Your father asks you to sit quietly in church.
- Your brother wants to watch a different TV program than you do.
- Your aunt fixes you a sandwich for lunch that you don't like.
- Your teacher asks you to wear your coat when you go out to play.
- Your mother says it is time to go to bed.

ACTING

1 Ask the children to turn to **page 45** in their books. Read it aloud. Have them do the activity. You might wish to play background music as they work. Walk around the room and ask individual children to tell you and the class about their pictures.

2 Show the children the wrapped present introduced on Day Two. Say:

- ***You have waited to see what is inside this box. We can open this box now.***

Invite volunteers to open the present. Inside the box are a sample empty-manger craft, which the children will make on Day Four, and copies of BLM 14 to help the children prepare to celebrate Jesus' birthday.

• ***This is an interesting gift. This is a manger, a feeding box for animals. What does this make you think of?*** (Christmas, a Nativity set, Jesus' birthday)

• ***This empty manger reminds us that during Advent we prepare to celebrate Jesus' birth at Christmas.***

• ***While we are waiting to celebrate Jesus' birthday, we can do things to get ready. You each drew a picture of something that you can do to prepare your heart for Jesus. More ideas are printed on this Advent calendar.***

Distribute copies of BLM 14 to the children and offer directions to the children about how they can use it as they wait and prepare for Christmas.

3 Invite the children to pray the adaptation of Psalm 25:5 with gestures:

Oh, Lord,
[Extend hand up.]
I wait for you
[Cross hands over heart.]
all day long.
[Bring crossed hands out in front and over to the sides.]

CHECKPOINT

• Do the children's pictures show that they understand ways to give loving service to others?

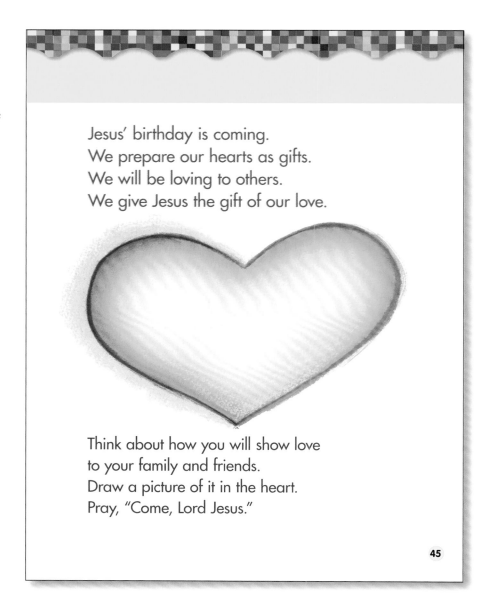

Jesus' birthday is coming.
We prepare our hearts as gifts.
We will be loving to others.
We give Jesus the gift of our love.

Think about how you will show love
to your family and friends.
Draw a picture of it in the heart.
Pray, "Come, Lord Jesus."

45

CHAPTER 11 | DAY FOUR

We Prepare Through Prayer

Student Book page 46

LEARNING OUTCOMES

The children will be able to

- realize that Advent is a special time of prayer as we prepare for Christmas.
- experience the joy in preparing for Christmas.
- anticipate bringing joy to others.

MATERIALS

- Poster 4
- For empty manger craft: brown-paper lunch bags; cotton balls, yarn, or strips of paper
- Bible enthroned, with note card on which you have written the adapted Scripture reading for SHARING #4, Luke 2:1–7

CENTERING

Link this lesson with the last one. Show Poster 4.

• ***Since our last lesson, did you remember to try to do loving acts to prepare for Christmas? Has anyone used his or her Advent calendar? Would some of you like to share what you have done to prepare your hearts for Jesus?*** [Allow time for the children to share their experiences.]

• ***During Advent we prepare our hearts for Jesus by the loving things we do for others. We also prepare our hearts for Jesus through prayer. The Advent wreath is one way we pray as we prepare our hearts for Jesus.***

• ***Today we will share a special prayer to prepare for Jesus' coming at Christmas.***

SHARING

1 Show the sample empty-manger craft from the wrapped present that was opened on Day Three.

• ***Who came at Christmas?*** (Jesus) ***Why is this manger empty?*** (During Advent we are preparing to celebrate Jesus' birthday at Christmas)

• ***Our loving deeds and our prayers will help make this manger a soft bed for Jesus when he comes.***

• ***We will use the empty manger as we prepare our hearts for Jesus with a prayer service.***

Place the empty manger on the table in the Prayer Center.

2 Invite the children to gather in the Prayer Center for the prayer service. Give each child a cotton ball, a small piece of yarn, or a strip of paper to be placed in the empty manger during the prayer service.

3 Invite the children to begin the prayer service by singing the song taught on Day Two (such as "Come, Lord Jesus" from *Hi God 2* or another from the song list on **page T137**).

• ***We prepare our hearts for Jesus by singing our prayer that Jesus will come to us soon.***

Sing the song together.

4 Take the Bible and open it to the Gospel according to Luke, Luke 2:1–7:

• ***Let's prepare ourselves to listen well to today's Bible reading.*** Hold the Bible with reverence and read:

• ***A reading from the holy Gospel according to Luke: "God told Mary and Joseph to prepare for Jesus' birth. Mary and Joseph said yes to God. When it was almost time for Jesus to be born, Mary and Joseph had to travel far from home. At the end of their journey, they looked for a place to rest. The only place they could find was a stable. A stable is the place where the animals sleep. Mary and Joseph rested there with the animals, waiting for Jesus to be born." The Word of the Lord.*** Invite the children to respond, "Thanks be to God."

5 Introduce a time for quiet prayer:

• ***Mary and Joseph prepared for Jesus' birth. They waited and prayed. We also prepare and pray as we wait for Jesus' birthday.***

6 Invite the children to sit quietly and to talk with God in the quiet of their hearts. Invite them to tell God one thing that they will do to prepare their hearts for Jesus. Tell the children that when they have finished their quiet prayer to God, they may place their cotton ball, piece of yarn, or strip of paper in the empty manger on the prayer table. Remind them to do this quietly so that others can continue to pray. When everyone has placed his or her object in the empty manger, conclude the prayer service.

7 Invite the children to stand and pray the adaptation of Psalm 25:5 with gestures:

> **Oh, LORD,**
> [Extend hand up.]
> **I wait for you**
> [Cross hands over heart.]
> **all day long.**
> [Bring crossed hands out in front and over to the sides.]

When finished, ask the children to quietly return to their seats.

ACTING

1 Help the children make an empty-manger craft to take home. Give the children brown-paper lunch bags to make their mangers. Have them cut the folded bags across the bottom third, just above the bottom flap. Ask the children to open the small remainder of the bag and then to fold the edges out. The result is a square miniature manger. Give each child a small envelope with cotton balls, 2- to 3-inch pieces of yarn, or strips of tissue paper to use as straw. Tell the children to take their mangers home and to add a piece of "straw" each day as they do a loving deed or say a prayer to prepare their hearts for Jesus.

2 Have the children take home the Family Page on **page 46** to share with their families.

CHECKPOINT

- Are the children enthusiastic about preparing for Jesus through loving deeds and prayer?

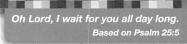

Oh Lord, I wait for you all day long.
Based on Psalm 25:5

Advent in Families

The Lesson Your Child Learned

Advent is the season of waiting and preparing to celebrate the threefold coming of Christ: his coming long ago as a man, his daily comings in grace through the sacraments and the events of our daily lives, and his future coming in glory. The children learned that Christmas commemorates the birth of God's Son, Jesus, who came for our salvation. Add "Come, Lord Jesus!" to your mealtime prayers.

Living the Lesson

Whenever someone utters the phrase, "He had his heart set on it," I think of young Ralphie Parker in the classic yuletide movie *A Christmas Story*. As Christmas approached, Ralphie absolutely ached to own the "Red Ryder, carbine-action, 200-shot, range model BB gun with a compass in the stock" that he saw on display at the local department store. Every time I see that film, I ache right along with Ralphie, because I can readily recall a number of Decembers I spent pining for a BB gun, a bike, or, when I was seven, a real pony.

If we're lucky, we never lose the habit of such Advent yearning; we simply change the object of our longing. Instead of the big-screen TV, diamond necklace, or holiday cruise that we "know" will finally satisfy us, we can learn to hope for a deeper experience with Jesus, the one who can truly make us whole, no matter what is under the tree.

Truth be told, aren't most of the things we set our hearts on bound to be disappointing if we don't have love at the center of our lives? That's the gift the Christ Child embodies—self-giving love for one and all. That's the gift to set your heart on through all the days of Advent.

–Tom McGrath, author of *Raising Faith-Filled Kids* (Loyola Press)

Bringing the Lesson Home

- Read with your child the pages from this chapter that were sent home.
- In your family's celebration of the winter holidays, try to keep the season of Advent distinct from the Christmas season.
- Set up a stable without the figures of Jesus, Mary, and Joseph. Put the animals in the stable. Place the shepherds and sheep a short distance away.
- On Christmas Eve let everyone help place the figures of Jesus, Mary, and Joseph in the stable. Read aloud as a family the story of Jesus' birth from the Bible and sing "Silent Night."

46

ENRICHING THE FAITH EXPERIENCE

Use the following activities to enrich a lesson, to replace an activity with one that better meets the needs of your class, or to create an additional lesson.

1 Teach a song to the melody of "God Is So Good."

Preparing is good.
(Two times)
Now we prepare
for a birthday.

God loves us so.
(Three times)
God gives his Son.

2 Have the children bring in new, unopened toys to be given to children of families in need.

3 Help the children prepare for Christmas by making a Christmas card for someone. Use copies of BLM 16 Christmas Card. • ***BLM 16 Christmas Card***

4 During Advent, we prepare for Jesus through prayer and acts of kindness. Help the children to make Advent Promise Cards that read: "I promise to prepare for Jesus' birthday." The children may write or draw a picture of what they will do during Advent to prepare for Christmas.

5 Show the children how to make an Advent table prayer card by folding one piece of paper in half so that it will stand. On each side of the table card, the children can copy or decorate a different Advent prayer (e.g., Lord, I wait for you all day long (Psalm 25:5); Prepare the way of the Lord (Isaiah 40:3); Rejoice, the Lord is near (Philippians 4:4–5 adapted); Come, Lord Jesus. (Rev. 22:20)

Songs

Play for the children any of these songs: "Mary's Cradle Song," (*Sing a Song of Joy!*) **CD 2 Track 12;** "Come, Lord Jesus," "We Are Little Gifts," "O Antiphons" (*Sing a Song of Joy!*); "Advent Song" (Dandelions); " "Come, Lord Jesus (*Hi God 2*); "O Come, O Come Emmanuel," "Stay Awake, Be Ready" (*Singing our Faith*); "Advent Song" (*Best of Mary Lu Walker*). For a list of all the music used in this program, see **page OV-39.**

Chapter 12

Choosing Is Good

FAITH FOCUS

We imitate Mary, Mother of God and our Mother, by saying yes to God. Luke 1:26–38

PREPARING THE FAITH EXPERIENCE

LISTENING

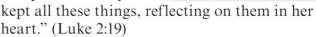

The vocation of a teacher is to communicate with joy the good news of God's love. Take some time to let yourself be refreshed by the good news found in the Bible. As you pray, hear God speak to you his good news of love and salvation.

Then the angel said to her, "Do not be afraid, Mary, for you have found favor with God. Behold, you will conceive in your womb and bear a son, and you shall name him Jesus. . . . The holy Spirit will come upon you, and the power of the Most High will overshadow you. Therefore the child to be born will be called holy, the Son of God."

Mary said, "Behold, I am the handmaid of the Lord. May it be done to me according to your word." Then the angel departed from her.

Luke 1:30–31,35,38

REFLECTING

God's preparations for the coming of his Son took thousands of years. Whatever time we might spend reflecting on God's ways cannot exhaust this mystery of our faith.

But when the fullness of time had come, God sent his Son, born of a woman, . . . so that we might receive adoption.

Galatians 4:4–5

God the Father chose a young Jewish virgin to be the mother of his Son. Yet wherever God enters people's lives, he respects their freedom. God respected Mary's freedom. She listened to God's word with complete openness and chose to respond in simple faith. She offered herself as the Lord's faithful handmaid. By her yes, she allowed God to fulfill his will through the promises made to her. With her consent, the Word became flesh through the power of the Holy Spirit. Jesus, the Son of God, entered human history. The profound fact overwhelmed Mary: "And Mary kept all these things, reflecting on them in her heart." (Luke 2:19)

Mary is our model in exercising human freedom. True freedom is being able to choose that which is pleasing to God. Mary shows us how, by total surrender to God's will in our lives, we are free to respond with love to each manifestation of God's love. Then, like Mary, we can fulfill what God calls each of us to do: welcome Christ into our hearts. Thankful for Mary's response to God, we try to imitate her yes and let God use us to bring the Savior to all people. We pray:

God of love and mercy,
Help us to follow the example of Mary,
always ready to do your will.

RESPONDING

God's Word moves us to respond in word and action. Let the Holy Spirit work within you as you prayerfully consider how you are being called to respond to God's message to you today.

- When do I call on Mary to help me make good choices?
- How can I foster love of Mary in the children?

God of love, help me and the children respond to you with a faith-filled yes.

Catechism of the Catholic Church

The themes of this lesson correspond to the following paragraphs: 494, 973, 1730–1732, 2676, 2679.

THE FAITH EXPERIENCE

DAY ONE
We Choose What Is Good

DAY TWO
Mary Chose to Say Yes to God

DAY THREE
We Pray to Mary

DAY FOUR
Mary Helps Us Say Yes to God

Scripture in This Chapter

- *Luke 1:46–55 Mary's song of thanksgiving for all that the Lord has done for her tells what we can expect when we open our hearts to God's action.*
- *Luke 2:22–35 In accordance with Jewish law, Jesus is presented in the Temple. Simeon meets his Savior and prophesies the sorrows Mary will encounter.*

Church Documents

General Directory for Catechesis #196.
National Directory for Catechesis #38, C.
Teaching about Mary should be done within the context of the Trinity, Christ, and the Church.

Pastoral Constitution on the Church in the Modern World #16.
Our consciences call us to love and do what is good and to avoid evil.

Bulletin Board At the left is a suggestion for a bulletin-board design. Distribute copies of BLM 17 Choices and guide the children to do the activity. Post their work on the bulletin board. You might include a banner with the words, "Choosing Is Good."
- ***BLM 17 Choices***

For a list of children's literature suggestions, please see **page OV-47.**

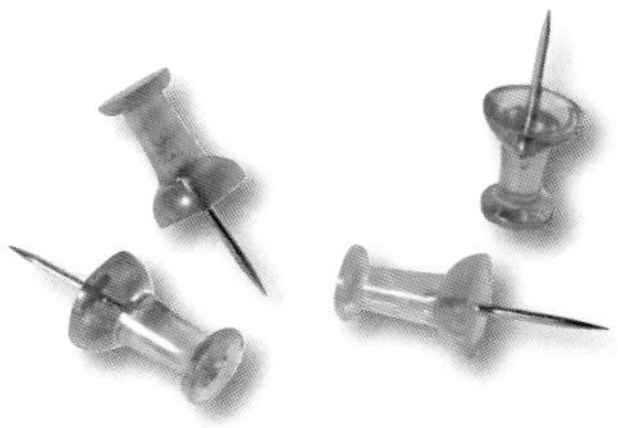

CHAPTER 12 | DAY ONE

We Choose What Is Good

Student Book page 47

LEARNING OUTCOMES

The children will be able to

- be aware that they should think before they choose.
- appreciate that choosing what pleases God brings joy.

MATERIALS

- Puppets made from Cutouts 51–58
- Two sticker designs, enough of each for each child

COMMENTS

1. Studies have shown that a child's preschool years are the most important for emotional, intellectual, and religious growth. It is important that the children learn to make decisions based on certain norms of conduct and to take responsibility for their choices.

2. Making choices can be difficult for very young children. When we provide opportunities for children to make everyday decisions, we prepare them for a lifetime of decision making.

CENTERING

Recall the last chapter.

- ***In the last chapter we talked about preparing. What do we do during the season of Advent?*** (We prepare to celebrate Jesus' birthday, Christmas.) ***What do we do to prepare for Christmas?*** (We prepare our hearts by performing loving deeds and by praying.)
- ***You can choose to prepare or not to prepare your hearts. Today we will think and talk about choosing.***

SHARING

1 Show the children two sheets of stickers, each sheet with a different design. Tell the children that they may each have one sticker and allow them to choose which sticker design they would like. Give each child the sticker he or she chooses.

2 Invite the children to talk about their experiences making choices.

- ***Was it easy for you to choose which sticker you wanted? Why did you choose one sticker and not the other?***
- ***Do you ever have a hard time choosing? Who would like to tell us about one of the times when it was hard for you to choose?***
- ***What are some choices you make every day? Who helps you make your choices?***

3 Ask the children to turn to **page 47** in their books. Read aloud the text. Discuss:

- ***What does it mean to make good choices?***

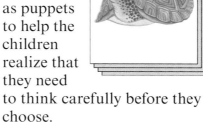

4 Use Cutouts 51–58 Animal Set as puppets to help the children realize that they need to think carefully before they choose.

- ***Some animal friends are talking about choices that they must make. Let's listen to what they say and decide whether or not they are making good choices. Be ready to tell why the choice is good or not good.***
- ***Herbie Horse says, "I can eat some hay, or I can have some candy. Hay is good for me. Which shall I choose?"*** (Hay, because it is good food for horses)
- ***Gilda Goldfish says, "I want a pair of shiny black shoes, but I also want some fish food to eat. The little girl who feeds me has pretty, shiny black shoes. Which shall I choose?"*** (Fish food) ***Will shoes be helpful to Gilda?*** (No. She can't do anything with them.) ***Is it always good to want what other people have? Why not?***
- ***Charlie Chick says, "I want a red bathing suit but I also want some birdseed. I like the color red a lot. Which shall I choose?"*** (Birdseed)
- ***Katie Kitten says, "I like to play with a toy mouse, but I also might like a computer. Which shall I choose?"*** (Toy mouse) ***Why wouldn't a computer be a good choice?*** (Kittens can't use computers.)

- ***Connie Cow says, "I want a pair of ice skates. Once I saw some children having lots of fun ice skating. I would also like some green grass to eat. Which shall I choose?"*** (Green grass) ***Why isn't ice skates a good choice?*** (She can't use them.)
- ***Rita Rabbit says, "I like carrots. But I also might like a basketball. Which shall I choose?"*** (Carrots)
- ***Betty Bird says, "I like needles because they are bright and shiny. I want to put them in my nest to make it look pretty. But I also like straw in my nest. Which shall I choose?"*** (Straw) ***Why shouldn't she choose needles for her nest?*** (She might get hurt if she puts needles in her nest.)
- ***Tillie Turtle says, "I would really like a rock to rest on. But I might also like to have a CD. Which shall I choose?"*** (A rock)

5 Discuss the importance of thinking carefully before choosing. Ask:

- ***Is it good to choose something that will hurt us?***
- ***Are we making a good choice if we know it will make someone upset or unhappy? Why not?***
- ***Is it good to choose something God would not want us to do?***
- ***Some choices are easier to make than others. Before we choose, we should think about what is really good. God knows what will make us happy. God lets us know what is really good. We show our love for God when we make good choices.***

ACTING

Invite the children to pray the psalm prayer adapted from Psalm 25:12:

God
[Extend arms up.]
shows me
[Put one hand on your heart.]
the way to choose.
[Point in three directions.]

CHECKPOINT

- What choices are the children invited to make on a daily basis?
- Are the children willing to accept the consequences of their choices?

CHAPTER 12

Choosing Is Good

We should think before we choose.

We want to make good choices.

When we make good choices, we are happy.

47

CHAPTER 12 | DAY TWO

Mary Chose to Say Yes to God

Student Book page 48

LEARNING OUTCOMES

The children will be able to

- know that God chose Mary to be the mother of Jesus.
- understand that Mary said yes to God.

MATERIALS

- Cutouts 21, 43
- Flashcard 5
- BLM 17
- Yes Card punchouts from the Student Book
- Drawing paper
- Pencils
- Crayons or markers
- Bible enthroned, with note card on which you have written the adapted Scripture reading for SHARING #1, Luke 1:26-38

COMMENTS

1. The scriptural account of the Annunciation in Luke's Gospel is evidence of a divine revelation to Mary regarding the birth of Jesus. It also substantiates Jesus' divine origin from the first moment of his existence on earth. He is both the Son of God and the Son of Mary.

2. Mary's response to the angel at the moment of the Annunciation was in keeping with the surrender she had already made to God and foreshadowed her responses throughout her life. Through her yes, she accepted God's plan for her. She was indeed the perfect follower of Jesus. She always listened to God's Word and lived it out in the ordinary events of her everyday life. Her yes to God made her the mother of God and of his Church. She is our model of discipleship.

CENTERING

Recall the last lesson and introduce today's lesson:

• ***Every day we have opportunities to make choices. Some choices are easy to make. Some choices are more difficult. What kinds of choices are easy for you to make? What are choices that are more difficult for you to make?***

• ***We want to make good choices. Making good choices helps us be happy.***

• ***Let's practice making some choices now by playing a game.***

Teach the children to play a simple game to practice making choices. Ask a series of questions, beginning with simple choices, such as "Which would you choose for dessert, vanilla ice cream or chocolate ice cream?" "Which would you choose to play, baseball or soccer?"

When the children show that they are comfortable with the game, move to more difficult choice questions, such as "If your friend asked to share your crayons, would you say yes or no?" "If your mom or dad asked you to pick up your toys, would you say yes or no?"

If you have not already done so, you might distribute copies of BLM 17 Choices for the children to complete.
• BLM 17 Choices

SHARING

1 Ask the children to open their books to **page 48** and prepare to tell the story of the Annunciation.

• ***Today I am going to tell you about Mary. This story about Mary is found in the Bible. Mary loved God very much. Her love for God helped her choose what was good.***

• ***This story tells us more about how God prepared the world for his Son, Jesus, to be born. When everything was ready for God our Father to send his Son Jesus into the world, God chose a mother for him. Whom did God choose to be the mother of Jesus?*** (Mary)

Introduce this Bible story by showing the Bible and opening it to the Gospel according to Luke, Luke 1:26–38. Enthrone the Bible.

• ***Let's prepare ourselves to listen well to today's Bible story.***

2 Tell the story of the Annunciation:

• [Show Cutout 43 Mary.] ***God sent an angel to ask Mary to be Jesus' mother.*** [Show Cutout 21 Angel.] ***The angel Gabriel came to Mary and said, "Hail Mary, full of grace. The Lord is with you! God wants you to be the mother of his Son. You will have a baby. You are to name him Jesus."***

• ***God let Mary choose if she would be Jesus' mother. She could say yes or no to God.***

• ***Mary loved God. She chose what God wanted. Mary said, "Yes."*** [Show Flashcard 5 *yes*.] ***I will be Jesus' mother. I will do what God wants."***

❸ Discuss the story of the Annunciation. Distribute the Yes Card punchouts and tell the children to raise their yes cards when the answer is *yes*.

• ***What did God ask Mary?*** (To be the mother of Jesus)

• ***What did Mary say?*** (Yes)

• ***Why did Mary say yes?*** (She chose to do what God wanted.)

• ***Did Mary choose what was good?*** (Yes.)

• ***Do you think that Mary was happy saying yes to God?*** (Yes.) ***Mary felt joy. Doing what God wants brings happiness. This special kind of happiness is called joy.***

• ***Who told Mary what God wanted her to do?*** (The angel)

• ***Who can help you learn what God wants you to do?***

❹ Read aloud **page 48.**

ACTING

❶ Have the children draw a picture of Mary.

❷ Invite the children to pray the psalm prayer adapted from Psalm 25:12 with gestures.

CHECKPOINT

• Do the children understand the story of the Annunciation?

God chose Mary to be the mother of Jesus.

Mary chose to do what God wanted.

Scripture

Mary said yes to God.

Based on Luke 1:38

48

CHAPTER 12 | DAY THREE

We Pray to Mary

Student Book page 49

LEARNING OUTCOMES

The children will be able to

- realize that Mary is their mother.
- understand and learn the first two lines of the Hail Mary.

KEY TERMS

grace—goodness, God's life and love

hail—hello

Mother Mary—the Mother of God and our mother

MATERIALS

- Statue of Mary (or the picture of Mary found on page 49)
- Blue cloth, white cloth for costumes (optional)
- Song about Mary (optional)
- Crayons or markers

COMMENT

The traditional form of the Hail Mary uses "thee" and "thou." In the scriptural form based on new translations, "you" is used. In teaching the prayer, follow the local usage. After this lesson, you can teach the remaining parts of the Hail Mary line by line until the children know it. As modeled in this chapter, teach a single line at time, explaining the words of the prayer and inviting the children to repeat the phrases after you. Then have the children pray the prayer from the beginning, adding the new line just learned. Proceed in this way until the children know the entire prayer. Continue to pray the Hail Mary with the children at the beginning or end of your time together. Children learn the prayers of our tradition best by praying them with others. Remind the children that they can also pray the Hail Mary at home with their families using the Hail Mary Prayer Card punchouts they will bring home at the end of this chapter. When the children know the prayer by heart they may color the cross by the Hail Mary on the inside front cover of their books.

CENTERING

Let the children dramatize the story of the Annunciation from SHARING in Day Two. Either have two children act it out without speaking as you read the account or read just the narration and have the children do the speaking parts. Let them respond spontaneously. You may whisper lines and directions. A blue cloth may be used for Mary's veil or shawl and a white cloth for the angel's robe.

SHARING

1 Introduce the Hail Mary.

- ***We can be happy like Mary when we choose what God wants. It is not always easy to do this, but Mary will help us. Mary is the mother of Jesus. She is also our mother in heaven. We call Mary our mother too.***
- ***There is a special prayer that the Church prays to Mary. Now that you are growing up and know that you belong to the Church, you can learn to pray it too. Listen carefully and see if you have heard the first part before.***

Hail Mary, full of grace,
the Lord is with you.

- ***Who was the first one to say these words to Mary?*** (The angel said them when he asked Mary if she would be the mother of God's Son.)

2 Show a statue or picture of Mary. Place it on a table in front (or in the Prayer Center) as you explain the meaning of these lines:

- **Hail Mary** ***is a greeting like "Hello, Mary." Say these words after me: "Hail Mary."***
- **Full of grace** ***means full of goodness or full of God's life and love. Say these words after me: "full of grace." What did we tell Mary she is filled with?*** (Goodness, God's life and love)
- **The Lord is with you** ***means God is with Mary. Say these words after me: "The Lord is with you."***
- ***Now say each line of the prayer after me: "Hail Mary,***

full of grace." [Have the children repeat.] ***"The Lord is with you."*** [Have the children repeat.]

• ***When we pray this prayer, we honor Mary, our Mother. When we honor Mary, we also honor her Son, Jesus.***

Songs

Play for the children any of these songs: "Immaculate Mary" **CD 1 Track 9**; "I Say 'Yes,' My Lord/Digo 'Si,' Señor" (*Singing Our Faith*); "Yes, We Will Do What Jesus Says" (*Stories and Songs of Jesus*); "Hail Mary" (*Dandelions*). For a list of all the music used in this program, see **page OV-39**.

ACTING

1 Ask the children to turn to **page 49.** Read it aloud and have the children do the activity. You might play a song about Mary as they work. (See the song list above.)

2 Invite the children to look at the picture on **page 49** and lead them into prayer.

• ***Mary was always happy because she chose what was good. Now she is happy with God in heaven. She will help us say yes to God if we ask her. Say these words after me as you look at the beautiful picture of Mary you colored: "Mary, our Mother, help us say yes to God."***

CHECKPOINT

• Can the children say the first two lines of the Hail Mary?

Yes

Mary is the mother of Jesus.

Mary is our mother too.

Mary helps us say yes to God.

Try This

Color and decorate the word Yes.

Color Mary's dress.

Ask Mary to help you say yes to God.

49

CHAPTER 12 | DAY FOUR

Mary Helps Us Say Yes to God

Student Book pages 50–52

LEARNING OUTCOMES

The children will be able to

- desire to imitate Mary's yes to God through loving deeds and kind words.
- be familiar with the story of the Visitation.

MATERIALS

- *A Child's Bible*, page 14
- BLM 18
- Hail Mary Prayer Card punchouts from the Student Book
- Scissors
- Crayons or markers
- Paper fasteners

CENTERING

Pray the first lines of the Hail Mary with the children. Ask them what Mary said to God. (Yes.) Tell them that today they will find out about another day that Mary showed her love for God.

SHARING

1 Explain that Mary said yes to God all her life.

- ***Mary was a person who loved God always. She was also a person who shared God's love with others. In her loving deeds for others, Mary showed her yes to God.***

2 Prepare to tell or to read "Mary's Visit" from *A Child's Bible*, **page 14.** Introduce this Bible story by showing the Bible and opening it to the Gospel according to Luke, Luke 1:36–56. Enthrone the Bible.

- ***Let's prepare ourselves to listen well to today's Bible story.*** Read the story "Mary's Visit" from *A Child's Bible*, **page 14.**

Discuss:

- ***What did Mary do after the visit from the angel?*** (She traveled to help Elizabeth, who was also going to have a baby.)
- ***Why do you think Mary went to help Elizabeth?*** (She knew it was a good, loving thing to do. She loved God. She loved Elizabeth.)

God shows me the way to choose.
Based on Psalm 25:12

Choosing in Families

The Lesson Your Child Learned

Mary, the perfect follower of Jesus, shows us that we attain happiness and self-fulfillment by loving surrender in obedience to God's will. By their choices, family members contribute to family unity or take away from it. The self-control and good habits your child learns now lay the foundation for a moral life. In this chapter the children learned the importance of making good choices. They learned that Mary is their mother and will help them do what God wants.

Living the Lesson

Over the years I've come to recognize the small decisions that loom large in my life at home. Do I empty the dishwasher or leave it for someone else to do? Do I make an effort to call when I'm going to be late? Do I think to send a no-special-occasion card to my wife, parents, or daughters during the year to say, "You're special to me every day"? I see these seemingly small decisions as indicators of the healthiness of my commitments and relationships. If I'm withholding the small things, I know that in some way I'm also withholding my heart, which can have potentially large consequences.

The same is true with God. Do I make time for God at the beginning of the day? Do I thank him throughout the day for all the help that he sends my way? Do I look for the presence of God in others and treat them accordingly? If you focus on the small decisions that will open your heart, your relationships with your family and with God will reap giant rewards.

–Tom McGrath, author of *Raising Faith-Filled Kids* (Loyola Press)

Bringing the Lesson Home

- Read with your child the pages from this chapter that were sent home.
- Assist your child with the Hail Mary prayer printed on the back of the Mary card he or she brings home.
- Point out the happiness your child's good actions bring the family and the pain bad actions cause.
- Let your child make decisions and encourage him or her to stand by them.
- Guide your child to take responsibility for his or her actions. Be sure to model this behavior too.
- Let your child know what is acceptable behavior at home and in public and expect conformity. Take the time early on to explain the reasons for what you ask your child to do.

50

• ***Our Mother, Mary, helps us do loving things too.***

❸ Let the children role-play endings to the following stories, making choices to please God.

• ***We will have some little plays. First I will tell you about one. Then I will ask who would like to be in it. These children will show how to finish the play by choosing something that God wants.***

• ***Dion and Carter are playing ball in the backyard. Keisha, Dion's sister, wants to play with them. What should the boys do?***

• ***Who would like to finish the play to show what happens?*** [Call on two boys and a girl to role-play.]

• ***Is God pleased with what Dion and Carter chose to do? Why?***

• ***After Casey finishes eating lunch in school, she tries to chase Min around the class-room. The teacher had said that they were to go outside after lunch to run and play on the playground.***

• ***Who would like to show us what Min does when Casey tries to chase her?*** [Call on two girls to role-play.]

• ***God asks Min to choose what is good. What does Min say to God?***

• ***The teacher calls the children to line up for a drink of water. Everyone is very thirsty.*** [Call groups of children to line up.]

• ***Does God want you to push other children when you get in line? Why not?***

• ***If you are very thirsty, is it all right to run to be first in line? Why not?***

• ***God asks you to be polite to other children when you line up. Think what you should do.*** [Pause.] ***What are you telling God when you are polite?***

❹ Help the children use BLM 18 Yes to God to make an "I Say Yes" dial. Invite the children to color the segments of the circle and the dial. Then have them cut out the segments. The circle and the dial can be glued to a circle of stiffer paper (like a file

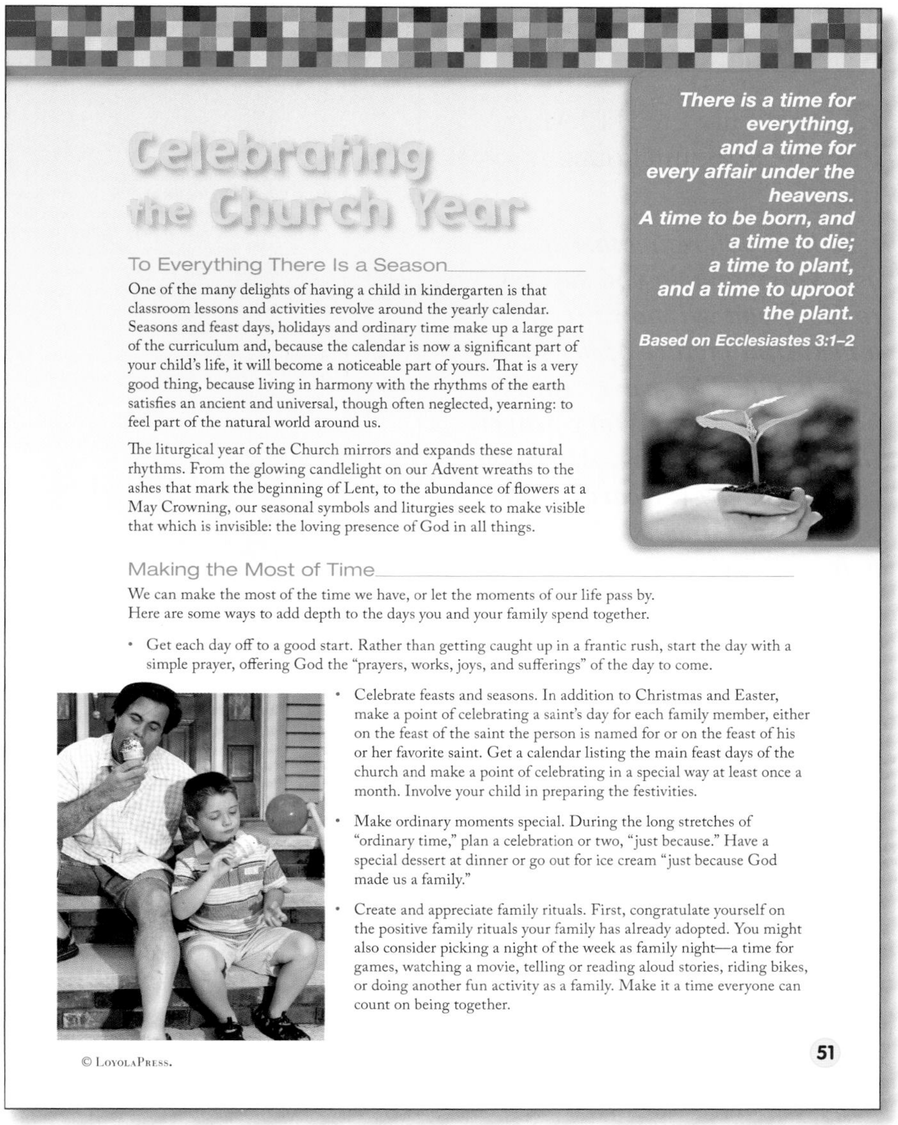

Celebrating the Church Year

There is a time for everything,
and a time for every affair under the heavens.
A time to be born, and a time to die;
a time to plant, and a time to uproot the plant.
Based on Ecclesiastes 3:1–2

To Everything There Is a Season

One of the many delights of having a child in kindergarten is that classroom lessons and activities revolve around the yearly calendar. Seasons and feast days, holidays and ordinary time make up a large part of the curriculum and, because the calendar is now a significant part of your child's life, it will become a noticeable part of yours. That is a very good thing, because living in harmony with the rhythms of the earth satisfies an ancient and universal, though often neglected, yearning: to feel part of the natural world around us.

The liturgical year of the Church mirrors and expands these natural rhythms. From the glowing candlelight on our Advent wreaths to the ashes that mark the beginning of Lent, to the abundance of flowers at a May Crowning, our seasonal symbols and liturgies seek to make visible that which is invisible: the loving presence of God in all things.

Making the Most of Time

We can make the most of the time we have, or let the moments of our life pass by. Here are some ways to add depth to the days you and your family spend together.

- Get each day off to a good start. Rather than getting caught up in a frantic rush, start the day with a simple prayer, offering God the "prayers, works, joys, and sufferings" of the day to come.
- Celebrate feasts and seasons. In addition to Christmas and Easter, make a point of celebrating a saint's day for each family member, either on the feast of the saint the person is named for or on the feast of his or her favorite saint. Get a calendar listing the main feast days of the church and make a point of celebrating in a special way at least once a month. Involve your child in preparing the festivities.
- Make ordinary moments special. During the long stretches of "ordinary time," plan a celebration or two, "just because." Have a special dessert at dinner or go out for ice cream "just because God made us a family."
- Create and appreciate family rituals. First, congratulate yourself on the positive family rituals your family has already adopted. You might also consider picking a night of the week as family night—a time for games, watching a movie, telling or reading aloud stories, riding bikes, or doing another fun activity as a family. Make it a time everyone can count on being together.

51

folder). Help them to attach the dial to the circle with a paper fastener. Each day they can spin the dial and choose to find ways to show their yes to God as indicated. Remind them that they can ask Mary to help them say yes to God through their actions. • ***BLM 18 Yes to God***

ACTING

1 Help the children pray the Hail Mary. Tell them that when they know the prayer by heart they may color the cross by the Hail Mary on the inside front cover of their books.

2 Distribute the Hail Mary Prayer Card punchouts. Explain:

• ***To help you remember to ask Mary to help you say yes to God, you will now receive a beautiful picture of her to take home. The prayer card has on it the Hail Mary prayer that we are learning. After you receive the prayer card, return to your seat and ask Mary to help you say yes to God.***

3 Have the children take home the Family Page on **page 50** to share with their families.

CHECKPOINT

- How did the children show that they love Mary as their mother in heaven?
- How will you continue to help the children make good choices?

FAMILY FEATURE

Help the children carefully tear out the Family Feature on **pages 51–52.** Ask them to take home the Family Feature to read and to work on with their families.

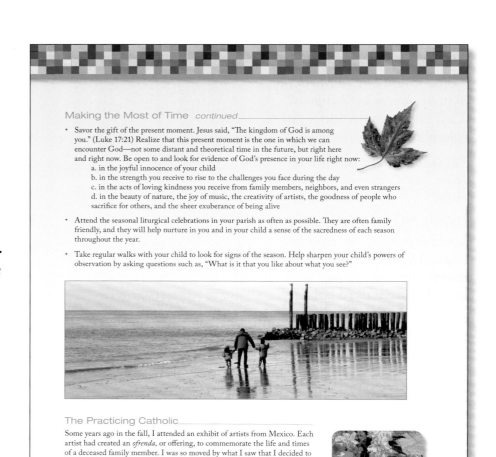

Making the Most of Time *continued*

- Savor the gift of the present moment. Jesus said, "The kingdom of God is among you." (Luke 17:21) Realize that this present moment is the one in which we can encounter God—not some distant and theoretical time in the future, but right here and right now. Be open to and look for evidence of God's presence in your life right now:
  a. in the joyful innocence of your child
  b. in the strength you receive to rise to the challenges you face during the day
  c. in the acts of loving kindness you receive from family members, neighbors, and even strangers
  d. in the beauty of nature, the joy of music, the creativity of artists, the goodness of people who sacrifice for others, and the sheer exuberance of being alive
- Attend the seasonal liturgical celebrations in your parish as often as possible. They are often family friendly, and they will help nurture in you and in your child a sense of the sacredness of each season throughout the year.
- Take regular walks with your child to look for signs of the season. Help sharpen your child's powers of observation by asking questions such as, "What is it that you like about what you see?"

The Practicing Catholic

Some years ago in the fall, I attended an exhibit of artists from Mexico. Each artist had created an *ofrenda,* or offering, to commemorate the life and times of a deceased family member. I was so moved by what I saw that I decided to make an *ofrenda* at home in memory of my father. I gathered photographs and a few other items that he had used and treasured during his life and placed them on the mantle in my living room. As I worked, long-forgotten incidents from my childhood came flooding back, and I remembered my father vividly in specific ways that I had not since he died—things like his twinkly eyes, his laugh, and especially the way his hands looked and felt. This ritual has become my treasured tradition on the Feast of All Souls, partly because of the powerful memories it evokes and partly because I can share them with my children.

Ann O'Connor, author of *The Twelve Unbreakable Principles of Parenting (ACTA Publications)*

Ofrenda for My Father, Ripot Garcia

52

ENRICHING THE FAITH EXPERIENCE

Use the following activities to enrich a lesson, to replace an activity with one that better meets the needs of your class, or to create an additional lesson.

1. Teach a song to the melody of "God Is So Good."

Choosing is good.
(Three times)
Mary said, "Yes, God."

Choose what God wants.
(Three times)
Mary will help us

2. Let the children enjoy listening to the poem "Choosing." You might show a picture of each object named as you read that line.

Choosing

Which will you have, a ball or
a cake?
A cake is so nice, yes, that's
what I'll take.
Which will you have, a cake or
a cat?
A cat is so soft, I think I'll take
that.
Which will you have, a cat or
a rose?
A rose is so sweet, I'll have that,
I suppose.
Which will you have, a rose or
a book?
A book full of pictures—oh, do
let me look!
Which will you have, a book or
a ball?
Oh, a ball! No, a book! No, a—
There! Have them all!

Eleanor Farjeon.

3. Teach a song about Mary, such as "Immaculate Mary" or "I Say 'Yes,' My Lord/ Digo 'Si,' Señor" (*Singing Our Faith*)

4. Invite the children to make ornaments that show Mary's yes to God. Give each child a dessert-size paper plate. Invite them to draw a picture of the angel's visit to Mary in the center of the plate. Have yarn, glue, glitter, and other material available for the children to decorate the outside of the plate. Punch a hole at the top of each paper plate and tie a loop of yarn through the hole.

unit three

Sharing God's Love

In this unit the children will learn to have a greater love for God and seek to share God's love with others through acts of kindness.

13 SHEPHERDS ARE GOOD

The children are led to understand what Jesus meant when he called himself the Good Shepherd, who calls his sheep by name.

14 HEARTS ARE GOOD

The children think about people who love them and how Jesus loves people. They are encouraged to show love as Jesus did.

15 HANDS ARE GOOD

The children explore ways that people help others with their hands. They are inspired to serve others as Jesus did.

16 FORGIVENESS IS GOOD

The children learn to handle their feelings, especially anger, in healthy ways. They are taught to be sensitive to the feelings of others and the importance of asking for forgiveness. They are introduced to the next part of the Our Father.

17 CHURCH IS GOOD

The children learn that a church is sometimes called God's house. They visit a church and learn about several of the furnishings, in particular the baptismal font where they became members of the Church. They discuss the people who make up the Church, which is God's family.

18 MEALS ARE GOOD

The children reflect on meals as a time for sharing love. They learn how bread and wine are made. Then they hear the story of Jesus' Last Supper and are introduced to the Eucharist as the Body and Blood of Jesus.

Chapter 13

Shepherds Are Good

FAITH FOCUS

Jesus, the Good Shepherd, loves and cares for his sheep. Psalm 23; John 10:2–5,14–16

PREPARING THE FAITH EXPERIENCE

LISTENING

Before you begin to prepare this week's lessons, take some time for prayer. Quiet yourself by taking several deep breaths. Become aware of God's presence, for God is with you always. Ask God to open your heart to hear his words to you today.

I am the good shepherd, and I know mine and mine know me, just as the Father knows me and I know the Father; and I will lay down my life for the sheep.

John 10:14–15

REFLECTING

Of all the psalms, possibly the best known is Psalm 23, the Good Shepherd psalm. Its double meaning of loving trust and tender compassion plumbs the very depths of the human soul, evoking a response born of humankind's collective experiences of fear and want, of weariness and dismay, of doubt and despair. The theme of this psalm is echoed throughout Scripture. The inspired Old Testament writers make several references to the love-trust association between a shepherd and his sheep, paralleling it to Yahweh's relationship with his chosen people, Israel:

For this is our God,
whose people we are,
God's well-tended flock.
Psalm 95:7

Centuries later the prophet Ezekiel wrote:

I myself will pasture my sheep; I myself will give them rest, says the Lord God. The lost I will seek out, the strayed I will bring back, the injured I will bind up, the sick I will heal.

Ezekiel 34:15–16

When Christ preached to the crowds and was met by hardened hearts or by incomprehension of his message, he lovingly devised the mercy parables. One of the most touching is the parable of the Good Shepherd. Echoing Ezekiel and the psalmist, Christ not only designated himself a shepherd, but he also proclaimed himself to be a model shepherd—the Good Shepherd, who would one day lay down his life for his sheep and so provide a model for all shepherds of souls throughout the centuries.

For the receptive, Christ's proclamation has been a source of hope, strength, and confidence.

RESPONDING

Having reflected upon God's Word, take some time now to continue to respond to God in prayer. You might wish to use a journal to record your responses throughout this year.

- What aspect of the image of the Good Shepherd appeals most to me?
- How am I like a shepherd for my flock? How do I try to imitate the Good Shepherd?

Good Shepherd, guard and guide me and the children.

Catechism of the Catholic Church

The themes of this lesson correspond to the following paragraphs: 545, 605, 896, 2586, 2602, 2665.

THE FAITH EXPERIENCE

DAY ONE
Shepherds Care for Sheep

DAY TWO
Jesus Is the Good Shepherd

DAY THREE
Jesus Is My Shepherd

DAY FOUR
We Celebrate the Good Shepherd

Scripture in This Chapter

- *Psalm 23:1–4 David claims Yahweh as his shepherd and expresses trust in God's loving care for his sheep.*
- *Ezekiel 34:11–16 God declares that he is the true shepherd of Israel.*

Church Documents

General Directory for Catechesis #219.
National Directory for Catechesis #48, E, 2.

Catechists are pastoral agents, shepherding young people in their growth in faith.

Constitution on the Church #6.
The Church is a flock, which is led and brought to pasture by Christ, who gave his life for his sheep.

Bulletin Board At the left is a suggestion for a bulletin-board design. Draw sheep, one for each child, using white construction paper. You might use Cutout 64–65 Sheep as a pattern. Write each child's name on a sheep. Post the sheep around the bulletin board. Post a picture of Jesus on the bulletin board. You might also post a banner with the words, "Jesus Is My Shepherd."

For a list of children's literature suggestions, please see **page OV-47.**

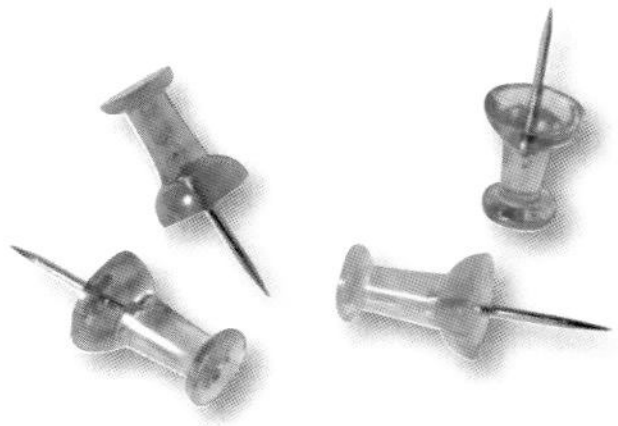

CHAPTER 13 | DAY ONE

Shepherds Care for Sheep

LEARNING OUTCOMES

The children will be able to

- know that shepherds care for sheep.
- realize that God is our shepherd.

KEY TERMS

flock—a group of sheep
pasture—grassy land where sheep eat
rod—club used for protection against wild animals
sheepfold—pen where the sheep stay during the night
shepherd—one who takes care of sheep
staff—long, slender stick, usually with a hook on the end, used in caring for sheep

MATERIALS

- For sheep craft:
  Paper plates (one dinner and one dessert plate for each child)
  Black construction paper
  Crayons or markers
  A handful of cotton balls for each child
  Glue
  Stapler
- Cutouts 13, 41, 59, 60, 62–65
- Green construction paper to represent a pasture
- Blue construction paper to represent a stream

COMMENTS

1. The parable of the Good Shepherd expresses the relationship of love and trust that is possible between humans and Christ. Although few children today have experiences with sheep or shepherds, this parable still interests them. It evokes a sense of peace and inner joy, indicating that the Christian message can satisfy deep needs. Children can relate God's love, as manifested through the Good Shepherd figure, to the love they experience through other people. Although the children will gradually appreciate the meaning of the parable, their eventual understanding of it is facilitated by their early appreciation of it.

2. Prepare a sample of the completed sheep craft before this lesson along with one set of materials for each child.

- Staple a dinner plate to a dessert plate to make the sheep's head and body
- Cut out of black construction paper triangles for ears and tails and rectangles for legs.

CENTERING

1 Recall the last chapter.

- ***We have been talking about choosing. What kinds of things should we choose?*** (What is good, what God wants) ***What word can we say to God?*** (Yes.)
- ***Today you will hear how God leads us to good things.***

2 Show Cutouts 64–65 Sheep to the children. Ask:

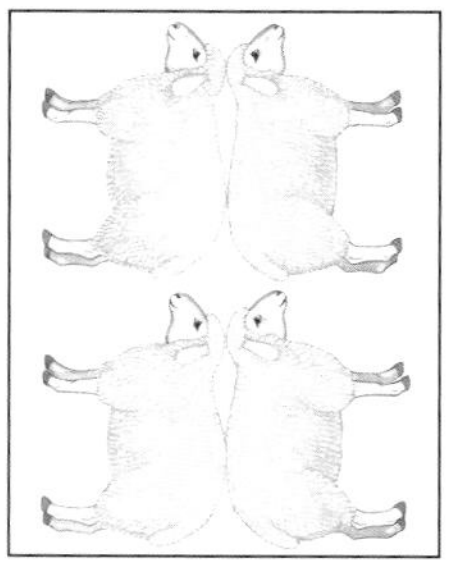

- ***What animals are these?*** (Sheep) ***What sounds do they make?*** (Baa) ***Has anyone ever seen sheep at a farm or in a zoo?***

Allow children to talk about their experiences with sheep.

- ***Why are sheep important to people?*** (People cut sheep's hair, or fleece, and use it to make wool yarn and cloth.) ***It does not hurt the sheep when their hair is cut off. Right away, it slowly starts growing back again.*** [Show the sample sheep craft.] ***Let's make this craft to help us learn more about sheep.***

3 Help the children make sheep from paper plates.

Distribute the necessary materials to each child. Help them glue the ears, legs, and tail in place. Have the children draw faces for their sheep on the small paper plate, using crayons or markers. Have them glue cotton balls to the large paper plate to make the sheep's fleece. Help the children to write their names on their sheep.

Collect and save the sheep craft for use on Day Four.

SHARING

1 Talk about sheep, using the green paper pasture, the blue paper stream, and the other cutouts.

- ***Sheep are very gentle and shy. A group of sheep is called a flock. In some countries, caring for sheep is a very important job. The person who cares for the sheep is called a shepherd.*** [Show Cutout 60 Shepherd.]

- [Set up Cutout 59 Sheepfold with Cutouts 64–65 Sheep.] ***Sheep live in a sheepfold, or sheep pen. They usually stay in the sheepfold at night.***

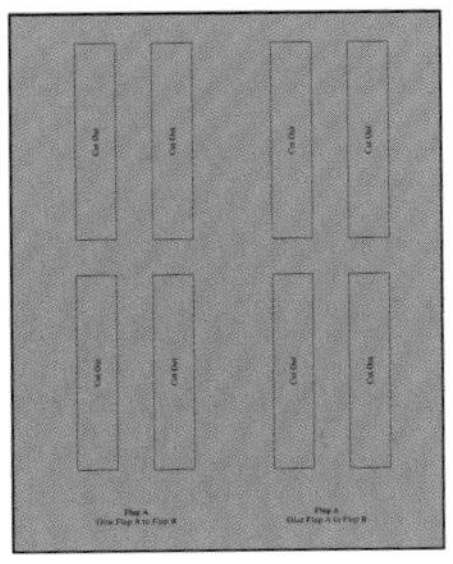

- ***In the morning, the shepherd leads his flock out to green pastures where they can feed on good grass. He calls the sheep by name, and they come because they know his voice.*** [Place the green construction paper down for the pasture.] ***When the sheep have eaten all the grass in one place, the shepherd leads them to a new pasture.***
- ***The shepherd knows where to find clean water. He leads the sheep there for a drink.*** [Place the blue construction paper down for the stream.]

2 Explain what good shepherds do.

- [Show Cutout 13 Wolves.] ***Sheep cannot defend themselves against wild animals. All they can do is run away. A good shepherd protects his sheep. Many shepherds carry a staff.*** [Show Cutout 62 Staff.] ***This is a long, slender stick that often has a hook on one end. A shepherd guides the sheep with his staff to keep them on the right path.***

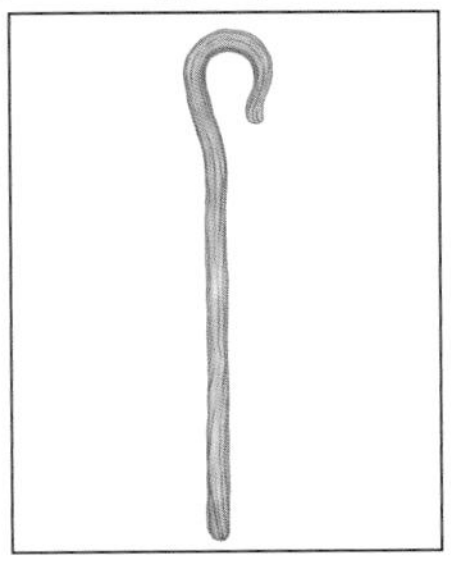

- [Show Cutout 63 Rod.] ***Sometimes a shepherd carries a rod, or club, to protect himself and his sheep from wild animals. Good shepherds sometimes risk their lives defending their sheep.***

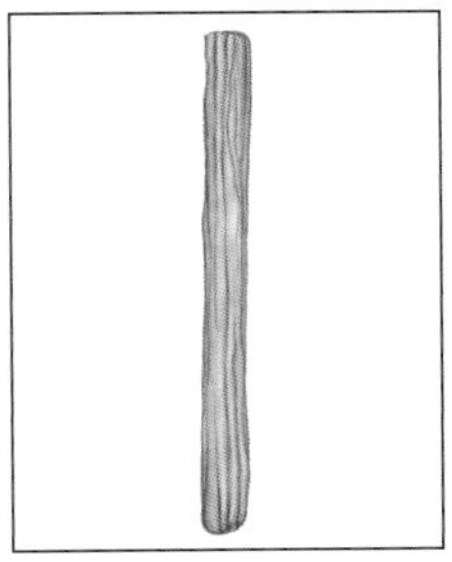

- ***If a sheep gets lost, a good shepherd searches for it until he finds it. He knows that the sheep is probably frightened to be all alone. When the shepherd finds the lost sheep, he brings it back to the flock.***
- ***A good shepherd is always very close to his sheep. They are calm and content when he is near. They know that their shepherd will take care of all their needs. The sheep are very lucky to have a good shepherd.***

3 Check the children's understanding of a shepherd.

- ***Sheep are very helpless animals. When they get lost or hurt, who do you think goes out and looks for these sheep or helps them?*** (The shepherd)

ACTING

Teach and pray with the children the adapted Psalm verse 23:1; including the gestures described below.

- ***We need someone to care for us too. Who cares for us?*** (God) ***David was a great king of God's people long ago. As a boy, he was a shepherd.*** [Show Cutout 41 David playing harp.] ***While he watched over his sheep, he thought about God's care. He prayed this prayer:***

The Lord
[Raise arms up.]
is my shepherd;
[Cradle arms in front. Look down lovingly.]
I shall not want.
[Open arms. Shake head no.]

- ***In this psalm, the words*** **to want** ***mean "to need something." When we pray this prayer, we are saying that God gives us everything that we need.***

CHECKPOINT

- Which part of the lesson most interested the children?
- Did the children demonstrate a new understanding of sheep and shepherds?

CHAPTER 13 | DAY TWO

Jesus Is the Good Shepherd

Student Book pages 53–54

LEARNING OUTCOMES

The children will be able to

- become familiar with Jesus' parable of the Good Shepherd.
- know what a good shepherd does for his sheep.

KEY TERM

Good Shepherd—Jesus

MATERIALS

- Bible enthroned, with note card on which you have written the adapted Scripture reading for SHARING #1, John 10:1–5,14–16
- Cutouts 1, 14, 59–65
- Green construction paper to represent a pasture
- Blue construction paper to represent a stream

COMMENT

When discussing the parable of the Good Shepherd, it is not necessary to tell the children that the sheep represent people. Allow them to come to this realization on their own. If any children mention it themselves, then comment on it.

CENTERING

Show Cutouts 64–65 and let the children tell what they remember about these animals. Ask what the people who care for sheep are called. (Shepherds)

SHARING

1 Read aloud **page 53.** Then show Cutout 1 Jesus. Prepare to tell the parable of the Good Shepherd. Introduce this Bible story by showing the Bible and opening it to the Gospel according to John, John 10:1–5,14–16. Enthrone the Bible. Say:

- ***Let's prepare ourselves to listen well to today's Bible story.*** [Read aloud the parable of the Good Shepherd as found on **page 54.**]

2 [Show Cutout 61 Good Shepherd.] Discuss the parable.

- ***How the Good Shepherd loves his sheep! He has so many sheep, yet he knows each one. He calls them each by name.*** [Pause.]
- ***He cares about each sheep so much that if one is lost, he will leave the rest to search for it. When he finds it, he will lead it back to the flock.*** [Show Cutout 14 lambs.] ***Sometimes, if he finds a lost lamb—or baby sheep—he will gently lift it up and, rejoicing, carry it back in his arms or on his shoulders.*** [Pause.]
- ***Do you know anyone in your family or among your friends who is like the Good Shepherd?*** (Parents, grandparents, teachers)
- ***Jesus' sheep must be very special and important. He knows all of them by name. He loves them so much that he is willing to die for them.***
- ***Why do you think Jesus calls himself a good shepherd who cares for his sheep?*** (He loves and cares for his sheep, just like a good shepherd.)
- ***What is Jesus telling us in this story?*** (He loves his sheep, and he knows them very well.)
- [Make the following comments if some of the children have realized that we are the sheep.] ***If we are the sheep Jesus is talking about, we are very happy indeed. Jesus really loves us. He knows us by name.***

3 Have the children look at **pages 54–55.** Welcome their comments.

4 Teach a song that tells the parable of the Good Shepherd or on the theme of the Good

Shepherd, such as "The Good Shepherd" (*Stories and Songs of Jesus*) or another chosen from the song list on this page.

ACTING

❶ Set up Cutouts 59–65 and the pasture and stream. Retell the story (based on John 10:1–5,14–16), moving the figures accordingly.

- ***Listen to Jesus' story again. Jesus said, "The shepherd enters the sheepfold through the gate. The sheep hear his voice as, one by one, he calls them by name. When the shepherd brings the sheep out, he goes ahead to lead them. The sheep follow because they know his voice. They never follow a stranger. The sheep run away from a stranger because they do not recognize his voice."***
- ***Jesus said, "I know my sheep and my sheep know me. I am willing to die for them. I am the Good Shepherd."***

❷ Invite the children to pray the adapted version of Psalm 23:1 with gestures:

The Lord
[Raise arms up.]
is my shepherd;
[Cradle arms in front. Look down lovingly.]
I shall not want.
[Open arms. Shake head no.]

Songs

Play for the children any of these songs: "The Lord, the Lord, the Lord is My Shepherd" (Singing Our Faith) **CD 1 Track 11**; "Caring," "I Wonder" (*Peaceable Kingdom*); "The Good Shepherd" (*Stories and Songs of Jesus*); "Lead Me, Shepherd, Lead Me" (*Dandelions*); "Psalm of the Good Shepherd" (*Color the World with Song*); "Lead Me, Guide Me," "You Are My Shepherd" (*Singing Our Faith*). For a list of all the music used in this program, see **page OV-39**.

CHECKPOINT

- How did the children respond to the parable of the Good Shepherd?
- Did the children identify themselves with the sheep?

UNIT THREE
CHAPTER 13
Shepherds Are Good
A shepherd loves and cares for his sheep.
53

CHAPTER 13 | DAY THREE

Jesus Is My Shepherd

Student Book page 54

LEARNING OUTCOME

The children will be able to

- appreciate more deeply the significance of the Good Shepherd parable.

MATERIALS

- Poster 6
- For Good Shepherd craft:
  9-inch aluminum pie plates
  Paper banners with the phrase "I am the Good Shepherd"
  Colored construction paper
  Glue
  Markers
- Cutout 65 or a sheep stuffed animal
- Good Shepherd Sets from the punchouts in the Student Book
- Envelopes for children to store their Good Shepherd sets

COMMENT

Before this lesson, prepare a sample of the Good Shepherd picture craft. Also, prepare paper banners for each child with the phrase, "I am the Good Shepherd."

CENTERING

❶ Display Poster 6 Jesus, the Good Shepherd. Let the children look at it quietly for a few moments, and then ask them who the shepherd is (Jesus). Let them comment on the picture.

❷ Tell them that today they will learn even more about the Good Shepherd. Invite them to make a Good Shepherd craft that they can take home to help them remember what they have learned.

Show the children a sample of the craft. Distribute the pie plates and paper banners. Invite the children to draw and cut out figures of a child and a shepherd, using construction paper. Remind them to make their figures small enough to fit on the inside of the pie plate. Help them to glue the figures and the banner to the inside of the pie plate.

SHARING

❶ Distribute the Good Shepherd Set punchouts and help the children set them up. In this activity, instill reverence for the figures, which represent something holy.

❷ Reread the story about the Good Shepherd on **page 54** and have the children move the figures accordingly. Then distribute the envelopes and tell the children to put the figures inside.

❸ Let the children take turns playing the shepherd looking for a lost sheep:

- One child, the shepherd, steps outside the room, while another child hides Cutout 65 or the sheep stuffed animal.
- When the shepherd returns, he or she searches for the lost sheep, and the other children bleat softly like lambs. As the shepherd nears the lost sheep, the children bleat more loudly as a sign that he or she is getting close to finding the sheep. Invite the children to rejoice together when the lost sheep is found.

ACTING

1 Invite the children to close their eyes and quiet their hearts while you read aloud this poem that is a prayer to the Good Shepherd.

Good Shepherd

Oh, Jesus, Good Shepherd,
You watch me with love
You know me by name
And call me with love.
You guard me from evil
And help me do right.
You guide me to safety
By day and by night.
You love and you care,
And give all that I need.
Forever and always
I'll go where you lead.
M. Kathleen Glavich, S.N.D.

2 Suggest that the children tell the story of the Good Shepherd at home, using their punchout sets. Have the children take home their Good Shepherd crafts.

CHECKPOINT

- Are the children becoming familiar with the parable of the Good Shepherd?
- Are more children identifying with the sheep in the parable?

Scripture

Jesus said, "The shepherd of the sheep enters the sheepfold through the gate. He calls the sheep by name.

When the shepherd brings the sheep out, he walks ahead to lead them. The sheep follow because they know his voice."
Based on John 10:1–5

Jesus said, "I am the good shepherd.
I know my sheep.
They know me.
I call them by name.
I am willing to die
for my sheep."
Based on John 10:14–16

54

CHAPTER 13 | DAY FOUR

We Celebrate the Good Shepherd

Student Book pages 55–56

LEARNING OUTCOME

The children will be able to

- experience joy in knowing they are loved by Jesus, the Good Shepherd, and in loving him.

MATERIALS

- Bible enthroned, with note card on which you have written the adapted Scripture reading for SHARING #2, John 10:3,11,27
- Nametags for the paper-plate sheep made on Day One
- Tape or stapler
- Poster 6
- Recording of a Good Shepherd song for SHARING #3 (suggestions found on page T155)
- Crayons or markers

COMMENTS

1. Scripture, liturgy, celebration, and prayer increase our receptiveness to the action of the Spirit. Become familiar with the flow and the mood of the prayer celebration in order to help the children fully enter into the spirit of the prayer.

2. Place Poster 6 where it can be easily removed for the procession and where the children can put their sheep around it.

CENTERING

1 Read aloud the text at the top of **page 55.** Have the children do the activity.

2 Tell the children that today they will celebrate the loving care of Jesus, the Good Shepherd. Redistribute the paper-plate sheep made on Day One. Explain that the children will use their sheep in today's prayer celebration. Ask them to take their sheep with them as they gather in the Prayer Center.

SHARING

1 Call the children to prayer:

- ***Jesus is our Good Shepherd. Today we celebrate his loving care. Close your eyes gently if you want to and make this prayer your own.***
- ***God Our Father, you sent Jesus to be our Good Shepherd. Help us listen to him and follow where he leads. We ask this in the name of Jesus the Lord.***

The LORD is my shepherd: I shall not want.
Psalm 23:1
Shepherding in Families
Jesus loves and cares for us.
We love Jesus, the
Good Shepherd.
Try This
Color the staff and the wolf.
Jesus, the Good Shepherd, knows
you and calls you by name.
What do you want to tell Jesus?
55

Invite the children to respond, "Amen."

2 Open the Bible and read the following passage adapted from John 10:3,11,27. Invite the children to remember what they learned about how to be good listeners.

• ***Let's prepare ourselves to listen well to today's Bible reading.***

• ***Jesus said, "I am the Good Shepherd. I know my sheep. I call them by name. My sheep know me. I am willing to die for my sheep." (John 10:3,11, 27)***

3 Lead the children in a procession in honor of the Good Shepherd. Hold Poster 6. Invite the children to follow you as they carry their sheep. Play a Good Shepherd song. If this is the song taught on Day Two, the children may choose to sing during the procession.

• ***Jesus, the Good Shepherd, knows his sheep and calls them, one by one, by name. Then he goes ahead, and they follow him. When I call your name, you may take your sheep and line up behind me. When all of you are in line, I shall lead you around the room with the beautiful Good Shepherd picture. Walk quietly or sing while following the Good Shepherd.***

Lead the procession around the classroom and return to the Prayer Center.

4 Invite the children to pray with you:

• ***God Our Father loves and cares for us. He gives us everything we need. He gives us Jesus to be our Good Shepherd.***

• ***We need never be afraid. Jesus will take care of us. We need never feel unloved. Jesus wants us and calls us by name. He loves us.***

• ***Now, you may put your sheep gently near the picture of Jesus, the Good Shepherd. As you do, you may choose to say something to Jesus.***

Call each child by name. Invite him or her to pray by asking questions such as What would you like to say to Jesus, the Good Shepherd? Would you like to thank Jesus for something?

ACTING

1 Invite the children to pray:

• ***Jesus, you love us and call us by name. Thank you for your loving care. We will try to follow your way of love. Amen.***

Invite the children to pray the adapted version of Psalm 23:1 with gestures:

The Lord
[Raise arms up.]
is my shepherd;
[Cradle arms in front. Look down lovingly.]
I shall not want.
[Open arms. Shake head no.]

2 Have the children take home the Family Page on **page 56** to share with their families.

CHECKPOINT

• How did the children respond to the celebration?

ENRICHING THE FAITH EXPERIENCE

Use the following activities to enrich a lesson, to replace an activity with one that better meets the needs of your class, or to create an additional lesson.

1 Instill in the children a love and respect for animals as creatures of God. Remind them that animals are creatures of God so we must never abuse them or hurt them. Each animal gives praise to God in its own way. God has placed the earth, including its plants and animals, in our care.

2 Let the children draw pictures of their pets and tell how they take care of them. Children who do not have pets may draw a favorite animal.

3 Invite the children to dramatize the story of the Good Shepherd.

4 Play a game such as "Follow the Leader" or "Simon Says." Remind the children that we follow Jesus, the Good Shepherd.

Chapter 14

Hearts Are Good

FAITH FOCUS

Jesus loves us and wants us to love others.

John 13:34; John 21:2–13

PREPARING THE FAITH EXPERIENCE

LISTENING

As you prepare to share God's Word of love with the children, spend some quiet time with God in prayer. Relax your body, quiet your mind, and let yourself be aware that you are filled with God's love. Ask God to speak to you his Word of love.

I give you a new commandment: love one another. As I have loved you, so you also should love one another. This is how all will know that you are my disciples, if you have love for one another.

John 13:34,35

REFLECTING

The author of the Johannine letters summed up his intimate relationship with Christ in one sentence: "God is love, and whoever remains in love remains in God and God in him."

(1 John 4:16)

To give oneself to another in love, however, can be risky. Rejection of one's ideas hurts deeply, but rejection of one's heart offered in love leaves a far deeper and longer-lasting wound. Rejection can be a source of lasting pain for the human person. Even the mere suspicion or fear of one's heart being spurned often paralyzes the human spirit. Since ancient times, the word *heart* has denoted not only the physical organ, but also the center of a person's intellect, will, and emotions.

Metaphorically, then, *heart* means "person." And so when one gives one's heart in love to another, the entire person is given, and the *entire* person, therefore, stands in danger of rejection.

As though to reassure his frightened, hesitant children, our loving Father tenderly tells us that we are to love because he has loved us first. He assures us that he loved us first, loved us into existence. He has loved us when we have wandered away from him in sin, loved us even to giving us his only Son as our savior, and he will love us unto eternity. His call is to not fear the risk, but to give our love, our hearts, in return.

It is precisely because this affectionate Father has taken the initiative and revealed his faithful love, preeminently through the heart of Christ his Son, that we are enabled to reciprocate that love and to share it with others. And it is this love for one another that has become the hallmark of true Christian discipleship.

RESPONDING

God's Word calls us to respond in love. Respond to God now in the quiet of your heart and perhaps through a journal that you are keeping this year.

- How can the children see in my actions an example of Christian love?

Spirit of Love, enkindle in me and in the children the fire of your love.

Catechism of the Catholic Church
The themes of this lesson correspond to the following paragraphs: 1931–1933, 1970.

THE FAITH EXPERIENCE

DAY ONE
We Are Loved

DAY TWO
Jesus Loves

DAY THREE
We Love

DAY FOUR
We Make a Love Gift

Scripture in This Chapter

- *Jeremiah 31:3 Yahweh reminds Israel of his age-old love and mercy.*
- *1 Corinthians 13 This entire chapter consists of Saint Paul's magnificent hymn about Christian love.*

Church Documents
General Directory for Catechesis #115.
National Directory for Catechesis #25, G.
The message transmitted by catechesis must include the double commandment of love of God and love of neighbor.

Decree on the Apostolate of the Laity #8.
Christ made love of neighbor his personal commandment and the distinguishing mark of his disciples.

In All Things Charity #III.
The great dual command to love God and neighbor forms the basis of all Christian morality.

The theme of this chapter corresponds well to Valentine's Day. This chapter can be taught during the week or two before Valentine's Day. Lesson 18 on Saint Valentine in SPECIAL SEASONS AND DAYS can be correlated with this chapter.

Bulletin Board At the left is a suggestion for a bulletin-board design. Have the children draw pictures of how they show love to others. Post their drawings on the bulletin board. You might include a banner with the words, "I Love You."

For a list of children's literature suggestions, please see **page OV-47.**

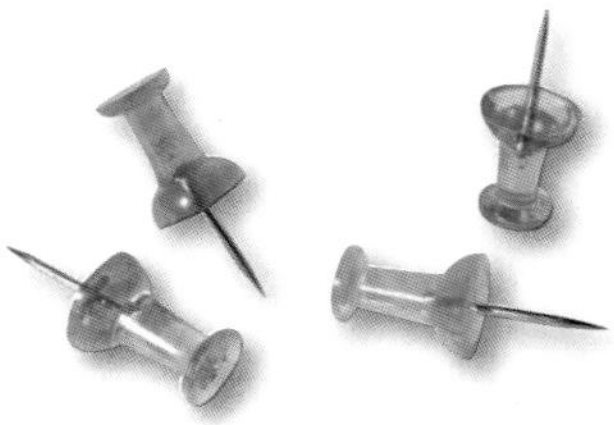

We Are Loved

Student Book pages 57–58

LEARNING OUTCOMES

The children will be able to

- look upon themselves as worthwhile persons who are loved by God and by others.
- realize that love is shown through actions.

MATERIALS

- Cutout 4
- Hearts cut from red construction paper, one for each child
- 1 large heart cut from red poster board
- Crayons or markers (several red and pink if possible)
- Tape
- Drawing paper

COMMENT

Children who love themselves and consider themselves individuals worthy of love will find it easier to reach out in love to God and to others. Therefore, in every meeting with the children, endeavor to instill attitudes of self-acceptance by affirming each child whenever the occasion presents itself. We help children become loving and lovable by loving them.

CENTERING

1 Recall the last chapter.

- ***You learned about sheep and shepherds. What kind of shepherd did Jesus call himself?*** (The Good Shepherd) ***Why is Jesus a good shepherd?*** (He loves and cares for us. He gave his life for us.)
- ***Today you will learn more about God's care for us.***

2 Show Cutout 4 Heart. Say:

- ***The gift of love is so precious that no amount of money can buy it.***
- ***Others can also give the gift of love to you. It makes you very happy.***
- ***You can give this gift to others. It makes others happy.***
- ***This gift cannot be seen.***
- ***The more of this gift you give away, the more of it you have.***

3 Distribute one paper heart to each child. Ask:

- ***The heart is a symbol of love. Do you know what the heart reminds us of?*** (God's gift of love)

Display the large heart cut from poster board.

SHARING

1 Tell the children about people who love you, and invite those children who wish to, to tell about people who love them. Ask them how they feel when someone gives them the gift of love. Say:

- ***We feel happy when we know that people love us. Our love for others also brings happiness.***

2 Invite the children to make this craft as a symbol of their loving hearts. Using the hearts you distributed above, have the children draw a picture of Jesus on one side. On the other side, have them draw pictures of family members, friends, and other people they love. Guide them to write their names on the hearts.

Have the children thank God for the people who love them. Let each child hold the heart he or she made as he or she says a prayer. Lead the children by saying:

- ***I would like to thank God for giving me people to love and for giving me people who love me.*** [Hold the heart.] ***Thank you, God, for*** (Names) ***who love me.***

When the children have finished their prayers, invite them to tape their craft hearts onto the large poster-board heart, which represents God's love.

3 Ask the children to open their books to **page 57.** Read aloud the text. Discuss:

- ***Jesus loved his Father in heaven. He prayed to him. He did what his Father wanted. Jesus showed God's love to people.***
- ***What are some things that Jesus did to show God's love to people?*** (He told them

about his Father. He blessed little children. He healed sick people. He forgave people.)

- ***Jesus loves all people.***

❹ Help the children understand that love extends beyond just words and feelings.

- ***Loving is more than just saying, "I love you," or having a happy feeling inside. Love is showing that you really mean the words you say.***
- [Show the picture on **page 58.**] ***How are the children showing love?*** (They are hugging each other.)
- ***What else do people do for others to show their love?*** (Do special things for them; help them; share things with them.)

ACTING

Teach and invite the children to pray the adapted version of Psalm 36:6 with gestures:

> **Lord,**
> [Raise arms outward.]
> **your kindness**
> [Cross hands over heart.]
> **reaches to heaven.**
> [Extend right arm up.]

CHECKPOINT

- Are the children aware of the people who love them and of God's great love for them?
- Are there children in this group who need extra attention because they seem to be insecure about their self-worth?

Songs

Play for the children any of these songs: "Love One Another" (*Singing Our Faith*) **CD 1 Track 6;** "Love One Another" (*Sing a Song of Joy!*) **CD 2 Track 4;** "We Are Little Gifts" (*Sing a Song of Joy!*) **CD 2 Track 6;** "God Loves Little People" (*Sing a Song of Joy!*) **CD 2 Track 8;** "God's Love" (*Sing a Song of Joy!*) **CD 2 Track 14;** "Handle with Care" (*Peaceable Kingdom*); "Happy the Heart," "I Like God's Love," "Love That Is Kept Inside," "Thank You, Lord" (*Hi God!*); "If I Were a Butterfly," "This Is My Commandment" (*Hi God 2*); "God's Circle of Love" (*Hi God 3*); "Put on Love," "Things That Money Can't Buy" (*Songs for Young Children*); "How Much God Loves Us" (*Stories and Songs of Jesus*); "God's Love" (*Big Steps for Little Feet*); "Jesus, You Love Us" (*Calling the Children*); "God Is Love" (*Sing a Song of Joy!*); "Jesus and His Friends Have Breakfast on the Beach," "Together We'll Share" (*More Stories and Songs of Jesus*); "This Is My Commandment" (*Singing Our Faith*); "Put on Love," "Things That Money Can't Buy" (*Best of Mary Lu Walker*). For a list of all the music used in this program, see **page OV-39.**

CHAPTER 14

Hearts Are Good

Love is a special gift God puts in our hearts.
God's love makes us happy.
God sent Jesus into the world to show us his love.

57

CHAPTER 14 | DAY TWO

Jesus Loves

Student Book pages 57–58

LEARNING OUTCOMES

The children will be able to

- become more aware of Jesus' love for them and for all people.
- know that God wants them to love others.

MATERIALS

- Bible enthroned, with note card on which you have written the adapted Scripture reading for SHARING #3, John 13:34
- *A Child's Bible*, page 27

COMMENT

Christian love is a gift from the Father given to us through Jesus Christ. Jesus gives this gift as a "new commandment": to love one another as he loves us. This love for one another is a sign of the continued presence of Jesus among us through the Holy Spirit. Jesus speaks of his love as a "new commandment" because God's love was fully revealed to us in Jesus. Only in him can we know what genuine love is.

CENTERING

1 Invite the children to pray the adapted version of Psalm 36:6 with gestures:

Lord,
[Raise arms outward.]
your kindness
[Cross hands over heart.]
reaches to heaven.
[Extend right arm up.]

2 Read aloud **page 57**. Discuss Jesus' love.

- ***What are some loving things Jesus did for people?*** (He blessed children. He gave bread to hungry people. He healed sick people. He was a friend to those who were in need and showed he cared about them. Jesus comforted those who were sad. He forgave those who were sorry for doing wrong.)
- ***You remember that Jesus called himself the Good Shepherd because he takes such good care of us.***
- ***What did Jesus say he was willing to do for his sheep?*** (Die for them)

SHARING

1 Prepare to read or to tell the story "Breakfast on the Beach" from *A Child's Bible*, **page 27.** Say:

- ***Jesus lived his life showing God's love to all people. The Bible has many stories about how Jesus helped people. In this story, Jesus helped his friends, the disciples, who were fishermen. Let's listen carefully to learn how Jesus helped his friends in this story.***

Introduce this Bible story by showing the Bible and opening it to the Gospel according to John, John 21:1–14. Enthrone the Bible.

- ***Let's prepare ourselves to listen well to today's Bible story.***

Read or tell the story "Breakfast on the Beach" from *A Child's Bible*, **page 27.** Discuss how Jesus showed love in action:

- ***What did Jesus do for his friends while they were in their fishing boats?*** (He told them where to throw the nets so that they could catch more fish.)
- ***What did Jesus and his friends do after they hauled in the fish?*** (They shared breakfast together.)

2 Have the children turn to **page 58** in their books. Read it aloud. Explain how Jesus shows us his love today.

- ***Jesus loves people today. He listens when they talk to him. He speaks to them in their hearts. He gives them all the good things they have.***
- ***We see the love of Jesus in the people who love us. He puts his love into the hearts of our mothers, fathers, teachers, brothers, sisters, friends, and many others. When others love us, they share Jesus' love with us.***

3 Introduce Jesus' teaching about love. Say:

- ***One of the most important things Jesus taught his disciples was about love. I want you to listen carefully to what Jesus told his disciples. This is found in the Bible. It is found in the part of the Bible called the Gospels. When we hear the Gospel, we respond by offering***

praise to Jesus with the words, "Praise to you, Lord Jesus Christ." Let's practice that so we can respond when we hear this Gospel reading. Have the children repeat the response.

Invite the children to remember what they learned about how to be good listeners.

- ***Let's prepare ourselves to listen well to this Bible reading.***

Read the new commandment based on John 13:34.

- ***Jesus said: "My little children, I give you a new commandment: Love one another, just as I have loved you. By this love you have for one another, everyone will know you are my friends." Let us praise Jesus for giving us a new commandment to love as he loves. Say after me, "Praise to you, Lord Jesus Christ."***

- ***Those who love us are doing what Jesus told everyone to do: "Love one another just as I have loved you." You can love with Jesus' love too.***

4 Tell the children that you would like to show them something very important about Jesus' love. One by one, invite the children to join you in making a circle. When all the children have joined the circle, observe how easy it was to make the circle bigger so that everyone could join in. Even now more people could easily be added to the circle. Tell the children that Jesus' love is like a circle:

- ***We can always make our circle bigger. Jesus' love never runs out. We can always share Jesus' love with others and still have a place in our circle.***

ACTING

While in the circle, teach a song about God's love, such as "Love That Is Kept Inside" (*Hi God!*) or "God's Circle of Love" (*Hi God 3*) or pray together the adapted version of Psalm 36:6 with gestures:

LORD,
[Raise arms outward.]
your kindness
[Cross hands over heart.]
reaches to heaven.
[Extend right arm up.]

CHECKPOINT

- How do the children show love for others?

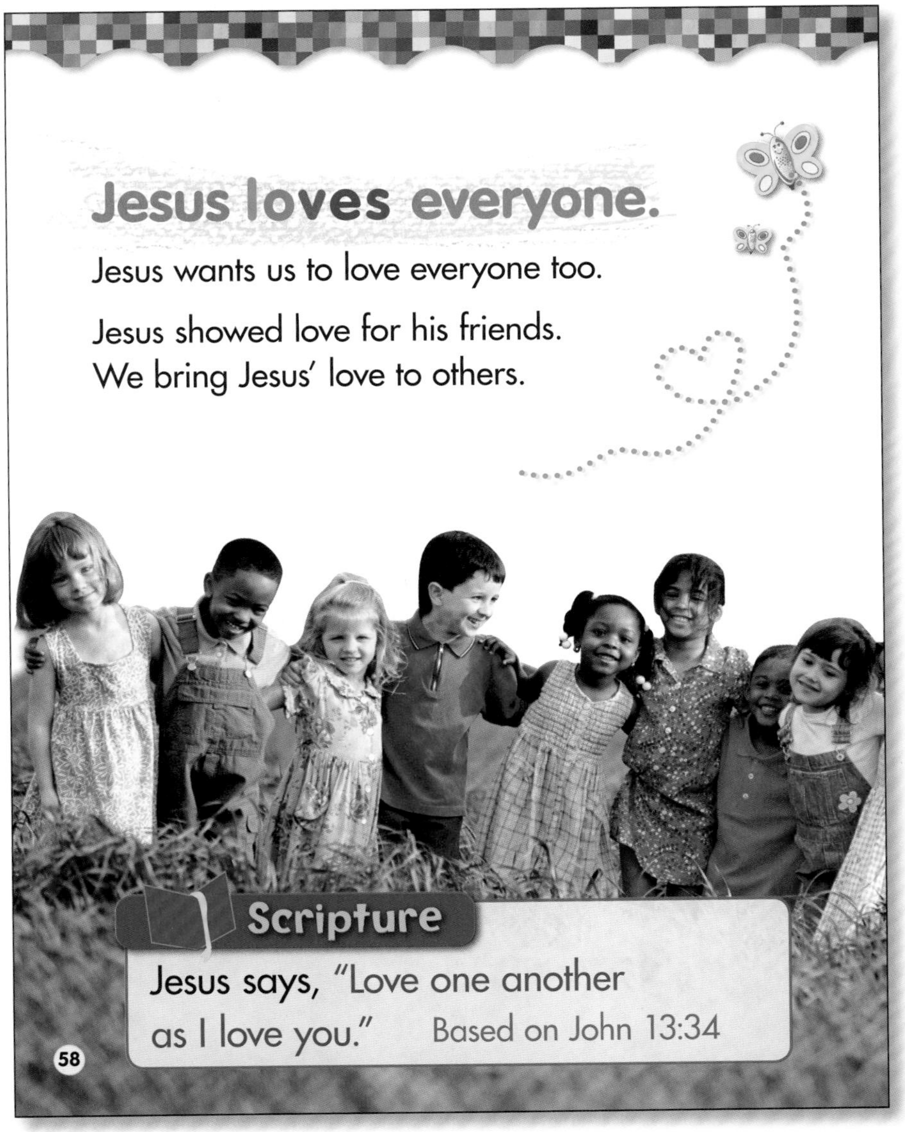
Jesus loves everyone.
Jesus wants us to love everyone too.
Jesus showed love for his friends.
We bring Jesus' love to others.
Scripture
Jesus says, "Love one another as I love you." Based on John 13:34
58

CHAPTER 14 | DAY THREE

We Love

Student Book pages 58–59

LEARNING OUTCOMES

The children will be able to
- be aware of specific ways they can show love.
- desire to be more loving in their words and deeds.

MATERIALS
- BLM 19
- Crayons or markers
- Song about love for ACTING #1 (See song list found on page T163)

CENTERING

❶ Recall the Bible story, "Breakfast on the Beach," from *A Child's Bible*, **page 27:**

- ***What did Jesus do for his friends while they were in their fishing boats?*** (He told them where to throw the nets so that they could catch more fish.)
- ***What did Jesus and his friends do after they hauled in the fish?*** (They shared breakfast together.)

❷ Read aloud **page 59** and guide the children in doing the activity.

SHARING

❶ Read **page 58** again for the children, leaving off the last three words of the Scripture quotation for them to finish. (I love you.) Comment:

- ***We have many chances to love like Jesus each day.***

❷ Have the children role-play people showing love. After each skit, ask the children who in the play showed love and how. Read aloud each play and call on volunteers to act it out.

- ***Amir's mother is very busy getting supper ready. The table needs to be set. Amir and his sister, Sari, are watching cartoons on TV. His mother asks him to set the table. What should he do to show love for his mother and his family?***
- ***Dawn likes to play with her toys, but she doesn't like to put them away. Dawn's family has a rule that everyone must put away his or her toys after playing with them. Dawn and her friends Joshua and Taylor have finished playing with the toys. How can Dawn and her friends show love for Dawn's family?***
- ***Andy likes to knock down blocks. When he knocked down Thea's castle yesterday, she started to cry. Today Thea made a very high tower. Andy feels like knocking it down. What should Andy do to show love for Thea?***
- ***Sarah, Elliot, and Miguel are having fun playing tag on the playground. They see Tim standing alone, with no one to play with. He looks sad. How can the children show love for Tim?***
- ***David is playing with a farm set. Jasmine and Maya want to play with the farm set too. What could David do to show love for Jasmine and Maya?***

❸ Distribute copies of BLM 19 Loving Hearts and help the children identify ways to show love.

- ***BLM 19 Loving Hearts***

ACTING

1 Teach the poem "Love" or sing a song about God's love (see the song list on **page T163** for suggestions).

Love

God loves me,
[Clap, clap, point to self.]
And I love you.
[Clap, clap, point forward.]
We show love
[Clap, clap, fold hands over heart.]
By what we do.
[Clap, clap, hold out hands.]
M. Kathleen Glavich, S.N.D.

2 Invite the children to enter into their quiet hearts and ask Jesus to help them be more loving. Introduce the closing prayer:

- ***Jesus loves you. He wants you to share his love with others. We can ask Jesus to help us.***

Guide the children to pray this prayer, asking Jesus to help them show love to others:

- ***Quiet helps us pray. We can meet Jesus deep within our quiet hearts. Let us prepare ourselves to meet Jesus.***
- ***Straighten your back.*** [Pause.]
- ***Rest your arms on your lap, hands open in front of you.*** [Pause.]
- ***You may gently close your eyes if you want to.*** [Pause.]
- ***Slowly breathe in and out, in and out, in and out.*** [Pause.]
- ***Deep within you, see Jesus sitting next to you.*** [Pause.]
- ***In the quiet of your heart, thank Jesus for his love. Tell Jesus how you feel when you think about his love for you.*** [Pause.]
- ***Ask Jesus to help you share his love with others. Tell Jesus one thing that you will do to share his love with someone else.*** [Pause.]
- ***When you are finished praying, open your eyes.***

CHECKPOINT

- Were the children able to identify ways to show love to others?

Try This

- Connect the dots from 1 to 10.
- See what Jesus gave his friends.
- Color it.
- Draw a fire on the sticks where Jesus cooked breakfast for his friends.

Thank God for the gift of love.

59

CHAPTER 14 | DAY FOUR

We Make a Love Gift

Student Book page 60

LEARNING OUTCOME

The children will be able to
- anticipate giving joy to others by presenting a gift of love.

MATERIALS
- Cutout 4
- Heart with Jesus' Name punchouts from the Student Book
- Hole punch
- Pieces of yarn 22 inches long, one for each child
- For each heart basket craft:
  - Two 6-inch circles cut from construction paper
  - A 1-inch by 8-inch strip of construction paper for handle
  - Glue or stapler
  - Crayons or markers
  - Sample heart-basket craft
  - Small treats for the heart baskets (optional)

COMMENT

Instead of making heart baskets, the children might make chains. of love. See ENRICHING THE FAITH EXPERIENCE #2.

CENTERING

1 Invite the children to pray the adapted version of Psalm 36:6 with gestures:

> **Lord,**
> [Raise arms outward.]
> **your kindness**
> [Cross hands over heart.]
> **reaches to heaven.**
> [Extend right arm up.]

2 Show Cutout 4 Heart and recall God's gift of love.

- ***What wonderful gift has God given us that makes us happy?*** (Love)
- ***What happens when we give love to others?*** (We grow in love. We are happy.)

3 Show the children a sample of the heart basket. Explain:

- ***Today you will make something that you can give to someone to show your love. Giving gifts to others is one way that we can show our love.***

SHARING

Show the children how to make a heart-shaped basket. Fold in half two 6-inch circles of construction paper. Join the folded circles together at one end to form a heart. Have the sides of one circle overlap the other to form a basket. Glue the circles together. Make a handle by cutting and gluing a 1-inch by 8-inch strip of paper to the inside of the basket where the two halves meet. The basket can be decorated with a message such as "Jesus loves you." Small treats can be added.

ACTING

1 Distribute the Heart with Jesus' Name punchouts. Have the children write their names on the blank side of the hearts. Punch a hole in the heart and string it with a loop of yarn to make a pendant. Collect the pendants for use in the closing prayer.

- ***Each of you will receive a heart pendant.*** [Show Jesus' name on one.] ***Whose name is on this side of the pendant?*** (Jesus') ***Your name is on the other side. Jesus has put his love into your heart. You can bring Jesus' love to others. Wearing the heart pendant can help you remember this.***

2 Invite the children to gather in the Prayer Center.

- Sing together a song chosen from the song list on **page T163.**

- Proclaim the Scripture, John 13:34:

Invite the children to remember what they learned about how to be good listeners.

- ***Let's prepare ourselves to listen well to this Bible reading.***

Read the new commandment based on John 13:34.

- ***Jesus said: "My little children, I give you a new commandment: Love one another, just as I have loved you. By this love you have for one another, everyone will know you are my friends." Let us praise Jesus for giving us a new commandment to love as he loves. Say after me, "Praise to you, Lord Jesus Christ."***

- Present the heart pendants: Call each child forward and present the heart pendants to the children as you say: "[Name], love others as Jesus loves you."

- Close by singing the song together again.

- Have the children take home their heart baskets as a gift for someone they love.

3 Have the children take home the Family Page on **page 60** to share with their families.

CHECKPOINT

- How have the children tried to show love?

Lord, your kindness reaches to heaven.
Based on Psalm 36:6

Loving in Families

The Lesson Your Child Learned

God's love was fully revealed to us in Jesus. The Christian religion is based on a love relationship between God and the human person. We want our children to realize that God loves them personally. They learn to accept themselves as persons worthy to be loved by God and by others. In this chapter the children heard again about God's great love for them as shown through Jesus and through the loving people God places in their lives. They were invited to share in Jesus' love by showing love for others. They heard about Jesus' love for his friends in the story of the large catch of fish and cooking breakfast. (John 21:1–14)

Living the Lesson

Think of all the books, movies, TV shows, songs, and soap operas that gain dramatic tension by observing two people on the verge of falling in love. They capture and convey a longing that seems universal, as if the whole world is holding its breath, waiting for love to erupt in their lives.

This great longing is holy. It's a manifestation of our desire to know and to experience God's love for us. God placed this desire to know, love, and serve him deep in our hearts. God also sent his Son, the embodiment of divine love, as the true response to our deepest longing.

As parents we are in a position to teach our children about love by simply loving them well. At our best, we model the love of God in our own love. When we tend to our children when they're sick, listen to them when they are troubled, share their joy during play, and nurture their bodies, minds, and souls, we are preparing them to live a life of love. They become ready to expect God's love and are more likely to see signs of it all around them.

–Tom McGrath, author of *Raising Faith-Filled Kids* (Loyola Press)

Bringing the Lesson Home

- Read with your child the pages from this chapter that were sent home.
- Ask your child to tell you about the heart pendant he or she received as a reminder to love as Jesus did.
- Encourage your child's efforts to show love and care for others at home, in the neighborhood, and at school. Notice times your child acts with loving kindness and commend him or her. Be specific.
- In secret, say or do something today to make every member of your family feel loved and appreciated.

60

ENRICHING THE FAITH EXPERIENCE

Use the following activities to enrich a lesson, to replace an activity with one that better meets the needs of your class, or to create an additional lesson.

1 Show pictures of people being loving. Let the children select one and tell who is being loved and how the person knows he or she is loved.

2 Teach the children how to make chains of love, which they may wear as a reminder to show love for others or which they may give away as a gift.

Materials for each chain:

- 30-inch piece of yarn, one end wrapped with transparent tape
- 2 drinking straws cut into 1 1/2-inch pieces for beads
- 10 small stickers

Directions:

- Put stickers on some of the straw pieces.
- String the beads, using the taped end of the yarn. Suggest that the children make patterns as they string the beads.

3 Teach the children the "Sharing Poem."

Sharing Poem

When we're munching on a
treat,
And our friend has none to eat,
What do we do?
We share. [Clap, clap]
We share. [Clap, clap]

When we're paging through
a book,
And our sister wants a look,
What do we do?
We share. [Clap, clap]
We share. [Clap, clap]

When we're watching the TV,
And there's a show Dad wants
to see,
What do we do?
We share. [Clap, clap]
We share. [Clap, clap]

When we're bouncing a
new ball,
And someone's playing not
at all,
What do we do?
We share. [Clap, clap]
We share. [Clap, clap]

When we're playing with a toy,
And here comes a girl or boy,
What do we do?
We share. [Clap, clap]
We share. [Clap, clap]

M. Kathleen Glavich, S.N.D.

4 Have the children create heart pictures. Distribute crayons or markers, glue, construction paper, and hearts cut from red construction paper. Show samples to give the children ideas of what they might make.

5 Plan a Senior Citizen's or Grandparent's Day. Prepare a simple program for the visitors, such as a skit, poems, or songs. Let the children make cards or another surprise to give their guests.

6 You might treat the children by giving them heart-shaped sugar cookies. Be sure to find out if any children have food allergies and take them into account when planning snacks.

Chapter 15

Hands Are Good

FAITH FOCUS

Jesus calls us to help others.

Matthew 20:29–34

PREPARING THE FAITH EXPERIENCE

LISTENING

Those who share God's Word with others must be fed themselves by God's Word found in Sacred Scripture. Share some time of quiet prayer with God, listening to God's word. Ask God to fill you with his presence and nourish you by his holy Word.

Rather, whoever wishes to be great among you shall be your servant; whoever wishes to be first among you shall be your slave. Just so, the Son of Man did not come to be served but to serve and to give his life as a ransom for many.

Matthew 20:26–28

REFLECTING

The human hand is a testimonial to God's creative genius. Hands can caress in love, clasp in friendship, fold in prayer, or clench in anger or withdrawal.

During his earthly life, Christ chose to use his hands to serve others, so much so that he was able to say of himself: "For the Son of Man did not come to be served but to serve." (Mark 10:45) Just before making this statement, Jesus had issued a challenge to his quarreling disciples on their aspirations to greatness: those who wished to rank first had to serve the needs of the rest.

By the gift of his hands in ministry to others, Christ set the example of service for his apostles and for all Christians. The work of Christ's hands also manifested his divine power. He took a dead girl by the hand and her life came rushing back; he touched blind eyes and deaf ears to restore sight and hearing. His raised hand calmed a raging sea; that same hand blessed a few loaves and some fish to provide food for hungry thousands. Today, Christ's ministry of healing, comforting, and caring continues through the dedicated hands of countless men and women the world over.

Paradoxically, Christ's supreme moment of service to the human race came when his hands were powerless, nailed to a cross. Perhaps through those motionless hands, Christ was telling his followers that, in addition to active ministry to others, for some the greatest service to humankind may be helpless immobility, accepted in love.

RESPONDING

Having been nourished by God's word, we are able to respond to his great love for us. In prayer, respond to God's call to you to share his word with others. You may also wish to respond in your prayer journal.

- How do I serve others in the course of my day?

Jesus, may the children and I imitate you in acts of loving service.

Catechism of the Catholic Church

The themes of this lesson correspond to the following paragraphs: 2208, 2444, 2447.

THE FAITH EXPERIENCE

DAY ONE
Hands Are Gifts

DAY TWO
People Use Their Hands to Help Others

DAY THREE
Jesus Helped People

DAY FOUR
We Can Have Helping Hands

Scripture in This Chapter

- *John 13:15–16 At the Last Supper, Christ reminded his apostles that their greatness would consist of serving others as he did.*
- *Romans 12:6–7 God has given us a variety of gifts to be used in ministering to others.*

Church Documents

National Directory for Catechesis #45, G.
Catechesis should encourage the practice of works of charity.

Pastoral Constitution on the Church in the Modern World #88.
The Church challenges us to volunteer our services in help to others and to make sacrifices so as to relieve the sufferings of others.

On Social Concern #39.
The virtue of solidarity enables us to see other people as our neighbors and helpers.

Bulletin Board At the left is a suggestion for a bulletin-board design. Have the children trace their hands or make handprints using finger paints. You might include a banner with the words, "Hands Are Good."

For a list of children's literature suggestions, please see **page OV-47.**

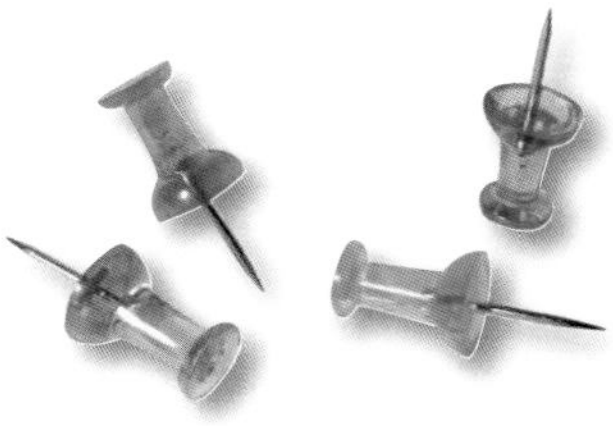

CHAPTER 15 | DAY ONE

Hands Are Gifts

LEARNING OUTCOMES

The children will be able to

- reflect on what their two hands enable them to do.
- appreciate the gift of their hands.

MATERIALS

- Washable stamp pads or finger paints
- Paper
- Crayons or pencils
- Cleaning supplies

COMMENT

Be sure that the stamp pads and finger paints the children will be working with are washable and that there are plenty of cleaning supplies available when the activities are completed.

CENTERING

1 Recall the last chapter.

- ***In the last chapter you learned that God gave us the gift of love. What does God ask us to do?*** (To give his love to others)
- ***Very often we give our love to others by doing things for them with our hands.***

2 Show the children how to make fingerprint pictures using stamp pads or finger paints. Show how these can be made into pictures. Show the children how to make hearts by joining two thumbprints together. Allow the children to make several fingerprint pictures and hearts. Guide them to write their names on their pictures.

SHARING

1 Lead the children to reflect on their hands.

- ***Who gave you your hands?*** (God)
- ***God made your hands just for you. No one has hands exactly like yours. Look at the lines on the palms of your hands and on your fingertips. God made your fingerprints your very own. No one in the whole world has fingerprints exactly like yours. This is one way God makes each person special.***

Allow time for the children to compare their fingerprint pictures to see their uniqueness.

2 Have the children think about what they can do with their hands.

- ***What are some good things you do with your hands?*** (Build or make things, draw or color a picture, help others)
- ***God gave us hands to do good things, loving things. But sometimes we let our hands do things that are not good. What might some of these things be?*** (Hurt others, take things without permission) ***What can we tell God when we use the gift of our hands to do things that are wrong?*** (I'm sorry.)

3 Encourage the children to learn some good things their hands can do. Teach them the following finger play or another familiar finger play such as "Where Is Thumbkin?"

I Can Knock with My Two Hands

I can knock with my two hands;
Knock, knock, knock!
[Pantomime knocking on a door.]
I can rock with my two hands;
Rock, rock, rock.
[Tap fists against each other.]
I can pat with my two hands;
Pat, pat, pat.
[Pat belly.]
I can clap with my two hands;
Clap, clap, clap.
[Clap hands.]

4 Read this poem to the children. Then read it again, inviting them to act out each line.

My Hands

My hands can clap or bounce
a ball,
Gently touch a furry kitten.
They help to feed me
chocolate cake
And sometimes find a fallen
mitten.
My hands put rubber boots
on me.
They write my name with
letters straight.
I lift them when I talk to God
To praise the one who is so
great.

ACTING

Invite the children to lift their hands in prayer and join in thanking God for the gift of their hands. Begin each sentence "Thank you, God, for my hands that let me . . ." Invite volunteers to complete each prayer.

CHECKPOINT

- Were there signs that the children appreciated the uniqueness of their hands?
- Were the children able to identify good, loving things that their hands can do?

Songs

Play for the children any of these songs: "Bless Our Hands" (*Sing a Song of Joy!*) **CD 2 Track 10;** "A Little Peace Song" (*Dandelions*); "Make a Joyful Noise" (*Color the World with Song*); "Peace to You and Me" (*Hi God 3*); "Yes, We Will Do What Jesus Says" (*Stories and Songs of Jesus*); "Fingerprints" (*Fingerprints*) "A Little Peace Song" (*Best of Mary Lu Walker*); "I am Wonderfully Made" (*Sing a Song of Joy!*). For a list of all the music used in this program, see **page OV-39**.

CHAPTER 15 | DAY TWO

People Use Their Hands to Help Others

Student Book page 61

LEARNING OUTCOME

The children will be able to

- be aware of people who help them in different ways.

KEY TERM

priest—one of God's helpers, who brings Jesus' love and care to us in special ways

MATERIALS

- Cutout 29
- Pictures of people doing something with their hands that benefits others. (Examples: doctors, farmers, artists, factory workers, a person praying)

CENTERING

Have the children open their books to **page 61.** Read aloud the poem and ask the children what it is telling us. (Our hands help us show our love for others and for God.)

Our Hands

Our helping hands are gifts of love.
[Have opened hands in front.]
With them, we give to others.
[Move hands out to side.]
We show the love that's in our hearts
[Put crossed hands on heart.]
For our sisters and our brothers.
[Move right hand outward, then left hand.]
Our hands can bring us blessings, too,
[Have opened hands in front.]
For they help us share our love,
[Put crossed hands on heart.]
Our loving deeds bring happiness,
[Point to self with both hands.]
And special joys from God above.
[Raise arms to sky.]

SHARING

1 Read aloud the poem again, letting the children perform the actions suggested here or their own.

2 Show pictures of people doing things for others. (Examples: doctors, farmers, artists, factory workers, a person praying) Tell the children that people use the gift of their hands to help make our world a better place. They use their hands to help others. Have the children select a picture and tell how the person in it is using his or her hands to help others. If pictures are not available, ask:

- ***What do gardeners do with their hands?*** (Plant bushes and flowers to make the world more beautiful)
- ***How do doctors and nurses use their hands to help others?*** (Help people who are sick feel better)
- ***What do artists do with their hands?*** (Create beautiful things) ***Musicians?*** (Create beautiful sounds) ***How do artists' pictures help us? How does music help us?*** (They each bring joy.)
- ***What are some things members of your family do with their hands to help you?*** (Prepare food, help tie our shoes)
- ***How does the person who is praying help others?*** (Praying shows love and care for people and for the world.)

• [Show Cutout 29 Priest.] ***How does a priest help us?*** (The priest uses his hands to bless and to lead God's people to be holy. With his hands, he offers up gifts to God for the people.) ***The bishop anoints the hands of a new priest with oil. Oil is a symbol of holiness and strength.***

3 Introduce the children to the idea that we use our hands to communicate. Say:

• ***Sometimes we use our hands to communicate with others.***

Invite the children to shake hands with one another as a sign that they are thankful for any help they have received and as a promise to offer help in times of need. Explore other actions that express gratitude and an offer to help, such as a high five.

ACTING

Teach and invite the children to pray the adapted version of Psalm 90:17 with gestures.

• ***God helps us serve others in love. We can ask God to help us with the words of this psalm prayer. In the psalm, the word prosper means "to bless" and "to make our work useful and helpful."***

Prosper the work
[Extend hands overhead.]
of our hands for us!
[Show both hands wide open.]

CHECKPOINT

• Were the children able to identify ways that people help others with their hands?

CHAPTER 15

Hands Are Good

Our helping hands are gifts of love. With them, we give to others.

We show the love that's in our hearts for our sisters and brothers.

Our hands can bring us blessings too, for they help us share our love.

Our loving deeds bring happiness and special joys from God above.

61

CHAPTER 15 | DAY THREE

Jesus Helped People

Student Book page 62

LEARNING OUTCOME

The children will be able to

- see Jesus as one who helped others.

MATERIALS

- Coats, sweaters, boots, or other items for CENTERING #2
- Bible enthroned, with note card on which you have written the adapted Scripture reading for SHARING #1, Matthew 20:30–34

COMMENTS

1. In Scripture, Jesus' concern and compassion for others is exemplified by his healing touch, communicated through the gentle laying on of his hands. During his life, Jesus spent himself as a total gift for us and culminated his loving service by his death on the cross.

2. In presenting the story of Jesus healing the blind men, do not stress the miracle as such, or the children may look upon the healing as a kind of magic. Rather, guide them to see Jesus' healing as a sign of his active concern in reaching out to people in need.

3. When discussing the story of Jesus healing the men who were blind, invite the children to imagine what it might be like to not be able to see. When you do so, the children will discover that certain activities may be more difficult for people without sight. Help them to understand that many of these activities are not impossible. We help teach the children about the dignity of the human person by acknowledging each person's many abilities and contributions.

CENTERING

1 Have the children open their books to **page 62.** Tell them it shows a Bible story about Jesus and two men who are blind. Ask:

- ***What do you think is happening?*** (The men who are blind are asking Jesus for help. Jesus is helping them.)
- ***Close your eyes. Think about what it might be like to not be able to see.***

2 Let the children experience doing a simple task without sight. They might try to put on their coats, sweaters, or boots with their eyes closed. Say:

- ***We use our eyes for many things. Many things might be more difficult for us if we could not see. Yet, people who are blind learn to do many things well without their sight.***
- ***Today you will hear a story from God's book, the Bible, about how Jesus used his hands to give sight to two men who were blind.***

SHARING

1 Prepare to tell the story of the healing of the two men born blind on **page T179.**

Introduce this Bible story by showing the Bible and opening it to the Gospel of Matthew, Matthew 20:30–34. Enthrone the Bible.

- ***Let's prepare ourselves to listen well to today's Bible story.***

2 Discuss the story.

- ***What do you think the men meant when they called out, "Lord, have mercy on us"?*** (They wanted Jesus to help them.)
- ***Why did Jesus want to help the men who were blind?*** (He cared for them.)
- ***How do you think the two men felt when they discovered that Jesus' touch had made them see?*** (Surprised, happy)
- ***What did the two men do when they knew Jesus had healed them?*** (They praised God.)

The Healing of the Two Men Who Were Blind

Once there were two men who couldn't see the blue sky or the green grass. They couldn't see pretty flowers growing. These men couldn't see anything at all. They were blind.

The two men were sitting by the side of the road. They heard that Jesus was passing by, so they shouted, "Lord, have mercy on us."

A crowd of people around Jesus scolded the men and told them to be quiet. But the two men shouted out even louder, "Lord, have mercy on us."

Then Jesus stopped and asked them, "What do you want me to do for you?" They said, "Lord, let us see."

Jesus wanted to help the men who were blind. He cared for them. He reached out his hand and touched their eyes. They could see. [Pause.] Then the two men followed Jesus, praising God. [Pause.]

ACTING

Lead the children to reflect on Jesus' care of people and invite them to pray the adapted version of Psalm 90:17 with gestures:

- ***Jesus cared about people and wanted to help them. That is why he reached out his hands and healed the men who were blind. They praised God for sending Jesus. Let us praise God for Jesus too. Let us pray that God will bless us and help us to serve others:***

Prosper the work
[Extend hands overhead.]
of our hands for us!
[Show both hands wide open.]

CHECKPOINT

- Do the children see Jesus as someone who cared for and helped others?

Scripture

Two men who were blind heard that Jesus was passing by.

They shouted, "Lord, have mercy on us!"

Jesus stopped and asked, "What do you want me to do for you?"

They said, "Lord, let us see."

He touched their eyes.

They could see.

The two men followed Jesus, praising God.

Based on Matthew 20:30–34

62

CHAPTER 15 | DAY FOUR

We Can Have Helping Hands

Student Book pages 63–64

LEARNING OUTCOMES

The children will be able to
- know that Jesus calls them to be helpers.
- desire to serve others.

MATERIALS
- BLM 20
- Crayons or markers
- Scissors

COMMENT

Throughout his life, Jesus was completely at the service of others. Sometimes he delayed meeting his own needs for rest and nourishment so that he could serve others. Jesus was in our midst as one who serves, and he asks his followers to be willing to give themselves in service of others. He taught self-giving as the way to human fulfillment.

CENTERING

Tell the children to listen carefully as you tell them something very important about Jesus.

- ***Jesus is God, but he did not come to earth as a great and powerful king. He came as a lowly servant who helped people. Jesus told his followers that they must be willing to be helpers too. Those who belong to Jesus' Church must be ready to help people in need.***

SHARING

1 Introduce this song activity:

- ***We belong to Jesus' Church. We must be willing to do things to help other people.***
- ***To help you think of things you can do for others, we will sing a song called "Ways to Help."***

Have the children sing verses such as "This is the way we pick up our toys, set the table, sweep the floor, etc." to the melody of "Here We Go 'Round the Mulberry Bush."

Ask the children to name things that they can do to help others and sing these as verses as well, for example "This is the way we share with our friends . . ."

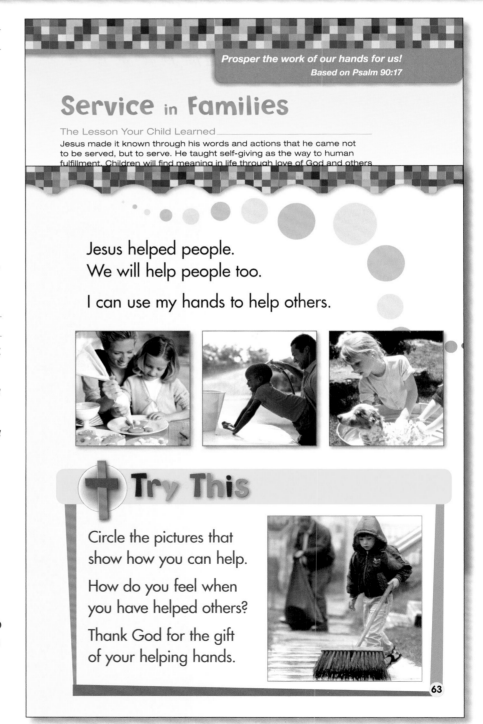

Prosper the work of our hands for us!
Based on Psalm 90:17

Service in Families

The Lesson Your Child Learned

Jesus made it known through his words and actions that he came not to be served, but to serve. He taught self-giving as the way to human fulfillment. Children will find meaning in life through love of God and others

Jesus helped people.
We will help people too.

I can use my hands to help others.

Try This

Circle the pictures that show how you can help.

How do you feel when you have helped others?

Thank God for the gift of your helping hands.

63

2 Help the children make a card from BLM 20 Helping Hands to give to someone as an offer of help.

• *BLM 20 Helping Hands*

• Show a sample that you made before today's lesson. Read the message inside.

• Have the children fold their paper in half and place the hand they do not write with along the fold so that their palm covers the message.

• Tell them to spread their fingers slightly apart and to trace around their hand.

• Have them cut out the hand. Be sure that they do not cut the hands apart on the fold.

• Help the children write their names on the line and refold the card so that the message is on the inside. They might color and draw on their cards.

• Encourage the children to take their cards home and talk with their families about how they might help people in need.

ACTING

1 Have the children turn to **page 63.** Read aloud the text at the top of the page and have the children repeat after you:

• ***I can use my hands to help others.***

Help the children do the activity.

2 Invite the children to pray the adapted version of Psalm 90:17 with gestures:

Prosper the work
[Extend hands overhead.]
of our hands for us!
[Show both hands wide open.]

3 Have the children take home the Family Page on **page 64** to share with their families.

CHECKPOINT

• Have the children shown a willingness to help others?

• How will you encourage the children to be more helpful?

ENRICHING THE FAITH EXPERIENCE

Use the following activities to enrich a lesson, to replace an activity with one that better meets the needs of your class, or to create an additional lesson.

1 Lead the children to express sorrow for not using their hands the right way.

• ***Jesus used his hands to help others. God has given us hands to help others too. Sometimes we have used our hands to hurt others. Let us tell Jesus that we are sorry for times we used our hands the wrong way and ask him to help us. Repeat "Lord, have mercy" after me.***

• ***Sometimes our hands have not helped those in need. Lord, have mercy . . .***

• ***Sometimes our hands have hurt parents, brothers, sisters, or friends. Lord, have mercy . . .***

2 Have the children draw someone doing something that makes our world a better place. Let the children show their pictures and offer a prayer of thanks to God for the people they drew.

3 Play the game "Helping Hands."

• ***To help you think of things you can do for others, we will play a game. I will name people. You think of how you could help them.***

• ***What could you do for your mother or father? your sisters or brothers? a friend? your neighbor?*** (Answers will vary.)

4 Have the children make handprints to give to their parents. Put out finger paints. Have the children place their hands in the finger paints. Then guide them to press their hands gently to a sheet of paper. Have the children write their names on their papers. Attach the following poem to their work.

Handprints

Sometimes you get
discouraged
Because I am so small
And always leave my
handprint
On furniture and wall

But everyday I'm growing
(I'll be all grown someday)
And all those tiny handprints
Will surely fade away.

So here's a final handprint
Just so you can recall
Exactly how my fingers looked
When they were very small.

© T. Lambert, Jr. May 1978

Chapter 16

Forgiveness Is Good

FAITH FOCUS

We seek forgiveness for doing wrong and forgive those who hurt us. Matthew 18:35; Luke 19:1–10

PREPARING THE FAITH EXPERIENCE

LISTENING

The vocation of a teacher is to communicate with joy the good news of God's love. Take some time to let yourself be refreshed by the good news found in the Bible. As you pray, hear God speak to you his good news of love and salvation.

All bitterness, fury, anger, shouting, and reviling must be removed from you, along with all malice. [And] be kind to one another, compassionate, forgiving one another as God has forgiven you in Christ.

Ephesians 4:31–32

REFLECTING

Spontaneity and candor are two of children's most endearing traits. Usually young children are quite uninhibited, particularly in showing their feelings. They display joy, sympathy, affection, or anger with little or no hesitation. At times, adults are both disconcerted and touched by the readiness of a child's sympathetic tears, the suddenness of an affectionate hug, or the sincerity of an apologetic smile. Their own behavior is frequently a marked contrast. Grown-ups more readily hide their emotions behind veneers of cool sophistication or indifference.

In children, Jesus saw a praiseworthy openness to the Kingdom of God. Jesus showed this openness to God throughout his life. Jesus was fully God and also fully human. Like us in all things but sin, Jesus accepted all the conditions of human nature. His thoughts and actions showed the fullness of his humanity. He also experienced a full range of emotions: joy during a wedding feast; grief at the death of a friend; sorrow over a sinful city; anger and righteous indignation at the desecration of his Father's house; fear at the prospect of death. He manifested all these feelings with full human dignity. Christ never evaded the risk of having his feelings hurt. Jesus suffered not only spiritually and physically, but also intellectually and emotionally. His life of loving atonement for the sins of humanity led inexorably to the bleak summit of Calvary, where he cried out, "My God, my God, why have you forsaken me?" (Mark 15:34)

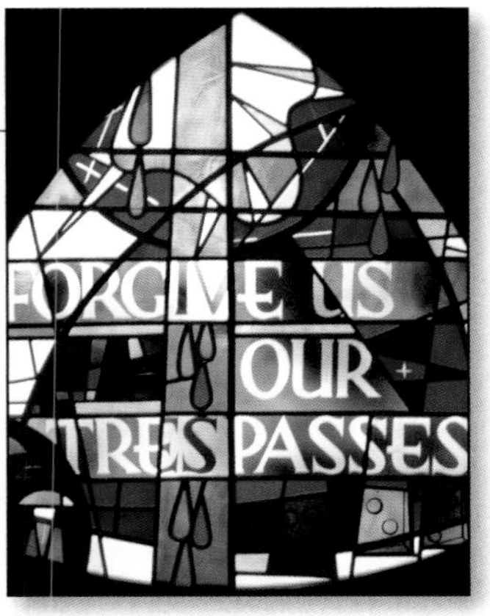

Inspired by the example of Jesus' vulnerability in that moment of supreme sacrifice, we find the courage to cry out, "I am sorry for doing wrong."

RESPONDING

God's Word moves us to respond in word and action. Let the Holy Spirit work within you as you prayerfully consider how you are being called to respond to God's message to you today.

- How do I feel when I am forgiven? When I forgive others?
- Do I teach the children by my example to be forgiving?

Holy Spirit, give us the courage to ask for forgiveness and the love to forgive others.

Catechism of the Catholic Church

The themes of this lesson correspond to the following paragraphs: 1431, 1441, 1451, 2838–2845.

THE FAITH EXPERIENCE

DAY ONE
We Have Feelings

DAY TWO
Others Have Feelings

DAY THREE
Jesus Forgives Us

DAY FOUR
We Forgive Those Who Have Hurt Us

Scripture in This Chapter

- *Matthew 18:21–22 Christ tells Peter that there is no limit to the number of times we should forgive others.*
- *Colossians 3:13 Paul urges the early Christians to imitate Christ's forgiveness.*

Church Documents

General Directory for Catechesis #86; *National Directory for Catechesis* #20, 5. The attitudes which catechesis should inculcate include the spirit of simplicity and humility, special concern for the least and the alienated, fraternal correction, common prayer, and mutual forgiveness.

Memory and Reconciliation #3.3. Because sin is present in the Church, the Church must constantly renew itself and pursue conversion as the People of God.

Bulletin Board At the left is a suggestion for a bulletin-board design. On one half of a sheet of paper, have the children draw a face to show how they feel when they have hurt someone. On the other half, have them draw a picture to show how they feel after saying they are sorry. Post the children's work on the bulletin board. You might include a banner with the words, "Forgiveness Is Good."

For a list of children's literature suggestions, please see **page OV-47.**

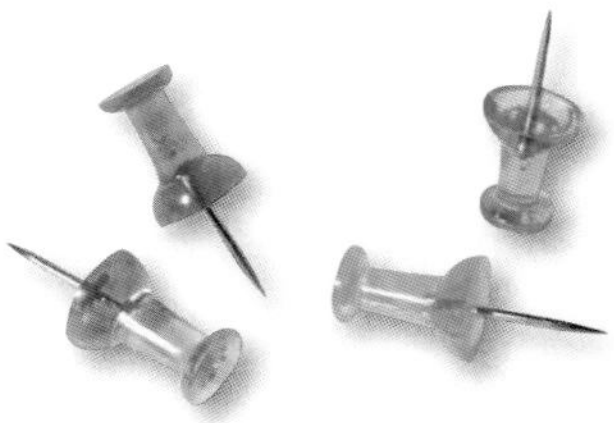

CHAPTER 16 | DAY ONE

We Have Feelings

LEARNING OUTCOMES

The children will be able to
- be more aware of their feelings.
- learn how to handle their negative feelings.

KEY TERM

feelings—happy, sad, afraid, angry

MATERIALS
- Cutouts 66–69
- Circles from the punchouts in the Student Book for feelings puppets
- Transparent tape
- Craft sticks
- Crayons or markers

COMMENT

Feelings are essential and enriching. However, repressing our feelings or responding to them inappropriately can be disruptive. It is important to help the children develop healthy attitudes toward their feelings and learn to respond to their feelings in ways that will foster a positive self-concept and good relationships with others.

CENTERING

1 Recall the previous chapters.

- ***We have talked about our hands. We said that God wants us to use our hands to do good things, things that show our love for other people. When we make good choices, we are happy, and we help to make other people happy. But we also said that sometimes we hurt people by the things we choose to do. Sometimes we become sad or angry, and we make choices that make others sad or angry as well.***
- ***Today you'll learn more about your feelings, which are also given to you by God.***

2 Display Cutouts 66–69 Feelings Set. Ask the children to identify the feelings expressed. Explain:

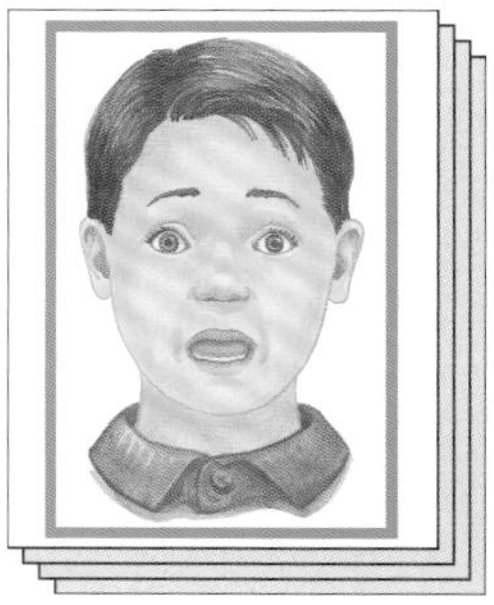

- ***God put different kinds of feelings within us when he made us as human persons. Sometimes feelings can lead us to choose to act in ways that are good and loving. Sometimes feelings can make us want to act in ways that are unloving.***

3 Ask the children to find the faces in the Cutouts that show the feelings of the children in the following situations:

- ***Find the face that shows how Mandy felt when her mother made her a beautiful birthday cake.***
- ***Find the face that shows how Juan felt when his dog was feeling sick.***
- ***Find the face that shows how Ashley felt when she couldn't find her mother in the big store.***
- ***Find the face that shows how Chen felt when his big brother said he was too little to play a game.***

SHARING

1 Show the children how to make stick puppets using the Circle punchouts. Tell them to decorate each side of the punchout as a face showing a different emotion. (Examples: happy, excited, hopeful, sad, mad, scared, angry, worried) Tape a craft stick to each decorated punchout circle to make a two-sided puppet.

2 Encourage the children to explore their own feelings using the puppets they have made. Have them take turns selecting which side of the puppet to show. As they hold the face, the children can describe experiences that made them feel the emotion on the face. Begin by sharing one or two examples of how you felt at a certain time.

3 Read the poem "Feelings" to the children and have them do the gestures with you.

Feelings

When I'm angry, you can tell,
For I stamp my feet and yell.
[Stamp feet.]

When I'm sad, I mope about,
Sigh and cry and don't go out.
[Put hands under chin, cupping face.]

When I'm scared by day or night,
I shake and hide, my eyes closed tight.
[Shake.]

When I'm happy, hear me sing,
I laugh at almost anything.
[Extend arms to sides.]

Whether I'm feeling good or bad,
God loves me. For this I'm glad!
[Clap.]

M. Kathleen Glavich, S.N.D.

4 Lead the children to an appreciation and acceptance of all their feelings.

- ***We have many different kinds of feelings. God made our feelings to help us show our love for him and for other people. It is all right to have different kinds of feelings. We like feeling happy. Sometimes we feel angry or sad. Sometimes we don't like these feelings. But our feelings of anger and sadness can also help us.***
- ***We can learn how to share our feelings with others. However, it is not all right to do bad or mean things when we have these kinds of feelings. We may not break someone else's things when we feel angry. We may not hurt others or ourselves because of the way we feel inside. To do such things is wrong.***

5 Discuss ways to respond to negative feelings.

- ***When you feel like doing mean things because you are angry, you can do something else to help you handle the angry feeling. I heard of a little boy named Sam who felt angry whenever someone took his toy without asking first. When people do things that are unkind or unfair, we get angry. But Sam knew that it would not be good to hit anyone or to break something because he was feeling angry. Whenever he felt angry, he tried to handle the angry feeling without doing something mean.***

Sometimes Sam could talk to his friend and tell him that he wanted his toy back. But sometimes Sam was so angry that he couldn't talk to his friend right away. When Sam was this angry, he walked away from his friend before he spoke so he wouldn't do or say something mean.

Sometimes Sam went outside and bounced his big ball as hard as he could. Sometimes he ran around the yard as fast as he could. Once he went into his bedroom and pounded on his pillow.

After he did these things, Sam felt less angry. When Sam was feeling less angry, he could talk to his friend who took his toy. When he talked with his friend, he told his friend that he didn't like it when someone took his toy without asking. Later, Sam and his friend were able to play with his toy together.

- ***Some people who suddenly become angry walk away or count to ten before they do or say anything. Why do you think they do this?*** (Sometimes we need time to calm down so that we don't do or say something unkind.)

ACTING

1 Encourage the children to put into practice one of the suggestions offered in this lesson for dealing with anger.

2 Invite the children to thank God for their feelings. Say:

- ***We can also talk to God about our feelings—happy, sad, angry, or scared. God wants to hear about all our feelings.***

Invite the children to offer thanks to God for their feelings as they hold their stick puppets as you pray:

- ***God, thank you for loving me when I am happy.***
- ***God, thank you for loving me when I am sad.***
- ***God, thank you for loving me when I am angry.***
- ***Happy, sad, or mad, help me***

CHECKPOINT

- How easily were the children able to identify feelings?
- Were the children able to identify good and loving things that they can do?

CHAPTER 16 | DAY TWO

Others Have Feelings

Student Book page 65

LEARNING OUTCOMES

The children will be able to
- become more aware of others' feelings.
- know that it is wrong to hurt themselves, others, or property.

KEY TERM

sin—an unkind or unloving act that offends God and hurts others or ourselves

MATERIALS

- Cutout puppets 51–57

COMMENT

If time allows at the end of the lesson, have the children demonstrate with the puppets how Charlie Chick, Katie Kitten, and Betty Bird could ask for and receive forgiveness from Tillie Turtle, Herbie Horse, and Rita Rabbit.

CENTERING

1 Teach the following game: One child covers his or her eyes while the others say the rhyme given here. The teacher motions for the children to be sad or glad, and the child who is "It" opens his or her eyes and must guess which feeling is being expressed. After this child guesses correctly, another child is chosen to be "It."

I'm very, very sad.
I'm very, very glad.
Sometimes sad.
Sometimes glad.
Which am I now?

Play the game several times, changing the words each time to reflect other emotions, such as surprise, fright, anger, or worry.

2 Comment that in the last lesson the children talked about their own feelings. Today they will think about the feelings of other people.

SHARING

1 Use Cutout puppets 51–57 Tillie Turtle, Charlie Chick, Herbie Horse, Gilda Goldfish, Katie Kitten, Betty Bird, and Rita Rabbit to help the children become sensitive to the feelings of others. Hold the puppets with speaking parts and ask a child to hold the third puppet in each group.

Gilda Goldfish, Charlie Chick, Tillie Turtle

Charlie Chick: Here comes slowpoke Tillie Turtle. Tillie's a slowpoke. Tillie's a slowpoke. [Tillie Turtle goes slowly away.]

Gilda Goldfish: That's mean, Charlie Chick. Tillie can't help being slow. God made her that way.

- ***How did Charlie Chick make Tillie Turtle feel?*** (Sad)
- ***Charlie Chick seemed to have forgotten that Tillie Turtle has feelings too.***

Charlie Chick, Katie Kitten, Herbie Horse

Katie Kitten: Herbie Horse, get out of my way. I want to chase that butterfly. [Because Herbie doesn't move fast enough, Katie scratches Herbie's leg with her claws.]

Charlie Chick: Katie, you hurt Herbie Horse's leg with your sharp claws. Herbie is crying.

- ***How did Katie Kitten feel about Herbie Horse?*** (Impatient, angry)
- ***What must Katie Kitten learn to do?*** (Wait patiently, say "I'm sorry")

Katie Kitten, Betty Bird, Rita Rabbit

Betty Bird: [Sees Rita Rabbit with a lettuce leaf.] What a nice lettuce leaf Rita Rabbit has. I'm going to fly down and take it to my nest. [Betty Bird snatches the leaf away from Rita Rabbit.]

Katie Kitten: Betty Bird, why did you do that to Rita Rabbit? She looked all morning to find a treat for her babies. Then you swooped down and took it.

• ***How do you think Rita Rabbit felt?*** (Upset, angry)

• ***Betty Bird didn't think about Rita Rabbit's feelings, did she? She was only thinking about herself.***

2 Help the children realize that others have feelings too.

• ***Sometimes we are like the animal friends. We forget that other people have feelings too. Our parents, teachers, friends, brothers, sisters, and even little babies have feelings. When we do unkind and unloving things to others, they hurt just as much as we do when someone does things like that to us.***

• ***Unkind and unloving things that hurt others and ourselves are called sins. God does not want us to do these things. He does not want us to sin. He wants us to love one another.***

• ***When we act mean or hurt others, we are also unhappy. What can we do about it?*** (Tell those we have hurt that we are sorry.)

3 Ask the children to open their books to **page 65**. Read it aloud.

ACTING

Introduce the psalm prayer:

• ***When we have hurt someone else's feelings, we tell them, "I'm sorry." We also say "I'm sorry" to God. God always forgives us.***

Invite the children to pray the following adaptation of Psalm 38:19 with gestures:

> **I am sorry**
> [Cross arms across chest.]
> **for doing wrong.**
> [Bow head.]

CHECKPOINT

- Are the children aware that others have feelings too?
- How can the children learn to show their feelings in ways that are respectful of others?

CHAPTER 16

Forgiveness Is Good

It is not easy to always be loving.
Sometimes we do things
that do not please God.

Sometimes we hurt others.
This is a sin.
When we sin, we are not happy.

But we can say "I'm sorry."
Then we will be happy again.

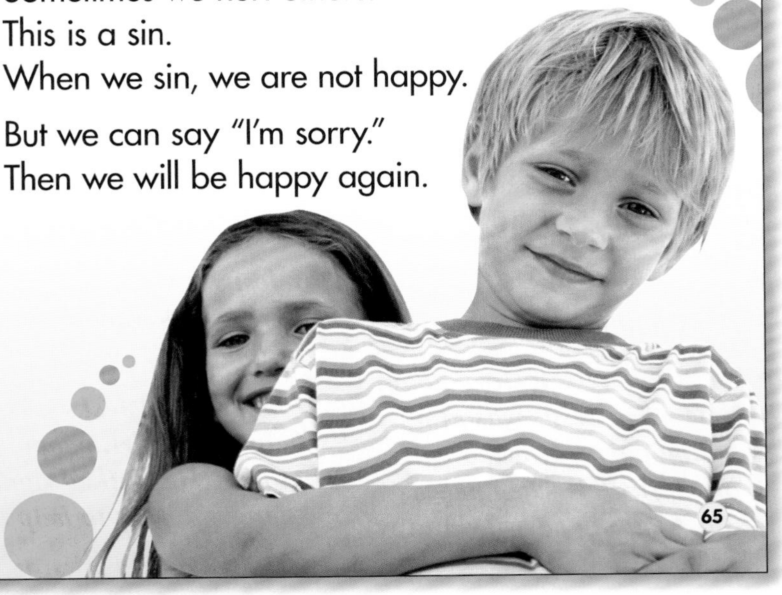

65

CHAPTER 16 | DAY THREE
Jesus Forgives Us

Student Book page 66

LEARNING OUTCOMES

The children will be able to

- know that Jesus had feelings.
- realize that Jesus forgives them when they are sorry.

MATERIALS

- Cutouts: 66–69
- Note cards with sample situations for SHARING #3

COMMENTS

1. The penitential rite at the beginning of Mass is a time for reflecting on our personal failings and on our corporate witness to the world as the Body of Christ. As a Christian community, we acknowledge our sins and ask God's forgiveness. In the Our Father, a meal prayer before communion, we ask to be reconciled with God and with one another before receiving the Bread of Life, the symbol of our unity with him and with one another.

2. For use in SHARING #3, prepare note cards with situations that might cause children to feel angry or hurt. Some examples of situations include the following:

- Someone tells you that your drawing isn't very good.
- Someone pushes in front of you in line.
- Someone takes your crayons without asking.
- Someone takes the last cookie on the plate, the one that you wanted.

CENTERING

1 Show Cutouts 66–69. Ask the children to recall some of the feelings they have been talking about. Help them to identify appropriate ways to express these feelings.

2 Teach a song about feelings or forgiveness from the suggestions on **page T192**, such as "Got to Get in Touch" (*Hi God!*), "I'm Sorry" (*Stories and Songs of Jesus*) or "Jesus, You Love Us" (*Calling the Children*). Invite the children to thank Jesus for being so loving.

SHARING

1 Discuss the feelings of Jesus.

- ***Jesus had feelings too.***
- ***The Bible tells a story about a time when Jesus was at a wedding party. How do you think Jesus felt when he was at the wedding party?*** (Happy)
- ***The Bible tells us the story about when Jesus saw people not showing respect for God's Temple. How do you think Jesus felt when people did not show respect for God, his Father?*** (Angry)
- ***The Bible tells us that many people who were sick asked Jesus for help. How do you think Jesus felt when he saw people who were suffering?*** (Sad)
- ***The Bible tells us about the sad days before Jesus died on the cross. How do you think Jesus felt when he knew he would die on the cross?*** (Sad)

2 Tell how Jesus handled anger.

- ***Jesus never did anything to hurt others when he was hurt or angry.***
- ***Once when Jesus was going to help a sick girl, people laughed at him. He walked right by them and went to help her.***
- ***Another time people called Jesus names. How might that have made Jesus feel?*** (Sad, angry) ***He just walked away. He was never mean to others when they were mean to him.***

3 Guide the children to role-play loving responses to situations that might cause children to feel angry or hurt, using the situations on the note cards you prepared in advance (See COMMENT #2). Let volunteers choose to role-play with partners how they will respond as you read each situation. Introduce the activity:

- ***Sometimes we feel angry or hurt by things that people do or say to us. When these things happen, it can be difficult to walk away or to keep from hurting those who have hurt us. It is good to practice how we might respond when these things happen.***

• ***On these cards, I have examples of situations that can sometimes happen that can make us feel hurt or angry. I will choose one at a time to read aloud. Then I'll ask two volunteers to show us how we can respond in this situation as Jesus would.***

Allow several pairs of volunteers to role-play responses to each situation.

4 Have the children look at the pictures on **page 66** while you read aloud the text, up to the passage from Scripture. Ask:

• ***What does Jesus do when we say that we are sorry?*** (Jesus forgives us.)

5 Tell the children how Jesus forgave his friends.

• ***Jesus had feelings too. Sometimes Jesus' friends hurt him. Peter was a good friend of Jesus. Jesus chose Peter to be one of his special helpers. But there was one time when Peter was not a good friend to Jesus. He told a lie and said he was not one of Jesus' helpers. He said, "I don't even know Jesus." Peter said this because he was afraid of Jesus' enemies. He was very afraid that they might put him in prison if they knew he was a friend of Jesus.***

• ***How do you think Jesus felt when Peter said he didn't know him?*** (Sad, hurt, angry)

• ***Jesus may have been hurt by what Peter said, but Jesus did not do or say anything that was mean. He knew that Peter was sorry. Jesus forgave Peter. He showed Peter that they were still friends.***

6 Acquaint the children with the Penitential Act at the beginning of the Mass and teach them to pray, "Lord, have mercy."

• ***When the Church comes together to worship God at Mass, we tell God and one another that we are sorry for not always living as children of God.***

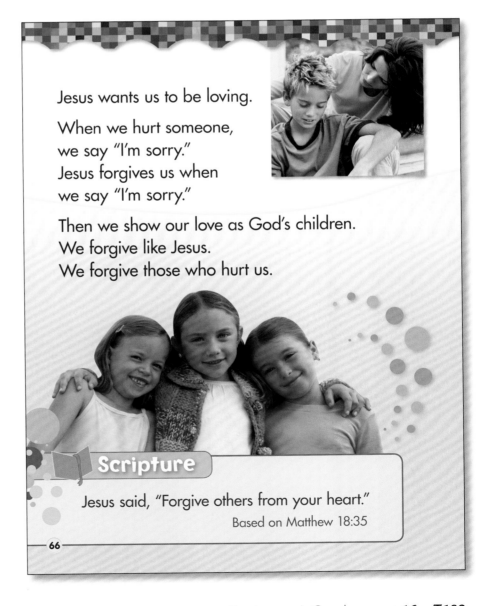

Jesus wants us to be loving.

When we hurt someone,
we say "I'm sorry."
Jesus forgives us when
we say "I'm sorry."

Then we show our love as God's children.
We forgive like Jesus.
We forgive those who hurt us.

Scripture

Jesus said, "Forgive others from your heart."

Based on Matthew 18:35

66

• ***Do you remember what the blind men said when they asked Jesus for help?*** ("Lord, have mercy on us.") ***"Lord, have mercy" are the words we say at the beginning of Mass to tell God and one another that we are sorry and to ask for help in being more loving. In this prayer, we also call Jesus "Christ." We say, "Christ, have mercy." We repeat the prayer after the priest prays it.***

• ***Pray the prayer with me as you do at Mass.***

Lord, have mercy.
[Repeat with the children.]
Christ, have mercy.
[Repeat with the children.]
Lord, have mercy.
[Repeat with the children.]

ACTING

❶ Invite the children to pray a simple prayer of sorrow with the response "Lord, have mercy."

• ***Jesus forgives us when we say, "I'm sorry." Repeat "Lord, have mercy" each time I say it.***

• ***Sometimes we show our anger in ways that are mean or hurtful. Lord, have mercy . . .***

• ***Sometimes we forget that our parents, brothers, sisters, or friends have feelings just like we do. Lord, have mercy . . .***

• ***Sometimes we forget to ask other people to forgive us. Lord, have mercy . . .***

❷ Invite the children to pray the following adaptation of Psalm 38:19 with gestures.

I am sorry
[Cross arms across chest.]
for doing wrong.
[Bow head.]

CHECKPOINT

- Were the children able to identify feelings that Jesus might have experienced?
- Do the children know that Jesus forgives them?

CHAPTER 16 | DAY FOUR

We Forgive Those Who Have Hurt Us

Student Book pages 66–68

LEARNING OUTCOMES

The children will be able to
- practice forgiving others.
- recognize that being loving and kind makes them happy.

KEY TERM

trespasses—wrong things that we do

MATERIALS
- *A Child's Bible*, pages 24–26
- Poster 7
- Bible enthroned, with note cards on which you have written the adapted Scripture reading for SHARING #1, Luke 19:1–10, and ACTING #1, Matthew 18:35

COMMENT

Many children would enjoy acting out the story of Zacchaeus.

CENTERING

1 Recall the last lesson:

- ***In the last class you heard that Jesus forgave one of his friends, the one who told a lie and said that he was not one of Jesus' helpers. Which friend did Jesus forgive?*** (Peter) ***Jesus always forgives us when we say, "I'm sorry."***

2 Have the children open their books to **page 66**. Read aloud the passage from Scripture. Ask:

- ***How do we show that we love God?*** (We forgive as Jesus did.)

SHARING

1 Prepare to tell the story "Zacchaeus Sees" found in *A Child's Bible*, **pages 24–26.** Show Poster 7 Zacchaeus in the Tree. Introduce the story:

- ***One day Jesus forgave a man no one else liked. This man showed how happy he was to be forgiven by Jesus by making other people happy. Listen to the story.***

Show the Bible, opening it to the Gospel of Luke, Luke 19:1–10. Enthrone the Bible.

- ***Let's prepare ourselves to listen well to today's Bible story.***

Read or tell the story "Zacchaeus Sees" **pages 24–26** of *A Child's Bible.*

2 Discuss the story:

- ***What did Zacchaeus do that was wrong?*** (He cheated people by stealing their money.)
- ***How did he show he was sorry?*** (He paid people back more than he took from them.)
- ***Why do you think Jesus forgave Zacchaeus?*** (Jesus forgives sinners; Jesus loved Zacchaeus.)
- ***Would you forgive Zacchaeus if he had stolen money from you?***
- ***How do you think Zacchaeus felt when Jesus said he would eat at his house?*** (Surprised, happy)
- ***We are happy too when Jesus forgives us. We can make other people happy by forgiving them after they have hurt us.***

3 Have the children turn to **page 67**. Read aloud the text. Guide the children in doing the activities.

4 Teach the part of the Our Father in which we ask for forgiveness.

- ***There is a part in the Our Father in which we ask God to forgive us for the times we have not been loving to others. We use a big word for the wrong things we do. The word is* trespasses. *Say it after me: "trespasses."***
- ***Here is the line of the prayer: "And forgive us our trespasses." We are asking God to forgive the wrong things we have done. Say the line after me.*** [Repeat with the children.]
- ***We ask God to forgive us the way we forgive those who hurt us. We say: "And forgive us our trespasses as we forgive those who trespass against us." Say the line after me.***
- ***Say each line after me again: "And forgive us our trespasses"***

[Repeat with the children.] ***"as we forgive those who trespass against us."*** [Repeat with the children.]

- ***Now say the two lines with me.***

5 Invite the children to pray the Our Father.

- ***Sometimes God's people join hands when they pray the Our Father. We want to show that we are all children of God Our Father. We are all brothers and sisters. Let us join hands now and pray this prayer.***

Songs

Play for the children any of these songs: "Love One Another" (*Sing a Song of Joy!*) CD 2 Track 4; "I'm Sorry," "Zacchaeus" (*Stories and Songs of Jesus*); "God Is Our Father," "Got to Get in Touch," "Peace Time" (*Hi God!*); "I Forgive You" (*Hi God 5*); "I Forgive, You Forgive," "I Am Sorry" (*Songs for Young Children*); "A Little Peace Song" (*Dandelions*); "Jesus, You Love Us" (*Calling the Children*); "Hold Us in Your Mercy" (*Singing Our Faith*); "A Little Peace Song" (*The Best of Mary Lu Walker*); "Zacchaeus" (*Wee Sing Bible Songs*). For a list of all the music used in this program, see page OV–39.

ACTING

1 Share Jesus' message of forgiveness from the Bible.

- ***Jesus asks his followers to be like him. Listen as I read what Jesus tells us to do.***

Invite the children to remember what they learned about how to be good listeners.

- ***Let's prepare ourselves to listen well to this reading from the Bible.*** [Reverently take the Bible and read the message adapted from Matthew 18:35.] ***Jesus said, "You are to forgive others from your heart."***
- ***"From your heart" means really forgiving. We don't keep any anger deep inside us.***

2 Tell the children that when they do something wrong, they can ask Jesus to forgive them. They can also ask Jesus to help them forgive others from their heart. Say:

- ***When Jesus forgives us, we are happy like Zacchaeus. We become better people, and we share Jesus' love and forgiveness with others.***

Invite the children to quiet themselves and to talk to Jesus in their hearts:

Try This

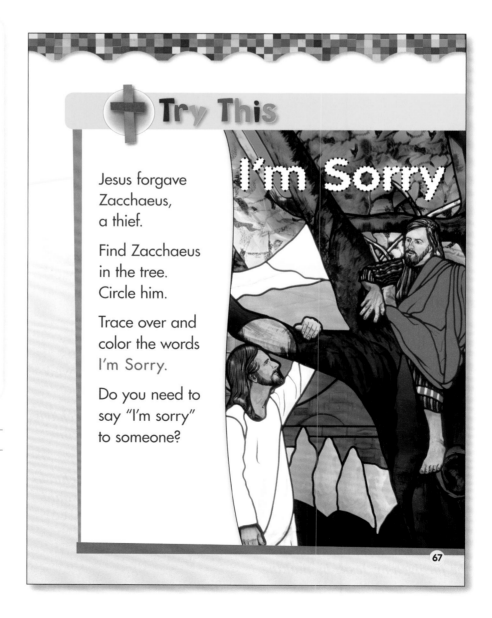

Jesus forgave Zacchaeus, a thief.

Find Zacchaeus in the tree. Circle him.

Trace over and color the words I'm Sorry.

Do you need to say "I'm sorry" to someone?

67

- ***Quiet helps us to pray. We can meet Jesus deep within our quiet hearts. Let us prepare ourselves to meet Jesus.***
- ***Straighten your back.*** [Pause.]
- ***Rest your arms on your lap, hands open in front of you.*** [Pause.]
- ***You may gently close your eyes if you want to.*** [Pause.]
- ***Slowly breathe in and out, in and out, in and out.*** [Pause.]
- ***Deep within you, see Jesus sitting next to you.*** [Pause.]
- ***In the quiet of your heart, tell Jesus you are sorry for something you have done wrong. Ask Jesus to forgive you.*** [Pause.] ***Ask Jesus to help you forgive others.*** [Pause.]
- ***When you are finished praying, open your eyes.***

3 Have the children take home the Family Page on **page 68** to share with their families.

CHECKPOINT

- How did the children react to the story of Zacchaeus?
- Do the children apologize and readily forgive one another?

ENRICHING THE FAITH EXPERIENCE

Use the following activities to enrich a lesson, to replace an activity with one that better meets the needs of your class, or to create an additional lesson.

1 On one side of a sheet of paper, have the children draw a picture to show what they do that others like. On the other side, they may draw a picture to show something they did that made others unhappy. Walk around as the children work and let them tell you about their pictures. When all are finished, lead the children in prayer.

- ***Dear Jesus, help us remember that others have feelings too. We are sorry for the times we hurt others.***

2 Read to the children "Joseph and His Brothers" on **page 5** of *A Child's Bible.*

3 Let the children practice saying "I'm sorry" and showing forgiveness. Have them use puppets to role-play situations in which one character does something that makes the other unhappy. Then have them show what the two characters might say to each other to make up.

I am sorry for doing wrong.
Based on Psalm 38:19

Forgiveness in Families

The Lesson Your Child Learned

Our ability to feel and to express emotions enriches our lives. In themselves, feelings are neither good nor bad. We all have a need to admit our feelings and to take responsibility for the way we express them. Children who live in families where forgiving and being forgiven are part of life easily learn to accept God's forgiveness. In this chapter, the children explored some of their feelings and were made aware of others' feelings. They learned that it is wrong to hurt themselves, to hurt others, or to damage property when angry. They learned how to say "I'm sorry" when they hurt someone's feelings, and they heard Jesus tell them to forgive those who hurt them.

Living the Lesson

Did you ever play the game "hot potato"? I remember both the joy and the fear we had as kids as we hurriedly passed the "hot potato" so we didn't end up with it and get eliminated from the game. Sometimes families treat feelings like hot potatoes. When an uncomfortable emotion arises, each person tries to pass along that charged feeling to someone else.

There are three steps families can take to short-circuit the hot potato game. One, become aware of your own emotional state. Two, ask for God's help in responding appropriately to the emotions you find the most troublesome. Three, respond rather than react. Responding means that you don't just pass along the emotional charge. Instead you might calmly say, "It sounds as though you are upset. Let's figure out what you're feeling." And if your child expresses his or her emotions in a way that goes against your values, use that as a teachable moment, saying, "We don't talk to one another like that. It's okay to have your feelings, but it's not okay to be mean."

–Tom McGrath, author of *Raising Faith-Filled Kids* (Loyola Press)

Bringing the Lesson Home

- Read with your child the pages from this chapter that were sent home.
- Make room in your family for one another's feelings. Do not encourage repressing feelings, but teach your child how to deal with the feelings that come up. Welcome the feelings and coach them about the behavior.
- Readily say "I'm sorry" when you have acted in ways that don't live up to your values of respect and care for others.

68

Chapter 17

Church Is Good

FAITH FOCUS

Jesus is present when the Church gathers to worship. Acts 2:42,46–47

PREPARING THE FAITH EXPERIENCE

LISTENING

Before you begin to prepare this week's lessons, take some time for prayer. Quiet yourself by taking several deep breaths. Become aware of God's presence, for God is with you always. Ask God to open your heart to hear his words to you today.

They devoted themselves to the teaching of the apostles and to the communal life, to the breaking of the bread and to the prayers. . . . Every day they devoted themselves to meeting together in the temple area and to breaking bread in their homes. They ate their meals with exultation and sincerity of heart, praising God and enjoying favor with all the people. And every day the Lord added to their number those who were being saved.

Acts 2:42,46–47

REFLECTING

It was the Holy Spirit who breathed life into the early Church. The Spirit attended to the disciples' needs, both physical and spiritual, through the building up of this community. Here the early Christians found love and companionship. They taught and welcomed new members into the fellowship of the believers. Above all, they worshiped God through the breaking of the bread and in communal prayer. Each Christian was taught to accept his or her full role in the community. Saints Peter and Paul described the result of this total commitment in almost identical words:

Come to him, a living stone, rejected by human beings but chosen and precious in the sight of God, and, like living stones, let yourselves be built into a spiritual house to be a holy priesthood to offer spiritual sacrifices acceptable to God through Jesus Christ.

1 Peter 2:4–5

So then you are . . . built upon the foundation of the apostles and prophets, with Christ Jesus himself as the capstone. Through him the whole structure is held together and grows into a temple sacred in the Lord; in him you also are being built together into a dwelling place of God in the Spirit.

Ephesians 2:19–22

The same Holy Spirit has never ceased to quicken the Church through the centuries. Under the Spirit's inspiration, today's Church community continues to pattern itself on the ideals so well described by the New Testament writers.

Under the leadership of their pastors, Christians celebrate the Eucharist, meet regularly for communal prayer, and share their lives with one another. Each man, woman, and child goes out to serve the needs of others, then returns with joy to the center, the very heart of life—the encounter with Christ celebrated by the Church.

RESPONDING

Having reflected upon God's Word, take some time now to continue to respond to God in prayer. You might wish to use a journal to record your responses throughout this year.

- Why is belonging to the Catholic Church important to me?
- How have I experienced God's grace through the Church today?

Holy Spirit, give us a love for the Church.

Catechism of the Catholic Church

The themes of this lesson correspond to the following paragraphs: 1071, 1179–1184, 2691.

THE FAITH EXPERIENCE

DAY ONE
The Church at Worship

DAY TWO
We Visit a Church

DAY THREE
Everyone Has a Role in Worship

DAY FOUR
We Make a Church

Scripture in This Chapter

- *Acts 2:41 The Church grows through the baptism of those who have accepted the words of the apostles.*
- *1 Corinthians 12:12–26 The Church is the body of Christ. There are many members and many gifts, but one body. All are united in the Spirit.*

Church Documents

General Directory for Catechesis #28.
Catechesis should serve to bring us together as church, based on a theology of the Church as communion. It should help develop in us a spirituality of belonging to the Church.

Constitution on the Church #6.
The Church is called the building of God, the house of God in which his family dwells, with Christ as the cornerstone and a foundation built by the apostles.

Built of Living Stones #16.
The building that we call church is both the house of God on earth and a house fit for the prayers of the community, and it must express the presence of God, help celebrate the sacrifice of Christ, and reflect the community that celebrates there.

Bulletin Board At the left is a suggestion for a bulletin-board design. Using construction paper, poster board, felt, or similar materials, make a church building. You might include people and symbols such as a cross, a Bible, and the Eucharist. Post a banner with the words, "Church Is Good."

For a list of children's literature suggestions, please see **page OV-47.**

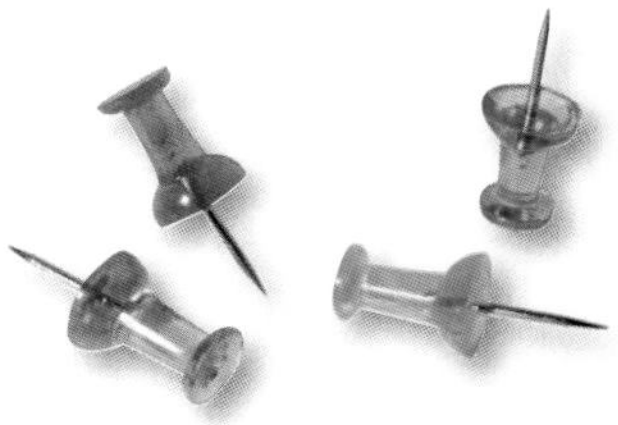

CHAPTER 17 | DAY ONE

The Church at Worship

Student Book page 69

LEARNING OUTCOMES

The children will be able to
- learn the two meanings of the word *church.*
- anticipate a visit to the church building.

KEY TERMS

Church—God's special family who believes in Jesus and tries to love as Jesus did

church—the building where God is present in a special way and where God's people gather together to worship

worship—to praise and thank God

COMMENT

All who are members of the Catholic Church profess the same creed and share the same sacraments—through which Jesus is really made present in the world—in union with their bishop and with the Holy Father in Rome. People become Catholic Christians through a process of initiation. They are brought into full membership through the sacraments of Baptism, Confirmation, and Eucharist. The journey in faith continues throughout a person's life as he or she comes to realize more fully the meaning of incorporation into Jesus' Passion, Death, and Resurrection.

CENTERING

Recall the last chapter.

- ***In the last chapter, we talked about how we try to follow God and to love one another. We also talked about times when we do not love as we should. What do we do when we do not love as we should or when we hurt one another?*** (We say that we are sorry, and we ask for forgiveness.)
- ***At our Baptism, Jesus shared his gift of forgiveness with us. We were also made members of the Church.***
- ***Today you will learn more about God's family, the Church.***

SHARING

1 You might write *church* and *Church* on note cards or on the board prior to this lesson to assist your explanation of their meanings. Invite the children to open their books to **page 69.** Discuss the picture found on this page.

- ***What do you see in the picture?*** (People in church)
- ***When was the last time you went to church? Who took you there? Why did you go? What did you do while you were in church?*** (Prayed, celebrated Mass)
- ***We have a special word for what we do when we gather at church. We gather at church to* worship *God. When we worship, we offer praise and thanks to God, who is so good to us. What do we do at church?*** (We worship God.)
- [Point to the word *church.*] ***A church is a place where God's people gather to worship God. This same word,* Church, *is also used to talk about the people who gather to worship God.*** [Point to the word *Church.*] ***We became members of the Church at our Baptism. The Church includes all the people who belong to Jesus. We believe in Jesus and try to follow his way of love. We are the Church, God's people, who worship in a building that is called a church.***

Read aloud **page 69**. Invite the children to follow along.

2 Tell the children the importance of the church building.

- ***God's people come together in a special building. We come to praise and thank God and to remember Jesus. The building where we meet is called a church because the people who gather in it are the Church. Sometimes people call the church building "God's house."***
- ***We go to church to worship God.***

3 Invite the children to worship God now by singing a song of praise, such as “Glory and Gratitude and Praise,” “Jesus in the Morning” (*Singing Our Faith*), “Alleluia, Praise God” (*Hi God 4*), or “Praise Him” (*Miracle Mud*).

4 Explain what the church means to God’s people.

- ***The church building is a very holy place. Jesus is present in the church building in a special way. It is the home of God’s people too. We gather to worship in this building. We love God and are happy to go to God’s house. We are happy to be with God’s family, the Church. When God’s people gather to worship, Jesus is with us as well.***

ACTING

1 Prepare the children for the church visit you will make in the next lesson.

- ***You belong to God’s people, the Church. You became a member of the Catholic Church when you were baptized. God’s house, the church building, is your home too. Because you are growing up in God’s family, you will want to be with its members when they gather to worship God.***
- ***We shall visit the church building where God’s people worship so that you will know more about this home of yours.***

2 Teach and pray the psalm prayer based on Psalm 122:1 with gestures:

I
[Point to self.]
am glad
[Bursting gesture out and up]
when I go
[Rolling movement with hands]
to God’s house.
[Join fingertips of both hands to form a roof.]

CHECKPOINT

- Were the children able to differentiate between the two uses of the word *church*?
- Did the children indicate familiarity with the church building?

CHAPTER 17

Church Is Good

At our Baptism, we became members of the Catholic Church.

The Church is a family of people who believe in Jesus.

God’s family, the Church, follows Jesus’ way of love.

God’s family gathers together to worship God our Father.

69

CHAPTER 17 | DAY TWO
We Visit a Church

LEARNING OUTCOMES
The children will be able to
- feel more a part of the Church.
- become acquainted with some aspects of the church building.

KEY TERMS
altar—the table in God's house on which the Eucharist is offered
ambo—the stand where God's Word is read
baptismal font—the place in church where we were baptized
crucifix—a cross that shows the body of Jesus; a special sign of God's love for us
holy-water font—container for blessed water that reminds us of our baptism
Lectionary for Mass—the book containing the readings from the Bible read at Mass
celebrant's chair—special seat for the priest who is leading or celebrating Mass
sanctuary light—the lamp in church that tells us Jesus is present in the Blessed Sacrament reserved in the tabernacle
stained-glass windows—colored windows that show pictures of Jesus, Mary, the saints, and our beliefs
tabernacle—place in church where Jesus is present in a special way, in the Blessed Sacrament

MATERIALS
- BLM 21A–B (optional)

COMMENTS
1. A church building is a sacred space designed to support and to deepen the faith of those who gather there. The prominence of the altar points to the centrality of our corporate worship—the celebration of the Eucharist. The ambo reminds us that God's Word is proclaimed at Mass. The tabernacle and burning sanctuary light speak of the presence of Christ, whose sacramental presence is with us always. The crucifix, statues, and windows testify to what we believe as Catholics.

2. The reverence and awe that small children experience when entering a church and being introduced to its sacred objects can have a lasting impression. As you visit the church building, help the children learn to show respect for our place of worship.

3. As you name the sacred objects found in church, be aware that many of these words will be new to the children in your group. Young children can easily mishear these new vocabulary words. Be sure that you are pronouncing these words clearly and distinctly. You may even choose to have the children repeat these words to confirm their understanding.

4. If a priest is to conduct the church tour, plan with him the route you will take so that the children can be briefed and the tour can proceed smoothly. If you are unable to take the children to church, you might use BLM 21A–B Sacred Church Objects to explain some of the features of a church building. • ***BLM 21A–B Sacred Church Objects***

CENTERING
Prepare the children for a visit to church.

• ***Many things in the church building are holy. They help us think of God and pray. We do not enter a church the way we enter other buildings. We walk in quietly and reverently. A church is the home of God Our Father and our home too. We show respect for God and God's house by talking and walking quietly and calmly when we are in a church.***

SHARING
1 Briefly tell the procedure for the church visit.

2 As you visit the church building, speak softly and show reverence as you describe the sacred objects. Allow the children to touch these objects gently and reverently. If time is short, you might choose to focus on only a few of the objects. (Examples: the altar, the ambo, the tabernacle, and the baptismal font)

Holy Water Font
• ***The water in this bowl, or font, is not ordinary water. It has been blessed by a priest. It is called holy water. As we enter the church, we dip our fingers into the holy water and make the Sign of the Cross, Jesus' special sign, on ourselves.*** [Demonstrate for the children.] ***The holy water reminds us that we became members of God's people, the Church, when we were baptized with water. God's house really is our home too***

because we belong to God's special family, the Church.

Altar

• ***Families have a table in their homes. The altar is a special table in God's house. It is the holy place where the Eucharist is offered. The altar is the Lord's table. It is a sign of Jesus. It is blessed with incense, and we bow before it. At the altar the Lord prepares a special meal for his people. God's people come to the altar to be fed with the Eucharist. The priest kisses the altar at the beginning and end of the Mass. He shows reverence and love for the holy table in God's house.***

Ambo

• ***This is a special stand where God's Word is read. The holy book that has readings from the Bible is placed here. This book is called the* Lectionary for Mass.**

Celebrant's Chair

• ***The priest sits on a special chair to show that he represents Christ and all of us when he leads, or celebrates, Mass.***

Cross

• ***A crucifix, or cross, is near the altar. The cross may have the figure of Jesus on it. It reminds us of God's great love for us.***

Candles

• ***These candles were blessed because they were to be used for Mass. The lighted candles remind us of God, the Giver of Life, and of Jesus, who came to be the light of the world.***

Tabernacle

• ***The Holy Bread that is Jesus is kept in a special place in church called a tabernacle. When we approach the tabernacle, we genuflect to show our love for Jesus. Holy Communion can be brought to people who are too sick to attend Mass so that Jesus will comfort and strengthen them.***

Sanctuary Light (Lamp)

• ***A sanctuary light burns near the tabernacle. It burns night and day. It tells us that Jesus is present in the tabernacle.***

Baptismal Font

• ***A baptismal font is where we were baptized, when water was poured over our heads and we became members of God's family, the Church. At our Baptism, we were also anointed with chrism, the special holy oil that made us belong to Jesus' royal family. We became Catholics because we were baptized into the Catholic Church.***

Statues

• ***Statues remind us of Jesus, Mary, and the saints. The saints also belong to God's family, the Church. Now they are living with God in heaven.***

Stained-Glass Windows

• ***Windows made up of pieces of brightly colored glass are called stained-glass windows. They help to make the church beautiful. Sometimes the pictures in these windows tell stories about Jesus, Mary, and the saints.***

3. Have the children stand around the altar or tabernacle and pray the psalm prayer based on Psalm 122:1 with gestures:

I
[Point to self.]
am glad
[Bursting gesture out and up]
when I go
[Rolling movement with hands]
to God's house.
[Join fingertips of both hands to form a roof.]

ACTING

1. Upon returning to the classroom, allow the children to talk about the church visit.

2. Invite the children to quietly thank God for being with us in church.

CHECKPOINT

- Did the children show reverence for the church building and the sacred objects it contains?
- What impressed and interested them most during the church visit?

CHAPTER 17 | DAY THREE

Everyone Has a Role in Worship

Student Book page 70

LEARNING OUTCOME

The children will be able to

- become familiar with the different roles within the Church.

MATERIALS

- Cutouts 1, 22–31

COMMENT

Make it a point to acknowledge the children you see at Sunday Mass, to smile at them, and to say a few words to them after Mass.

CENTERING

Talk about the different roles of family members.

- ***The people in your family share many jobs that need to be done in your household. What are some jobs your family members do? What are some jobs you do?***
- ***When God's family, the Church, gathers to worship, there are many different jobs that must be done too.***

SHARING

1 Talk to the children about the Church today. Place Cutout 1 Jesus and Cutouts 22–31 People Set on display around the room. Have a child get each cutout as you name it and put it in a special place to form a group.

- ***The Church is the family of people who belong to Jesus. It is a family made up of babies, boys and girls, teenagers, mothers and fathers, grandmothers and grandfathers, sisters and brothers, deacons, priests, bishops, and the pope. We are all part of God's family, the Church.***
- [Gesture toward the cutouts.] ***All people who have been baptized belong to the Church. All of us love Jesus and share his love with others. We come together in a church building to pray and to worship God. We ask God to help us to become better Christians. Then we go out and spread Jesus' love everywhere.***

2 Have the children open their books to **page 70.** Read aloud the text. Discuss the pictures. Describe the following people and explain what each person does when we gather for worship. You might choose to provide props as appropriate. (Examples: a Lectionary or Bible, robes, song books, a Sacramentary)

- ***A priest is the person who leads us when we celebrate Mass. The altar servers assist the priest on the altar. The lector reads God's Word. The choir is a group of people who lead us in song at Mass. The choir director leads the choir. Greeters are people who welcome us when we enter the church building for Mass.***
- ***Everyone takes part in the Church's worship. Different people do different things, but everyone is needed.***
- ***Jesus, the Good Shepherd, is the head of the Church. But he has special helpers on earth to lead and to shepherd the Church for him. Do you know who these special helpers are?*** (Priests, bishops, cardinals, the pope) Name for the children the priests who serve in your parish.

3 With the children standing in place as for Mass, invite the children to sing a song about God's Church (such as "We Are the Church" (*Singing Our Faith*), another from the song list on **page T201,** or the song of praise taught on Day One.

ACTING

1 When the children have returned to their seats, ask them how they can add to the Church's worship as members of God's family. (Pray, sing, be quiet so others can worship)

2 Invite the children to pray the psalm prayer based on Psalm 122:1 with gestures:

I
[Point to self.]
am glad
[Bursting gesture out and up]
when I go
[Rolling movement with hands]
to God's house.
[Join fingertips of both hands to form a roof.]

Songs

Play for the children any of these songs: "Come and Go with Me," "God Is Building a House" (*Hi God 2*); "Let Everyone Be Happy" (*Color the World with Song*); "Where I Am, God Is!" (*Songs for Young Children*); "God Has Made Us a Family" (*Hi God 3*); "Holy House" (*Sing a Song of Joy!*); "A Place in the Choir" **CD 1 Track 1**; (*The Best of Joe Wise: Music for Kids, Volume 2*); "Spirit-Friend" and "We Are the Church" (*Singing Our Faith*). For a list of all the music used in this program, see **page OV-39**.

CHECKPOINT

- How familiar are the children with the different roles of Church members?

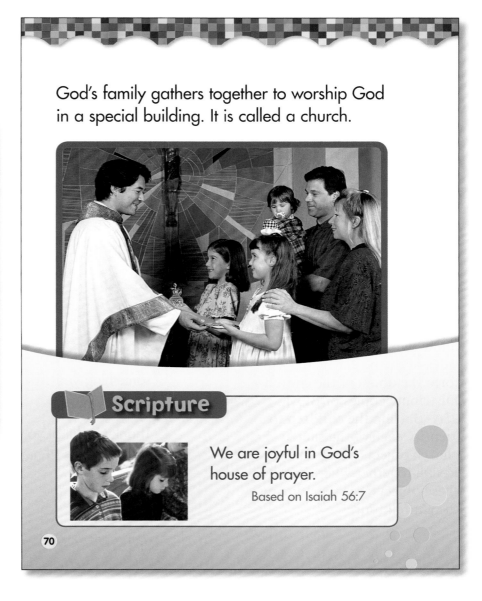

God's family gathers together to worship God in a special building. It is called a church.

Scripture

We are joyful in God's house of prayer.

Based on Isaiah 56:7

70

CHAPTER 17 | DAY FOUR

We Make a Church

Student Book pages 71–72

LEARNING OUTCOME

The children will be able to

- enjoy making a triptych of a church.

MATERIALS

- Sample church craft
- Small poster board or tag board, folded as a triptych, one for each child
- BLM 21A–B
- Crayons or markers
- Pictures of people from magazines (optional)
- Scissors
- Glue

CENTERING

1 Recall the visit to the church building and last lesson's discussion of the different roles within the Church. Ask the children to describe their favorite part about going to church.

2 Read aloud **page 71.** Have the children do the activities.

3 Prepare a sample of the church craft prior to this lesson. Show the sample to the children. Tell them they will each be making one.

SHARING

1 Distribute the small poster board, prefolded as a triptych. Have the children locate the parts that will be the front, back, and sides of the church. Show them how the folded sides of the poster board will form the doors of the church. Distribute copies of BLM 21A–B. Help the children to identify each of the sacred church objects pictured. Recall together where each of these objects was seen during the church tour.

2 Give directions for making the church craft:

- ***The front of your church opens, just like the doors of a church. You may draw a stained-glass window on either side. Or you might color, cut, and glue the picture of the***

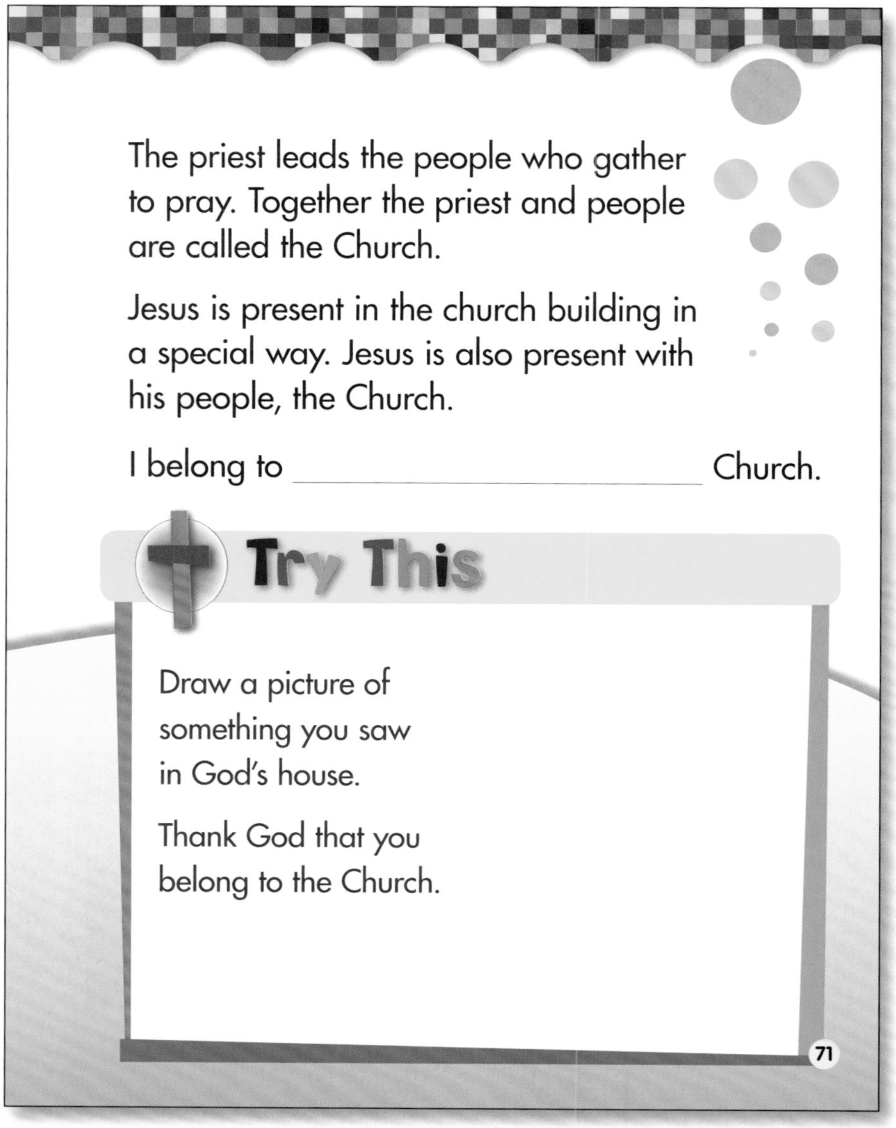
The priest leads the people who gather to pray. Together the priest and people are called the Church.

Jesus is present in the church building in a special way. Jesus is also present with his people, the Church.

I belong to ______________________ Church.

Try This

Draw a picture of something you saw in God's house.

Thank God that you belong to the Church.

71

stained-glass window from the set of pictures I gave you.

- ***On the inside of your church doors, you can draw some of the people who belong to Jesus, gathering to worship God. You can draw yourself as one of the people gathering.***

The children might cut out pictures of people from magazines instead of drawing them.

- ***Color, cut, and glue the pictures of sacred church objects inside your church.***
- ***Color, cut, and glue the picture of the cross to the highest point of your church.***

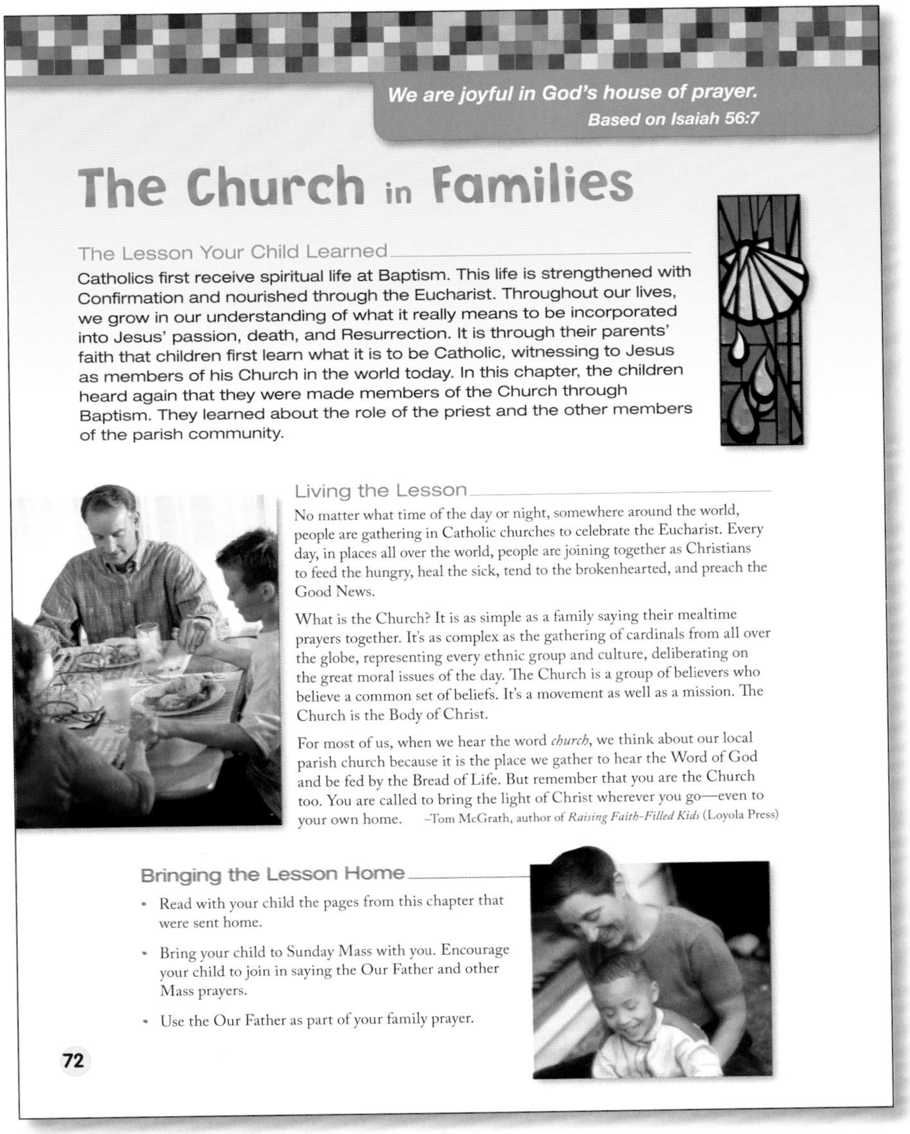

We are joyful in God's house of prayer.
Based on Isaiah 56:7

The Church in Families

The Lesson Your Child Learned

Catholics first receive spiritual life at Baptism. This life is strengthened with Confirmation and nourished through the Eucharist. Throughout our lives, we grow in our understanding of what it really means to be incorporated into Jesus' passion, death, and Resurrection. It is through their parents' faith that children first learn what it is to be Catholic, witnessing to Jesus as members of his Church in the world today. In this chapter, the children heard again that they were made members of the Church through Baptism. They learned about the role of the priest and the other members of the parish community.

Living the Lesson

No matter what time of the day or night, somewhere around the world, people are gathering in Catholic churches to celebrate the Eucharist. Every day, in places all over the world, people are joining together as Christians to feed the hungry, heal the sick, tend to the brokenhearted, and preach the Good News.

What is the Church? It is as simple as a family saying their mealtime prayers together. It's as complex as the gathering of cardinals from all over the globe, representing every ethnic group and culture, deliberating on the great moral issues of the day. The Church is a group of believers who believe a common set of beliefs. It's a movement as well as a mission. The Church is the Body of Christ.

For most of us, when we hear the word *church*, we think about our local parish church because it is the place we gather to hear the Word of God and be fed by the Bread of Life. But remember that you are the Church too. You are called to bring the light of Christ wherever you go—even to your own home. –Tom McGrath, author of *Raising Faith-Filled Kids* (Loyola Press)

Bringing the Lesson Home

- Read with your child the pages from this chapter that were sent home.
- Bring your child to Sunday Mass with you. Encourage your child to join in saying the Our Father and other Mass prayers.
- Use the Our Father as part of your family prayer.

72

ACTING

1 Display the completed church crafts in the Prayer Center and gather the children there to pray. Lead them to respond to each of the prayer statements below with the psalm prayer based on Psalm 122:1 with gestures:

I
[Point to self.]
am glad
[Bursting gesture out and up]
when I go
[Rolling movement with hands]
to God's house.
[Join fingertips of both hands to form a roof.]

- ***We belong to God's people, the Church.*** [Respond with the psalm prayer.]
- ***The house of God is our home too.*** [Respond with the psalm prayer.]
- ***We meet God in church.*** [Respond with the psalm prayer.]
- ***We praise and thank God in church.*** [Respond with the psalm prayer.]

2 Encourage the children to show their church crafts to their families and to tell them about the many people who make up the Catholic Church.

3 Have the children take home the Family Page on **page 72** to share with their families.

CHECKPOINT

- What have the children learned about the church and the roles for God's people, the Church?

ENRICHING THE FAITH EXPERIENCE

Use the following activities to enrich a lesson, to replace an activity with one that better meets the needs of your class, or to create an additional lesson.

1. Invite a priest and other parish members to talk to the children about their particular roles in the parish community. They should help the children understand how, as Catholics, they bring Jesus' love to others. Remind them to keep their presentations simple.

2. Have the children draw pictures of different members of the parish whom they know: priests, sisters, catechists, and others.

3. Have the children draw a picture of their visit to the church.

4. Invite some of the people identified on **page T200** to talk to the children about their roles in the Eucharistic Liturgy.

5. Teach the following finger play.

Finger Play

Here is the church.
[Interlace fingers with knuckles showing upwards and with thumbs pointing up.]

Here is the steeple.
[Point index fingers up together to make a steeple.]

Open the doors
[Turn hands over with fingers still interlaced.]

And see all the people.
[Wiggle fingertips.]

Chapter 18
Meals Are Good

FAITH FOCUS

Jesus gives himself to us in the Eucharist. John 6:1–13; 1 Corinthians 11:23–26

PREPARING THE FAITH EXPERIENCE

LISTENING

As you prepare to share God's Word of love with the children, spend some quiet time with God in prayer. Relax your body, quiet your mind, and let yourself be aware that you are filled with God's love. Ask God to speak to you his Word of love.

When the hour came, he took his place at table with the apostles. He said to them, "I have eagerly desired to eat this Passover with you before I suffer, for, I tell you, I shall not eat it [again] until there is fulfillment in the kingdom of God." . . . Then he took the bread, said the blessing, broke it, and gave it to them, saying, "This is my body, which will be given for you; do this in memory of me." And likewise the cup after they had eaten, saying, "This cup is the new covenant in my blood, which will be shed for you."

Luke 22:14–16,19–20

REFLECTING

All over the world, meals have a special significance. Almost universally, people observe life's milestones with some type of meal: birthday meals or parties, graduation dinners, victory banquets, wedding feasts, even simple meals after a funeral service. The predominant theme of each is a celebration of life. The very act of eating is itself a sign of life. It is humanity's tacit declaration that life must go on.

Some of the most important events in the life of Christ were also associated with meals. In John's Gospel we read that at a wedding feast, Jesus worked his first miracle and sanctified marriage by his presence there. At a banquet he showed the Father's great mercy toward sinners when he forgave and praised the penitent woman kneeling at his feet. It was immediately after a huge outdoor meal that Christ first promised the Eucharist. And it was at the Last Supper that Christ not only kept that promise and instituted the Eucharist but also gave us the means to perpetuate this heavenly food.

It is with grateful wonder and love that we receive this sacrificial meal that unites and strengthens the whole Body of Christ.

RESPONDING

God's Word calls us to respond in love. Respond to God now in the quiet of your heart and perhaps through a journal that you are keeping this year.

- How do I prepare myself to receive Jesus in the Eucharist?

Lord, prepare the hearts of the children to receive your Body and Blood in the Eucharist.

Catechism of the Catholic Church

The themes of this lesson correspond to the following paragraphs: 1333, 1337–1339, 1368.

Scripture in This Chapter

- *1 Corinthians 10:16–17 Members of the Church are united in the Body and Blood of Christ.*
- *John 6:53 Eternal life comes through the eucharistic meal.*

THE FAITH EXPERIENCE

DAY ONE
We Share Meals with Others

DAY TWO
Bread and Wine Are Gifts of God

DAY THREE
Jesus Shares a Special Meal

DAY FOUR
Jesus Shares Himself at Mass

Church Documents

General Directory for Catechesis #115.
The Holy Eucharist occupies a unique place to which all of the other sacraments are ordained. Catechists should present the Eucharist as the "sacrament of sacraments."

National Directory for Catechesis #39.
The liturgy helps us live the Christian faith through dedication to the teaching of the apostles, the communal life, the breaking of the bread, and prayer.

Letter to Families #18.
Jesus instituted the Eucharist in a family-like setting during the Last Supper. When families meet for meals and are together in harmony, Christ is close to them.

Bulletin Board At the left is a suggestion for a bulletin-board design. Using construction paper, poster board, felt, or similar materials, craft a chalice and a host. You might also include a banner with the words, "Meals Are Good."

- ***BLM 1 Jesus***

For a list of children's literature suggestions, please see **page OV-47.**

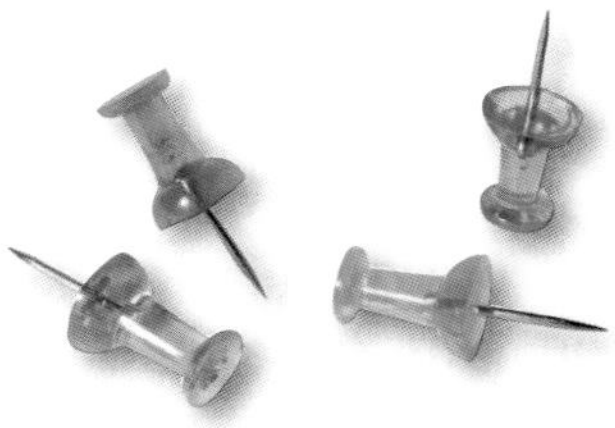

CHAPTER 18 | DAY ONE

We Share Meals with Others

LEARNING OUTCOMES

The children will be able to

- learn the values expressed when we share meals.
- become acquainted with the Bible story of the multiplication of the loaves and fishes.

KEY TERM

meal—eating, usually with others

MATERIALS

- *A Child's Bible*, page 18
- Place mat, plate, knife, fork, spoon, napkin, and drinking cup
- Drawing paper
- Crayons or markers
- Magazine picture of a table set for a meal or of a family sharing a meal
- Bible enthroned, with note card on which you have written the adapted Scripture reading for SHARING #3, John 6:1–15

COMMENTS

1. What Christ did once and for all in his Paschal Mystery (passion, death, Resurrection, and ascension) is made present again under the sign of a holy meal. The Eucharist is both a sacrifice and a meal. It is a memorial celebration of the Paschal Mystery; it is a celebration that involves us in the present moment; and it joyfully looks forward to the fulfillment of this mystery at the end of time. It presupposes our Christian unity, while helping to strengthen it.

2. The children might enjoy role-playing a family meal. Have them pray grace, pass the food, eat, and carry on conversations.

CENTERING

1 Recall the last chapter.

- ***In the last chapter we talked about the special place where we gather to worship God. What do we call the building where we gather to worship God?*** (church)
- ***Today you will begin to learn more about what God's people do when we gather to worship God in church.***

2 Set a place mat on a table in front of the class, keeping the items needed to finish the place setting out of sight. Ask the children to identify items that are needed to complete the place setting. As each item is named (Plate, fork, knife, spoon, napkin, and drinking cup), invite a volunteer to set each one in place. Ask the children when a place setting such as this might be used. (At a meal) Discuss:

- ***All of us eat because food keeps us healthy and strong. Besides food, what do we need for a meal?*** (Table, dishes, utensils, people) ***It is good when people gather around a table for a meal.***
- ***With whom do you eat your meals at home? What are some of your favorite foods?***

3 Distribute drawing paper and crayons. Have the children draw a picture of their family eating a meal. When finished, invite volunteers to describe what they have drawn in their pictures.

SHARING

1 Show a magazine picture of a table set for a meal or of a family sharing a meal. Discuss meals as times for sharing love.

- ***Sharing a meal with others is special. People become closer to one another when they sit down and eat together. Sharing food reminds us to share our love. How can you help make your family's mealtime a happy time?*** (Smile. Listen to others. Tell something interesting or funny. Say nice things. Be thankful for the food that was prepared. Help by setting the table or drying the dishes.)
- ***As your family shares food at a meal, you also share your love with one another.***

❷ Ask the children who gives us our daily bread. (God) Tell the children that the Bible has a story about how Jesus provided food for a huge crowd of people.

❸ Prepare to tell or to read the story of the multiplication of the loaves and fishes, "Jesus' Wonderful Picnic," from *A Child's Bible*, **page 18.** Introduce this Bible story by showing the Bible and opening it to the Gospel according to John, John 6:1–15. Enthrone the Bible.

- ***Let's prepare ourselves to listen well to today's Bible story.*** Tell or read the story.

❹ Discuss the story.

- ***Why were the people hungry?*** (They had been listening to Jesus teach, and it was now late in the day.)
- ***What did Jesus use to feed the people?*** (Five loaves of bread and two fish)
- ***How do you think the people felt after they ate?*** (Satisfied, happy)
- ***What was surprising about the meal?*** (Jesus fed a huge crowd of people with just five loaves of bread and two fish. There were twelve baskets of food left over.)

❺ Ask the children how they would act at a family meal if Jesus were at their table. Remind them that he is with them, even though they can't see him.

ACTING

Teach and pray the prayer based on Psalm 104:14–15 with gestures.

LORD,
[Raise arms slightly.]
you give us bread
[Lower arms. Open hands in front.]
to make us strong.
[Move arms to side. Make fists.]

Songs

Play for the children any of these songs: "Plant Love" (*I See a New World*) **CD 2 Track 7;** "Tell Them, Feed Them Well" (*Stories and Songs of Jesus*); "Friends All Gather 'Round" (*Singing Our Faith*); "Gathered Together" (*Songs for Young Children*); "God Is So Good" (*Color the World with Song*); "His Banner over Me Is Love" (*Hi God!*); "We Come to Your Table" (*Hi God 2*). For a list of all the music used in this program, see **page OV-39.**

CHECKPOINT

- What did you learn about the children's experiences of sharing family meals?
- How did the children respond to the story of the multiplication of the loaves and fishes?

CHAPTER 18 | DAY TWO

Bread and Wine Are Gifts of God

LEARNING OUTCOME

The children will be able to
- identify the importance of the bread and wine used at Mass.

KEY TERMS

flour—grain that is ground for baking

grain—the seed or fruit of certain food plants

MATERIALS

- Loaf of bread
- Cup of grape juice
- Flour
- Grapes
- Picture of wheat field, picture of a vineyard, samples of a variety of breads, grains of wheat (optional)
- Ingredients and supplies to bake bread in SHARING #6 (optional)

COMMENTS

1. Make the necessary preparations to bake bread as a group using the recipe found on page T217 or using the pretzel recipe found in Chapter 6.

2. Alternative activities include drawing pictures of various kinds of bread; making a bread-and-wine collage by gluing pictures of bread, wine, and happy people on a large sheet of paper, and adding a caption such as "Bread and wine are gifts from God."

CENTERING

Help the children retell the story from the last lesson about the multiplication of the loaves and fishes. Explain that bread means something special to us as members of the Catholic Church.

SHARING

1 Show a loaf of bread and comment:

- ***Bread is one of the most important foods we eat. People almost everywhere eat bread. It helps us grow strong and healthy.*** [Show a cup of grape juice.] ***Wine is a drink made from grapes that is sometimes used to celebrate at special meals.***

2 You might show the children samples of different kinds of bread. Let them talk about their differences and name other breads.

3 Describe how bread is made.

- ***All bread is a gift from God. All bread comes from God's gift of grain.*** [You might pass among the children a few grains for them to examine.]
- ***The grain seeds are planted in the ground. God sends sun and rain to help the seeds grow. Have you ever seen a field of golden grain?*** [Show the picture of a wheat field.]
- ***The ripe grain is picked and ground into flour.*** [Show the flour.] The flour is made into bread.
- ***Have you ever made bread with someone or watched someone make bread? What are some things mixed with the flour to make bread?*** (Water, salt, egg, yeast)

4 Describe how wine is made.

- [Show the grapes.] ***Grapes are a fruit that grows on vines. Have you ever seen a grapevine or picked grapes?*** [Show the picture of a vineyard.]
- ***When the grapes are pressed, we get grape juice. When the juice of grapes becomes fermented (or aged), it turns into wine. What colors of grape juice have you seen? (Red, white) Just like grape juice, wine can be red or white depending on the kinds of grapes used to make the wine.***

❺ Teach this song of thanks and praise to the melody of "The Farmer in the Dell."

Thank You, God

God makes the wheat seeds grow,
God makes the grapevines grow.
Let's give God thanks and praise
For wheat and grapes that grow.

❻ Make bread together using the recipe found on **page T217**. Alternatively, you could make pretzels as found in Chapter 6. If you bake bread as a group, save enough to share on Day Four. Be sure to find out if any children have food allergies and take these into consideration when planning this activity.

ACTING

❶ Recall the petition of the Our Father in which we ask for bread.

- ***Families give each other what they need. We ask God, our heavenly Father, for what we need when we say, "Give us this day our daily bread."***
- ***When we ask God for bread, we are actually asking for all the things we need each day to be happy and healthy children of God.***

❷ Invite the children to pray "Give us this day our daily bread" with hands extended in front of them. Invite the children to pray together the Our Father.

CHECKPOINT

- How have the children shown a greater understanding of God's gifts of bread and wine?

CHAPTER 18 | DAY THREE

Jesus Shares a Special Meal

Student Book page 73

LEARNING OUTCOMES

The children will be able to

- develop a simple understanding of the Mass and its relationship to Jesus' Last Supper.
- begin to recognize the gift of Jesus in Holy Communion.

KEY TERMS

apostles—followers of Jesus, Jesus' special helpers

Last Supper—the last meal Jesus ate with this apostles before he died, during which he offered himself to the Father for us and gave us the Eucharist

Mass—the meal Catholics celebrate in which we hear God's Word, remember the death and Resurrection of Jesus, offer ourselves to God the Father, and receive the bread and wine that have become Jesus

MATERIALS

- Poster 8
- Serving plate and wine goblet
- Tablecloth or white shelf paper, large enough for all the children to sit around
- Small paper plates and cups, one for the catechist and for each child

COMMENT

If the children are familiar with the parts of the Mass, you might point out the meal elements of the Mass. (Examples: washing hands before eating, setting the table, bringing food to the table, saying grace, passing the food, talking together)

CENTERING

Link this lesson to the last one.

- ***What food and drink did you learn about in the last lesson?*** (Bread and wine)
- ***Today you will hear about a special meal of bread and wine that Jesus shared with his friends.***

SHARING

1 Prepare the children to hear the story of Jesus' Last Supper. Tell them that this story is found in the Bible. Introduce this Bible story by showing the Bible and opening it to the Gospel according to Luke, Luke 22:14–16,19–20. Enthrone the Bible.

2 Tell the children that on the night before Jesus died on the cross for us, he had a very special meal with his friends, the apostles. Ask for volunteers to prepare your Prayer Center:

- Invite two volunteers to place the tablecloth or white shelf paper on the floor to represent the table.
- Invite two volunteers to set the "table" with paper plates and cups.
- Invite a volunteer to set the serving plate and wine goblet in the center of the tablecloth.
- Display Poster 8 The Last Supper.

- Ask the children to join you in the Prayer Center and pretend to be Jesus' apostles seated around the table.

3 Read aloud the story "The Last Supper" on **page T213.** Use the serving plate and wine goblet as you tell the story.

4 Explain the significance of the Last Supper.

- ***At this meal Jesus shared himself in a new way. He gave himself with all his love to his apostles.***
- ***He wanted his friends to remember him by having this special meal.***
- ***Now we call this special meal, in which Jesus offers himself for each of us, the Mass or the Eucharist.***

The Last Supper

On the night before Jesus died, he had supper with his apostles, his special friends. This was a holy supper. Jesus said to his apostles, "I have wanted so much to share this meal with you before I die." [Pause.]

During the meal, Jesus took bread from the table. He gave God praise, saying, "Thank you, heavenly Father, for this bread made from many grains of wheat."

Then Jesus broke the bread, gave it to his friends, and said, "Take this, all of you, and eat it: This is my body which will be given up for you." [Pause.]

[Tell the children to close their eyes and to imagine Jesus speaking these words to them. Tell them to imagine that they are taking and eating the bread that Jesus shared at his Last Supper. Pause.]

When Jesus shared this bread with his apostles, he was sharing the gift of himself in a very special way. [Pause.]

Then Jesus took a cup that was filled with wine. He gave God thanks, praying, "Thank you, heavenly Father, for this wine made from many grapes."

Then Jesus gave the cup to his friends and said, "Take this, all of you, and drink from it: [Raise the cup.] My blood will be shed for you and for all people so that sins may be forgiven." Then Jesus passed the cup around for his apostles to drink. [Pause.]

[Tell the children to close their eyes and to imagine Jesus speaking these words to them. Tell them to imagine that they are taking and drinking from the cup that Jesus shared at his Last Supper. Pause.]

When Jesus shared this cup of wine with his apostles, he was sharing the gift of himself in a very special way. Jesus offered himself up for us. [Pause.]

Then Jesus said, "Do this in memory of me." We do this when we celebrate Mass with the priest.

ACTING

Read aloud **page 73.** Encourage the children to talk about what happened at Jesus' Last Supper.

CHECKPOINT

- Did the children connect the story of the Last Supper with the Mass?
- Are the children aware that the bread and wine shared at Mass are special?

CHAPTER 18

Meals Are Good

On the night before he died, Jesus ate a meal with the apostles. It was Jesus' last supper with them.

At this meal, Jesus gave thanks and praise to his Father. Jesus offered himself to his Father for us. Jesus gave himself to us as bread and wine.

73

CHAPTER 18 | DAY FOUR

Jesus Shares Himself at Mass

Student Book pages 74–78

LEARNING OUTCOMES

The children will be able to

- become more familiar with the Eucharist.
- enjoy sharing a meal made from wheat and grapes.

MATERIALS

- The Last Supper Triptych punchouts from the Student Book
- Crayons or markers
- If you made bread on Day Two, use the bread you saved for today. Otherwise, prepare freshly baked brown-and-serve rolls (one roll for every three or four children).
- Cups of grape juice, one cup for each child.

COMMENT

Be sure to find out if any children have food allergies and take these into consideration when planning the lesson.

CENTERING

Have the children sing the song learned in Day Two:

Thank You, God

God makes the wheat seeds
grow,
God makes the grapevines
grow.
Let's give God thanks and
praise
For wheat and grapes that
grow.

SHARING

1 Ask the children what is happening in the picture on **page 74.** (A child is receiving Holy Communion.)

2 Encourage the children to follow along as you read aloud the page. Comment:

- ***Because God our Father loves us, he invites us to his table to receive the bread and wine that have become the Body and Blood of Christ. The picture shows God's people doing this at Mass. The Mass is a holy meal that God's family shares.***

As God's family, we come together at Mass. We give God thanks and praise.

We hear God's Word in the Bible.

We remember Jesus' Last Supper.

We remember that Jesus died for all of us. Jesus gives himself to us in the Eucharist.

At Mass the bread and wine become the Body and Blood of Jesus. Jesus gives us the gift of himself in Holy Communion.

Scripture

Jesus said, "Do this in memory of me."

Based on Luke 22:19

74

- ***When we receive Holy Communion, we remember how much Jesus loves us.***

- ***Because you belong to God's special family, the Catholic Church, one day God will call you to receive Jesus at the altar table. God will fill you with his love and joy when you receive Jesus in Holy Communion.***

3 Introduce the snack of bread and grape juice:

- ***You cannot yet receive Holy Communion at Mass. You must wait until you are older. But you can share this bread and juice. As we share this food that God has given to us, we can think about the day when you will receive Jesus in Holy Communion.***

4 Serve the children bread and grape juice. Carefully break the rolls into pieces. Tell the children you will pass the plate around. They may each take a piece, but should wait until everyone has been given their juice before eating. Give each child a small cup of grape juice. When all have taken a piece of bread and have a cup of grape juice, invite the children to pray grace before they eat:

- ***Bless us, O Lord, and these your gifts which we are about to receive from your goodness, through Christ our Lord. Amen.***

5 Invite the children to enjoy the bread and the grape juice.

6 Teach a song to help the children anticipate the day they will receive Jesus at their First Communion, such as "Friends, All Gather 'Round" (*Singing Our Faith*) or "We Come to Your Table" (*Hi God 2*), or another song from the song list on **page T209.**

7 Have the children turn to **page 75** and talk about the cup and the bread. Read aloud the text and the directions. Guide the children in doing the activity. Encourage the children to thank Jesus for giving himself to us as food.

ACTING

1 Distribute the Last Supper Triptych punchouts. Help the children fold it on the lines so that it stands up. Invite the children to look at the triptych and to thank God for giving us the holy bread and the holy wine that is Jesus. Invite them to think about the time when they will receive

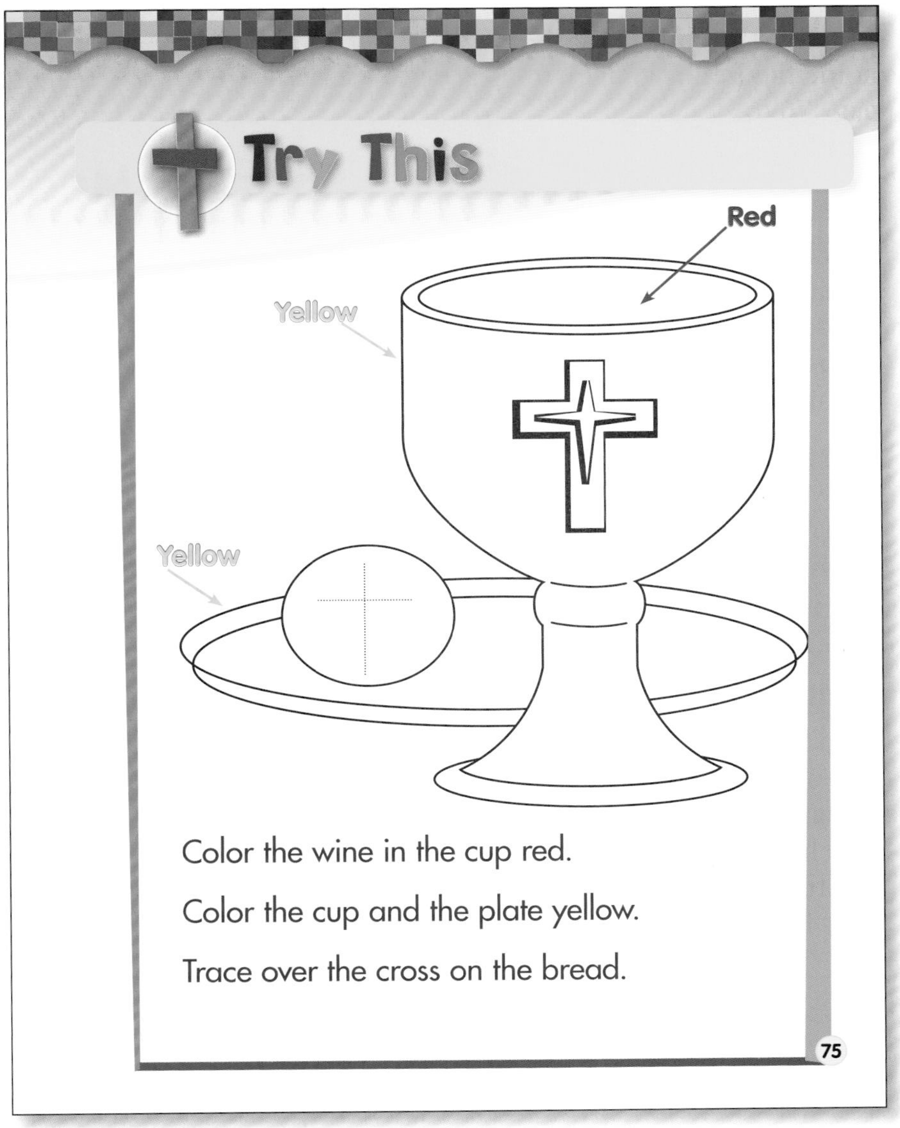
Try This
Red
Yellow
Yellow
Color the wine in the cup red.
Color the cup and the plate yellow.
Trace over the cross on the bread.
75

Jesus in the Eucharist at their First Communion. Pray together the prayer based on Psalm 104:14–15:

> **Lord,**
> [Raise arms slightly.]
>
> **you give us bread**
> [Lower arms. Open hands in front.]
>
> **to make us strong.**
> [Move arms to side. Make fists.]

2 Have the children take home the triptych of the Last Supper as a reminder of Jesus' wonderful meal.

3 Have the children take home the Family Page on **page 76** to share with their families.

CHECKPOINT

- What is the children's understanding of the Last Supper, Mass, and Holy Communion?
- Are the children looking forward to the day when they will receive Jesus at their First Communion?

FAMILY FEATURE

Help the children carefully tear out the Family Feature on **pages 77–78.** Ask them to take home the pages to read and to work on them with their families.

ENRICHING THE FAITH EXPERIENCE

Use the following activities to enrich a lesson, to replace an activity with one that better meets the needs of your class, or to create an additional lesson.

1 Have the children make place mats showing God's gift of bread. Distribute sheets of construction paper. Tell the children that they may draw bread or cut out pictures of bread from magazines that can be glued to the construction paper. Help the children to write a simple meal prayer on their place mat. When finished, the place mats can be covered with clear contact paper or laminated.

2 Talk with the children about good meals and the importance of eating a variety of foods. Invite volunteers to pantomime eating different

***Lord*, you give us bread to make us strong.**
Based on Psalm 104:14–15

Sharing Meals in Families

The Lesson Your Child Learned

At the Last Supper Jesus gave us the everlasting gift of himself. He offered his life as a sacrifice to his Father. He gave himself as food to strengthen us, to unite himself with us, and to unite us with one another. The Mass, then, is both a sacrifice and a meal. In this chapter, the children learned that meals are times for sharing love as well as for sharing food. They heard the story of Jesus' Last Supper and learned that at Mass Jesus offers himself up for us and feeds us with the bread and wine that are his Body and Blood. Through the love and friendship shared at family meals, children experience the human values found in the Eucharist.

Living the Lesson

Do you want to strengthen your family? Eat meals together regularly. Recent studies have shown that children whose families eat together regularly get better grades, enjoy better nutrition, and have a lower incidence of drug use and other problematic behavior. They're also more likely to practice their faith.

When we come together at the kitchen table, we bring not only our physical hunger, but also our social, emotional, and spiritual hungers. At the family meal, all these hungers are fed. In a time when children are being tossed about on the stormy seas of life, the family meal provides an anchor within a safe harbor—the family.

The biggest benefit of the family meal is that it prepares us all to come to the table of the Lord in the Eucharist. The more we can be present to one another at our own kitchen table, the more we will be able to experience the Real Presence of Jesus in the Eucharist.

–Tom McGrath, author of *Raising Faith-Filled Kids* (Loyola Press)

Bringing the Lesson Home

- Read with your child the pages from this chapter that were sent home.
- Discuss the day's activities as a family at mealtime.
- Have a family baking project and enjoy the results at your family meal.
- Give your child the job of setting the table.
- Begin each family meal with a prayer. Let your child lead the prayer from time to time.

76

foods, such as an ice-cream cone, spaghetti, and a lollipop. Have the class guess the food.

3 Make the children aware that there are people who are hungry.

• ***There are people who have no bread to eat. We who have food must thank God and not waste it. If we have more than we need, God wants us to share with those who don't have enough. Sometimes you might not buy candy or another snack and give your money to those who have less than you.***

4 Make bread together as a group.

Recipe

Bread in a Bag

(Measurements and directions given are for one child)
¼ cup pancake mix
1 tablespoon milk
1 small resealable plastic bag

Put ¼ cup of pancake mix in the resealable plastic bag. Add 1 tablespoon milk. Seal the bag securely and mix by kneading the bag until dough forms. Remove the dough from the bag and place on an ungreased cookie sheet. Bake at 450° until golden brown.

Alternatively, use the pretzel recipe in Chapter 6.

[A]s the Lord has forgiven you, so must you also do.
Colossians 3:13

To Forgive and to Serve

Forgiveness in the Family

The movie *Home Alone* may remain so popular because it shows what happens when a mom and her young son are not behaving at their best. This is not an unusual situation in families, so we can all relate to this family's dilemma. Tension in the household is running high, and Kevin McAllister and his mom say things they both end up regretting. The golden moment of the film is when mother and son are reunited by sharing the simple words, "I'm sorry." Some of the very best moments in a family come when forgiveness is freely offered and received all around.

The *Catechism of the Catholic Church* says, "[T]he home is the first school of Christian life...." It is the place where we "learn endurance and the joy of work, fraternal love, [and] generous—even repeated—forgiveness...." (*CCC* #1657) As fallible human beings, we need to learn to forgive as well as how to ask to be forgiven. What a blessing it is to live in a home where forgiveness is generously given and received. Forgiveness is a hallmark of Christian life.

When we recite the Our Father, the prayer Jesus taught us, we say, "Forgive us our trespasses as we forgive those who trespass against us." In that short passage, Jesus described forgiveness as an essential part of Christian life. Forgiveness is like a river; its nature is to flow and we know that it flows first and foremost from the heart of God. Because we are forgiven, we are able to

Getting Started

Some lessons are best learned by practice. Here are a few suggestions on how you can make your home a school of Christian life by modeling the virtue of forgiveness.

- When your child has done something you need to correct, ask in an unshaming way, "Do you understand what you did wrong?" or "Do you understand how your behavior hurt your sister?" The point is not punishment as much as it is helping your child grow in awareness.
- When correcting your child, be sure to make a distinction between the behavior and the person. For example, say, "Hitting other people is wrong because it will hurt them." instead of "You're a bad boy for hitting Jason." This is not to let the child "off the hook" but will help him or her, over time, build empathy and understand the consequences of his or her actions.
- When you've acted in a way you regret, model for your child the way to ask forgiveness:
  1. Say you are sorry.
  2. Be specific as to what you are sorry for.
  3. Make an honest promise to do better in the future. This might sound something like this: "Jennifer, I'm sorry that I yelled at you in the car. I was worried I was going to be late, and I didn't take time to listen to your questions. I hope you'll forgive me. I will try to leave more time between errands next time so that I'll have time to listen to your questions."

- Let your child see you give and receive forgiveness with other family members. Apologizing is not a sign of weakness. It is an acknowledgement that we adults can fail, and that forgiveness is important to us too.
- The next time you pray the Our Father as a family, point out to your child the phrase, "Forgive us our trespasses as we forgive those who trespass against us." Explain that Jesus wants us to forgive one another and to ask for forgiveness when we haven't been loving to one another. Forgiveness is a sign that God is in our home.
- Tell your child the story of the Good Shepherd who seeks out the lost sheep. (Luke 15:3–7) This is a good opportunity to let your child know that Jesus is always ready to forgive us no matter what we do. We just need to tell him we're sorry.

78

unit four

Celebrating God's Love

In this unit the children will learn to celebrate God's gift of love with others.

19 SEEDS ARE GOOD

Through the life of a seed, the children are introduced to the mystery of life and death. They learn that through the cross they received new life in Baptism to live as Jesus did. They learn to make the Sign of the Cross.

20 BUTTERFLIES ARE GOOD

The children recall how spring brings forth new life. They compare the life cycle of a butterfly to Jesus' death and Resurrection. They hear that through Baptism they participate in Jesus' new life. They learn that *alleluia* means "Praise the Lord!"

21 LIGHT IS GOOD

The children are led to appreciate light as a gift of God. They learn that Jesus called himself the light of the world and are introduced to the Easter candle as a symbol of the risen Jesus. They learn that they received a candle at Baptism as a sign of their share in Jesus' life. They are encouraged to pass on the love of Jesus.

22 CELEBRATING IS GOOD

The children discover the meaning of gifts and are shown how to thank God for the gifts of his love at the celebration of the Mass. They learn that they are invited, by reason of their Baptism, to join in the Mass.

23 AIR IS GOOD

The children compare air, an invisible reality needed for life, to the Holy Spirit. They hear that the Holy Spirit will help them live as Christians. They learn the last line of the Our Father.

24 JOY IS GOOD

The children learn that the risen Jesus is the source of Christian joy and that they are invited to share this joy. They are encouraged to reach out to others in self-sacrificing love and to bring joy to those they meet.

25 LIFE IS GOOD

The children recall that new life comes through death. They reflect on the joys of this world and learn about the joys of heaven. They learn that the greatest joy comes from experiencing God's love.

Chapter 19
Seeds Are Good

FAITH FOCUS

Jesus died to give us new life.

John 12:23–25

PREPARING THE FAITH EXPERIENCE

LISTENING

Those who share God's Word with others must be fed themselves by God's Word found in Sacred Scripture. Share some time of quiet prayer with God, listening to God's word. Ask God to fill you with his presence and nourish you by his holy Word.

"Amen, amen, I say to you, unless a grain of wheat falls to the ground and dies, it remains just a grain of wheat; but if it dies, it produces much fruit. Whoever serves me must follow me, and where I am, there also will my servant be."

John 12:24,26

REFLECTING

Suffering leads to growth, and death leads to life. Nature reflects this paradox: the planted seed dies and only then becomes a flower; the cocooned caterpillar is slowly transformed into a beautiful butterfly. Human experience is also marked by this mysterious pattern. In each person's life there are "small deaths"—sufferings, separations, misunderstandings. Saint Francis of Assisi had this in mind when he prayed:

> For it is in giving that we receive,
> it is in pardoning that we are pardoned,
> it is in dying that we are born to eternal life.

Through the mystery of his death and Resurrection, Christ himself experienced this same paradox. He transformed suffering, death, and evil into a glorious new life. And he did so freely. Strengthened by prayerful union with his Father, he willingly accepted the consequences of humanity's sin. He countered hatred with love, arrogant pride with humble docility, death with life. The response of Jesus is the ideal for anyone who characterizes himself or herself as his follower. Imitation of Christ—even unto death—is the standard of perfection for the Christian. It is our response to Jesus' words, "Do this in remembrance of me."

RESPONDING

Having been nourished by God's Word, we are able to respond to God's great love for us. In prayer, respond to God's call to you to share his word with others. You may also wish to respond in your prayer journal.

- How do I respond to the suffering, death, and evil that are part of human life?
- How will I present the story of Jesus' death and Resurrection in a way appropriate to the maturity level of the children in my class?

Holy Spirit, help us appreciate the new life Jesus won for us.

Catechism of the Catholic Church

The themes of this lesson correspond to the following paragraphs: 617–618, 654, 2157.

THE FAITH EXPERIENCE

DAY ONE
Plants Grow from Seeds

DAY TWO
Seeds Die to Give Plants Life

DAY THREE
Jesus Died to Give Us New Life

DAY FOUR
The Cross Is a Sign of Jesus' Love

Scripture in This Chapter

- *Isaiah 52:13 The suffering servant will prosper.*
- *Mark 10:45 The Son of Man came to serve and to ransom many.*

Church Documents

General Directory for Catechesis #16.
All of reality is marked by the dynamism which bursts forth from the Resurrection of Christ, the seed which renews believers in the hope of a definitive fulfillment.

Directory on Popular Piety and the Liturgy #128.
Christians see the Cross as an expression of the triumph of Christ over the powers of darkness. They adorn the cross with precious stones and use it as a sign of blessing on one's self, on others, and on objects.

The Church in the Modern World #18.
Christ won the victory of eternal life for us when he rose from the dead, for by his death he freed us from death.

The theme of this chapter corresponds to the beginning of the season of Lent. This chapter is best taught after the first Sunday of Lent. Lesson 5 of SPECIAL SEASONS AND DAYS is an additional Lent session. Refer to the ENRICHING THE FAITH EXPERIENCE section of this chapter and Lesson 5 of SPECIAL SEASONS AND DAYS for additional ideas to expand upon the themes of Lent.

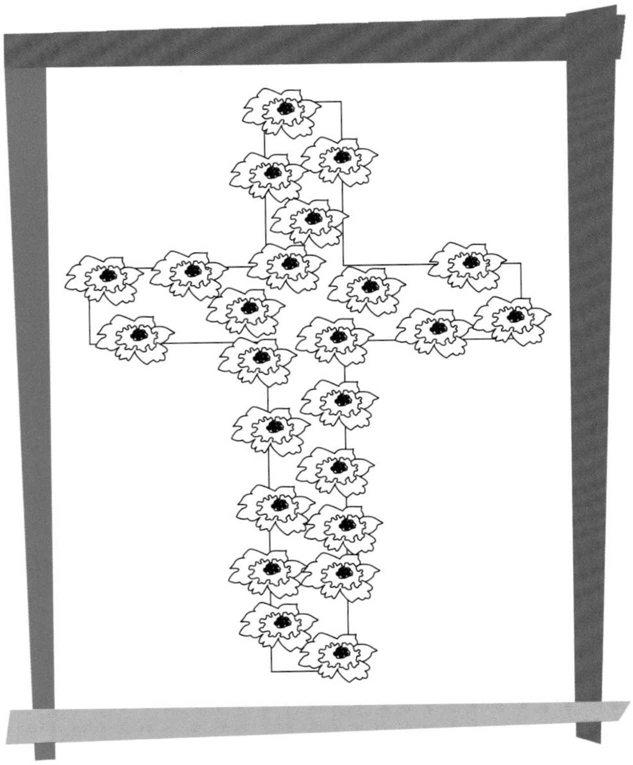

Bulletin Board At the left is a suggestion for a bulletin-board design. Let the children make flowers from construction paper. Pin or tape their flowers to the cross.

For a list of children's literature suggestions, please see **page OV-47.**

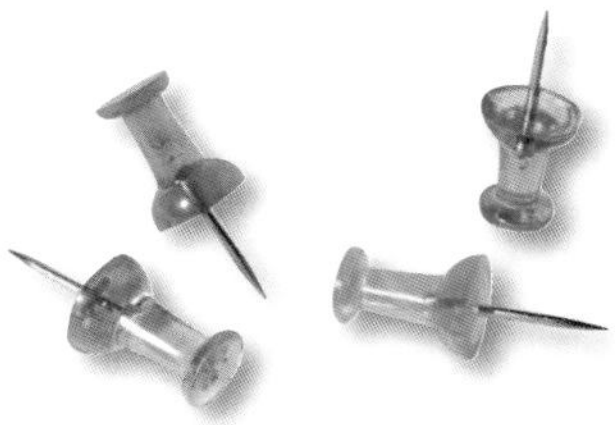

Plants Grow from Seeds

Student Book page 79

LEARNING OUTCOMES

The children will be able to

- know that plants come from seeds.
- marvel at the wonder of God's gifts of seeds and plants.

MATERIALS

- Cutout 33
- Small paper cups each containing a few seeds with a picture of the appropriate plant taped to it
- Fruits or vegetables that contain seeds (cucumber, pepper, apple, orange)
- Knife
- Plant with a flower
- Lima bean soaked overnight, one for each child
- Drawing paper prefolded into thirds
- Crayons or markers

COMMENTS

1. By his Passion, Death, Resurrection, and Ascension, Jesus freed us from slavery to sin and became the source of our eternal life. This is the Paschal Mystery, the Good News of salvation. And so the Church proclaims the Paschal Mystery in the celebration of the Eucharist. The Paschal Mystery is the source of the preaching and teaching of the Christian message, which is broadened and deepened by catechesis. We continue to proclaim this "mystery of our faith" at every Mass.

2. Remind the children that much of the food we eat grows from seeds. All our food is a gift from God for all people. We can share our abundance with people who are hungry in our community and around the world. Lead the children to pray that people will share their food with those who do not have enough to eat.

CENTERING

1 Recall the last chapter.

- ***In the last chapter we learned about Jesus' Last Supper with his friends, the apostles. What did Jesus tell us to do in memory of him?*** (Share the bread and wine that are his Body and Blood; celebrate Mass.)
- ***Today you will begin to learn more about the great act of love that Jesus did for us.***

2 Let the children examine seeds. Have them form small groups. Give each group three cups, each containing a different kind of seed with a picture of the plant the seeds will become. Ask:

- ***What do the seeds look like? What colors are they?***
- ***Are all these seeds the same? Why do they look different?***
- ***Do the seeds look like the plants they will become?***
- ***Where did these seeds come from?***

Cut a piece of fruit or a vegetable to show the seeds inside. If you cut an apple horizontally, you will see that the seeds are in the shape of a star.

- ***Seeds can help us understand what Jesus did for us.***
- ***God made seeds in a very wonderful way. Inside each seed is a tiny plant. The seed also holds food for the little plant.***
- ***Very carefully peel off the seed coat or thin lining that keeps the seed together. Gently break the seed open. Look inside.***
- ***See the little plant with tiny leaves. See the food around the little plant.***
- ***Each seed is a gift from God that can grow into a plant.*** Collect the seeds.

SHARING

1 Show the children a plant. Tell them that they will learn more about how a seed grows into a plant. Give each child a lima bean that has been soaked overnight to examine.

2 Show a flower. Explain:

- ***This beautiful flower came from a little seed. But the little seed is not alive anymore. It had to die so the new plant could grow.***

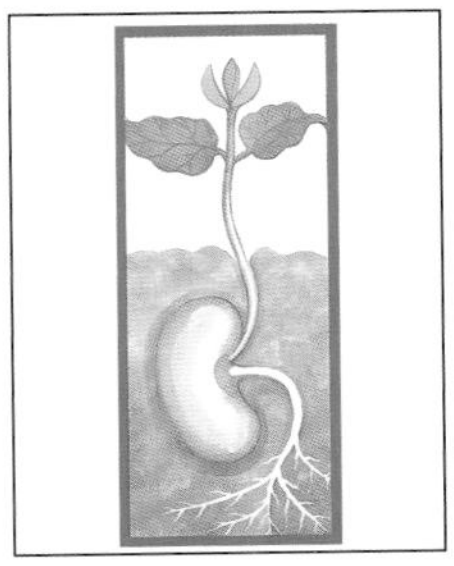

• [Show Cutout 33 Growing seed.] ***This is what all seeds do when they are planted. They die to give new life to a plant.***

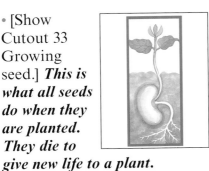

3 With the children, dramatize how a seed grows.

• ***The seed is deep down in the ground.*** [Kneel, hands hugging knees, head touching floor and hands.] ***The little plant in the seed is waking up.*** [Raise head very slowly.] ***The plant is beginning to grow.*** [Rise slowly and stand up.] ***The sun shines and the plant grows up.*** [Smiling, slowly raise arms and reach up to the sun.]

4 Have the children draw pictures of a seed growing. Distribute paper that has been folded into three sections. Tell the children to draw in the left section a picture of the seed planted in the ground. In the middle section they should draw the seed sprouting roots beneath the ground while green leaves grow above the ground. In the right section they should draw the blossoming plant.

ACTING

1 Have the children open their books to **page 79.** Invite them to describe the picture. Ask what happens to seeds when they are planted in the ground. Have the children listen and follow along as you read aloud the poem.

2 Place all the seeds that the children studied in today's lesson on a table near the Bible in the Prayer Center. Tell the children that seeds and plants are gifts from God. Many plants provide food for us to eat. Invite the children to pray that seeds being planted all around the world will grow to produce much food for people who are hungry. Invite the children to thank God for seeds, which are a sign for us of God's

CHECKPOINT

- What knowledge of seeds and plants did the children demonstrate?
- What signs were there that the children were awed by the miracles of nature?

UNIT FOUR
CHAPTER 19

Seeds Are Good

Put a seed into the ground
To die so a plant can grow.
With sun and water from God,
New life sprouts and starts to show.
Apple seeds make apple trees,
Potato seeds, potatoes.
Radish seeds grow radishes,
Tomato seeds, tomatoes.
Flower seeds grow marigolds,
Violets, and roses, too.
Each seed that dies and grows
Tells God's love for me and you.

79

CHAPTER 19 | DAY TWO

Seeds Die to Give Plants Life

Student Book page 80

LEARNING OUTCOMES

The children will be able to

- be aware of the death-to-new-life cycle of a seed.
- know that Jesus died on a cross and rose to new life to give them new life.

MATERIALS

- Bible, with note card on which you have written the adapted Scripture reading for SHARING #2, John 12:24
- Cutout 1
- Poster 9
- Grain of wheat, brown rice, or another seed that looks like wheat
- Cross or crucifix
- Seeds, potting soil, and clear plastic cups for SHARING #6

COMMENT

Our lives are a continuous series of deaths and resurrections, from the moment we leave our mother's womb to begin a new life in a new world to the ultimate moment we leave this world in death to enter the realm of eternal life.

CENTERING

Reread to the children the poem on **page 79**. Let them join in on any lines they remember. Alternatively, teach the children the finger play "I Had a Little Cherry Stone."

I Had a Little Cherry Stone

I had a little cherry stone
And put it in the ground.
[Pretend to put cherry in left hand using right thumb and forefinger.]

And when next year I went to look,
A tiny shoot I found.
[Raise right forefinger from clenched left fist.]

The shoot grew upward day by day,
[Raise both hands slowly to imitate growth.]

And soon became a tree.
I picked the rosy cherries then,
[Keep left hand raised to imitate tree; right hand picks cherries.]

And ate them for my tea.
Here's some for you and me.
[Gesture outward, then point to self.]

SHARING

1 Display Cutout 1 Jesus and tell how Jesus' death brings new life the way a grain of wheat does.

- ***The week before Jesus died, he told a story about a wheat seed dying. We find Jesus' words in the Bible.***

2 Show the Bible and open the Bible to the Gospel of John, John 12:24. Invite the children to remember what they learned about how to be good listeners.

- ***Let's prepare ourselves to listen well to today's Bible reading.***
- ***This is what Jesus said: "Unless a grain of wheat*** [Show the seed.] ***dies, it remains just a grain of wheat. But if it is put into the ground to die, it grows into a stalk of wheat with many grains on it."***

3 Explain how a seed dies to give new life to the plant and how this is like Jesus' death and Resurrection:

- ***If the seed is to grow, it must be pushed down into the ground. You have to bury it, cover it up with dirt, and let it die. Then it grows and becomes a stalk of wheat with many seeds on it.*** [Pause.]
- ***But Jesus was talking about more than a grain of wheat. He was really talking about himself.*** [Reverently show a cross. Allow a moment of silence.] ***Jesus knew he would soon die on a cross.*** [Pause.] ***He loves us. He wanted to save us and give us new life.***
- ***When Jesus died, his body was put into the ground—buried in a tomb, or grave.*** [Pause.]
- ***A seed does not stay in the ground. It comes up with new life. Jesus did not stay in the tomb. He rose with new life.***
- ***A seed dies to give new life to a plant.*** [Display Poster 9 Jesus on the Cross.] ***Jesus died to give new life to us so that we can grow more like him. You received this new life when you were baptized. The new life helps you live in love as Jesus did.***

4 Lead the children in hand actions for the reading based on John 12:24. Let a child hold the Bible as you read.

• ***Unless a grain of wheat*** [Pinch forefinger and thumb together as if holding a grain of wheat.] ***dies, it remains just a grain of wheat.*** [Hold up right forefinger.] ***But if it is put into the ground to die,*** [Make a fist with the left hand. Push right forefinger into the hole with a planting action.] ***it grows into a stalk of wheat*** [Slowly raise fists, touching each other, in an upward growing movement.] ***with many grains on it.*** [Open fists and wiggle fingers to show many grains.] ***The Gospel of the Lord.***

• ***Let us praise Jesus for telling us about himself when he told about a grain of wheat. Say after me, "Praise to you, Lord Jesus Christ."*** [Have the children repeat after you.]

5 Direct the children to **page 80.** Read aloud the page as the children follow along. Read the following sentence together as a class:

• ***Jesus gave his life for us!***

6 Have each child plant a seed to take home to care for and to watch grow. Plant the seeds in clear plastic cups so that the children can observe the plant growth beneath the soil as well as the sprouting plant.

ACTING

1 Invite the children to pray.

• ***A little seed dies to give life to a new plant. Jesus died to give new life to us. He wanted us to know how much God Our Father loves us.***

2 Teach and pray together a prayer based on John 3:17 with gestures:

• ***The Bible tells us about the new life Jesus gives to us:***

God, you sent your Son
[Kneel on one knee and bow head.]
that we might live.
[Rise and lift arms.]

CHECKPOINT

• Are the children familiar with the life cycle of a seed?

• What do the children seem to know about Jesus' death and Resurrection?

A seed dies to give a plant new life. Jesus died to give us new life so that we can live in love as Jesus did.

Jesus gave his life for us!

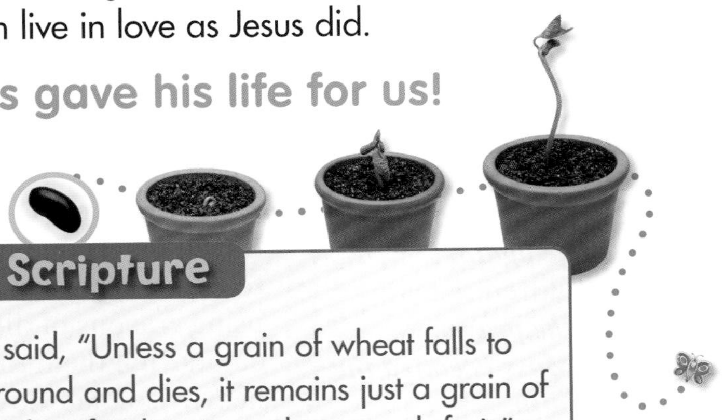

Scripture

Jesus said, "Unless a grain of wheat falls to the ground and dies, it remains just a grain of wheat; but if it dies, it produces much fruit."

Based on John 12:24

80

CHAPTER 19 | DAY THREE

Jesus Died to Give Us New Life

LEARNING OUTCOME

The children will be able to

- appreciate the cross as a special sign of God's love for them.

KEY TERM

crucifix—a cross that shows the body of Jesus; a special sign of God's love for us

MATERIALS

- Poster 9
- Cross or crucifix
- Crayons
- Drawing paper
- Cross pattern for tracing (or pretrace the cross on the drawing paper)
- Black tempera paint mixed with water
- Paintbrushes
- Scissors

COMMENT

A crucifix is to be on the altar or near it during the celebration of Mass. A cross or crucifix in a home is traditionally a sign of the Catholic faith. Many people wear a cross or crucifix to witness their commitment to Jesus.

CENTERING

Have the children focus on Poster 9 and pray the verse based on John 3:17 with gestures:

God, you sent your Son

[Kneel on one knee and bow head.]

that we might live.

[Rise and lift arms.]

SHARING

1 Introduce the Mystery of Faith. Explain:

- ***Jesus loves us. He was willing to die for us. When we come together for Mass, we remember that Jesus died to give us new life. We sing or say this prayer:***
"We proclaim your Death,
O Lord,
and profess your Resurrection
until you come again."
[Have the children repeat.]
This part of the prayer we pray during Mass is called the Mystery of Faith.

2 You might teach a sung Mystery of Faith that is frequently sung during Mass in your parish.

3 Show a cross. Explain:

- ***A cross is a special sign of God's love for us. Jesus died on a cross.***
- ***Some crosses show Jesus' body on the cross. When an image of Jesus is on the cross, it is called a crucifix.***
- ***Some crosses are beautifully decorated. Some are decorated with jewels. Some have an image of the risen Jesus on them. These crosses show that Jesus died on the cross, but he rose and is alive again. They show us we have new life too.***

4 Have the children make a jeweled cross. Give them a cross pattern to trace on paper or have the cross already traced for them. Direct them to make shapes on the cross using crayons of different colors. Tell them to press heavily so that the colors shine. Have them outline the cross with crayon and then paint over it with black tempera paint mixed with water. The colors will shine through the black paint. When the crosses are dry, have the children cut them out.

ACTING

1 Invite the children to gather in the Prayer Center. Display a cross. Invite the children to pray as they look at the cross:

- ***As you look at the cross, think about the new life that Jesus gives us. Tell Jesus in your heart that you love him.***

2 Invite the children to pray together the prayer based on John 3:17 with gestures:

God, you sent your Son

[Kneel on one knee and bow head.]

that we might live.

[Rise and lift arms.]

CHECKPOINT

- What was the children's response when they learned that Jesus died on the cross to give us new life?

The Cross Is a Sign of Jesus' Love

Student Book pages 81–82

LEARNING OUTCOME

The children will be able to
- make the Sign of the Cross reverently.

KEY TERM

Sign of the Cross—the prayer with gestures that shows we are followers of Jesus

MATERIALS
- Construction-paper cross, 9 inches by 12 inches, with the four ends numbered to show how to make the Sign of the Cross
- Crayons or markers
- Cross punchouts from the Student Book
- Seeds
- Glue
- Holy water

COMMENTS

1. The Sign of the Cross is a profession of our belief in the Trinity. Through this sign, we express our belief that we are saved through Jesus' death on the cross.

2. You might wish to make numbered paper crosses similar to the one described in Materials to pin on the children to help them as they learn to make the Sign of the Cross.

3. Standing with your back to the class or facing the class and making the Sign of the Cross backwards (from right to left) may help the children learn to make the Sign correctly.

CENTERING

Link the last lesson to this one.

- ***Why is the cross so special?*** (Jesus died on the cross. He gives us new life.)
- [Make the Sign of the Cross.] ***When have you seen people make this special sign?*** (At Mass, when praying)

SHARING

1 Tell the children about the Sign of the Cross.

- ***We make a cross sign to show that we love God.***
- ***Making the Sign of the Cross is a prayer. The Sign of the Cross is also an offering of ourselves to God. When we sign our forehead, we give God our mind. When we sign our chest, we give God our heart. When we sign our body from shoulder to shoulder, we give God our whole self. This is***

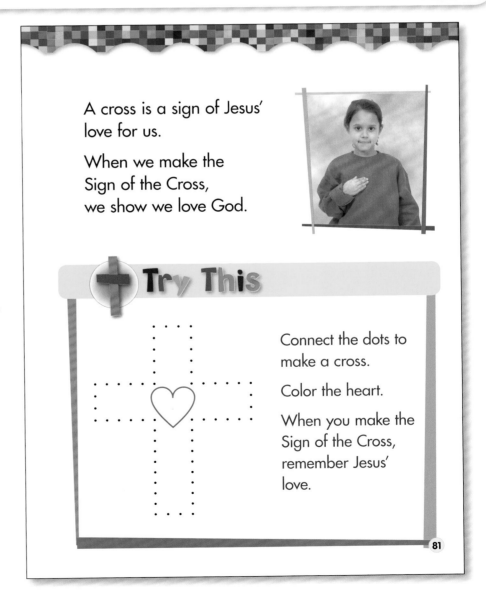

A cross is a sign of Jesus' love for us.

When we make the Sign of the Cross, we show we love God.

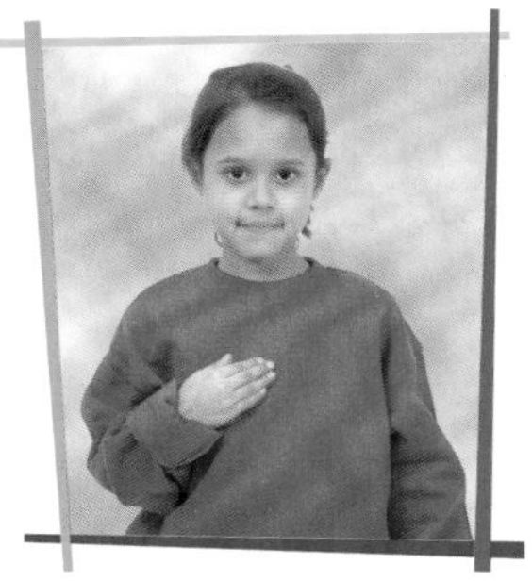

Try This

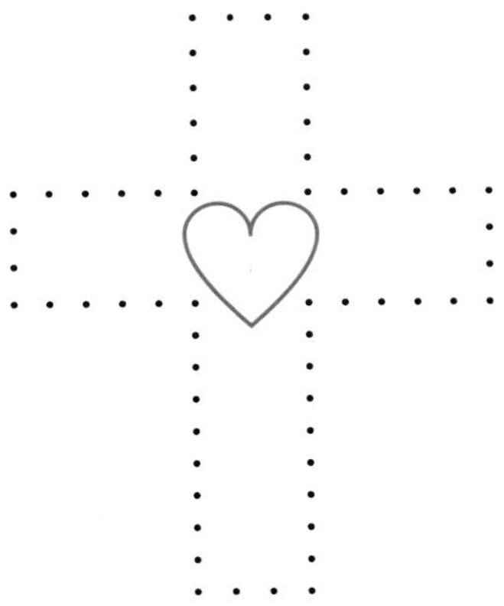

Connect the dots to make a cross.

Color the heart.

When you make the Sign of the Cross, remember Jesus' love.

81

how we do it. [Pin the paper cross on yourself and make the Sign of the Cross. Remove the paper cross.]

• ***Watch carefully as I make the Sign of the Cross again and say the words of the prayer: In the name of the Father, and of the Son, and of the Holy Spirit. Amen.***

2 Have the children make the Sign of the Cross with their right hands.

3 Have the children turn to **page 81.** Read it to them and help them do the activity. Practice with the children making the Sign of the Cross. Help them learn the words. When they know it, let them color the cross next to the prayer on the inside front cover of their books.

ACTING

1 Distribute the Cross punchouts and the seeds. Invite the children to put glue on the small inner cross and carefully place seeds on the glue. Have the children take home their crosses to help them remember that just as the seed dies so the plant can grow, Jesus died to give them new life.

2 Invite the children to thank God for showing us such great love by reverently making the Sign of the Cross using holy water. Pray together the prayer based on John 3:17 with gestures:

God, you sent your Son [Kneel on one knee and bow head.]

that we might live. [Rise and lift arms.]

3 Have the children take home the Family Page on **page 82** to share with their families.

CHECKPOINT

• How will you help the children continue to learn to make the Sign of the Cross slowly, prayerfully, and reverently?

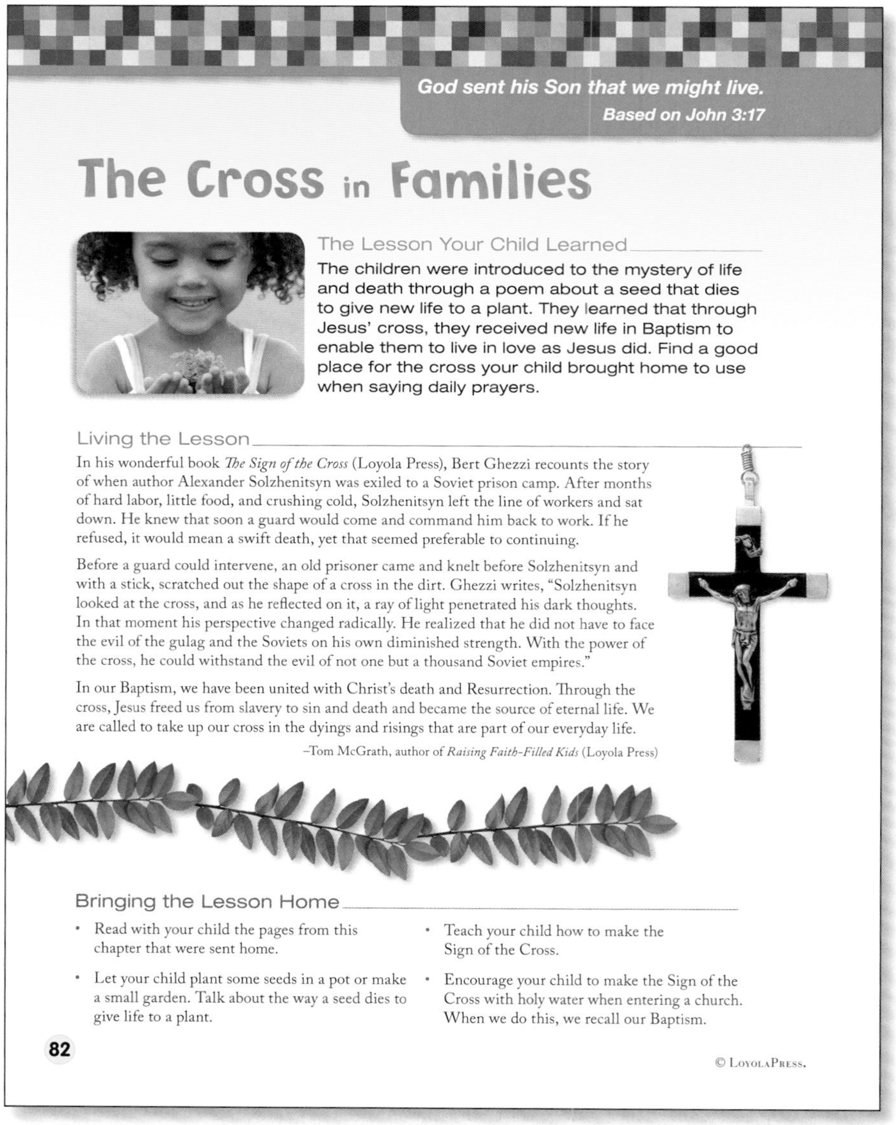

God sent his Son that we might live.
Based on John 3:17

The Cross in Families

The Lesson Your Child Learned

The children were introduced to the mystery of life and death through a poem about a seed that dies to give new life to a plant. They learned that through Jesus' cross, they received new life in Baptism to enable them to live in love as Jesus did. Find a good place for the cross your child brought home to use when saying daily prayers.

Living the Lesson

In his wonderful book *The Sign of the Cross* (Loyola Press), Bert Ghezzi recounts the story of when author Alexander Solzhenitsyn was exiled to a Soviet prison camp. After months of hard labor, little food, and crushing cold, Solzhenitsyn left the line of workers and sat down. He knew that soon a guard would come and command him back to work. If he refused, it would mean a swift death, yet that seemed preferable to continuing.

Before a guard could intervene, an old prisoner came and knelt before Solzhenitsyn and with a stick, scratched out the shape of a cross in the dirt. Ghezzi writes, "Solzhenitsyn looked at the cross, and as he reflected on it, a ray of light penetrated his dark thoughts. In that moment his perspective changed radically. He realized that he did not have to face the evil of the gulag and the Soviets on his own diminished strength. With the power of the cross, he could withstand the evil of not one but a thousand Soviet empires."

In our Baptism, we have been united with Christ's death and Resurrection. Through the cross, Jesus freed us from slavery to sin and death and became the source of eternal life. We are called to take up our cross in the dyings and risings that are part of our everyday life.

–Tom McGrath, author of *Raising Faith-Filled Kids* (Loyola Press)

Bringing the Lesson Home

- Read with your child the pages from this chapter that were sent home.
- Let your child plant some seeds in a pot or make a small garden. Talk about the way a seed dies to give life to a plant.
- Teach your child how to make the Sign of the Cross.
- Encourage your child to make the Sign of the Cross with holy water when entering a church. When we do this, we recall our Baptism.

82

ENRICHING THE FAITH EXPERIENCE

Use the following activities to enrich a lesson, to replace an activity with one that better meets the needs of your class, or to create an additional lesson.

1 Teach the children this finger play:

God Made a Flower

I pushed a seed into the ground.
[Push right forefinger into hole made by left fist.]

It was round and small and hard.
[Pinch right forefinger against thumb to form circle.]

Out of it God made a flower.
[Slowly raise folded hands.]

Right there in my own backyard!
[Open folded hands into a flower.]

Janice Driscoll
Religion Teacher's Journal

2 Draw and cut out of poster board crosses, 8 inches by 10 inches, one for each child. Cut several different colors of yarn into 12-inch lengths, several pieces for each child. Distribute the crosses and the pieces of yarn. Invite the children to spread glue on the vertical bar of their crosses and then, starting with the outside edge of the cross, press the yarn to the poster board and spiral it inward. Allow the children to experiment with their yarn patterns. Have them trim excess yarn with scissors and supply more pieces of yarn as necessary. Invite them to continue their yarn patterns on the horizontal bar of their crosses. When they have finished, punch a hole at the top of each cross and loop a piece of yarn through the hole. Hang up the crosses and allow them to dry.

3 Set up an observation center in your classroom where the children can watch and monitor seeds as they sprout and grow into plants. Soak large seeds (beans, peas, corn) overnight. Fill a glass jar with pieces of crumpled paper towels. Place the soaked seeds between the glass and the rolled paper towels. Add an inch of water to the jar. Set the jar in a sunny spot and watch the seeds sprout over the next few weeks. When the sprouts are large enough, plant the seedlings in potting soil.

Songs

Play for the children any of these songs: "O How Good Is Christ the Lord" (*Singing Our Faith*) **CD 1 Track 10;** "The Seed" (*The Best of Joe Wise*); "Bloom Where You're Planted" (*Bloom Where You're Planted*); "The Flower Song" (*Songs for Young Children*); Memorial Acclamation A from the Eucharistic Prayer (various versions found in Singing Our Faith). For a list of all the music used in this program, see page OV-39.

Chapter 20

Butterflies Are Good

FAITH FOCUS

Jesus rose from the dead and gave us new life.

Mark 16:1–7

PREPARING THE FAITH EXPERIENCE

LISTENING

The vocation of a teacher is to communicate with joy the good news of God's love. Take some time to let yourself be refreshed by the good news found in the Bible. As you pray, hear God speak to you his good news of love and salvation.

"Do not be amazed! You seek Jesus of Nazareth, the crucified. He has been raised; he is not here. Behold, the place where they laid him."

Mark 16:6

REFLECTING

As they walked to the tomb where Jesus lay, the women could not have felt more sorrowful. They were probably thinking of the years they had followed Jesus. The hope that he stirred in them seemed to disappear in the catastrophe of his death. Now they were preparing to do a final act of service for their master and friend. Imagine how startled they were to discover the empty tomb and to encounter the angel, who gave them a message of hope. In the midst of their sorrow came words of hope and resurrection.

We can all be drawn into periods in which just getting up in the morning is a heavy burden. We can wonder if it is worth the effort—whether anyone cares how we feel or about the work we face each day. The Gospel story tells us that it is in the midst of our sorrow that we can discover hope for resurrection. It can be a small sign of appreciation, a kind word, or support from someone from whom we least expect it. These are signs of the hope of resurrection at work in our lives.

Children of every age experience mood swings, with moments of elation followed by moments of sorrow. As we reflect on the theme of this chapter, we have the opportunity to share with them the words that can help them to see the emergence of the butterfly from the cocoon, to watch expectantly for the happiness beyond the sorrow.

RESPONDING

God's Word moves us to respond in word and action. Let the Holy Spirit work within you as you prayerfully consider how you are being called to respond to God's message to you today.

- How is Jesus' Resurrection and the new life he shares with us a source of hope and joy for me?

Risen Lord, fill me and the children with hope, joy, and peace.

Catechism of the Catholic Church

The themes of this lesson correspond to the following paragraphs: 654–655, 1020.

THE FAITH EXPERIENCE

DAY ONE
Butterflies Have New Life

DAY TWO
Jesus Has New Life

DAY THREE
We Have New Life

DAY FOUR
We Celebrate New Life

Scripture in This Chapter

- *Luke 24 Luke joyfully relates the experiences of the disciples who are the witnesses to the presence of the risen Jesus Christ.*
- *1 Corinthians 6:14 God will raise us by his power just as he raised his Son.*

Church Documents

General Directory for Catechesis #91. The Easter Vigil is the focal point of the Christian liturgy, and its spirituality of Baptism should inspire all catechesis.

Constitution on the Church #7. By overcoming death through his own death and resurrection, Jesus redeemed us and changed us into a new creation.

The theme of this chapter corresponds to Easter and the Easter Season. It is best taught just before or just after Easter. Lesson 6 of SPECIAL SEASONS AND DAYS is an additional Easter session. Refer to the ENRICHING THE FAITH EXPERIENCE sections of this chapter and Lesson 6 of SPECIAL SEASONS AND DAYS for additional ideas to expand upon the themes of Easter.

Bulletin Board At the left is a suggestion for a bulletin-board design. Recreate the four stages of the butterfly's life cycle (egg, caterpillar, chrysalis, butterfly). You might include a banner with the word "Alleluia!"

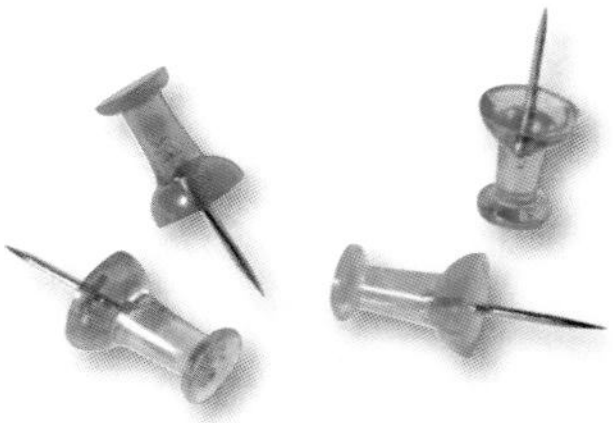

For a list of children's literature suggestions, please see **page OV-47.**

CHAPTER 20 | DAY ONE

Butterflies Have New Life

LEARNING OUTCOMES

The children will be able to

- know the life cycle of a butterfly.
- realize that new life can come from death.

KEY TERM

chrysalis—the hard silk blanket inside which a caterpillar changes into a butterfly

MATERIALS

- Cutouts: 18, 70–71
- Craft stems to attach to Cutout 71 as antennae (optional)
- Dinner-size paper plates, two for each child
- Brass paper fasteners
- Crayons or markers

COMMENTS

1. Jesus' Resurrection is the basis of our faith. He is gloriously enthroned as king over the kingdom he came to establish. But his triumph is ours as well. By reestablishing for us a loving relationship with the Father, he made it possible for us to have the fullness of life for which we yearn. Through the Resurrection of Jesus, all things are made new. Although we experience suffering and daily dying, the power of the Resurrection will transform our pain into new life and glory. We are able to overcome sin and live Jesus' new life because we died and rose with him in Baptism. In the Eucharist, through the mystery of faith, we are united with Christ's dying and rising.

2. Although young children are not yet able to understand the theology of Jesus' death and Resurrection, they can become aware of death and resurrection in the world around them and begin to accept these realities of life. In time they will grasp the mystery of faith that we glimpse in these realities.

CENTERING

Recall the last chapter.

- ***In the last chapter you learned how what happens to seeds is like what happened to Jesus. What does a seed have to do before it becomes a flower?*** (Be buried and die.)
- ***Today you will find out about something else that changes into a new form of life.*** [Show the children Cutout 18 Butterflies.]

SHARING

1 Explain the life cycle of a butterfly using Cutouts 70 Caterpillar/Chrysalis and 71 Butterfly.

- ***Do you know where butterflies come from?***
- ***A butterfly was not always this beautiful. It was not always free to fly high in the sky or to flit from flower to flower. Once the beautiful butterfly was a caterpillar. It crawled like a worm.*** [Cover the caterpillar so that only the leaf with the tiny eggs is visible.]
- ***Butterflies do not begin as baby butterflies. A butterfly begins as a tiny egg. Its mother lays the egg on a plant. When the little caterpillar hatches from the egg, it has good food to eat.*** [Show the caterpillar.] ***As the baby caterpillar chews and chews on the plant, it grows bigger and bigger.***
- ***When the caterpillar is grown, it attaches itself to a twig or branch with a silk thread it spins from its own body. As it hangs upside down, the caterpillar spins a blanket of silk around itself.*** [Show the chrysalis.] ***Soon the blanket hardens and is called a*** **chrysalis** (KRIS-a-lis).
- ***Then inside the chrysalis something wonderful happens. The wormlike caterpillar turns into a beautiful butterfly.***

• ***When the butterfly is ready, the chrysalis splits open, and the butterfly comes out. Its wings are flat and useless until the butterfly pumps them up with its body.*** [Fold Cutout 71 and unfold it so its wings are upright. Hold the butterfly on the fold. Make the wings open and close by tightening and releasing your thumb and forefingers.] ***Then the butterfly carefully opens and closes its wings to strengthen them.***

• ***Soon the butterfly is ready to fly away to places it never saw when it could only crawl as a caterpillar.*** [Open the butterfly to show its wings outspread.] ***It has a wonderful new life.***

2 Dramatize with the children the life cycle of a butterfly.

[Egg stage]
Curl into a tight ball.

[Caterpillar]
Crawl like a caterpillar.

[Chrysalis]
Stand very still, arms tight at your sides.
[Butterfly]

Place your hands on your hips. Exercise your wings by moving your elbows back and forth. Move lightly on tiptoe like a dancing butterfly flying away.

3 Help the children show the life cycle of a butterfly by making charts from paper plates. Prepare a set of two plates for each child. Cut off the rims from each plate. Cut a one-quarter pie shape from one plate. Using a pen or crayon, divide the other plate into four quadrants. Distribute the plate sets. Have the children draw the four stages of the butterfly's life cycle (egg, caterpillar, chrysalis, butterfly), one in each of the four quadrants. Ask the children to place the plate with the pie-shape cutout on top of the plate with their drawings. Put a brass paper fastener through the center of both circles. As the children turn the story wheel, ask volunteers to describe each of the four stages of the butterfly's life cycle.

ACTING

Lead the children to pray Psalm 149:1 with gestures.

• ***When the butterfly flies, it is doing something it didn't do as a caterpillar. A butterfly flying is like singing a new song to God.***

• ***Jesus gave us new life to help us live his love. We can sing a new song. Our new song will be to live Jesus' love. The psalm prayer this week reminds us to live Jesus' love.***

Sing to the LORD
[Move arms slightly outward.]

a new song.
[Frame mouth with fingers.]

Songs

Play for the children any of these songs: "People of God/Alleluia" (*Singing Our Faith*) **CD 1 Track 13;** "God Loves the Animals" (*I See a New World*) **CD 2 Track 15;** "All Men on Earth Rejoice and Sing" (*Songs for Young Children*); "A Celebration of Sunshine" (*Dandelions*); "New Hope," "O, Yes! Lord Jesus Lives" (*Hi God 2*); "Signs of New Life" (*Bloom Where You're Planted*); "Jesus Lives," "Take My Hand," "We Believe" (*Stories and Songs of Jesus*); "Alleluia, Alleluia, Give Thanks," "Easter Alleluia" (*Singing Our Faith*); "The Butterfly Song" (*Best of Mary Lou Walker*); the Alleluia from the Mass (various versions found in Singing Our Faith). For a list of all the music used in this program, see **page OV-39.**

CHECKPOINT

- What new information can the children now share about the life cycle of a butterfly?
- Were the children filled with wonder and delight at the butterfly's life?

CHAPTER 20 | DAY TWO

Jesus Has New Life

Student Book page 83

LEARNING OUTCOMES

The children will be able to

- appreciate spring as a time of new life and a time to rejoice that Jesus is risen.
- see the comparison between the life cycle of a butterfly and the death and Resurrection of Jesus.

KEY TERM

Resurrection—Jesus' new life after dying on the cross

MATERIALS

- Poster 10
- Cutouts: 9, 14–15, 17–18, 70–71
- Cross made from yellow construction paper
- Drawing of a tomb
- Yarn to tie around the waist to identify characters in the Easter story: white (angel), several blue (holy women), yellow (Mary Magdalene)
- Bible enthroned, with note card on which you have written the adapted Scripture reading for SHARING #2, Mark 16:1–7

CENTERING

Discuss with the children the new life that emerges in spring. Show the appropriate cutouts as you describe the new life that begins in spring.

- ***Spring is a special time of year. The whole world is singing a new song to the Lord. The butterflies we talked about in the last lesson come out of their chrysalises. What else is new in spring?*** (Trees, bushes, and the ground have new life. Birds build nests for baby birds. Other animals have babies.)

- ***Today you will learn about another kind of new life, the new life of Jesus.***

SHARING

1 Relate the butterfly's life cycle to Jesus' Resurrection. Show Cutouts 70–71.

- ***The butterfly was once a caterpillar inside a chrysalis. Inside the chrysalis its old caterpillar life died. It came out of the chrysalis with a wonderful new butterfly life.***

- [Show the paper cross and the drawing of a tomb.] ***Jesus died on a cross. His friends were very sad. They put his body into a tomb. A tomb is a place where people are buried when they are dead. Then God raised Jesus from the dead. He came back to life! Jesus came out of the tomb with a wonderful new life.*** [Show Poster 10 Jesus Is Risen.]

2 Introduce the Easter story dramatization based on Mark 16:1–7. Show the Bible and open it to the Gospel according to Mark, Mark 16:1–7. Enthrone the Bible. Invite volunteers to help dramatize as you tell the Easter story.

- ***Today I will tell you more about this wonderful Easter story. I will need help to tell the story. Who would like to help?*** Name the characters in "The Story of Easter": several women, Mary Magdalene, and the angel. As the children volunteer, give them the respective color yarn to tie around their waists.

- ***The story will tell you when it is time for your parts. Listen carefully as I tell the wonderful story of Jesus' Resurrection.***

3 Read "The Story of Easter" on **page T233.** While telling the story, say the characters' lines in addition to your narration. Then have the characters repeat after you.

The Story of Easter

• Teacher: [Show the paper cross and the drawing of a tomb.] The happy story of Easter begins sadly.

• After Jesus died on the cross, his friends buried him in a grave, called a tomb. It was like a cave in a hillside.

• A big, heavy rock was rolled in front of the cave. Early in the morning, some women who were Jesus' friends brought some sweet smelling spices to put on Jesus' body. [Call Mary Magdalene and the women to dramatize as you tell the story. Guide them by quietly giving directions.]

• On the way to the tomb, the women were wondering who would roll away the stone, because it was too heavy for them to move. The women said to one another,

• Women: [Women repeat after teacher.] Who will roll away the stone? It is too heavy to move.

• Teacher: When the women reached the tomb, they looked up and saw that the stone had already been rolled away. [Women show shock and surprise.]

• Women: [Point to the tomb and repeat after teacher.] Look, the stone has been rolled back! Who rolled it back?

• Teacher: So the women entered the tomb. They did not know what to think. In the tomb, they saw a figure dressed in a white robe sitting on the right side. [Call the angel.] The women were scared. But the angel said,

• Angel: [Repeat after teacher.] Do not be scared! You are looking for Jesus. He has been raised. He is not here. Go and tell his disciples and Peter, "You will see him in Galilee, as he told you."

• All: [Repeat after teacher.] Jesus has been raised!

• Teacher: This is the wonderful Easter story. Jesus' disciples found the stone rolled away from the tomb where Jesus had been buried. They did not find Jesus' body. Jesus was raised from the dead. Jesus was raised to new life. There are other stories in the Bible that tell us that Jesus' disciples saw Jesus after he was raised from the dead. They saw Jesus with the new, glorious life of heaven. Jesus wants us to share in his glorious life too.

4 Discuss Jesus' Resurrection:

• ***Jesus' followers were full of joy. Jesus will never die again. Now he is risen and is with us always.***

• ***The beautiful new life of a butterfly fills us with wonder and joy. The life of the risen Jesus fills us with even more wonder and joy.***

• ***Every spring we celebrate Jesus' Resurrection on Easter.***

5 Have the children turn to **page 83**. Encourage the children to follow along as you read aloud the text.

6 Acquaint the children with the word *alleluia*.

• ***Have you ever been so surprised or so full of wonder that you could barely talk? All you could do was open your mouth wide and say, "Wow!"***

• ***God's people, the Church, celebrate Jesus' Resurrection this way. We are so full of joy because Jesus is risen that we shout out the Easter joy word* alleluia. Alleluia *means "Praise the Lord."***

• ***We rejoice in Jesus' new life because it means he is with us always. We rejoice because we know if we live his life of love, we too shall be changed with the glory life of heaven. We will live forever.***

ACTING

Invite the children to pray the Easter joy word, *Alleluia*: Teach and pray a simple sung alleluia, such as "People of God/Alleluia" or "Easter Alleluia" (*Singing Our Faith*), or teach and pray the Easter Cheer:

Easter Cheer

Jesus is risen.
[Take two steps forward on the beats.]

Al-le-lu-ia
[Raise arms up and down twice.]

Jesus is risen.
[Take two steps backward on the beats.]

Al-le-lu-ia
[Raise arms up and down twice.]

Jesus is risen.
[Take two steps forward on the beats.]

Al-le-lu-ia
[Raise arms up and down twice.]

That's gr—rr—
[Swing right arm around twice as if winding up for a pitch.]

—eat!
[Jerk right elbow back. Clap twice.]

M. Kathleen Glavich, S.N.D.

CHECKPOINT

- Were the children able to identify signs of new life that emerge in spring?
- What understanding of Jesus' Resurrection are the children able to demonstrate?

CHAPTER 20

Butterflies Are Good

A butterfly gives us joy. It has new life.
On Easter, Jesus rose from
the dead with new life.
We celebrate his new life with great joy.
We sing ALLELUIA!

Scripture

"You are looking for Jesus.
He has been raised."
Based on Mark 16:6

83

CHAPTER 20 | DAY THREE

We Have New Life

Student Book page 84

LEARNING OUTCOMES

The children will be able to

- be aware that they have new life through the death and resurrection of Jesus.
- identify ways to show Jesus' love.

MATERIALS

- Pieces of colored felt, 6 inches by 9 inches, one for each child
- Sets of precut letters to spell ALLELUIA! (craft foam or felt)
- Precut butterflies (craft foam or felt)
- 9-inch pieces of yarn, one for each child's banner
- Sample of completed Good News banner, for SHARING #4.

CENTERING

1 Play a game with the children using the word *alleluia*. Explain:

- ***I am going to whisper a special word to one of you. That child will whisper it to someone else. The word will be passed this way until everyone has heard it. Then when I count to three, we will all say the word three times, putting as much joy in our voices as we can.***

2 Recall the meaning of *alleluia*.

- ***Who remembers what alleluia means?*** (Praise the Lord.)
- ***We say alleluia because we are very happy. Why are we happy?*** (Because Jesus rose and has new life; because we can share his new life)

SHARING

1 Discuss how Jesus shares new life with them.

- ***On Easter morning, Jesus rose gloriously with new life. Because Jesus died and rose for us, we can share in his new life. We shared Jesus' new life when we were baptized. We continue to live this new life as we live Jesus' love.***

2 Recall the Easter story from the last lesson.

- ***Last time we heard the wonderful Easter story.***
- ***What did the women find when they went to the tomb on Easter morning?*** (The stone was rolled away. An angel told them that Jesus was raised from the dead.)
- ***What did the angel tell the women to do?*** (To tell Jesus' disciples that they would see him in Galilee)
- ***The angel asked the women to tell amazing, wonderful news. We call this Good News. We also share good news when we live Jesus' love.***

3 Have the children look at **page 84.** Read aloud the text and have the children tell about the people in the picture who are living Jesus' love. Ask the children to name ways that they can live Jesus' love at home, at school, on the bus, in the library, and on the playground.

4 Tell the children that they will make Good News banners to help them remember to share good news by living Jesus' love. Show a sample. Help the children make Good News banners, which say "Alleluia!" and have a butterfly as a symbol of Easter. Provide each child with a 6-inch by 9-inch piece of colored felt, precut letters to spell "Alleluia!" and precut butterflies. Allow the children to glue the symbols onto their banners. When finished, staple a 9-inch length of yarn to each banner to make a hanger.

ACTING

Teach and pray the poem "Jesus Is Risen" with gestures.

Jesus Is Risen

Birds are singing,
[Press forefingers up and down on thumbs.]

Church bells ringing,
[Fold hands. Swing arms back and forth.]

New life springing,
[Stoop down. Spring up.]

All around.
[Touch chest with fingertips. Open hands in wide outward movement.]

Tell the Good News,
[Frame mouth with cupped hands.]

Jesus is risen,
[Touch chest with fingertips. Open hands in wide outward movement.]

Alleluia
[Touch shoulders with fist. Raise fists in cheering gesture.]

Is our song.
[Frame mouth with fingertips.]

M. Kathleen Glavich, S.N.D.

CHECKPOINT

- How have the children demonstrated awareness that Jesus gives them new life?
- Were the children able to identify ways to live Jesus' love?

Jesus rose to new life.
We can share the good news.
We can live Jesus' new life.

We can show love for God and others.
How will you show love?

In springtime, signs of new life are everywhere.
They tell us to live Jesus' life of love.
Butterflies remind us of Jesus' new life.

84

CHAPTER 20 | DAY FOUR

We Celebrate New Life

Student Book pages 85–86

LEARNING OUTCOMES

The children will be able to
- be happy because Jesus rose.
- identify the butterfly as a reminder of new life in Jesus.

MATERIALS
- Poster 10
- Sample butterfly craft
- Butterfly wings precut from construction paper
- Glue
- Glitter
- 6-inch craft stems
- Song about life for SHARING #2, such as "Jesus Lives" from *Stories and Songs of Jesus*
- Bible, with note card on which you have written the adapted Scripture reading for SHARING #3, Mark 16:6
- Butterfly Pendant punchouts from the Student Book
- 22-inch pieces of yarn, two for each child
- Happy song for ACTING #4

COMMENT

Before the lesson, remove the Butterfly Pendant punchouts. Make two butterfly pendants for each child. Punch out the hole in each pendant and string it with a loop of yarn.

CENTERING

1 Tell the children that they will celebrate the new life of Jesus and the new life he won for them. Display Poster 10.

2 Introduce the butterfly craft that the children will make as a reminder of the new life of Jesus. Ask:

- ***What new life found in spring have we said reminds us of Jesus' new life?*** (Butterflies)
- ***Today you will make a butterfly craft to take home to remind you to live Jesus' new life.*** [Show a sample butterfly craft.]

Distribute butterfly wings precut from construction paper. Help the children decorate the wings. Show them how to apply glue and to shake on glitter. Help them to bend in half the craft stems. Show the children how to wrap the craft stems around the middle lengthwise to make the butterfly body. Help them to twist the ends of the craft stems at the top to make antennae.

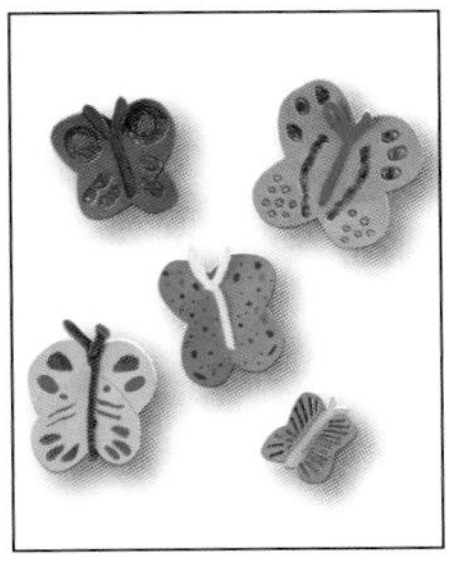

3 Read aloud **page 85** and guide the children in doing the activity.

SHARING

1 Ask the children to close their eyes gently to quiet themselves so that they are ready to celebrate.

2 Sing an Easter song or play a recording of one. See song list on **page T231.**

3 Prepare to proclaim the Scripture. Introduce the reading:

- ***We like good news. Jesus' rising from the dead is Good News. We call the books written about Jesus* Gospels, *or "Good News," because the books tell that God raised Jesus from the dead. Let us stand and listen carefully to the Good News.***

Introduce this Bible reading by showing the Bible and opening it to the Gospel according to Mark, 16:6.

Invite the children to remember what they learned about how to be good listeners.

- ***Let's prepare ourselves to listen well to today's Bible reading.***
- ***A reading from the book of Mark: "You seek Jesus of Nazareth, the crucified. He has been raised; he is not here.***

Behold, the place where they laid him." The Gospel of the Lord. (Based on Mark 16:6)

4 Let the children respond by singing or saying alleluia.

5 Invite the children to recite the Easter Cheer on **page T234** or the poem "Jesus Is Risen" on **page T236.**

ACTING

1 Explain the butterfly pendants displayed on the table.

- ***We have new life too. When did we receive it?*** (At Baptism) ***What will the new life help us do?*** (Live in love.) ***These butterfly pendants will remind you to live Jesus' love. Think about one way you will share Jesus' love with someone. If you want, you may tell us what you will do to show Jesus' love.***

2 Present two butterfly pendants to each child. Explain:

- ***One butterfly pendant is for you to wear as a reminder to live Jesus' love.*** [Allow the children to put on one butterfly pendant now.]
- ***The other butterfly pendant is for you to take home. Give it to someone to wish them new life in Jesus' love. When you give away the butterfly, you may say, "Jesus is alive. Live in his love."*** [Let a few children show how they will do this.]
- ***Let us pray: Heavenly Father, we have celebrated Jesus' new life. Help us live his love. We ask this through Jesus, our risen Lord.***

3 Close with a song during which the children may make their butterflies dance.

4 Have the children take home the Family Page on **page 86** to share with their families.

CHECKPOINT

- How have the children shown they know Jesus is alive?
- Are the children eager to give their second butterfly pendant as a gift?

Try This

Find the 11 hidden butterflies.
Circle them.
Praise God that Jesus is risen.
Pray the Easter word Alleluia.

85

ENRICHING THE FAITH EXPERIENCE

Use the following activities to enrich a lesson, to replace an activity with one that better meets the needs of your class, or to create an additional lesson.

1 Take the children outside for a walk to look for signs of new life. (Examples: flowers, eggs, birds, butterflies) Then have them draw pictures of what they see. Invite volunteers to share their drawings with the class.

2 Direct the children to draw or paint something from spring. They might draw with a crayon and then watercolor over their drawings with a spring color. Let them feel free to create their own impressions of spring. Play music as they work. Have the children take turns showing their pictures and thanking God for the new life they have depicted.

3 Give the children art materials and have them decorate the word *Alleluia.*

4 Teach the children the action rhyme "Roly-Poly Caterpillar."

Roly-Poly Caterpillar

Roly-Poly Caterpillar
Into a corner crept,
Spun around himself a blanket,
[Spin around.]
Then for a long time slept.
[Place head on folded hands.]
Roly-Poly Caterpillar
Wakening by and by—
[Stretch.]
Found himself with beautiful wings
Changed to a butterfly.
[Flutter arms like wings.]

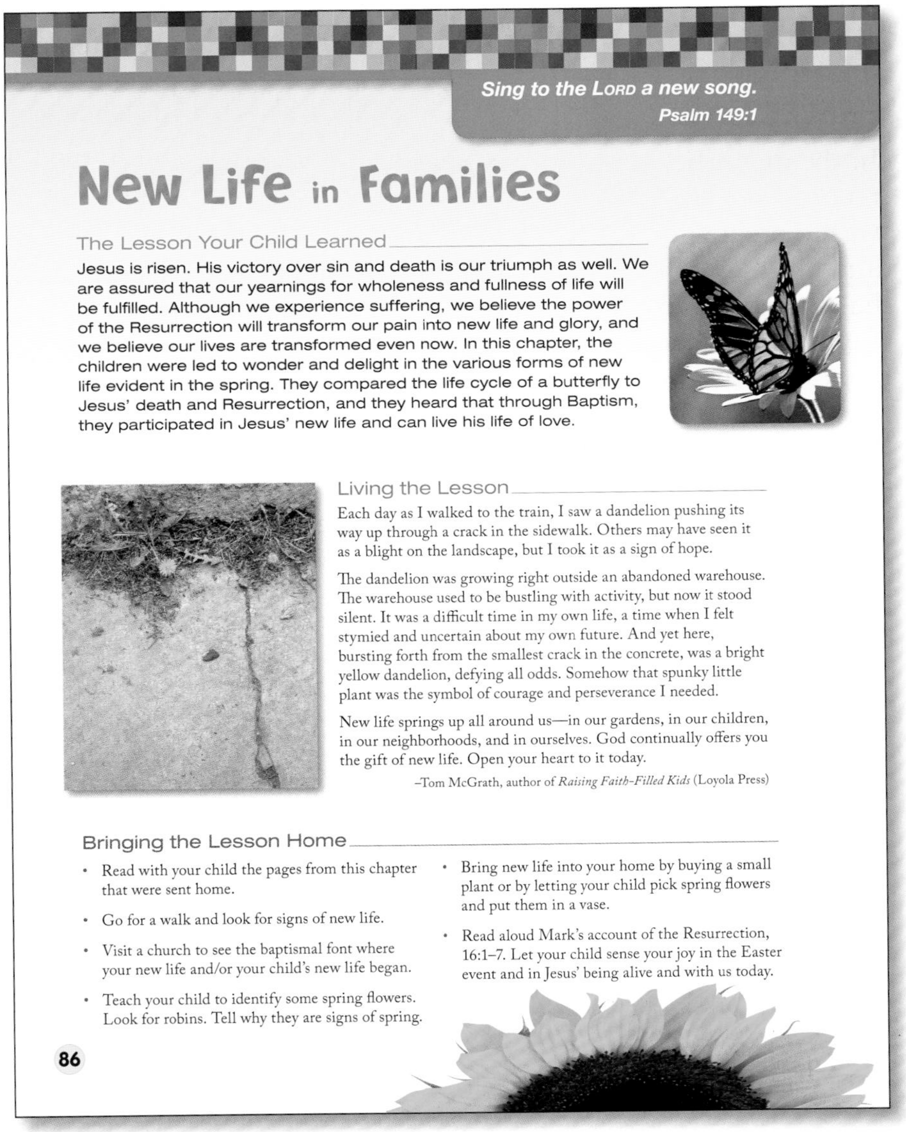

Sing to the Lord a new song.
Psalm 149:1

New Life in Families

The Lesson Your Child Learned

Jesus is risen. His victory over sin and death is our triumph as well. We are assured that our yearnings for wholeness and fullness of life will be fulfilled. Although we experience suffering, we believe the power of the Resurrection will transform our pain into new life and glory, and we believe our lives are transformed even now. In this chapter, the children were led to wonder and delight in the various forms of new life evident in the spring. They compared the life cycle of a butterfly to Jesus' death and Resurrection, and they heard that through Baptism, they participated in Jesus' new life and can live his life of love.

Living the Lesson

Each day as I walked to the train, I saw a dandelion pushing its way up through a crack in the sidewalk. Others may have seen it as a blight on the landscape, but I took it as a sign of hope.

The dandelion was growing right outside an abandoned warehouse. The warehouse used to be bustling with activity, but now it stood silent. It was a difficult time in my own life, a time when I felt stymied and uncertain about my own future. And yet here, bursting forth from the smallest crack in the concrete, was a bright yellow dandelion, defying all odds. Somehow that spunky little plant was the symbol of courage and perseverance I needed.

New life springs up all around us—in our gardens, in our children, in our neighborhoods, and in ourselves. God continually offers you the gift of new life. Open your heart to it today.

–Tom McGrath, author of *Raising Faith-Filled Kids* (Loyola Press)

Bringing the Lesson Home

- Read with your child the pages from this chapter that were sent home.
- Go for a walk and look for signs of new life.
- Visit a church to see the baptismal font where your new life and/or your child's new life began.
- Teach your child to identify some spring flowers. Look for robins. Tell why they are signs of spring.
- Bring new life into your home by buying a small plant or by letting your child pick spring flowers and put them in a vase.
- Read aloud Mark's account of the Resurrection, 16:1–7. Let your child sense your joy in the Easter event and in Jesus' being alive and with us today.

86

Chapter 21

Light Is Good

FAITH FOCUS

Jesus, the light of the world, calls us to share his light with others. John 8:12; Matthew 5:14–16

PREPARING THE FAITH EXPERIENCE

LISTENING

Before you begin to prepare this week's lessons, take some time for prayer. Quiet yourself by taking several deep breaths. Become aware of God's presence, for God is with you always. Ask God to open your heart to hear his words to you today.

"I am the light of the world. Whoever follows me will not walk in darkness, but will have the light of life."

John 8:12

REFLECTING

In the magnificent account of creation recorded in Genesis, God's first creative act was to create light. Light is a symbol of God and God's goodness. Like God himself, light has the power to change all that it touches. Light from the sun casts out darkness, dries the rain after a storm, and melts the winter snow. Christ himself acknowledged the power of light when he spoke to his disciples: "You are the light of the world. Just so, your light must shine before others, that they may see your good deeds and glorify your heavenly Father." (Matthew 5:14,16)

On another occasion, referring to himself, he said: "For God did not send his Son into the world to condemn the world, but that the world might be saved through him. And this is the verdict, that the light came into the world, but people preferred darkness to light, because their works were evil." (John 3:17,19)

Paradoxically, we can often appreciate light better if we have known darkness. This is true not only on the spiritual plane, but also on all human levels: material (or physical), emotional, intellectual. Mysteriously, the patches of light that dapple the pathway of every human life are often made brighter by the contrasting patches of shadow. And led by the very Light of the World, we are confidently able to cry out in the midst of our darkness: "The LORD is my light!" (Adapted from Psalm 27:1)

RESPONDING

Having reflected upon God's Word, take some time now to continue to respond to God in prayer. You might wish to use a journal to record your responses throughout this year.

- Do I depend upon prayer to Christ to bring enlightenment to the children in my care?

Spirit of Light, brighten our days with your presence.

Catechism of the Catholic Church

The themes of this lesson correspond to the following paragraphs: 655, 782, 864.

THE FAITH EXPERIENCE

DAY ONE
Light Is a Gift of God

DAY TWO
Jesus Is the Light of the World

DAY THREE
The Light of Jesus Shines in Us

DAY FOUR
We Bring the Light of Jesus to Others

Scripture in This Chapter

- *John 9:1–41 Christ cures physical blindness, but he explains that there is a far worse blindness: a deliberate spiritual blindness of turning away from the light of Christ.*
- *John 8:12 Christ declares himself the light of the world.*

Church Documents

General Directory for Catechesis #17. Catechesis should emphasize the social teaching of the Church so that its presence may be a light that shines on the world.

The Church in the Modern World #40. The Church communicates divine life to humanity and casts the reflected light of that divine life over all the earth.

The theme of this chapter continues to elaborate and to teach a predominant theme of Easter and the Easter season. In particular, this chapter teaches about the service of light, which is an integral part of the Easter Vigil. The children will be invited to participate in a celebration modeled on this part of the Easter Vigil. This chapter is best taught one or two weeks after Easter.

Bulletin Board At the left is a suggestion for a bulletin-board design. Refer to BLM 22 Stained-Glass Window if you wish to make a photocopy or transparency. Trace the design from BLM 22 onto wax paper. Then design and color the wax paper with crayons. When held up to the light, the colors will shine through like stained glass. You might include a banner with the words, "Light Is Good."

- ***BLM 22 Stained-Glass Window***

For a list of children's literature suggestions, please see **page OV-47.**

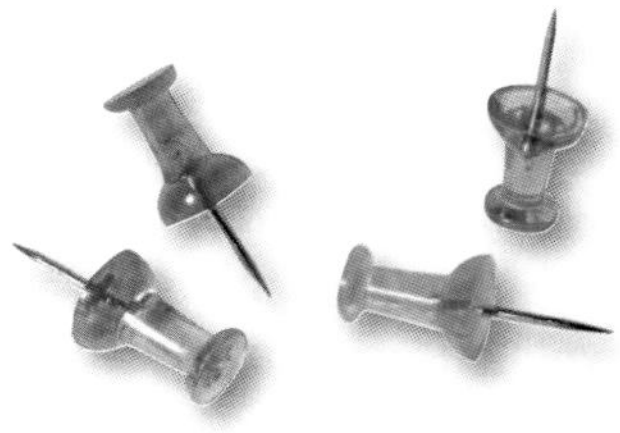

CHAPTER 21 | DAY ONE

Light Is a Gift of God

LEARNING OUTCOMES

The children will be able to

- appreciate light as a gift of God.
- learn that light is a symbol of God for us.

MATERIALS

- Cutouts 2, 41
- Sheet of black construction paper
- Sheet of yellow construction paper
- Flashlight
- Bible enthroned, with note card on which you have written the adapted Scripture reading for SHARING #3
- Pictures from magazines of different kinds of light (Examples: candles, the moon and the stars, fire burning in a fireplace, fireworks, neon lights in stores, lamps and night-lights at home, a campfire, car headlights, and candles)

COMMENT

In both the Old and New Testaments, light is a symbol of God's presence. The theme of light is important during the Advent liturgy, when we celebrate the Divine Light shining through the darkness of our world and becoming visible among us. Our Easter service of light celebrates the risen Jesus, "rising in shining splendor to dispel the darkness of our hearts and minds." The Easter candle burns each day for 50 days after Easter to remind us that "Christ, the morning star, who is risen, has shed his peaceful light on us." *(Liturgy of Holy Saturday)*

CENTERING

1 Recall the last chapter.

- ***We have talked about Jesus' new life that he gives to us. How do we show we have Jesus' new life?*** (By loving others)
- ***Today you will learn that Jesus taught us ways to love.***

2 Lead the children to appreciate light.

- ***When it's nighttime and you go into your room, what do you need to do in order to see everything in the room?*** [Turn on the light.]
- ***When you go outside and the sun is shining, what do you like best?*** [Show Cutout 2 Sun.]
- ***How does the sunlight make you feel?***

SHARING

1 Discuss light.

- ***What does our world look like during the night?*** [Show the black paper.]
- ***What happens to the darkness when the sun rises?*** [Show the yellow paper.]
- ***The light changes the darkness into brightness. The sun warms the earth after the darkness of night. Everything becomes bright and beautiful in the morning sun. The sunlight starts a new day.***

2 Guide the children to understand that light transforms things.

- ***Light is good. It changes what it touches.*** [Shine the flashlight.] ***What will happen to the darkness if I put this light in a dark room?*** (The darkness will be gone.) ***The light changes darkness into brightness.***

Turn off the lights in your classroom and shine a flashlight on objects in the room. Invite volunteers to take turns with the flashlight, experimenting with how the light of the flashlight changes the way things appear.

- ***Light changes things in many different ways.***
- ***How does sunlight change a plant?*** (It helps it grow.)
- ***How does it change the wet world after a rain?*** (It dries the puddles.)
- ***Sunlight changes our feelings too. How do you sometimes feel on a dark, rainy day? How do you feel when you see the sun come out?***

3 Lead the children to appreciate light as a gift of God.

- ***Who gave our world the gift of light?***

• ***A story in the Bible tells us that God gave us light. I would like to share this Bible reading with you.***

Introduce this Bible reading by showing the Bible and opening it to the Book of Genesis, Genesis 1:14–15.

Invite the children to remember what they learned about how to be good listeners.

• ***Let's prepare ourselves to listen well to today's Bible reading.***

• ***God said, "Let there be light to shine on the earth. And so it was."*** (Based on Genesis 1:14–15) Comment:

• ***God is good to create the light so that we do not have to be in darkness all the time.***

❹ Show the pictures cut from magazines showing different kinds of light. (Examples: candles on a birthday cake, the moon and the stars, fire burning in a fireplace, fireworks, neon lights in stores, lamps and night-lights at home, a campfire, car headlights, and candles) Invite volunteers to tell about these different kinds of lights and tell why each is good.

ACTING

Introduce Psalm 27:1. Teach and pray this prayer with the children, using gestures. Show Cutout 41 David playing harp.

• ***God gives us the gift of light. David knew that God was good and wonderful like the light. He called God his light. He prayed:***

The Lord
[Raise arms up.]
is
[Turn palms outward.]
my light.
[Lower arms in circular motion while moving fingers.]

Songs

Play for the children any of these songs: "We Are Marching" (*Singing Our Faith*) **CD 1 Track 14;** "We Are Walking in the Light" (*Singing Our Faith*) **CD 1 Track 2;** "A Celebration of Sunshine" (*Dandelions*); "Light," "Lightning Bug" (*Songs for Young Children*); "How Much God Loves Us" (*Stories and Songs of Jesus*); "Bring Forth the Kingdom," "Walk, Walk in the Light" (*Singing Our Faith*). For a list of all the music used in this program, see **page OV-39.**

CHECKPOINT

- Do the children understand light to be a gift from God?
- Are the children able to identify the ways that light can be a symbol of God for us?

CHAPTER 21 | DAY TWO

Jesus Is the Light of the World

Student Book page 87

LEARNING OUTCOMES

The children will be able to

- know that Jesus is "the light of the world."
- realize that they share in Jesus' light through Baptism.

MATERIALS

- Bible enthroned, with note card on which you have written the adapted Scripture reading for SHARING #2, John 8:12
- Flame punchouts from the Student Book
- Styrofoam cups, 4- or 6-ounce size with slit in bottom, one for each child
- Thick white candle and matches (Remember to check with the proper authority regarding local regulations for using candles in a classroom setting. If lighted candles are not permitted, you might use an electric candle.)
- Sheet of black construction paper
- Sheet of yellow construction paper
- Crayons or markers

COMMENT

After sunset on the night before Easter, the Church gathers in darkness for the Easter Vigil. The Vigil begins with the service of light. The Easter candle (also known as the paschal candle) is lit from the newly blessed Easter fire. We celebrate Christ, the Light of the World, soon to be risen from the dead. The community praises "Christ our Light" three times as the congregation lights taper candles from the Easter candle. By the light of these candles, the great Exultet—or Easter proclamation—is sung. The Vigil continues with the Liturgy of the Word as the story of salvation history is proclaimed. Finally, light triumphs over darkness as we begin our celebration of Christ's resurrection with the Gloria, New Testament epistle, and Gospel. Young children are unlikely to participate in this Easter Vigil until they are older. However, in this chapter, they will be introduced to the wonder of this great night as they share a prayer celebration based on the Easter Vigil's service of light.

CENTERING

1 Place the candle on a table in front of the children. Light (or turn on) the candle without speaking. Watch it for a moment.

• ***The light is very beautiful. It makes us happy to see the brightness. The light spreads warmth and joy. It helps us see. It seems almost alive.***

2 Invite the children to pray Psalm 27:1 with gestures:

The Lord
[Raise arms up.]
is
[Turn palms outward.]
my light.
[Lower arms in circular motion while moving fingers.]

Extinguish (or turn off) the candle.

SHARING

1 Have the children turn to **page 87.** Ask:

• ***What do you see in the picture?*** (Trees; people; sunlight)

Encourage the children to follow along as you read aloud **page 87.**

2 Introduce this Bible reading by showing the Bible and opening it to the Gospel according to John, John 8:12.

Invite the children to remember what they learned about how to be good listeners.

• ***Let's prepare ourselves to listen well to today's Bible reading.*** Read John 8:12:

• ***Jesus calls himself a light. He says: "I am the light of the world. Whoever follows me will not walk in darkness."*** [Pause.]

3 Lead the children to reflect on how Jesus is our light.

• ***How do you think Jesus is a light for us?*** (He shows us how to bring light to others by being loving and kind.)

• ***When we think only of ourselves, we are in the darkness of selfishness.*** [Show black paper.] ***When we think of others, Jesus is leading us out of the darkness into the brightness of his love.*** [Show yellow paper.]

• ***Jesus is our light. He shows us how to be loving and kind.***

❹ Teach a song about following Jesus our Light, such as "We Are Marching" (*Singing Our Faith*), or another from the song list on **page T243**.

❺ Tell the children about the Easter candle.

• ***On Easter, when we celebrate Jesus' rising from the dead, we remember that Jesus is our light. The night before Easter, there is a big celebration at church. The celebration begins with everyone standing in the dark. Then the priest lights a large decorated candle called the Easter candle.***

• ***The Easter candle stands for Jesus. It is carried into the dark church. Three times the priest sings, "Christ our light," and everyone answers, "Thanks be to God." They thank God for giving Jesus to be our light. Then everyone lights his or her small candle from the Easter candle. This makes the whole church bright with light.***

❻ Show the children how to make candles to remind them that Jesus is our light. Distribute the cups and the Flame punchouts. Show the children how to turn the cup upside down and carefully insert the flame into the slit at the bottom of the cup. Have them write their names on the upside-down cups.

ACTING

❶ Demonstrate the candle rite of the Easter Vigil.

• ***Let us imagine we are at the Easter celebration on the night before Easter. I will hold this candle and say, "Christ our light." You say after me, "Thanks be to God."*** [Raise the candle and say (or sing) "Christ our light" three times.]

❷ Have the children put their candles on the worship table or in a safe place for the next two lessons.

CHECKPOINT

- Do the children now recognize that we call Jesus "the light of the world"?
- How did the children respond to the Easter Vigil activity?

CHAPTER 21

Light Is Good

God knows we need light.

He gives us the gift of the sun.

Jesus is a light for us too.

Jesus helps us see how to love God by loving others.

Scripture

Jesus said, "I am the light of the world." Based on John 8:12

87

CHAPTER 21 | DAY THREE

The Light of Jesus Shines in Us

Student Book page 88

LEARNING OUTCOME

The children will be able to

- be aware that they are called to share Jesus' love.

MATERIALS

- Bible enthroned, with note card on which you have written the adapted Scripture reading for SHARING #2, Matthew 5:14–16
- Candles the children made on Day Two
- Large white candle
- Flashlight
- A sun catcher, stained-glass ornament, prism, and other objects that show the effects of light
- Wax paper or other transparency paper
- Crayons
- BLM 22

CENTERING

1 Recall the last lesson:

• ***Last time we learned about the special way we celebrate Jesus our Light at the Easter Vigil. Let's pray this prayer together.***

Invite the children to pray the candle rite of the Easter Vigil:

• ***Remember, as I raise this candle, I will say, "Christ our light." You say, "Thanks be to God."*** [Raise the candle and say "Christ our light" three times.]

2 Distribute candles or have the children find the candles they made in the last lesson. Tell them to keep their candles in front of them during this lesson.

SHARING

1 Discuss spreading Christ's light.

• ***Light has the power to change whatever it touches.*** [Show how light changes the look of a sun catcher or stained-glass ornament, or how light changes when viewed through a prism, or show other objects that change in the light.]

• ***Jesus gave us the light of his love when we were baptized. He wants his love to shine through us to others.***

2 Introduce this Bible reading:

• ***I want to share with you a reading from the Bible that tells us something Jesus said about light.***

Show the Bible and opening it to the Gospel according to Matthew, Matthew 5:14–16. Invite the children to remember what they learned about how to be good listeners.

• ***Let's prepare ourselves to listen well to today's Bible reading.***

• ***Jesus said, "You are the light of the world. Don't put your light under a bushel basket so no one can see it. Let your light shine so people see the good things you do and praise our Father in heaven."*** (Based on Matthew 5:14–16)

3 Demonstrate what happens when light is covered up or blocked. Shine a flashlight through the sun catcher. Then let a child cover the flashlight with a piece of cardboard or a book. Discuss:

• ***What happened to the light?***

• ***Does the covered light help you see the colors of the sun catcher?***

• ***Jesus tells us to let our light shine.***

• ***At your Baptism, your baptismal candle was lit from the light of the Easter candle. This showed that you now had the light of Jesus within you. You can spread the light that Jesus gave you to people all around you. You can share the warmth of Jesus' love with others, or you can keep it hidden.***

4 If you have not already done so, help the children make stained glass windows. Distribute copies of BLM 22 Stained-Glass Window. Invite the children to trace onto wax paper the design from BLM 22. Then help them design and color the wax paper with crayons. Show the children how the light shines through their colored designs.
- ***BLM 22 Stained-Glass Window***

- ***We can let the light of Jesus' love shine through us.***

5 Let the children suggest ways the light of Jesus' love might shine through them.

- ***How do you let the light of Jesus' love shine through you?*** [You might prompt the children by asking, What happens when you smile at someone? What happens when you ask someone, "Can I help you?"]

6 Have the children turn to **page 88.** Read aloud the text as the children follow along. Ask:

- ***What is Jesus doing?*** (Talking; teaching the people)

- ***What do you think he is telling the people?***

ACTING

Teach the children to sing "This Little Light of Mine." Have them act out the words, using the candles they made. At the end, have the children put away their candles for the next lesson.

This Little Light of Mine

This little light of mine, I'm gonna let it shine. [Three times]
Let it shine, let it shine, all the time, all the time.

Put it under a bushel? No! I'm gonna let it shine. [Three times]
Let it shine, let it shine, all the time, all the time.

CHECKPOINT

- Were the children able to identify ways they can let Jesus' love shine through them?

Our hearts are bright with Jesus' love.

Jesus wants his love to shine through us.
We light up the world with Jesus' love.

We show love for God and others.

CHAPTER 21 | DAY FOUR

We Bring the Light of Jesus to Others

Student Book pages 89–90

LEARNING OUTCOMES

The children will be able to

- realize ways they might let their light shine.
- resolve to let their light shine in a particular way at home.

MATERIALS

- BLM 23
- Puppets from Cutouts 38–39
- Candles made by the children on Day Two
- Crayons or markers
- For Light of Jesus craft:
  Glue
  Photos of each child collected before the lesson (his or her school photo or one from home)
  9-inch metal pie plates
  4-inch by 4-inch squares of colored felt
  Paper banners with the phrase "The Light of Jesus Shines Through Me"
- Sample Light of Jesus craft

COMMENT

For the puppets in SHARING #1, you might use Cutouts 38–39 or other puppets you may have.

CENTERING

1 Recall the last lesson.

- ***When you were baptized, you received a lighted candle. The candle flame looked alive. It told everyone you had new life. Jesus shared his life of love with you. He gave you new life.***
- ***Today you will think about ways to let your light shine.***

2 Distribute candles or have the children find their candles.

SHARING

1 Use puppets made from Cutouts 38–39 Carlos and Ana to show ways of spreading light and ways of keeping light hidden. After each line, have the children raise their candles if the line showed a way to spread Jesus' light.

Girl: My mom is taking us to the beach. Would you like to come? (Yes.)

Boy: Did you forget your lunch? Here, have half of mine. (Yes.)

Girl: You look funny without your front teeth. Funny face. Funny face. (No.)

Boy: Let me be first. I'm the biggest. (No.)

Girl: Here's your crayon. It fell on the floor. (Yes.)

Boy: I like the picture you drew. The colors are very pretty. (Yes.)

Girl: Teacher, teacher! Billy's not listening. (No.)

Boy: Give me that ball or I'll push you. (No.)

Girl: We're playing tag. Do you want to play? (Yes.)

Boy: I'll help you find your mitten. (Yes.)

2 Distribute copies of BLM 23 Rays of Light and guide the children in identifying ways to share Jesus' light.

- *BLM 23 Rays of Light*

3 Have the children turn to **page 89.** Read it aloud and have them do the activity.

4 Invite the children to make a Light of Jesus craft that they can take home to help them remember what they have learned. Show the children a sample of the craft. Distribute the pie plates, felt squares, and paper banners with the phrase "The Light of Jesus Shines Through Me." Have the children glue the felt squares to the inside of the pie tin. Then have each child glue their photo on top of the felt. Help them glue the banner on the rim of the pie plate.

ACTING

1 Encourage the children to make a resolution.

- ***When you carry your candles and Light of Jesus crafts into your homes, carry the light of Jesus' love into your families. Let Jesus' light shine through you to make your homes brighter and happier.***
- ***Think of one thing you will do at home to let your light shine.***
- ***Pray with me: God Our Father, help us that we may let***

Jesus' love shine through us. We ask this through Jesus, our risen Lord.

Sing together "This Little Light of Mine."

2 Have the children take home the Family Page on **page 90** to share with their families.

CHECKPOINT

- Are the children aware that when they show love to others, they are also sharing Jesus' love?
- How do the children show they are letting Jesus' love shine through them?

ENRICHING THE FAITH EXPERIENCE

Use the following activities to enrich a lesson, to replace an activity with one that better meets the needs of your class, or to create an additional lesson.

1 Have the children draw pictures of sunshine and thank God for the gift of light.

2 Take the children outside to feel the warmth of the sun and to observe sunlight shining on plants and flowers. Tell the children that sunlight helps the plants grow. It helps the leaves make food for the plants. It also makes the leaves green. Without sunlight, the leaves would be yellow or white. Experiment with plants and light. Show how plants grow toward the direction of the sunlight by moving plants and observing their growth.

3 Have the children draw or paint pictures to show how they will spread Jesus' light by being loving toward others.

The Lord is my light.
Adapted from Psalm 27:1

Light in Families

The Lesson Your Child Learned

In this chapter the children were led to appreciate light as a gift of God. They heard Jesus call himself the light of the world and learned that the Easter candle is a symbol of the risen Jesus. The children were told about the candle they received at Baptism to show that they share in Jesus' life. They took home candles that they made as reminders to let their light shine by being loving to their families.

We let the light of Jesus' love shine through us.

Try This

Make the light shine through the darkness. Color the rays bright colors.

How will you share the light of Jesus' love?

89

Chapter 22

Celebrating Is Good

FAITH FOCUS

We celebrate God's love and give thanks at Mass. Luke 22:19–20

PREPARING THE FAITH EXPERIENCE

LISTENING

As you prepare to share God's Word of love with the children, spend some quiet time with God in prayer. Relax your body, quiet your mind, and let yourself be aware that you are filled with God's love. Ask God to speak to you his Word of love.

Then he took the bread, said the blessing, broke it, and gave it to them, saying, "This is my body which will be given for you; do this in memory of me." And likewise the cup after they had eaten, saying, "This cup is the new covenant in my blood, which will be shed for you."

Luke 22:19–20

REFLECTING

The Book of Genesis records that after six days of creative work, God set aside the seventh day as a period of rest—a time to view with satisfaction the results of his handiwork. By putting aside work, the Creator expressed control over it. In this, God serves as a model. God ordained that his people should also work for six days and preserve the seventh day as a Sabbath day, a time for worship, leisure, and relaxation, a change of pace. Human beings control their work lest it control them, and they celebrate to show their mastery over it. In addition to showing that we have control over our work, freeing one day of the week for other activities fulfills a deep need within our nature: the need for rest from tension and worry. The scriptural statement that God too rested on the seventh day is like a divine seal of approval: Yes, it is good for us to savor a day of leisure and enjoyment between periods of intense labor.

Celebration is necessary for all peoples; history attests to this truth. Every nation has days of work and special days of rest and of festivity. From the earliest days of the Church, Christians celebrated Sunday as a day to give glory to God, to refresh the spirit, and to renew the body. Liturgically, Sunday begins on Saturday evening with Evening Prayer (Vespers) and the Vigil Mass.

There are five characteristics of the Christian celebration of the Lord's Day: joyful remembrance of Christ's Resurrection; active family participation in the Eucharist; prayer and reflection; physical renewal through relaxation, leisure, and family meals shared in mutual love; and good works and service to the sick, the elderly, and others in need.

The Second Vatican Council has urged a universal return to this model so that the celebration of the Eucharist, uniquely associated with the solemnization of Sunday, may truly be for Christians a foretaste of the eternal joys of heaven—eternal rest.

RESPONDING

God's Word calls us to respond in love. Respond to God now in the quiet of your heart and perhaps through a journal that you are keeping this year.

- How are my Sundays a joyful remembrance of the Resurrection?

Father, help me always to honor Sunday as a day of rest and to celebrate your day with expectation and joy.

Catechism of the Catholic Church

The themes of this lesson correspond to the following paragraphs: 1359–1360, 1382, 2174–2188.

THE FAITH EXPERIENCE

Scripture in This Chapter

- *Exodus 20:8–11 God commanded his people to keep the Sabbath holy and to rest on that day.*
- *Acts of the Apostles 2:46–47 The early Christian community's celebration of the Eucharist was an occasion of joy.*

Church Documents

National Directory for Catechesis #36, A, 3.
Catechesis should clarify the roles and ministries in Mass so that everyone may participate fully in the celebration of Mass.

Constitution on the Liturgy #10.
The goal of apostolic work is to bring together all the baptized so that they can take part in the Sacrifice and eat the Lord's Supper.

The Day of the Lord #41.
The Mass is a dialogue between God and his people, in which God proclaims the wonders of salvation and the people respond by giving thanks and praise.

Bulletin Board At the left is a suggestion for a bulletin-board design. Invite the children to draw pictures of themselves and their families going to church for Sunday Mass. You might post a banner with the words, "Sunday Is Special!"

For a list of children's literature suggestions, please see **page OV-47.**

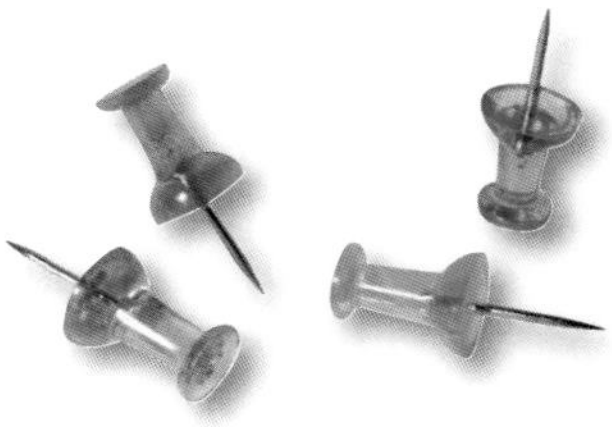

CHAPTER 22 | DAY ONE

We Celebrate with Thanks

Student Book page 91

LEARNING OUTCOMES

The children will be able to

- know the meaning of saying thank you.
- understand that at the celebration of the Eucharist we give thanks to God.

KEY TERM

celebration—a happy gathering of people in honor of someone or something

MATERIALS

- A thank-you card
- Large sheets of construction paper, one for each child
- Magazines
- Scissors
- Glue
- Crayons or markers

COMMENT

The Church has shown special concern for the instruction and participation of children in the Eucharist through the publication of the document *Directory for Masses with Children* in 1973 by the Sacred Congregation for Divine Worship. The *Directory* points out that by reason of their Baptism, children have both the right and the duty to participate in the Church's liturgy. It is the hope of the Church that young Christians who participate in the eucharistic sacrifice will learn to proclaim Christ by expressing love for others. (#55) The *Directory* recommends that from their early years children take part in the Mass with their families.

CENTERING

1 Recall the last chapter.

- ***In the last chapter, what did you learn that Jesus called himself?*** (The light of the world)
- ***Jesus gives us light, life, and love. Today you will learn how we celebrate Jesus.***

2 Lead the children in a discussion about gifts.

- ***When people give us gifts, they give us their love. They give us a part of themselves. When we give gifts to others, we do the same thing. We give them our love. We give them a part of ourselves.***
- ***Tell us about someone who has given you a gift. Who was it? What was the gift? When did you receive it?*** Allow volunteers to tell about gifts that they have been given.
- ***Tell us about someone to whom you gave a gift.*** Allow volunteers to tell about gifts that they have given to others.

SHARING

1 Point out the importance of saying thank you.

- [Show the thank-you card.] ***When we receive gifts from people, we thank them. What are some ways that we can show our thanks?*** (Give them a hug or kiss, say thank you, send a thank-you card.)
- ***How do you feel when a friend thanks you for a gift you have given to him or her? It is important to thank people because it brings them joy.***

2 Have the children open their books to **page 91.** Lead the children to realize that God's gifts are signs of love.

- ***God has given us many gifts because God loves us very much. What are some gifts that God has given to us?***
- ***God has given us people who love us too. Who are they?*** (Our family, our friends)
- ***God loves us so much that he gave us the very best gift, his Son Jesus. Jesus showed us how much God our Father loves us when he died on the cross for us and rose to new life.***

3 Let the children make thank-you cards for all of God's gifts. Distribute large sheets of construction paper, folded in half. Help the children write a message on the front of the card, such as: "For all your gifts, we thank you God." Inside the card, have the children make a collage that shows some of the things for which they are most thankful. Allow the children to draw or cut from magazines pictures of things for which they are thankful.

Encourage them to include drawings of their families and friends. Have the children sign their cards.

4 Explain that we thank God at Mass.

- ***God has been so good to us. There are many ways that we can thank God for his gifts. What are some ways that we can thank God for all his gifts, especially for the gift of Jesus?*** (Say thank you when we pray. Do good things.)
- ***There is a celebration we share with others in which we thank God in a very special and important way. This important way that we thank God is by celebrating Mass. Mass is a special celebration of God's love. At Mass we give God our love.***
- ***We call the Mass a celebration because we come together with other people to thank and praise God for his wonderful gifts. We come together to pray and sing our thanks to God.***
- ***At Mass Jesus thanks God our Father with us by offering himself as a gift. We thank God by offering ourselves with Jesus.***
- ***At Mass Jesus also gives himself to the people as food in Holy Communion. When you are older, you will receive this wonderful gift. This gift of Jesus in Holy Communion is the best gift of God's love.***

Encourage the children to follow along as you read aloud **page 91.**

ACTING

Invite the children to pray the prayer based on Psalm 89:2 with gestures:

I will
[Move hands up, backs of fingers touching.]
celebrate
[Move fingers as you bring hands down in a circle.]
your love
[Cross hands on heart.]
forever, LORD.
[Raise crossed hands, then open them outward.]

CHECKPOINT

- Were the children able to identify some of God's many gifts and to offer thanks?
- How do the children show they understand the Mass as a celebration?

CHAPTER 22

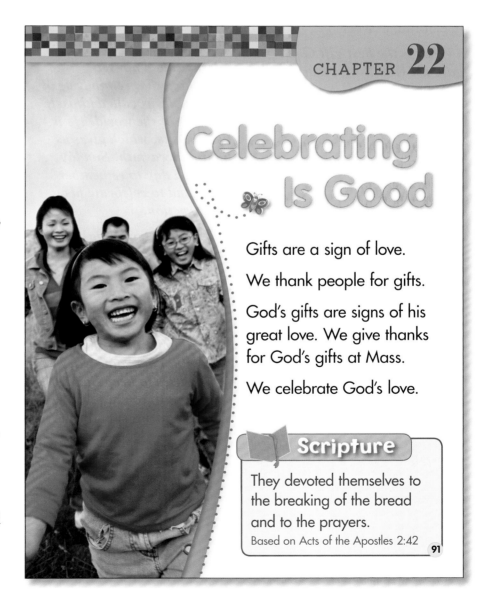

Celebrating Is Good

Gifts are a sign of love.

We thank people for gifts.

God's gifts are signs of his great love. We give thanks for God's gifts at Mass.

We celebrate God's love.

Scripture

They devoted themselves to the breaking of the bread and to the prayers.
Based on Acts of the Apostles 2:42

91

CHAPTER 22 | DAY TWO

Sunday Is Special

LEARNING OUTCOMES

The children will be able to

- realize that Sunday is a special day.
- know ways to celebrate Sunday.

KEY TERM

Sunday—the day on which Jesus rose from the dead, a special day for Christians to worship God

MATERIALS

- Cutout 2
- Calendar
- Paper plates
- Crayons or markers

CENTERING

1 Recall the last lesson.

• ***In the last lesson we talked about God's gifts to us and how we can give thanks to God.***

• ***What is the special way we say thank you to God?*** (Celebrate at Mass.)

• ***What is the best gift God gave us?*** (His Son, Jesus)

2 Show a calendar and invite volunteers to name the days of the week. Ask if anyone knows which of the seven days is a special day for God's people, the Church. (Sunday)

SHARING

1 Show Cutout 2 Sun and tell the children about Sunday.

• ***The sun has always been very important to people. Long ago, when people named the days of the week, they called one day* Sunday, *or "day of the sun."***

• ***Sunday is holy to Christians because Jesus, our Lord, rose from the dead on a Sunday. We call Sunday "the Lord's Day." On Sunday Christians come together to remember Jesus' dying and rising from the dead. We thank God for his great love. We thank Jesus for sharing his new life with us.***

• ***Jesus called himself something that reminds us of the sun. Jesus called himself the light of the world. He is like the sun, which gives us light and warmth. Sunday is a good day to remember Jesus and to celebrate his Resurrection.***

• ***Christians try to make Sunday a special day. You do not go to school on Sunday. We try not work on Sunday unless it is necessary. God wants us to have time to go to church, to rest, and to be with those we love. What are some ways your family tries to keep Sunday special?*** (Go to church, share a special meal, spend time having fun together.)

• ***You are young Christians. You can go to church with your family to sing and pray. Catholics begin celebrating Sunday on Saturday evening so you might go to church on Saturday.***

2 Have the children make paper-plate suns. Distribute the paper plates. Have the children draw a sun on the inner part of the plate and rays on the outer rim. Tell them to show the sun shining brightly, full of light and warmth. On the back of the plates, have the children draw a church. Ask the children where they might put their suns to remind their families to celebrate Sunday by going to church.

3 Have the children draw a heart on each of the Sundays on your classroom calendar. Ask why we put a heart on the Sundays. (We celebrate God's love on Sunday.)

ACTING

Invite the children to pray the following adaptation of Psalm 89:2 with gestures:

- ***We can say this psalm prayer to celebrate God's love:***

  I will
  [Move hands up, backs of fingers touching.]
  celebrate
  [Move fingers as you bring hands down in a circle.]
  your love
  [Cross hands on heart.]
  forever, LORD.
  [Raise crossed hands, then open them outward.]

Songs

Play for the children any of these songs: "Jesus in the Morning" (*Singing Our Faith*) **CD 1 Track 4;** "Sing, Sing, Praise and Sing!" (*Singing Our Faith*) **CD 1 Track 12;** "Make a Wonderful Noise" (*Sing a Song of Joy!*) **CD 2 Track 16;** "Thank You, Lord," "His Banner Over Me Is Love" (verse 1), "Celebrate God" (*Hi God!*); "Purim Song" (*Dandelions*); "Uyai Mose/Come All You People," "We Are the Church," "All You Works of God," "Rejoice in the Lord Always," "Glory and Gratitude and Praise" (*Singing Our Faith*); Into the House of God (*Young People's Glory and Praise*). For a list of all the music used in this program, see **page OV-39.**

CHECKPOINT

- Are there signs that Sunday is special for the children?
- Do the children know ways to honor Sunday as a Sabbath day of rest?

CHAPTER 22 | DAY THREE

The Mass Is a Celebration

Student Book page 92

LEARNING OUTCOMES

The children will be able to

- deepen their understanding of the Eucharist.
- experience joy in belonging to the Church and in being invited to the eucharistic celebration.
- desire to celebrate Mass with their families.

KEY TERM

Mass—the sacramental celebration of Jesus' Last Supper; At Mass we hear God's Word, we commemorate Jesus' sacrifice on the Cross and his Resurrection from the dead, we offer ourselves to God the Father, and we receive Holy Communion

MATERIALS

- Poster 8
- Sample of BLM 24A–B, colored and cut out
- Sample set of Priest, Altar, and Candle punchouts from the Student Book
- Paper plate
- Priest, Altar, and Candle punchouts
- BLM 24A–B
- Envelopes
- Song for ACTING #2 (see song list on page T255)

CENTERING

Recall the last lesson.

- ***What makes Sunday special?*** (We celebrate the Mass.)
- ***Today we will talk about what happens at that celebration. Then you will be able to take part more fully when you go to Mass.***

SHARING

1 Show Poster 8 The Last Supper. Use the sample punchout set to explain the Mass. [Set up the Priest and Altar punchouts. Fold the Priest punchout so it stands. Put the altar cloth from BLM 24A Mass Set on the Altar punchout, matching the slits. Put the Mass book on the altar.]

- *BLM 24A Mass Set*

- ***When Jesus had the Last Supper with his apostles, he was celebrating a holy meal. We remember and celebrate this meal every Sunday. We pray special prayers to praise and thank God. We receive Holy Communion. The priest leads us in the celebration.***
- ***We like to be invited to celebrations. You were invited to the Mass celebration when you were baptized. You were invited to come together every Sunday with all of God's family, the Church.***
- ***Because the Mass is a celebration, it is a time to wear dress-up clothes. The priest wears special clothes for the celebration too.*** [Put a stole and chasuble from BLM 24A and BLM 24B Mass Set on the Priest punchout. Put the chasuble on the model, front-to-back through the slits. Put the stole on the model, back-to-front through the slits.]
  - *BLM 24B Mass Set*
- ***At the Mass celebration, we remember God's goodness and love in Jesus, who died and rose for us. What will the candles lit at Mass help you remember?*** (Jesus is alive. He is the light of the world.) [Insert the Candle punchouts into the slits on top of the altar.]
- ***Gifts are often a part of a celebration. The best gift at Mass is Jesus. He gives himself to his heavenly Father for us at every Mass. We give gifts too. We give bread and wine to God. This is a sign that we are giving ourselves to our Father along with Jesus' offering.*** [Show the bread and chalice from BLM 24A and set them on the altar.] ***Our gifts of bread and wine remind us of all the good things God has given us. It is our way of showing that we are ready to make a gift of ourselves to God.***
- [Show a paper plate.] ***Special food is part of a celebration. The food at Mass is very special. The priest takes our gifts of bread and wine and does what Jesus did at the Last Supper. When he says the words that Jesus said, the bread and wine become the Body and Blood of Christ.***

When we eat and drink this bread and wine, we are joined together with Jesus and his family, the Church.

2 Distribute the Priest, Altar, and Candle punchouts. Help the children prepare these punchouts as follows:

- Fold Priest punchout in thirds. This will make the priest stand.
- Fold Altar punchout on the dotted lines to make it stand.
- Place Altar punchout in front of the priest.
- Place Candle punchouts in the slits on top of the altar.

3 Distribute copies of BLM 24A–B. If time allows, the children can color the pieces and cut them out. Provide envelopes so that the children can keep all the pieces together. If time is short, the children can take their envelopes home and ask family members to help them. Give these directions:

- Place the chasuble on the priest from the front. Carefully put the tabs through the slits.
- Place the stole on the priest from the back. Carefully push the ends of the stole through the slits from the back.
- Place the altar cloth on the altar, removing the candles, then placing them in the slits. Then put the Mass book, cup, and bread on the altar.

ACTING

1 Have the children turn to **page 92**. Read it aloud.

- ***What do the pictures show?*** (A priest and children at Mass) ***During Mass, we pray the prayer that Jesus taught us, the Our Father.*** Invite the children to pray together the Our Father.

2 Invite the children to learn and sing a song they might sing at Mass or a song chosen from the song list on **page T255.**

CHECKPOINT

- What understanding of the Eucharist have the children demonstrated?
- Have the children indicated familiarity and comfort with Sunday Mass?
- Do the children look forward to being with the community at Sunday Mass?

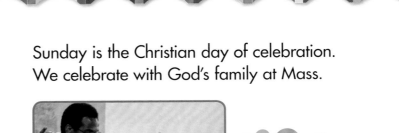

Sunday is the Christian day of celebration.
We celebrate with God's family at Mass.

A priest leads the celebration.

We hear God's Word.

We sing and pray and give gifts.

We remember that Jesus died and rose to new life.

We thank Jesus for his great love.

92

CHAPTER 22 | DAY FOUR

We Prepare to Celebrate Mass

Student Book pages 93–94

LEARNING OUTCOMES

The children will be able to

- become more familiar with the celebration of the Eucharist.
- be able to respond to some of the prayers of the Eucharist.

MATERIALS

- BLM 25
- Scissors
- Stapler
- Crayons or markers

COMMENT

Children at this age can benefit by joining a group of older children who are planning a eucharistic celebration. Arrange with an upper-grade teacher to include the kindergarten class. The songs, readings, and intentions should be explained to the children before the celebration. Pictures or banners the children have made can be used. The Mass can be planned with a theme to relate it to the children's daily lives. If such a eucharistic celebration is being planned, take this lesson to prepare the children for their participation by practicing Mass responses and songs and preparing readings, prayers, or posters.

CENTERING

1 Recall the last lesson.

- ***What is the wonderful celebration that God's family, the Church, shares every Sunday?*** (Mass)
- ***What do we celebrate?*** (God's goodness and love; that Jesus died and rose.)
- ***What gifts are given?*** (Jesus gives himself to the Father. We give bread and wine. We give ourselves. We unite our offering with Jesus' gift of himself.)
- ***Today you will do some things to help you celebrate Mass with God's family.***

2 Have the children open their books to **page 93.** Read aloud this page and help them do the activities.

SHARING

1 Distribute BLM 25 Mass Booklet and discuss what happens when God's people gather for Mass. Help the children cut out the booklet and fold the pages. Staple together the pages of each child's booklet.

- *BLM 25 Mass Booklet*

Ask the children to turn to page 1 of their Mass booklets:

- ***Mass begins with the Introductory Rites. We sing a song to praise God as we gather for Mass.***

Sing a song of praise to God that the children may be familiar with from Mass or choose a song from the song list on **page T255.**

- ***We ask for God's forgiveness. We pray, "Lord have mercy." We praise God and say "Glory to God."***

Practice the "Lord, have mercy" response by having the children repeat after you:

Lord, have mercy.
Christ, have mercy.
Lord, have mercy.

Have the children turn to page 2 of their Mass booklets:

- ***During the Liturgy of the Word we listen to God's Word. We respond, "Thanks be to God."***

Remind the children that when God's Word is proclaimed, we listen attentively. Practice the response to the readings.

- ***After each reading, the reader says, "The Word of the Lord" and we respond, "Thanks be to God."***

Have the children draw a picture of themselves at Mass listening to God's Word on page 2 of their Mass booklets.

Have the children turn to page 3 of their Mass booklets:

• ***During the Liturgy of the Eucharist, we offer God our gifts of bread and wine. We ask God to bless our gifts. They become the Body and Blood of Jesus. We pray Hosanna, the Mystery of Faith, and the Amen.***

Practice the Mystery of Faith taught in Chapter 19:
"We proclaim your Death,
  O Lord,
and profess your Resurrection
until you come again."
(If a sung Mystery of Faith was taught, then sing this together.)

Have the children draw the gifts of bread and wine that become the Body and Blood of Jesus on page 3 of the Mass booklets.

Tell the children to turn to page 4 of their Mass booklets:

• ***Before Holy Communion, we pray the Our Father and share a sign of peace. Then we see God's people receive Jesus in Holy Communion. We pray that one day we will also receive Jesus in Holy Communion. We sing a song about Jesus. At the end of Mass, the priest sends us in peace to glorify the Lord by our lives. We pray, "Thanks be to God."***

2 Encourage the children to participate in Mass.

• ***At every celebration of Jesus' dying and rising at Mass, candles are lit. What do the candles remind us of?*** (Jesus is alive. He is the light of the world.) ***You can look at the beautiful candles during the celebration. You can watch the flames burn brightly. You can pray to Jesus.***

• ***If you do not already go to church with your family every Sunday, you might ask your parents to take you. Your Mass booklet can help you remember how to participate in the celebration of the Mass.***

God wants us to celebrate his love and goodness at Sunday Mass.

Try This

Draw an altar for the priest celebrating Mass.	Draw a candle on each end. Draw a cross in the center.	Thank God for inviting you to Mass.

93

ACTING

1 Invite the children to pray the adaptation of Psalm 89:2 with gestures:

- ***The Mass celebration is a very special celebration. We thank God that we belong to the Catholic Church and are invited to the Mass celebration every Sunday. Let us pray the psalm prayer together:***

  I will
  [Move hands up, backs of fingers touching.]
  celebrate
  [Move fingers as you bring hands down in a circle.]
  your love
  [Cross hands on heart.]
  forever, LORD.
  [Raise crossed hands, then open them outward.]

- Let us join hands and pray the Our Father together.

2 Have the children take home the Family Page on **page 94** to share with their families.

CHECKPOINT

- Are the children showing greater familiarity with the responses we pray at Mass?
- How does the children's participation in the Eucharist reflect their deeper understanding and appreciation of it?

I will celebrate your love forever, LORD.
Based on Psalm 89:2

Celebrating in Families

The Lesson Your Child Learned

Studies show that children are profoundly affected by early religious experiences. Habits of prayer are best learned by praying with others and joining in the celebration of the Mass. In this chapter the children discovered the meaning of gifts and were shown how to thank God at Mass for the gifts of his love. The children learned that they are invited, by reason of their Baptism, to join in the Sunday Mass celebration.

Living the Lesson

And the band sang, "Celebrate good times, come on!" We were at a family wedding, and everyone was on the dance floor. Old and young, limber and lame, great dancers and klutzes, we all joined the dance and everyone belonged. My wife and I were dancing with our young daughters, but we knew we were really dancing with the whole extended family, and it felt like we were dancing with every person in the world. In that moment I sensed the oneness that Jesus prayed we might all achieve.

Celebrating is a deeply human trait. Unlike God's other earthly creatures, people celebrate birthdays and weddings, anniversaries and achievements. In doing so, we grow in awareness that all good gifts—love, fidelity, longevity, and life itself—come from God. Make sure to celebrate family events both large and small. Be aware of the One who makes it all possible.

–Tom McGrath, author of *Raising Faith-Filled Kids* (Loyola Press)

Bringing the Lesson Home

- Read with your child the pages from this chapter that were sent home.
- Use the Mass cutouts your child brought home.
- Take your kindergartner to church to celebrate Sunday Mass. Continue with a special meal or activity that shows Sunday is special.
- Let your child see that singing, praying, and receiving Holy Communion at Mass are important to you.
- Go through a family photo album and look at pictures of family celebrations, such as weddings, Baptisms, and reunions. Tell stories about how you celebrated these events.

94

ENRICHING THE FAITH EXPERIENCE

Use the following activities to enrich a lesson, to replace an activity with one that better meets the needs of your class, or to create an additional lesson.

1. Let the children make large drawings or paintings to symbolize the Mass or to illustrate the reading used at a Mass they attend.

2. Have the children draw a picture of their favorite part of the Mass.

3. Invite a priest to visit the class to talk about his role at Sunday Mass and how he prepares for Mass. Consider visiting the church together to learn more about the Mass. (Refer to Chapter 17.)

4. To add to the celebration of the Mass, invite the children to make rhythm maracas. Distribute two plastic cups and a handful of dried beans to each child. Guide the children to put the beans in one cup. Then have them place the second cup upside down on top of the first cup. Help the children tape the cups together. Then wrap the maracas in aluminum foil or plastic wrap. Invite the children to decorate their maracas and write their names on them. You might encourage the children to shake their maracas when singing songs during a lesson.

Chapter 23
Air Is Good

FAITH FOCUS

Jesus sent his Spirit to help us love like him.

Romans 5:5

PREPARING THE FAITH EXPERIENCE

LISTENING

Those who share God's Word with others must be fed themselves by God's Word found in Sacred Scripture. Share some time of quiet prayer with God, listening to God's word. Ask God to fill you with his presence and nourish you by his holy Word.

. . . the love of God has been poured out into our hearts through the holy Spirit that has been given to us.

Romans 5:5

REFLECTING

We human beings are very much at home when perceiving the world through our five senses. We gaze in awe at the grandeur of a sunset; music can stir us deeply; instinctively we stop to smell the fragrance of a rose and to touch its petals; we savor the taste of good food.

However, in all these sensate experiences, our response is not triggered solely by the external reality. Rather, it seems to well up from deep within, a movement stirred by an inner reality. We learn in Genesis how God, in infinite wisdom, decreed that living creatures be a composite of the material and the nonmaterial. In Adam's case, however, God's love did not stop there. God further decreed that the spirit of this new creature be an image of himself. Genesis 2:7 tells how this was accomplished: God breathed a breath of his own life into Adam's body. And it is this breath of God within all people that not only gives life itself but also enables us to feel kinship with things of the spirit.

The spiritual life is sustained and renewed by the Holy Spirit. We do not know where the wind comes from or where it is going. Yet we feel its effects. So it is with the life of the Holy Spirit whose effects we can see in our lives. Wind can both fan and extinguish fire; as a gentle wind, the Holy Spirit can enkindle in us the fire of God's love or can extinguish the fire of raging passion. Wind cannot be perceived as any definite shape or form. Rather, it fills out and then is limited only by the size of its container. Similarly, the Holy Spirit has no definite shape or form. The Holy Spirit's presence in our lives, though, is surely discernible as God brings us to completion, limited only by our finite capacity.

RESPONDING

Having been nourished by God's Word, we are able to respond to God's great love for us. In prayer, respond to God's call to you to share his word with others. You may also wish to respond in your prayer journal.

- How strong is my relationship with the Holy Spirit?

Holy Spirit, prompt us to strive for what is good.

Catechism of the Catholic Church

The themes of this lesson correspond to the following paragraphs: 689, 733–736, 739, 2415.

Scripture in This Chapter

- *Genesis 2:7 God breathed his own breath of life into Adam's body.*
- *2 Corinthians 3:6–9 Paul discusses the life-giving effects of the Holy Spirit.*

THE FAITH EXPERIENCE

DAY ONE
God Gives Us the Gift of Air

DAY TWO
Jesus Gives Us the Gift of the Holy Spirit

DAY THREE
The *Holy Spirit Is the Spirit of Love*

DAY FOUR
A Dove Stands for the Holy Spirit

Church Documents

General Directory for Catechesis #43.
The Holy Spirit increases the Church's understanding of the Gospel and helps her proclaim the Gospel throughout the world.

Constitution on the Church #4.
The Holy Spirit was sent to sanctify the Church so that those who believe might have access through Christ in one Spirit to the Father.

The theme of this chapter corresponds to Pentecost, the conclusion of the Easter season. Lesson 7 of SPECIAL SEASONS AND DAYS is an additional Pentecost session. Refer to the ENRICHING THE FAITH EXPERIENCE section of this chapter and Lesson 7 of SPECIAL SEASONS AND DAYS for additional ideas to expand upon the themes of Pentecost.

Bulletin Board At the left is a suggestion for a bulletin-board design. Use BLM 26 Pinwheel and prepare a pinwheel craft and post it in the center of the bulletin board. You might post other pictures and/or symbols of air around it. • *BLM 26 Pinwheel*

For a list of children's literature suggestions, please see **page OV-47.**

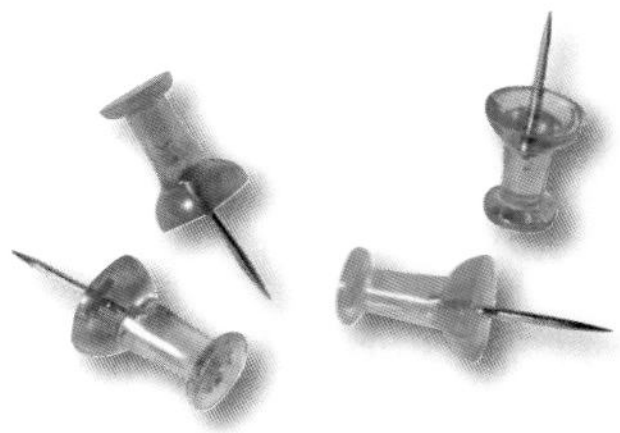

CHAPTER 23 | DAY ONE

God Gives Us the Gift of Air

Student Book page 95

LEARNING OUTCOMES

The children will be able to

- appreciate and respect air as a gift from God.
- learn that Jesus gave us the gift of the Holy Spirit.

KEY TERM

Holy Spirit—God, the Third Person of the Trinity; the Spirit of Jesus that we received at Baptism

MATERIALS

- Cutout 1
- For pinwheel craft:
  BLM 26
  Crayons or markers
  Scissors
  Plastic straws
  Hole punch
  Tape
  Brass paper fasteners
- Glue
- Paints (optional)
- Sample pinwheel craft

COMMENT

The Hebrew word *ruah* means both "wind" and "spirit," and the Greek word *pneuma* can be used for both words as well. In this lesson the children are introduced to the Holy Spirit by first learning about air/wind, an invisible reality they need to live. Then they learn that they need the invisible reality of the Holy Spirit to live in love as Christians.

CENTERING

1 Recall the last chapter.

- ***Last time, we learned about a special way that we, as members of the Catholic Church, celebrate God's love.***
- ***What do we call the special celebration of God's love that we celebrate on Sunday?*** (Mass)
- ***Today you will learn who brings Jesus' love into our hearts.***

2 Show the class the sample pinwheel craft.

- ***What should we do to make this toy work?*** (Use our breath to make the pinwheel turn.) [Demonstrate.]
- ***What made this pinwheel turn?*** (The air from my breath)
- ***What are some other toys that are moved by air or the wind?*** (Bubbles, balloons, kites, paper airplanes, paper fans)

SHARING

1 Discuss air.

- ***Where did the air to turn the pinwheel come from?*** (Our breath)
- ***We have air inside us. We breathe it into our lungs. Then we breathe it out again.*** [Ask the children to take a deep breath and then slowly exhale. Have them put their hands in front of their faces as they breathe out, so they can feel the air.]
- ***Animals and plants need air too. Air is a mixture of many things we cannot see. One of these is oxygen. We need oxygen to live.***
- ***Why can't we see the air?*** (It is invisible. It is colorless.)

2 Help the children to make pinwheels, using BLM 26 Pinwheel. Allow time for the children to play with them. If time allows, spend this playtime outdoors. Look for evidence of the wind. If possible, engage in the next discussion about air while outdoors.

To make the pinwheels, have the children color the pattern found on BLM 26 Pinwheel. Help the children cut out the patterns. Using the hole punch, punch out holes in the corners and the center, as shown on the pattern. Show the children how to gently fold up each section from the tip to the center. Punch a hole through the top of the straw. Insert a paper fastener through the holes in the pinwheel and the straw and spread the fastener's prongs to secure them in place. Keep them loose enough so that the pinwheel turns easily.

- ***BLM 26 Pinwheel***

3 Compare air and wind to the Holy Spirit. If you are not able to have this conversation outdoors, then have the children open their books to **page 95.** Have them look at the picture and tell what it feels like to be out in the fresh air and to feel a cool breeze.

- ***Air and wind are mysterious. We can hear the wind.*** [If outdoors, invite the children to listen for the effects of the wind.] ***We can feel the wind blow against us.*** [If outdoors, invite the children to attend to the air as it touches their skin.] ***We can see what the wind can do.*** [If outdoors, invite the children to look for evidence of the wind.] ***What have you seen the wind do?*** (Blow the leaves on the trees; blow through tall grass; blow leaves along the ground.)
- ***But we cannot see the wind.***
- ***We cannot completely understand the Holy Spirit because the Holy Spirit is God, and God is so great.***

If you have held this discussion outdoors, return to the classroom.

4 Have the children turn to **page 95.** Recall the effects of the wind that were observed outdoors. Read aloud **page 95.**

ACTING

Teach and pray this verse based on Wisdom 1:7. Show Cutout 1 Jesus.

- ***Jesus has sent the Holy Spirit into our world. His Holy Spirit is everywhere, just as air is everywhere. We can pray:***

The spirit of the LORD fills the whole world.
[Make large circular motions with your arms, upward, then downward.]

CHECKPOINT

- Do the children understand that air is a gift from God?
- Do the children recognize the Holy Spirit as a gift from Jesus?

CHAPTER 23

Air Is Good

God gives us the gift of air.
We cannot see air.
We can see what moving air does.
We need air to live.

Jesus gives us the gift of the Holy Spirit.
We cannot see the Holy Spirit.
The Holy Spirit fills us with love.
We can see what love does.

We need the Holy Spirit to love as Jesus does.

95

Jesus Gives Us the Gift of the Holy Spirit

Student Book page 96

LEARNING OUTCOMES

The children will be able to

- know that Jesus sent the Holy Spirit to us.
- be aware of the mysterious, hidden presence of the Holy Spirit.
- be familiar with the Gospel story of how Jesus raised the daughter of Jairus.

MATERIALS

- *A Child's Bible*, page 20
- Cutout 1
- Bible enthroned, with note card on which you have written the adapted Scripture reading for SHARING #3, Luke 8:40–56

COMMENT

Love is the most powerful force in the world. Before his Ascension, the risen Jesus promised the gift of the Holy Spirit to enable the Church to fulfill its mission. The Holy Spirit enables us to put on the mind of Christ and to follow in his way of love.

CENTERING

1 Recall the last lesson:

- ***Last time, we learned that we cannot see the wind. Still, we know that the wind is there. How do we know the wind is there if we cannot see it?*** (We can see the effects of the wind.)

Read aloud the poem "Who Has Seen the Wind?"

Who Has Seen the Wind?

Who has seen the wind?
Neither I nor you;
But when the leaves hang trembling,
The wind is passing through.
Who has seen the wind?
Neither you nor I;
But when the trees bow down their heads,
The wind is passing by.

Christina Rossetti

2 Show Cutout 1. Comment:

- ***Like the wind, Jesus is with us, even though we can't see him. Today we will talk about how he is with us.***

SHARING

1 Discuss how Jesus gives us the Holy Spirit and is present with us.

- ***Before Jesus went back to be with God in heaven, he told us he would be with us always. We have learned that Jesus is with us in a special way at Mass. How is Jesus with us at Mass?*** (He changes bread and wine into his Body and Blood through the priest at Mass.) ***Jesus also gives us his Holy Spirit and stays with us in the Holy Spirit. We cannot feel his touch the way people did when Jesus walked on earth. But Jesus is with us.***
- ***We received the Holy Spirit when we were baptized. The Holy Spirit helps us think and feel and love as Jesus did.***
- ***Jesus loved his Father in heaven. He prayed to him and did what God wanted. The Holy Spirit in our hearts helps us pray and say yes to what God wants us to do.***

2 Teach and sing a song about Jesus' gift of the Holy Spirit, such as "Spirit-Friend" (*Singing Our Faith*) or another from the song list on **page T267.**

3 Read the story "The Girl Who Came Back to Life" from *A Child's Bible*, **page 20,** to show how Jesus loved. Introduce this Bible story by showing the Bible and opening it to the Gospel according to Luke, Luke 8:40–56. Enthrone the Bible.

- ***Let's prepare ourselves to listen well to today's Bible story.*** Read the story. Discuss:

- ***What loving things did Jesus do in this story?*** (He brought Jairus's daughter back to life.)
- [Have the children look at the picture on **page 96.**] ***How do you think the little girl felt when she came back to life and saw Jesus?*** (Surprised)
- ***How do you think Jairus and his wife felt?*** (Happy, overjoyed, surprised, thankful)

4 Let the children act out the story of the daughter of Jairus, as you read aloud **page 96.**

ACTING

Invite the children to pray the verse based on Wisdom 1:7 with gestures:

> **The spirit of the Lord fills the whole world.** [Make large circular motions with your arms, upward, then downward.]

Songs

Play for the children any of these songs: "Hold My Hand" (*I See a New World*) **CD 2 Track 9**; "Alleluia Round," "A Psalm for All Seasons" (*Color the World with Song*); "Jesus Always Helps Us" (*Stories and Songs of Jesus*); "Kathy's Special Day" (*Dandelions*); "Our God Is a God of Love" (*Hi God 2*); "Sing Praise," "The Wind Song" (*Songs for Young Children*); "Spirit-Friend," "If You Believe and I Believe" (*Singing Our Faith*). For a list of all the music used in this program, see **page OV–39.**

CHECKPOINT

- How have the children demonstrated awareness that Jesus shared the gift of the Holy Spirit at their Baptism?
- What have the children said or done that shows they are aware that loving actions are prompted by the Holy Spirit?
- How did the children respond to the story of the raising of the daughter of Jairus?

Scripture

Jairus's little girl was very sick. He asked Jesus for help.
Jesus went with Jairus to his house.
Before they got there, the little girl died.
Jesus entered the house. He brought the little girl back to life.

Based on Luke 8:40–56

Jesus is with us always.
He is with us in his spirit of love.

96

CHAPTER 23 | DAY THREE

The Holy Spirit Is the Spirit of Love

Student Book pages 96–97

LEARNING OUTCOMES

The children will be able to

- desire to follow the Holy Spirit by showing Jesus' love.
- learn the last line of the Our Father.

KEY TERM

temptations—thoughts or feelings that make us feel like doing something wrong

MATERIALS

- Cutouts 4–7, 9, 12–13, 15–16, 22–31
- A kite, or a picture of a kite
- A large shape, such as a heart, cut out of poster board
- 3-inch by 5-inch pieces of construction paper
- Hole punch
- Yarn
- Crayons or markers
- Stapler

COMMENTS

1. With the help of the Holy Spirit, we willingly submit to God's designs on our behalf. We understand our interdependence with all peoples and are concerned about doing our part to bring about a more equitable sharing of the goods of the earth. We gratefully use the gifts of the earth with reverence and respect.

2. Make plans for a class project. See ENRICHING THE FAITH EXPERIENCE #5 for project ideas.

CENTERING

1 Recall the last lesson. Have the children turn to **page 96.** Ask a volunteer to tell the story that goes with the picture.

2 Explain that today the children will think more about ways they can love like Jesus.

SHARING

1 Tell how Jesus had love for the earth.

- ***Jesus respected the gift of the earth, with all the wonderful gifts of nature in it.*** [Show the appropriate Cutouts of nature (see list in MATERIALS) as you talk.]
- ***Jesus enjoyed the beauty of the flowers and the green grass. He liked to look up and see birds flying across the blue sky and to smell the fresh, clean air. He liked to walk along a sandy beach and watch the waves break on the shore. He often went alone up a green mountainside where he could enter into his quiet heart and talk to his heavenly Father.***
- ***What gifts of nature help you think about God?***

2 Show the Cutouts of people (see list in MATERIALS) and ask the children to choose one, hold it, and tell how they can show love to that person like Jesus. Let them do the same for the Cutouts of the gifts of nature. Conclude:

- ***When you love and pray to God our Father as Jesus did, respect and love other persons, and care for the gifts of the earth as Jesus did, the Holy Spirit is spreading Jesus' love in the world through you.*** [Show Cutout 4 Heart.]

3 Help the children see that the Holy Spirit helps us live in simplicity like Jesus.

- ***Jesus lived a simple life. He did not own many things. The Holy Spirit helps us realize that having lots of things does not make us happy. We do not need everything that other people have. If we do have more than we need, the Holy Spirit invites us to share with others.***

4 Show the children a kite or a picture of a kite. Ask,

- ***If I wanted to make this kite fly high in the air, what would I need?*** (Wind)
- ***If I want to love as Jesus did, what do I need?*** (Holy Spirit)

As a class, make a kite as a reminder that the Holy Spirit works through us to spread Jesus' love. Distribute the pieces of construction paper. Tell the children to write or draw a picture of an action that shows how the Holy Spirit might work in them to spread Jesus' love in the world. Invite the children to tell what they put on their papers as you collect them. Punch a hole at the top and the bottom of the poster-board heart. Tie a loop of yarn through the top hole. Knot one end of a length of yarn through the bottom hole. Attach the children's papers in a row to the yarn at the bottom of the kite, making a tail. Explain that just as a kite needs wind to fly high up into the air, we need the Holy Spirit working in us so that we can show the love of Jesus. Hang up the kite by the loop at the top and display it in the classroom.

5 Teach the last line of the Our Father.

- ***The Holy Spirit helps us be good and love like Jesus. However, sometimes we do not feel like doing the right thing. Sometimes we feel like doing something wrong. Thoughts and feelings that make us feel like doing wrong are not from the Holy Spirit. Things that lead us to do something wrong are called temptations. Temptations can lead us to disobey God.***
- ***At the end of the Our Father, we pray, "And lead us not into temptation, but deliver us from evil." We want to be good and loving like Jesus.***
- ***Say the line after me: "And lead us not into temptation, but deliver us from evil."*** [Have the children repeat.]

6 Read **page 97** to the children and help them do the activity. Ask:

- ***What does the kite need to fly?*** (Wind)
- ***What do we need to love as Jesus did?*** (Holy Spirit)

ACTING

Invite the children to pray the Our Father together. Tell the children that when they know the prayer, they may color the cross next to it on the inside front cover of their books.

CHECKPOINT

- Do the children know ways to show love?
- Are the children becoming more familiar with the Our Father?

Try This

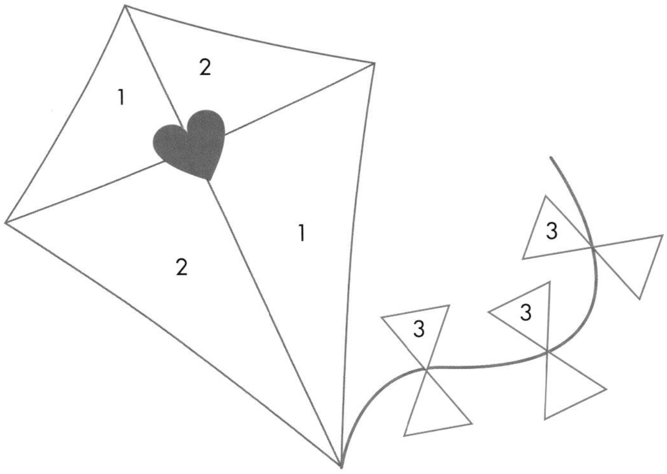

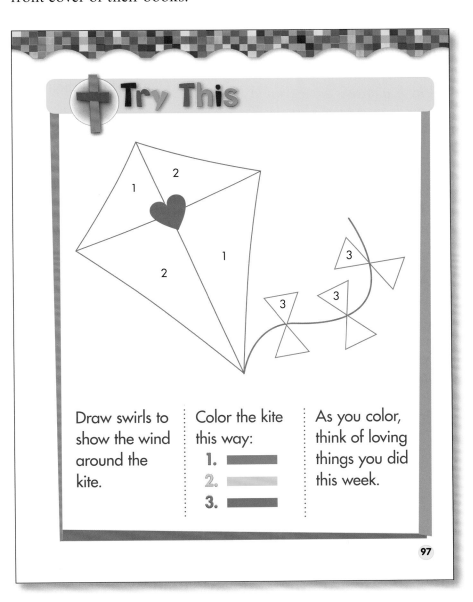

Draw swirls to show the wind around the kite.

Color the kite this way:
1.
2.
3.

As you color, think of loving things you did this week.

97

CHAPTER 23 | DAY FOUR

A Dove Stands for the Holy Spirit

Student Book page 98

LEARNING OUTCOMES

The children will be able to
- understand why the dove is a symbol for the Holy Spirit.

MATERIALS

- Sample dove craft
- BLM 27
- Glue
- Crayons or markers

CENTERING

Show the sample dove and tell about it.

- ***Because we cannot see the Holy Spirit, we have symbols to stand for Jesus' Holy Spirit. One symbol of the Holy Spirit is a dove. When Jesus was baptized, the Holy Spirit came down like a dove. A dove is a very gentle bird. It is a symbol of love and peace.***
- ***Why is a dove a good symbol for the Holy Spirit?*** (The Holy Spirit brings Jesus' love into the world.)
- ***Today you will make a dove like this. Then we will celebrate the Holy Spirit, who is with us always.***

SHARING

1 Have the children make doves from copies of BLM 27 Dove. Read the prayer on the dove to the children.
- *BLM 27 Dove*

2 Teach the children to pray, "Holy Spirit, fill me with love." They might sing it to the melody of the first two lines of "Father, We Adore You" (*Hi God 2*). Have them gently wave the dove symbols as they sing.

ACTING

1 Invite the children to the Prayer Center. Lead them to pray.

- ***Air is good. The Holy Spirit is good. We cannot see the Holy Spirit, but we can see the loving actions that the Holy Spirit helps people do.***
- ***The Holy Spirit helps us love as Jesus did.***
- ***The response to each prayer petition is "Holy Spirit, fill me with love."***
- ***Holy Spirit, help us do what God wants.*** [Response]
- ***Holy Spirit, help us love God and pray.*** [Response]
- ***Holy Spirit, help us respect and love everyone.*** [Response]
- ***Holy Spirit, help us respect the gifts of air, water, earth, and living things that God has given us.*** [Response]
- ***Holy Spirit, help us be happy having what we need.*** [Response]

Close with the verse from Wisdom 1:7, "The spirit of the LORD fills the whole world" or sing the song about the Holy Spirit taught on Day Two.

2 Suggest that the children take home the dove to put in a place where it will remind them of the Holy Spirit's presence, inviting them to live in Jesus' love.

3 Have the children take home the Family Page on **page 98** to share with their families.

CHECKPOINT

- Do the children recognize the dove as a symbol of the Holy Spirit?

ENRICHING THE FAITH EXPERIENCE

Use the following activities to enrich a lesson, to replace an activity with one that better meets the needs of your class, or to create an additional lesson.

1 Use a fan or let the children make fans by accordion-pleating a decorated piece of paper in order to experience wind. Staple one end to make a handle.

2 Let the children put on skits showing children following the Holy Spirit.

3 Teach the children the song "Jesus Always Helps Us" (*Stories and Songs of Jesus*) or the following song.

I'm Gonna Sing When the Spirit Says Sing
G
I'm gon - na sing when the spi - rit says
sing; I'm gon-na sing when the spi - rit says
D7 G
sing; I'm gon-na sing when the spi - rit says
C G D7 G
sing, and o - bey the spi - rit of the Lord.

4 Read the poem "God Is There." Invite the children to echo the repeated lines and join in on the last line.

God Is There

When I run in the sun,
God is there, God is there.
When I fall playing ball,
God cares, God cares.
When I'm sad or I'm glad,
God knows, God knows.
When I mind or I'm kind,
God sees, God sees.
God is with me day and night,
Helping me to do what's right.
I love you, God!

M. Kathleen Glavich, S.N.D.

5 Introduce a class project to spread God's love:

- clean an area of the parish or school building
- collect money for the missions
- perform a Bible story for another class
- collect food donations for a local food pantry

Tell the children about the plans to work on this class project.

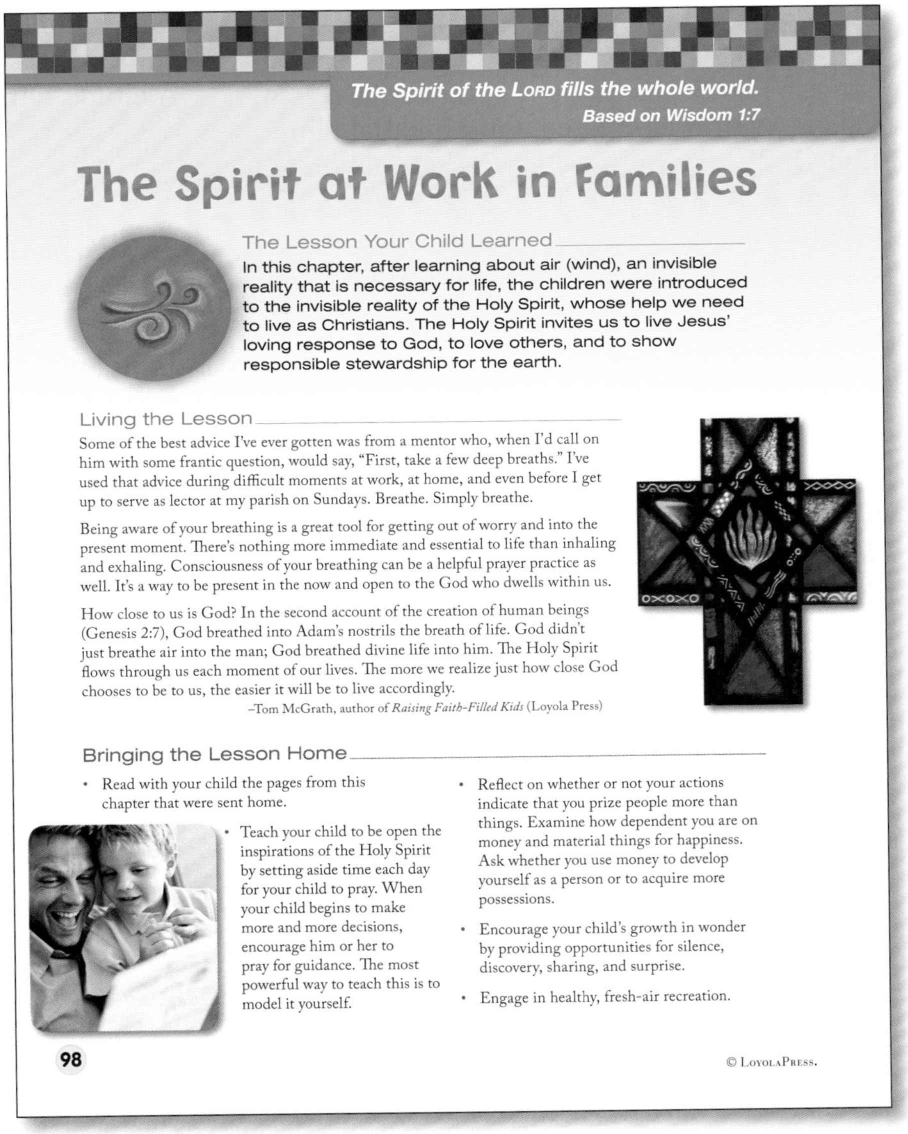

The Spirit of the LORD fills the whole world.
Based on Wisdom 1:7

The Spirit at Work in Families

The Lesson Your Child Learned

In this chapter, after learning about air (wind), an invisible reality that is necessary for life, the children were introduced to the invisible reality of the Holy Spirit, whose help we need to live as Christians. The Holy Spirit invites us to live Jesus' loving response to God, to love others, and to show responsible stewardship for the earth.

Living the Lesson

Some of the best advice I've ever gotten was from a mentor who, when I'd call on him with some frantic question, would say, "First, take a few deep breaths." I've used that advice during difficult moments at work, at home, and even before I get up to serve as lector at my parish on Sundays. Breathe. Simply breathe.

Being aware of your breathing is a great tool for getting out of worry and into the present moment. There's nothing more immediate and essential to life than inhaling and exhaling. Consciousness of your breathing can be a helpful prayer practice as well. It's a way to be present in the now and open to the God who dwells within us.

How close to us is God? In the second account of the creation of human beings (Genesis 2:7), God breathed into Adam's nostrils the breath of life. God didn't just breathe air into the man; God breathed divine life into him. The Holy Spirit flows through us each moment of our lives. The more we realize just how close God chooses to be to us, the easier it will be to live accordingly.

–Tom McGrath, author of *Raising Faith-Filled Kids* (Loyola Press)

Bringing the Lesson Home

- Read with your child the pages from this chapter that were sent home.
- Teach your child to be open the inspirations of the Holy Spirit by setting aside time each day for your child to pray. When your child begins to make more and more decisions, encourage him or her to pray for guidance. The most powerful way to teach this is to model it yourself.
- Reflect on whether or not your actions indicate that you prize people more than things. Examine how dependent you are on money and material things for happiness. Ask whether you use money to develop yourself as a person or to acquire more possessions.
- Encourage your child's growth in wonder by providing opportunities for silence, discovery, sharing, and surprise.
- Engage in healthy, fresh-air recreation.

98

Chapter 24

Joy Is Good

FAITH FOCUS

Jesus is our source of joy.

John 5:1–8; John 15:11

PREPARING THE FAITH EXPERIENCE

LISTENING

The vocation of a teacher is to communicate with joy the good news of God's love. Take some time to let yourself be refreshed by the good news found in the Bible. As you pray, hear God speak to you his good news of love and salvation.

"I have told you this so that my joy might be in you and your joy might be complete."

John 15:11

REFLECTING

When Adam was created, God breathed into him God's own Spirit, a Spirit that brought Adam not only life but also a rich variety of gifts, among them joy and happiness. Accompanying these gifts was the ability to laugh and to smile. In those idyllic days of long ago, when God walked through the garden side by side with Adam and Eve, Eden certainly must have echoed with the delightful sounds of human joy and laughter. But then sin entered, and everything changed. No longer did happiness flow spontaneously. Worry and fear became part of the human experience.

The Gospels describe Jesus as one who experienced the full range of human emotions. Among these was the full depth of human joy. With his gentle humor, Jesus teased the learned Nicodemus. When celebrating with family and friends at a wedding, Jesus worked his first miracle to sustain the happiness of the celebration. Jesus brought smiles and deep joy to those he encountered. More importantly, he taught people how to laugh at their own self-importance, how to see things as they really are, and how to bring joy to others, even at the cost of personal inconvenience and suffering.

Many adults experience wistful nostalgia when witnessing a child's innocent joy and laughter. A child's happiness is a potent reminder that the loving Father made us and sent his Son to show us the way home again.

RESPONDING

God's Word moves us to respond in word and action. Let the Holy Spirit work within you as you prayerfully consider how you are being called to respond to God's message to you today.

- Would people describe me as a joyful person?
- Are my lessons joyful experiences for the children?

Spirit of Joy, fill our hearts with your love that brings everlasting joy.

Catechism of the Catholic Church

The themes of this lesson correspond to the following paragraphs: 1718, 1723, 2548.

THE FAITH EXPERIENCE

DAY ONE
Happy People Bring Joy

DAY TWO
Jesus Brings Joy

DAY THREE
Ways to Bring Joy

DAY FOUR
We Spread Joy

Scripture in This Chapter

- *Psalm 104 This entire psalm is a hymn of joy about God's revelation of himself as Creator.*
- *Romans 14:17 Joy is a characteristic of the heavenly kingdom.*

Church Documents

National Directory for Catechesis #54, B, 8. Catechists should faithfully practice the faith in a spirit of faith, charity, hope, courage, and joy.

Constitution on the Church in the Modern World #1. The joy and hope of the people of the world as well as their grief and anguish are the joy, hope, grief, and anguish of the followers of Christ.

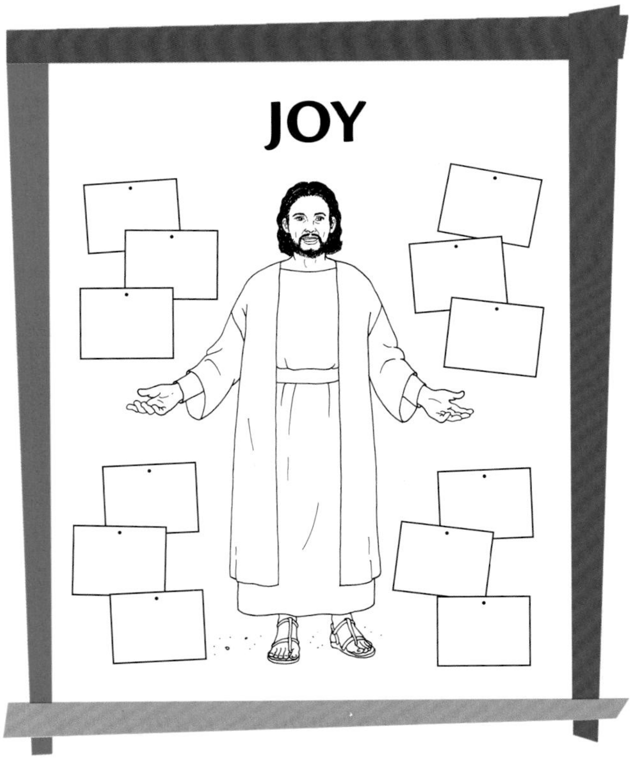

Bulletin Board At the left is a suggestion for a bulletin-board design. Use BLM 1 Jesus if you wish to make a photocopy or transparency. Invite the children to draw the people and things that bring them joy. Post their drawings on the bulletin board, with the picture of Jesus in the center. You might also post a banner with the word "Joy."

- ***BLM 1 Jesus***

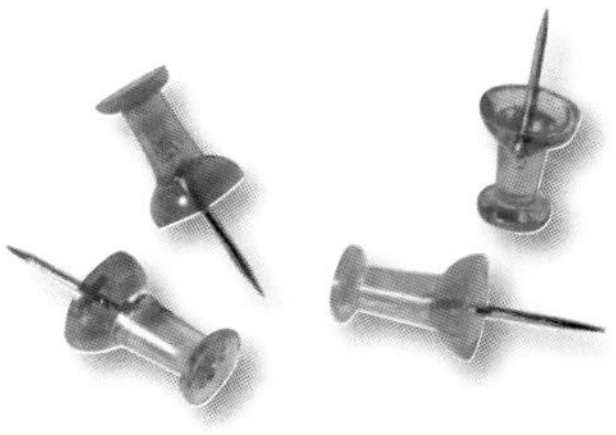

For a list of children's literature suggestions, please see **page OV-47.**

CHAPTER 24 | DAY ONE

Happy People Bring Joy

Student Book page 99

LEARNING OUTCOME

The children will be able to

- know that God wants them to be joyful.

MATERIALS

- A drawing of a face with a detachable paper frown
- A set of dominos
- Picture of a person smiling

COMMENT

Of all the creatures God has made, people alone have been endowed with the ability to smile and to laugh. We are made to experience joy. Catechesis should be imparted within an atmosphere of joy and reverence because our faith proclaims the joy of our salvation. The Gospel is Good News. Christians have every reason to rejoice. Through his Resurrection, Jesus has conquered death for all time. He has assured our reconciliation with the Father. Jesus assures us too that we can live forever in endless joy. He sent his Spirit to be with us and to fill us with joy.

CENTERING

1 Recall the last chapter.

- ***We have been talking about the Holy Spirit. Who sent the Holy Spirit to us?*** (Jesus) ***What does the Spirit help us do?*** (Love like Jesus)
- ***Today you will learn about another gift from Jesus.***

2 Show the children a face with a frown taped to it. Ask:

- ***How do people feel when they look like this?*** (Sad) ***How do you know?*** (The expression on our face often shows how we are feeling.)
- ***Who can come and change the person's frown into a smile?*** [Let a volunteer turn the frown into a smile.]
- ***If you turn a frown upside down, you will have a smile.***
- ***Everyone frown.***
- ***Now turn your frowns into smiles.***
- ***When do people smile?*** (When they are happy)
- ***What makes you smile or laugh?*** (Playing with friends; when people do something nice for us)

SHARING

1 Read aloud **page 99.** Talk about happy people.

- ***How are these people showing that they are happy?***
- ***Being with people who are happy can make us feel happy too. Their smiles can make us smile too.***
- ***Has someone done something lately that made you happy? What was it?*** [Allow volunteers to tell about things that made them feel happy.]
- ***All of us can be happy, because God loves us.***

2 Teach and sing a song about Christian joy, such as "Sing, Sing, Praise and Sing!" (*Singing Our Faith*) **CD 1 Track 12**, another from the song list on **page T281,** or "If You're Happy and You Know It."

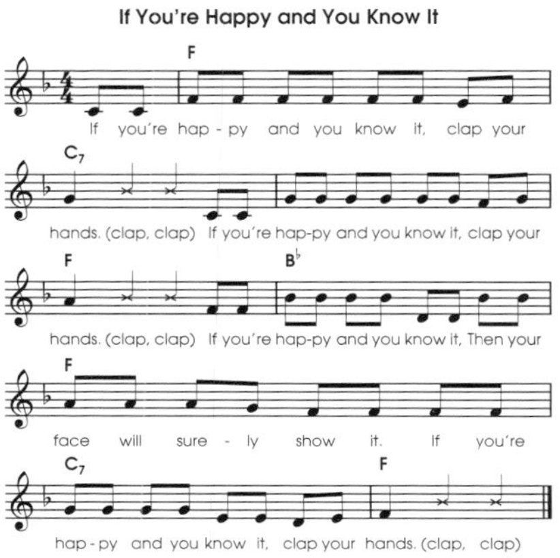

2. Stamp your feet.
3. Nod your head.
4. Do all three.

3 Explain that only God makes us completely happy.

- ***God wants us to be joyful. People who are really happy make us smile and share joy***

with us. But only God can fill us with the fullness of joy. Only God can make us completely happy.

4 Demonstrate how simple actions can spread joy to others. Give each child a domino. Set up a few dominos on a table in the front of the classroom and, one at a time, invite the children to add their dominos to those you have set up. When all the dominos have been set up, adjust the dominos as needed so that when the first one is pushed over, a chain reaction will make all the dominos fall. Tell the children that God's joy is a little bit like these dominos. Say:

- ***God gives us joy and wants us to share his joy with others. Sharing God's love and joy with others is a little bit like these dominos. Each smile or act of love spreads from one person to another. God can take the joy we share with just one person and extend that joy to many others. Watch.*** [Gently make the first domino fall so that all the dominos fall in turn.]

Have the children form groups of two or three. Give each group some dominos and allow them to set up the dominos again, taking turns to make the dominos fall.

5 Talk about ways to spread joy. Show the picture of a person smiling.

- ***What are some things that you might do to bring a smile to someone's face?*** (Greet the person, do something to help the person, tell the person something funny or something happy.)

ACTING

Invite the children to pray the following adaptation of Psalm 16:11 with gestures:

You
[Stretch arms out.]
fill me
[Touch chest with fingertips, backs of hands together.]
with joy.
[Move arms outward in an explosive gesture.]

CHECKPOINT

- Do the children look forward to your lessons as times of joy?
- How do the children show they understand the joy God gives us?

CHAPTER 24

Joy Is Good

Jesus brought joy to the world.

He wants us to share his joy.

Loving and helping others brings them joy.

It brings us joy too.

99

CHAPTER 24 | DAY TWO

Jesus Brings Joy

LEARNING OUTCOME

The children will be able to

- recall how Jesus brought joy to people.

MATERIALS

- *A Child's Bible*, page 22
- Sample New Year cracker
- For New Year cracker craft:
  - Cardboard tubes
  - Tissue paper to wrap the cardboard tubes, precut to size
  - Twist ties, tape, or ribbon
  - Small wrapped treats, such as hard candy
  - BLM 28
  - Crayons or markers
- Bible, with note card on which you have written the adapted Scripture reading for SHARING #1, John 5:1–8
- Stickers (optional)

COMMENTS

1. Tell the children that some people need help to know the joy that God wants us all to experience. Have the children pray for those who are sad or lonely. When someone helps these people and relieves their misery, they too can experience the joy that Jesus has promised.

2. The children will make a small gift of messages of hope for people who are sick as a way to share Jesus' love and joy. Arrange to give these gifts to those in your parish who bring Holy Communion to people who are sick.

CENTERING

Talk about how the Bible tells us that Jesus brought joy to people.

- ***How did Jesus bring joy to people?*** (He told people of God's love and care for them. He forgave people. He fed them. He opened the eyes of the blind and the ears of the deaf.)
- ***Today you will hear another story of how Jesus made someone happy.***

SHARING

1 Introduce the story "The Man by the Pool" from *A Child's Bible*, **page 22.** Show the Bible and open it to the Gospel according to John, John 5:1–8. Enthrone the Bible.

Invite the children to remember what they learned about how to be good listeners.

- ***Let's prepare ourselves to listen well to today's Bible story.*** Read the story "The Man by the Pool" from *A Child's Bible*, **page 22.**

2 If time allows, have the children act out the story of the man by the pool who was healed by Jesus.

3 Discuss the story.

- ***How do you think the man at the pool felt when he couldn't get into the pool?*** (Frustrated, sad)
- ***Why was he happy after Jesus cured him?*** (He had been sick for a very long time and now he was well.)
- ***Could someone have made the man happy earlier?*** (Yes.) ***How?*** (By helping him to the pool)
- ***How can you help people who are sick feel better?*** (Pray for them, do nice things for them, send get-well cards, show care for them.)

4 Tell the children that, like Jesus, the Church cares for people who are sick. Church members and priests visit people who are sick every week. They bring Jesus in the Eucharist to people who are not able to come to Mass. They pray with them and share Jesus' love with them. Show the sample New Year cracker. Say:

• ***We can also show our love and care and bring joy to people who are sick. One way we can do this is to make gifts for people in our community who are sick. The priests and Church members who visit the people who are sick can take our gifts with them when they visit.***

Show the children how to make the New Year crackers as gifts for people who are sick. Distribute copies of BLM 28 Psalms. Have the children color and decorate the Scripture verse message. Tell them to put the message and a few candy treats into the cardboard tube. Help the children wrap the filled cardboard tubes with the tissue paper, securing the tissue paper at the ends with tape, twist ties, or ribbon. Allow each child to have one treat. Stickers can be added to the wrapped tubes as decoration. When finished, have the children bring their gifts to the Prayer Center.
• ***BLM 28 Psalms***

ACTING

1 In the Prayer Center, invite the children to pray for people who are sick, especially those people who will receive their gifts. Let them place their gifts next to the Bible. Invite the children to pray together:

• ***Jesus, heal those people who are sick. Send them your peace, your love, and your joy.***

Invite the children to name people they know who are sick and in need of prayer.

2 Conclude by inviting the children to pray the following adaptation of Psalm 16:11 with gestures:

You
[Stretch arms out.]
fill me
[Touch chest with fingertips, backs of hands together.]
with joy.
[Move arms outward in an explosive gesture.]

CHECKPOINT

• Were the children able to identify ways that Jesus brought joy to people?

Look at the pictures above.

Who is giving joy to others?
Who needs joy?
How would you bring joy to them?

Christians bring joy to others.
We show that we love God.

100

CHAPTER 24 | DAY THREE

Ways to Bring Joy

Student Book page 100

LEARNING OUTCOMES

The children will be able to

- know that Jesus is the source of their joy.
- know ways to bring joy to others.

MATERIALS

- Bandana or handkerchief
- Bible, with note card that has the adapted Scripture reading for SHARING #2, John 15:11
- Poster 10
- Crayons or markers
- Drawing paper
- Hole punch
- Yarn
- Music for ACTING #1

COMMENT

Jesus has made it clear that our joy does not arise from having our selfish desires fulfilled. Rather, it is in sharing the gift of self through unselfish love and service to others that we experience the joy Jesus promised.

CENTERING

1 Play a game that is sure to make the children laugh and smile, such as the "giggle game." To play this game, tell the children to stand in a circle. Have the children take turns tossing a bandana or handkerchief into the air. Tell the children that as long as the bandana is in the air, they can laugh as loud as they want. When the bandana lands on the floor, they must stop laughing and stay completely silent. Play the game until everyone has had a turn tossing the bandana.

2 Discuss things that bring us joy and happiness.

- ***Games can make us laugh and smile. What are some others things that make you laugh or smile?*** (Telling jokes and riddles, sharing good times with family and friends, music, sports)
- ***When we laugh and smile, we are filled with joy.***

SHARING

1 Show Poster 10 Jesus Is Risen and discuss the joy Jesus brings us.

- ***Jesus fills us with the special kind of happiness called joy. When we are joyful, we may laugh or smile. But more importantly, our hearts are filled with peace and love.***
- ***After his Resurrection, Jesus brought great joy to his friends by showing them that he was really alive. He told his friends that he would be with them always. He sent the Holy Spirit, who gives his followers a joy that remains even during hard times.***

2 Reverently take the Bible and prepare to read the passage adapted from John 15:11. Say:

- ***Jesus taught his friends how to live with joy always. Let's listen to what Jesus said.***

Introduce this Bible reading by showing the Bible and opening it to the Gospel according to John, John 15:11. Enthrone the Bible.

Invite the children to remember what they learned about how to be good listeners.

- ***Let's prepare ourselves to listen well to today's Bible reading.***
- ***Jesus said, "I have told you how to love others so that my own joy may be in you, and your joy may be complete."*** [Pause.]
- ***Jesus wants us to be as full of joy as he is now after his Resurrection. He wants us to bring his joy to others.***

3 Have the children turn to **page 100.** Read it aloud and invite volunteers to answer the questions.

4 Have the children make Joy banners.

- Distribute paper and drawing materials.
- Write the word *joy* on the board. Guide the children to copy the word on their banners.

- Let the children decorate their banners with symbols of joy. (Examples: butterflies, flowers, sun, smiling faces, or balloons)
- Use a hole punch to punch holes at the top of the banners. String them with a loop of yarn so they can be hung up.
- Tell the children that they can give away their joy banners to bring joy to others.

ACTING

1 Have the children experience joy by listening to joyous music, such as: "Entr'acte No. 1" from *Rosamunde* (Schubert); "Miniature Overture," "Dance of the Flutes," or "Waltz of the Flowers" from *Nutcracker Suite* (Tchaikovsky); "Viennese Musical Clock" from *Háry János* (Kodály).

2 Invite the children to pray the following adaptation of Psalm 16:11 with gestures:

You
[Stretch arms out.]
fill me
[Touch chest with fingertips, backs of hands together.]
with joy.
[Move arms outward in an explosive gesture.]

CHECKPOINT

- Do the children know Jesus to be the source of their joy?
- Were the children able to identify ways they can bring joy to others?

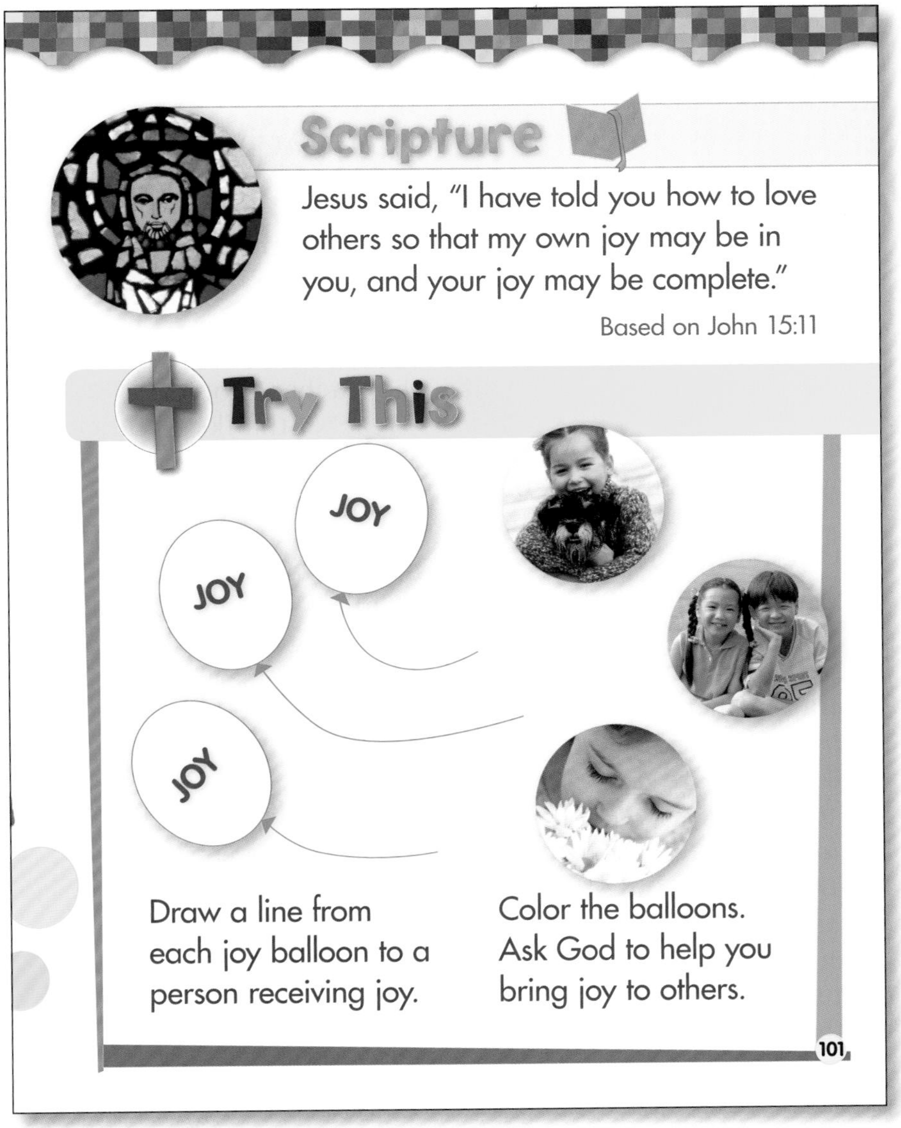
Scripture

Jesus said, "I have told you how to love others so that my own joy may be in you, and your joy may be complete."

Based on John 15:11

Try This

Draw a line from each joy balloon to a person receiving joy.

Color the balloons. Ask God to help you bring joy to others.

101

CHAPTER 24 | DAY FOUR

We Spread Joy

Student Book pages 101–102

LEARNING OUTCOME

The children will be able to

• desire to bring joy to others.

MATERIALS

• Crayons or markers

COMMENT

If possible, for the skits in SHARING #1, assign a parent or older student to help each group.

CENTERING

1 Ask the children what kinds of things make other people happy.

2 Draw on the board a face without a mouth. Have a child come up and draw a large smile on the face. Tell the children that today they will be learning about more ways we can share joy with others.

SHARING

1 Let the children prepare and perform skits about joyful times, then discuss the words and actions that made these times joyful.

At a Birthday Party

Toby is celebrating his birthday. He is happy because his mother, father, brothers, and sisters are having a little party for him.

Characters: Toby, his parents, several brothers and sisters

Setting: Cake time. Father and children are seated, waiting for the cake.

Action:

• Mother brings the cake to the table and says, "Happy birthday, Toby."

• Family sings "Happy Birthday." Toby says, "Thank you," and gives Father a big hug.

• All at the table smile and wish Toby a happy birthday.

In the Classroom

The children were asked to draw pictures of people or things that make them happy. The children are arriving with the pictures in the morning.

Characters: Teacher, several children

Setting: Arrival time

Action:

• Child #1 arrives. Teacher and child greet each other with a smile.

• Child #1 gives teacher a drawing of a rainbow and tells the teacher about it.

• Teacher thanks Child #1 and then posts the drawing.

• Child #2 arrives and gives the teacher a drawing of his or her family.

• Child #3 brings the teacher a drawing of the classroom and the teacher.

On the Playground

A group of children are taking turns on the swing at recess.

Characters: Five or six children, school nurse or mother who acts as nurse

Setting: Recess time. Two children are playing with a ball. One child is on the swing (chair) and another is pushing the swing. Other children are lined up for turns.

Action:

• Child #1 and Child #2 laugh and talk as they pretend to throw a ball to each other.

• Child #3 laughs and swings. Child #4 pushes the "swing."

• Child #3 jumps off the "swing," falls, and skins his or her knee. Child #4 goes to pick up and console Child #3. Others go for help.

• Child #5 gets the nurse. She comes, hugs the child, cleans the cut, and puts a bandage on it. Child #3 smiles and thanks the nurse.

2 Guide the children in doing the activity on **page 101.**

ACTING

1 Invite the children to pray the following adaptation of Psalm 16:11 with gestures:

You
[Stretch arms out.]
fill me
[Touch chest with fingertips, backs of hands together.]
with joy.
[Move arms outward in an explosive gesture.]

2 Have the children take home the Family Page on **page 102** to share with their families.

Songs

Play for the children any of these songs: "Sing, Sing, Praise and Sing!" (*Singing Our Faith*) **CD 1 Track 12;** "Make a Wonderful Noise" (*Sing a Song of Joy!*) **CD 2 Track 16;** "Color the World with Song," "Let Everyone Be Happy" (*Color the World with Song*); "Come and Go with Me," "Our God Is a God of Love" (*Hi God 2*); "Joy, Joy, Joy," "The Joy of the Lord," "Rejoice in the Lord Always," "Thank You, Lord" (*Hi God!*); "This Is the Day" (*Sing a Song of Joy!*); "Give It Away" (*Fingerprints*); "Shout for Joy" (*Singing Our Faith*). For a list of all the music used in this program, see **page OV-39.**

CHECKPOINT

- How did the children experience joy during this class?

ENRICHING THE FAITH EXPERIENCE

Use the following activities to enrich a lesson, to replace an activity with one that better meets the needs of your class, or to create an additional lesson.

1 Read the poem "Family Laughs" to the children.

Family Laughs

My mother usually giggles.
The baby squeals with glee.
My father laughs so his
stomach shakes.
Aunt Rose just goes "Tee hee."
I laugh so much I hurt.
I laugh until I cry.
I laugh so hard I roll on the
ground.
And sometimes don't even
know why.

M. Kathleen Glavich, S.N.D.

2 Teach the children to be aware of the natural joy that comes from performing a task well, being faithful to a duty, sharing with others, or serving others.

3 Music is a source of joy. Many psalms tell us to "sing joyfully to God" (Psalms 66:1; 81:1; 95:1; 98:4; 100:1). Allow the children to make simple instruments to add joy to their songs and prayers.

You fill me with joy.
Based on Psalm 16:11

Joy in Families

The Lesson Your Child Learned

Christians have every reason to rejoice. Through his glorious Resurrection, Jesus has assured us that we can live in endless joy. In this chapter the children learned that the risen Jesus is the source of Christian joy and that they are called to be joy-bringers. They were encouraged to go beyond self-centeredness, to reach out to others in self-sacrificing love, and to bring joy to those whom they meet.

Living the Lesson

When I think of the word *joy*, I think of my elderly neighbor walking hand in hand toward the park with his three-year-old granddaughter. As they toddle along together, she is wonder-struck by all she sees, and my neighbor beams with the sheer joy of her presence in his life.

Before her arrival in the world, he was a gruff guy, a hard-nosed sales manager who barked orders at those around him. Now we see the softer side of our neighbor. He has joy in his life, and it has transformed him.

Joy can transform us too. The world encourages us to grasp at pleasure. But joy arrives not as something to be pursued but as a gift to be received with gladness. All we need to do is make room for joy. Sometimes that takes the form of slowing our hectic pace and leaning down to hold the hand of innocence. Tonight, spend a few moments silently watching your child sleep as you let joy seep into your life.

–Tom McGrath, author of *Raising Faith-Filled Kids* (Loyola Press)

Bringing the Lesson Home

- Read with your child the pages from this chapter that were sent home.
- Help your child realize that disappointments and hardships are part of everyone's life and can take away our deep inner joy only if we let them.
- Do something this week as a family to bring joy to someone outside your immediate family.
- Tell your child that seeing him or her happy gives you joy and pleases Jesus. Being happy is one way of spreading Jesus' joy.
- Let your child be a child. Too often parents and guardians rush their children to take on activities and ways of dressing that are beyond their years. Letting your child enjoy childhood provides a solid foundation for a more joyful life in years to come.

102

Chapter 25

Life Is Good

FAITH FOCUS

After we die, we can live happily forever in heaven with God. 1 Corinthians 2:9; Matthew 22:1–2

PREPARING THE FAITH EXPERIENCE

LISTENING

Before you begin to prepare this week's lessons, take some time for prayer. Quiet yourself by taking several deep breaths. Become aware of God's presence, for God is with you always. Ask God to open your heart to hear his words to you today.

But as it is written:
"What eye has not seen, and ear has not heard,
and what has not entered the human heart,
what God has prepared for those who love him."

1 Corinthians 2:9

REFLECTING

It is interesting to note that all the things God made during the first five days of Creation were unlike himself: light and dark, earth and sky, land and water, plants and animals. Then came the sixth and last "working" day. Initially, God simply made another creature on this day. But then, God gave this new creature something no previous one had been given: a share in his very own life. God breathed into it a breath of life, and humankind came into existence—and "God saw that it was good."

Just how valuable is this breath of God, this gift of human life? It is so priceless that it is safeguarded in the Ten Commandments, under penalty of serious sin: "Thou shalt not kill." It is so dear that those who beget new life in cooperation with God are protected by a special commandment—Honor thy father and thy mother—the only commandment with a reward promised for its observance. It is so precious that a loving Father decreed that death itself would not take it away, but merely change it. It is so costly that the same good Father sent his only Son to share our humanity and to ensure the quality of that life for eternity. Is it any wonder, then, that after contemplating earthly life with all its beauty, its nobility, and its many joys, the psalmist cried out, "LORD, what are mortals, that you notice them; human beings, that you take thought of them?" (Psalm 144:3)

Yet the wonders we experience on earth are only a shallow foretaste of what we will experience in heaven. There we will find Jesus fully alive at the right hand of the Father. There Mary will welcome us in the name of her Son. And in the Communion of Saints we will find the community that has always cared for us, prayed for us, and interceded with God for us. There we will find our true home.

RESPONDING

Having reflected upon God's Word, take some time now to continue to respond to God in prayer.

- What measures do I take to protect and to promote my natural life? my supernatural life?

Life-giving Spirit, deepen our appreciation of life.

Catechism of the Catholic Church

The themes of this lesson correspond to the following paragraphs: 1023–1026, 1932, 1934–1937.

Scripture in This Chapter

- *Genesis 9:5–6 God safeguards the sacredness of human life.*
- *John 10:10 Jesus explains that he came to give us the fullness of life.*

THE FAITH EXPERIENCE

DAY ONE
Being Alive Is Good

DAY TWO
We Will Live Forever

DAY THREE
New Life Comes Through Death

DAY FOUR
Jesus Shows Us the Path to Life

Church Documents

General Directory for Catechesis #102.
Our life is not a journey to nowhere. Human history is on pilgrimage toward the Father's house and already offers a foretaste of the world to come.

The Dignity of Older People #11.
Jesus reversed the significance of death, which is no longer a condemnation but a moment of hope of coming face to face with the Lord.

Bulletin Board At the left is a suggestion for a bulletin-board design. Let the children draw pictures of their favorite things or cut out pictures from magazines. You might post a banner with the words, "Life Is Good."

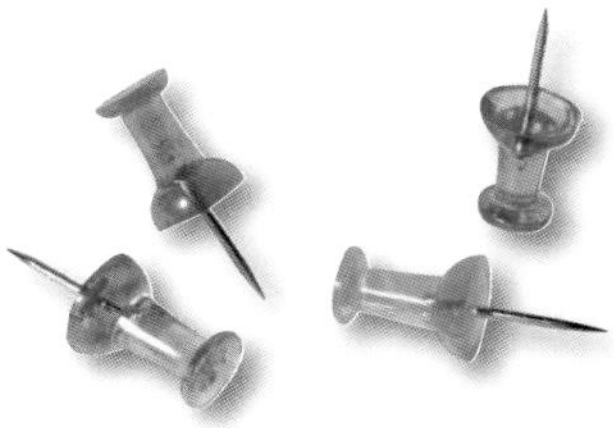

For a list of children's literature suggestions, please see **page OV-47.**

CHAPTER 25 | DAY ONE
Being Alive Is Good

LEARNING OUTCOMES

The children will be able to
- recognize life as a gift from God.
- appreciate the joys of life.
- have respect for all people.

MATERIALS

- Cutouts 22–28, 31
- Sample blessings banner
- For blessings banner craft:
  Index cards
  Ribbon
  Crayons or markers
  Magazines
  Scissors
  Glue
  Hole punch
- Two identical holy cards: one in an attractive box with a bow, the other in a simple box with no bow
- Pictures of beautiful things (optional)
- Recording of music that would appeal to children, such as a dance from the *Nutcracker Suite* (optional)

COMMENTS

1. Life reaches its fullness in heaven. Our sharing in divine life, which begins on earth with the Sacrament of Baptism, will be perfected in the beatific vision. We will finally be able to reflect Christ perfectly because we will see him as he is. We will be together with Mary, the angels, and all the blessed, including the loved ones with whom we shared our lives on earth. However, the fullness of glory will be reserved until after the Second Coming, when our bodies will also be glorified. Then we will rejoice in a renewed, glorified universe.

2. Prepare a sample blessings banner, showing things in your life that you recognize as blessings from God.

CENTERING

Recall the last chapter.

- ***We have been talking about the joy Jesus gives. Why are we joyful?*** (God loves us. Jesus is risen and is with us.) ***What makes us joyful?*** (Bringing joy to others)
- ***Today you will learn about the joy that never ends.***

SHARING

1 Teach the children to sing or to chant the words for this action game. After the children have learned these words, they may wish to suggest words for other actions. Gestures can and should be adapted when necessary to accommodate different needs. Introduce the game:

- ***One of the ways we find joy is by using the gifts that God has given to us. Let's play this game together and think about the wonderful things we can do because God has given us the gift of life.***

I can walk on two legs, two legs, two legs.
I can walk on two legs, round and round and round.
2. Can you hop on one leg? . . .
3. Can you wave with one hand? . . .

Ask the children to suggest additional actions to continue the game.

2 Lead the children to appreciate life:

- ***How did you feel when we were playing the game together?*** (Happy, joyful)
- ***Why were you happy when playing this game?*** (We enjoy singing and learning about all the wonderful things that we can do with the gift of life that God has given us.)
- ***Why is life good?*** (God has given us many wonderful gifts. We can use the gifts that God has given us to share joy with others.)

• ***Being alive is good. It is good to feel ourselves breathing.*** [Let the children be conscious of their breathing.] ***It is fun to be able to move—to hop and skip and jump. It feels good to smile and to laugh.***

• ***There are other things that give us deeper joy in life.***

3 Describe an experience that brought you joy, such as watching a sunset, listening to music, being with a friend. Invite the children to relate experiences that gave them joy. You might show pictures of beautiful things and/or play music. Comment:

• ***Knowing that someone loves us and cares for us is the greatest joy of all.***

• ***Why is the life of a person the most precious gift?*** (God made us like himself. We are able to think and love and choose what is good. We can live forever with God if we choose to love as God asks.)

• ***Sometimes life is hard. Sad things happen. No matter how hard life may be, we know that if we choose to love God, we will be happy forever with God in heaven.***

4 Show the sample blessings banner and help the children make this craft. Prepare a stack of index cards by punching a hole at the top of each card. Distribute several index cards to each child. Invite the children to draw or to cut pictures from magazines of some of the things in their lives that they recognize as blessings from God. Tell them to draw or to glue one picture on each index card. Show the children how to thread a piece of ribbon through the hole in the index card and help them fasten the index cards to a longer ribbon.

Tell the children that they can display their blessing banners at home as a reminder to thank God for the blessings of life.

5 Lead the children to respect life in all people. Show the children the two boxes, each containing the same holy card. (One box should be wrapped with a bow, and the other box should be plain, with no bow.) Ask:

• ***Which package do you think has the more precious gift inside?*** [The children will probably be inclined toward the attractive box.]

• [Call on two volunteers to unwrap the gifts.] ***Were you surprised to see that both gifts were the same?***

• ***Can you tell by the wrapping how precious a gift is?*** (No.)

• ***Which is more important, the gift or the wrapping?*** (The gift)

Invite the children to share other experiences in which they were surprised to find a wonderful gift not in fancy packaging.

6 Show the Cutouts of people (see list in MATERIALS). Comment:

• ***People are like the two packages. Although people look different on the outside, God has given each one the same precious gift of life. God loves everyone because he has given each of us the gift of life.***

• ***God gave people different abilities and talents. Some people can run very fast. Some people cannot hop, skip, or even walk because they cannot use their legs. God loves all people, fast runners and people who cannot walk at all.***

• ***Some people can throw and catch a ball. Some people can use their hands to draw beautiful pictures. Some people's hands do not work at all. God loves all people—those who can play ball, those who can draw beautiful pictures and those who cannot use their hands at all.***

- ***Some people can see beautiful colors with their eyes. Some people need glasses to see clearly. Some people can't see at all. Some people hear birds chirping far in the distance. Some people use hearing aids so they can hear the person talking next to them. Some people cannot hear anything at all. God loves everyone—those with sharp eyes or ears and those who cannot see or hear at all.***
- ***God has given everyone so many wonderful gifts. Even when there are some things a person cannot do, there are many others things that a person can do.***
- ***All people can experience the best joy of all—the joy of loving and being loved.***

ACTING

1 Invite the children to pray to God in thanksgiving for all the ways that they can enjoy the life that God has given them. Invite volunteers to mention one thing they like to do to enjoy life, and then invite all to pray together, "Thank you, God."

2 Invite the children to pray the adapted version of Psalm 16:11 with gestures:

You show me
[Point to self.]
the path
[Extend right arm.]
to life.
[Raise both arms.]

CHECKPOINT

- Do the children realize that life is God's gift to us?
- How have the children demonstrated an appreciation of the joy of life?
- Do the children show respect for others?

CHAPTER 25

Life Is Good

Jesus gave us a life that will never end.

We have this life now.

We will have it forever in heaven.

Jesus lives in heaven with the Father and the Holy Spirit.

Jesus lives in us too.

Scripture

Jesus said, "I came so that they might have life."

Based on John 10:10

103

CHAPTER 25 | DAY TWO

We Will Live Forever

Student Book pages 103–105

LEARNING OUTCOMES

The children will be able to

- understand that in heaven they will live forever in happiness with God.
- look forward to the perfect joy of heaven.

KEY TERMS

eternal life—living forever with God in glory

saints—people who loved God on earth and who live now and forever with God in heaven

MATERIALS

- Poster 10
- Drawing paper
- Crayons or markers
- Song celebrating life

COMMENT

In discussing heaven with the children, do not make comments that are not grounded in truth. If you are unable to answer a question, admit simply that you do not know, rather than answer in a way that will mislead the children.

CENTERING

1 Have the children do the "Easter Cheer" from Chapter 20.

Easter Cheer

Jesus is risen.
[Take two steps forward on the beats.]
Al-le-lu-ia
[Raise arms up and down twice.]
Jesus is risen.
[Take two steps backward on the beats.]
Al-le-lu-ia
[Raise arms up and down twice.]
Jesus is risen.
[Take two steps forward on the beats.]
Al-le-lu-ia
[Raise arms up and down twice.]
That's gr—rr—
[Swing right arm around twice as if winding up for a pitch.]
—eat!
[Jerk right elbow back. Clap twice.]

M. Kathleen Glavich, S.N.D.

2 Ask the children why it is great that Jesus is risen. (He is still with us.) Comment:

- ***Jesus' rising from the dead means something very great for us too.***

SHARING

1 Tell the children that Jesus is alive and will live forever. Show Poster 10 Jesus Is Risen.

- ***Jesus is alive. He lives forever in glory with the Father and the Holy Spirit. We call living forever in glory* eternal life. *Jesus died on the cross for us and rose from the dead so that we would have eternal life with him.***
- ***When did you receive Jesus' new life?*** (At Baptism) ***With Jesus' new life, we can live forever with him in heaven.***

2 Have the children open their books to **page 103.** Encourage the children to follow along as you read aloud the text.

3 Talk about heaven. Develop these points:

- ***Saint Paul told us that heaven is so wonderful that we can't even imagine the beautiful things God has prepared there for those who love him.***
- ***We do not know what heaven is, but in heaven, Jesus will make our joy complete.***
- ***Jesus told us that heaven is like a wedding feast. Weddings celebrate the love between the bride and groom. That is why they are such happy times. Love is the greatest joy that God gives us.***
- ***In heaven we will see God face to face. God's radiant beauty will fill us with great joy, and our hearts will overflow with love.***
- ***It will also make us happy to be with Mary, the angels, and the saints. We will know our guardian angels and our patron saints. We will be with our family and friends.***
- ***Everyone will have deep joy that will last forever and ever.***

4 Let the children draw pictures of what they think heaven is like. Invite volunteers to talk about their pictures.

5 Direct the children to the picture on **pages 104–105.** Comment:

- ***We believe that Jesus will bring to heaven all people who love God. We call these people* saints. *Saints are people who loved God on earth and who live now and forever with God in heaven.***
- ***The saints in heaven are people who helped and cared for others as Jesus did. They are happy to be living now with God forever.***
- Identify the following for the children: (1) Saint Elizabeth Ann Seton, (2) Saint Thérèse of Lisieux, (3) Our Lady of Guadalupe, (4) Mary, (5) Saint Patrick, (6) Saint Julie, (7) Saint Joseph, (8) Jesus, (9) Saint Nicholas, (10) Saint Bernadette, and (11) Saint Francis of Assisi. (See the Calendar of Saints on **page T296** for more information.)

6 Read aloud **page 104.**

ACTING

1 Sing "Eternal Life Song" in celebration of life.

Eternal Life Song
(Melody: "Are You Sleeping?")

I have new life.
I have new life.
Thanks to God.
Thanks to God.
I will live with Jesus.
I will live with Jesus.
Forever, forever.

M. Kathleen Glavich, S.N.D.

2 Invite the children to pray the adapted version of Psalm 16:11 with gestures:

You show me
[Point to self.]
the path
[Extend right arm.]
to life.
[Raise both arms.]

CHECKPOINT

- What understanding of heaven have the children demonstrated?
- Have the children shown awareness that they will share life with God forever in heaven?

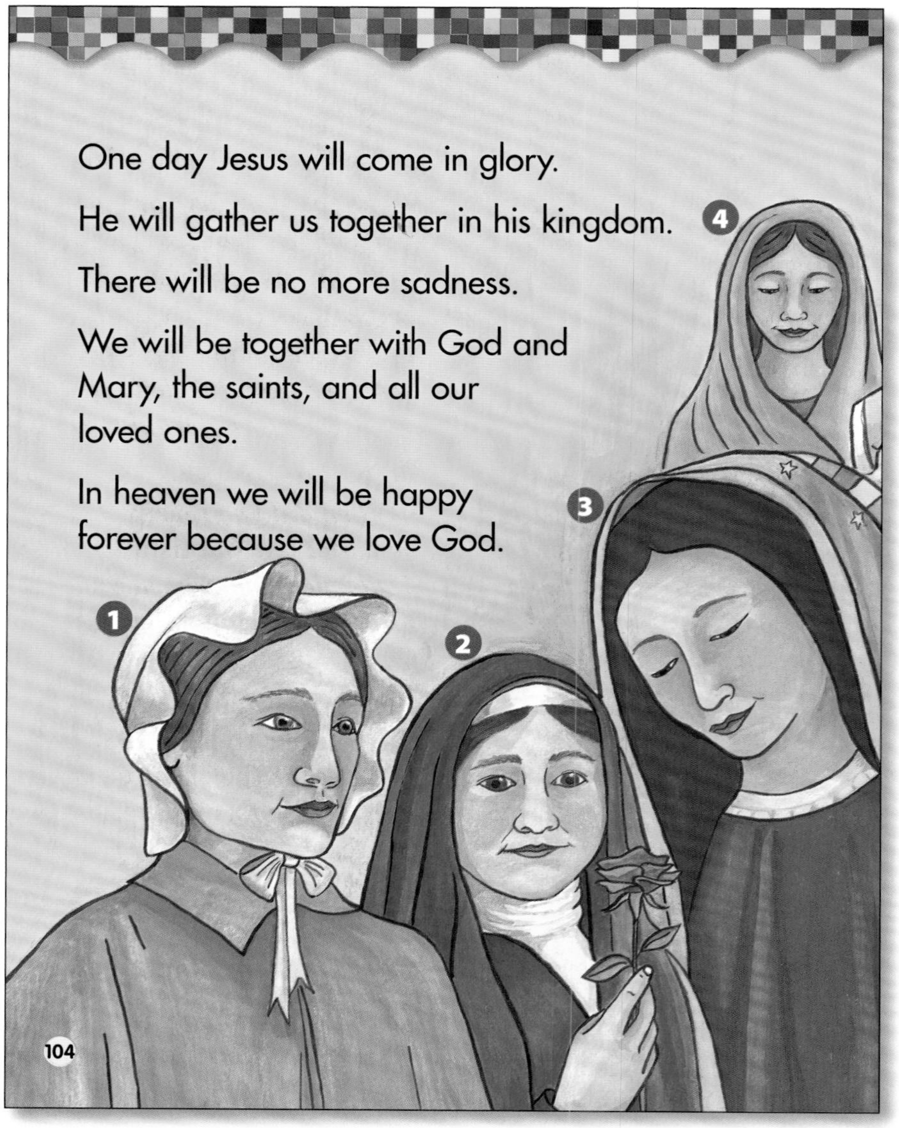
One day Jesus will come in glory.
He will gather us together in his kingdom.
There will be no more sadness.
We will be together with God and Mary, the saints, and all our loved ones.
In heaven we will be happy forever because we love God.
1
2
3
4
104

CHAPTER 25 | DAY THREE

New Life Comes Through Death

LEARNING OUTCOMES

The children will be able to

- know that those who die can be happy with God forever in heaven.
- look forward to the promise of new life in heaven.

MATERIALS

- Poster 10
- Cutouts 9, 18, 33, 70–71
- Strips of stiff felt, 8 inches by 2 inches, one for each child
- Precut felt butterflies and/or flowers
- Glue
- Scissors
- Ribbon (optional)
- Hole punch (optional)

COMMENTS

1. Death is a mystery. Because Jesus willingly suffered and "died" in many different ways throughout his life, he was prepared for Calvary, where he died as he had lived. Because of his death and Resurrection, death has been changed for those who believe in him. Now death leads to everlasting life in God. Jesus has shared with us his triumph over death. At the moment of death, we surrender ourselves to our loving Father, ready to accept the ultimate destiny that will complete the meaning of our lives.

2. Be very sensitive to any child who has recently experienced the death of a relative or friend.

CENTERING

Show Cutouts 70–71 Caterpillar/Chrysalis and Butterfly. Discuss:

- ***This is a butterfly. What was it before it was a butterfly?*** (A caterpillar)
- ***What had to happen before the butterfly grew wings and could fly?*** (It made a chrysalis and died to new life as a caterpillar.)
- ***Today we'll talk about what happens to us before we can have new life.***

SHARING

❶ Help the children recall that new life comes through death. Show the Cutouts (see list in MATERIALS) as you talk about them. Display Poster 10.

• ***New life comes through death. Jesus had to die before he could live his new heavenly life.***

• ***The caterpillar had to die to life before it could be a butterfly. What else on earth has to die in order to have new life?*** (Flowers and seeds)

• ***People die to the life they have on earth so that they can live the glorious life of Jesus in heaven. We feel sad when those we love die, because we will miss them. We are still with them through our prayers and love. We believe that those who have died can be happy with God forever in heaven.***

2 You might share your experience of the death of a friend or relative. Then let the children share their experiences if they wish.

3 Help the children look forward to the promise of new life in heaven.

• ***Jesus taught us that when people die their life is changed, but it is not ended.***

• ***When a seed becomes a flower, the seed dies to its life as a seed in order to become a beautiful flower.***

• ***When a caterpillar becomes a butterfly, the caterpillar dies to its life as a caterpillar in order to become a beautiful butterfly.***

• ***When Jesus died, he died to his life on earth in order to live his new, wonderful resurrected life.***

• ***When people die, they die to their life on earth in order to enjoy the wonderful new life with God in heaven. To live in heaven, we live in love now as Jesus did.***

4 Show the children how to make a bookmark with a reminder of the wonderful new life that we hope to share one day with God in heaven. Say:

• ***We have learned two symbols of the wonderful new life we can share with God in heaven: a flower and a butterfly. Let's use these symbols to decorate bookmarks to remind us of Jesus' promise of new life in heaven.***

Give each child a piece of stiff felt and a precut butterfly or flower. Guide the children to glue the symbol onto the piece of felt. The bookmark can be decorated by tying a ribbon through a hole punched at the top. Fringe can be added to the bottom by cutting slits into the felt.

ACTING

1 Invite the children to pray in thanks to God for the promise of new life in heaven. You might invite them to offer prayers for people who have died. Pray:

• ***God, thank you for the promise of new life in heaven.***

2 Invite the children to pray the adapted version of Psalm 16:11 with gestures:

You show me
[Point to self.]
the path
[Extend right arm.]
to life.
[Raise both arms.]

CHECKPOINT

- What did the discussion reveal about the children's understanding of death?
- Do the children understand the promise of new life in heaven?

CHAPTER 25 | DAY FOUR

Jesus Shows Us the Path to Life

Student Book pages 106–108

LEARNING OUTCOMES

The children will be able to

- realize that Jesus shows the way to eternal life.
- know that we can ask the saints to pray for us.

MATERIALS

- Prizes, such as small treats, holy cards, or other small gifts, one for each child
- *A Child's Bible*, page 28
- For Our Treasure Is in Heaven craft:
  BLM 29
  Crayons or markers
  Scissors
  Glue
  Paper plates with equally spaced holes prepunched around the rims
  Yarn
  Tape
  Pencils
- Bible, with note card on which you have written the adapted Scripture reading for SHARING #1, Matthew 13:44

CENTERING

Let the children enjoy a treasure hunt, finding the prizes you have hidden in the room. Each child may continue searching until he or she finds a prize. When a child finds a prize, he or she takes it to his or her seat. Continue the treasure hunt until all have found a prize. Then have everyone return to his or her seat. Ask:

- ***How did you feel when you found the prize?*** (Happy)
- ***What is the greatest prize you can ever get?*** (Heaven)

SHARING

1 Prepare to read to the children "The Buried Treasure" in *A Child's Bible*, **page 28.**

- ***Jesus told us how wonderful heaven is by telling us a story.***

Introduce this Bible story by showing the Bible and opening it to the Gospel according to Matthew, Matthew 13:44. Enthrone the Bible.

Invite the children to remember what they learned about how to be good listeners.

- ***Let's prepare ourselves to listen well to today's Bible story.***

Read "The Buried Treasure" in *A Child's Bible*, **page 28.**

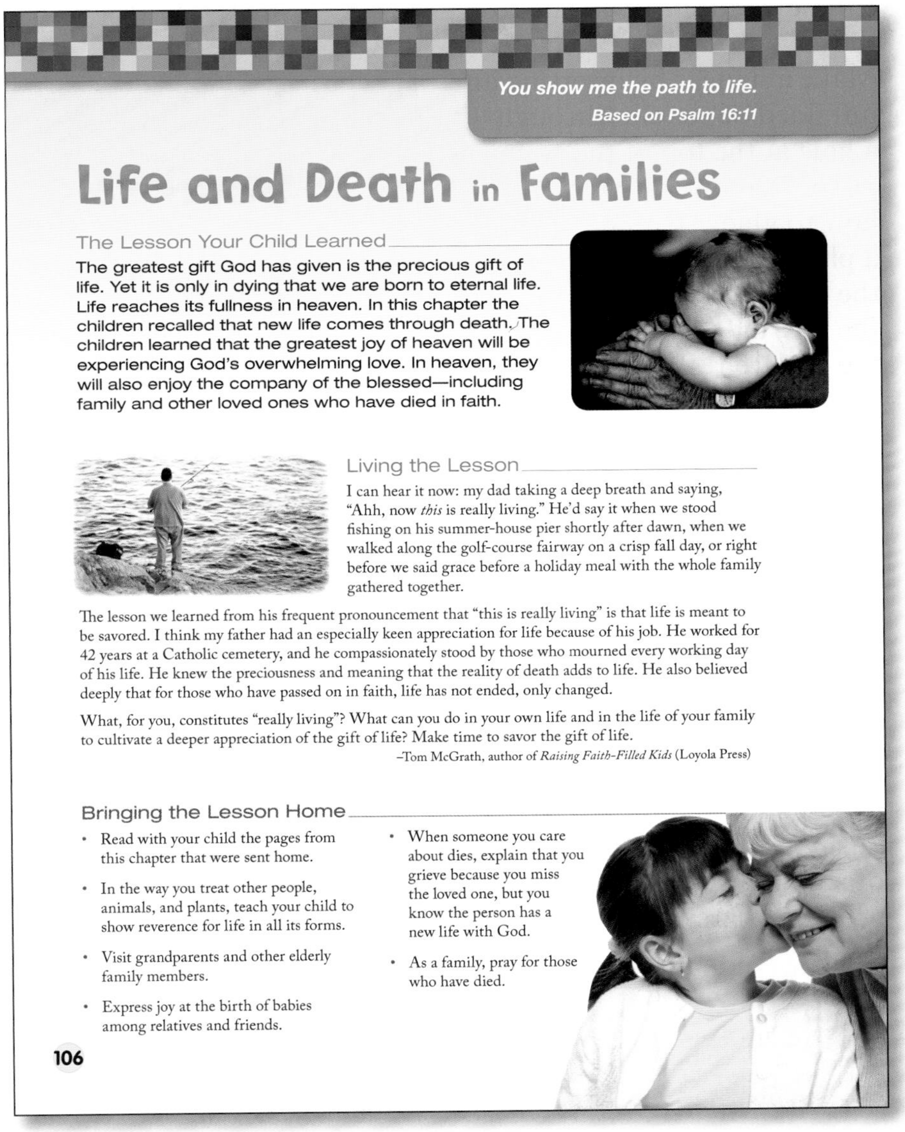

You show me the path to life.
Based on Psalm 16:11

Life and Death in Families

The Lesson Your Child Learned

The greatest gift God has given is the precious gift of life. Yet it is only in dying that we are born to eternal life. Life reaches its fullness in heaven. In this chapter the children recalled that new life comes through death. The children learned that the greatest joy of heaven will be experiencing God's overwhelming love. In heaven, they will also enjoy the company of the blessed—including family and other loved ones who have died in faith.

Living the Lesson

I can hear it now: my dad taking a deep breath and saying, "Ahh, now *this* is really living." He'd say it when we stood fishing on his summer-house pier shortly after dawn, when we walked along the golf-course fairway on a crisp fall day, or right before we said grace before a holiday meal with the whole family gathered together.

The lesson we learned from his frequent pronouncement that "this is really living" is that life is meant to be savored. I think my father had an especially keen appreciation for life because of his job. He worked for 42 years at a Catholic cemetery, and he compassionately stood by those who mourned every working day of his life. He knew the preciousness and meaning that the reality of death adds to life. He also believed deeply that for those who have passed on in faith, life has not ended, only changed.

What, for you, constitutes "really living"? What can you do in your own life and in the life of your family to cultivate a deeper appreciation of the gift of life? Make time to savor the gift of life.

–Tom McGrath, author of *Raising Faith-Filled Kids* (Loyola Press)

Bringing the Lesson Home

- Read with your child the pages from this chapter that were sent home.
- In the way you treat other people, animals, and plants, teach your child to show reverence for life in all its forms.
- Visit grandparents and other elderly family members.
- Express joy at the birth of babies among relatives and friends.
- When someone you care about dies, explain that you grieve because you miss the loved one, but you know the person has a new life with God.
- As a family, pray for those who have died.

106

2 Discuss the story.

- ***What did the man do to get the treasure?*** (Sold all he had)
- ***What must we do to get the treasure of heaven?*** (Live as Jesus showed us; be loving.)

3 Have the children make laced picture frames entitled: "Our Treasure Is in Heaven." Distribute copies of BLM 29 Heart and have the children color and cut out the heart. Distribute the paper plates. Show the children how to lace yarn through the holes around the rim. Have each child glue his or her heart to the center of the paper plate. Make a hanger by inserting an unfolded paper clip through a hole at the top of the paper plate. Demonstrate how to glue a photo to the center of the heart. Tell the children that they can add a photo to their frames and display them at home as reminders to live as Jesus showed us.

- *BLM 29 Heart*

4 Ask the children how they will follow the path of life during the summer and live as Jesus showed them. (Help our parents, play nicely with others, pray, go to church, do what our parents ask)

ACTING

1 Lead the children in a Litany of the Saints based on the drawing on **pages 104–105**.

- ***The saints in heaven are people who have reached the treasure of heaven. They did their best to live like Jesus.***
- ***The saints are part of the Church too. If we ask them, they will help us love God as they did. Then, one day, we will join them in heaven and be happy forever. Let us ask Mary and the saints to help us now. After each name I say, respond, "Pray for us."***

Mary, Mother of Jesus and our Mother . . .
Saint Joseph . . .
All you angels and saints . . .

2 Lead the children to pray the adapted version of Psalm 16:11 with gestures.

You show me
[Point to self.]
the path
[Extend right arm.]
to life.
[Raise both arms.]

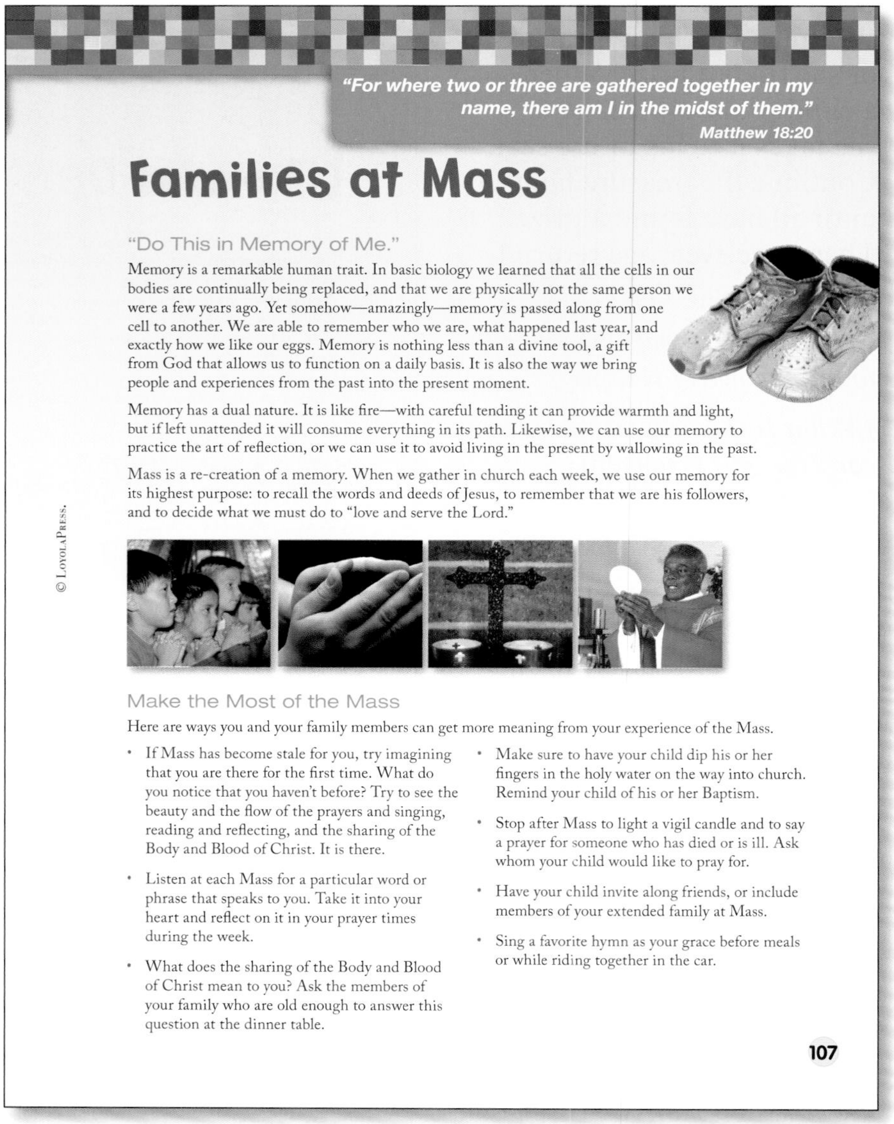

"For where two or three are gathered together in my name, there am I in the midst of them."
Matthew 18:20

Families at Mass

"Do This in Memory of Me."

Memory is a remarkable human trait. In basic biology we learned that all the cells in our bodies are continually being replaced, and that we are physically not the same person we were a few years ago. Yet somehow—amazingly—memory is passed along from one cell to another. We are able to remember who we are, what happened last year, and exactly how we like our eggs. Memory is nothing less than a divine tool, a gift from God that allows us to function on a daily basis. It is also the way we bring people and experiences from the past into the present moment.

Memory has a dual nature. It is like fire—with careful tending it can provide warmth and light, but if left unattended it will consume everything in its path. Likewise, we can use our memory to practice the art of reflection, or we can use it to avoid living in the present by wallowing in the past.

Mass is a re-creation of a memory. When we gather in church each week, we use our memory for its highest purpose: to recall the words and deeds of Jesus, to remember that we are his followers, and to decide what we must do to "love and serve the Lord."

Make the Most of the Mass

Here are ways you and your family members can get more meaning from your experience of the Mass.

- If Mass has become stale for you, try imagining that you are there for the first time. What do you notice that you haven't before? Try to see the beauty and the flow of the prayers and singing, reading and reflecting, and the sharing of the Body and Blood of Christ. It is there.
- Listen at each Mass for a particular word or phrase that speaks to you. Take it into your heart and reflect on it in your prayer times during the week.
- What does the sharing of the Body and Blood of Christ mean to you? Ask the members of your family who are old enough to answer this question at the dinner table.
- Make sure to have your child dip his or her fingers in the holy water on the way into church. Remind your child of his or her Baptism.
- Stop after Mass to light a vigil candle and to say a prayer for someone who has died or is ill. Ask whom your child would like to pray for.
- Have your child invite along friends, or include members of your extended family at Mass.
- Sing a favorite hymn as your grace before meals or while riding together in the car.

107

3 Suggest that the children pray for one another during the summer.

4 Have the children take home the Family Page on **page 106** to share with their families.

CHECKPOINT

- Are the children able to identify Jesus as the source of our eternal life?
- Are the children familiar with our tradition of prayer to the saints?

FAMILY FEATURE

Help the children carefully tear out the Family Feature on **pages 107–108.** Ask them to take home the pages to read and to work on with their families.

ENRICHING THE FAITH EXPERIENCE

Use the following activities to enrich a lesson, to replace an activity with one that better meets the needs of your class, or to create an additional lesson.

1 Review the year and show the posters one at a time. Go through the Student Book and ask the children what they remember about the lesson that goes with each poster. You might display all the posters and ask the children which was their favorite lesson and why.

2 Have the children draw or paint pictures of what they can enjoy doing during the summer because they have the gift of life.

3 Let the children offer spontaneous prayers to thank God for the gift of life.

Songs

Play for the children any of these songs: "All Night, All Day" (*Singing Our Faith*) **CD 1 Track 7**; "Father We Adore You" (*Hi God!*); "All Your Gifts of Life," "If I Were a Butterfly" (*Hi God 2*); "On Holy Ground" (*When Children Gather*); "Soon and Very Soon," "Over My Head," "Behold, I Make All Things New," "Blest Are They," "Circle Round for Freedom" (*Singing Our Faith*). For a list of all the music used in this program, see **page OV-39.**

Make the Most of the Mass *continued*

- Give your child a short tour of your church. Try to convey a sense of the sacredness of the space. Notice any seasonal decorations and talk about why they are there. Look at a few stained-glass windows and see if you can tell what or whom they portray. Point out the lit candle next to the tabernacle that indicates the presence of the Blessed Sacrament. On your way out, draw your child's attention to the holy-water fonts at the doors and talk about why they are there.

A Practicing Catholic

Like many Catholics, I stopped going to Mass as soon as I began living on my own. But after my first child was born, I decided to give it another try. As I sat there week after week, a passage from 1 Corinthians came to mind; the one that begins "when I was a child, I used to talk as a child, think as a child, reason as a child. When I became a man, I put aside childish things." (13:11) It dawned on me that my view of the Mass had remained unchanged since high school. I had never stopped to think that as an adult and a parent, the prayers and readings might touch me in a different way. From that point on, I became more interested in what was happening. Then one Sunday I was sitting in the pew listening to the opening prayer when I felt an overwhelming wave of emotion run through my whole body. It was as though I was hearing the words for the first time and yet it was all so familiar, I started crying and couldn't stop. That was sixteen years ago. I've stopped crying since then, but I haven't stopped coming to Mass.

–Ann O'Connor, author of *The Twelve Unbreakable Principles of Parenting* (ACTA Publications)

Mass and Your Family

Families can face a variety of hurdles on the way to Mass each week—a stalling, whining child, our own fatigue, or ordinary inertia. But like all the other obstacles we overcome to ensure our child's well-being, getting to Mass is worth the effort we put into it. Nothing is as important to our child's spiritual welfare as being part of a faith community. The rhythm it establishes for the week, the hour of (relative) quiet, and simply being in the presence of a group of people while they sing, pray, reflect, ask forgiveness, and share the Body and Blood of Christ all have a powerful impact on a child. This is true even if it seems (and he or she claims) that your child is getting nothing out of the experience. It's just one more thing your child might not appreciate until he or she is grown up. Keep at it. You're giving your child a gift that can last an eternity.

108

Special Seasons and Days

In these lessons the children will learn about the seasons, feast days, and saints' days that are part of the Church's liturgical year. They will be encouraged to deepen their commitment to Jesus through their celebration of the liturgical year.

Special Seasons

1 All Saints Are Good
The children learn about the saints. They are encouraged to choose favorite saints or learn about their patron saints.

2 Advent Is Good
The children are introduced to our preparation for Christmas during the season of Advent. They learn about and make an Advent wreath.

3 Christmas Is Good
The children act out the Christmas story.

4 The Wise Men Are Good
The children hear the story of the Wise Men. They discuss the message of the story of Epiphany and how God wants all people to know and love him.

5 Lent Is Good
The children are introduced to Lent as a time to grow in God's love. They are encouraged to pray and to do good deeds during Lent so that by Easter they will be full of love. They note their progress by coloring a picture.

6 Easter Is Good
The children hear how the disciples found Jesus' tomb empty on Easter morning. They learn that we celebrate the good news of Jesus' Resurrection at Easter.

7 Pentecost Is Good
The children are introduced to the Holy Spirit, Jesus' gift to the Church.

Special Days

8 Jesus Our Light Is Good
The children learn about the Presentation and consider how they can be a light for others like Jesus.

9 Mary Is Good
The children celebrate Mary's birthday. They learn that she is Jesus' mother and theirs.

10 Saint Joseph Is Good
The children are introduced to Saint Joseph, his role in the Holy Family, and his role in the Church.

11 The Holy Family Is Good
The children imagine what the Holy Family's life was like. They think of ways to be helpful.

12 **Angels Are Good**
The children are introduced to guardian angels as special helpers. They are encouraged to pray to their guardian angels.

13 **Saint Thérèse Is Good**
The children learn why Saint Thérèse is called the Little Flower of Jesus. They are encouraged to pray to her.

14 **Saint Francis Is Good**
The children learn that Saint Francis loved God and saw God's goodness in all creation.

15 **Saint Elizabeth Ann Is Good**
The children are introduced to Saint Elizabeth Ann Seton. They learn from her to practice acts of love and kindness.

16 **Saint Nicholas Is Good**
The children hear about the goodness of Saint Nicholas. They are led to imitate him.

17 **Saint Bernadette Is Good**
The children hear the story of Mary's appearance to Saint Bernadette at Lourdes, France. They learn the hymn "Immaculate Mary."

18 **Saint Valentine Is Good**
The children learn about Saint Valentine and then make valentines for special people.

19 **Saint Patrick Is Good**
The children hear the story of Saint Patrick and his devotion to the Trinity.

20 **Saint Julie Is Good**
The children learn about Saint Julie Billiart and her sisters and their work of telling the world about the goodness of God.

21 **Our Lady of Guadalupe Is Good**
The children learn about Mary's appearance to Saint Juan Diego. They are encouraged to pray to Mary for help.

22 **Mary Our Mother in Heaven Is Good**
The children are led to appreciate Mary's role as God's Mother and their mother. They participate in May devotions in honor of Mary.

Calendar of Saints

John Neumann

DATE	NAME	DESCRIPTION
January		
January 4	Elizabeth Ann Seton	She was the first American-born saint. She started Catholic schools in the United States.
January 5	John Neumann	He was the first American bishop to become a saint. He worked hard to start many Catholic schools.
January 21	 Agnes	She was a young girl who died for Jesus when she was only 12 years old. She loved Jesus very much.
January 24	Francis de Sales	He was a priest and bishop. He learned to control his bad temper and became very kind. He tried to be gentle like Jesus.
January 26	Timothy & Titus	They were missionaries with Saint Paul. They told people about Jesus.
January 27	Angela	She started a group of sisters who taught poor girls how to be good Christians.
January 28	Thomas Aquinas	He liked to study and became a teacher. He wrote many great books about God.
January 31	John Bosco	He was a priest who wanted to help homeless boys. He made homes for them and started schools to teach children how to be good Christians.
February		
February 3	Blase	He was a bishop put in prison and killed for his beliefs. While in prison, he healed a boy who was choking by praying for him.
February 8	Jerome Emiliani	At first he was a soldier, but later he worked helping orphans and the poor.
February 11	Our Lady of Lourdes	The Blessed Virgin Mary appeared to young Bernadette and showed her where to dig to find a spring of healing water. People make pilgrimages to the site of Mary's appearance in Lourdes, France, seeking physical and spiritual healing.
February 14	 Valentine	He was a Roman priest who was imprisoned and sentenced to death for his beliefs and practices of the faith. While in prison, he wrote letters to all his friends telling of his love for them.
March		
March 9	Frances of Rome	She was a widow who gave her belongings to the poor and took care of sick people. She was so lovable that people liked to be near her.
March 17	Patrick	As a young man, he was captured and sold as a slave in Ireland, where he was made to work as a shepherd. After he escaped, he became a priest and bishop. He taught the Irish people about God.
March 19	Joseph 	He was the husband of Mary and the foster father of Jesus. He worked as a carpenter and took care of Jesus and Mary. He had great trust in God. Now he cares for the Church.

DATE	NAME	DESCRIPTION
April		
April 5	Vincent Ferrer	He was a preacher who traveled to many countries to tell people about the Church. He helped many people change their lives and become good followers of Jesus.
April 8	 Julie Billiart	She is called "The Smiling Saint" because she was cheerful and hopeful even when she had many troubles. She started a group called the Sisters of Notre Dame who carry her message "How good God is!" to people around the world.
April 11	Stanislaus	He was born in Poland and became a bishop who helped the poor. Because he told the king to stop being so wicked, he was killed.
April 16	Bernadette	When the Blessed Virgin Mary appeared to her, Bernadette shared Mary's messages about prayer and sacrifice. It was a long time before people believed Bernadette and obeyed the messages from Mary.
April 23	George 	He was a soldier who gave away all he had to the poor in order to follow Jesus. He died for Jesus.
April 25	Mark	He traveled around telling the story of Jesus. Then he wrote a book about him. Mark's book about Jesus is part of the Holy Bible.
April 29	Catherine of Siena	She was filled with love for God and wrote books to help people pray and love God. She tried to bring peace to cities that were at war with one another.
May		
May 1	Joseph the Worker	The foster father of Jesus is honored as the patron of all workers.
May 3	Philip & James	They were two of Jesus' special helpers who taught people about God's love. They began churches in the places they taught. Later they died for Jesus.
May 15	Isidore	He was a farmer in Spain. He prayed a lot. He shared his food with hungry people.
May 25	Gregory	He was a pope who was born in Italy. He loved the Church and worked hard to help it.
May 26	Philip Neri	He was a priest who served God joyfully. He showed great love for others by caring for the poor and sick.
June		
June 13	Anthony of Padua 	He was a priest who went to Africa to tell the people about Jesus. He also helped many people in France and Italy believe in Jesus.
June 19	Romuald	He was a holy man who wanted to be alone with God and pray.

DATE	NAME	DESCRIPTION
June 21	Aloysius Gonzaga	He was rich, but he gave his riches to his brother and studied to become a priest. While taking care of sick people, he became sick and died.
June 22	John Fisher & Thomas More	They were two brave men who were killed because they told the king that he was doing something that did not please God.
June 24	John the Baptist	He was Jesus' relative, and he baptized him—but he knew that Jesus was greater than he was. A wicked king killed John the Baptist.
June 28	Irenaeus	He was a priest who wrote books to help Catholic Christians know more about Jesus' Church.
June 29	Peter	Peter was a fisherman when Jesus called him to be his special helper. Jesus made him the head of his Church on earth. Later Peter died for Jesus.
June 29	Paul	Paul started many churches in cities where he traveled. Then he wrote letters to the churches. These letters are part of the Holy Bible. Paul died for Jesus.
July		
July 3	 Thomas	Thomas was another of Jesus' helpers. He went to India to tell the people about Jesus.
July 4	Elizabeth of Portugal	She was a mother and a queen who brought food to the poor and cared for the sick. When her husband died, she became a sister.
July 11	Benedict	He lived in Italy a long time ago. He started a monastery, which is a place where men go to live a quiet life of prayer for God.
July 13	Henry	He was a German king who did not care about being rich. He tried to serve God by working for the Church and keeping peace.
July 14	 Blessed Kateri Tekakwitha	A Native American girl from the Mohawk tribe in what is now New York State, Kateri was baptized when she was 20 years old. She showed her love for Jesus and prayed for her people even when she was treated meanly. She is called the "Lily of the Mohawks."
July 25	James	He was one of Jesus' special helpers called apostles. He was the first of Jesus' apostles to die for him.
July 26	Joachim & Ann	They were the parents of Mary and the grandparents of Jesus. They were holy and taught Mary how to love God and say yes to him.
July 29	Martha	She was a good friend of Jesus. She often prepared meals for him.
July 31	 Ignatius of Loyola	He was a soldier who came to know Jesus when he was getting well after being wounded in battle. He started a group of men called Jesuits, who work in all parts of the world teaching about God and the Church.

Rose of Lima

DATE	NAME	DESCRIPTION
August		
August 8	Dominic	He studied and became a priest. He started a group of men called Dominicans, who help the Church by teaching about Jesus and by trying to be like him.
August 10	Lawrence	Lawrence lived at a time when many Christians were killed for believing in Jesus. Lawrence died for Jesus.
August 11	Clare	Clare started a group of sisters who showed love for Jesus by being poor. Saint Francis of Assisi helped Clare.
August 15	Mary	On the Feast of the Assumption we celebrate Mary's being taken body and soul into heaven, where she now shares in the joy of her Son, Jesus.
August 16	Stephen of Hungary	He was a king of Hungary many years ago. He was a good king who tried to do what was best for his people.
August 18	Jane Frances de Chantal	After her husband died, she became a sister and took care of the poor and sick. She started a group of sisters to help in this work.
August 20	Bernard	He was a holy man who helped others become holy too. He also traveled to many places, trying to bring the peace of Jesus wherever he went.
August 21	Pius X	He was the pope who made it possible for young children to receive Jesus in Holy Communion when they are ready, instead of waiting until they are older.
August 23	Rose of Lima	Rose lived in Lima, Peru. She loved God so much that she wanted to belong to God alone and not get married. She showed her love for God by caring for children, old people, and the sick.
August 24	Bartholomew (Nathanael)	He was one of Jesus' special helpers called apostles. He went to India to tell people about Jesus. Bartholomew died for Jesus in India.
August 25	Louis	He became king of France when he was only 22 years old. He tried to be a good king. He kept peace in his country and helped the people be good Christians.
August 27	Monica	She was a good mother who prayed many years for her son, Augustine, who was not leading a good life. Because of her prayers, he changed his ways and became a saint.
August 28	Augustine	He did not know and love God until his mother, Monica, prayed for him. After he became a Christian, he became a bishop and worked hard to teach people about Jesus and his Church.

Blessed Teresa of Calcutta

DATE	NAME	DESCRIPTION
September		
September 3	Gregory the Great	He was a pope who lived a very long time ago. He wrote many books about God and about how to live a good life.
September 5	Blessed Teresa of Calcutta	Mother Teresa was called by God to care for the people who were poor in Calcutta, India. She is known for treating the people she served with great dignity. Others joined in her work, leading to the founding of a new religious order, the Missionaries of Charity.
September 8	Mary	Mary is the mother of God, so the whole Church celebrates her birthday on September 8.
September 9	Peter Claver	He was a missionary priest who spent his life caring for slaves and teaching them about Jesus.
September 17	Robert Bellarmine	He was a priest who taught about God in a college in Rome, Italy.
September 21	Matthew	He was a tax collector when Jesus called him to be one of his special helpers, an apostle. Matthew left all his money and gladly followed Jesus.
September 27	Vincent de Paul	He and some other priests formed a group whose main work was to help the poor.
September 28	Michael, Gabriel, and Raphael	They are archangels whom God chooses to take important messages to people on earth.
September 30	Jerome	He was a priest who wrote many books about the Holy Bible.
October		
October 1	Thérèse	She loved Jesus so much that she wanted to become a sister when she was still a young girl. She did everything for the love of God.
October 2	Guardian Angels	They guide and care for us in a special way.
October 4	Francis of Assisi	He gave away all his riches to follow Jesus as a poor man. He loved everything God made and called God's creatures his brothers and sisters.
October 11	Blessed John XXIII	Elected pope at the age of 76, he called all of the world's bishops to gather in Rome at the Second Vatican Council. He called for the bishops to help the Church better address the needs of the modern world.
October 15	Teresa of Jesus	She loved Jesus greatly and grew close to him in prayer.
October 16	Margaret Mary	She loved Jesus very much and became a sister. She prayed to the Sacred Heart of Jesus after he showed her his great love.
November		
November 3	Martin de Porres	He lived in Lima, Peru. He became holy by loving all people—even those who were unkind to him—as his brothers and sisters. He did all he could to help the poor and sick.

DATE	NAME	DESCRIPTION
November 4	Charles Borromeo	He was a bishop who worked very hard to help his people live as good Christians.
November 13	Frances Xavier Cabrini	She started a group of sisters to work in schools, hospitals, and orphanages. She was the first U. S. citizen to be called a saint by the Church.
November 15	Albert the Great	He was a great teacher who wrote many books to help people learn more about God and our world.
November 16	Margaret of Scotland	She was a mother and queen who had a special love for the poor.
November 16	Gertrude	She became a nun and lived close to God by studying about God and praying often.
November 17	Elizabeth of Hungary	She was a queen and mother. After her husband died, she spent the rest of her life taking care of sick people.
November 22	Cecilia	She lived a long time ago. She suffered bravely for love of Jesus. She is the special saint for musicians.
November 30	Andrew	He was Peter's brother. Both of them left their fishing boat and nets to follow Jesus as helpers. Andrew was one of Jesus' apostles.
December		
December 3	Francis Xavier	He was a priest who spent 10 years in India and Japan telling people about Jesus. Many came to believe in Jesus because of what Saint Francis taught.
December 6	Nicholas	He is a bishop who is remembered for his kindness. Some children receive gifts from him on his feast day. They hang up stockings or put their shoes out for him to fill with presents.
December 9	Juan Diego	The Blessed Virgin Mary showed her great love for people who are poor when she appeared to Juan Diego as a beautiful lady, an Aztec princess. Juan Diego was surprised because he was an Aztec. He brought Mary's message of love and care to the bishop and all the people.
December 12	Our Lady of Guadalupe	When Juan Diego gave the Blessed Virgin Mary's message to the bishop, she left her image on Juan Diego's cloak, called a *tilma*. Because of the miracle, the bishop listened to Juan Diego. To this day, Mary's image can be seen on the *tilma*. Our Lady of Guadalupe is the patroness of Mexico.
December 13	Lucy	She is the patron saint of schoolgirls in Sweden. Her name means "light." She died for Jesus.
December 26	Stephen	He loved Jesus very much and was the first follower of Jesus to die for him.
December 27	John	He was one of Jesus' apostles, or helpers. John is said to have written some of the books in the Bible, including two books about Jesus and three letters that tell how much God loves us.

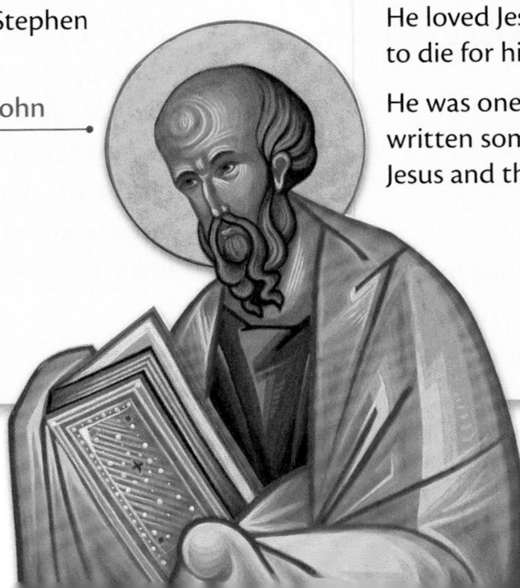

LESSON 1

All Saints Are Good

FEAST OF ALL SAINTS, NOVEMBER 1
Matthew 5:1–12

Student Book pages 111–112

CATECHISM OF THE CATHOLIC CHURCH
The themes of this session correspond to the following paragraphs: 956–957, 2030.

LEARNING OUTCOMES
The children will be able to
- identify a favorite saint or a patron saint.
- ask the saints to pray for us.

KEY TERM
saints—people who loved God on earth and who live now and forever with God in heaven

MATERIALS
- Crayons or markers
- Pictures of saints (optional)

COMMENTS
1. When sunlight shines through crystal, we are dazzled by the profusion of rich colors. By God's grace, saints are like crystal; they reflect the divine qualities uniquely embodied in Jesus Christ. Saints reveal to the world Christ's light that has penetrated their very beings. The Lord's light shines through their words and actions. Each person's particular and personal appreciation of God prompts a unique response that reflects his or her understanding of divine love. However varied the individual expressions, they all reveal divine goodness and divine love. Divine light is diffused through the saints as they stand before the Lord, totally open to his love.

2. The Church names a person to be a saint through a process called *canonization*. The lives of those declared saints provide an exemplary witness of Christian living, and the intercession of these saints is known to be efficacious. These are the saints we know by name and honor with special days on the liturgical calendar. However, many people—men, women, and children—who have not been canonized by the Church are also living in heaven with God. These people are also saints.

On the feast of All Saints, we celebrate our communion with the saints. We honor all the saints—those officially named by the Church and those not officially declared—and pray that their prayers and examples will encourage us to respond more faithfully to God's love.

CENTERING

Prepare the children to learn about saints.

- ***When you were born, you became the newest member of your family. But there were people in your family before you were born. Who were they?*** (Mom, dad, brother, sister) ***When you were born, you also were born into a larger family of relatives. Who are some members of your larger family of relatives?*** (Grandparents, aunts, uncles, cousins)
- ***When you became members of the Church in Baptism, you became members of God's family. God's family, the Church, is a very big family. It includes people living all around the world. God's family also includes people no longer living on earth, people who lived their lives following Jesus and loving God and all people. These people are living now with God in heaven. They are called*** **saints.** ***The saints continue to love and care for those of us living on earth.***

SHARING

1 Tell the children about saints.

- ***Saints are members of God's family who are now living with God in heaven. They are happy there. The saints are filled with God's love.***
- ***The saints like to help God's family on earth. They help us love God and others so that one day we can be with them in heaven. Saints help us when we ask them to pray for us.***
- ***Sometimes a person is named after a saint. If you are named after a saint, that saint is called your*** **patron saint.** ***Sometimes people choose a favorite saint to be their patron saint. When you pray, you can ask your patron saint to help you and to pray for you.***

2 Discuss with the children the lives of the saints. With the help of the CALENDAR OF SAINTS on **pages T296–T301,** comment briefly on some saints that might be of special interest. Include the patron saint of your parish, saints for whom children in the group have been named, and your favorite saint. You might show pictures of saints or provide additional books about the saints. Help the children learn more about saints who interest them or may already be familiar to them.

3 Tell the children about the feast of All Saints.

• ***November 1, the day after Halloween, is the feast of All Saints. On this day we honor all the saints, all the good people in heaven, by a special celebration in church. We ask the saints to pray for us. They are our special friends in heaven.***

4 Have the children open their books to **page 111.** Read aloud the text as the children follow along. Give the children time to draw pictures of themselves with their patron saint.

ACTING

1 Pray a Litany of the Saints. Have each child hold up his or her drawing and name aloud the saint he or she drew. Invite the group to respond, "Pray for us."

2 You might also teach and sing a song about the saints, such as "All Night, All Day" *(Singing Our Faith)* **CD 1 Track 7** or "When the Saints Go Marching In." For a list of all the music used in this program, see **page OV-39**.

3 Have the children take home the Family Page on **page 112** to share with their families.

CHECKPOINT

- What knowledge of the saints have the children demonstrated?
- Are the children aware that they can call upon the saints to pray for them?

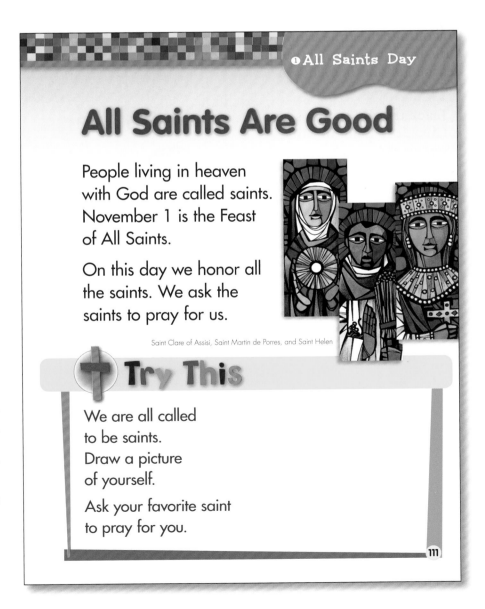

1 All Saints Day

All Saints Are Good

People living in heaven with God are called saints. November 1 is the Feast of All Saints.

On this day we honor all the saints. We ask the saints to pray for us.

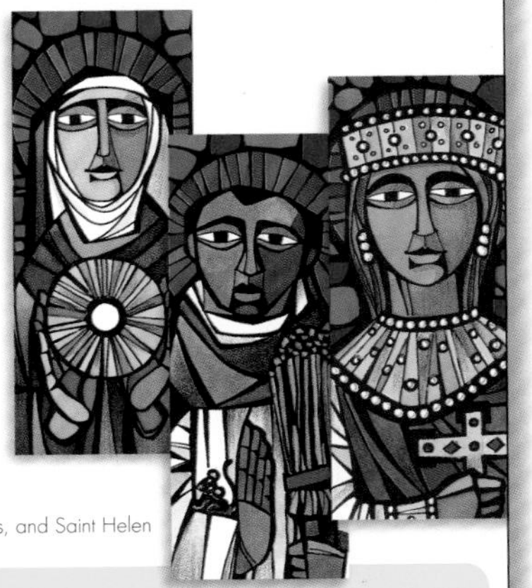

Saint Clare of Assisi, Saint Martin de Porres, and Saint Helen

Try This

We are all called to be saints.
Draw a picture of yourself.

Ask your favorite saint to pray for you.

111

ENRICHING THE FAITH EXPERIENCE

1 Plan to celebrate the feast of All Saints by making crowns and teaching the children a song. To prepare:

- Have the children make and decorate crowns using construction paper. Cut a triangular pattern along one edge of each sheet of construction paper. Fit each crown to a child's head and then staple the ends together. Help the children print the name of their patron saint on their crown. Invite them to decorate their crowns. Encourage the children to talk about what they have learned about their chosen saint.
- Teach the children to sing "This Little Light of Mine" *(Singing Our Faith)* on **page T247.**
- Let the children wear the crowns as they sing.

2 Make a mural showing favorite saints. Invite each child to draw a picture of a saint on a large piece of shelf paper. Display this mural in the classroom.

3 The *Saints Kit* (Loyola Press) contains cards with pictures and biographies for saints in the Roman calendar. Use the cards to talk about the saints.

Since we are surrounded by so great a cloud of witnesses, let us rid ourselves of every burden and sin that clings to us. *Hebrews 12:1*

Halloween in Families

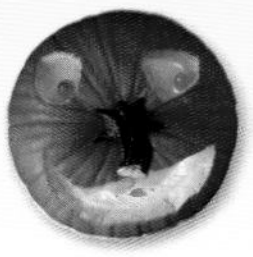

Halloween Blends the Holy and the Horrifying

Each year Halloween seems to receive more attention in our culture. It's a billion-dollar-a-year industry involving decorations, candy, costumes, and fun and scary activities for people of all ages. The holiday is rich in history and meaning, much of it religious, making it a great opportunity to combine fun with teaching our children about values.

A Quick History

Halloween as we know it today is a mixture of pagan, Christian, civic, and cultural influences. Various cultures have associated the day with witches, ghosts, and goblins. Many people trace its roots to an old Celtic festival, when the Celts believed the veil between the living and the dead was particularly thin. It was thought that on this night, the souls of those who had died could cross over into our mortal world. When Christian missionaries won over the hearts of the Celts, the popular feast was moved from spring to fall and celebrated as the feast of the eve of All Saints Day. Halloween comes from the word *hallowed* meaning "blessed" or "holy." So Halloween is the night where we eagerly anticipate the celebration of our living connection with the saints—all the faithful who have lived and died before us. It is fitting, then, that on the night before All Saints Day, our families remember and celebrate in a special way our belief in the Communion (close connection) of Saints.

Celebrating Your Values on Halloween

- Help your child research the saint he or she is named after or his or her favorite saint. Encourage your child to dress up as that favorite saint for Halloween.
- Tell your child that celebrating Halloween is a festive way to kick off the celebration of All Saints Day. We ask the saints to pray for us and to help us be good.
- At breakfast, recite a short litany of the family members who have died and whom you remember in your prayers. After each name, have everyone say, "Pray for us."
- Have fun! Make a special meal for dinner. Here's a quick idea for a healthy meal to offset the abundance of candy. Give each family member a paper plate. Put out bowls of olives, cucumbers, radishes, raisins, dried apricots or cranberries, cheese sticks, and cold cuts. Then have everyone make faces on his or her plate with the food. You can make scary faces or funny faces or both. Then everyone gets to eat what he or she created.

112

LESSON 2

Advent Is Good

SEASON OF ADVENT

Mark 13:33–37

The season of Advent is the beginning of the Church's liturgical year. Advent includes the four Sundays before Christmas. This session is best taught during the first week of Advent.

Student Book pages 113–114

CATECHISM OF THE CATHOLIC CHURCH

The themes of this session correspond to the following paragraphs: 522–524.

LEARNING OUTCOMES

The children will be able to
- realize that Advent is a special time to prepare for Christmas.
- experience joy in preparing for Christmas.

KEY TERMS

Advent—the four weeks before Christmas, a time when we prepare our hearts for Jesus' coming
Advent wreath—an evergreen wreath, with four candles, that reminds us to prepare for Jesus' coming

MATERIALS

- Monthly calendar
- Poster 4
- Advent wreath
- Advent Wreath punchouts from the Student Book
- Father in Heaven Prayer Card punchouts from the Student Book
- Crayons or markers

Remember to check with the proper authority regarding local regulations for using candles in a classroom setting.

COMMENT

The Advent wreath, whose four candles are lit successively on the four Sundays of Advent, is a sign of preparation for Christmas, when the Light of the World was born. The lighting of candles is accompanied by Scripture readings, hymns, and prayers. Usually three of the candles are violet and one is pink. Violet is the color the Church often uses in preparation for a feast. Pink or rose is a symbol of joy. The pink candle is lit on the third Sunday of Advent to tell us that the time of waiting is almost over and that Christmas is near. You might keep an Advent wreath on a table in the Prayer Center to use during prayer throughout the season of Advent.

CENTERING

Introduce the season of Advent. Together with the children look for December on a calendar. Together find December 25, Christmas. Ask:

• ***What do we celebrate on Christmas?*** (Jesus' birthday)

Ask for a volunteer to help you find the Sunday before Christmas. Ask the children to help you count back to the fourth Sunday before Christmas. Say:

• ***Jesus' birthday is so important to us that we start preparing for our celebration four Sundays before Christmas. We call this time of preparation Advent.***

• ***Today you will make something that will help you remember to prepare for Jesus' coming.***

SHARING

1 Show Poster 4 Advent Wreath. Show an Advent wreath.

• ***This is an Advent wreath. It reminds us to get ready for Christmas. The time we wait and prepare for Christmas is called Advent. The word* advent *means "coming." Who came at Christmas?*** (Jesus)

2 Explain the Advent wreath. Have the children sit in a circle so that they form a wreath.

• ***The Advent wreath is made of evergreen branches. Evergreen branches are always green. They do not change color as the leaves of some trees do. The evergreen reminds us that God's love for us never changes. God always loves us.*** [Have the children join hands.]

• ***How many candles do you see on the wreath?*** (Four) ***There are four candles on the wreath because there are four weeks of Advent. Usually three candles are purple and one is pink. The candles remind us that God's people waited a long time for Jesus. They prayed and tried to do what God wanted them to do. The candles remind us to prepare our hearts too. Each week of Advent we light one candle. When I point to you, stand in your place and hold your hands together above your head as though you were a lighted candle.*** [Point to four children in the position of the four candles on the wreath.]

• ***By Christmas, all the candles will be lit. If we have filled our hearts with love by trying to do what God wants, we will be ready to celebrate Jesus' birthday.***

❸ Distribute the Advent Wreath and Father in Heaven Prayer Card punchouts. Help the children trace the word COME in the box on the Advent wreaths and fold it up so that it can be read. Tell the children that each Sunday during Advent they can stand up one of the candles on their wreath and ask their parents to help them pray the prayer on the prayer card.

Alternatively, the children can make a simple Advent wreath. See ENRICHING THE FAITH EXPERIENCE, #1.

❹ Let the children hold their wreaths. Ask:

• ***What do we call this wreath?*** (Advent wreath)

• ***What does God's family do during Advent?*** (Prepares to celebrate Jesus' birthday)

• ***For how many weeks do we get ready for Christmas?*** (Four)

• ***What is the most important thing that we get ready?*** (Our hearts)

• ***How do we prepare our hearts?*** (By being loving)

• ***Remember, on each Sunday of Advent, we add one more candle to our Advent wreath by standing it up.***

ACTING

❶ Have the children open their books to **page 113.** Read it aloud. Have them do the activity.

❷ Invite the children to gather in the Prayer Center where the Advent wreath is displayed. Tell the children that during Advent we pray,

❷ Advent

Advent Is Good

During Advent, God's family prepares to celebrate Jesus' birthday.

We light the Advent wreath. We pray, "Come, Lord Jesus."

Try This

Color the candles and the Advent wreath.

Count the number of Sundays until Christmas.

113

"Come, Lord Jesus." Invite the children to repeat this prayer after you as you light the first candle of the Advent wreath. You might use electric candles instead, or you could tape a construction-paper flame to the wick of each candle.

Teach and sing an Advent song, such as "Come, O Come Emmanuel" or conclude by praying the adaptation of Psalm 25:5 with gestures (taught in Chapter 11):

Oh, Lord,
[Extend hand up.]

I wait for you
[Cross hands over heart.]

all day long.
[Bring crossed hands out in front and over to the sides.]

3 Have the children take home the Family Page on **page 114** to share with their families.

CHECKPOINT

- Do the children know that Advent is a time of preparation?
- Are the children looking forward to using their Advent wreaths?

ENRICHING THE FAITH EXPERIENCE

1 Invite the children to make their own Advent wreaths with green modeling clay. Have them mold the clay into a round, donut-shaped wreath. Allow the children to decorate their wreaths with beads and sequins. Distribute four birthday candles to each child to stand up in their wreaths. Remind the children that only adults are allowed to light the candles.

2 Help the children prepare for Christmas by making Christmas cards, using copies of BLM 16 Christmas Card.

- ***BLM 16 Christmas Card***

Songs

Play for the children any of these songs: "Leap Like a Deer" *(I See a New World)* **CD 2 Track 3;** "Mary's Cradle Song" *(Sing a Song of Joy!)* **CD 2 Track 12;** "Advent Song" *(Dandelions);* "Come, Lord Jesus," " 'O' Antiphons" *(Sing a Song of Joy!);* "Advent Song" *(Best of MaryLu Walker);* "Come Lord Jesus" *(Hi God 2).* For a list of all the music used in this program, see **page OV-39.**

Advent and Christmas in Families

"Behold, the virgin shall be with child and bear a son, and they shall name him Emmanuel," which means "God is with us."
Matthew 1:23

Advent Helps Prepare Our Hearts

Sometimes the demands of preparing for Christmas can be such that we miss out on the joy of the season. This is a special year to observe and enjoy your child because he or she is beginning to learn more about the story of Jesus and the reason why we celebrate this special time. So set aside a night for family togetherness.

Celebrating Your Values at Christmastime

After a simple meal, bring out some favorite snacks and gather near the Christmas tree. Turn off all the lights in the room except the lights on the Christmas tree. Get comfortable and cozy. Here are some ideas to spur conversation and togetherness:

1. Take turns naming your favorite Christmas song and then sing it as a solo or all together. If you enjoyed it, sing it again.
2. Each person points to a favorite ornament on the tree and tells why he or she likes it. Maybe there's a special story about how it came to be on your tree.
3. Tell your child about a favorite Christmas memory from your childhood. Be sure to tell lots of details about how it felt when you were that age. Share any special lessons you learned "back in the olden days" of your youth.
4. Read aloud to the family. Pick a seasonal favorite such as Clement Moore's "'Twas the Night Before Christmas", Charles Dickens's *A Christmas Carol,* or the picture book *Who's That Knocking on Christmas Eve?* by Jan Brett.
5. Finish the reading with the following section from the Gospel of Luke 2:1–20, which tells about the birth of Jesus in Bethlehem.

114

LESSON 3

Christmas Is Good

CHRISTMAS DAY, DECEMBER 25
Matthew 1:18—2:12; Luke 2:1–20

This lesson is best taught as close to Christmas Day as your school calendar allows.

Student Book page 115

CATECHISM OF THE CATHOLIC CHURCH
The themes of this lesson correspond to the following paragraph: 525.

LEARNING OUTCOMES
The children will be able to
- identify Christmas as the day we celebrate Jesus' birthday.
- share the Christmas story with others.

MATERIALS
- Poster 5
- Nativity Scene punchouts from the Student Book
- Crayons or markers
- Costumes for the play (optional):
  Mary—blue scarf (tie around waist or wear as a shawl)
  Joseph—colorful woolen scarf (tie across shoulder to waist); yardstick or pointer for walking stick
  Shepherds—colorful scarves (put over heads)
  Angels—halos (strips of yellow construction paper stapled together and sprinkled with glitter)
  Wise Men—crowns (cut from yellow construction paper)
  Big star—paper star (taped to yardstick or pointer)
  Innkeepers—scarves (tie around waists)
  Sheep—bell (cut from construction paper) pendant
- Props:
  Doll representing the baby Jesus
  Doll blanket for swaddling clothes
  Small rug for stable
  Gifts for the Wise Men to offer to the Christ Child
  Chair for manger
  Large piece of cardboard or poster board to use as a screen to block stable
  Recording of "Silent Night" (optional)

COMMENTS

1. Our Savior was born among us in the most quiet and humble of circumstances. Only Mary and Joseph and a few shepherds were there to welcome the Lord at his birth. The shepherds hurried to find their Savior and "returned, glorifying and praising God for all they had heard and seen." (Luke 2:20) In Matthew's Gospel we read that "magi from the east arrived in Jerusalem" seeking the infant king and bringing gifts of gold, frankincense, and myrrh. (Matthew 2:1) Our God had come to meet and to save all people through his Son, Jesus. He is with us today, waiting for us to acknowledge his presence and his saving help.

2. Invite parents or another class to join the children as guests as they present their play.

CENTERING

1 Display Poster 5 Nativity Scene. Tell the children that they will be in a Christmas play today. Explain that as you tell the story of the first Christmas they will act it out.

2 Involve every child in the play by assigning the following parts: Mary, Joseph, shepherds, angels, three Wise Men, star, innkeepers, and sheep.

3 Have the children help select sections of the class-room to represent the road to Bethlehem, inns of Bethlehem, cave or stable, hills where shepherds watched their sheep, the faraway country of the Wise Men, and heaven.

4 Place the doll representing the baby Jesus in the place designated as the stable. Cover it with the doll blanket. Instruct the child who is play-ing Mary to take the doll out from under the blanket after the screen is put in front of the stable.

5 Distribute costumes (if they are being used), and have the children put them on. Assist when necessary and encourage the children to help one another.

6 Instruct the children to remain in their places until you narrate their part of the play. Then they can go to the designated section of the room and act out the part while you read.

SHARING

1 Tell the story of the first Christmas based on Matthew 1:18—2:12 and Luke 2:1–20. Help the children act out the story as you tell it. Pause briefly after each section so that the children can act out the narration if they did not do so as you told the story. Whisper any necessary directions to the children during the dramatization to minimize distraction from the narration. Introduce the story by showing the Bible. Say:

• ***The story of the first Christmas is told in the Bible. It is the beautiful story of Jesus' birthday. When we tell this story, we learn about God's great love for us.*** [Enthrone the Bible.]

Invite everyone to listen carefully as you and the children tell the story of the first Christmas:

• ***When the time was ready for God to send his Son into the world, the emperor, or ruler, ordered all people to go to their hometowns to write their names in a large book. Then the emperor would count the names and know how many people he ruled.***

• ***Joseph and Mary left for the town of Bethlehem because they belonged to the family of King David. It was very close to the time for Jesus to be born.*** [Mary and Joseph walk to Bethlehem.]

• ***When Joseph and Mary reached Bethlehem, they went from place to place trying to find somewhere to stay for the night. But there was no room for them. The inns, places where people stay overnight, were already filled.*** [Mary and Joseph knock on doors, seeking shelter. Innkeepers respond by shaking their heads or by saying, "We're sorry, no room."]

3 Christmas

Christmas Is Good

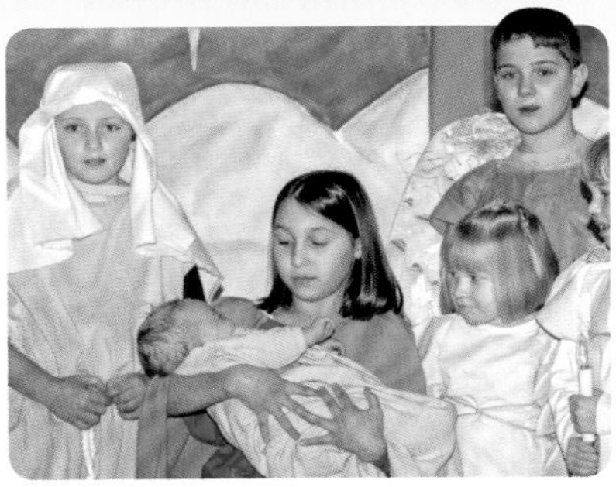

Christmas is Jesus' birthday. God our Father sent Jesus to us on the first Christmas.

Jesus came to show us how to love God.

Try This

Draw baby Jesus in the manger.

Thank God for sending us Jesus.

115

• ***So Mary and Joseph went to a stable for the night and slept on the straw that was there for the animals.*** [Mary and Joseph go to the stable and sit down on the rug. Move screen in front of the stable.]

• ***That night Jesus, the Son of God, was born.*** [Remove the screen.] ***Mary wrapped him carefully in swaddling clothes, which are bands of cloth, and laid him gently in a manger, an open box that holds food for animals. Mary and Joseph looked at Jesus with love. They knew he was the one promised by God.*** [Mary and Joseph act out the narration.]

• ***In the hills nearby, there were shepherds. They took turns watching each other's flocks during the night.*** [Shepherds and sheep take their places.]

• ***An angel of the Lord appeared to them, and the glory of the Lord shone around them. The shepherds were frightened.*** [Angel appears.]

• ***But the angel said to them, "Do not be afraid. Listen, I bring you news of great joy. Today in Bethlehem a Savior has been born. He is Christ the Lord. You will find the baby wrapped in swaddling clothes and lying in a manger."***

• ***Suddenly, there were many heavenly angels praising God and singing, "Glory to God in the highest and peace to his people on earth."*** [The rest of the angels appear.]

• ***After the angels went back to heaven, the shepherds were excited. They said to one another, "Let us go to Bethlehem and see what has happened there."***

• ***So they hurried away and found the stable. They saw Mary and Joseph and the baby Jesus lying in the manger. The shepherds understood what the angels had told them about Jesus. They knelt down and honored him.***

• ***The shepherds left the stable, praising God for all they had seen and heard.*** [The shepherds return to the fields, praising God.]

• ***Wise Men from the East saw Jesus' star as it rose in the sky.*** [Child with star raises it slowly. Wise Men point at it excitedly.] ***The Wise Men wanted to see Jesus and worship him, so they set out. The star went before them to lead them on their way. It stopped over the place where Jesus was.*** [Child with star walks slowly toward Bethlehem. The Wise Men, carrying their gifts, follow.]

• ***The Wise Men went in and saw Jesus with Mary, his mother. Falling to their knees, they worshiped him.*** [The Wise Men kneel in front of Mary and baby Jesus.]

• ***Then opening their treasures, they offered him gifts of gold, frankincense, and myrrh.*** [The Wise Men present their gifts to baby Jesus and place them in front of the manger.] ***They knew that Jesus was the Messiah, the one God had promised to send.***

2 Invite all the children to the stable. Lead everyone in singing "Silent Night."

3 When the children have returned to their places, have them open their books to **page 115.** Read it aloud. Have the children do the activity.

4 Tell the children that you have something special to help them remember that Christmas is Jesus' birthday. Distribute the Nativity Scene punchouts. Explain:

• ***Some people put a manger scene under their Christmas tree. You can use it to tell others the story of Christmas.***

• ***Take your manger scene with you to show relatives and friends when you visit during the holidays. The story of the first Christmas is such a beautiful one that people like to hear it over and over again.***

Have the children fold the sides of their punchouts so that the scenes stand.

5 Invite a few children to take turns telling their favorite part of the Christmas story as they show their manger scenes.

ACTING

Let the children reverently hold their manger scenes as you lead them in prayer.

- ***Christmas is good. Christmas shows how much God loves us. God loves us so much that he sent his Son, Jesus. Jesus came to help us love God so that we can be happy, not just on Christmas day, but every day.***

- ***Let us pray, thanking God for sending Jesus to us. Take a few minutes to thank God quietly in your heart.*** [Pause and let the children pray quietly.]

- ***Jesus is not a baby anymore. Now he is with us in a different way. He is with us in the Mass, even though we cannot see him with our eyes. He is with us in our churches in the tabernacle. He is with us in our love for one another.***

- ***Let us sing a Christmas song and remember God's great love for us.*** [Sing a favorite Christmas hymn, such as "Joy to the World" or "The First Noel."]

CHECKPOINT

- Do the children recognize the significance of Christmas as the day we celebrate Jesus' birthday?
- Are the children eager to share the Christmas story with others?

ENRICHING THE FAITH EXPERIENCE

1 Teach the children this prayer based on Psalm 108:2, using the gestures to tell God that their hearts are ready to celebrate Jesus' birthday.

My heart
[Hands crossed over heart]
is ready,
[Extend crossed hands away from body.]
O God.
[Move opened hands outward to sides.]

2 Help the children learn parts of traditional Christmas carols, such as "Joy to the World," "O Come, All Ye Faithful," and "The First Noel." Explain the meaning of the lyrics as you teach them.

3 Use puppets or pictures to tell or review the Christmas story, or include a children's Nativity set at an activity center in your classroom and allow the children to use it to tell the Christmas story.

4 Use old Christmas cards to make a story wheel to tell the story of how Mary and Joseph prepared for Jesus. Cut two large identical circles from heavy-weight paper. Cut a wedge out of one of the circles, about one-quarter the size of the circle. Draw light lines on the bottom circle to indicate the four quarters. Glue four pictures, each in a different quarter, showing four events leading up to Jesus' birth. Examples:

- the angel's visit to Mary
- Joseph's dream
- Mary and Joseph's journey to Bethlehem
- Jesus' birth in a stable

Place the cut-out circle on top of the circle with the pictures. Place a brass paper fastener in the center to join the two circles together. The story of Jesus' birth can be told by rotating the open wedge to each of the four pictures.

Songs

Play for the children any of these songs: "We Are Little Gifts" *(I See a New World)* **CD 2 Track 6;** "Mary's Cradle Song" *(Sing a Song of Joy!)* **CD 2 Track 12;** "Glory to God" *(Stories and Songs of Jesus).* For a list of all the music used in this program, see **page OV-39.**

LESSON 4

The Wise Men Are Good

EPIPHANY, JANUARY 6
Matthew 2:1–12

This lesson is best taught on the first day back to school after Christmas break or as close to January 6 as possible.

Student Book page 116

CATECHISM OF THE CATHOLIC CHURCH
The themes of this lesson correspond to the following paragraph: 528.

LEARNING OUTCOMES
The children will be able to
- know that Jesus wants all people to know and to love him.
- come to a simple appreciation of the meaning of the gifts the Magi offered and the gifts they themselves can offer to Jesus.

MATERIALS
- Poster 5
- Statues or picture of the Wise Men offering their gifts
- Cutouts 42–44, 47, 50
- Star of yellow paper taped to yardstick or pointer
- Crayons or markers
- Background music such as "We Three Kings" (optional)

COMMENT
In Matthew 2:1–12, we read the story about the Magi—the Wise Men or astrologers—who traveled to Jerusalem from the East to find the newborn king of the Jews. Traditionally, they have been called kings. Studies by modern scholars stress the richness of the doctrine that is revealed by Matthew's story of the Magi and their gifts. The Wise Men represent all nations, and their adoration of Jesus reveals that all people are called to believe in Jesus as Lord and to share in the salvation he came to bring. In this first presentation of the Magi to the children, it is important to emphasize the message rather than the details.

CENTERING

Show Cutout 50 Wise Men or another depiction of the Wise Men offering their gifts to the baby Jesus.

• ***Here are the Wise Men who came to visit Jesus after his birth. They have also been called kings.***

• ***What are they giving to Jesus?*** (Gifts)

• ***What are they doing that shows they believe Jesus is a king?*** (They are bowing, kneeling, and giving him gifts.)

SHARING

1 Set up Cutouts 42 Infant Jesus, 43 Mary, 44 Joseph, and 47 Manger and tell the story of the Wise Men.

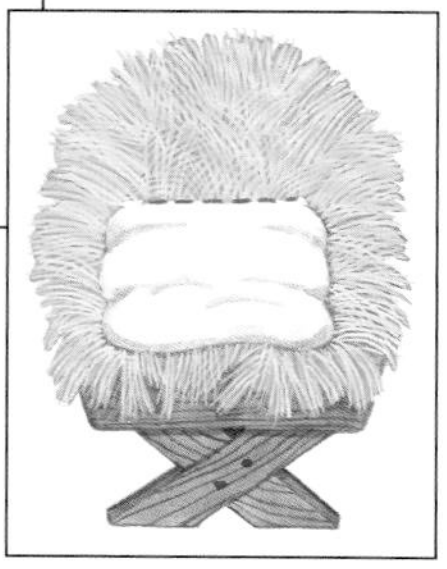

• ***The story of the Wise Men is found in God's holy book, the Bible.*** [Show the Bible and open it to the Gospel according to Matthew, Matthew 2:1–12. Enthrone the Bible.] ***As I tell the story, listen carefully so that you can share it with your family.***

Invite the children to remember what they learned about how to be good listeners.

Tell the "The Wise Men" story on **page T313.**

The Wise Men

After Jesus was born, the Wise Men, who lived in countries far away, noticed a very large bright star in the sky. It was a sign that a new king had been born. How happy the Wise Men were! Immediately they chose gifts to take to the new king and prepared for a long journey.

The Wise Men reached Jerusalem. They stopped there to ask King Herod where they could find the new king. Herod did not know, but others told him that the new king was to be born in Bethlehem. So Herod told the Wise Men to go to Bethlehem. He asked them to return and tell him where they had found the new king because he wanted to visit him too. After leaving Herod's palace, they followed the huge, bright star to where Jesus was.

The Wise Men entered the place and, with love, bowed before Jesus. How happy they were to give him their gifts! They gave him gold because that is a gift for a king. They gave him incense. Maybe you have smelled incense burning in church. As the sweet-smelling smoke rises, it reminds us to honor God. The Wise Men also gave Jesus myrrh. This is a thick liquid, like syrup. It comes from trees and was used as perfume when people were buried.

God told the Wise Men in a dream to go back to their own countries a different way because Herod wanted to harm the newborn king. So the Wise Men did not return to Herod. Instead they went directly back to their homes.

2 Help the children understand the message of the story of the Wise Men.

- ***The Wise Men came from faraway countries to honor Jesus. In this story, God tells us that he wants all people—young, old, no matter who they are or where they live—to know Jesus and to love him. Jesus wants all people to come to heaven and live with him, his Father, and the Holy Spirit.***
- ***How can we help people all over the world know and love Jesus?*** (Pray for them, give food and clothing to those who are in need, be kind)
- ***The Wise Men gave gifts to Jesus to show that they loved and honored him. Like the Wise Men, we can show our love for Jesus and honor him by our gifts of love. Our prayers are like incense. Our kind words and actions are like gold. The loving things we do are like myrrh.***

3 Have the children find the Wise Men on Poster 5 Nativity Scene.

4 Let the children retell the parts of the story they especially like and remember. Others can act it out as the story is told. Give one child a star on a yardstick to lead the Wise Men. Let the children take turns approaching the manger cutouts and imitating the Wise Men—bowing low, kneeling, standing, and offering gifts.

ACTING

1 Explain that the feast day of the Wise Men is called Epiphany. Read aloud **page 116.** Have the children do the activity. You might play soft music while the children work.

2 Conclude in prayer by singing a song, such as "We Are Little Gifts" *(I See a New World)* **CD 2 Track 6.** For a list of all the music used in this program, see **page OV-39.**

CHECKPOINT

- Do the children know that God sent Jesus to be the savior of all people?
- How have the children demonstrated awareness that they can offer Jesus the gift of their love?

ENRICHING THE FAITH EXPERIENCE

1 Teach "The Star Song," sung to the melody of "Twinkle, Twinkle, Little Star."

The Star Song

Twinkle, twinkle, guiding star,
Calling Wise Men from afar.
Underneath your shining light,
Jesus came for all one night.
Twinkle, twinkle, guiding star,
Calling Wise Men from afar.

M. Kathleen Glavich, S.N.D.

2 Continue to keep a children's Nativity set at an activity center in your classroom through the feast of the Epiphany. Allow the children to use it to retell the Christmas story and the visit of the Magi.

3 Help the children prepare a special gift of love to give to someone in their family. Have the children draw a picture showing a good deed that they can do to show love to a family member. (Examples: help set the table, help shovel the snow, let a sibling choose the game at playtime.) Show the children how to roll up each of their pictures into a scroll and help them tie it with a ribbon. Tell the children that when they give this special gift to a family member, they are also giving this gift to Jesus.

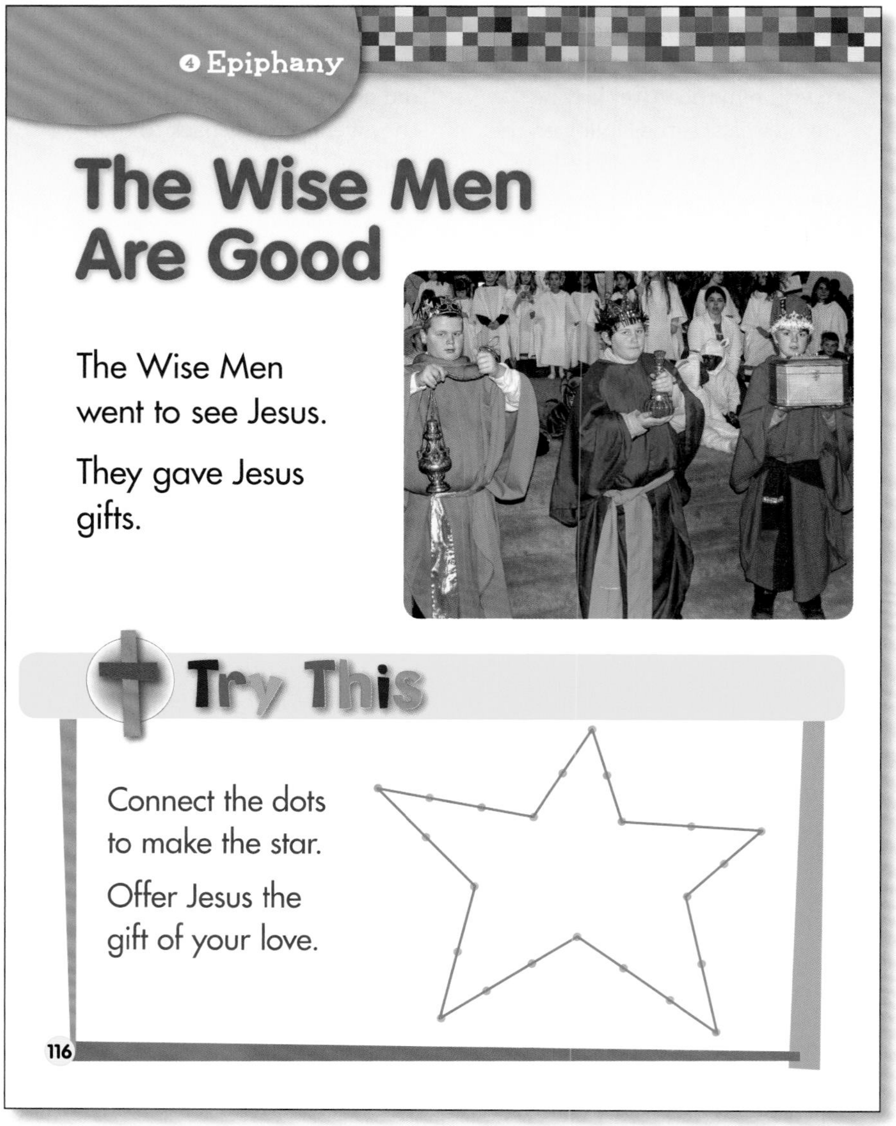

4 Epiphany

The Wise Men Are Good

The Wise Men went to see Jesus.

They gave Jesus gifts.

Try This

Connect the dots to make the star.

Offer Jesus the gift of your love.

116

LESSON 5

Lent Is Good

THE SEASON OF LENT
Matthew 6:1–6,16–18

This lesson is best taught on the Monday or Tuesday before Ash Wednesday, the first day of Lent.

Student Book pages 117–118

CATECHISM OF THE CATHOLIC CHURCH
The themes of this lesson correspond to the following paragraphs: 1168, 1438, 2014–2015.

LEARNING OUTCOMES
The children will be able to
- understand the meaning of Lent.
- resolve to pray and to perform good deeds during Lent.

MATERIALS
- Cutout 33
- Crayons or markers

COMMENTS

1. We eagerly await the signs of spring after the barren and cold winter months. In spring, new life bursts forth and shows us a transformed world—a world filled with beauty and song. The season of Lent often corresponds to the change of seasons from winter to spring. The word *Lent* is derived from an Old English word meaning "springtime" and may be a reference to the lengthening of the daylight hours that occurs during this time of year. During the weeks of Lent, we let the warmth of God's love permeate our hearts and transform our lives. In this lesson, the children learn that Lent is a time for them to grow in God's love. They are encouraged to pray and to do good deeds during the season of Lent so that when Easter arrives, their hearts will be full of love.

2. For centuries, the Church has placed ashes on Christians' foreheads on Ash Wednesday. Since the ashes are blessed by a priest, they are among the sacramentals of the Church. The Sign of the Cross made with ashes on the forehead is a reminder of the good news of salvation, of God's love manifested to us through Jesus. It expresses the great love of Jesus for his Father and for each of us. It reminds us to return his love through prayer, penance, and good deeds during the season of Lent.

3. You can use the ENRICHING THE FAITH EXPERIENCE activities throughout the season of Lent. Chapter 19 also focuses on the season of Lent.

CENTERING

Lead the children in a discussion of the things that have happened to them during the school year.

- ***Let's count together the number of months we have been in school so far.*** [Name and count the months with the children.]
- ***What are some new things you have learned so far in this school year?***
- ***Since you started kindergarten, you have learned many, many things. You have also grown older in age and bigger in size. You will continue to grow in these ways.***

SHARING

1 Explain that Lent is a special time for growing.

- ***Soon we will begin a special time of the year. It is a time for growing as God's children. During this time, we grow in loving God and in loving others. This growing helps us get ready to celebrate the great feast of Easter. This special time is called Lent.***

2 Help the children understand why Lent is like springtime.

- ***We have four seasons a year. What are they?*** (Spring, summer, fall, winter)
- ***What season do we have right now?*** (Winter) ***What does it look like outside at this time of the year?*** (The ground in many areas is cold and hard. In some parts of the country, there is snow and ice on the ground.)
- ***What season will come next?*** (Spring) ***What will happen in spring?*** (The ground will become soft. Rain will fall. The sun will shine more. Seeds will be planted and begin to grow.)
- ***Lent is like springtime. We call Lent a season because it lasts for 40 days. It begins on Ash Wednesday.***

• ***During Lent, we try to plant the seeds of God's love in our hearts by our prayers and good actions. Jesus will help his love grow in our hearts. Then by Easter, we will be more like Jesus.*** [Show Cutout 33 Growing seed.]

• ***Our kind words and deeds will help God's love grow in our hearts. What are some kind words you can say?*** (May I help you? Thank you. Please.) ***What are some kind deeds you can do?*** (Share toys. Give others a smile and greet them. Help at home.)

• ***Our prayers can help God's love grow in our hearts. When can we pray?*** (Before we go to bed; when we are in school; when we wake up in the morning; when we are in church)

• ***Sometimes we sing our prayers. Let's sing a prayer to God now.*** Have the children sing a song they know or teach a new song for Lent such as, "God's Love" *(Sing a Song of Joy!)* **CD 2 Track 14.** For a list of all the music used in this program, see **page OV-39.**

ACTING

1 Have the children turn to **page 117**. Read it aloud. Let the children color one of the petals on a flower as a sign that they have just said a prayer with their song. Review the directions provided about how to finish coloring the picture at home as they observe the season of Lent.

2 Invite the children to pray together this prayer based on John 3:17 with gestures:

God, you sent your Son
[Kneel on one knee and bow head.]
that we might live.
[Rise and lift arms.]

B Lent

Lent Is Good

Lent is like springtime.

It is a time for us to grow. During Lent, we grow in God's love. We pray and do good deeds.

By Easter our hearts should be full of love.

Try This

Color the leaves.

Each time you pray or do a good deed, color one flower petal.

117

3 Have the children take home the Family Page on **page 118** to share with their families.

CHECKPOINT

- What understanding of the season of Lent have the children demonstrated?
- Are the children eager to increase their observance of prayer and good deeds during the season of Lent?

ENRICHING THE FAITH EXPERIENCE

1 Prepare the children to receive ashes on Ash Wednesday, the first day of Lent. Explain how ashes will be distributed. Say:

- ***When we go to church together on Ash Wednesday, we will see the priest bless ashes.***
- ***We will walk up to the priest to receive a blessing with the ashes. The priest will dip his thumb into the ashes and make a cross on the forehead of each person. As he does this, he will say a prayer.*** [Demonstrate by making a cross on your own forehead and saying the prayer that might be used, "Turn away from sin and be faithful to the Gospel."]
- ***When we walk back to our places in church, we think about the Good News that Jesus brought us. We remember that Jesus loves us and that he died for us. We thank him for his***

Yet even now, says the LORD, return to me with your whole heart. Joel 2:12

Lent in Families

Lent Offers Three Ways to Grow Spiritually

Parents are busy people, and busy people usually don't like disruptions. We've got our plans made and our schedules set. Then comes Lent. Lent is a season of interruptions, a disturber of complacency. It begins with Ash Wednesday, a day in which we bear upon our foreheads a sign that something different is happening to us. And it goes on for 40 days—a symbolic time echoing Moses' 40 years in the desert and Jesus' 40 days of preparation before beginning his public ministry. In Lent we take up practices that purposely disrupt our lives. We fast rather than feast. We add more prayer to our day. And we give to others rather than gather for ourselves.

Lent is a time to return to God with our whole heart. It's important to introduce your child to appropriate Lenten practices so that he or she will know the spiritual benefits of these sacred days of the Church year.

Celebrating Your Values During Lent

Fasting: We fast so that we might come to know a deeper hunger, our hunger and thirst for God. If we are always satisfied, we will not be moved to seek the one who truly satisfies our deepest longings. There are many ways to fast. We can

- fast one evening a week from television and video games. Play board games, read uplifting books, or tell stories to your child about the spiritual heroes from your own childhood.
- fast from criticizing family members, classmates, and coworkers. Find only good things to say about others, or hold your tongue.

Praying: Once we awaken our spiritual hunger, we can nurture it by spending more time in prayer. Here are some ways your family can add prayer to their day:

- Begin each morning with prayer together, offering God all your "prayers, works, joys, and sufferings of this day."
- Teach your child to pray while washing his or her hands. Point out that the water, like God's grace, pours freely to help cleanse us and refresh us.

Almsgiving: As we grow in awareness of our reliance on God, we are moved to generosity toward others.

- With your child, go through your closets and toy bins, and bring unwanted goods to the Saint Vincent De Paul Society or Goodwill.
- Give of your time together to visit a sick relative, neighbor, or fellow parishioner. Your child can brighten the day of someone who is homebound.
- Have your child help you prepare a bag of non-perishable food and household supplies for a local food pantry or shelter.

118

love and tell him how much we love him too. We remember that Jesus rose from the dead to a new life and that some day we will live with him forever in heaven.

Distribute copies of BLM 30 We Celebrate Ash Wednesday and read it aloud. Suggest that as they color it, they thank Jesus for his love and tell him that they love him too.

- ***BLM 30 We Celebrate Ash Wednesday***

2 Place a small box of seeds or beans and an empty box in a special place in the classroom. Invite the children to put a seed in the empty box each time they do something kind for someone.

3 Use the following activities with popcorn to show the children how God's love can change us during Lent. Be sure to find out if any children have food allergies and take these into consideration when planning the activities.

- Let the children touch some unpopped kernels of popcorn to feel how hard they are. Tell them that these hard kernels remind us of people who do not love God and others. People without love have hard hearts. Then let the children touch some popped kernels. Explain that God's love can change our hearts and make them full of love if we pray and do good things.
- Give the children drawing paper and show them how to make beautiful spring blossoms with the popped kernels. Invite the children to draw a stem and leaves. Then have them glue kernels of popcorn in a pattern at the top of the stem to create a blossom. Have the children take home their popcorn blossoms and tell their parents how God's love can change our hearts.

4 Teach the children the following poems.

Celebrate

Let's celebrate today.
[Throw arms up high.]
It's such a happy day.
[Stoop down.]
The flowers all are growing.
[Gradually grow taller.]
See them swing and sway!

A Tiny Seed

A tiny seed died.
[Stoop and pretend to die.]
A new plant grew.
[Rise up.]
Jesus died for us.
[Extend arms to the side in the form of a cross.]
He gave us new life too.
[Raise arms high and stand on tiptoe.]

LESSON 6

Easter Is Good

EASTER SUNDAY
John 20:1–18

This Easter lesson is best taught as close to Easter Sunday as allowed by your schedule.

Student Book pages 119–120

CATECHISM OF THE CATHOLIC CHURCH
The themes of this lesson correspond to the following paragraphs: 654, 655.

LEARNING OUTCOMES
The children will be able to
- know the story of how Jesus' disciples found his tomb empty on Easter morning.
- share the good news of Easter with others.

MATERIALS
- Plastic Easter eggs, 2 for each child
- Stickers or other small treats to fill the Easter eggs
- Poster 10
- Crayons or markers

Be sure to find out if any children have food allergies and take these into consideration when planning the lesson.

COMMENT
Christians are, first and foremost, Easter people. Jesus' Resurrection is the basis of our faith and the source of our hope. Through the Resurrection of Jesus, all things are made new. Although we experience suffering and daily "dying," the power of the Resurrection will transform our pain into new life and glory. Through our Baptism, we died with Jesus and rose with him to new life. During the Easter Season, which lasts 50 days, we renew the promises of our Baptism. *Alleluia* is our Easter song.

CENTERING

Introduce the egg as a symbol of Easter. Give each child an empty plastic Easter egg. Invite the children to talk about how their families have used plastic Easter eggs like these in their celebration of Easter. Say:

- ***Many of you found candy or small gifts hidden inside these plastic Easter eggs. How did you feel when you found treats inside the eggs?*** (Happy, joyful, surprised)
- ***These plastic Easter eggs remind us of something very important about Easter. They remind us of the happiness, joy, and surprise of Jesus' disciples on Easter morning. They also remind us about what Jesus' disciples discovered about Jesus' tomb. Let's learn more about the story of Easter.***

SHARING

1 Introduce the story of the first Easter morning from the Gospel according to John, John 20:1–9.

Show the Bible and introduce the Gospel:

- ***Today I will tell you one of the most important stories in the Bible. It is the wonderful Easter story.*** [Show Poster 10 Jesus Is Risen.] ***Because this story is so important, I want you to listen carefully.***

Open the Bible to John 20:1–9. Enthrone the Bible. Invite the children to remember what they learned about how to be good listeners:

- ***Let's prepare to listen well to today's Bible story.***

Read aloud "The Story of Easter" on **page T320,** based on John 20:1–9.

2 Summarize the story so far and introduce the next part of the story:

- ***This is the wonderful Easter story. Jesus rose from the dead. The disciples found his tomb empty. Our empty Easter eggs remind us of this. But the disciples did not yet understand what had happened. There's more to the story. Let's learn about what happened next.***

Continue the Easter story by reading "Jesus Appears to Mary Magdalene" on **page T320,** based on John 20:10–18.

The Story of Easter

(Based on John 20:1–9)

After Jesus died on the cross, his friends were saddened. They buried him in a grave called a tomb. It was a cave in a hillside. Then a big, heavy rock was rolled in front of the cave to seal the tomb.

Early Easter morning, while it was still dark, Mary Magdalene, one of Jesus' friends, went to the tomb. She saw that the stone had been removed from the tomb.

Mary Magdalene ran from the tomb and found two of Jesus' friends, Simon Peter and another disciple. Mary Magdalene told them what she thought had happened at Jesus' tomb:

"They have taken the Lord from the tomb, and [I] don't know where they put him." (Mary Magdalene thought that Jesus' body had been stolen.)

Ask:

- ***How do you think Mary Magdalene felt when she saw that the stone had been removed from the tomb?*** (Curious, scared, angry)

Simon Peter and the other disciple ran to the tomb. The other disciple got to the tomb first and looked in. He saw the burial cloths, but he did not see Jesus' body. He did not go into the tomb. When Simon Peter arrived at the tomb, he ran right into the tomb. He saw the burial cloths, but Jesus' body was not there. The tomb was empty! Then the other disciple entered the tomb also.

Mary Magdalene, Simon Peter, and the other disciple were confused. The large stone had been rolled away. The tomb was empty. Jesus' body was not there, only the burial cloths. The cloths were rolled up and thrown aside. They did not yet understand that Jesus had risen from the dead.

Jesus Appears to Mary Magdalene

(Based on John 20:10–18)

Mary Magdalene had followed Simon Peter and the other disciple when they ran to the tomb. She stayed there after they left. She was very sad. She was crying. But, then she looked into the tomb and she saw two angels in white. They asked, "Why are you crying?" Mary said, "They have taken Jesus away. I do not know where he is." Then she turned to leave.

As she turned, she saw Jesus. But she did not know it was Jesus. Jesus said to her, "Why are you crying?" Mary thought he was the gardener, so she said, "If you took Jesus away, tell me where you put him." Then Jesus said, "Mary!"

Then Mary knew it was Jesus. She said, "Rabboni!" *Rabboni* means "teacher." Mary fell down at Jesus' feet and hugged them. Jesus said: "Do not hold on to me. Go and tell my friends that I am going to my Father."

So Mary ran out and told the disciples that she had seen the Lord. Mary said, "I have seen Jesus! He is alive! He is risen!"

3 Discuss the story:

- ***Why was Mary Magdalene weeping at the tomb?*** (She was sad and confused. She didn't know what had happened to Jesus' body.)
- ***What happened next? Why did Mary Magdalene stop crying?*** (She saw Jesus alive. She learned that Jesus had risen from the dead.)
- ***How do you think Mary Magdalene felt when she saw Jesus?*** (Joyful, happy, excited)
- ***What did Jesus tell her to do?*** (Jesus sent Mary Magdalene to tell the disciples the good news that Jesus was alive.)
- ***Our empty Easter eggs remind us that Jesus' empty tomb was the first sign of good news. Jesus rose from the dead. His life has changed. He is filled with the new, glorious life of heaven. Jesus is alive. Jesus wants us to share in his glorious life too.***
- ***Let's fill our empty Easter eggs with small treats to remind us of the good news that Jesus is alive and lives with us still. We can fill a second Easter egg to share with someone else to remind that person of the good news of Easter.***

Give the children stickers or other small treats to fill their eggs. Give each child a second egg to fill so that they can share the good news of Easter with someone else.

4 Have the children open their books to **page 119.** Read it aloud. Help the children do the activity.

ACTING

1 Invite the children to bring their filled Easter eggs to the Prayer Center. Tell the children that on Easter we pray and sing a special prayer word: Alleluia. *Alleluia* is a word that we pray to offer our praise to God. Encourage them to say Alleluia with great joy and enthusiasm.

2 Teach and pray a simple sung Alleluia, such as "People of God/Alleluia" or "Easter Alleluia" (*Singing Our Faith*), or teach and pray the "Easter Cheer" above.

3 Have the children take home the Family Page on **page 120** to share with their families.

CHECKPOINT

- What understanding of Easter have the children demonstrated?
- Are the children eager to share the good news of Easter with others?

Easter Cheer

Jesus is risen.
[Take two steps forward on the beats.]
Al-le-lu-ia
[Raise arms up and down twice.]
Jesus is risen.
[Take two steps backward on the beats.]
Al-le-lu-ia
[Raise arms up and down twice.]
Jesus is risen.
[Take two steps forward on the beats.]
Al-le-lu-ia
[Raise arms up and down twice.]
That's gr—rr—
[Swing right arm around twice as if winding up for a pitch.]
—eat!
[Jerk right elbow back. Clap twice.]

M. Kathleen Glavich, S.N.D.

6 Easter Sunday

Easter Is Good

On Easter morning, Jesus' disciples were surprised. They saw that the stone had been rolled away from the tomb. Jesus' tomb was empty. Jesus is alive! On Easter we pray Alleluia!

Try This

1 3 2

Put in order the events of the Easter story.

119

ENRICHING THE FAITH EXPERIENCE

1 Decorate Easter eggs by gluing pompoms, pieces of tissue paper, and other decorations onto plastic eggs. Fill the Easter eggs with messages of Easter joy, such as "Jesus is alive!" and "Alleluia!"

2 Make an Easter basket by weaving ribbon through the sides and bottom of a plastic produce container. Tie a ribbon from one side to the other to make a handle. Fill with Easter grass.

3 The Easter season lasts for 50 days, from Easter Sunday until the feast of Pentecost. On each day of the Easter season, greet the children with an Easter greeting, such as "Christ is risen! Alleluia! Alleluia!" Teach them to reply, "He is risen! Alleluia! Alleluia!"

Songs

Play for the children any of these songs: "Halle, Halle" *(Singing Our Faith)* **CD 1 Track 3;** "People of God/Alleluia" *(Singing Our Faith)* **CD 1 Track 13;** "The Butterfly Song" *(Best of Mary Lu Walker)*; "All Men on Earth Rejoice and Sing," "The Butterfly Song" *(Songs for Young Children)*; "A Celebration of Sunshine" *(Dandelions)*; "New Hope," "O, Yes, Lord Jesus Lives" *(Hi God 2)*; "Signs of New Life" *(Bloom Where You're Planted)*; "Jesus Lives," "Take My Hand," "We Believe" *(Stories and Songs of Jesus)*; "Alleluia, Alleluia, Give Thanks," "Easter Alleluia" *(Singing Our Faith)*; or the Alleluia from the Mass (various versions found in *Singing Our Faith*). For a list of all the music used in this program, see **page OV-39.**

Holy Week and Easter in Families

God indeed is my savior; I am confident and unafraid. My strength and my courage is the LORD, and he has been my savior.
Isaiah 12:2

Enter Into the Sacred Mysteries

Holy Week is the time each year when we enter into the sacred mysteries of Jesus' suffering, death, and Resurrection. The Church gathers to face the deepest questions that we have as human beings and to open our hearts to the lessons from the life and the example of Jesus. The events we observe this week are at the very heart of our faith and are the foundation on which we can build a life of faith for our families and ourselves.

Celebrating Your Values During Holy Week and Easter

The rituals and the retellings of the stories of our salvation are powerful. Participate in the Holy Week rites at your parish, and they will open up for you a sense of how these same sacred mysteries play out in our lives at home with our families.

Washing of the Feet: A lot of what parents teach is conveyed by example. Jesus followed this model, too, when he surprised his disciples by getting down on his knees and washing their feet. Think of the ways you serve your family by tending to their physical needs in feeding them, clothing them, and caring for them.

At the Last Supper, which we celebrate on Holy Thursday, Jesus used the sharing of the bread and wine to make real his continuing presence with us and for us in the Eucharist. Think of all the meals you share with your family and how you can make them a source of real presence to one another and a point of awareness of God's presence in your home.

The Agony in the Garden: Jesus agonized over the consequences he knew would come from his faithfulness to the Father's will. Think of the times you struggle with standing firm on doing what you know is best for your family. Know that you are not alone.

Jesus Is Put to Death: Life in a family teaches us that there are many moments of dying to ourselves when we choose to respect, honor, and serve the needs of others and not just our own.

Jesus Is Raised to New Life: The reward for being faithful is new and abundant life, and we experience that in families too, when we experience forgiveness, connection, joy, and hope.

120

LESSON 7

Pentecost Is Good

PENTECOST, 50 DAYS AFTER EASTER
John 20:19–23

Student Book page 121

CATECHISM OF THE CATHOLIC CHURCH
The themes of this lesson correspond to the following paragraphs: 731–732, 733–736, 739, 1287, 2623.

LEARNING OUTCOMES
The children will be able to
- know that the Holy Spirit is Jesus' gift to the Church.
- pray for the Holy Spirit's gift of peace.

MATERIALS
- Cutouts 66, 68–69
- Crayons or markers

COMMENT
Pentecost is the Greek word for the Jewish Festival of Weeks celebrated 50 days after Passover. It was originally a celebration of thanksgiving for the grain harvest. It later became a celebration of God's gift of the Law, given at Mount Sinai. Pentecost is also the name given to the day Christians celebrate the first outpouring of the Holy Spirit on Jesus' disciples because it happened on the Jewish feast of Pentecost. Christians celebrate Pentecost as the birthday of the Church. On this day, the gift of the Holy Spirit transformed the fearful disciples, making them bold witnesses to the good news. Jesus, the Crucified One, had been raised from the dead and was revealed as Lord and Savior. We pray for the Holy Spirit's gifts of peace and joy.

CENTERING

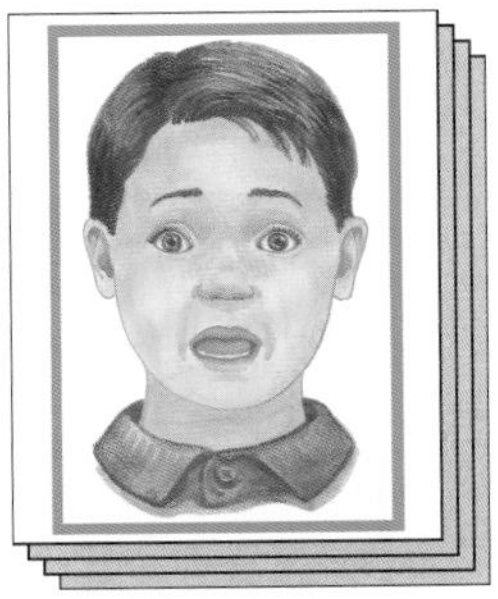

Show the children Cutout 66 Scared Face and Cutout 68 Sad Face. Ask:

- ***How do people feel when they look like this? (Scared, sad) How do you know?*** (A facial expression often shows how we are feeling.) ***Have you ever felt like this? Why?***

Show Cutout 69 Happy Face:

- ***When you felt sad, what helped you feel better? When you felt scared, what helped you feel better? What helped make you feel happy again?***

- ***After Jesus died, Jesus' friends were sad and afraid.*** [Show Cutouts 66 and 68.] ***But something wonderful happened that brought them joy and peace.*** [Show Cutout 69.]

SHARING

1 Tell the children about Jesus' promise to send his friends a helper, the Holy Spirit:

- ***Jesus knew that one day he would die and that his friends would be sad and afraid. Jesus did not want his friends to stay sad and afraid. He promised to send his friends a helper. This helper would bring the disciples peace and joy. This helper would aid Jesus' friends continue to live in love as Jesus taught. This helper is called the Holy Spirit. The Holy Spirit is Jesus' gift to us.***

2 Tell the children that after Jesus died and rose from the dead, he appeared to his disciples.

- ***How do you think Jesus' friends felt when they saw Jesus alive?*** (Happy, joyful, surprised)

- ***The Bible tells us a story about a gift that Jesus gave to his friends. This gift helped Jesus' friends continue to feel joyful and peaceful even when they no longer saw him. Jesus gave them the gift he promised, the Holy Spirit.***

Introduce this Bible story by showing the Bible and opening it to the Gospel according to John, John 20:19–23. Enthrone the Bible.

Invite the children to remember what they learned about how to be good listeners.

- ***Let's prepare ourselves to listen well to today's Bible story.***

Read "Jesus Sends the Holy Spirit," based on John 20:19–23.

Jesus Sends the Holy Spirit
(based on John 20:19–23)

After Jesus had died, Jesus' friends were gathered together in a locked room. They were afraid. Suddenly, Jesus stood before them. Jesus said, "Peace be with you." The disciples were confused. Was this really Jesus?

Jesus showed his friends his hands and his side. His friends could see the wounds from when Jesus was crucified. Jesus' friends now knew that the person standing before them was Jesus, raised from the dead and alive!

Jesus said to his friends, "Peace be with you. As the Father has sent me, so I send you." Then Jesus breathed on them and said, "Receive the holy Spirit."

Jesus' friends were no longer afraid. They were filled with peace and joy because they knew that Jesus was risen from the dead. Jesus would be with them always!

Discuss the story:

- ***How did Jesus' friends feel after Jesus had died?*** (Sad, afraid)
- ***What changed their sadness and fear to joy?*** (They saw Jesus alive.)
- ***What gift did Jesus give to his friends?*** (The Holy Spirit)
- ***The Holy Spirit brought Jesus' friends peace and joy.***

3 Remind the children that Jesus greeted his friends with the words "Peace be with you." Tell the children that they can also share words of peace with others. Help the children identify such words and thoughts that might help a person who is sad, scared, or worried feel better. (Examples: That's okay, I care about you; Things will get better.) Encourage the children to use such expressions when friends or family are feeling sad, scared, or worried.

4 Have the children open their books to **page 121.** Read it aloud. Have the children do the activity. Ask for Jesus' gift of peace. Pray, "Come, Holy Spirit."

ACTING

1 Invite the children to the Prayer Center. Tell them that they can pray to the Holy Spirit when they are worried, fearful, or sad. Jesus promised that the Holy Spirit will strengthen us and bring us peace.

7 Pentecost

Pentecost Is Good

Jesus promised that he would send the Holy Spirit. On Pentecost, we celebrate the Holy Spirit, Jesus' gift to us. The Holy Spirit brings us peace.

Try This

Peace be with you.

Trace over the missing letters to complete the sentence.

Read together Jesus' words to his friends.

121

2 Invite the children to pray this verse based on Wisdom 1:7 with gestures:

The spirit of the LORD fills the whole world.

[Make large circular motions with your arms, upward, then downward.]

CHECKPOINT

- Do the children know that the Holy Spirit is Jesus' gift to us?
- How have the children demonstrated an awareness that they can pray to the Holy Spirit to find peace and joy?

ENRICHING THE FAITH EXPERIENCE

1 Help the children make bookmarks from construction paper with the word *peace.* Suggest that the children decorate the bookmarks with a symbol of the Holy Spirit, such as a dove. Suggest that the children keep these bookmarks where they can see them and be reminded to pray to the Holy Spirit when they need the gift of peace.

2 Tell the children that there are many ways we see the Holy Spirit working in our lives. Read aloud Galatians 5:22, the Fruits of the Holy Spirit. Discuss the list identified in the reading (Love, joy, peace, patience, kindness, generosity, faithfulness, gentleness, and self-control). Show the children how to make a windsock to remind them of the many Fruits of the Holy Spirit that are in their lives. Roll a piece of construction paper and staple the sides together to make a large tube. Tape colored paper streamers onto one end of the tube. Tape a piece of yarn across the other end of the tube to hang the windsock. Hang the windsocks in the classroom (or suggest that the children hang them at home) as a reminder that the Holy Spirit is active in our lives.

Songs

Play for the children any of these songs: "Peace Is Flowing Like a River" *(Hi God 2)*; "Peace to You and Me" *(Hi God Gesture Book Recording)*; "Peace Chant," "Peaceable People" *(Sing a Song of Joy!)*; "We Will Bring Your Peace" *(Great Stories and Songs)*; "Peace of the Lord" *(Child of God)*; "Prayer of Peace" or "Go Now in Peace" *(Singing Our Faith)*. For additional song suggestions, see the song list for Chapter 23. For a list of all the music used in this program, see page OV-39.

LESSON 8

Jesus Our Light Is Good

THE PRESENTATION OF THE LORD, FEBRUARY 2
Luke 2:22–38

FEAST OF SAINT BLASE, FEBRUARY 3

Student Book page 122

CATECHISM OF THE CATHOLIC CHURCH
The themes of this lesson correspond to the following paragraph: 529.

LEARNING OUTCOMES
The children will be able to
- know that Mary and Joseph offered Jesus in the Temple.
- consider how they can each become a light for others as Jesus was.

MATERIALS
- Picture of the Presentation (optional)
- Blessed candle with appropriate decorations
- BLM 31
- Crayons or markers
- Matches

Remember to check with the proper authority regarding local regulations for using candles in a classroom setting.

COMMENTS

1. The Gospel of Luke reports that when Jesus was 40 days old, Mary and Joseph presented him to God in the Temple at Jerusalem. As an offering, they gave two doves. Lovingly, they gave Jesus to Simeon, a holy man, who received him into his arms. The venerable old man was enlightened by the Holy Spirit. He recognized, received, and blessed the infant as the Savior. Daily, he had prayed to live until his eyes saw the Messiah. When Simeon gave Jesus back to Mary, he foretold Jesus' redemptive mission and Mary's suffering.

2. The feast of the Presentation of the Lord is celebrated on February 2. Because this day recalls the infancy of Jesus, its theme is closely connected with the Christmas season. Because Simeon called Jesus a "light of revelation," the Church has a candlelight procession on this feast day and calls all of us to be lights by our lives and ministry. The lighted candle represents the dispelling of darkness and the presence of Christ our Light. Traditionally, the candles that will be used at liturgies throughout the year are blessed on this day. Thus, this feast day is sometimes called Candlemas Day.

3. On February 3, the feast of Saint Blase, the Church honors Saint Blase as the patron saint of throat diseases and celebrates his feast by blessing throats. Little is known about Saint Blase. The Church tells us that he was the Bishop of Sebaste (now central Turkey) in the early fourth century, a time of persecution. He was martyred for his faith in 317. It is said that his intercession resulted in many miracles. In one story, he healed a boy who was choking to death from a fishbone stuck in his throat.

On the feast of Saint Blase the priest blesses two crossed, unlighted candles, touches them to people's throats, and prays that God will bless the people and protect them from diseases of the throat and every other illness. You may wish to teach the children about Saint Blase and the blessing of throats using ENRICHING THE FAITH EXPERIENCE, #1.

CENTERING

Discuss with the children their experience of going to church.

- ***Think about the last time you went to church. Why did you go to church? What did you do in church?***
- ***Did your parents take you to church as a baby? What sacrament might you have celebrated as a baby?*** (Baptism)
- ***Today we remember when the baby Jesus was taken to the Temple, a place where Jewish people pray.***

SHARING

1 Show the children the picture of the Presentation and discuss it. Then tell "The Presentation" story.

The Presentation

When Jesus was a still a small baby, his parents took him to the Temple. They also carried a birdcage containing two doves as an offering.

When they arrived at the Temple, they met a holy man named Simeon. They let Simeon take Jesus in his arms. The Holy Spirit told Simeon that the child was the Savior that he had been waiting to see. With great joy, Simeon held the infant and then gave him back to his mother.

Mary heard Simeon say that Jesus was a light for the world. She also heard Simeon say that Jesus and she would suffer.

Lovingly, Mary took her child back home. She thought about what Simeon had said, and she prayed a lot. Together, she and Joseph thanked God for the wonderful gift that he had given them. They took good care of Jesus, the light of the world.

2 Have the children turn to **page 122** in their books. Read it aloud. Have the children do the activity.

3 Show the candle and explain the feast of the Presentation.

- ***We call this the feast of the Presentation because Jesus was presented to God the Father in the Temple on this day.***

On this day there is a candlelight procession in some churches. Candles used in church and in our homes are blessed on this day.

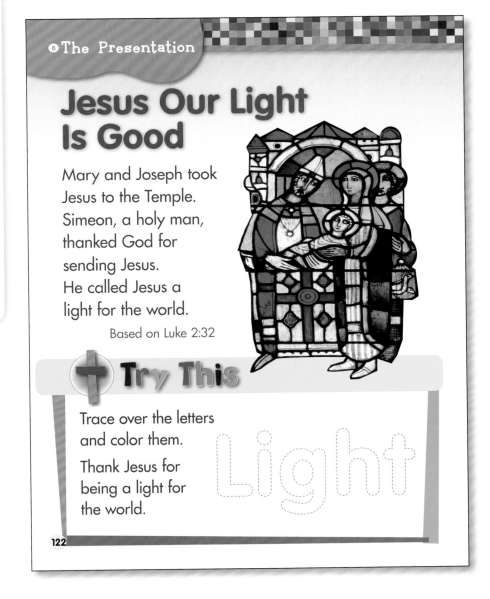

8 The Presentation

Jesus Our Light Is Good

Mary and Joseph took Jesus to the Temple. Simeon, a holy man, thanked God for sending Jesus. He called Jesus a light for the world.

Based on Luke 2:32

Try This

Trace over the letters and color them.

Thank Jesus for being a light for the world.

Light

122

ACTING

1 Place the candle on a table in the Prayer Center and have the children gather there. Raise the candle and invite the children to pray by repeating each prayer petition after you.

Jesus, you are light.
Jesus, you are the light of the world.
Jesus, you help us see.
Jesus, you show us the way.
Jesus, you are my light.
Jesus, you make me happy.
Jesus, you keep me safe.

If you wish, hold a procession with the lighted candle while you sing a song about following Jesus our Light, such as "We Are Walking in the Light" **CD 1 Track 2,** "We Are Marching" *(Singing Our Faith)* **CD 1 Track 14,** or "Walk, Walk in the Light" *(Singing Our Faith)*. For a list of all the music used in this program, see **page OV-39.**

2 Encourage the children to be a light for others like Jesus by their good actions.

CHECKPOINT

- Is each child now familiar with the story of the presentation of Jesus in the Temple?
- Is each child eager to be a light for others as Jesus was?

ENRICHING THE FAITH EXPERIENCE

1 Prepare the children for the blessing of throats on the feast of Saint Blase, February 3. Tell the children the story of "Saint Blase."

Saint Blase

Long, long ago, Blase was a good bishop, the leader of the Church, in faraway Asia. At that time the Christians were hated by some people. They were put in prison and sometimes put to death just because they loved and served the Lord. Blase went to prison and was killed because he believed in Jesus and loved him.

People told a story about the time when Blase was in prison. In this story, a little boy who was choking on a fishbone was brought to him. Blase blessed him, and the boy was healed by God.

Now on the feast of Saint Blase, the priest blesses our throats with two unlit candles. The priest prays over each person, asking God to protect him or her from diseases of the throat and from every other illness. He asks this through the prayers of Saint Blase.

Explain the blessing of throats and demonstrate with each child individually. Use two candles, crossed in front of the throat. Show how the priest uses the candles and says the words of the blessing.

- ***Through the intercession of Saint Blase, bishop and martyr, may God deliver you from every disease of the throat and from every other illness: In the name of the Father, and of the Son, and of the Holy Spirit.*** (Amen.)

Distribute copies of BLM 31 Blessings Are Good. Have the children trace around the crossed candles and color the ribbons. You might wish to have them do this during the practice for the blessing of the throats.

- *BLM 31 Blessings Are Good*

2 Invite the children to offer examples of good things they can do and have them draw one of their ideas.

3 Let the children retell parts of the story of the Presentation or act out parts as you retell it.

4 Have the children decorate candles to be blessed on February 2 by gluing sequins, beads, and pompoms onto large white candles.

LESSON 9

Mary Is Good

BIRTHDAY OF MARY, SEPTEMBER 8

Student Book page 123

CATECHISM OF THE CATHOLIC CHURCH

The themes of this lesson correspond to the following paragraph: 488.

LEARNING OUTCOME

The children will be able to

- honor Mary as the mother of Jesus and their mother.

MATERIALS

- Statue of Mary
- Crayons or markers
- Treats (optional)

Find out if any children have food allergies and take these into consideration when planning snacks.

COMMENT

The Bible reports nothing about Mary's life before the Annunciation. However, ancient tradition tells us that Joachim and Ann were Mary's parents. Because they were entrusted with the initial spiritual formation of the mother of God, they must have been holy persons of deep faith. Mary was probably born in the village of Nazareth, where the Annunciation took place. If derived from the Egyptian, her name could mean "beloved." Her birth brought joy to the whole world; she was destined to be the mother of the Savior who would redeem humankind.

Because Mary was to be the mother of God, she was free of all sin from the first moment of her conception. This grace is called her Immaculate Conception. Through her total surrender to the Holy Spirit, she grew in holiness and became the perfect disciple of Christ. She is an example for the entire Church—a model of what each of us is called to be.

CENTERING

Interest the children in Mary's birthday.

- ***What do you like about birthdays?***
- ***Today we celebrate the birthday of someone very special.*** [Show a statue of Mary and display it.] ***Can you guess whose birthday it is?*** (Mary)

SHARING

1 Tell the story of Mary's birth.

- ***Who is Mary?*** (The mother of Jesus)
- ***I have a story to tell you about Mary. Listen carefully. When I finish the story, we will talk about all the things you learned about her.***
- ***A long, long time ago there lived a good man named Joachim, who was married to a holy woman named Ann. They loved each other and were happy together. They wanted to share their happiness with a baby, so they prayed to God to give them a child. God answered their prayers and gave them a beautiful baby girl. They named her Mary.***
- ***Mary was very good. She loved God. She obeyed her mother and father. God chose Mary to be the mother of Jesus. Even before she was born, God prepared Mary to be the mother of Jesus.***
- ***We honor Mary because she is the mother of Jesus. She is our mother too. She is our heavenly mother. We can ask Mary to help us at any time.***
- ***We say hello to Mary in a special way. We say, "Hail Mary." This is what the angel Gabriel said to Mary when he asked her to be the mother of Jesus. Say them after me: "Hail Mary."*** [Have the children repeat.] ***Saying "Hail Mary" is like saying "Hello, Mary."***

2 Invite the children to tell what they have learned or what they already know about Mary.

3 Have the children open their books to **page 123.** Read aloud the text and guide them in doing the activity.

ACTING

1 Lead the children in singing "Happy Birthday" to Mary. If you have treats, distribute them.

- ***What song do people sing to you on your birthday?*** ("Happy Birthday")

• ***Let's sing "Happy Birthday" to Mary now.***

2 Invite the children to pray the Hail Mary:

• ***We say a special prayer to honor Mary. This prayer is called the Hail Mary. Look at the statue of Mary as I pray the words of this prayer for us.*** Pray aloud the Hail Mary.

CHECKPOINT

- Do the children honor Mary as the mother of Jesus and their mother?

3 Tell the children that Ann and Joachim were Jesus' grandparents. Let the children tell about their own grandparents. Allow the children to make a card for a grandparent.

4 Hold a simple procession in honor of Mary's birthday. Carry the statue of Mary and lead the children while singing a hymn to Mary, such as "Immaculate Mary."

5 Make paper lilies to honor Mary on her birthday. The lily is traditionally associated with Mary. Have the children trace their hands on construction paper and cut them out. Then roll each paper hand so the pinky meets the thumb and tape or staple it together. Secure a green craft stem at the bottom opening (where the wrist would be) of each paper hand. The result will resemble a lily.

ENRICHING THE FAITH EXPERIENCE

1 Play the song "Immaculate Mary" *(Singing Our Faith)* **CD 1 Track 9** or "Jesus, I Will Stay with You" *(Stories and Songs of Jesus)*. For a list of all the music used in this program, see **page OV-39.**

2 Teach and pray the following prayer:

To Mary

Mary, my mother in heaven above,
This day I thank you and show you my love.
Help me to grow up to be like your Son,
Kind and loving to everyone.

M. Kathleen Glavich, S.N.D.

9 Birthday of Mary

Mary Is Good

Mary is the mother of Jesus.

She is our heavenly mother.

We celebrate her birthday on September 8.

Try This

Color and decorate Mary's cake.

Wish Mary a happy birthday.

123

LESSON 10

Saint Joseph Is Good

SOLEMNITY OF SAINT JOSEPH, HUSBAND OF MARY, MARCH 19

SAINT JOSEPH THE WORKER, MAY 1

Student Book page 124

CATECHISM OF THE CATHOLIC CHURCH

The themes of this lesson correspond to the following paragraphs: 437, 532, 534, 1014.

LEARNING OUTCOME

The children will be able to

- identify Saint Joseph as the foster father of Jesus and husband of Mary.

MATERIALS

- Picture or statue of Saint Joseph
- Picture of a carpenter (optional)
- Piece of wood or something made of wood (optional)

COMMENT

Little is known about Saint Joseph other than the few brief references to him in the Infancy Narratives of the Gospels of Matthew and Luke. However, the one short statement from Matthew telling us he was "righteous" carries with it a wealth of meaning. (1:19) It emphasizes the good relationship that Joseph had with God in terms of keeping the Law of the Covenant. The narratives reveal both his perplexity and his faith during his betrothal to Mary, as well as his concern and obedience in the journey to Bethlehem and the flight into Egypt. We see him clearly as a man attuned to the voice of the Spirit and the will of God, and wholly attentive to the care of his loved ones. Small wonder then that he is God's choice as head of the Holy Family and our choice as patron of the universal Church.

CENTERING

Introduce Saint Joseph to the children.

- ***God gave you families and gave them the important job of loving and caring for you. What are some important things that your families do to help you?***
- ***God is Jesus' father. God chose Mary to be Jesus' mother. God also chose someone to be Jesus' foster father, someone to care for Jesus on earth. This person's name is Joseph.***
- ***Joseph worked as a carpenter. A carpenter is someone who makes things out of wood. Many things can be built out of wood.*** [Show a picture or statue of Saint Joseph.]

SHARING

1 Tell the children about Saint Joseph by reading them the story, "Saint Joseph the Carpenter," on **page T332.**

- ***Today I have a story to tell you about Joseph, who was the foster father of Jesus and a carpenter.***

2 Discuss:

- ***How did Joseph show his love for God?*** (He prayed to God. He obeyed God's laws. He took care of Mary and Jesus.)
- ***What did Joseph do to take care of Jesus and Mary?*** (He loved Jesus and Mary. He worked hard at his job. He prayed with them.)
- ***Because Saint Joseph took such good care of his family, we are sure that he will take care of all of us who belong to God's family, the Church. In fact, he is called the guardian and protector of the Church.***

3 Teach the poem "Saint Joseph Is Good" using the following gestures.

Saint Joseph was a carpenter.
[Show hands, palms outward.]
He worked the whole day long.
[Make circular movement with arms.]
His shop was filled with many tools.
[Make sawing and hammering motions.]
And he was very strong.
[Show muscles.]

First he sawed and sawed and sawed.
[Make a sawing motion.]
He held the wood with care.
Then he hammered: bang, bang, bang.
[Make a hammering motion.]
He made a wooden chair.

Swishy, swishy went the plane.
[Make a back-and-forth motion.]
The boards were really rough.
Back and forth and back and forth
[Make a back-and-forth motion.]
Until there were enough.

Joseph worked so very hard
[Wipe brow.]
To get his day's work done.
[Make a sawing and hammering motion.]
He was glad to have the help
[Cup hands around smiling face.]
Of Jesus, God's own Son.
[Point upward.]

4 Read **page 124** and let the children talk about the picture. Have them do the activity.

Saint Joseph the Carpenter

Joseph lived long ago in a little town called Nazareth. He was Mary's husband and the foster father of Jesus. "Foster father" means that he took care of Jesus like a father. God Our Father in heaven is the true father of Jesus.

Joseph, Mary, and Jesus were a happy and holy family. They prayed together every day and went to the synagogue (like our church) every Sabbath day (like our Sunday) with their relatives, neighbors, and friends. Once a year, they took a long trip to the Temple in Jerusalem. Joseph, Mary, and Jesus prayed for many hours in the Temple with all the other people. They loved God and wanted to obey all of God's laws.

At home, Joseph took good care of Mary and Jesus. He had a carpentry shop and made things out of wood for his neighbors. He made furniture, tools, farm equipment, and other things. Joseph always did his work well. He did not charge too much money for the things he made. He was an honest and loving man.

ACTING

Lead the children in prayers of petition to Saint Joseph.

- ***Let's fold our hands in prayer now and lift our hearts to God. Let's ask that, through the help of Saint Joseph, God may bless us. I'll say the first part of the prayer. You answer, "Saint Joseph, pray for us."***

For blessings on our families . . .
For blessings on our neighbors . . .
For blessings on all carpenters . . .
For blessings on our school . . .
For blessings on our priests . . .
For blessings on our Church . . .
For blessings on all who are sick . . .

CHECKPOINT

- Do the children know that Saint Joseph is Mary's husband and Jesus' foster father?

ENRICHING THE FAITH EXPERIENCE

1 On the board, draw a large frame of a building to represent Saint Joseph's carpenter shop. Allow the children to sketch the people, the furniture, the tools, and all the items that would belong in this picture. Don't forget the neighbors coming to buy some items. This activity can also be done by each child on drawing paper.

2 Read aloud the poem "Saint Joseph."

Saint Joseph

When God was looking for
a man
To be the foster father of
his Son,
He thought a Jewish carpenter
Named Joseph would be just
the one.

Now Joseph made a super dad,
For he was always just
and good.
With Mary, he raised Jesus well
And taught him how to work
with wood.

Because Saint Joseph was
the head
Of Jesus' family from its birth,
In heaven he still guards
and helps
The family Jesus has on earth.

M. Kathleen Glavich, S.N.D.

3 Saint Joseph is the patron for workers. Have the children draw pictures of themselves as adults doing a job that they might like to do. Put these pictures together in a career book. Talk about the importance of the work that people do. Invite the children to pray for people who work and for people who are looking for a job.

4 Invite someone whose career or hobby is carpentry to visit the classroom. This person can talk about working with wood, show some items he or she has made, and show and tell about some of the tools that are used.

10 Saint Joseph

Saint Joseph Is Good

Joseph took care of Jesus and Mary.

Joseph was a good man.

Jesus helped Joseph.

Try This

Draw something that Joseph and Jesus might have built together from wood.

124

LESSON 11

The Holy Family Is Good

FEAST OF THE HOLY FAMILY, SUNDAY AFTER CHRISTMAS
Luke 2:51–52

Student Book pages 125–126

CATECHISM OF THE CATHOLIC CHURCH
The themes of this lesson correspond to the following paragraphs: 531–533.

LEARNING OUTCOMES
The children will be able to
- know why the Holy Family is called holy.
- be helpful members of their families.

MATERIALS
- Cutouts 36–39

COMMENT
The family is the basic social unit and, as such, determines the well-being of society in general. Family life has been profoundly affected by the dramatic changes of the modern world and consequently faces many new challenges. Recognizing this, the synod of bishops, meeting in Rome in 1980, reaffirmed the value of Christian family life and addressed some of these new challenges. In his apostolic exhortation *The Role of the Christian Family in the Modern World*, Pope John Paul II enlarges upon certain basic family values mentioned by the bishops. Among these are the sanctity and integrity of marriage, the precious gift of children, the rights and obligations of family members, and the necessity and privilege of both corporate and private prayer.

Because of the challenges faced by the modern family, the feast of the Holy Family, strategically placed near the great family feast of Christmas, assumes greater importance than ever.

CENTERING

Use Cutouts 36–39 to present a scene in the life of the Garcia family. Then relate the scene to the lives of the children.

- ***Do you remember the Garcia family? Let's see what the Garcia family is doing today.***

Mother: Ana, please pick up your toys.

Ana: Okay, Mom.

Father: Carlos, some of the toys belong to you, so please help your sister.

Carlos: Yes, Dad.

Ana: [Whispers to Carlos] Let's surprise Mom and Dad and wash the dishes after we clean up.

Carlos: All right. I'll help you.

- ***Did you do something for a member of your family this week? What was it?***
- ***How does your family feel when you help at home?***
- ***Today you will hear a story about Jesus and his family.***

SHARING

1 Tell the children about the Holy Family.

- ***Jesus grew up in a little town called Nazareth with Mary, his mother, and Joseph, his foster father. They loved one another, and they did many things together. They prayed and worked together. They ate meals and had good times together. They were a happy family. We call this family the Holy Family because Jesus belonged to it and because Mary and Joseph were holy people.***
- ***Like other people living in Nazareth at that time, Jesus, Mary, and Joseph lived in a plain, small home. They did not have all the furniture that we have today. They did not have running water, electric lights, or microwave ovens.***
- ***When Jesus lived, women had the important job of taking care of the home. Mary probably tended the garden, cooked the meals, cleaned the house, and washed the clothes. Jesus probably helped his mother many times around the house. What do you think he might have done?*** (Swept the floor, worked in the garden, got water from the well, washed or dried the dishes)

• ***Joseph worked as a carpenter. He used simple tools. He sawed wood and made things for people to use in their homes. How do you think Jesus could have helped Joseph?*** (He might have held the wood while Joseph sawed. He might have cleaned up the shop at the end of the day.)

2 Discuss how Jesus helped at home.

• ***Like other little boys, Jesus liked to play and have fun with his friends. Sometimes he had to give up his playtime to help his mother and father. Jesus loved Mary and Joseph very much and helped them often.***

• ***Sometimes we have to give up playtime or something else we like to do to help our families. Has this ever happened to you? What did you give up? Why did you give it up to help them?***

3 Guide the children in pantomiming acts of helpfulness that Jesus might have performed. Here are some suggestions:

- carrying a bucket of water
- washing or drying dishes
- planting seeds
- hammering nails
- sawing wood
- sweeping the floor
- digging in the ground

4 Have the children open their books to **page 125.** Encourage the children to follow along as you read aloud the text. Help the children do the activity.

ACTING

1 Have the children think of one way they will help their families tonight or tomorrow.

2 Invite the children to pray for their families. Pray aloud:

• ***God bless my family. Help us love and take care of one another as did the Holy Family, Jesus, Mary, and Joseph. Help us be holy too.***

3 Have the children take home the Family Page on **page 126** to share with their families.

CHECKPOINT

- Do the children know why the family of Jesus, Mary, and Joseph is called the Holy Family?
- Did the children identify ways to make helpful contributions to their family life?

11 The Holy Family

The Holy Family Is Good

God chose Mary to be the mother of Jesus. God chose Joseph to be the foster father of Jesus.

Jesus, Mary, and Joseph cared for one another. They are called the Holy Family.

Try This

Draw a picture of your family.

125

ENRICHING THE FAITH EXPERIENCE

❶ Let the children role-play the following scenes:

Scene One

At noontime Jesus is playing with his friends. Mary comes to call him.

Mary: Jesus, Jesus, it's time for lunch.
Jesus: [Turning toward her with a smile] Yes, Mother, I'm coming.

Scene Two

Jesus, Mary, and Joseph are eating lunch.
Mary: After lunch I'm going out in the garden to finish planting the rest of the seeds.
Jesus: You don't have to, Mother. I finished it yesterday when you went in to fix supper.
Joseph: I'm glad you helped your mother, Jesus. Can I count on you today to help me in the shop?
Jesus: Yes, Father, I'll be there.

❷ Let the children make cards for their families, thanking them for their love and care.

❸ Put together a family album for the Holy Family. Let the children draw pictures of events in the life of the Holy Family. Encourage them to use their imaginations to show what daily life might have been like for the Holy Family. Collect these drawing and put them together as a family album.

❹ Read the poem "The Holy Family." Have the children discuss it.

The Holy Family

Jesus, Mary, and Joseph
Lived in Galilee.
They seemed to all the neighbors
A normal family.

Mary, Jesus' mother,
Worked hard all day long:
Baked bread, sewed clothes, fetched water.
She often sang a song.

Joseph, Mary's husband,
Loved her and her boy.
By working as a carpenter,
He cared for them with joy.

Jesus was a good son.
He did as he was told,
And helped his mom and dad
Until he was quite old.

Jesus, Mary, and Joseph,
They're a special three—
For Jesus was God's Son
In the Holy Family.

M. Kathleen Glavich, S.N.D.

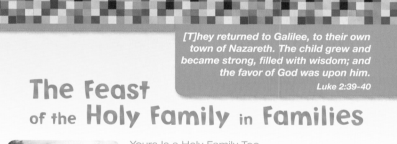

[T]hey returned to Galilee, to their own town of Nazareth. The child grew and became strong, filled with wisdom; and the favor of God was upon him.
Luke 2:39-40

The Feast of the Holy Family in Families

Yours Is a Holy Family Too

The feast of the Holy Family is celebrated each year on the Sunday after Christmas. It's good timing. With the birth of Jesus, a family was born too. But this day is not only for Jesus, Mary, and Joseph. By entering creation as an infant, God made all families holy. And while it might be hard to visualize one's own family as holy amid all the comings and goings—the laundry and the dishes, the obligations of work and school, not to mention the inevitable power struggles, misunderstandings, and conflicts—it is true nevertheless. Families are indeed holy. The dictionary defines the word *holy* as "belonging to, derived from, or associated with a divine power." That sounds like the definition of a family! Moreover, there is no better way to learn about ourselves, discover our weaknesses, and develop our strengths than in the sometimes calm and sometimes chaotic rhythms of family life. For this powerful spiritual workout, we can be truly grateful.

Celebrating Your Values with the Holy Family

- In every argument, see the opportunity for reconciliation.
- On every birthday, see the opportunity to celebrate the unfathomably marvelous gift of life.
- In every difficult family situation, see the opportunity to use your imagination and choose a new response.
- In every new experience for your child, see the opportunity to reexperience your own childhood with the awareness of God's grace.
- In every sickness, see the opportunity to show compassion.

One of the ways families thrive is by having a clear identity. Have each family member choose a virtue or characteristic that describes your family as a whole. Create a symbol for each one and together design a crest that represents your highest ideals and aspirations as a family. Mount it where everyone can see it.

Be vigilant about keeping your family traditions. Through their elements of ritual and symbol (however simple), along with the memories they create, traditions act powerfully to keep families working and striving together.

126

LESSON 12

Angels Are Good

FEAST OF THE GUARDIAN ANGELS, OCTOBER 2

Exodus 23:20–21
Matthew 18:10
Acts of the Apostles 12:15

Student Book page 127

CATECHISM OF THE CATHOLIC CHURCH

The themes of this lesson correspond to the following paragraphs: 328–330, 336.

LEARNING OUTCOMES

The children will be able to

- know who guardian angels are.
- know that their guardian angels guide and protect them.

KEY TERM

guardian angel—a good spirit who serves God by taking care of us

spirit—a person who has no body

MATERIALS

- Cutout 21
- Crayons or markers
- Angel food cake (optional)

Find out if any children have food allergies and take these into consideration when planning snacks.

COMMENTS

1. The word *angel* means "messenger" or "one who is sent." The Catholic Church teaches that angels are spiritual creatures who are superior to human beings in the celestial hierarchy. God sends them to earth to perform tasks for him. People have guardian angels who protect and direct them.

Good and evil spirits exist in the world. The good angels have been faithful to God and dwell in heaven; the evil spirits once refused to listen to God and suffer eternal punishment.

2. You might pray the Prayer to the Guardian Angel with the children daily at dismissal time.

CENTERING

Introduce guardian angels as special helpers God has given us.

- ***God gives us many good things. What are some good things God has given to you?***
- ***Today we will talk about the special helpers God has given us. We cannot see these helpers, but they are with us all the time. They are our guardian angels.***

SHARING

1 Tell the children why God has given us guardian angels.

- ***Our world is beautiful. Heaven, the home of our heavenly Father, is even more beautiful because we will see God there. God plans for us to live there with him forever. God has given each of us a guardian angel to care for us, to help us love God, and to lead us one day to our heavenly home.***

2 Explain how angels are different from us.

- ***Although angels are all around us, we do not see or feel them because angels are different from us. They do not have bodies, but they do think and choose. We call angels*** **spirits.**
- [Show Cutout 21 Angel.] ***Artists sometimes draw angels with wings to show that they are messengers of God. They bring messages from heaven to earth.***

3 Lead the children to pray to their guardian angels.

- ***Our guardian angels are special friends to us. They want to help us and protect us from harm. Our angels are ready to take our prayers to God in heaven.*** [Pause.]
- ***Ask your guardian angel to help you with something today.*** [Pause.]
- ***It is good to know that you always have a special angel friend nearby who protects you from danger. Thank your guardian angel for being your personal friend.*** [Pause.]

4 Have the children turn to **page 127.** Help the children do the activity.

ACTING

1 Discuss praying to guardian angels.

• ***We can ask our guardian angels to guard and protect us every day. When might you pray to your guardian angel?*** (At bedtime, in the morning)

• ***There is a special guardian angel prayer in your books on page 127 and on the inside back cover.*** [Help the children find the prayer to the Guardian Angel.]

• ***Let's pray this prayer together. I'll pray it aloud. You can pray with me by following along as I read.***

2 If you wish, share a treat of angel food cake.

CHECKPOINT

• What new knowledge of guardian angels do the children now demonstrate?

• Are the children eager to learn the prayer to their guardian angel?

ENRICHING THE FAITH EXPERIENCE

1 Explain the prayer to guardian angels.

• **Angel sent by God to guide me—*Who made the angels?*** (God) ***Why did God give them to us?*** (To guide us; God loves us.) ***God gave us guardian angels to watch over us. They guide us by leading us to do what God wants.***

• **Be my light and walk beside me—*What does a light help us do?*** (See) ***We ask our angels to help us see what God wants us to do. Why do we ask them to walk beside us?*** (To be there when we need them)

• **Be my guardian and protect me—*A guardian is someone who looks after and protects us. Our angels are powerful guardians. Their special job is to take care of us and to guard us from evil.***

• **On the paths of life direct me—*On earth, we have important decisions to make. We ask our angels to help us know and do what is good so that we can please God. We ask them to show us how to get to heaven.***

Tell the children that when they know the prayer by heart, they may color the cross by the Prayer to the Guardian Angel on the inside back cover of their books.

2 Have the children draw pictures of times when they need the help of their guardian angels.

3 Teach the children a song about angels, such as "All Night, All Day" *(Singing Our Faith)* **CD 1 Track 7.** For a list of all the music used in this program, see **page OV-39.**

12 Angels

Angels Are Good

Prayer to the Guardian Angel

Angel sent by God to guide me,
be my light and walk beside me;
be my guardian and protect me;
in the paths of life direct me.
Amen.

Try This

Follow the path guided by your guardian angel.

127

LESSON 13
Saint Thérèse Is Good

FEAST OF SAINT THÉRÈSE, OCTOBER 1

Student Book page 128

CATECHISM OF THE CATHOLIC CHURCH
The themes of this lesson correspond to the following paragraphs: 956, 2030.

LEARNING OUTCOMES
The children will be able to
- know the story of Saint Thérèse.
- ask Saint Thérèse to pray for us.

KEY TERM
sister—one who gives herself to God and loves and serves God in a special way

MATERIALS
Flower

COMMENTS
1. The lives of the saints show us how to be followers of Christ. As Christians, we are part of a family of saints. The lives of our ancestors inspire us to live lives of holiness. We can help children appreciate the example of the lives of the saints. However, we can also teach that we do not copy the lives of the saints but rather respond to God's love in our own lives, as the saints did in theirs.

2. Saint Thérèse was born in Lisieux, France, in 1873 and grew up in a devout, loving family. She entered the Carmelite monastery at the age of 15 and led an obscure, cloistered life until her death from tuberculosis at the age of 24. Although she was naturally a self-willed child, she gradually attained sanctity by offering herself in love to God. Her love and care for others extended to the entire human family. Before she died, she said, "I want to spend my heaven doing good upon earth." In our era of concern for self-fulfillment, she challenges us by her surrender to God's love. She inspires us to forget ourselves in the service of others. In 1997, Pope John Paul II recognized the importance of Saint Thérèse's teachings by naming her a Doctor of the Church.

CENTERING

1 Introduce the story of Saint Thérèse. Show a flower.

- ***How many of you like flowers? Today I have a story to tell you about a girl who called herself a little flower.***

2 Tell the story "The Little Flower" about Saint Thérèse.

The Little Flower

Long ago, when Thérèse Martin was only four years old, her mother died. After that, her big sisters and her father took care of her. She knew that God loved her and that she loved Jesus. Thérèse loved all the flowers God made. She knew that although some kinds of flowers may seem more beautiful than others, God loves them all. Thérèse learned too that even though God made all people different, he loves each person very much.

Thérèse decided that she was one of God's little ones, so she called herself the Little Flower of Jesus. She loved to go to church with her father, and she listened carefully even though she did not understand much of what the priest said. Every night she prayed before she went to bed. She often asked her sisters, "Have I been good? Is God pleased with me?"

Once Thérèse became very sick. She and her whole family prayed to Mother Mary that she would be well. Mother Mary answered their prayers, and Thérèse became well again.

Thérèse loved God so much that she wanted to give herself to him in a special way. She became a sister. She did everything for love of Jesus, even if it was washing dishes.

When Thérèse became sick again, she knew it was time for Jesus to take her to heaven. She looked at the figure of Jesus on her cross and said, "Oh, how I love him." Now that Thérèse is in heaven, we call her Saint Thérèse.

3 Have the children turn to **page 128.** Let them retell the story of the Little Flower by looking at the pictures, starting at the upper left. A suggested text follows.

- Thérèse loved Jesus very much. She called herself the Little Flower of Jesus.
- Thérèse loved going to church with her father.
- Once Thérèse became very sick. She prayed, "Mother Mary, help me get well."
- Thérèse wanted to give herself to God. She became a sister.

4 Explain Saint Thérèse's promise to help us.

- ***Now Thérèse is in heaven with Jesus. Sometimes we see pictures of her with roses. She promised that when she got to heaven she would continue to do good for all people by sending roses to earth. She meant that she would ask God to give special blessings to people who ask her to pray for them.***

ACTING

Encourage the children to think of Saint Thérèse when they pray.

- ***God wants all of us to be saints. We do this by loving God and others. Yes, we can be saints too. The saints show us how to love God so that we can be saints.***
- ***We can ask the saints in heaven to take our prayers to God.***
- ***What do you want to ask Saint Thérèse the Little Flower to pray for?*** [Let several children respond. Offer suggestions if necessary.]
- ***Look at the picture of Saint Thérèse and whisper a prayer. She will take your prayer to Jesus for you.***

CHECKPOINT

- Were the children able to tell the story of Saint Thérèse?
- Are the children familiar with our tradition of prayer with the saints?

Saint Thérèse Is Good

A picture story

Try This

Ask Saint Thérèse, the Little Flower of Jesus, to help you love God.

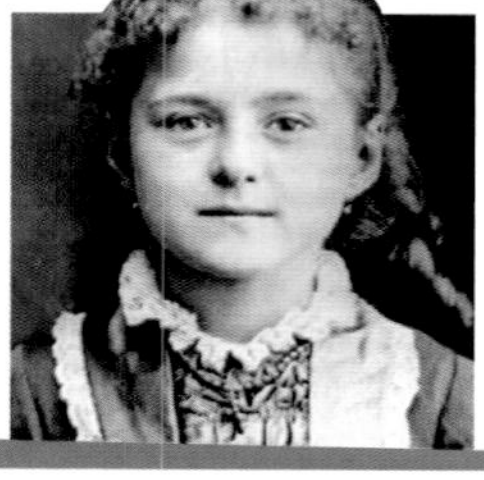

ENRICHING THE FAITH EXPERIENCE

1 Explain that Saint Thérèse is usually shown carrying a bouquet of roses because of her promise to "send roses to earth" by taking our prayers to God. Have the children cut out pictures of roses from magazines. Have the children glue these pictures on one side of a sheet of drawing paper. On the other side, tell the children to write or draw a prayer request that they would like Saint Therese to take to God.

2 Tell the children that Saint Thérèse is known for offering her work on everyday chores for the love of Jesus. To help the children remember this, teach and sing this song to the tune of "Here We Go 'Round the Mulberry Bush":

> **"This is the way we** [sing and do everyday actions],
> **all for the love of Jesus."**

Let the children fill in the words and actions with examples such as the following: wait our turn, say our prayers, and pick up our toys.

LESSON 14
Saint Francis Is Good

FEAST OF SAINT FRANCIS, OCTOBER 4

Student Book page 129

CATECHISM OF THE CATHOLIC CHURCH
The themes of this lesson correspond to the following paragraphs: 2415–2418, 2683.

LEARNING OUTCOME
The children will be able to
- know the message of Saint Francis.

MATERIALS
- Cutouts 13, 17
- Crayons or markers

COMMENT
Saint Francis of Assisi is said to have been the most Christlike person our world has known. Francis was totally convinced of the goodness of God's creation. He felt his oneness with all of God's creatures, even going so far as to call them his brothers and sisters. He loved God and shared God's love wherever he went. Even animals sensed his sincerity, lost their natural timidity or ferocity, and responded to him with trust. In simplicity, Francis led all God's creatures to render to their Creator. He invites us to open our eyes to the beauty and wonder of nature around us and to bring simplicity, love, and peace to a restless world that needs so much and loves so little.

CENTERING

Introduce Saint Francis to the children as one who loved animals. Say:

- ***Raise your hand if you like animals. What are some of your favorite animals?***
- ***Today I will tell you about a saint who liked all the creatures God made so much that he called them his brothers and sisters. His name is Saint Francis.***

SHARING

1 Tell the children about Saint Francis.

- ***Saint Francis lived a long time ago in a country called Italy. His parents were quite rich, so as a boy he had many nice clothes and went to fancy parties. But Francis discovered that clothes, parties, and good things to eat did not make him happy.***
- ***Francis knew that God wanted him to help the Church by being more like Jesus. So Francis gave away his beautiful clothes and wore simple clothes like Jesus. He began to love, as Jesus did, everyone and everything God made. Because Francis saw God's love and beauty in the creatures God made, he called the sun, moon, water, fire, flowers, and all the different animals his brothers and sisters. He spoke of sister sun, brother rabbit, and sister swallow.***
- ***People tell many stories about Saint Francis. They say Francis became so much like Jesus that even the wild animals were not afraid of him. In fact, they came to him when he called them.*** [Show Cutout 13 Wolves.]

- ***In one story, when Francis was trying to tell people about Jesus, some swallows were chirping so noisily that the people could not hear him.*** [Show Cutout 17 Birds.] ***So Francis said, "My sister swallows, you have talked enough. It is now time for me to speak." And the swallows were quiet until Francis finished talking about God.***

- ***Another time, Francis told the birds, "My brother birds, you should praise God and always love him. He has given you feathers to wear and wings to fly. He gives you food to eat." When the birds heard this, they began singing to thank God for being so good to them.***

• ***Now Francis is in heaven with God. We call him Saint Francis. He helps us know that all the things God made are good. We can call God's creatures our brothers and sisters as he did. Saint Francis helps us know that we too should love God, because God has been good to us. God loves all his creation.***

2 Have the children turn to **page 129**. Read aloud the page and guide the children in doing the activity.

ACTING

Invite the children, in the spirit of Saint Francis, to thank God for all his creations. If time allows, have the children show how animals praise God, by imitating each animal's sound or special feature. (Examples: barking like a dog, hissing like a snake, flapping arms like a bird)

CHECKPOINT

• How did the children respond when they learned of Saint Francis's love for all of God's creation?

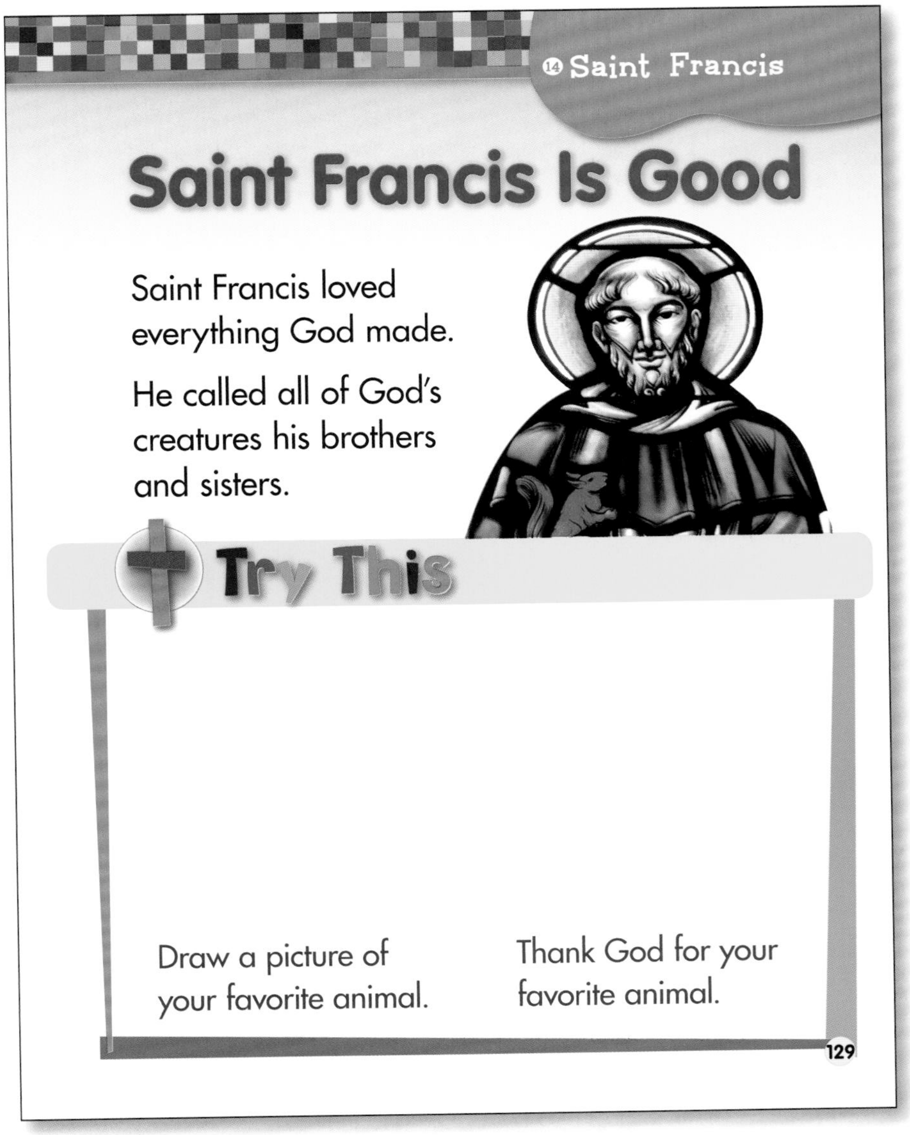
14 Saint Francis

Saint Francis Is Good

Saint Francis loved everything God made.

He called all of God's creatures his brothers and sisters.

Try This

Draw a picture of your favorite animal.

Thank God for your favorite animal.

129

ENRICHING THE FAITH EXPERIENCE

❶ Teach the children to sing a song that praises God for creation, such as "Canticle of the Sun" *(Singing Our Faith)* **CD 1 Track 15,** or "All You Works of God" *(Singing Our Faith)*. For a list of all the music used in this program, see **page OV-39.**

❷ Arrange for a blessing of pets in your parish on the feast of Saint Francis.

❸ Have the children clap and sing "God Our Father" to the melody of "Old MacDonald Had a Farm."

God Our Father

God our Father made the world. E-I-E-I-O.
And in this world God put some birds. E-I-E-I-O.
With a tweet, tweet, here and a tweet, tweet, there.
Here a tweet. There a tweet.
Everywhere a tweet, tweet.
God our Father made the world,and everything was good.
[Other verses: Lions—roar, sheep—baa, water—splash, trees—rustle.]

M. Kathleen Glavich, S.N.D.

❹ Tell the children that Saint Francis is also known as a peacemaker. Discuss ways in which the children can be peacemakers in the classroom, on the playground, and within their families. Teach and sing a song about peace or one based on the Peace Prayer of Saint Francis, for example, "A Means of Your Peace" *(Singing Our Faith).*

LESSON 15

Saint Elizabeth Ann Seton Is Good

FEAST OF SAINT ELIZABETH ANN SETON, JANUARY 4

Student Book page 130

CATECHISM OF THE CATHOLIC CHURCH

The themes of this lesson correspond to the following paragraphs: 2030, 2443.

LEARNING OUTCOMES

The children will be able to

- be familiar with the life of Saint Elizabeth Ann Seton.
- desire to be kind like Saint Elizabeth Ann.

MATERIALS

Crayons or markers

COMMENT

Elizabeth Ann, or Betsy, as she was called, was born in New York City in 1774 to Catherine and Dr. Richard Bayley. Though she saw little of her father, she loved him dearly. Surrounded by all the advantages that love could provide, Elizabeth grew into an attractive young lady, a deeply religious and devoted Episcopalian. At 19 she married Will Seton. After her husband's early death, Elizabeth took an interest in Catholicism and embraced the faith in spite of the resistance of her family and friends. She was then faced with the responsibility of making a living for herself and her children. Her husband's business had failed before his death, her father had died, and her other relatives and friends rejected her because she had become a Catholic. Even with these challenges, she succeeded in opening the first U.S. parochial school in Baltimore in 1808.

A year later, Elizabeth took religious vows with several companions and founded the Sisters of Charity of Saint Joseph. Soon a free private academy was established at Emmitsburg, Maryland. Today this site is cherished and visited by countless people. Mother Seton died at the age of 46, but her spirit lives on in the six North American religious orders that trace their beginnings to her. She was canonized in 1975, the first native-born American saint.

CENTERING

Introduce the story of Elizabeth Ann Seton by having the children recall their experiences with kind words and deeds.

- ***Were you kind to someone at home or school today? What did you do or say?***
- ***Was someone kind to you today? Tell us about it.***
- ***Today I have a story to tell you about the first American-born saint. She was known to be a very kind person. She learned kindness from her father. The saint's name is Elizabeth Ann Seton.***

SHARING

1. Show the children **page 130.** Point out the picture of Saint Elizabeth Ann Seton.
2. Tell the story "Saint Elizabeth Ann" on **page T346.**
3. Lead the children to practice acts of love and kindness.
   - ***Who might need a kind word or deed today at home? at school? at play? What will you do to show kindness today?***
4. Have the children open their books to **page 130.** Read it aloud. Have the children do the activity.

ACTING

Invite the children to pray together asking Saint Elizabeth Ann Seton to pray for them as they try to show kindness to others at home and at school.

Songs

Play for the children any of these songs: "Love One Another" *(Singing Our Faith)* CD 1 Track 6; "Bless Our Hands" *(Sing a Song of Joy!)* CD 2 Track 10; "Jesus' Hands Were Kind Hands," "This Is My Commandment," "Love One Another" *(Singing Our Faith).* For a list of all the music used in this program, see page OV-39.

Saint Elizabeth Ann

Elizabeth Ann was born in New York City. Her mother died when she was only three years old. Her father was a well-known doctor. He often helped sick people who could not afford treatment. He taught his little daughter to be kind to those who needed help.

When Elizabeth grew up, she married Will Seton and became the mother of five children. She stayed in New York City, and she often imitated her father's love for people in need. One cold winter day, she saw a group of little boys shivering as they drew their thin coats closer to themselves. She knew that many people in the city went to bed hungry each night. She had to do something to help. Because Elizabeth had been so blessed, she knew she had to share with people in need. Immediately she and a group of women began to gather clothing, food, and money for people in need. Elizabeth often visited with people in need and helped nurse sick people back to health.

While she was growing up, Elizabeth did not belong to the Catholic Church. But after her husband died, she became a Catholic. Later she became a sister and helped start Catholic schools in the United States. A sister is a woman who gives herself to God and loves and serves God in a special way. Many of the children who came to Elizabeth's school were from families in need. Elizabeth showed special love for those children. She taught the children in her school to love God and others.

People could see that Elizabeth's love and concern for all of God's people gave her a feeling of much peace and joy. They wanted to imitate her kind ways. We too can imitate Elizabeth's kindness. Then someday, like her, we too will be saints in heaven.

CHECKPOINT

- What new knowledge about the life of Saint Elizabeth Ann Seton do the children demonstrate?
- Are the children eager to imitate the kindness of Saint Elizabeth Ann Seton?

ENRICHING THE FAITH EXPERIENCE

1 Let the children take turns being a teacher. Ask them what they would teach about Jesus.

2 Saint Elizabeth Ann Seton was the mother of five children. She continued to love and pray for her children throughout her life. Talk about the important job that parents have of raising their children. Have the children draw pictures showing scenes from a day in the life of a parent or other caregiver.

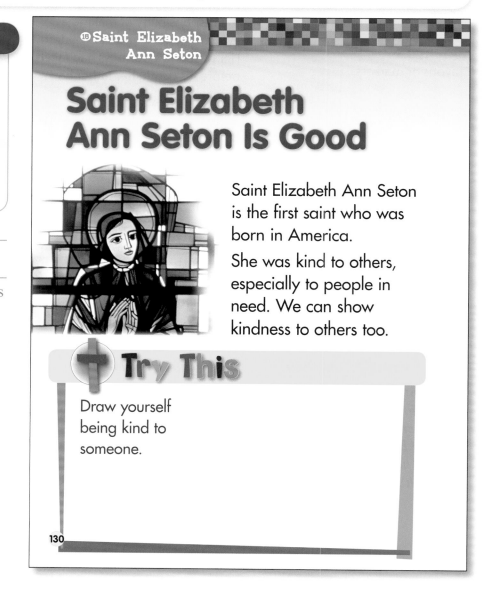

19 Saint Elizabeth Ann Seton

Saint Elizabeth Ann Seton Is Good

Saint Elizabeth Ann Seton is the first saint who was born in America.

She was kind to others, especially to people in need. We can show kindness to others too.

Try This

Draw yourself being kind to someone.

130

LESSON 16

Saint Nicholas Is Good

FEAST OF SAINT NICHOLAS, DECEMBER 6

Student Book pages 131–132

CATECHISM OF THE CATHOLIC CHURCH

The themes of this lesson correspond to the following paragraphs: 1932, 2030, 2443.

LEARNING OUTCOME

The children will be able to

- know that Saint Nicholas was a holy and kind bishop.

MATERIALS

- Crayons or markers
- Treats

Be sure to find out if any children in your classroom have food allergies and take these into consideration when planning snacks.

COMMENT

Although Nicholas is one of the most venerated saints in both the East and the West, little is known about him. He was born on the southeast coast of Asia Minor. Nicholas was ordained a priest and later became a bishop, known for his great piety and charity and for his miracles. The institution of Santa Claus may be one of the factors contributing to the popularity of Saint Nicholas. Because he was the patron saint of children, a custom developed in northern Europe of giving children presents on his feast day. This custom spread to North America where it is expressed in its current form, often dominating the celebration of Christmas.

CENTERING

Introduce to the children Saint Nicholas.

- ***How many of you have heard of Santa Claus?***
- ***How many of you have heard of Saint Nicholas?***
- ***Because* Santa *means "saint" in some languages, some people think that the name* Santa Claus *comes from* Saint Nicholas. *Would you like to hear a story about Saint Nicholas?***

SHARING

1. Read aloud the story "Saint Nicholas."

2. Explain the custom of putting out shoes for Saint Nicholas Day.

- ***In some countries, on the evening before his feast day, children put their shoes beside***

Saint Nicholas

Saint Nicholas lived a long, long time ago. His parents wanted a baby, so they prayed to God. When God answered their prayers and gave them a son, they called him Nicholas.

As Nicholas grew taller and stronger, he also grew in goodness. His mother and father died when he was young. They left him a lot of money. Nicholas wanted to use the money to help the poor.

When Nicholas grew up, he became a priest and then a bishop. A bishop helps God's people know and love God in many ways. As a bishop, Nicholas was able to help even more people.

Once Nicholas helped a man who had three daughters. In those days when a girl married, her father had to give a gift of money to her husband. The man didn't have money for his daughters, so they could not be married. Nicholas knew this. When it came time for the oldest girl to be married, he secretly went to the man's house at night. He threw a bag of gold coins in the window. Later he did the same thing for the second and the third daughters. Nicholas brought joy to everyone in the family.

Nicholas was especially kind to children. After he died and became a saint with God in heaven, he was named the patron saint of children.

their bedroom door for Saint Nicholas to fill. Our tradition of hanging stockings at Christmas is similar.

❸ Have the children open their books to **page 131.** Read aloud the text as the children follow along. Help the children do the activity. Then let them tell how they can be like Saint Nicholas.

- ***People in heaven are saints because they were like Jesus when they lived on earth. How was Saint Nicholas like Jesus?*** (He was kind and helped people in need.)
- ***What did Saint Nicholas try to do when he helped others?*** (Surprise them.)
- ***How can you be like Saint Nicholas?*** (Surprise others by doing something kind for them.)
- ***We can prepare for Christmas by imitating Saint Nicholas and surprising others with our kind deeds and our help.***
- ***Who can you surprise today? What kind deed will you do? How will you do the kind deed without anyone seeing you?***

ACTING

❶ Have the children bring their completed **page 131** to the Prayer Center. Tell the children to place it near the enthroned Bible as a sign of their commitment to surprising others with their kind deeds. Teach the children the following song to the tune of "Jolly Old Saint Nicholas."

Saint Nicholas

Holy, kind Saint Nicholas,
friendly, good, and wise—
When he could, he helped
the poor,
always by surprise.
We can be like Nicholas
and have a lot of fun,
Showing by our words
and deeds
love for everyone.

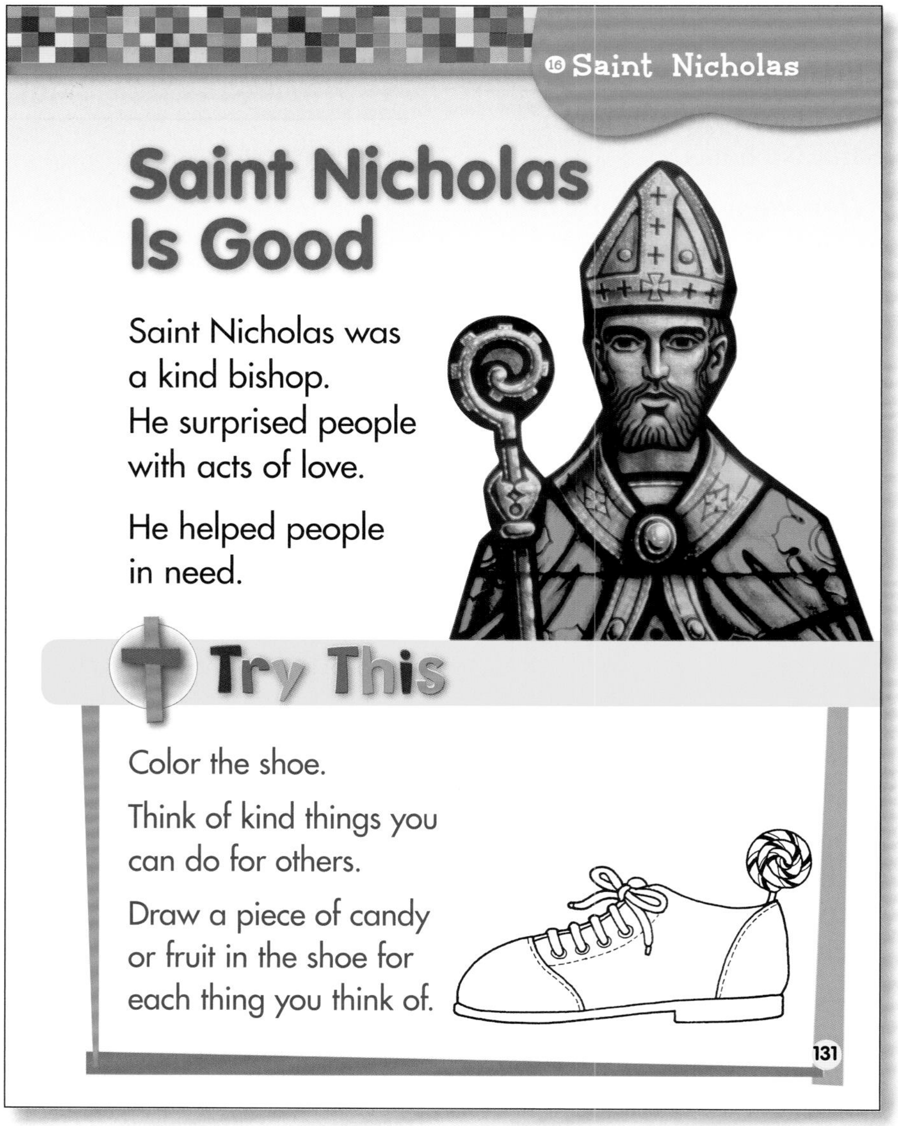
16 Saint Nicholas

Saint Nicholas Is Good

Saint Nicholas was a kind bishop.
He surprised people with acts of love.

He helped people in need.

Try This

Color the shoe.

Think of kind things you can do for others.

Draw a piece of candy or fruit in the shoe for each thing you think of.

131

2 Invite the children to pray together that God will bless their kind deeds as they prepare their hearts for Christmas. Pray the Advent Prayer, "Come Lord Jesus."

3 Share a small treat with the children in honor of Saint Nicholas.

4 Have the children take home the Family Page on **page 132** to share with their families.

CHECKPOINT

- What new knowledge about Saint Nicholas can the children demonstrate?

ENRICHING THE FAITH EXPERIENCE

1 Let the children make a card or a picture to give as a surprise gift to someone.

2 Decorate and fill stockings with treats to be distributed with holiday food baskets for people in need or to be delivered to those who are sick or homebound.

"Rescue the lowly and poor; deliver them from the hand of the wicked." Psalm 82:4

The Feast of Saint Nicholas in Families

Saint Nicholas: Model of Selfless Generosity

The story of Saint Nicholas is full of suspense, intrigue, and mystery. It is the story of three young girls in dire circumstances, their limited choices, and a last-minute anonymous rescue by a generous and holy man.

Legend has it that a man with three daughters fell on hard times. With each passing day the young women's prospects looked more and more bleak. It seemed that their only alternative was to sell themselves into a miserable life of servitude. Upon hearing of their plight, Nicholas, a fourth-century bishop of Myra, in what is now Turkey, secretly tossed a bag of gold into the girls' home on three consecutive nights. On the third night, the grateful father waited in hopes of learning the identity of this generous benefactor. But Nicholas outsmarted him by dropping the bag down the chimney. (We can see how the spirit of this generous man was adapted over time into the story of Santa Claus.)

History is full of stories of people who have been rescued from difficult circumstances. What makes this story so compelling is that the gifts were delivered in secret, under the cover of darkness. Nicholas's only desire was to be helpful, not to be recognized or thanked. And though his act of secret generosity eventually became known, people were inspired by his example to engage in secret acts of generosity and gift giving, even after his death. Saint Nicholas exemplified Jesus' advice to "Keep your deeds of mercy in secret." (Matthew 6:4)

Celebrating Your Values With Saint Nicholas

1. In many cultures children celebrate the feast of Saint Nicholas by putting their shoes near the front door on the evening of December 5 (the eve of his feast day), in the hope that their shoes will be secretly filled with treats during the night, such as gold-wrapped chocolate coins or an age-appropriate book that extols the virtue of generosity.

2. Tell your child the story of Saint Nicholas and have each family member put his or her name on a slip of paper. Then have each person secretly pick one of the names and do at least one secret good deed a day for that person during the following week.

3. Think of someone your family knows who could use encouragement. Send a note saying that you are thinking of and praying for that person and sign it, "Your secret friends." Remember that person in your prayers before meals during the coming week.

132

LESSON 17
Saint Bernadette Is Good

FEAST OF OUR LADY OF LOURDES, FEBRUARY 11

FEAST OF SAINT BERNADETTE, APRIL 16

Student Book page 133

CATECHISM OF THE CATHOLIC CHURCH

The themes of this lesson correspond to the following paragraphs: 966, 1674.

LEARNING OUTCOMES

The children will be able to
- know the story of Mary's appearance to Saint Bernadette at Lourdes.
- recognize that Mary helps us when we ask.

KEY TERMS

hymn—a holy song
Lourdes—place where Mary appeared to Saint Bernadette
procession—many people walking, usually in honor of someone or something
sacrifice—something difficult one chooses to do for the love of God
shrine—a place where people pray in honor of God, Mary, or a saint

MATERIALS

Crayons or markers

COMMENT

Bernadette Soubirous lived in Lourdes, France. Her parents had little money. On February 11, 1885, Bernadette went to collect firewood with her sister and a friend. Because Bernadette was not as strong as the other two girls, she stopped to rest while they walked ahead. Suddenly Bernadette saw a beautiful lady standing in a grotto in the rocks above her. The lady, who was the Blessed Mother, asked Bernadette to return to the cave again and again. Though Bernadette's parents did not believe her story, they allowed her to go back. During 18 visits, Mary made several requests of Bernadette, who was then only 14 years old. Mary told her to dig in the ground; she did and a spring of healing water came forth. Mary asked that a church be built on the site of the cave. She asked that people pray and sacrifice and have processions there. Bernadette gave all these messages to her parish priest and to the bishop, but they hesitated a long time because they did not believe her. Finally, they obeyed the messages. Several years later, Bernadette entered the convent of the Sisters of Charity and Christian Instruction at Nevers, France.

Now thousands of people each year make a pilgrimage to the Shrine of Our Lady of Lourdes in France. Many cures, some spiritual and some physical, still take place there. The Church has proclaimed more than 50 of these cures to be miraculous.

CENTERING

Let the children talk about surprise visits from relatives or friends.

- ***Have you ever had a surprise visitor? Who came? Tell us about it.***
- ***Today I have a story about a girl named Bernadette, who had a surprise visit from Mary, Jesus' mother.***

SHARING

1. Tell the children the story "Our Lady of Lourdes" on **page T351.**

2. Teach the Marian song "Immaculate Mary."

- ***Here is a song that people all over the world sing to honor Mary. Listen to the words while I sing the song for you.*** [Sing the song or play a recording of the song.]

Immaculate Mary

Immaculate Mary, your praises
we sing;
You reign now with Christ, our
Redeemer and King.
Ave, ave, ave Maria!
Ave, ave Maria!

- ***We call Mary* Immaculate Mary *because she always said yes to God. She never sinned but always showed her love for God.***

• ***When we say that Mary* reigns, *we mean that she is queen of heaven and earth.***

• ***We call Jesus* our Redeemer *because he saved us from sin.***

• **Ave Maria *means "Hail Mary."***

❸ Have the children open their books to **page 133.** Read aloud the text and encourage the children to follow along. Have the children color the picture. Tell them to pray as they color, asking Mary to help them think of good things to do to show their love for Jesus.

ACTING

Invite the children to prepare for prayer:

• ***Mary wants us to love God and others just as Jesus taught us. Mary will help us when we ask. We pray a special prayer in honor of Mary called the* Hail Mary. *Let's pray that prayer together now.***

Have the children open their books to the inside front cover. Invite them to pray the Hail Mary together.

CHECKPOINT

- How did the children respond to the story of Saint Bernadette's visions of Mary?
- How familiar are the children with Mary?

Our Lady of Lourdes

Long ago, Bernadette lived with her family in Lourdes, France. Her parents had very little money. They lived in a small, two-room home that was often cold and damp.

One day Bernadette went with her sister and a friend to gather firewood. They came to a cave near a flowing river. Bernadette was not strong and healthy. Her sister and friend left her behind to rest as they went farther on.

Suddenly, Bernadette's eyes grew wide with wonder as she looked at the small entrance to the cave. There she saw a beautiful lady dressed in blue and white. Stars were around her head and roses about her feet.

When Bernadette got home, she told her parents and friends, but they did not believe her. Bernadette went to the cave many times and saw the lovely lady again and again. The lady, who was really our Mother Mary, asked her to do a number of different things.

Mary told Bernadette to dig in the ground. When Bernadette did this, a cool, fresh spring of water came bubbling up. Mary told her to have the priests build a church at Lourdes. She wanted people to pray and to do kind and loving things even when they are hard to do. She also asked for processions. In processions people walk from one place to another, praying and singing to honor God.

After Bernadette had given all the messages to people who could do what Mary asked, she became a sister. A sister is someone who gives herself to God and loves and serves him in a special way.

Today thousands of people visit the beautiful Shrine of Our Lady of Lourdes. Sick people who have bathed in the waters have been made well again. Some people who were blind have been able to see, and some people who could not walk can walk again. Best of all, many, many people are healed in their hearts.

Processions take place every evening. While walking together in procession, the people sing a special song, "Immaculate Mary," to Our Lady. For many people this is a favorite hymn.

ENRICHING THE FAITH EXPERIENCE

❶ Teach the children the second verse of "Immaculate Mary" and explain the words. Then sing the song again, inviting the children to join in.

> **In heaven the blessed your glory proclaim;**
>
> **On earth we, your children, invoke your fair name.**
>
> **Ave, ave, ave Maria!**
>
> **Ave, ave Maria!**

• ***Who are the blessed in heaven?*** (Saints)

• ***When we say "proclaim," we mean to praise Mary.***

• ***When we say "invoke your fair name," we mean that we call upon Mary.***

❷ Help the children compose short prayers, such as the following:

> Saint Bernadette, pray for us.
>
> Jesus, bless us.
>
> Mary, we love you.

❸ Have the children suggest some good things they could do for Jesus as sacrifices. These might include letting someone go ahead of them in line, doing what their parents tell them right away, or sharing something with someone else.

❹ One of Mary's messages to Saint Bernadette was to pray the Rosary. Introduce the Rosary to the children. Show them a set of rosary beads. Tell them that we pray the Rosary by praying the Our Father, the Hail Mary, and the Glory Be to the Father. As we pray, we reflect on events in the lives of Jesus and Mary.

17 Saint Bernadette

Saint Bernadette Is Good

Mary visited Bernadette long ago.

Mary asked for prayers and sacrifices.

We do what Mary asks.

Try This

Color the rays yellow.

Color Mary's dress blue.

133

LESSON 18

Saint Valentine Is Good

SAINT VALENTINE'S DAY, FEBRUARY 14

Student Book page 134

CATECHISM OF THE CATHOLIC CHURCH

The themes of this lesson correspond to the following paragraphs: 1822–1823, 2030.

LEARNING OUTCOMES

The children will be able to

- know the story of Saint Valentine.
- imitate Saint Valentine by showing love to others.

MATERIALS

- Valentine or Cutout 4
- Construction paper
- Crayons or markers
- Scissors

COMMENT

Saint Valentine was a Roman priest who lived during the persecutions of the third century. He served God and his people by living the Gospels. Like so many Christians of his time, he was imprisoned and sentenced to death for his beliefs and practice of the faith. Tradition has it that while Valentine was in prison, he wrote letters to all his friends, telling of his love for them. It is believed that the custom of sending valentines began with these little messages from Saint Valentine.

CENTERING

Introduce Saint Valentine as a person who loved God and other people. [Show a valentine or Cutout 4 Heart.]

- ***Do you like to send valentines? Why?***
- ***Do you like to get valentines? Why?***
- ***What messages do you like to find in your valentines?***
- ***Valentines are named after a saint, Saint Valentine.***
- ***I have a story to tell you about Saint Valentine, who showed that he really loved God and other people as Jesus did.***

SHARING

1. Have the children open their books to **page 134.** Encourage the children to follow along as you read aloud the text. Have the children do the activity.

2. Tell the story of Saint Valentine.

- ***Valentine was a priest who loved God and worked hard for God's people. He read the Bible, in which Jesus tells us, "Love one another as I have loved you." Valentine found ways to do this. But like other Christians at that time, he was put in prison and sentenced to death by people who did not love God or believe in God.***
- ***A story has come down to us that while Valentine was in prison, he wrote letters to his friends telling of his love for them. We think that Saint Valentine's messages started the custom of sending valentines.***
- ***Saint Valentine's Day is a day when we can do something special for people we love. Love is from God. God shows us how we are to love. Let's celebrate Saint Valentine's Day in a special way today.***

ACTING

1. Ask the children to name some people they can thank this Valentine's Day for kindness they have shown them.

- ***Can you think of someone who has been kind to you?*** (Custodian, traffic guard, teacher's aides, volunteers in the cafeteria or playground) ***Let's make that person happy with a thank-you valentine.***

2 Distribute sheets of construction paper. Guide the children to draw and color valentines. Then help the children cut out the valentines and print their names on the back. As they work, play a song such as "I Like God's Love" *(Hi God!)*.

3 Tell the children to give their valentines to special people in their lives.

Songs

Play for the children any of these songs: "Love One Another" *(Singing a New Song)* CD 2 Track 4; "We Are Little Gifts" *(Sing a Song of Joy!)* CD 2 Track 6; "God's Love" *(Sing a Song of Joy!)* CD 2 Track 14; "Happy the Heart," "I Like God's Love," "Love That Is Kept Inside," *(Hi God!)*; "If I Were a Butterfly," "This Is My Commandment" *(Hi God 2)*; "God's Circle of Love" *(Hi God 3)*; "God Is Love" *(Sing a Song of Joy!)*; "This Is My Commandment," *(Hi God 2)*; "Love One Another" *(Sing a Song of Joy!)*. For a list of all the music used in this program, see page OV-39.

CHECKPOINT

- How did the children respond to the story of Saint Valentine?
- Are the children eager to share their valentine messages of thanks?

ENRICHING THE FAITH EXPERIENCE

1 Teach the poem "Love."

Love

God loves me,
[Clap, clap, point to self.]
And I love you.
[Clap, clap, point forward.]
We show love
[Clap, clap, fold hands over heart.]
By what we do.
[Clap, clap, hold out hands.]

M. Kathleen Glavich, S.N.D

2 On Valentine's Day, we send messages to our friends and families. Tell the children that people show their love for God by loving and caring for each other and for their families. Invite the children to pray for one another and for their families.

18 Saint Valentine

Saint Valentine Is Good

Saint Valentine showed his love for others by sending letters.
We honor Saint Valentine by sending valentines to loved ones.

Jesus said, "Love one another as I have loved you." Based on John 13:34

Try This

Color the valentine message.

Pray that God will help you love others.

134

LESSON 19
Saint Patrick Is Good

FEAST OF SAINT PATRICK, MARCH 17

Student Book page 135

CATECHISM OF THE CATHOLIC CHURCH
The themes of this lesson correspond to the following paragraphs: 234, 253–255, 1173.

LEARNING OUTCOMES
The children will be able to
- know the life of Saint Patrick.
- review the Three Persons of the Trinity.

MATERIALS
- Cutouts 6, 29
- Large shamrock cut from green construction paper (or outline of a shamrock drawn with chalk on the board)
- Picture of Saint Patrick
- Crayons or markers
- Background music for SHARING #3 (optional)

COMMENT
In many areas of the country, especially those with a significant population that has an Irish heritage, the feast of Saint Patrick needs no introduction. Parades, parties, cards, music, jigs, and leprechauns continue to be popular, even among those who are not of Irish descent. These festivities can help focus our attention on the missionary labors of this well-loved saint.

CENTERING

Introduce the shamrock by showing one.

- ***Does anyone know what this is?*** (A shamrock) ***Some people call it a three-leaf clover, and others say it could be a reminder of God. Some people say that Saint Patrick used a shamrock to teach the people of Ireland about God. Today I'd like to tell you a story about Saint Patrick.***

SHARING

1 Show a picture of Saint Patrick and tell the story "Saint Patrick" about him.

Saint Patrick

More than a thousand years ago in Britain, a country far away from here, there lived a 16-year-old boy named Patrick. One day something sad happened to him. He was captured by some soldiers and taken to live in an island country where he had never been before. The country he was taken to is called Ireland. Patrick was forced to work as a slave for six years. His job was to watch and to guard sheep day after day on the hillsides. Patrick found Ireland to be a beautiful country, and he often praised God for all its beauties. [Show Cutout 6 Mountains and hills.]

At the end of six years, Patrick escaped from Ireland by boat and managed to get back to Britain. By this time, he was 22 years old, old enough to decide that he wanted to become a priest. [Show Cutout 29 Priest.] After years of study, Patrick was ordained a priest, but he never forgot about the people in Ireland. He wanted to go back to teach them about God.

When Patrick was 42, he became a bishop. Soon after that, he decided to return to Ireland to help the people there learn about God. He took some missionary friends with him, and together they went from town to town, preaching the Good News about Jesus. They baptized the people in the name of the Father, and of the Son, and of the Holy Spirit. People say that Patrick used the shamrocks, which grew all over the fields and hillsides, to teach the people that we believe in God the Father, God the Son, and God the Holy Spirit. We say these words when we make the Sign of the Cross. [Make the Sign of the Cross, saying: "In the name of the Father, and of the Son, and of the Holy Spirit. Amen."]

2 Discuss the story and comment:

• ***Many of the people in Ireland were grateful that Patrick had come to tell them about God's love. They loved Patrick very much and when he died, they decided to remember him and to honor him by celebrating his feast in a special way every year. That is why this day is called Saint Patrick's Day.***

3 Have the children open their books to **page 135.** Encourage them to follow along as you read aloud the page. Guide them in doing the activity. You might wish to play appropriate music during this time, such as "All the Time" *(Bloom Where You're Planted)* or "Father, We Adore You" *(Hi God 2).*

ACTING

Invite the children to pray the following prayer with the gestures of the Sign of the Cross.

God the Father
[Right forefingers on forehead]

God the Son
[Right forefingers on heart]

God the Holy Spirit
[Right forefingers cross from left shoulder to right]

You are One.
[Both hands joined together as one]

With Saint Patrick, we pray for your blessing every day.
[Keep hands folded.]

CHECKPOINT

• How did the children respond to the story of Saint Patrick?

• Do the children show an initial familiarity with our belief in the Trinity?

19 Saint Patrick

Saint Patrick Is Good

A missionary travels to another country to tell people about God's love.

Saint Patrick was a missionary.

He taught the people of Ireland about God.

Try This

Color the cross.

Pray the Sign of the Cross.

135

ENRICHING THE FAITH EXPERIENCE

1 Tell the children that Saint Patrick is the patron saint of Ireland. Invite the children to pray for the people of Ireland. Have them respond with "Saint Patrick, pray for them."

That God may always bless the people of Ireland . . .

That God may give them peace . . .

That they may always live in God's love . . .

That faith may live in their hearts . . .

That they may always believe in God the Father, God the Son, and God the Holy Spirit . . .

2 Read a portion of the prayer from the Breastplate of Saint Patrick (the Lorica). Help the children make and decorate a breastplate or shield with a simple prayer of their own.

3 Teach and sing a song based on a prayer attributed to Saint Patrick, such as "Song of Saint Patrick" *(Singing Our Faith).* For a list of all the music used in this program, see **page OV-39.**

LESSON 20
Saint Julie Billiart Is Good

FEAST OF SAINT JULIE BILLIART, APRIL 8

Student Book page 136

CATECHISM OF THE CATHOLIC CHURCH
The themes of this lesson correspond to the following paragraphs: 925–927, 1123, 2030.

LEARNING OUTCOMES
The children will be able to
- become familiar with the life of Saint Julie Billiart.
- know more about what it means to have a vocation.

KEY TERMS
Notre Dame—"Our Lady," a name for Mary
vocation—God's plan for a person's life

MATERIALS
- Cutouts 29–30
- Flash card 2
- Crayons or markers

COMMENT
Julie Billiart was born on July 12, 1751, in Cuvilly, France. When she was only a child, God singled her out for the special work of spreading the Good News to his people. Teaching small children was the work dearest to Julie's heart. Even though crippled with a serious illness, she offered to prepare children's hearts for receiving first Holy Communion. Because of the great love for God that radiated from her countenance, she attracted both children and adults. Soon some young women joined her to help carry on her work. Together as religion teachers, they began to teach young girls. Julie was able to begin a new community of sisters that still exists today—the Sisters of Notre Dame de Namur. Saint Julie is also the spiritual mother of the Sisters of Notre Dame. Julie's spirit lives on in the sisters and in their work, especially in their ministry to people in need.

CENTERING

Introduce Saint Julie Billiart as one who was asked by Jesus to do something special for him.

- ***Have your friends ever asked you to do something special? What was it?***
- ***Today I have a story to tell you about a saint who was asked to do something special by Jesus. Listen to find out what it was.***

SHARING

1 Tell the story, "Saint Julie," that follows.

Saint Julie

Julie, or the "Smiling Saint" as she is often called, began at the age of nine to teach children "how good God is." [Show Flash card 2 *good*.]"I want plenty of little souls to teach them how to love and serve the good God," she said over and over. In her teens, Julie worked on a neighbor's farm. During the lunch break, she would tell stories of Jesus and sing songs. One day, she became very sick. This illness lasted many years. There were many days when Julie could not walk or talk. Yet she was happy that she could still prepare the parish children for their first Holy Communion. Little children gathered around to hear her explain how to receive Jesus in their hearts. The joy beaming from her face made all who met Julie love her. Already Jesus was calling her to help him spread his love to many people here on earth. Julie listened to Jesus and gladly did what he asked her to do.

Other women liked to be with Julie. They wanted to do good things for others and love God the way she did. God called Julie to become a sister and to begin a new group of sisters, the Sisters of Notre Dame. *Notre Dame* is a French phrase that means "Our Lady," another name for Mary. The sisters' special work was to spread the news of God's love among all people, but especially among people in need; they still do this today. "The good God loves the poor and so do I," Julie said. With all her heart, Julie always wished to teach others to live and to serve God. She had the joy of doing this throughout her life in many different ways.

2 Talk about God's call to people to be priests, deacons, sisters, and brothers and also to vocations to the married life and the single life.

- ***When you are older, some of you girls may hear Jesus call you and ask you to be sisters. The boys may be called and asked to be priests, deacons, or brothers.*** [Show Cutouts 29 Priest and 30 Sisters.] ***Some of you may hear Jesus call you to be married. Some will hear Jesus' call to follow him as a single person. Even now, you can pray that you will listen to Jesus and gladly do what he wants. We call this praying about one's vocation.***

3 Direct the children to **page 136** and read it aloud. Guide them to write the letter *O* in the empty blocks under the picture. Then read the completed sentence together. (God is good.)

20 Saint Julie Billiart

Saint Julie Billiart Is Good

Saint Julie Billiart was a Sister. She taught children to love God.

Sisters have a special love for God. Sisters share God's love with others.

Try This

G☐D IS G☐☐D

Write the letter O in the empty blocks.

Read what Saint Julie taught.

136

ACTING

Teach the children to sing and pray "Julie's Psalm" (by Sr. Melanie Svoboda, S.N.D.). Sing it for them and explain the words, and then have them sing along.

CHECKPOINT

- How did the children respond to the story of Saint Julie?
- Are the children eager to learn more about their vocations?

ENRICHING THE FAITH EXPERIENCE

1. Invite a sister or brother and a priest or deacon to speak to the children. Have him or her explain in simple terms his or her call and response to Jesus.

2. Discuss people's jobs and what leads people to know their vocation. Have the children draw pictures showing what they might do as adults.

3. Tell the children that Saint Julie is known as the "Smiling Saint" and explain why. Discuss the importance of being cheerful. Talk about things that the children can do to bring happiness to others.

Julie's Psalm

Let us sing a song to our Fa - ther.
As we walk a - long to our Fa - ther.
He is al - ways there; God is
ta - king gen - tle care; God is
love be - yond com - pare; God is
good. He is al - ways there; God is
ta - king gen - tle care; God is
love be - yond com - pare; God is good.

LESSON 21

Our Lady of Guadalupe Is Good

FEAST OF OUR LADY OF GUADALUPE, DECEMBER 12

FEAST OF SAINT JUAN DIEGO, DECEMBER 9

Student Book page 137

CATECHISM OF THE CATHOLIC CHURCH
The themes of this lesson correspond to the following paragraphs: 487, 971, 1674, 2619, and 2675.

LEARNING OUTCOMES
The children will be able to
- be familiar with the story of Our Lady of Guadalupe.
- learn to pray to Mary for help.

KEY TERMS
Aztec—a native people of Mexico
pilgrimage—a journey to visit a holy place
tilma—the Aztec word for cloak

MATERIALS
- Statue or picture of Mary, preferably of Our Lady of Guadalupe
- A rose or a picture of roses
- Crayons or markers

COMMENT

1. On December 9, 1531, Juan Diego, a 57-year-old Aztec man, was walking across the hills to church, as was his custom. On his way, he was surprised by the appearance of a beautiful lady. Dressed as an Aztec princess, she spoke to him and told him that she was the Immaculate Virgin Mary. She spoke of her desire for a shrine to be built on that very hill. She also spoke of her desire to help Juan Diego and his people: "Ask for my help. Here I will listen to people's prayers and I will help them."

The Lady asked Juan Diego to speak with the bishop on her behalf. Juan Diego spoke with the bishop several times, but was repeatedly rebuffed. The Lady told Juan Diego to persevere, finally offering to give him a sign to take to the bishop. Delayed by the illness of his uncle, Juan Diego saw the Lady again. She told him not to worry about his uncle; she had already healed him. She told Juan Diego to go and gather flowers from the hill. Juan Diego did as she said, even though he knew the place to be a rocky hill on which flowers never grew, especially in winter. On the hill he was surprised to find beautiful roses! He gathered the roses for the Lady and she arranged them in his *tilma*, the cloak he wore. Juan Diego took the roses to the bishop as the Lady directed. However, when he let the roses fall from his tilma, the bishop gasped as he saw an image of the Lady who had been appearing to Juan Diego. The bishop recognized the Lady immediately as the Blessed Virgin Mary. The bishop honored her request that a shrine be built at the site of her appearance on Tepeyac Hill. The image of Mary found on Juan Diego's tilma is called Our Lady of Guadalupe. To this day, the tilma is displayed in the basilica dedicated in her honor in Mexico City. Our Lady of Guadalupe is the patron saint of Mexico.

2. From the prayer of Mary found in the Gospel of Luke (Luke 1:46–55), we learn that Mary, the mother of Jesus, identifies herself with those who are poor. Mary's prayer, the Magnificat, sings the praises of God as the "Almighty" who does great things. God is praised because he has "lifted up the lowly." Mary's appearance to Juan Diego is further evidence of her special care for those who are in need.

CENTERING

Introduce the idea of Mary's care for us by talking about the need for help:

- ***Everybody asks for help from others sometimes. When you were younger and you needed help tying your shoes, whom did you ask? If you need help reading a book, whom might you ask? If you need help picking up your things, whom might you ask?***
- ***Adults ask others for help sometimes too. Moms and dads ask for help cleaning the house or setting the table for dinner. Teachers ask for help passing out papers or supplies.*** [Offer other examples as appropriate to your classroom setting.]
- ***Today you will learn about a saint who received a special visit from Mary. Mary asked this saint to help her because she wanted all people to know that they could turn to her for help.***

SHARING

1 Introduce the story of Our Lady of Guadalupe by talking about Juan Diego:

- ***Juan Diego lived long ago in Mexico. His family had lived on that land for a long time. He was from a community of people called the Aztecs. He had learned about Jesus from the Spanish people who had come to his land. Juan Diego became a Catholic.***

- ***Juan Diego was surprised by an amazing thing that happened to him. This event changed his life and the lives of many of the Aztec people. Let's listen carefully to his story.***

2 Tell the following story of "Our Lady of Guadalupe."

3 Tell the children about some of the ways in which people honor Our Lady of Guadalupe:

- ***December 12, the feast of Our Lady of Guadalupe, is an important day, especially to the people of Mexico. This is a day of prayer and celebration. People build altars in honor of Mary and bring their prayers to Mary. People travel to visit the church in Mexico dedicated to Our Lady of Guadalupe. When people travel to visit a holy place, it is called a*** **pilgrimage.** ***Sometimes people sing songs as they journey. They ask Mary to pray for them.***

Our Lady of Guadalupe

Juan Diego loved Jesus very much. He walked many miles to go to Mass each Saturday and Sunday to show Jesus his love. One day an amazing thing happened on his walk. It changed his life forever.

As Juan Diego walked, a beautiful lady appeared to him. She was dressed like one of his people, the Aztecs. He knew that she was a very important lady because she was dressed like an Aztec princess! The Lady spoke to him in his own language. She told him that she was the Virgin Mary, the Mother of God. She told Juan Diego that she wanted a beautiful church built on the hill because she wanted to help Juan Diego and his people. She said, "Ask for my help. Here I will listen to people's prayers, and I will help them." The Lady sent Juan Diego to tell the bishop, the Church leader, what she wanted.

Juan Diego did as the Lady asked. But the bishop did not believe him. Many times Juan Diego tried to convince the bishop to do as the Lady asked. Many times the bishop said no. Finally, the bishop told Juan Diego to ask the Lady for proof that she was the Mother of God. If Juan Diego brought proof of this, then the bishop would build the church as she asked.

Juan Diego left the bishop. However, before he could see the beautiful Lady again, his uncle got very sick. Juan Diego took good care of his uncle, but it looked like his uncle would die. Juan Diego ran to get the priest to help his uncle as he lay dying. On his way to get the priest, the beautiful Lady appeared again. She told Juan Diego that she would help his uncle. In fact, she had already made him well.

The Lady then told Juan Diego to gather flowers from the top of the hill. Juan Diego thought that this was a funny thing to ask. It was winter, and he knew that flowers do not grow in winter. He also knew that the hill was very rocky. Even in summer, flowers did not grow there. But Juan Diego did as the Lady asked. Imagine his surprise when he found roses at the top of the hill! He gathered the roses and brought them to the Lady.

The Lady put the roses in his cloak, which the Aztec people called a *tilma*. Juan Diego took the roses to the bishop. The roses, which Juan Diego found in the middle of winter, would convince the bishop that the Lady was Mary, the Mother of God. When Juan Diego opened his cloak to show the bishop the roses, the bishop looked even more surprised that Juan Diego expected. When he looked to see what the bishop saw, Juan Diego gasped too. On the tilma they saw a picture of the Lady that Juan Diego had met. The bishop knew immediately that the Lady was indeed Mary, the Mother of God.

The bishop agreed to build the church as Mary had asked. Today people continue to celebrate Mary's appearance to Juan Diego. People continue to visit the place where the church was built. They visit the church to ask Mary for her help. They also visit the church to see the cloak that Juan Diego wore. Even though the cloak is more than 450 years old, people can still see the picture of the Lady on the cloak. Mary, Our Lady of Guadalupe, will help us if and when we ask.

4 Discuss some times we might ask Mary for help:

- ***Mary is our Mother in heaven. She wants to help us. Mary helps us follow Jesus.***
- ***What are some things for which you might ask Mary's help?*** (Obeying parents and teachers, playing fairly with friends or brothers and sisters, making good choices.)

5 Ask the children to turn to **page 137** and read it aloud. Have them do the activity.

ACTING

Share a procession in honor of Our Lady of Guadalupe. Teach the children to sing a song in honor of Mary, such as "Holy Is Your Name" or "Magnificat/Sing Out, My Soul" *(Singing Our Faith).* Carry the statue or picture of Our Lady of Guadalupe and lead the children around the classroom as you sing the song.

Lead the procession to the Prayer Center and finish by praying together the Hail Mary.

CHECKPOINT

- How did the children respond to the story of Our Lady of Guadalupe?
- Are the children comfortable asking for Mary's help in prayer?

Our Lady of Guadalupe Is Good

Mary appeared to Juan Diego.

She spoke to him.

Mary told Juan Diego, "Ask for my help."

Mary will help us when we ask.

Try This

Color the picture of Our Lady of Guadalupe.

Ask Mary to help you.

ENRICHING THE FAITH EXPERIENCE

❶ Make tissue-paper flowers in honor of Our Lady of Guadalupe. Help the children cut a variety of flower shapes from colored tissue paper. Layer these flower shapes. Push a craft stem through the center of the layered flower shapes. Curl the craft stem to form the center of the flower. Twist and shape the tissue paper around the craft stem to form a flower. Have the children take the flowers home to remind them to turn to Mary when they are in need of help.

❷ Help the children dramatize the story of Mary's appearance to Juan Diego. Roles can include Mary, Juan Diego, Juan Diego's uncle and family members, the bishop, the bishop's servants, and onlookers.

❸ Mary's special concern for people in need is first evidenced in her prayer, the Magnificat (Luke 2:46–55). Pray this prayer with the children or teach and sing a song based on this prayer, such as "Holy Is Your Name" or "Magnificat/Sing Out, My Soul" *(Singing Our Faith)*. For a list of all the music used in this program, see **page OV-39.**

❹ Mary's special love for those in need is an important lesson of Our Lady of Guadalupe. Talk with the children about ways in which they can help those in need in their community. Plan and carry out a food drive or fundraiser for your parish food pantry or another local organization.

LESSON 22
Our Mother in Heaven Is Good

MARY'S MONTH, MAY

THE ASSUMPTION OF THE BLESSED VIRGIN MARY, AUGUST 15

Student Book page 138

CATECHISM OF THE CATHOLIC CHURCH
The themes of this lesson correspond to the following paragraphs: 964, 967–971.

LEARNING OUTCOMES
The children will
- know why we honor Mary.
- join in May devotions wholeheartedly.

KEY TERMS
Assumption—Mary's being taken to heaven, body and soul
queen—female ruler with great power

MATERIALS
- Altar with a picture or statue of Mary on it
- Empty vases on the altar
- One flower for each child (may be brought by the children)
- Crown of flowers for Mary
- Marian song (optional)
- BLM 32
- Crayons or markers

COMMENT
1. The practice of having special devotions in honor of Mary during May goes back many centuries. Pope Pius VII approved that special prayers be offered to Mary during May, and later Popes Leo XIII and Pius XII issued significant documents concerning devotions to Mary, including the custom of May devotions. Traditionally, May devotions include processions, the ceremony of crowning Mary as our Queen, and the setting up of May altars.

2. Mary's assumption into heaven, body and soul, was defined as a truth of faith by Pope Pius XII in 1950. In this doctrine, the Church teaches that when the Virgin Mary's earthly days were completed, she was taken up to heaven—body and soul. Since Mary was the Mother of God and shared in the redemptive mission of her Son, Catholics believe that God granted her this privilege. Truly this day must have been the most joyous of all days for Mary. As she entered heaven, we can well imagine that she proclaimed, "God who is mighty has done great things for me, holy is his name."

In the United States, the Church rejoices with Mary and celebrates with her by setting aside the feast of the Assumption as a Holy Day of Obligation on August 15. At Mass on this day, Catholic people celebrate this privilege given to Mary. We rejoice with all the angels and proclaim Mary as our Queen and Mother.

CENTERING

Show the picture or statue of Mary.

- ***Whose mother is this?*** (Jesus' mother)
- ***Mary became the mother of Jesus when she said yes to God. It was at the time when the angel visited her and told her that God wanted her to be the mother of his Son, Jesus.***

SHARING

1 Explain why we honor Mary as our Queen and Mother during the month of May.

- ***Jesus loved his mother very much. Joseph, who was Mary's husband and Jesus' foster father, loved Mary too.***
- ***Jesus wants us all to love Mary as he did, for she is our mother too.***
- ***Jesus loved his mother so much that he took her to heaven to be with him forever. He made her the queen of heaven and earth.***
- ***Because she was God's mother and had loved God so much, God took her to heaven, body and soul. God welcomed her and made her the queen of heaven and earth.***
- ***The angels and all the people in heaven welcomed her. They sang and rejoiced because she was with them. The celebration was a very happy one.***
- ***We celebrate this day of Mary's joy on August 15.***

We call it the feast of the Assumption.* Assumption *means "taken up to heaven." This is a Holy Day of Obligation for us, and we go to church to celebrate Mary's joy at Mass.

2 Discuss Mary's importance to us:

- ***Do you know anything about a queen?*** [Accept all reasonable responses.] ***In some countries the people have a queen, who is the greatest and first lady of the land. She can do many things for her people because she is queen. The people love her and show their love in special ways. When she visits them, they cheer, clap, and sing for her. They have parades for her, and bands play in her honor.***
- ***Mary is our Queen and our Mother. We show our love for her in special ways. The best way to show our love for her is to try every day to become like her Son, Jesus. How can we become like Jesus?*** (Pray and ask God to help us; do what God wants; show love for other people.)
- ***Because May is Mary's month, we do special things during May to show our love for Mary. Some ways in which we honor Mary in May are through special processions, songs, and May altars. We honor her as our Queen by placing a crown made from flowers on a statue of Mary.***

3 Have the children open their books to **page 138**. Read aloud the text and encourage the children to follow along. Help the children do the activity.

4 Prepare the children for a May procession in honor of Mary.

- Point out the May altar you have set up.
- Have each child carry a flower to the altar as a gift for Mary.
- Show the children how to process around the room to the altar and how to place their flowers in the vases.
- Appoint one child to carry the crown and show him or her where to put it. If you have a statue, the crown can be placed on Mary's head. If a picture is used, lay the crown in front of it.
- Teach the song you will sing during the procession, for example, "Immaculate Mary."

22 Mary

Our Mother in Heaven Is Good

During the month of May, we honor Mary.

Mary is our Queen and Mother.

Mary prays to God for us.

Try This

Connect the dots to make a shrine for Mary.

Color the picture.

138

ACTING

Pray together this May devotion:

Procession and Song

All: Immaculate Mary, your praises we sing;
You reign now with Christ, our Redeemer and King.
Ave, ave, ave Maria!
Ave, ave Maria!

After the procession, the children stand around the altar. They take turns putting their flowers in the vases. Then the child carrying the crown places it on the statue of Mary. A recording of a Marian song may be played during this time.

Prayer

Teacher: Let's pray together to Mary. After each prayer petition, we'll pray together, "Mary, our Queen and our Mother, pray for us." [Have the children repeat this response with you.]

Teacher: Dear Jesus, we thank you for giving us Mary as our Queen and Mother. Help us love her as you did. Help us love God Our Father and others as Mary did. When God asks us to obey, we will go to Mary and pray . . .

All: Mary, our Queen and our Mother, pray for us.

Teacher: When God asks us to share with others, we will go to Mary and pray . . .

All: Mary, our Queen and our Mother, pray for us.

Teacher: When God asks us to be helpful at home, we will go to Mary and pray . . .

All: Mary, our Queen and our Mother, pray for us.

Teacher: When God asks us to say that we are sorry for something we did, we will go to Mary and pray . . .

All: Mary, our Queen and our Mother, pray for us.

Song

All: Immaculate Mary, your praises we sing;
You reign now with Christ, our Redeemer and King.
Ave, ave, ave Maria!
Ave, ave Maria!

CHECKPOINT

- Do the children know why we honor Mary?
- Did the children enjoy the celebration honoring Mary?

ENRICHING THE FAITH EXPERIENCE

1 Give the children copies of BLM 32 May Altar and let them talk about May altars. Then read the directions to them and have them color Mary's dress and the flowers. Direct them to cut out the altar, take it home, and hang it in a place where they pray.

- ***BLM 32 May Altar***

Remind the children to pray to Mary whenever they look at the May altar. Suggest that they ask their parents about making a real May altar in their homes.

2 Teach one of the Marian hymns sung in your parish, for example "Virgin, Full of Grace," "Hail, Holy Queen Enthroned Above," "Sing of Mary," or "Yes, We Will Do What Jesus Says" (*Stories and Songs of Jesus*). For a list of all the music used in this program, see **page OV-39.**

3 Have the children draw pictures of themselves doing something to become like Jesus or to show love for Mary.

4 Pray the Hail Mary.

5 Help the children compose short prayers to Mary, such as the following:

Mary, Queen of Angels, pray for us.

Mary, Queen of Heaven, pray for us.

Mary, our Queen and Mother, pray for us.

Mary, full of joy, pray for us.

GUIDELINES FOR MEETING WITH PARENTS

REASONS FOR THE MEETING

- To help parents realize their important role in shaping their children's religious lives
- To suggest ways parents can make the most of the ordinary opportunities that abound at home to nurture family faith
- To afford parents an opportunity to reflect on their experience in the family, to share with other parents, and to begin to see other parents as a resource and a community with shared values
- To help parents understand their children's level of human growth and become aware of factors contributing to their religious development
- To explain the kindergarten religion program and parental involvement

NUMBER OF MEETINGS

The number of meetings will vary according to the parents' needs and interest. The following suggestions are for one meeting. Scheduling meetings at two different times provides more opportunities for all parents to attend.

PRACTICAL POINTS TO CONSIDER

1. Schedule a meeting near the beginning of the year. Select a convenient time for the parents. Invite a parish priest to participate.

2. Create a comfortable atmosphere for the meeting.

- Select a suitable meeting place.
- Plan to welcome each person while committee members attend to registration, name tags, and so on.

3. Decide how to publicize your meeting. Announce the meeting in parish bulletins, letters to parents. Highlight its benefits to parents and clearly state the following details:

- why it is being held
- who is involved
- what will be included
- when and where it will take place
- how long it will last
- whom to contact for further information

Always follow up written announcements with a personal invitation.

4. Plan the way you will pray together during the meeting.

- Use scriptural or liturgical prayer.
- Include a media presentation, such as slides with music or narration.

5. Provide time for adequate exchange of thoughts and feelings.

6. Include parents in an evaluation of the meeting. You may wish to distribute a form for written comments.

Parent-Catechist Meeting

Ordinary Opportunities to Nurture Family Faith at Home

PROPOSED MEETING OUTLINE

I. Introduction
- **A.** Welcome
- **B.** Focus on the parents' unique and important role
- **C.** Brief overview of the meeting
- **D.** Prayer

II. Presentation of "How to Make Our Homes Places of Life and Love"

Refreshments

III. Presentation of "Fostering the Religious Growth of Kindergartners"

IV. Discussion

V. Closing prayer

CONSIDERATIONS WHEN PLANNING THE PRESENTATIONS

1. Families come in many forms and styles. One thing attending families will have in common is a strong love for their kindergarten child. This concern and care make this meeting a great opportunity to nurture the faith of each family member.

2. Family schedules are demanding. Respect the parents' time by preparing well and starting and ending as scheduled.

3. Many adults in attendance will not have had a thorough catechetical formation. They may even be indifferent to religion.

4. Parents typically value gaining insight into how families function and the developmental stages their children are going through.

5. Raising children in the faith often demands a willingness to make choices as a family that go against the culture.

6. Many parents crave support and authorization to step into their role as spiritual leaders in their families.

7. Parents crave what's best for their children. They may need help in seeing how good moral and spiritual development are essential elements in providing what's best.

8. Families may be aware of their own story of faith, but will benefit from understanding how our own stories are tied into the larger story of the Church. They have a noble mission to bring Christ to their homes, workplaces, neighborhoods, and the world.

SAMPLE MEETING

Part I: Introduction (15 minutes)

A Welcome the parents.

- Express your joy in seeing them.
- Thank them for coming; recognize the difficulties they may have encountered in arranging to be present. Invite them to settle quietly in their seats, take a few deep breaths, and let go of the cares of the day.
- Have the parents introduce themselves to the people sitting around them.
- Introduce the catechists in the kindergarten program.

B Focus on the parents' unique and important role.

- Express your awareness of the parents' deep concern for their children.
- Remind them that they are all recipients of God's grace throughout the day, especially through the sacraments—Baptism first of all, Eucharist, Reconciliation, Confirmation, and possibly Matrimony. Remind them that as their children's first teachers of the faith, they have already been involved in the religious development of their children. Give specific examples of how parents help shape their children's faith through actions of love, acceptance, respect, as well as by praying and worshiping together.
- Remind them that their children have received the gift of faith through Baptism and are, therefore, open to God and capable of perceiving his presence. Parents are in a unique position to guide them to encounter God in the ordinary moments of daily life.
- Explain that parents teach the faith in many ways, most powerfully through their example. When they respond to Christ's call in their daily lives, their children learn to love Christ and listen to him. Parents are given a sacred trust to nurture the tender faith of their children.

C Briefly outline the meeting and your expectations for it.

D Pray together.

• Set the tone of the meeting with a prayer experience that will heighten the parents' appreciation of the family as a community of life and love. Create a prayerful environment by fashioning a small prayer center on which you place an open Bible, some back-to-school items like crayons and pencils, a copy of the *God Loves Us* Student Book, and a candle. Use lighting, music, and visual effects to enhance the mood and the message.

• As you or a designated person lights the candle, explain that Jesus is the light of the world, the one who lights our way on the path to peace.

Part II: How to Make Our Homes Places of Life and Love (20 minutes)

A As a way of introducing the theme and helping parents get to know one another, have them think back to when they were the same age as their kindergartners. If this is too much of a strain on the memory, they can recall themselves at any grammar-school age. Ask them to recall a person in their life at that time who had a major positive influence on their spiritual life.

As they think about that person, have them consider three questions: What was the main spiritual lesson this person taught me? What methods did that person use to pass on that lesson? What lesson does that hold for me as someone called to nurture the faith of my child? Give them a chance to consider these questions privately first and then have them gather in groups of three or four to talk about the three questions. Give each person a few minutes to share. When time is up, solicit a few responses from the group to underscore that

• many of us were influenced by family members, particularly our parents.

• the methods they used were most likely the ordinary opportunities of daily family life.

• the lesson for parents is that we, too, can use our life as a family as a means of nurturing our child's faith.

(If you are going to split this material into two sessions, you might read the story "The Shoelace" from John Shea's *Elijah at the Wedding Feast and Other Tales* (ACTA Publications, 1999, www.actapublications.com, 800-397-2282) on **page T373.**)

B Explain the purpose of a family and how it functions. An excellent source for this topic is the apostolic exhortation of Pope John Paul II entitled *On the Role of the Christian Family in the Modern World* (1981). In it the Pope describes the Christian family as an intimate community of life and love whose mission is to guard, reveal, and communicate love. In this way the family will be a living reflection of God's love for his people and his Church. The document is divided into four sections:

• Bright Spots and Shadows for the Family Today

• The Plan of God for Marriage and the Family

• The Role of the Christian Family

• Pastoral Care of the Family

You might also refer to Pope Benedict XVI's encyclical *God Is Love* (2006), John Paul II's *Letter to Families* (1994), and the United States bishops' statement *Follow the Way of Love: A Pastoral Message to Families* (1993). These are available from the United States Conference of Catholic Bishops, 3211 Fourth Street N.E., Washington, DC 20017; www.usccb.org.

C Suggest ways in which parents can make their homes a domestic church. Combine ideas from the apostolic exhortation of Pope John Paul II and the following outline.

1. Describe the modern home environment.

- centers for supplying basic needs of food, clothing, shelter, and rest
- electronic media centers for TV, the Internet, electronic games, and entertainment
- single-parent families, blended families, multigenerational families

2. Explain how the home can be a domestic church, a school of virtues, and a place where faith is nurtured.

- center of religious life in the early Christian tradition
- place where family members recognize and celebrate God's presence in their lives
- faith-filled homes that strengthen the parish church and help bring Christ to the world

3. Have parents name factors in modern life that can be a threat to families. (List them for all to see.) They will likely list such topics as time pressures, economic stresses, the effect of media on family life, and peer pressure. Have a few of your own ideas ready to mention to get the sharing started or to include if they are not mentioned.

4. Now have parents name factors that encourage faith sharing in the home. You will likely get answers such as mutual respect, family prayer, good communication, the faith example of the parents, and signs and symbols of the faith in the home (e.g., crucifixes, statues, religious art, a family Bible.)

Break for Refreshments (10 minutes)

Part III: Fostering the Religious Growth of Kindergartners (20 minutes)

A Explain the characteristics of kindergarten children and how they affect religious development. The chart "Kindergartners . . ." on **page OV-20** may provide ideas for this part of the presentation. The use of slides that exemplify each trait would enhance this segment.

B Present a brief overview of the *God Loves Us* kindergarten program. Show how it fosters the religious growth of kindergarten children by recognizing their characteristics and meeting their needs.

C Give examples of the different types of activities included in the kindergarten program.

- prayer with gestures
- dramatization
- singing and listening to religious music
- creative movement
- storytelling
- psalm prayers
- art activities that express religious concepts
- joyful celebrations
- group sharing
- sensory experiences
- fun activities that encourage self-control and quieting the self as an important aspect of prayer
- symbols as reminders of religious experiences and truths learned

Show children's art projects and explain their purpose.

D Describe parental involvement.

- Point out the location of the Family Pages and show a sample page in the Student Book.
- Explain that the Family Pages tell what the children were taught in that chapter. They also include a brief story for the parent to reflect on and suggest home activities to extend the concepts and experiences of each class session.
- Ask parents to commit to reading the Family Pages and to use some of the suggestions for the chapter as a way to nurture their children's faith.
- Point out the Note to Families on **pages v–vi** of the Student Book and stress the importance of this message.
- Call attention to the Family Feature pages at the end of each unit and encourage the families to read and use them.
- Encourage the parents to explore the support information and resources for families available at www.ChristOurLife.org and www.FindingGod.org.

Part IV: Discussion (15 minutes)

Gather the people into their groups again. You may want to ask some parents before the meeting to serve as group leaders to facilitate discussion. Use the following questions to begin discussion.

- When and how does your family pray together?

- What kind of faith sharing takes place in your family?
- Name one or more ordinary ways you nurture faith in your home.
- How can you help your family be more aware of God's presence?
- What challenges do you foresee in trying to make your home a place in which to celebrate God's presence? What responses to those challenges have you found to be the most effective?

Part V: Closing (10 minutes)

A Evaluation

Give parents an evaluation form on which they can assess the strengths and weaknesses of the different parts of the meeting. Include a question that asks them to identify the part of the meeting they found most valuable. Use the responses as guides to improve the next meeting.

B Closing Prayer

Give parents a copy of the following prayer. Invite them to join you in a closing prayer. Have the left side of the room read aloud *Side 1.* Have the right side of the room read aloud *Side 2.* Ask a volunteer to read aloud the passage from the Letter of Saint Paul to the Ephesians.

Leader: Let us conclude this time together by pausing to give thanks for the graces we receive from God each day. We begin our prayer in the name of the Father, and of the Son, and of the Holy Spirit.

All: Amen.

Leader: We give you praise and thanks, O God, for all the ways, large and small, in which you reveal yourself to us. We ask you to help us recognize you in the ordinary moments of daily life and use the grace you bestow on us in service of others.

Side 1: Lord, help us know you in the breaking of the bread at Mass and also in the meals we share around our kitchen table.

Side 2: Lord, help us hear you in the Word of God proclaimed in Scripture and also in the word you speak through the little ones we nurture and cherish.

Side 1: Lord, help us see you in the faces of our Church leaders and also in the faces of each member of our families, and in the face we see in the mirror each day.

Side 2: Lord, help us touch you in the sacraments we celebrate and also in the tears we wipe away, the hands we hold, and the goodnight kisses we give.

Leader: As we listen to the following reading from Saint Paul, imagine that he is addressing these words directly to you.

Reader: A reading from the Letter of Saint Paul to the Ephesians 1:15–21.

Leader: Let's pause for a moment and reflect silently on the richness of God's grace that dwells in us. [Pause.] Remembering that we are all children of the one Father, let us pray together in the words that Jesus taught us—Our Father, . . .

All: God our Father, you promised to dwell among us. Help us recognize you at our kitchen table, welcome you into our family fun, and discover you whenever we show love for one another. May we grow in awareness of your presence and cherish it always. We ask this in confidence because we know you love us. Amen.

The Shoelace

By John Shea

In a moment of madness, I agreed to do a series of workshops on storytelling in Ireland. On the sleepless plane ride to Dublin, I pondered the real folly captured by the phrase "bringing coals to Newcastle." What idiocy was I undertaking—telling and talking about stories in the spiritual home of storytelling?

But the people were gracious and forgiving, and the humble truth soon became evident. I was there to learn, not to teach.

On the first day, I sat in a small group as a woman of about seventy-five told a story from her childhood. This is her story, flattened by print and my memory lapses, but impoverished most of all by the absence of her wonderful, soft, lilting voice.

"I was one of fourteen children," she said, "and my mother tried to put order in everything that had to do with our brood. Every Sunday we would walk to the church about three miles away. But before we set out, there was a home ritual every bit as set in its ways as what the priest did at Mass.

"There was only one mirror in the house, and my mother would stand in front of it. Then each of us would queue up and pass between my mother and the mirror. As we did, she would straighten us up and comb our hair. After this combing we could go out and play. When everyone was done we would gather and walk to church.

"One Sunday, I was about third in the queue. My mother looked down the line and saw that my little sister did not have a shoelace in her shoe. My mother looked at me and said. 'Go back and get your sister a shoelace.'

"But I did not want to lose my place, so I didn't budge. When my turn came, I stepped between my mother and the mirror. My mother said nothing. She simply combed my hair and off I went to play.

"I came in a little while later. My little sister—the one without the shoelace—was between my mother and the mirror. My mother bent down and took a shoelace out of her own shoe and put it in the shoe of my little sister. When I saw this, I went into the back of the house and got a shoelace. I came out and knelt at my mother's feet and put the shoelace in her shoe. As I did this and while she was combing the hair of my little sister, she reached down with her free hand and stroked my hair."

The woman stopped telling her story and looked down. The people in the group said nothing until one man asked, "Are you done?"

She nodded. Then the man began to tell one of his stories.

After the session, I was walking around outside when the woman who had told the story walked by. I stopped her and said, "Your story blew me away."

"What?" she asked, and I realized that my "Yankism," as they called them, was causing her bewilderment.

"It was rich and moving," I explained. "I don't know what it means but I was moved by it."

"It was stupid," she said. "I shouldn't have told it."

"No," I replied. "We are all better for having heard it."

"Thank you," she said, and then she walked on.

Coda

While I was conducting the workshops I would pass the long, civilized Irish afternoon breaks sitting under a tree smoking a cigar. On the fourth day, the woman who had told the story approached me.

"Where is your cigar?" she asked.

"It's in my room," I answered, "but I am too tired to go get it."

"I noticed you didn't have one, so I bought you a cigar," she said. She handed me a cigar.

"Thank you," I said.

I looked down and fiddled with the cellophane wrapper. When I looked up, the woman was gone. As I am smoking the cigar—thinking of nothing in particular—it suddenly dawns on me: the cigar is the shoelace, the cigar is the shoelace.

During the next session, I saw the woman seated in the back of the room. As soon as I was finished, I pushed through the crowd and found her. I loomed over her and said with way too much enthusiasm, "The cigar is the shoelace, the cigar is the shoelace!"

She looked up at me and stuck out her chin. "I know that," she said. She looked down and then looked back up at me. "It was a pact with my mother," she said with emotion. "It was a pact with my mother."

And as she said this, she hit her heart twice.

Ave Maria Press
P.O. Box 428
Notre Dame, IN 46556
(800) 282-1865
www.avemariapress.com

The Center for Learning
P.O. Box 910, Evergreen Road
Villa Maria, PA 16155
(800) 767-9090
www.centerforlearning.org

Coronet, the Multimedia Company
A Division of Phoenix Learning
2349 Chaffee Dr
St. Louis, MO 63146
(800) 221-1274
www.phoenixlearninggroup.com

The Crossroad Publishing Company
16 Penn Plaza, Suite 1550
New York, NY 10001
(212) 868-1801
www.cpcbooks.com

Daughters of St. Paul
See Pauline Books & Media

Educational Activities, Inc.
P.O. Box 87
Baldwin, NY 11510
(800) 797-3223
www.edact.com

Franciscan Communications
See St. Anthony Messenger Press

G.I.A. Publications, Inc.
7404 S. Mason Avenue
Chicago, IL 60638
(800) GIA-1358(442-1358)
www.giamusic.com

Liguori Publications
1 Liguori Drive
Liguori, MO 63057-9999
(800) 325-9521
www.liguori.org

The Liturgical Press
P.O. Box 7500
St. John's Abbey
Collegeville, MN 56321
(800) 858-5450
www.litpress.org

Liturgy Training Publications
1800 N. Hermitage Avenue
Chicago, IL 60622-1161
(800) 933-1800
www.ltp.org

Live Oak Media
P.O. Box 652
Pine Plains, NY 12567-0652
(800) 788-1121
www.liveoakmedia.com

Loyola Press
3441 N. Ashland Avenue
Chicago, IL 60657
(800) 621-1008
www.loyolapress.com

National Catholic Educational Association
1077 30th Street NW, Suite 100
Washington, DC 20007-3852
(202) 337-6232
www.ncea.org

National Conference for Catechetical Leadership
125 Michigan Ave., NE
Washington, DC 20017
(202) 884-9753
www.nccl.org

New City Press
202 Cardinal Road
Hyde Park, NY 12538-2903
(800) 462-5980
www.newcitypress.com

North American Liturgy Resources (NALR)
See Oregon Catholic Press

Oblate Media and Communication
1509 Washington Avenue, Suite 550
St. Louis, MO 63103
(800) 233-4629
www.videoswithvalues.org

Orbis Books
Walsh Building, Box 308
Maryknoll, NY 10545
(800) 258-5838
www.maryknollmall.org

Oregon Catholic Press (OCP)
P.O. Box 18030
Portland, OR 97218-0030
(800) 548-8749
www.ocp.org

Our Sunday Visitor Publishing
200 Noll Plaza
Huntington, IN 46750
(800) 348-2440
www.osv.com

Pauline Books & Media
50 St. Paul's Avenue
Boston, MA 02130
(800) 876-4463
www.pauline.org

Paulist Press
997 Macarthur Boulevard
Mahwah, NJ 07430
(800) 218-1903
www.paulistpress.com

Paulist Productions
Box 1057
17575 Pacific Coast Highway
Pacific Palisades, CA 90272
(310) 454-0688
www.paulistproductions.org

Resource Publications, Inc.
160 E. Virginia Street, # 290
San Jose, CA 95112-5876
(888) 273-7782
www.rpinet.com

Sacred Heart Kids' Club
869 South Rimpau Blvd.
Los Angeles, CA 90005
(323)935-2372
www.sdsh.org/kidsClub/kidsclub.html

St. Anthony Messenger Press
Franciscan Communications
28 W. Liberty Street
Cincinnati, OH 45202-6498
(800) 488-0488
www.catalog.americancatholic.org

St. Mary's Press
702 Terrace Heights
Winona, MN 55987-1318
(800) 533-8095
www.smp.org

Sheed & Ward
Rowman & Littlefield Publishers, Inc.
4501 Forbes Blvd., Suite 200
Lanham, MD 20706
(800) 462-6420
www.rowmanlittlefield.com/Sheed

Sophia Institute Press
P.O. Box 5284
Manchester, NH 03108
(800) 888-9344
www.sophiainstitute.com

Spoken Arts, Inc.
195 South White Rock Road
Holmes, NY 12531
(800) 326-4090
www.spokenartsmedia.com

Treehaus Communications, Inc.
906 West Loveland Ave. P.O. Box 249
Loveland, OH 45140
(800) 638-4287
www.treehaus1.com

Twenty-Third Publications
1 Montauk Ave Suite 200
New London, CT 06320
(800) 321-0411
www.twentythirdpublications.com

United States Conference of Catholic Bishops
3211 Fourth Street, NE
Washington, DC 20017
(800) 235-8722
www.usccbpublishing.org

Vision Video
P.O. Box 540
Worcester, PA 19490
(800) 523-0226
www.visionvideo.com

Weston Woods Studios
143 Main Street
Norwalk, CT 06851
800-243-5020
www.teacher.scholastic.com/products/westonwoods

World Library Publications
J.S. Paluch Company, Inc.
3708 River Rd, Suite 400
Franklin Park, IL 60131
(800) 566-6150
www.wlp.jspaluch.com

MUSIC SOURCES

G.I.A. Publications, Inc.
7404 S. Mason Avenue
Chicago, IL 60638
(800) 442-1358
www.giamusic.com

World Library Publications (WLP)
J.S. Paluch Company, Inc.
3708 River Rd, Suite 400
Franklin Park, IL 60131
(800) 566-6150
www.wlp.jspaluch.com

Oregon Catholic Press Publications (OCP)
P.O. Box 18030
Portland, OR 97218-0030
(800) 548-8749
www.ocp.com

Pauline Books & Media
50 St. Paul's Avenue
Boston, MA 02130
(800) 876-4463
www.pauline.org

Mary Lu Walker Albums & Songbooks (MLW)
http://home.stny.rr.com/maryluwalker

A

B

C

I

J

Q

R

S

T

U

V

W

Y

Z

M

P

R

S

T

W

ACKNOWLEDGMENTS FOR GIA CD

The Best of Joe Wise: Music for Kids Volume II.
© 2003 **GIA Publications, Inc.**
Available at www.giamusic.com
CD #578

Singing Our Faith. © 2002 **GIA Publications, Inc.**
Available at www.giamusic.com
CD #495

Track 1: "A Place in the Choir" by Joe Wise. ***The Best of Joe Wise: Music for Kids Volume II.*** © 2003 **GIA Publications, Inc.**

Track 2: "We Are Walking In the Light." Text: traditional. Tune: James Moore, Jr. © 1987 GIA Publications, Inc. ***Singing Our Faith.*** © 2002 **GIA Publications, Inc.**

Track 3: "Halle, Halle." Music: Traditional Caribbean, arr. by John L. Bell. © 1990 Ional Community, GIA Publications, Inc. Agent verses and acc. by Marty Haugen. © 1993 GIA Publications, Inc. ***Singing Our Faith.*** © 2002 **GIA Publications, Inc.**

Track 4: "Jesus in the Morning." Text and Tune: African-American folk song. ***Singing Our Faith.*** © 2002 **GIA Publications, Inc.**

Track 5: "You Have Put On Christ." Text: Rite of Baptism for Children. © ICEL. Music: Howard Hughes, SM. © 1977 ICEL. ***Singing Our Faith.*** © 2002 **GIA Publications, Inc.**

Track 6: "Love One Another." Text: Matthew 5:38–48; Rob Glover b.1950. Tune: Rob Glover, b.1950. © GIA Publications, Inc. ***Singing Our Faith.*** © 2002 **GIA Publications, Inc.**

Track 7: "All Night, All Day." Text: African-American spiritual. Tune: All Night, All Day with refrain, African-American traditional. Acc. by Robert J. Batastini, b. 1942. © 2000 GIA Publications, Inc. ***Singing Our Faith.*** © 2002 **GIA Publications, Inc.**

Track 8: "Over My Head." Text: African-American spiritual. Tune: African-American spiritual. Arr. by John L. Bell, b. 1949. © 1998 Iona Community, GIA Publications, Inc., agent. ***Singing Our Faith.*** © 2002 **GIA Publications, Inc.**

Track 9: "Immaculate Mary." Text: st. 1, Jeremiah Cummings, 1814-1866; alt. st. 2–7, Brian Foley, b.1919. © 1971 Faber Music, Ltd. Tune: Lourdes Hymn, 11 11 with refrain; Grenoble, 1882. ***Singing Our Faith.*** © 2002 **GIA Publications, Inc.**

Track 10: "O How Good is Christ the Lord" Text: Puerto Rican traditional. Tune: Oh Que Bueno Es Jesus, 7 7 7 6 6 6 7 6 Puerto Rican traditional. Acc. by Robert J Batastini, b. 1942. © 2000 GIA Publications, Inc. ***Singing Our Faith.*** © 2002 **GIA Publications, Inc.**

Track 11: "The Lord, the Lord, the Lord Is My Shepherd" Text: African-American spiritual. Tune: The Lord Is My Shepherd, irregular; African-American spiritual. Harm. by Austin C. Lovelace, b.1919. © 1956 GIA Publications, Inc. ***Singing Our Faith.*** © 2002 **GIA Publications, Inc.**

Track 12: "Sing, Sing, Praise and Sing!" Text: Elizabeth Syré, South Africa, alt. Tune: Sing, Sing, Praise and Sing, 6 6 with refrain; South African traditional. Adapt. by Elizabeth Syré; acc. by Robert N. Roth. © 2000 GIA Publications, Inc. ***Singing Our Faith.*** © 2002 **GIA Publications, Inc.**

Track 13: "People of God/Alleluia." Text: David Haas, b.1957. Tune: refrain by Fintan O'Carroll; verses by David Haas, b.1957. © 1982, 1991, 1997 GIA Publications, Inc. ***Singing Our Faith.*** © 2002 **GIA Publications, Inc.**

Track 14: "We Are Marching." Text and tune: South Africa. © 1984 Utryck, Walton Music Corporation, agent. ***Singing Our Faith.*** © 2002 **GIA Publications, Inc.**

Track 15: "Canticle of the Sun." Text and tune: Marty Haugen, b.1950. © 1980 GIA Publications, Inc. ***Singing Our Faith.*** © 2002 **GIA Publications, Inc.**

ACKNOWLEDGMENTS FOR WLP CD

CD ***I See a New World*** by *Juliana Howard*
©2002 **World Library Publications**
Available at www.wlpmusic.com
CD #7518

CD ***Sing a Song of Joy*** by *Jack Miffleton*
©1999 **World Library Publications**
Available at www.wlpmusic.com
CD #6109

Track 1: Greatest Show on Earth by Juliana Howard from CD ***I See a New World*** by *Juliana Howard* ©2002 **World Library Publications**

Track 2: To Give Thanks by *Jack Miffleton* from CD ***Sing a Song of Joy*** by Jack Miffleton ©1999 **World Library Publications**

Track 3: Leap Like A Deer by *Juliana Howard* from CD ***I See a New World originally recorded in What Would Jesus Do?*** by *Juliana Howard* **©Juliana Howard. Used by permission.**

Track 4: Love One Another by Jack Miffleton from CD ***Sing a Song of Joy*** by *Jack Miffleton* ©1999 **World Library Publications**

Track 5: Here I Am God by Juliana Howard from CD ***I See a New World*** by *Juliana Howard* ©2002 **World Library Publications**

Track 6: We Are Little Gifts by Jack Miffleton from CD ***Sing a Song of Joy*** by *Jack Miffleton* ©1999 **World Library Publications**

Track 7: Plant Love by Juliana Howard from CD ***I See a New World*** by *Juliana Howard* ©2002 **World Library Publications**

Track 8: God Loves Little People by Jack Miffleton from CD ***Sing a Song of Joy*** by *Jack Miffleton* ©1999 **World Library Publications**

Track 9: Hold My Hand by Juliana Howard from CD ***I See a New World*** by *Juliana Howard* ©2002 **World Library Publications**

Track 10: Bless Our Hands by Jack Miffleton from CD ***Sing a Song of Joy*** by *Jack Miffleton* ©1999 **World Library Publications**

Track 11: Glory in the Light by Juliana Howard from CD I See a New World by *Juliana Howard* ©2002 **World Library Publications**

Track 12: Mary's Cradle Song by Jack Miffleton from CD ***Sing a Song of Joy*** by *Jack Miffleton* ©1999 **World Library Publications**

Track 13: In the Presence of the Angels by Juliana Howard from CD ***I See a New World*** by *Juliana Howard* ©2002 **World Library Publications**

Track 14: God's Love by Jack Miffleton from CD ***Sing a Song of Joy*** by *Jack Miffleton* ©1999 **World Library Publications**

Track 15: God Love the Animals by Juliana Howard from CD ***I See a New World*** by *Juliana Howard* ©2002 **World Library Publications**

Track 16: Make A Wonderful Noise by Jack Miffleton from CD ***Sing a Song of Joy*** by *Jack Miffleton* ©1999 **World Library Publications**

#29 **Priest**
People Set

#1 **Jesus**

Jesus

#2 **Sun**

#1 **Jesus**
Flash card

good

#3 **Smiling Face**

#2 **Good**

Flash card

amen

#4 **Heart**

#3 **Amen**
Flash card

thank you

yes

#4 **Thank you**
Flash card

#5 **Yes**
Flash card

#5 **Seas and rivers**
Creation Set

#10 **Pumpkin**
Creation Set

#6 **Mountains and hills**
Creation Set

#9 **Flowers**
Creation Set

#7 **Apple tree**
Creation Set

#8 **Fir tree**
Creation Set

#11 **Moon and stars**
Creation Set

#12 **Dolphins and other water creatures**
Creation Set

#13 **Wolves**
Creation Set

#14 **Lambs**
Creation Set

#15 **Kittens**
Creation Set

#16 **Puppies**
Creation Set

#17 **Birds**
Creation Set

#18 **Butterflies**
Creation Set

#19 **Rain**
Creation Set

#21 **Angel**
Creation Set

#20 **Adam and Eve**
Creation Set

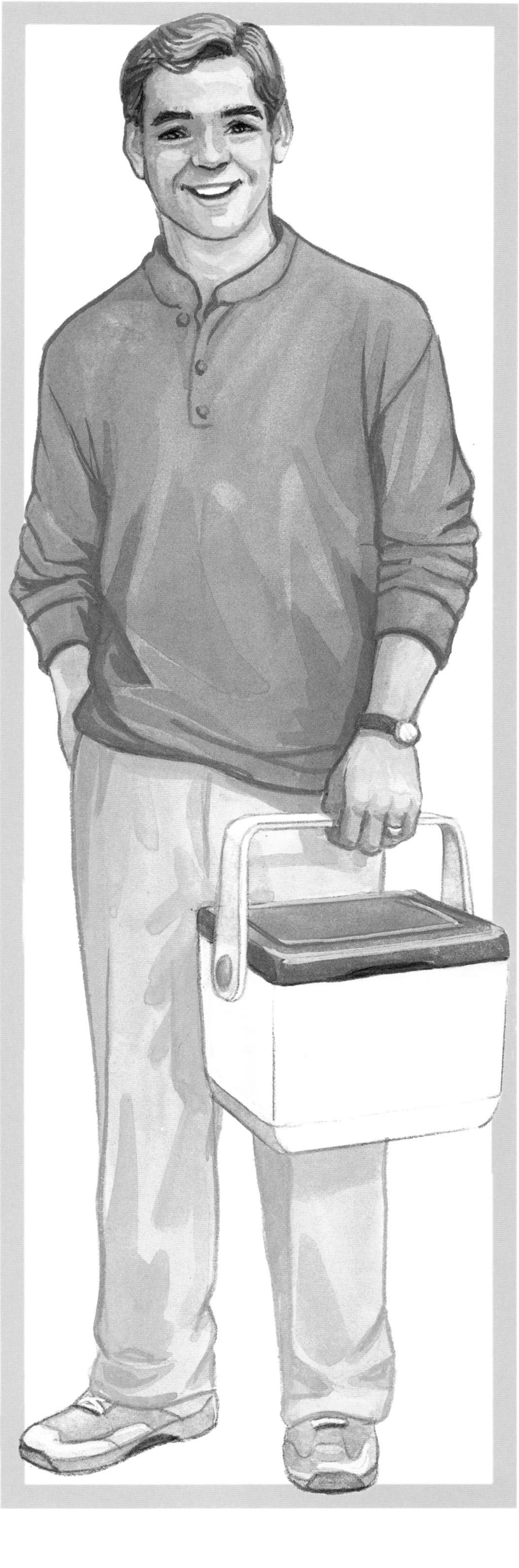

#23 **Father**
People Set

#22 **Mother**
People Set

#24 **Grandmother**
People Set

#25 **Grandfather**
People Set

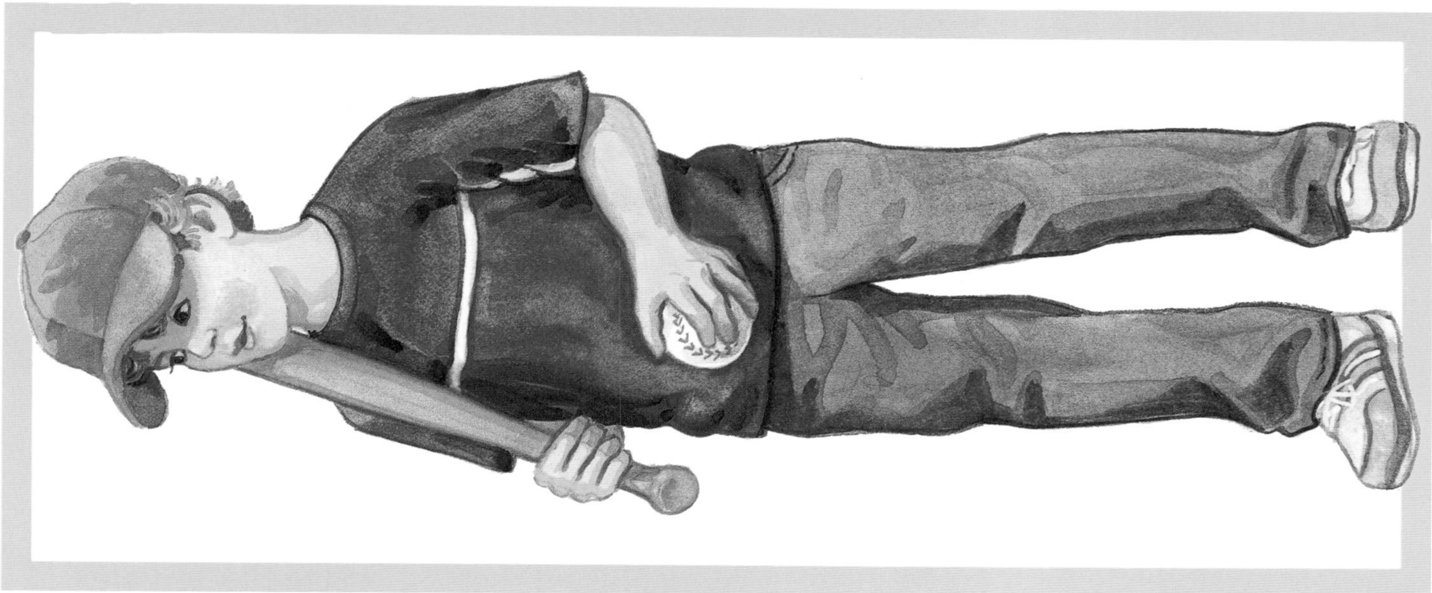

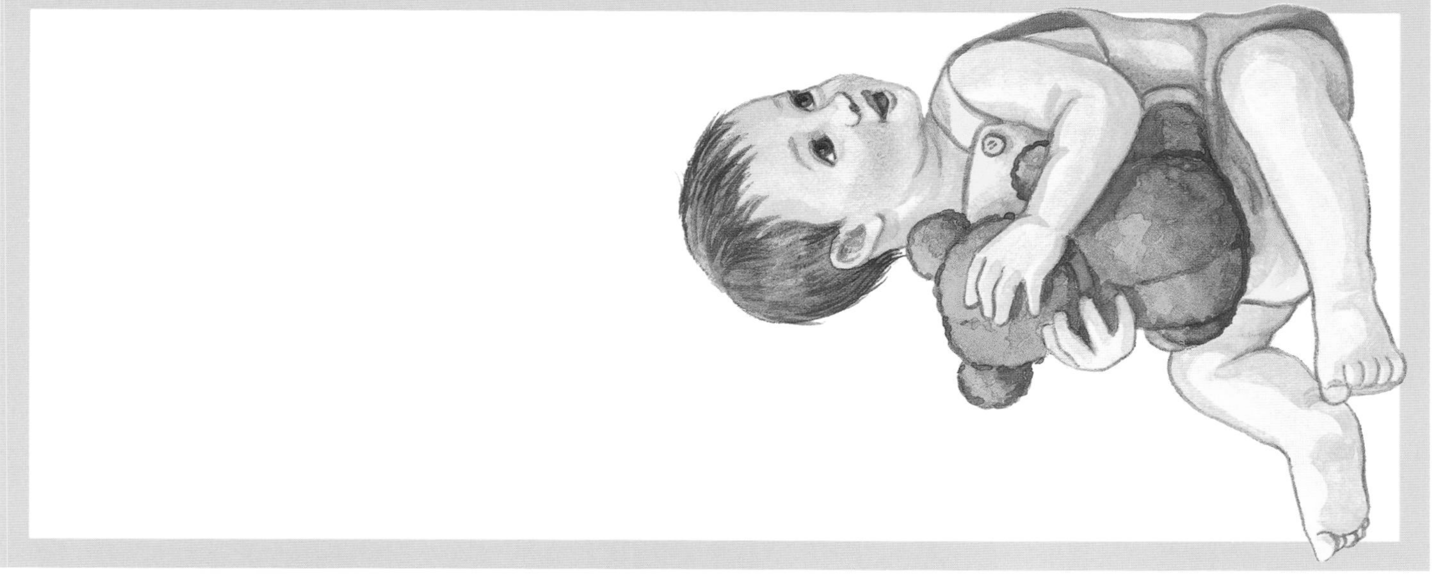

#26 **Boy**
People Set

#27 **Girl**
People Set

#28 **Baby**
People Set

#30 **Sisters**
People Set

#31 **Teenagers**
People Set

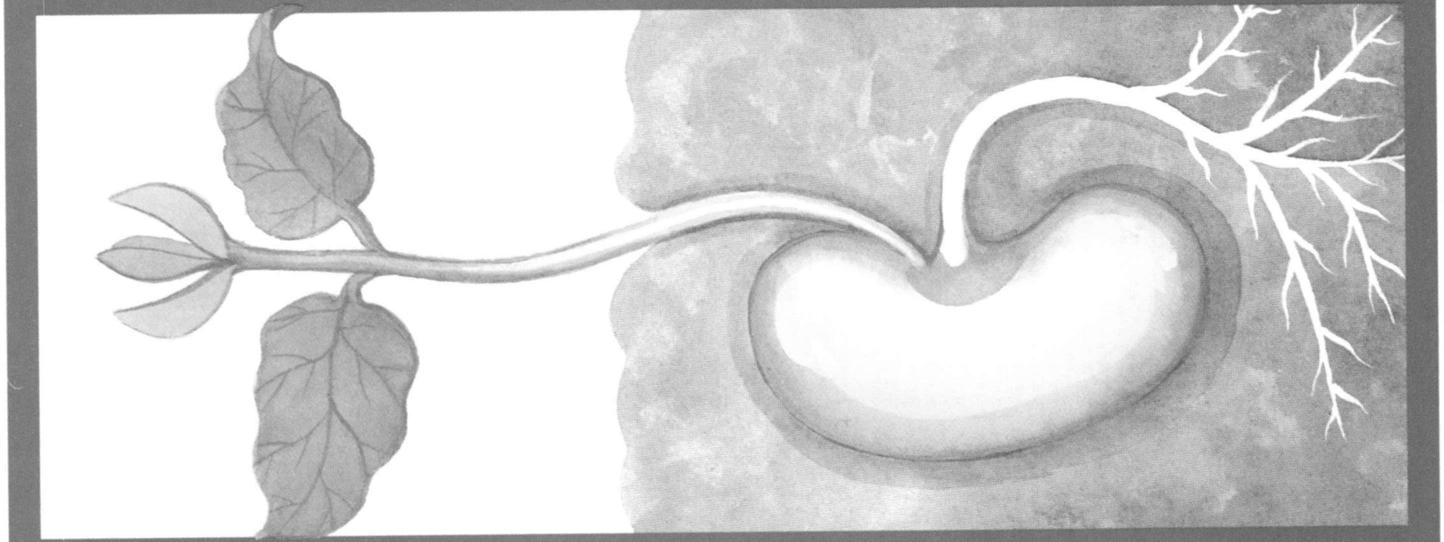

#32 **Prayer posture**

#33 **Growing seed**

#34 **Cat**
Puppet Set

#35 **Dog**
Puppet Set

#36 **Mrs. Garcia**
Puppet Set

#37 **Mr. Garcia**
Puppet Set

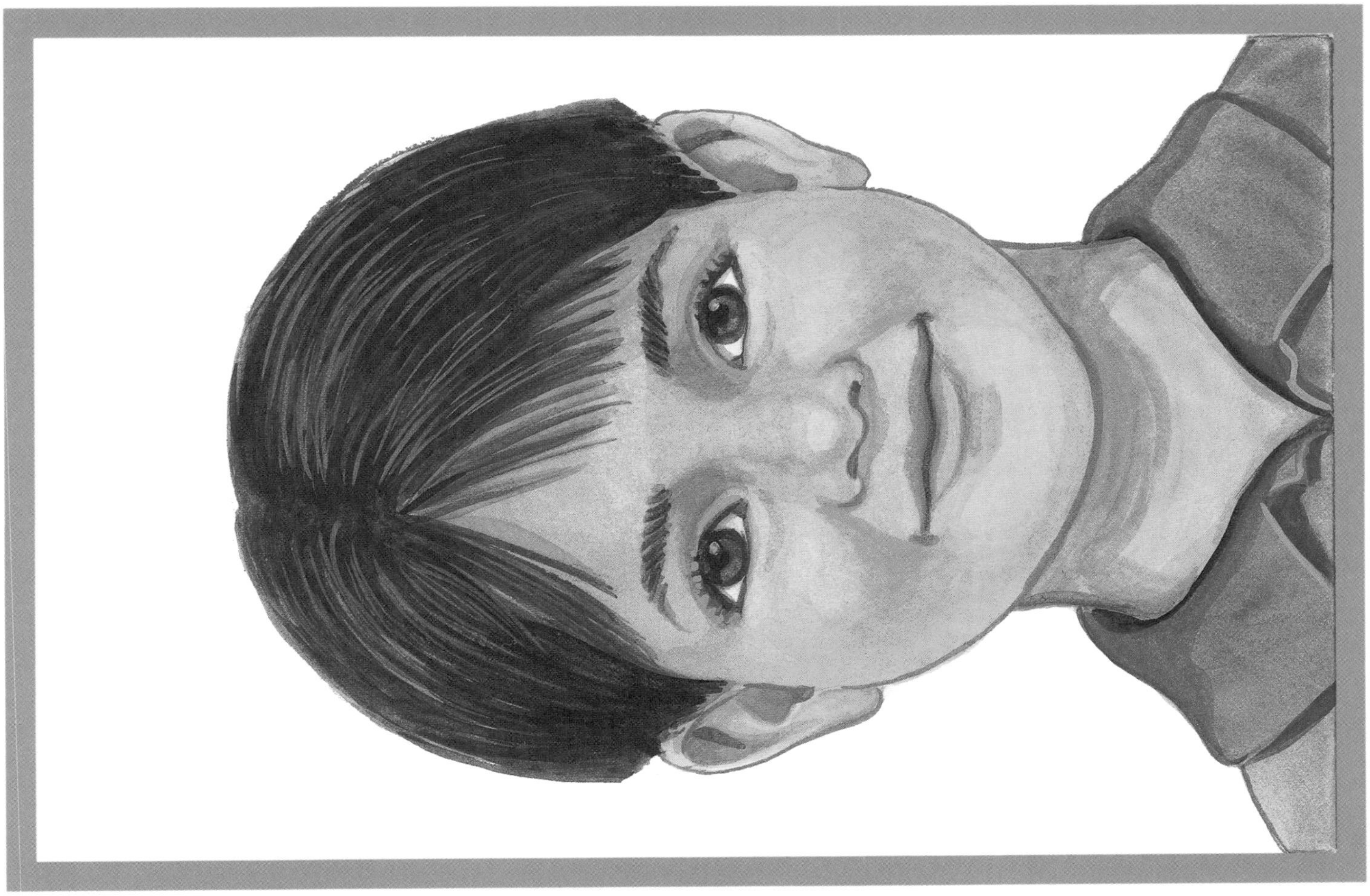

#38 **Carlos**
Puppet Set

#39 **Ana**
Puppet Set

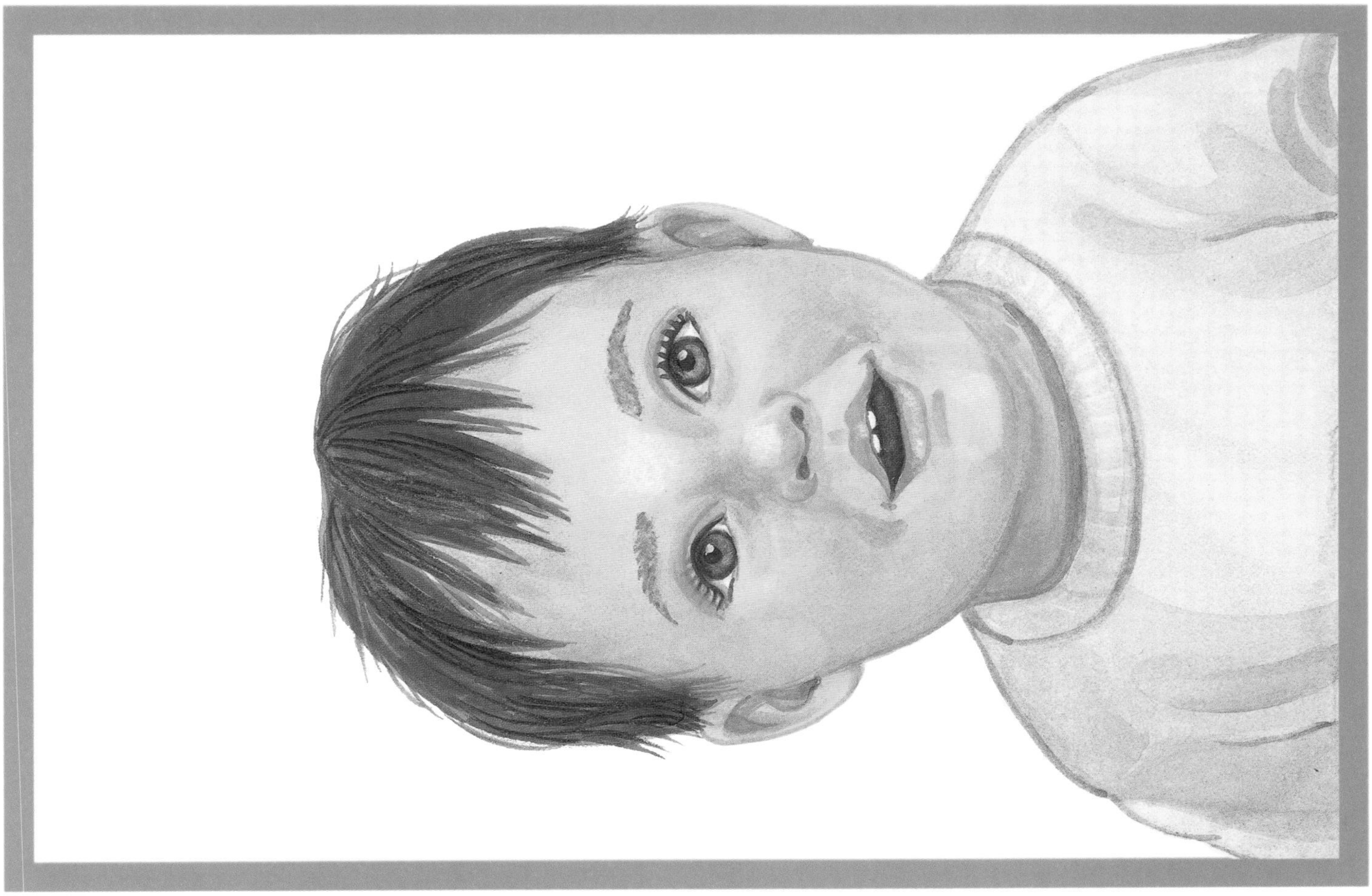

#40 **Baby Raul**
Puppet Set

#43 **Mary**
Christmas Set

#41 **David playing harp**
Christmas Set

#44 **Joseph**
Christmas Set

#45 **Shepherds**
Christmas Set

#50 **Wise Men**
Christmas Set

#46 **Angel**
Christmas Set

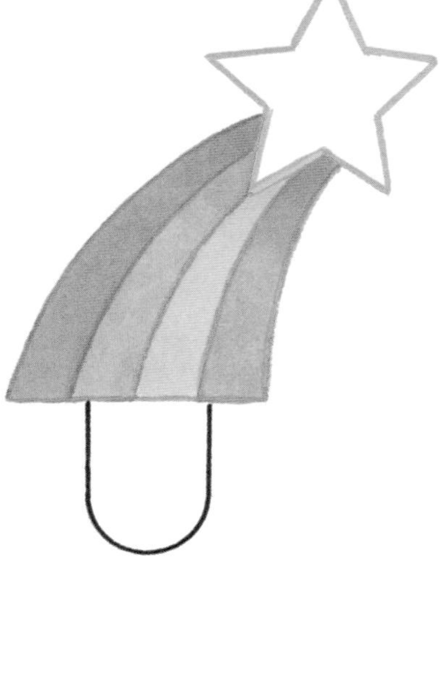

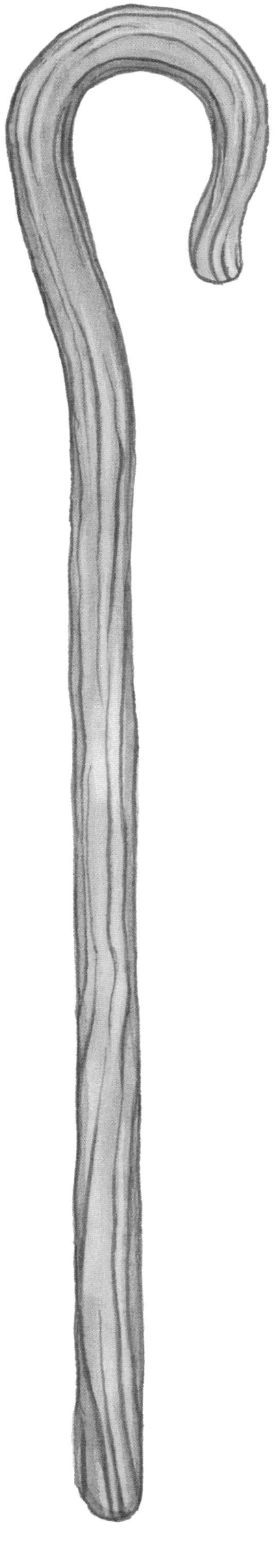

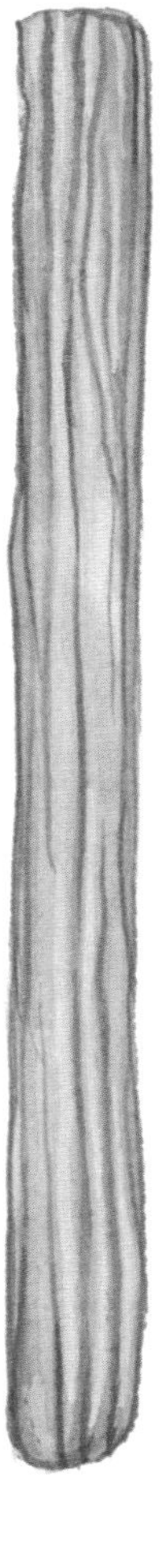

#47 **Manger**
Christmas Set

#42 **Infant Jesus**
Christmas Set

#63 **Rod**
Shepherd Set

#62 **Staff**
Shepherd Set

#48 **Star**
Christmas Set

#49 **Stable**
Christmas Set

#52 **Charlie Chick**
Animal Set

#54 **Gilda Goldfish**
Animal Set

#53 **Herbie Horse**
Animal Set

#55 **Katie Kitten**
Animal Set

#56 **Betty Bird**
Animal Set

#57 **Rita Rabbit**
Animal Set

#51 **Tillie Turtle**
Animal Set

#58 **Connie Cow**

Animal Set

Cut Out

Cut Out

Cut Out

Cut Out

Cut Out

Cut Out

Cut Out

Cut Out

Flap A
Glue Flap A to Flap B

Flap A
Glue Flap A to Flap B

Flap B
Glue Flap B to Flap A

Flap B
Glue Flap B to Flap A

#59 Sheepfold

Shepherd Set

Directions:
1. Tear OUT FOUR SIDES.
2. Cut out all windows.
3. Fold A flaps and glue them to B flaps.
4. Leave one end open for a gate.

Cut Out

Cut Out

Cut Out

Cut Out

Flap A
Glue Flap A to Flap B

Cut Out

Cut Out

Cut Out

Cut Out

Flap A
Glue Flap A to Flap B

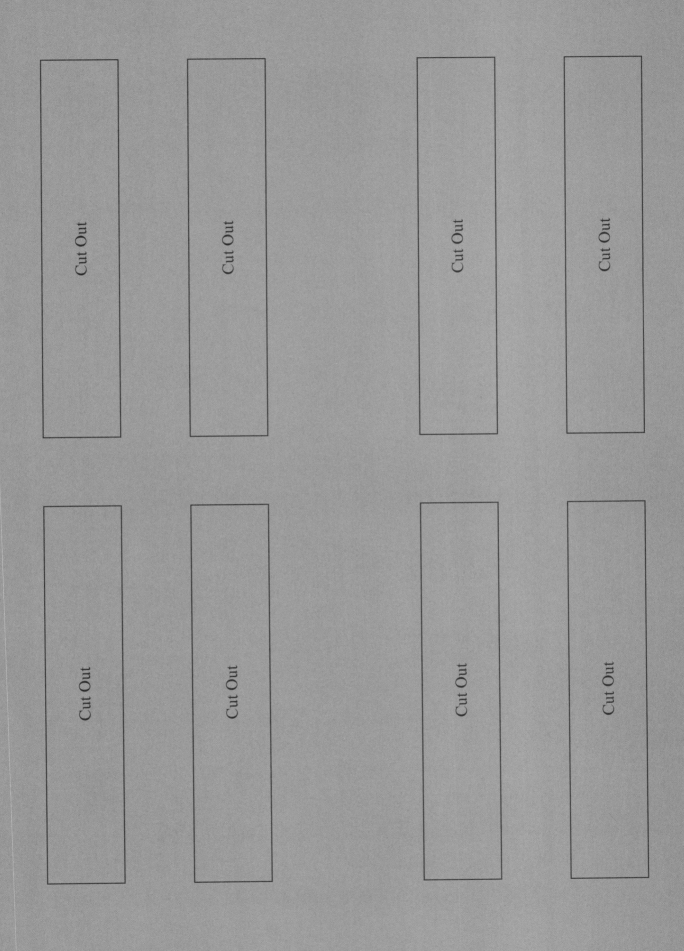

Flap B
Glue Flap B to Flap A

Flap B
Glue Flap B to Flap A

#59 Sheepfold

Shepherd Set

Directions:

1. Tear out four sides.
2. Cut out all windows.
3. Fold A flaps and glue them to B flaps.
4. Leave one end open for a gate.

#61 **Good Shepherd**
Shepherd Set

#60 **Shepherd**
Shepherd Set

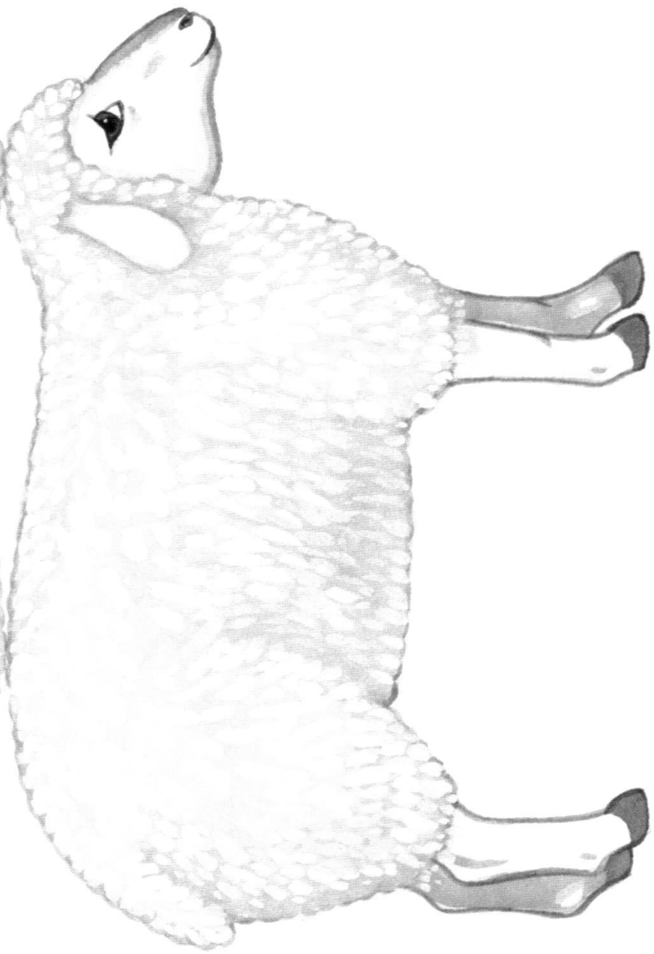
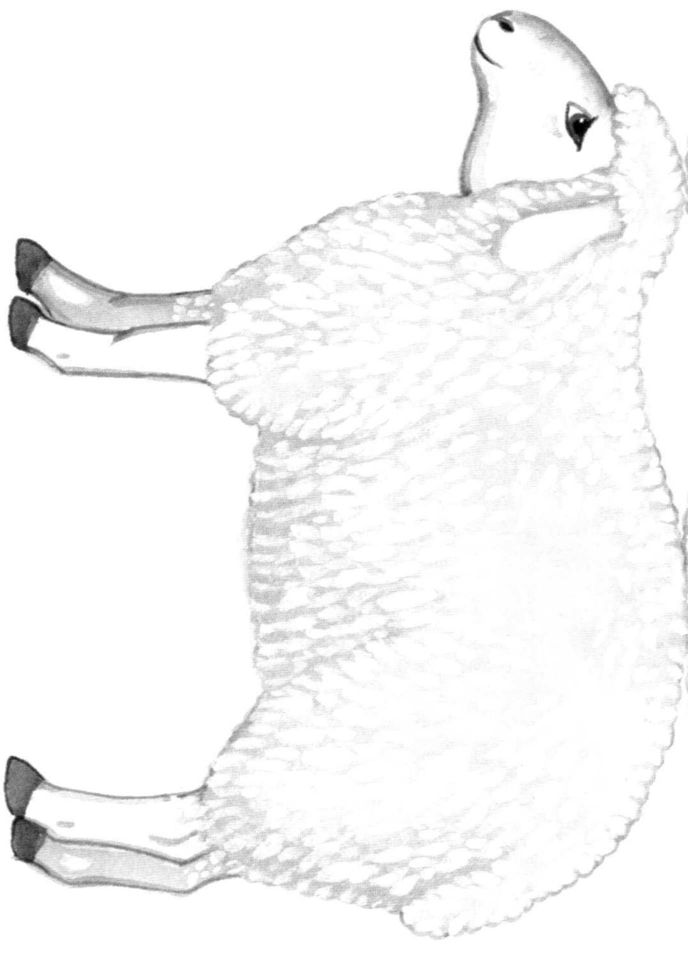
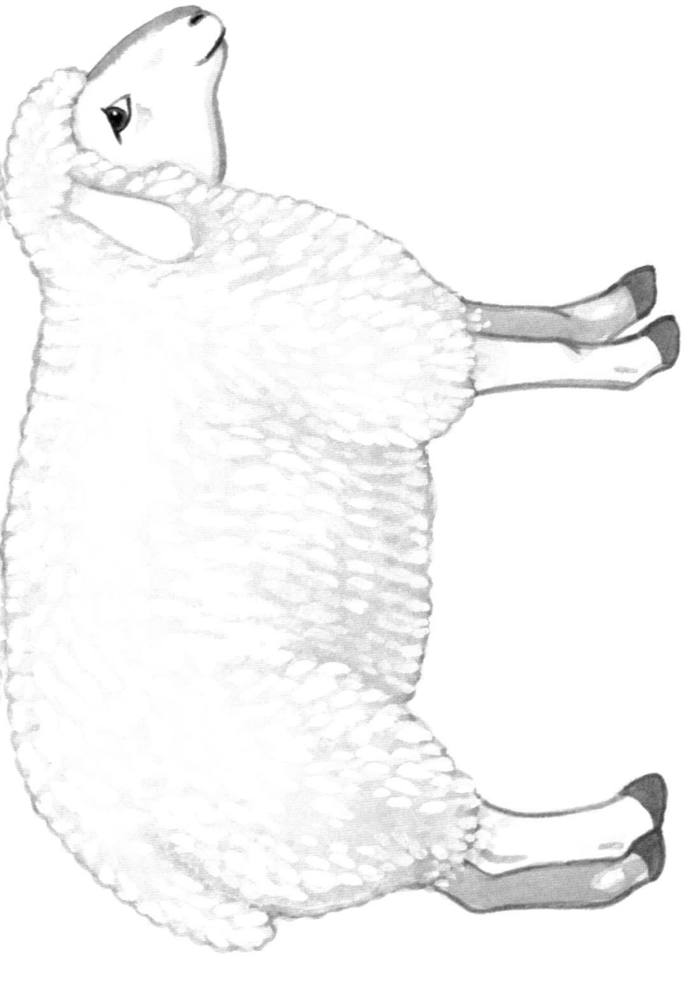

#64–65 **Sheep**
Animal Set
Fold the sheep along the dotted line.

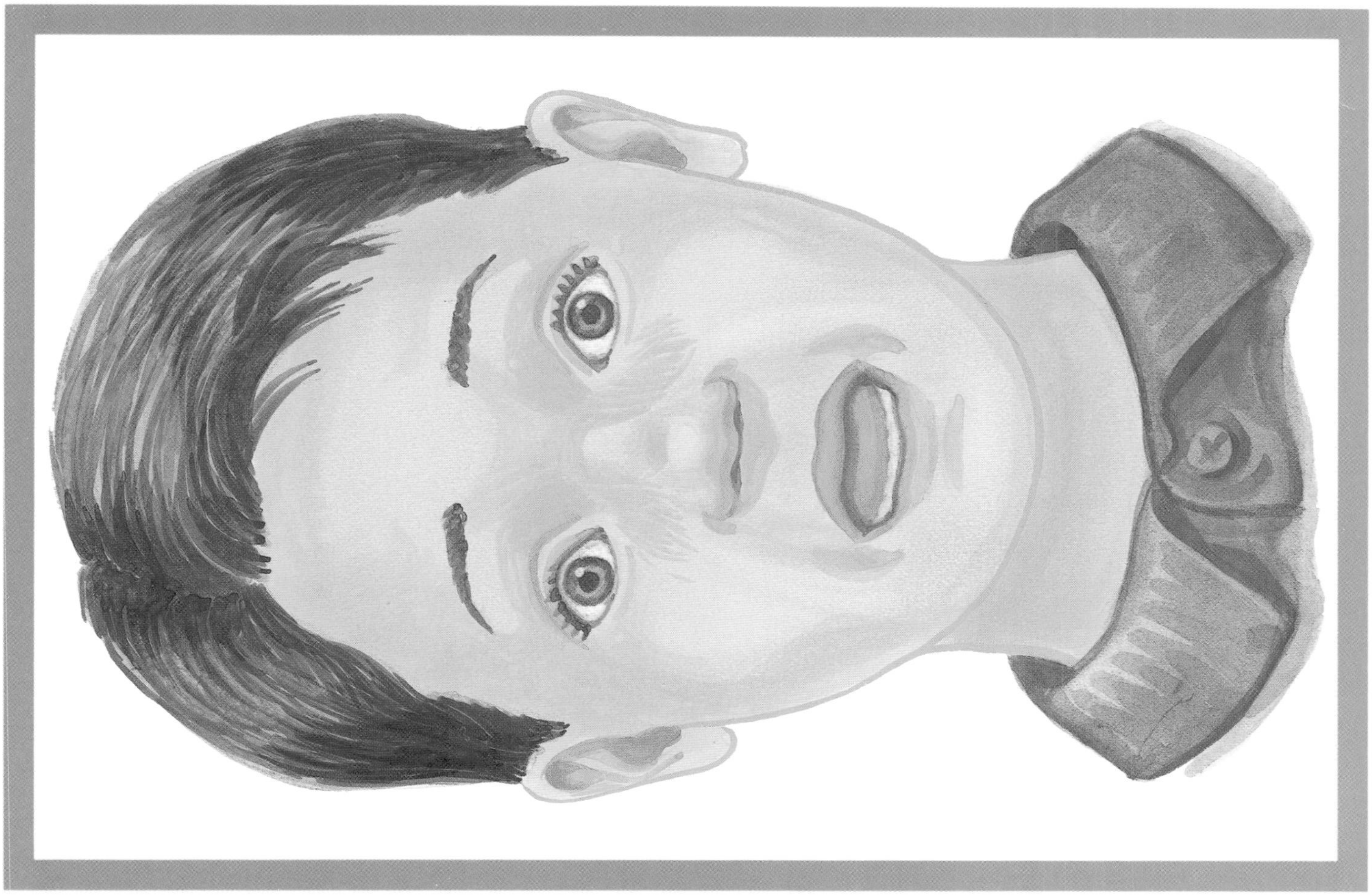

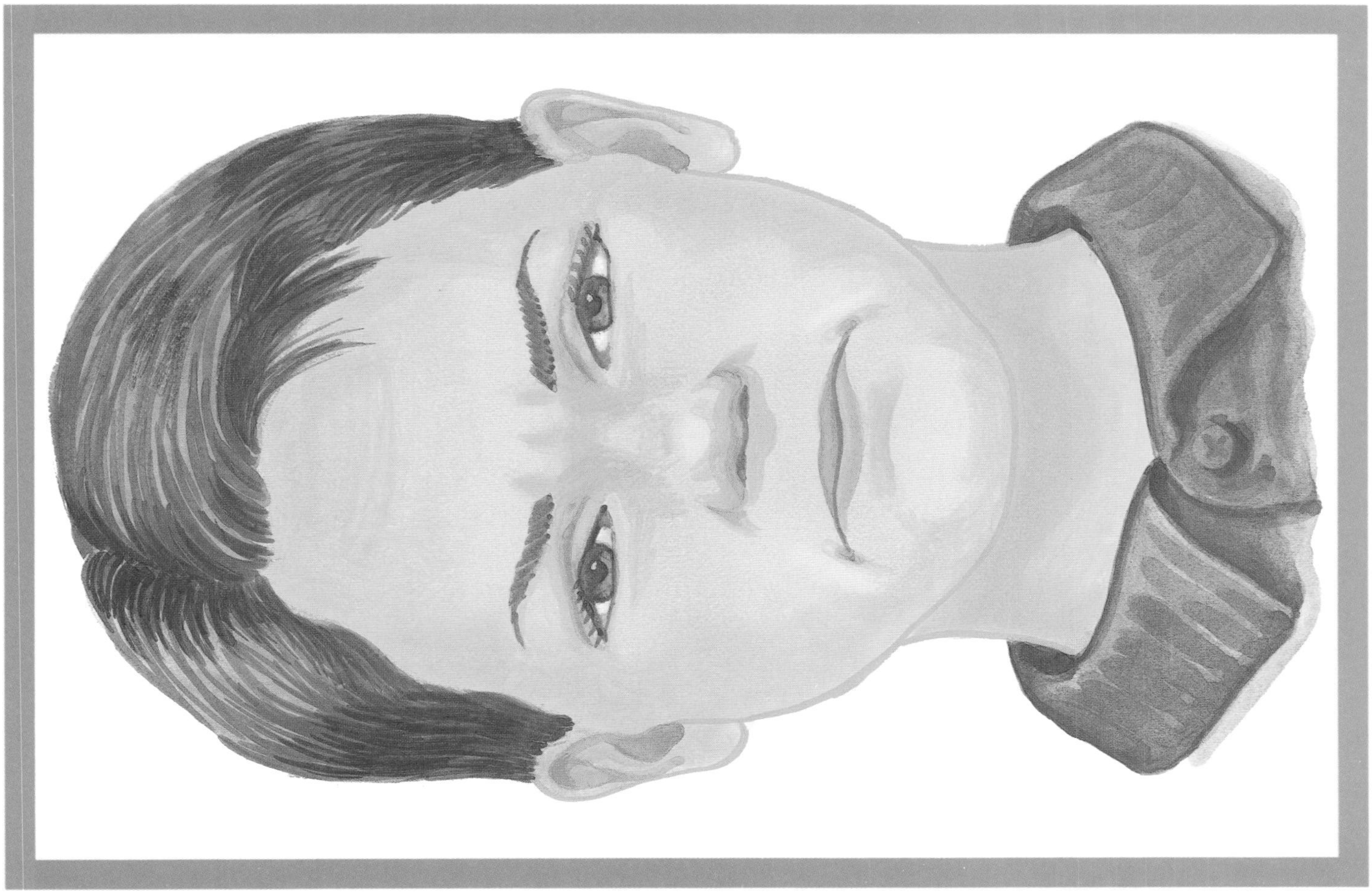

#66 **Scared Face**
Feelings Set

#67 **Angry Face**
Feelings Set

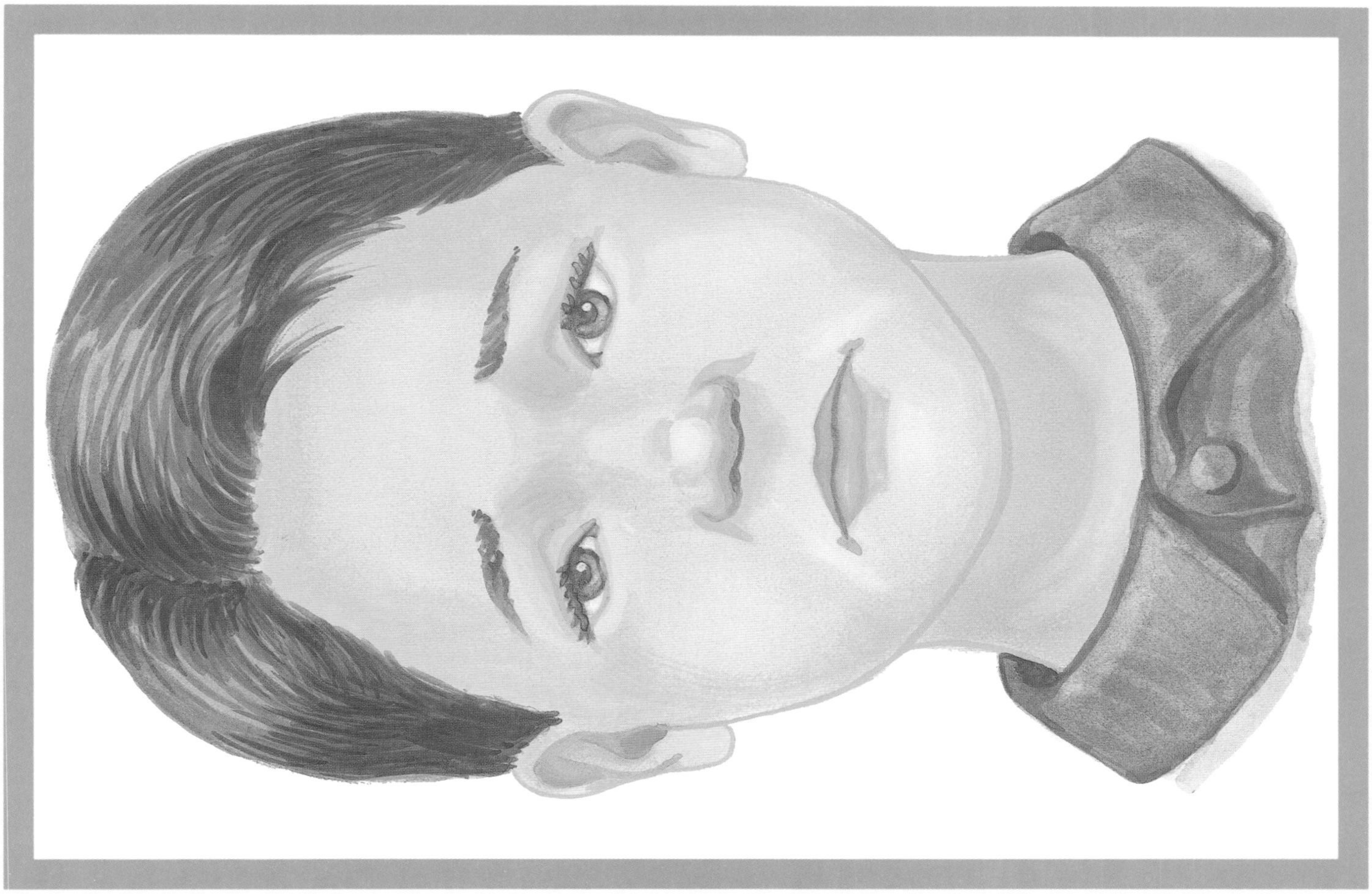

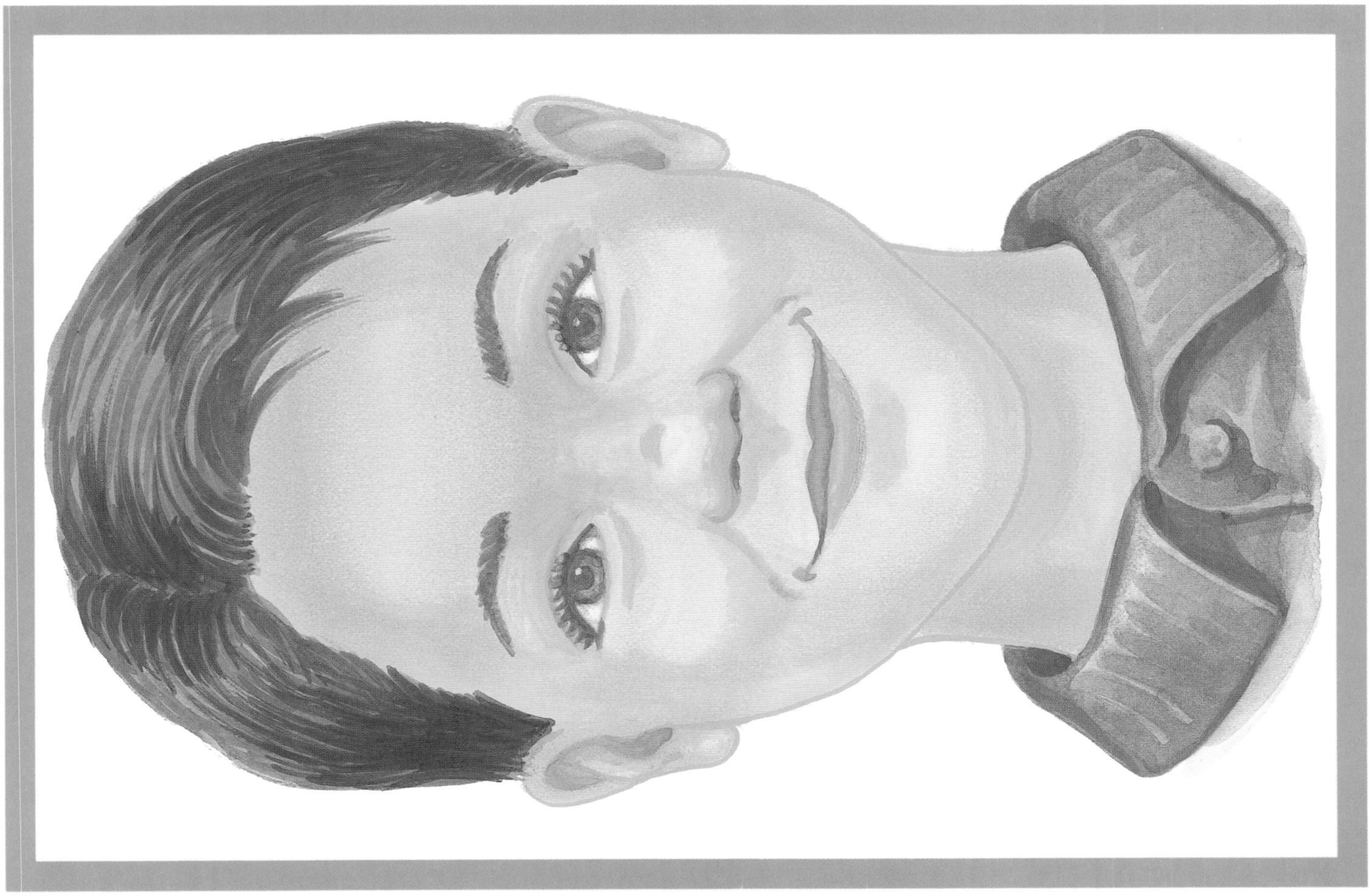

#68 **Sad Face**
Feelings Set

#69 **Happy Face**
Feelings Set

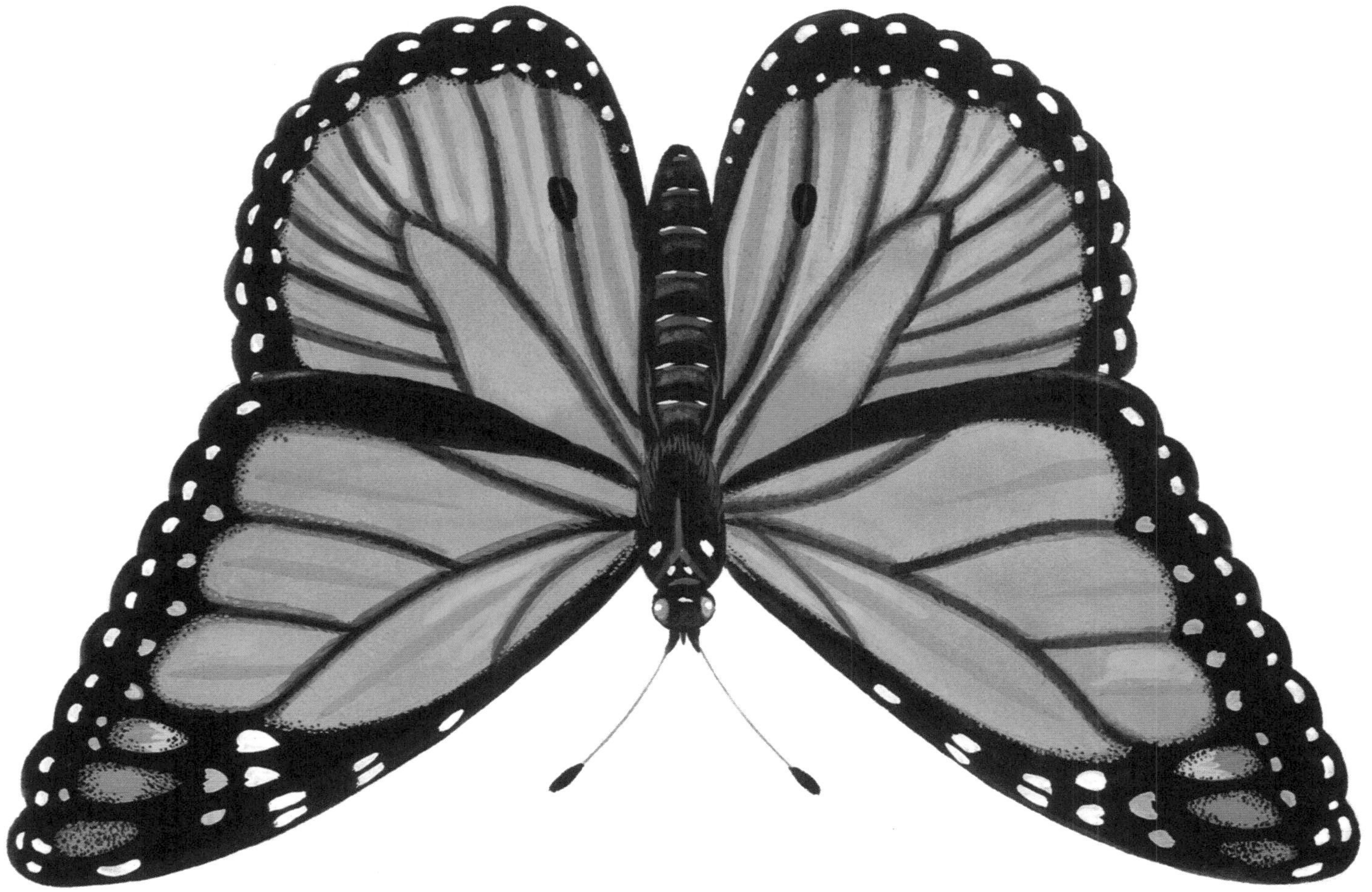

#70 **Caterpillar/Chrysalis**
Butterfly Life Cycle Set

1. Cut out the butterfly outline that encloses the caterpillar and chrysalis. Then cut out the butterfly.
2. Glue or tape the cutouts back to back.

#71 **Butterfly**
Butterfly Life Cycle Set

© LoyolaPress.